Cisco CID Exam Certification Guide

Michael Crane

Reggie Terrell

Cisco Press

Cisco Press
201 W 103rd Street
Indianapolis, IN 46290

Cisco CID Exam Certification Guide

Michael Crane

Reggie Terrell

Copyright © 2001 Cisco Press

Cisco Press logo is a trademark of Cisco Systems, Inc.

Published by:
Cisco Press
201 West 103rd Street
Indianapolis, IN 46290 USA

Printed in the United States of America 1 2 3 4 5 6 7 8 9 0

Library of Congress Cataloging-in-Publication Number: 2001-086618

ISBN: 1-58720-033-3

Warning and Disclaimer

This book is designed to provide information about Cisco Internetwork Design. Every effort has been made to make this book as complete and as accurate as possible, but no warranty or fitness is implied.

The information is provided on an "as is" basis. The author, Cisco Press, and Cisco Systems, Inc., shall have neither liability nor responsibility to any person or entity with respect to any loss or damages arising from the information contained in this book or from the use of the discs or programs that may accompany it.

The opinions expressed in this book belong to the author and are not necessarily those of Cisco Systems, Inc.

Trademark Acknowledgments

All terms mentioned in this book that are known to be trademarks or service marks have been appropriately capitalized. Cisco Press or Cisco Systems, Inc., cannot attest to the accuracy of this information. Use of a term in this book should not be regarded as affecting the validity of any trademark or service mark.

Feedback Information

At Cisco Press, our goal is to create in-depth technical books of the highest quality and value. Each book is crafted with care and precision, undergoing rigorous development that involves the unique expertise of members of the professional technical community.

Reader feedback is a natural continuation of this process. If you have any comments regarding how we could improve the quality of this book or otherwise alter it to better suit your needs, you can contact us through e-mail at feedback@ciscopress.com. Please make sure to include the book title and ISBN in your message.

We greatly appreciate your assistance.

Publisher	John Wait
Editor-in-Chief	John Kane
Cisco Systems Management	Michael Hakkert
	Tom Geitner
	William Warren
Executive Editor	Brett Bartow
Acquisitions Editor	Amy Lewis
Managing Editor	Patrick Kanouse
Development Editor	Howard Jones
Project Editor	Marc Fowler
Copy Editor	Gayle Johnson
Technical Editors	A. Anthony Bruno
	Warren Heaton
	Anthony Kwan
	Andre Paree-Huff
Team Coordinator	Tammi Ross
Cover Designer	Louisa Klucznik
Compositor	Steve Gifford
Indexer	Tim Wright

CISCO SYSTEMS

Corporate Headquarters
Cisco Systems, Inc.
170 West Tasman Drive
San Jose, CA 95134-1706
USA
http://www.cisco.com
Tel: 408 526-4000
     800 553-NETS (6387)
Fax: 408 526-4100

European Headquarters
Cisco Systems Europe
11 Rue Camille Desmoulins
92782 Issy-les-Moulineaux
Cedex 9
France
http://www-europe.cisco.com
Tel: 33 1 58 04 60 00
Fax: 33 1 58 04 61 00

Americas Headquarters
Cisco Systems, Inc.
170 West Tasman Drive
San Jose, CA 95134-1706
USA
http://www.cisco.com
Tel: 408 526-7660
Fax: 408 527-0883

Asia Pacific Headquarters
Cisco Systems Australia,
Pty., Ltd
Level 17, 99 Walker Street
North Sydney
NSW 2059 Australia
http://www.cisco.com
Tel: +61 2 8448 7100
Fax: +61 2 9957 4350

Cisco Systems has more than 200 offices in the following countries. Addresses, phone numbers, and fax numbers are listed on the Cisco Web site at www.cisco.com/go/offices

Argentina • Australia • Austria • Belgium • Brazil • Bulgaria • Canada • Chile • China • Colombia • Costa Rica • Croatia • Czech Republic • Denmark • Dubai, UAE • Finland • France • Germany • Greece • Hong Kong • Hungary • India • Indonesia • Ireland Israel • Italy • Japan • Korea • Luxembourg • Malaysia • Mexico • The Netherlands • New Zealand • Norway • Peru • Philippines Poland • Portugal • Puerto Rico • Romania • Russia • Saudi Arabia • Scotland • Singapore • Slovakia • Slovenia • South Africa • Spain Sweden • Switzerland • Taiwan • Thailand • Turkey • Ukraine • United Kingdom • United States • Venezuela • Vietnam • Zimbabwe

About the Authors

Michael Crane, CCIE #5531, CCNA/CCNP/CCDP, is a network architect with Dimension Data since July 2000 and specializes in the designing, implementation, and troubleshooting of global area networks. Dimension Data is one of the six global partners of Cisco Systems, Inc.. Mike Crane has more than 20 years of experience in the computer industry. He maintains several Cisco certifications, including all the Cisco Specialization tracks, as well as Novell and Microsoft certifications. Prior to working at Dimension Data, Mike was a consultant to Science Applications International Corporation (SAIC) and has supported large federal agencies, including the Department of Transportation, the National Institutes of Health, and the White House.

Reginald Terrell is currently employed as a Senior Telecommunications Engineer for Science Applications International Corporation (SAIC), and has been in the networking and computer industries for the past fifteen years. Throughout his career, he has worked as a systems design engineer, network architect, integrator, certified trainer, technical consultant, and project manager. His experience in telecommunications dates back to the 110-baud modem. His experience has given him the opportunity to address real-world problems, and the opportunity to develop sound strategies for network design. Mr. Terrell holds several network certifications in Microsoft and Novell. He also holds several Cisco certifications, which include the CCDP and CCNP, and is currently pursuing the CCIE certification. Reggie received his Bachelor of Science degree in Computer Science and his Master of Science degree in Telecommunications Management from the University of Maryland.

About the Technical Reviewers

A. Anthony Bruno is a principal consultant with 10 years of experience in the internetworking field. His network certifications include CCIE #2738, CCDP, CCNA-WAN, Microsoft MCSE, Nortel NNCSS, and Certified Network Expert (CNX) Ethernet. As a consultant, he has worked with many customers in the design, implementation, and optimization of large-scale multi-protocol networks. Anthony has worked on the design of large company network mergers, wireless LANs, Voice over IP/Frame Relay, and Internet access. He formerly worked as an Air Force captain in network operations and management. He received his MS in electrical engineering from University of Missouri-Rolla in 1994 and his B.S. in electrical engineering from the University of Puerto Rico-Mayaguez in 1990. Anthony is the co-author of the Cisco Press book *CCDA Exam Certification Guide* and was a contributor and the lead technical reviewer for the Cisco Press book *Cisco CCIE Fundamentals: Network Design and Case Studies*, Second Edition. He also performed a technical review of Cisco Press' *CID Exam Certification Guide* and *Internetworking Troubleshooting Handbook*.

Warren Heaton, CCNA, CCDA, CCNP, CCDP, is currently a chief operating officer for A Technological Advantage in Louisville, Kentucky. He has been responsible for the Cisco Training, Reseller and Consulting Division, as well as performed Cisco pre-sales work, including design, implementation, and support of enterprise networks.

Anthony Kwan, CCDA, CCDP, is a network architect for Ignite Tek, Corp.

Andre Paree-Huff, CCNP, CCDA, MCSE+I, ASE, A+, Network+, I-Network+, Server+, has been working in the computer field for more than nine years. He is currently working for Compaq Computer Corporation as a network support engineer level III for the North America Customer Support Center in Colorado Springs, Colorado. He handles troubleshooting of network hardware, specializing in Layer 2 and 3 of the OSI model. Andre has co-authored five network-related books and has been a technical editor on more then two dozen others. He is currently working toward his CCDE and CCIE.

Dedication

Michael Crane:

This book is dedicated to my wife and best friend, Connie, for her support during this project. She makes it all worthwhile.

And to my lovely daughters, Holly and Melissa, for putting up with the absence of their father for nine months.

Reggie Terrell:

To my parents, Emma and Welton Terrell. To Mom, who early on taught me a love of God and a respect and appreciation for knowledge, and to Dad, who early on taught me the value of hard work.

Acknowledgments

Michael Crane:

I would like to express my sincere appreciation to Steven Horr, Carol Peake, and Wesley D. Smith for giving me the opportunity to participate in and contribute to the design of the Arinc Global Network, which coincided with the writing of this book and provided ideas for the chapters.

To Amy Lewis, Howard Jones, and Anthony Bruno. Words would fail me if I were to seek an expression of appreciation. Thanks!

Also, I would like to extend a personal thank you to Kathy and Scott Russell, Chuck Spotts, and Treva Terrell.

Finally, to Reggie Terrell, you are one of a kind and please stay that way. I always enjoy working with you.

Reggie Terrell:

You would not be reading this book were it not for the able and capable guidance of Amy Lewis. Amy, if it were up to me, you would get a promotion and a raise. Thanks again for your patience and diligence. Our primary reviewer, Howard Jones, shepherded us through every step with his thorough reviews, insightful comments, and attention to detail. Howard, please accept my gratitude. Our primary technical reviewer, Anthony Bruno, contributed mightily to the technical accuracy and depth of this book. I am certain that the reader will doubly benefit from the wisdom that Anthony has added to the words that we have written. Anthony, I am grateful for what you have done.

A tender special thanks to my wife, Treva, who was a model of support throughout this project.

Finally, my genuine and heartfelt appreciation goes to the author of this book, Mike Crane. Mike, you are a special person. Simply knowing you is a privilege and a pleasure.

Contents at a Glance

Contents

Introduction

Professional certifications have been an important part of the computing industry for many years and will continue to become more important. Many reasons exist for these certifications, but the most often cited reason is credibility. All other considerations held equal, the certified employee/consultant/job candidate is considered more valuable than one who is not.

Goals and Methods

The most important and somewhat obvious goal of this book is to help you pass the Cisco Internetwork Design exam. However, the methods used in this book to help you pass the exam are also designed to make you much more knowledgeable about how to do your job. Although this book and the accompanying CD have more than enough questions to help you prepare for the exam, the intent is not to make you memorize as many questions and answers as you possibly can.

The key methodologies used in this book are to help you discover the exam topics that you need to review in more depth, to help you fully understand and remember those details, and to help you prove to yourself that you have retained your knowledge of those topics. This book does not try to help you pass by memorization. Instead, it helps you truly learn and understand the topics. The Cisco Internetwork Design exam is just one of the foundation topics in the CCDP certification. The knowledge contained within is vitally important if you are to consider yourself a truly skilled routing/switching design engineer or specialist. This book would do you a disservice if it didn't attempt to help you learn the material. To that end, this book helps you pass the Cisco Internetwork Design exam by using the following methods:

* Helping you discover which test topics you have not mastered
* Providing explanations and information to fill in your knowledge gaps
* Supplying exercises and scenarios that enhance your ability to recall and deduce the answers to test questions
* Providing practice exercises on the topics and the testing process via test questions on the CD

Who Should Read This Book?

This book is not designed to be a general networking topic book, although it can be used for that purpose. This book is intended to tremendously increase your chances of passing the Cisco Internetwork Design exam. Although other objectives can be achieved from using this book, it was written with one goal in mind: to help you pass the exam.

So why should you want to pass the Cisco Internetwork Design exam? Because it's one of the milestones toward getting the CCDP certification—no small feat in itself. What would getting the CCDP mean to you? A raise, a promotion, recognition? How about enhancing your resume? Demonstrating that you are serious about continuing the learning process and that you're not content to rest on your laurels? Pleasing your reseller-employer, who needs more certified employees for a higher discount from Cisco? Or one of many other reasons.

Strategies for Exam Preparation

The strategy you use for Cisco Internetwork Design might be slightly different from strategies used by other readers, mainly based on the skills, knowledge, and experience you already have obtained. For instance, if you have attended the Cisco Internetwork Design course, you might take a different approach than someone who learned to design networks on the job. Chapter 1 includes a strategy that should closely match your background.

Regardless of your strategy or background, this book is designed to help you get to the point where you can pass the exam in the least amount of time possible. For instance, there is no need for you to practice or read about IP addressing and subnetting if you fully understand this topic already. However, many people like to make sure that they truly know a topic and thus read over material they already know. Several book features will help you gain the confidence you need to be convinced that you know some material already, and also help you know what topics you need to study more.

How This Book Is Organized

Although this book could be read cover-to-cover, it is designed to be flexible. You can easily move between chapters and sections of chapters to cover just the material you need more work on. Chapter 1 provides an overview of the CCNP and CCDP certifications and offers some strategies for how to prepare for the exam. The chapters can be covered in any order. If you intend to read them all, the order in the book is an excellent sequence to use.

Chapters 1 through 16 cover the following topics:

- **Chapter 1, "Design Goals and Models"**—This chapter focuses on design goals and also discusses the recommended steps for designing an internetwork, seven steps for designing internetworks, concerns facing designers, disaster recovery, fault-tolerant media implementations, controlling broadcasts, and full mesh versus partial mesh. Core, access, and distribution layer strategies are discussed.
- **Chapter 2, "Business and Technical Requirements"**—This chapter discusses the evolution of campus LAN design and issues that CCDPs should consider when designing campus LANs. Virtual LANs (VLANs) and their role in a successful campus LAN design strategy are discussed, along with customer availability requirements and selecting the right products for WAN design.
- **Chapter 3, "Campus LAN Technologies"**—This chapter discusses campus LAN technologies from a design perspective and defines LAN interconnection methods. A discussion of logical and physical connections that exist at OSI Layer 2 is included. You'll read about the role of LAN switching technology in campus networks and get an overview of wireless networks.
- **Chapter 4, "ATM Design Models"**—This chapter discusses the ATM protocol stack and how ATM uses virtual circuits for data transmission. It includes an overview of the ATM adaptation layer. Routing protocols and methods used to define ATM addresses are discussed. Design models for ATM, including campus, LAN, and the WAN core, are mentioned. Designing an ATM address plan is detailed. You also will read about the Cisco/StrataCom family of ATM switches and where they fit into a network design.
- **Chapter 5, "Designing TCP/IP Addressing"**—Addressing choices and the decisions to be faced when designing a TCP/IP network are covered in detail in this chapter. Also, the definition of classful and classless addressing and their role in optimizing TCP/IP design concerns are discussed. This chapter also covers network addressing guidelines and managing addresses with DHCP, route summarization, and CIDR blocks.

- **Chapter 6, "Routing Concepts"**—This chapter discusses static and dynamic routing, path determination, and how routing protocols use metrics to determine the best path. Also discussed are route redistribution between dissimilar protocols, routing algorithms, enabling and disabling split horizon for IP networks, Cisco Express Forwarding, host routing, and Tag Switching.
- **Chapter 7, "OSPF"**—This chapter examines the Open Shortest Path First (OSPF) protocol, OSPF network types, and categories. You'll see how OSPF propagates link state advertisements with summarization and area definition. You'll read about the network design that maximizes stability and scalability, design models for the OSPF backbone, IGRP routing characteristics, and how the IGRP metric works. You'll also read about EIGRP and the enhancement features that make it superior to IGRP. Other topics include OSPF protocols and area assignments, OSPF summarization and scalability, designated and backup designated routers, and determining OSPF convergence.
- **Chapter 8, "Desktop Design"**—This chapter discusses the AppleTalk protocol and considerations to remember when designing AppleTalk networks. It also covers Novell's IPX routing and issues that relate to how SAP and RIP broadcasts are controlled on the network. You'll see an examination of a client's requirements and read about constructing a design solution using Windows Networking. RTMP, EIGRP convergence, IPX Protocol, IPX Routing, and encapsulation types are discussed, as well as NetWare Link Services Protocol and IPX/IP gateways.
- **Chapter 9, "WAN Design Considerations"**—This chapter discusses the various options available and helps you choose the optimum technology to use. It covers the goals for designing the WAN core, including redundancy, partitioning, load balancing, and convergence. You'll read about the various performance-related options available in Cisco IOS in terms of design trade-offs such as compression, queuing, and Quality of Service (QoS). You'll also read about managing the backbone with single protocol versus multiprotocol, as well as tunneling features.
- **Chapter 10, "X.25/Frame Relay Topologies"**—This chapter provides a brief overview of the X.25 protocol, which is used extensively in areas outside the United States. You'll see where it fits into today's networks. You'll read about X.25 over TCP/IP (XOT), X.25 over ISDN, hub and spoke Frame Relay, common terms used with Frame Relay, and Frame Relay service characteristics. Additionally, oversubscription, determining the measurement interval, split horizon, and Frame Relay interaction with routing protocols are discussed.
- **Chapter 11, "Remote Access"**—This chapter reviews analog and ISDN services available today, as well as the common methods of accessing remote sites, remote node and remote control. Also covered are options for remote routers and access servers, functions and reference points used with ISDN, ISDN Primary Rate Interface, IP Unnumbered and where to use it, Point-to-Point Protocol, HDLC and LAPB, multilink PPP, and where various remote-office routers fit into the network design.
- **Chapter 12, "SNA Technoogies"**—This chapter discusses the types of gateways available in the SNA arena, the LLC2 and SDLC connection-oriented protocols, SNA frame types, the SNA model, subarea nodes, peripheral nodes, establishing LU-LU sessions, boundary nodes, dependent and independent LU sessions, explicit and virtual routing, and downstream physical units.
- **Chapter 13, "SNA Interworking"**—This chapter discusses serial tunneling of SDLC (STUN) and some of the transport protocols for the SDLC frames, the evolution of DLSw+ and some of its options, Advanced Peer-to-Peer Networking (APPN), Channel Interface Processor (CIP) and where it fits into the SNA design, CIP features and terminology, Cisco enhanced DLSw+ features, choosing a transport protocol for DLSw+, and avoiding timeouts with LLC2.

- **Chapter 14, "SNA Topologies"**—This chapter discusses some common Token Ring designs, various DLSw+ designs and methods of controlling broadcasts with border peers, and various methods of implementing QoS with DLSw+. You'll read descriptions of the different timers available and when it might be practical and effective to apply them. Also covered are redundancy and load balancing, dual-backbone Token Ring design, DLSw+ design, minimizing explorer replication, border peer design, configuring traffic priority, queuing algorithms, and priority and custom queuing for DLSw+.

- **Chapter 15, "Network Security Technologies"**—This chapter examines the underlying security technologies and their components, the common firewalls available, where firewalls fit into a corporate design, and Cisco IOS features for firewalls. Also covered are the concept of IPSec and some of the algorithms it uses, including DES and SHA encryption technologies, VPN concepts and tunneling mechanisms, L2TP and L2F protocols, technology weaknesses, and configuration weaknesses. You'll read about firewall design, packet-filtering routers, application proxy, stateful filtering, the Demilitarized Zone (DMZ), Network Address Translation (NAT), IP spoofing, inbound and outbound access lists, Content-Based Access Control (CBAC), IP Security (IPSec), Authentication Header (RFC 2402), Public Key Technology (PKI), hashing algorithms, digital signatures, MD5 (Message Digest 5), Internet Key Exchange (IKE), Data Encryption Standard (DES), Virtual Private Networks (VPNs), Layer 2 Tunneling Protocol (L2TP), and L2TP Access Concentrator (LAC).

- **Chapter 16, "Voice"**—This chapter reviews the traditional voice environment, addresses the challenges that the design professional faces when engineering voice over data, and addresses QoS for voice and why voice traffic needs guarantees to ensure timely delivery. You'll read about PBX and key systems, designing voice over data networks, analog and digital signaling, tandem switching, Signaling System 7, addressing and dial plans, voice over ATM, VoATM addressing, Voice over Frame Relay, VoIP and delay, the H.323 family, Cisco CallManager version 3.0, QoS for packetized voice, Cisco end-to-end QoS services, traffic engineering, traffic measurement units, and calculating the number of trunks.

Sample test questions and the testing engine on the CD offer simulated exams for final practice.

Each of these chapters uses several features to help you make the best use of your time in that chapter:

- **"Do I Know This Already?" Quiz and Quizlets**—Each chapter begins with a quiz that helps you determine the amount of time you need to spend studying that chapter. The quiz is divided into parts called "quizlets" that correspond to a section of the chapter. If you follow the directions at the beginning of each chapter, the "Do I Know This Already?" quiz will direct you to study all or particular parts of the chapter.

- **Foundation Topics**—This is the core section of each chapter. It explains the protocols, concepts, and configuration for the topics in the chapter.

- **Foundation Summary**—Near the end of each chapter, a summary collects the most important tables and figures from the chapter. The Foundation Summary section is designed to help you review the key concepts in the chapter if you score well on the "Do I Know This Already?" quiz. This section is an excellent tool for last-minute review.

- **Q&A**—These end-of-chapter questions focus on recall, covering topics in the Foundation Topics section by using several types of questions. Because the "Do I Know This Already?" quiz questions can help increase your recall, they are restated in the Q&A section. Restating these questions, along with offering new questions, provides a larger set of practice questions for when you finish a chapter and for final review when your exam date is approaching.

- **Scenarios**—Located at the end of the chapter, the scenarios allow a much more in-depth examination of a network implementation. Rather than posing a simple question asking for a single fact, the scenarios let you design and build networks (at least on paper) without the clues inherent in a multiple-choice quiz format.
- In addition, the companion CD contains a large number of questions not included in the book. You can answer these questions by using the simulated exam feature or by using the topical review feature. This is the best tool for helping you prepare for the test-taking process.

Approach

Retention and recall are the two features of human memory most closely related to performance on tests. This exam preparation guide focuses on increasing both retention and recall of the topics on the exam. The other human characteristic involved in successfully passing the exam is intelligence. This book does not address that issue!

Adult retention is typically less than that of children. For example, it is common for 4-year-olds to pick up basic language skills in a new country faster than their parents. Children retain facts as an end unto itself. Adults typically either need a stronger reason to remember a fact or must have a reason to think about that fact several times to retain it in memory. For these reasons, a person who attends a typical Cisco course and retains 50 percent of the material is actually quite an amazing student.

Memory recall is based on connectors to the information that needs to be recalled. The greater the number of connectors to a piece of information, the better chance and better speed of recall.

Recall and retention work together. If you do not retain the knowledge, it will be difficult to recall it. This book is designed with features that help you increase retention and recall. It does this in the following ways:

- By providing succinct and complete methods of helping you decide what you recall easily and what you do not recall at all.
- By giving references to the exact passages in the book that review the concepts you do not recall so that you can quickly be reminded about a fact or concept. Repeating information that connects to another concept helps retention, and describing the same concept in several ways throughout a chapter increases the number of connectors to the same piece of information.
- By including exercise questions that supply fewer connectors than multiple-choice questions. This helps you exercise recall and avoids giving you a false sense of confidence, as an exercise with only multiple-choice questions might do. For example, fill-in-the-blank questions require you to have better recall than multiple-choice questions.
- Finally, accompanying this book is a CD-ROM that has exam-like multiple-choice questions. These are useful for you to practice taking the exam and to get accustomed to the time restrictions imposed during the exam.

Icons Used in This Book

Command Syntax Conventions

Throughout the book, you will see the following icons used for networking devices:

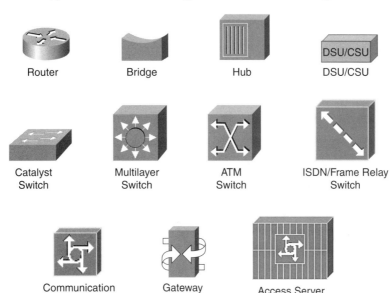

Throughout the book, you will see the following icons used for peripherals and other devices.

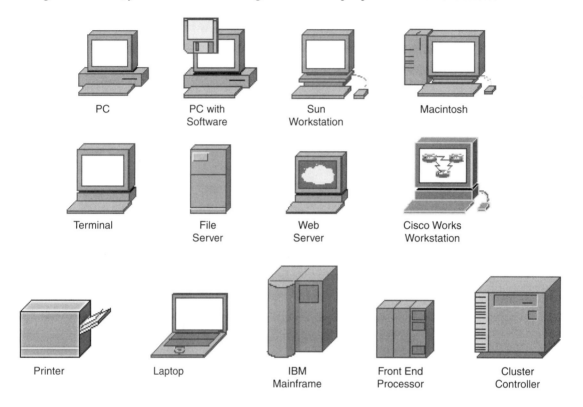

PC

PC with
Software

Sun
Workstation

Macintosh

Terminal

File
Server

Web
Server

Cisco Works
Workstation

Printer

Laptop

IBM
Mainframe

Front End
Processor

Cluster
Controller

Throughout the book, you will see the following icons used for networks and network connections.

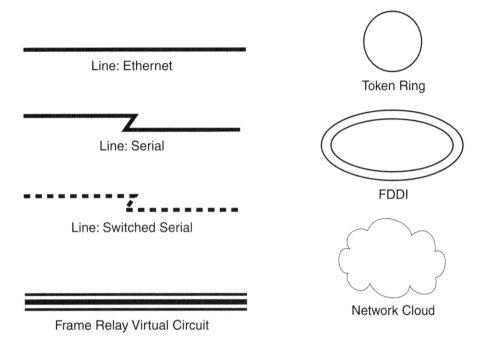

Line: Ethernet

Line: Serial

Line: Switched Serial

Frame Relay Virtual Circuit

Token Ring

FDDI

Network Cloud

The conventions used to present command syntax in this book are the same conventions used in the *IOS Command Reference*. The *Command Reference* describes these conventions as follows:

- Vertical bars (|) separate alternative, mutually exclusive elements.
- Square brackets ([ ]) indicate optional elements.
- Braces ({ }) indicate a required choice.
- Braces within brackets ([{ }]) indicate a required choice within an optional element.
- **Boldface** indicates commands and keywords that are entered literally as shown. In actual configuration examples and output (not general command syntax), boldface indicates commands that are manually input by the user (such as a **show** command).
- *Italics* indicates arguments for which you supply actual values.

This chapter covers the following topics that you will need to master as a CCDP:

- **Internetwork design goals**—This section focuses on design goals and also discusses the recommended steps for designing an internetwork.

- **Design models**—This section discusses campus design models that apply to the CCDP.

Cisco expects the successful CCDP candidate to be able to use the steps recommended in this chapter to incorporate an internetwork design. In addition, the CCDP should be able to integrate Cisco products into the hierarchical model.

CHAPTER 1

Design Overview

How to Best Use This Chapter

By following these steps, you can make better use of your study time:

- Keep your notes and the answers for all your work with this book in one place for easy reference.

- Take the "Do I Know this Already?" quiz, and write down your answers. Studies show that retention is significantly increased through writing down facts and concepts, even if you never look at the information again.

- Use the diagram shown in Figure 1-1 to guide you to the next step.

Figure 1-1   *How to Use This Chapter*

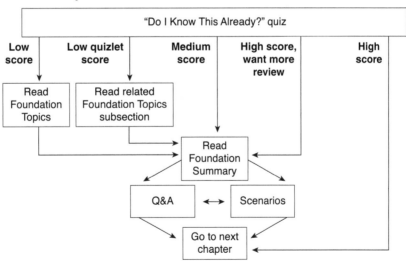

If you skip to the Foundation Summary, Q&A, and Scenarios sections and have trouble with the material there, you should go back to the Foundation Topics section.

"Do I Know This Already?" Quiz

The purpose of the "Do I Know this Already?" quiz is to help you decide which parts of this chapter to use. If you already intend to read the entire chapter, you do not necessarily need to answer these questions now.

This 14-question quiz helps you determine how to spend your limited study time. The quiz is divided into two smaller "quizlets" that help you select the sections of the chapter on which to focus. Figure 1-1 outlines suggestions on how to spend your time in this chapter. Use Table 1-1 to record your score.

Table 1-1 *Score Sheet for Quiz and Quizlets*

Quizlet Number	Foundation Topics Section Covering These Questions	Questions	Score
1	Internetwork design goals	1, 2, 6, 8, 9, 10, 11, 15	
2	Design models	3, 4, 5, 7, 12, 13, 14	

1 What are the goals of an internetwork design?

_____

_____

_____

2 What trade-off is present in every network design?

_____

_____

_____

3 What are the three layers of the hierarchical model?

_____

_____

_____

4 Where should redundancy be prioritized?

_____

_____

_____

5 What layer acts as the intermediate layer in the hierarchical model?

_____

_____

_____

6 True or false: After implementing the network, the CCDP should consider the task complete.

_____

_____

_____

7 What Cisco router is recommended for the Core layer?

_____

_____

_____

8 What is the simplest internetwork design model?

_____

_____

_____

9 What is the most significant cost component of an internetwork over time?

_____

_____

_____

10 Why is protocol selection important with regard to network design?

_____

_____

_____

11 What are the recommended steps for designing an internetwork?

_____

_____

_____

12 What benefits can be gained by using the hierarchical model?

_____

_____

_____

13 Name a Cisco router that can be employed at each layer of the hierarchical model.

_____

_____

_____

14 What layer of the network is primarily concerned with high-speed transport of data?

_____

_____

_____

The answers to the "Do I Know this Already?" quiz are found in Appendix A. The suggested choices for your next step are as follows:

- **6 or fewer overall score**—Read the chapter. This includes the "Foundation Topics," the "Foundation Summary," and the "Q&A" sections, as well as the scenarios at the end of the chapter.

- **2 or less on any "quizlet"**—Review the subsection(s) of the "Foundation Topics" part of this chapter based on Table 4-1. Then move into the "Foundation Summary," the Q&A section, and scenarios at the end of the chapter.

- **7, 8, or 9 overall score**—Begin with the "Foundation Summary" section and then go to the Q&A section and scenarios at the end of the chapter.

- **10 or more overall score**—If you want more review on these topics, skip to the "Foundation Summary" section, then go to the Q&A section and scenarios at the end of the chapter. Otherwise, move on to the next chapter.

Foundation Topics

Designing an internetwork requires a certain mix of art and science. Design purists can spend hours debating the merits of one design versus another, but in the real world, issues of self-interest, background, pride, politics, and personal ego sometimes play a role in the acceptance of the design process.

For test purposes, the CCDP candidate need only be concerned with matching the business and technical requirements to the engineering, availability, time, and cost constraints. The successful network design marries the best technical solution with the needs of the business.

With the advent of e-commerce and e-business, companies face increasingly complex challenges to deliver profit to the shareholders and value to the customers. Their requirements for network performance are becoming more and more demanding. Add those requirements to the changing technical issues of the day, and it is easy to see why the task of CCDP is a very demanding professional assignment. In addition to having a strong technical foundation, the CCDP must articulate technical ideas to a primarily nontechnical audience. The CCDP must display a great deal of versatility. Indeed, through the life cycle of a network design, the CCDP can expect to serve in the role of project manager, consultant, integrator, technical liaison, troubleshooter, and problem solver.

Defining the Problem

A design cannot provide an effective solution to a problem that has not been defined. The CCDP who attempts to design a network before the problem is understood will be as successful as a painter who attempts to paint a moving bus. The design will never satisfy the customer, because there is no general agreement on what was needed in the first place.

NOTE   No problem—no solution!

Know problem—know solution!

The CCDP's first mission is to define the problem. All design requests start with a problem as perceived by someone.

After the problem has been defined, the business requirements must be stated and needs must be prioritized. Then a technical solution can be implemented. A good network design is optimized to meet the requirements of the business at hand. Therefore, a design that is ideal for one business might be woefully lacking for another. One business might have higher security concerns, and another business might be more concerned about disaster recovery. Still another business might share these concerns but might not have the available funds to implement those features. For each client, there is an optimum design that provides a best-fit solution for his or her situation and circumstances.

Internetwork Design Goals

Designing an internetwork can be a challenging task. Despite improvements in equipment performance and media capabilities, internetwork design is becoming more difficult. The trend is toward increasingly complex environments involving multimedia, multiple protocols, and interconnections to networks beyond an organization's domain of control. To render a successful design, the CCDP must realize stated objectives while designing the internetwork.

Here are the goals of internetwork design:

- Functionality
- Scalability
- Adaptability
- Manageability
- Cost-effectiveness

The CCDP should realize that these goals are interrelated and must strike a balance to ensure an optimum design. As an example of the balance that is needed, let's look at the relationship between the goals of network design. Of course, it would be desirable to have adaptability and scalability incorporated into the network design. However, if an abundance of adaptability and scalability exists, the design might be very expensive and might compromise the goal of rendering a cost-effective solution.

The foremost goal of an internetwork design is a working system that meets a client's business and technical objectives. Of all the goals listed, there can be no flexibility on this one. The design's success will ultimately be measured by whether the network works. The design should ensure adaptability and compatibility between old and new technologies. The design should allow scalability and flexibility as the client's business and technical requirements change. Although the design should be efficient, it should also be predictable enough to allow others to manage and troubleshoot. Even though the CCDP will understandably want to display brilliance when designing the network, it is important to keep in mind that the network design must be straightforward enough for other network personnel to grasp its concepts.

Of all the goals listed, the one the other goals must be compared is cost. The CCDP must always strike a balance with the other goals in regard to cost. In a perfect world, network design would allow each user to have voice, video, and data on the desktop. Companies, which have profit as one of their business requirements, would not want to use the fastest technology available if the price was unreasonable. The CCDP must be careful to consider cost as the most important metric. An extravagant design might look good on the dream board but, when implemented, would be wasteful and could represent a stranded investment.

If the design meets the criteria for functionality, scalability, and technological advancement while satisfying the all-important metric of cost, the design should be considered a success.

Seven Steps for Designing Internetworks

Figure 1-2 shows a recommended methodology for designing a network. The first three steps should remain static, but the remaining steps will require revisions as dictated by the business's changing needs and requirements.

The following steps are recommended for designing internetworks:

1 Gather information

2 Analyze requirements

3 Develop the internetwork structure

4 Estimate network performance

5 Assess costs and risks

6 Implement and monitor the network

Figure 1-2   *Design Methodology*

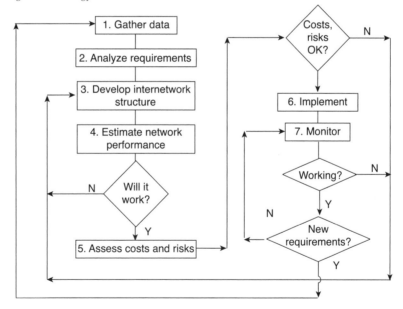

Gather Information

The first step in network design should involve data gathering. Learn about the corporate structure. Find out what applications are being used and what plans exist in the future for change. Obtain a baseline of current network performance. Determine who will play a key role in the decision-making process. Find out how the customer assigns authority with regard to information resources. Do your best to understand the customer and their needs.

NOTE   The best source of information about performance requirements is the people who use the system. Be sure to include user groups to ensure that no one is left out of the design process.

Analyze Requirements

Determine the customer's business requirements. As soon as you understand the business goals, you can determine the type of technology that is needed. Determine the network availability requirements and the acceptable mean time between failures. Each customer will have a different definition of availability. Adding more resources can increase availability. However, resources increase cost. At some point, greater availability yields a lower output because of the increased cost of providing it. Internetwork design provides the greatest availability for the least cost.

Other requirements include the following:

- **Security**—Determine the amount of security that this design requires.

- **Disaster recovery**

- **Application characteristics**—Determine the types of applications that the network will serve:

    — Which ones are bandwidth-intensive, and how much bandwidth do they require?

    — Do any applications require multicasting?

- **Users**—Determine the number of users who will access the network.

    — Which customers have special needs?

    — What are the peak times for network usage and its load?

NOTE   Be aware of the corporate culture and how it impacts the decision-making process. The best-planned network design might not be accepted if the president's uncle is in the network business and has different ideas.

Develop the Internetwork Structure

This stage of design lays out the internetwork's overall topology and structure. At this stage, the CCDP does the following:

- Designs the internetwork topology
- Chooses the internetwork technology
- Chooses a network management strategy

The hierarchical model, which is discussed later in this chapter, is the recommended choice for building a scalable internetwork. This model can demystify a complex network.

You should determine the network's protocols and addressing conventions during this step. Each protocol has different advantages and disadvantages. It might not be obvious which protocol is best. Although TCP/IP might be an easy selection because of its universal acceptance, the choice of a routing protocol, such as EIGRP or OSPF, might take more consideration. Addressing and naming should be planned in advance. You should choose names that add value to the network's design. You should choose addresses that properly subdivide network traffic flow and allow for routing summarization.

You should provision resources with regard to hardware, host servers, LAN resources, and WAN resources. For example, a typical hierarchical design might use a Cisco 7200 router to handle the heaviest traffic requirements at the core, a Cisco 3600 router to handle the medium traffic requirements at the distribution layer, and a Cisco 2500 router to handle the lightest loads at the access layer. At this stage, the CCDP should have a reasonably good idea about where the greatest and least amount of traffic will be generated throughout the network.

Estimate Network Performance

Determining the amount of traffic load in a network is vital to ensuring network performance. Use network simulation and modeling tools to determine the estimated network performance. Estimate the performance of the internetworking device. Determine what devices could cause latency in an internetwork. You can use a sniffer to monitor the actual network traffic information. You can obtain trend information by observing the data from day to day.

Network monitoring tools let you monitor, analyze, manage, and forecast network performance.

By gathering and aggregating performance data from routers, WAN links, and network devices, network monitoring tools can help users benchmark network behavior, efficiently and easily isolate and resolve bottlenecks, verify carrier compliance with established service-level agreements (SLAs), and minimize WAN costs while improving overall performance.

Assess Costs and Risks

There is a natural trade-off between cost and availability. A good design can create availability but can cost extra money. Over time, internetwork support is the most significant cost component in an internetwork. The next-biggest costs are the wide-area network links. An ideal assessment of the risks involved should result in a cost-effective network. When you assess the risks, the network's benefits must be greater than the costs.

Implement and Monitor

Implement the design in phased increments. If possible, test the design in a lab environment before rollout. As the design is implemented, verify and validate each phase of the rollout. After implementing, monitor the network.

Monitoring is listed as the last phase, but it can also be viewed as the first phase in managing the network's ongoing changes. In the context of this step, consider the following actions:

- Using network management tools for monitoring

- Performing proactive data gathering

- Knowing when to scale the network to meet new demands

    — Upgrading hardware

    — Adding faster circuit speeds

Use network management tools and protocol analyzers to maintain a snapshot of the network. Monitor traffic patterns at determined intervals. One thing is certain: Change is inevitable. Network applications will continue to demand more bandwidth. It is essential that the CCDP measure the network under normal conditions to determine how to plan for changes in network capacity. You should monitor the network for growth before the network slows to a crawl.

Network management applications that use Simple Network Management Protocol (SNMP) provide a useful array of tools to control internetwork support costs:

- Cisco **debug** and **show** commands

- Syslog

- Protocol analyzers

- DNS

- TFTP and FTP

- DHCP and BOOTP

- Telnet

- TACACS

- Cisco Works (router configuration management and network analysis)

Cost Versus Availability

Internetwork costs fall into two general categories:

- One-time fixed costs

- Recurring costs

Fixed costs are equipment purchases, such as hardware and software network management tools. Recurring costs are the monthly circuit fees from the service provider. The ongoing salaries of the information technology personnel who support and maintain the network must be considered a recurring cost.

A well-designed internetwork can help balance the issues of cost and availability. The best design optimizes application availability while maximizing the cost-effective use of network resources. The goal is to minimize cost based on these elements while delivering service that does not compromise established availability requirements. These design factors will always be at odds. When used at its maximum, each becomes a trade-off of the other. Any increase in availability must generally be reflected as an increase in cost. As a result, the CCDP must carefully weigh the relative importance of resource availability and overall cost.

TIP   Communicate, communicate, communicate! Keep everyone who needs to know informed about the status of the design project. When the lines of communication are open, a customer is more likely to be supportive of an idea or concept that might be difficult to embrace.

Concerns Facing Designers

An effective design must ensure that network processes continue to run smoothly in the event of a natural or human-caused disaster. An effective design should include a disaster recovery plan that covers both the hardware and software required to run critical business applications. To design successfully, first assess the mission-critical business processes and associated applications. The following sections discuss issues related to disaster recovery.

Disaster Recovery

The CCDP should be concerned with ensuring that the network is available to the users. The issue of availability must be measured against the issue of cost. If you could make a network completely fault-tolerant, this could be done only at a cost that most businesses would consider unacceptable. Beware of designing redundancy just for the sake of redundancy. Duplicating a component that has a very low likelihood of failure could represent a stranded environment. The CCDP must determine the appropriate amount of cost-effective fault tolerance to be included in a network.

Fire, storms, floods, earthquakes, chemical accidents, and an airplane crash (loss of key staff) are just a few examples of disasters that can happen that are external to the network that can impact business.

Establish Priorities for Your Network and Applications

Identify the important business processes, and assign each one a priority. Priorities can be based on the following levels:

- **Mission-critical**—A network or application outage or destruction that would cause an extreme disruption to the business, cause major legal or financial ramifications, or threaten someone's health and safety. The targeted system or data requires significant effort to restore, or the restoration process is disruptive to the business or other systems.

- **Important**—A network or application outage or destruction that would cause a moderate disruption to the business, cause minor legal or financial ramifications, or cause problems with access to other systems. The targeted system or data requires a moderate effort to restore, or the restoration process is disruptive to the system.

- **Minor**—A network or application outage or destruction that would cause a minor disruption to the business. The targeted systems or network can easily be restored.

Assess Network Resiliency

Assess the resiliency of the network with regard to the following three levels of availability: reliable networks, high-availability networks, and nonstop networks. Doing so helps you prioritize risks, set requirements for higher levels of availability, and identify the mission-critical elements of your network.

Be sure to evaluate the following areas of the network:

- Network links

    — Carrier diversity

    — Local loop diversity

    — Facilities resiliency

    — Building wiring resiliency

Resiliency and backup services form a key part of disaster recovery. Resiliency can be defined as the ability to recover from a network failure or issue, whether it is related to a disaster, link, hardware, design, or network services. Diversity relates to having alternative choices in the event that the primary source is unable to render the desired service.

- Hardware resiliency

  — Power, security, and disaster

  — Redundant hardware

  — Mean time before replacement (MTTR)

  — Network path availability via multiple hardware devices

Redundant Power Systems

Power faults occur from time to time. Redundant power supplies connected to different power sources can prevent some power failures. A site could connect one power system to the local power grid and another to an uninterruptible power supply.

If the router power supply fails, the router cannot continue to provide connectivity to each connected network.

For organizations that have the greatest need for availability, providing a duplicate corporate data center can protect the company from potential power failures. Organizations could locate a redundant data center in another city, or in a part of the same city that is at some distance from the primary data center. All back-end services can be duplicated, and transactions coming in from remote offices can be sent to both data centers. This configuration would require duplicate WAN links from all remote offices, duplicate network hardware, duplicate servers and server resources, and leasing another building. Because this approach is so costly, it is typically the last step taken by companies that want the ultimate in fault tolerance.

To render this design more cost-effective, partial duplication of the data center might be an attractive alternate design. Instead of full duplication, you could duplicate several selected critical servers and links to those servers.

Fault-Tolerant Media Implementations

Media failure can cause the network to fail. Included in this category are all problems associated with the medium and its link to each individual end station. Under this classification, media components might include network interface controller failures, lobe or attachment unit interface (AUI) cable failures, transceiver failures, hub failures, and all failures associated with media components such as the cable or terminating devices.

One way to reduce the confusion caused by failed media is to segment existing media and support each segment with different hardware. If 100 stations are attached to a single switch, some of the stations can be moved to other switches. This reduces the effect of a hub failure and some subnetwork failures. If a router is placed between segments, the CCDP can protect against additional problems and cut subnetwork traffic. NICs, hub ports, and interface cables can be redundant.

This approach doubles the cost of network connectivity for each end station as well as the port usage on all internetworking devices and is therefore recommended only in situations in which complete redundancy is required. It also assumes that end-station software, including both the network and the application subsystems, can handle and effectively use the redundant components. The application software or the networking software or both must be able to detect network failures and initiate the use of the other network. Hot Standby Router Protocol (HSRP) is an example of an application that can detect a router failure. For IP, HSRP allows one router to automatically assume the function of the second router if the second router fails.

Certain media access protocols have some fault-tolerant features built in. Token Ring multistation access units (MAUs) can detect certain media connection failures and bypass the failure internally. FDDI dual rings can wrap traffic onto the backup ring to avoid portions of the network that have problems.

From a router's standpoint, many media failures can be bypassed as long as alternative paths are available. Using various hardware detection techniques, routers can sense certain media-level problems. If routing updates or routing keepalive messages have not been received from devices that would normally be reached through a particular router port, the router will soon declare that route down and will look for alternate routes. Meshed networks provide these alternate paths, allowing the router to compensate for media failures.

NOTE   Everything has a price! At some point, a network that is designed for maximum redundancy will exceed a company's capacity to stay within budget. The key is striking a happy medium between cost and disaster protection.

Backup Hardware

Like all complex devices, routers, switches, and other internetworking devices can develop problems. When catastrophic failures occur, the use of dual devices can effectively reduce the adverse effects of a show-stopping hardware failure. After a failure, discovery protocols help end stations choose new paths with which to communicate across the network. If each network connected to the failed device has an alternative path out of the local area, complete connectivity is still possible.

When backup routers are used, routing metrics can be set to ensure that the backup routers will not be used unless the primary routers are not functioning.

Controlling Broadcasts

Broadcasts serve a necessary function in network communications. All stations listen and accept broadcasts. As long as the amount of broadcast traffic remains low, they do not negatively impact the network. Desktop protocols, which are discussed in detail later, typically use broadcasts to launch services and find neighbors. These protocols can produce an excessive number of broadcasts. When stations spend too much time processing broadcasts and a significant amount of network bandwidth is devoted to processing broadcasts, the network can become inefficient. The CCDP must ensure that broadcasts do not impede the transmission of vital data.

Strategic Internetwork Design

Strategic internetwork design is also called *macro internetwork design.*

Macro internetwork design includes the following:

- Capacity planning
- Overall internetwork topology
- Budget
- Network applications requirements
- Network management
- Policy decisions
- Planning for
    - Growth
    - Change
    - Disaster
    - Phased implementation
- Choosing vendors and platforms

Design Models

Several design models have been proven to work when implemented properly. The following paragraphs discuss the campus LAN design models that are recommended by Cisco.

The Flat Earth Model

The flat earth model is the simplest model and is easy to explain. Everyone is connected to a Layer 2 device. In the early days, the flat earth model consisted of hubs and repeaters. Today's flat earth model can consist of bridges and switches. One feature, though, has not changed: The network remains one large broadcast domain, so it has no protection from broadcasts that run amok.

The CCDP would consider the flat earth model for only the smallest and least-complicated network scenario. For example, when designing for a Home Area Network (HAN), the flat earth model could work. In fact, the flat earth model design (three computers and a hub) works well for me at home. For other networks that require scalability and adaptability, the flat earth model is not a wise choice. The flat earth model should not be used for networks that have more than 50 nodes. Figure 1-3 depicts the flat earth design model.

Figure 1-3   *Flat Earth Design Model*

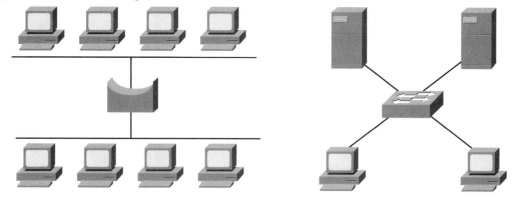

The Star and Ring Models

The star model, shown in Figure 1-4, represents an uncomplicated design concept. A single router, which is typically located at the company's central point of focus, the headquarters, interconnects the other locations. Although the star model achieves the goal of a cost-effective working network and is relatively easy to administer and troubleshoot, it fails the goals of scalability and adaptability and offers little relief in the area of disaster recovery. This model could be a good fit for a small business with limited capital that is willing to assume single-point-of-failure risks.

Figure 1-4   *Star Model*

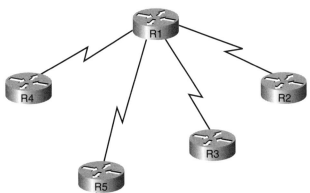

The ring model, shown in Figure 1-5, is the successor to the star model. It offers redundancy and multiple paths to protect the WAN from a single point of failure. As a small business begins to grow and becomes more concerned about protecting its network investments, it might want to spend the extra money for the protection that a ring model provides. The features and benefits of this model can be realized on a wide-area network.

Figure 1-5   *Ring Model*

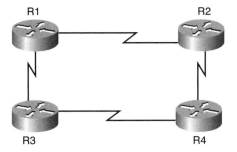

The star and ring models have serious limitations when addressing the issues of scalability and adaptability. With a large network, it is easy to see why the star model is undesirable. First, the core router represents a single point of failure. Second, the core router limits overall performance for access to backbone resources because it is a single pipe through which all traffic intended for the backbone must pass. Finally, the port density limitations of the star router restrict its scalability. The CCDP would not utilize these models in a large network environment.

The Two-Tier Model

The two-tier model, shown in Figure 1-6, builds on the star model design and is beneficial in certain settings. It allows two sites to serve as primary feeds to the remote branches. The primary sites are also connected to each other. This solution can be effective for an organization that has a limited budget but that still wants connectivity between its units.

Figure 1-6 *Two-Tier Model*

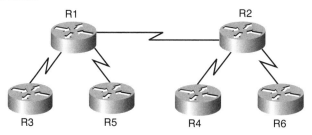

The Mesh Network

A mesh network exists in two flavors: partial mesh and full mesh. A full mesh provides full connectivity between all systems on a WAN, and a partial mesh provides full connectivity for some, but not all, devices connected to the WAN.

Although the full-mesh design represents the ideal solution with regard to scalability and adaptability, it might cost too much to implement for a network that has many nodes. In an ideal scenario, in which each device has unlimited capacity and cost is not an issue, everything could be connected to everything.

Full mesh is a design concept that requires every device to have connectivity to every other device (see Figure 1-7). Although the full-mesh design might be ideal for connecting two or three devices in a small environment, it is not cost-effective to design large networks that require all routers to behave as peers. As the number of links increases, the number of subnets and routing peers also grows, and the complexity increases. The disadvantages of the full-mesh topology revolve around two issues: cost and quantity. If the routers are far apart, the link costs can quickly become prohibitively expensive because adding routers creates a geometric explosion in links required. Also, the routers have a finite number of ports. When the number of links surpasses a certain number, the routers will not have enough ports to support this topology.

Figure 1-7   *Full-Mesh Design*

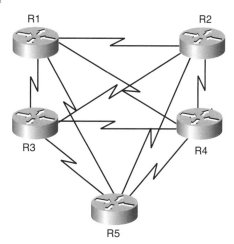

The number of links required for connectivity in a full mesh can be calculated using the following formula, where *n* equals the number of routers:

$$[n(n-1)/2]$$

Under a full-mesh design, if there were 20 sites, 190 links would be required.

NOTE   As the number of sites increases, the issues of management and administration increase as well. For a large site, a full mesh could easily become an administrative *full mess!*

The partial-mesh design, shown in Figure 1-8, appears to strike the balance among scalability, adaptability, and cost. The CCDP can designate certain sites to be hubs and less-critical sites to be spokes. There are no hard requirements as to which sites must be hubs and which must be spokes. Likewise, there are no requirements as to the absolute number of sites. Therefore, the design can easily adapt to any cost constraints.

Figure 1-8 *Partial-Mesh Layer*

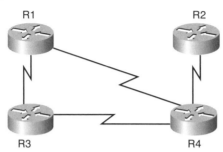

Hierarchical Design

In a real-world environment, the hierarchical design of core, distribution, and access represents the practical approach to network design. Hierarchical design, which is also referred to as the multilayered approach, makes operational management, network upgrades, and troubleshooting more simple. Upgrades are simpler and cost-effective because the hierarchical design allows for a phased-in approach. In order to upgrade one device in a WAN link from a full-mesh design, all the other modules must be upgraded at the same time where they mesh. Therefore, upgrades and changes are required everywhere. Troubleshooting is simpler because each layer can isolate the problems encountered.

If the right network design approach is followed, performance and reliability are easy to achieve. Other network design approaches can result in a network with lower performance, reliability, and manageability. With so many features available, and with so many choices and combinations possible, it is easy to go astray. For example, deploying a Cisco 7206 at the core working in tandem with a Cisco 4500 at the distribution layer and a Cisco 2500 at the access layer would offer maximum scalability and performance but would be impractical for a remote office with 25 users. The CCDP should take a commonsense approach to multilayered network design that will result in simple, reliable, and manageable networks.

Some benefits of a hierarchical model include the following:

- Scalability

- Ease of troubleshooting

- Protocol support

- Manageability

The three hierarchical layers are

- Core

- Distribution

- Access

These are discussed in detail in the following sections.

The Core Layer

The core layer, shown in Figure 1-9, is a high-speed switching backbone and should be designed to switch packets as fast as possible. The core layer should provide high-speed, robust connectivity among remote sites. The core layer can be likened to an interstate highway that allows traffic to flow between major arteries. A telecom service provider usually provides services at the core layer. Like an interstate highway, the core should be designed to provide optimized transport. In addition, the core should be designed for availability and reliability. To ensure reliability, the core layer should have fault tolerance. Because this layer must have low latency, it does not filter packets, which would slow down throughput.

Figure 1-9   *Core Layer*

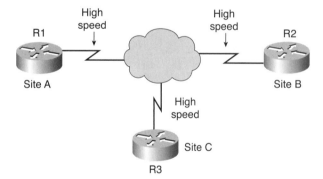

The Distribution Layer

The distribution layer of the network, shown in Figure 1-10, is the midpoint between the access and core layers. The purpose of this layer is to provide boundary definition between the core and the access layers, and it is the place where packets can be filtered. The distribution layer can be a point for redistribution of routing protocols. It can be the first point of entry for a remote site into the corporate network. It can also provide connectivity based on policy.

Figure 1-10 *Distribution Layer*

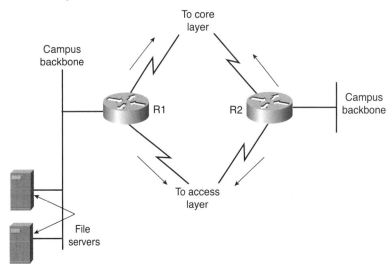

The distribution layer connects networks that can also connect access layer networks that are located in the same corporate/campus network. The distribution layer can be compared to a boulevard or thoroughfare that provides a link to the existing infrastructure. Implement policy at the distribution layer.

The following issues might be determined by the network administrator and controlled at the distribution layer:

- Access to parts of the internetwork
- Access to services on the internetwork
- Definition of path metrics

Security is an example of policy that should be defined at the distribution layer. Cisco IOS features implement security by:

- Filtering by source or destination address
- Filtering on input or output ports
- IP accounting
- SNMP traps
- Hiding internal network numbers by route filtering
- Static routing

The Access Layer

The access layer, shown in Figure 1-11, is the point at which local end users are allowed into the network. This layer may also use access lists or filters to further optimize the needs of a particular set of users. The access layer connects a group of LANs and workstations. The access layer can be compared to a road or street on which houses reside. The access layer allows for network segmentation based on logical needs, and it isolates broadcast traffic between workgroups and LANs. User traffic and services should be connected at the access layer.

Figure 1-11 *Access Layer*

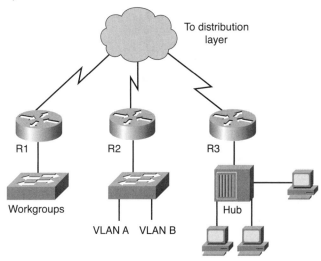

Access router functions include the following:

- Extended media filtering
- Segmentation into networks or subnetworks
- Proxy services
- Naming services
- Broadcast forwarding
- Router discovery and hot standby
- Connectivity on demand
- Connection to multicast networks

Other Design Models

Depending on the business requirements, all three tiers might not be required. Small and medium businesses might be able to use models that implement only one or two tiers of the hierarchical model.

NOTE   When using the one- or two-tier model, be sure to incorporate scalability and adaptability for network expansion. As the business grows, the three-tier design might be required in the future.

One-Tier

In a one-tier design, the router operates at the core layer, providing connectivity between the users and the WAN. Routers connected to the core in the one-tier model are typically the same routers that might be used at the access layer of the hierarchical model. For a low-speed WAN backbone, slow performance can be a factor. Use available features on the Cisco router to improve WAN performance and utilization:

- Header, link, and payload compression

- Priority queuing and bandwidth reservation

- Proxy services between the router and clients

- Encapsulation and tunneling across the WAN core

Figure 1-12 shows examples of the one- and two-tier models.

Figure 1-12   *One- and Two-Tier Models*

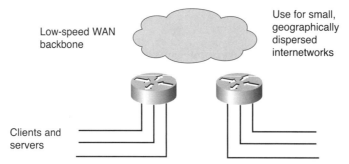

Low-speed WAN backbone

Use for small, geographically dispersed internetworks

Clients and servers

Two-Tier

In a two-tier design, core routers provide access to the WAN, and access routers give client LANs access to corporate resources. Core routers use features that take advantage of expensive WAN resources.

Redundant Two-Tier

The core LAN backbone is duplicated with total redundancy. This model provides cost-effective LAN redundancy. Figure 1-13 shows the redundant two-tier model.

Figure 1-13   *Redundant Two-Tier Model*

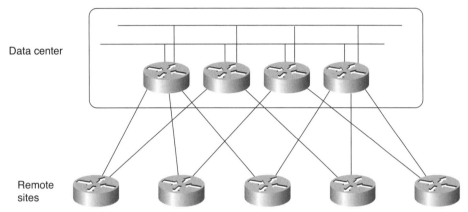

Use for cost-effective LAN redundancy

Routers at Different Layers

The CCDP should know where the router is located in the hierarchy and what the key needs are for a given layer so that the router can be configured to meet the layer's specific needs. Routers at a given layer have dedicated purposes. Router features should be comparable at each layer:

- Core routers must be reliable because they carry information about all the routes in an internetwork. If one of these routers goes down, it affects routing on a larger scale than when an access router goes down.

- Distribution routers need to be able to select the best path to different locations to make efficient use of bandwidth.

- Access routers are typically where you provide security and filtering. Access routers reduce the amount of overhead by keeping unnecessary traffic out of the network's core.

Here are some examples of Cisco routers that can be used at each layer of the hierarchy:

- **Core**—Cisco 7000 and 12000 series routers

- **Distribution**—Cisco 4000 series routers

- **Access**—Cisco 1000 and 2500 series routers

Figure 1-14 shows the three-tier model.

Figure 1-14 *Three-Tier Model*

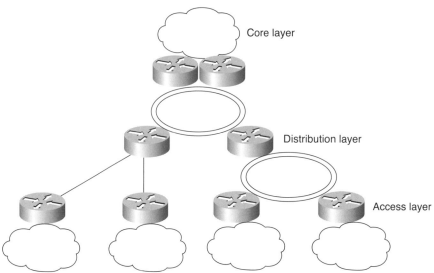

Remote Access

With the booming popularity of the Internet, telecommunications, e-commerce, and centralized data farms, the wide-area network is replacing the local-area network as the first point of access. On many corporate networks, a user will soon be more likely to access a file from a centrally located remote server via the WAN as a first choice. Almost every PC now has wide-area access through dialup. DSL allows remote access via the existing LAN card. In addition, the ranks of telecommuters and mobile users are growing every day, and they expect to use the same multimedia applications at home and on the road.

To reduce costs and to ease management and administrative burdens, networks are beginning to consolidate their servers. Before long, the majority of traffic from the client networks is expected to travel across the WAN backbone. The majority of the traffic will flow between subnets. These new traffic patterns mean that Layer 3 devices will handle more and more traffic. High-speed switches that can handle Layer 3 and Layer 4 requirements will be needed to handle the new remote access requirements.

NOTE   In the 21st century, most network data will be accessed via the WAN. The CCDP should expect at least 80 percent of the traffic to travel out of the local network.

Static and Snapshot Routing for Remote Access

Conserving bandwidth is a way to make the design more efficient.

Routing protocols consume bandwidth for overhead and service advertisements.

Static routes can be used across the WAN to conserve bandwidth. Snapshot routing allows peer routers to exchange routing information upon initial connection, and then only after specified intervals.

Getting Information About Network Design

Cisco provides information on the Cisco Connection documentation CD and at http://www.cisco.com/univercd/home/home.htm. The Web site is updated regularly.

A huge amount of current data can be accessed. Here is some of the information that can be found:

- The documentation set for the Cisco Internetwork Operating System software
- The Internetwork Design Guide
- Internetworking case studies
- New product information
- Technical tips
- Software images
- Installation help
- Service and support

Foundation Summary

This section is a collection of tables and figures that provide a convenient review of many key concepts in this chapter. If you are already comfortable with the topics in this chapter, this summary might help you recall a few details. If you have just read this chapter, this review should help solidify some key facts. If you are doing your final preparation before the exam, these tables and figures are a convenient way to review the day before the exam.

Every network design should anticipate growth and change. The best-managed scalable internetworks are typically designed following the recommended design steps and using one of the models recommended by Cisco (see Table 1-2). The hierarchical model (see Tables 1-3 and 1-4) has been successful because it can be applied to any network. For small networks, a tier or two can be omitted without compromising the model's design goals.

Here are the steps for designing internetworking solutions:

1 Gather information.

2 Analyze requirements.

3 Develop the internetwork structure.

4 Estimate network performance.

5 Assess costs and risks.

6 Implement the network.

7 Monitor the network.

Table 1-2 *Design Models*

Design Models	Advantages	Disadvantages
Flat earth	Inexpensive and easy to set up	Network does not regulate or control broadcasts.
		Network performance is impacted.
		Scalability is limited by the number of broadcasts. Is not scalable for medium to large networks.
Star	Easy setup and administration	Allows for a single point of failure.
		Does not scale for medium to large networks.
Ring	Network does not have a single point of failure.	Higher cost
	Allows for limited scalability (more than star).	

Table 1-2   *Design Models (Continued)*

Design Models	Advantages	Disadvantages
Full mesh	Maximum scalability	Higher cost
	Maximum adaptability	As the network grows, administration requirements increase significantly.
	Redundancy	
Partial mesh	An effective solution, striking a balance between scalability, adaptability, and cost	Some circuits might not be protected with redundancy.
Three-tier model	Scalability	Model might be too costly for a small network.
	Ease of troubleshooting	
	Ease of administration and management	

Table 1-3   *Hierarchical Model*

Hierarchical Model Layer	Functions
Core	High-speed transport layer between geographically remote sites
Distribution	Connects multiple networks within a network environment.
	Establishes route filtering, route summarization, and network policy.
	Provides network naming and numbering conventions.
	Provides network security.
Access	Connects a LAN or a group of LANs. Gives users access to network services.
	Provides network segmentations.
	Isolates broadcast traffic.
	Distributes services.

Table 1-4   *Recommended Equipment for Hierarchical Design*

Layer	Recommended Equipment
Core	Cisco 7000, 12000 series
Distribution	Cisco 3600, 4000, 5000 series
Access	Cisco 1000, 1600, 2500 series

Q&A

The questions and scenarios in this book are more difficult than what you will experience on the actual exam. The questions do not attempt to cover more breadth or depth than the exam; however, they are designed to make sure that you know the answer. Rather than allowing you to derive the answer from clues hidden inside the question, the questions challenge your understanding and recall of the subject. Questions from the "Do I Know this Already?" quiz from the beginning of the chapter are repeated here to ensure that you have mastered this chapter's topic areas. Hopefully, these questions will help limit the number of exam questions on which you narrow your choices to two options and then guess. Be sure to use the CD and take the simulated exams.

The answers to these questions can be found in Appendix A.

1 What are the goals of an internetwork design?

_____

_____

_____

2 What are the seven steps for designing an internetwork?

_____

_____

_____

3 What trade-off is present in every network design?

_____

_____

_____

4 What are the three layers of the hierarchical model?

_____

_____

_____

5 What benefits can be gained by using the hierarchical model?

_____

_____

_____

6 Name two methods of redundancy that are available to the CCDP.

_____

_____

_____

7 Where should redundancy be prioritized?

_____

_____

_____

8 Name a Cisco router that can be employed at each layer of the hierarchical model.

_____

_____

_____

9 Explain the processes involved in gathering information.

_____

_____

_____

10 What layer acts as the intermediate layer in the hierarchical model?

_____

_____

_____

11 What tools can be used to estimate network performance?

_____

_____

_____

12 What are two methods of reducing bandwidth on a remote access link?

_____

_____

_____

13   True or false: After implementing the network, the CCDP should consider the task
complete.

_____

_____

_____

14   Why is a partial mesh more cost-effective than a full-mesh design?

_____

_____

_____

15   What layer of the network is primarily concerned with high-speed transport of data?

_____

_____

_____

16   How have the latest technology advances changed the 80/20 rule?

_____

_____

_____

17   At what step of designing the internetwork should a protocol be selected?

_____

_____

_____

18   What Cisco router is recommended for the Core layer?

_____

_____

_____

19   List five elements of strategic internetwork design.

_____

_____

_____

20 What is the simplest internetwork design model?

_____

_____

_____

21 Where can information on network design be found?

_____

_____

_____

22 True or false: To save the customer money, an immediate cutover is recommended as the first option of implementation.

_____

_____

_____

23 What is the most significant cost component of an internetwork over time?

_____

_____

_____

24 What area of the network usually is the most dominant cause of latency in the wide-area network? What area usually contributes the least?

_____

_____

_____

25 When provisioning hardware, what do you need to consider in addition to node capacity?

_____

_____

_____

26 Why is protocol selection important with regard to network design?

_____

_____

_____

27 What is typically the largest cost not related to support?

_____

_____

_____

28 Your design will require compression, congestion, control, and security. At what layer should this be implemented?

_____

_____

_____

29 Why has the hierarchical layer been a successful factor in network design?

_____

_____

_____

30 What Cisco IOS features can improve WAN utilization and performance?

_____

_____

_____

Scenarios

Scenario 1

Each chapter presents challenges to your internetwork design skills. At its simplest level, the internetwork must provide functionality so that the desired applications and resources of each network are available to the users and machines connected to the other networks. The internetwork will very likely include some or all of the following three components:

- Campus networks, which consist of multiple interconnected local-area networks (LANs), where users in a building or group of buildings have a network connection with each other

- Wide-area networks (WANs), which connect campuses

- Remote connections, which link branch offices and single users (mobile users and telecommuters) to a local campus or the Internet

To help design the optimum solution and address the issues presented in each chapter, you have contracted with the design professionals at RouteitRight to help you.

RouteitRight provides internetworking design solutions to small businesses and corporate clients. For more than 20 years, RouteitRight has been recognized as being at the vanguard of internetwork design solutions.

RouteitRight's key personnel are as follows:

Chief Executive Officer (CEO)	Billy Broadcast
Chief Information Officer (CIO)	Megg A. Bight
Senior Telecommunications Engineer	Peter Packett
Director of Sales	Freddy Forklift
Information Systems Manager	Harry Helpnot
Help Desk Manager	Millie Sekkons
Network Specialist	Roddy Routebegone

A team of RouteitRight professionals is looking at the existing network at radio station WSOL. WSOL would like to discuss faster network performance for its support branches and believes that it might be time to upgrade the existing network infrastructure. WSOL currently has a wide-area topology that resembles the star model, connecting its headquarters to its two satellite branches.

The folks at RouteitRight are having a discussion about the WSOL network. Billy had a meeting with the CEO of WSOL to determine some business requirements. He knows that they need a high-speed line for some killer apps that they presently have and that WSOL has plans for additional applications. He has spoken to the CEO of WSOL, who indicated a preference for the type of desktop video that is equal to or better than what is being used by radio station WBIG, a competitor, which currently has the number-one audience in the city. WSOL's CEO also wants a network that is stable and scalable, in addition to being compatible with its current network applications. Freddy, director of sales, recommends the hierarchical model. He says that this model will solve just about any problem. Megg thinks the team should take a closer look at the business requirements before making a technical recommendation. Millie recommends that the network have lots of bandwidth to satisfy the users' desktop application requirements.

1   What business issues at WSOL are relevant to this network design?

2   What customer and technical requirements need to be obtained from WSOL?

3   What performance and application requirements need to be obtained from WSOL?

4   What network management issues need to be addressed?

5   What security concerns need to be addressed?

Scenario 2

WSOL has just purchased four other radio stations to create a regional radio conglomerate called Radio 1000:

WSOL headquarters, New York
Satellite branch, Manhattan
Satellite branch, Queens
WLAN (purchase 1), Boston
WNET (purchase 2), Baltimore
WCAP (purchase 3), Washington
WGAS (purchase 4), Atlanta

WSOL wants to establish full connectivity between all sites. WSOL would like one site to be able to back up the main site in the event of equipment failure. WSOL requires that the submitted design be scalable, because it expects to purchase additional stations in the future as soon as Congress passes an amendment to the Telecommunications Act. WSOL also wants the network to be cost-effective, to ensure that the investment will yield a good return to its investors.

Freddy Forklift, Director of Sales at RouteitRight, has proposed a full-mesh solution for WSOL. He says this solution will provide the redundancy and scalability that WSOL has requested. Figure 1-15 depicts the full-mesh design.

As you will see in chapters that follow, RouteitRight is an unconventional group. In this instance, the Director of Sales does not recommend the model because he believes it to be technically sound. He simply wants to sell the hierarchical model because sales of the hierarchical model will mean big money for the sales team.

1   Is the full-mesh solution the best one for WSOL?

2   If not, what solution might work better?

Figure 1-15   *Full-Mesh Design Methodology for WSOL*

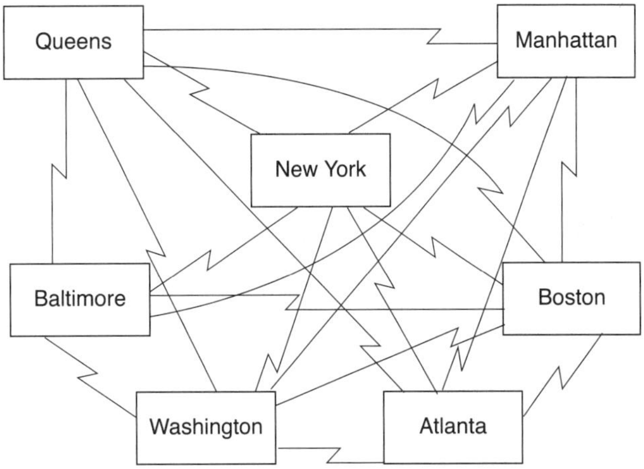

Answers to Scenario 1

1 What business issues at WSOL are relevant to this network design?

- Cost effectiveness
- Scalability
- Security
- Compatibility
- Manageability
- Performance
- Identification of potential business constraints that could compromise the technical solution—political, organizational, dedicated vendor, financial, and so on

2 What technical requirements need to be obtained from WSOL?

- Network addressing methodology
- Protocols used
- Behavior of current network traffic and performance, and expected performance after the network scales with company growth

3 What performance and application requirements need to be obtained from WSOL?

- Name of application

- Type of application

- Number of users

- Protocol requirements

- Approximate bandwidth requirements

4 What network management issues need to be addressed?

- Identifying potential bottlenecks

5 What security concerns need to be addressed?

- Technology weaknesses

- Configuration weaknesses

- Security policy weaknesses

Answers to Scenario 2

1 Is the full-mesh solution the best one for WSOL?

No. The disadvantage of the full-mesh topology centers on one primary issue: There are too many physical links. If the routers are far apart, the link costs can quickly become prohibitively expensive, because adding routers creates an exponential increase in the number of links required.

Under a full-mesh solution, the number of permanent virtual circuits (PVCs) equals $[n (n–1)]/2$. If $n = 7$, the number of PVCs would equal 21 connections. With 21 PVCs, the routers will not have enough ports to support this topology.

This number of connections would not be cost-effective for WSOL. In addition, routers currently available would have density available for 21 port connections. Although this full mesh provides a great deal of redundancy, it might prove prohibitively expensive to implement.

2 What solution might work better?

A partial-mesh solution would be more effective for WSOL. A partial-mesh solution (see Figure 1-16) could allow New York and Manhattan to operate in a full-mesh topology, while the other station routes can be connected as a partial mesh. Providing complete redundancy for WSOL could represent a stranded investment for WSOL's capital investors. A partial mesh will provide enough redundancy to satisfy WSOL's business requirements and is less expensive to implement. A partial mesh ensures that at a minimum, only a small part of the network is down at any one point, not the entire network.

Figure 1-16   *Partial-Mesh Design Methodology for WSOL*

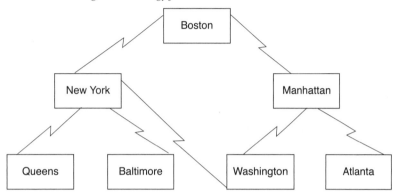

This chapter covers the following topics that you will need to master as a CCDP:

- **Campus LAN design evolution**—This section discusses the evolution of campus LAN design.

- **Issues facing campus LAN designers**—This section discusses issues that CCDPs should take into account when designing campus LANs.

- **Selecting the right device**—This section defines virtual LANs (VLANs) and discusses their role in a successful campus LAN design strategy.

Cisco expects the successful CCDP candidate to be able to use campus LAN design models to render a cost-effective solution that will meet the client's requirement for scalability and stability. The CID exam tests your knowledge of how OSI Layer 2 functionality can be integrated into a successful network design.

CHAPTER 2

Business and Technical Requirements

How to Best Use This Chapter

By following these steps, you can make better use of your study time:

- Keep your notes and the answers for all your work with this book in one place for easy reference.

- Take the "Do I Know This Already?" quiz, and write down your answers. Studies show that retention is significantly increased through writing down facts and concepts, even if you never look at the information again.

- Use the diagram shown in Figure 2-1 to guide you to the next step.

Figure 2-1 *How to Use This Chapter*

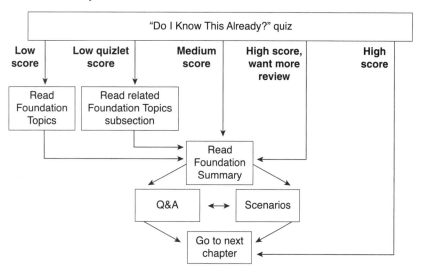

If you skip to the Foundation Summary, Q&A, and Scenarios sections and have trouble with the material there, you should go back to the Foundation Topics section.

"Do I Know This Already?" Quiz

The purpose of the "Do I Know This Already?" quiz is to help you decide what parts of this chapter to use. If you already intend to read the entire chapter, you do not necessarily need to answer these questions now.

This 15-question quiz helps you determine how to spend your limited study time. The quiz is divided into three smaller "quizlets" that help you select the sections of the chapter on which to focus. Figure 2-1 outlines suggestions on how to spend your time in this chapter. Use Table 2-1 to record your score.

Table 2-1   *Score Sheet for Quiz and Quizlets*

Quizlet Number	Foundation Topics Section Covering These Questions	Questions	Score
1	Campus LAN design evolution	1, 2, 5	
2	Issues facing campus LAN designers	3, 4, 11	
3	Selecting the right devices	6, 7, 8, 9, 10, 12, 13, 14	

1   What is the first step in campus network design?

_____

_____

_____

2   What two backbones are the recommended models for the campus LAN design?

_____

_____

_____

3   What business issues govern the design acceptance process?

_____

_____

_____

4   What three categories of problems do most networks fall into?

_____

_____

_____

5 What are the two largest factors in determining network design?

_____

_____

_____

6 Why are desktop protocols least desirable for a large network?

_____

_____

_____

7 What solution should the CCDP employ when addressing a network with media contention?

_____

_____

_____

8 When might an ATM switch improve an internetwork's design and performance?

_____

_____

_____

9 What device should be used to filter broadcasts and multicasts?

_____

_____

_____

10 What is the difference between a broadcast domain and a bandwidth domain?

_____

_____

_____

11 What issues should you address when designing a campus LAN?

_____

_____

_____

12 How can a VLAN improve network performance?

_____

_____

_____

13 What device controls broadcasts and multicasts?

_____

_____

_____

14 Name two protocols that are not recommended for wide-area network (WAN) design.

_____

_____

_____

15 What protocol is recommended for use on the Internet?

_____

_____

_____

The answers to the "Do I Know this Already?" quiz are found in Appendix A. The suggested choices for your next step are as follows:

- **6 or fewer overall score**—Read the chapter. This includes the "Foundation Topics," the "Foundation Summary," and the "Q&A" sections, as well as the scenarios at the end of the chapter.

- **2 or less on any "quizlet"**—Review the subsection(s) of the "Foundation Topics" part of this chapter based on Table 4-1. Then move into the "Foundation Summary," the Q&A section, and scenarios at the end of the chapter.

- **7, 8, or 9 overall score**—Begin with the "Foundation Summary" section and then go to the Q&A section and scenarios at the end of the chapter.

- **10 or more overall score**—If you want more review on these topics, skip to the "Foundation Summary" section, then go to the Q&A section and scenarios at the end of the chapter. Otherwise, move on to the next chapter.

Foundation Topics

In the early days of local-area networking, campus LANs consisted of thick or thin Ethernet or star-wired Token Ring. In the late '80s and early '90s, networks adopted unshielded twisted-pair (UTP) as the LAN cabling standard. A typical cabling infrastructure consisted of UTP cabling to the desktop and multimode fiber in the backbone. As networks continued to grow and user applications continued to demand more bandwidth, something had to be done about controlling the extra traffic. Bridges were developed to segment traffic and minimize congestion. Routers and switches were introduced to isolate broadcast traffic and to allow better traffic-flow management. With the addition of Apple's and Novell's operating systems to the network arena, AppleTalk and IPX protocols were introduced to the network environment. As you will see, each protocol brings different challenges to the issues of network traffic management. As the needs of users and applications continue to evolve, so will the issues of campus LAN design. See Figure 2-2.

Figure 2-2   *Change from Shared to Switched Networks*

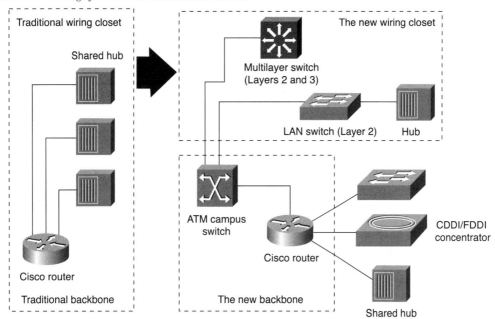

No matter what the size of the current network, there is one thing the CCDP should always expect: change. As the customer grows and changes, so will the demands placed on the network. Users will move to different locations. Branches will relocate to different cities. Business and Web applications will become more powerful and demanding. Changing business and technical requirements mandate that flexibility be a primary requirement of internetwork design.

Today's internetworks are becoming increasingly congested and overworked. In addition to an ever-growing population of network users, several factors have combined to put stress on the capabilities of traditional LANs:

- **Faster CPUs**—In the mid-'80s, the most common desktop workstation was a PC. At the time, most PCs could execute one million instructions per second (MIPS). Today, workstations with 500–750 MIPS of processing power are common, and I/O speeds have increased accordingly. Two modern engineering workstations on the same 10 Mbps LAN can easily saturate it.

- **Faster operating systems**—During the first generation of network design, operating systems had limited network access. Of the three most common desktop operating systems, only UNIX could allow users to initiate simultaneous network transactions. With the release of Microsoft Windows, PC users could multitask, create peer-to-peer networks, and increase their demands for network resources. Presently, most network users are expected to depend on the WAN as their primary source of resources.

- **Network-intensive applications**—Use of client/server applications is now more the norm than the exception. The CCDP should expect his users to obtain 80 percent of their applications or data from a remote server or network. Client/server applications allow administrators to centralize information, thus making it easy to maintain and protect. Client/server applications free users from the burden of maintaining information and the cost of providing enough hard disk space to store it. Given the cost benefit of client/server applications, such applications are likely to become even more widely used in the future.

Campus VLAN Design

The first step in campus network design is to identify the business and technical requirements. The primary objective of a network design is to ensure efficient delivery of the right information at the right time to the right person. The determination of what information has preference on the network and which users have network access priority must be defined by the business requirements.

To overcome the bandwidth limitations and shortcomings of the router and hub design, many designers embraced the campus VLAN design. Today's applications are designed to be more powerful. More power demands more network horsepower. The campus VLAN design provides additional bandwidth, giving users a dedicated 10 or 100 Mbps to the server. A VLAN isolates bandwidth segments. Therefore, one user or a group of users who require large amounts of bandwidth will not impact network performance for the rest of the network. The development of Layer 2 switching in hardware several years ago led to network designs that emphasized Layer 2 switching.

Bridges and switches are data-link layer communications devices that operate at Layer 2 of the OSI reference model. Bridges connect and enable packet forwarding between different networks. Three types of bridging dominate the bridging environment:

- Transparent

- Translational

- Source-route

Transparent bridging is found, for the most part, in Ethernet environments. Source-route bridging is found primarily in Token Ring environments. Translational bridging provides a means of translation between the formats and transit requirements of Ethernet and Token Ring. Source-route transparent bridging combines the algorithms of transparent bridging and source-route bridging to enable communication in mixed Ethernet/Token Ring environments.

Today, switching technology has emerged as the next-generation successor to bridge-based internetworking solutions. Switching implementations dominate applications in which bridging technologies were once implemented. Superior throughput performance, higher port density, lower per-port cost, and greater flexibility are several factors that have contributed to the emergence of switches as replacement technology for bridges. See Figure 2-3.

Figure 2-3   *Campus VLAN Design*

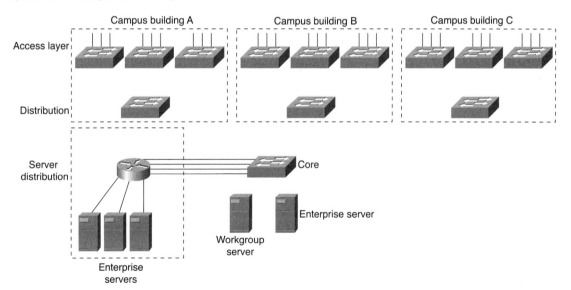

Issues Facing Campus LAN Designers

The CCDP must take several things into account when designing a campus LAN. These issues can be categorized into the following general areas:

- Traffic patterns

- Server and client end stations

- Network infrastructure

- Reliability and resiliency

- Network management

- Business concerns

- Security

- Change and growth

Traffic Patterns

To optimize the network design, the CCDP must understand the traffic flow. In many ways, analyzing traffic flow on an internetwork is much like looking at commuter traffic patterns in a busy metropolis. During rush-hour traffic, bottlenecks slow traffic and affect commuters. During periods of heavy usage, bottlenecks slow network traffic and affect network users. To regulate traffic flow, large vehicles such as transfer trucks are restricted to certain highways and certain lanes. To regulate traffic flow, bandwidth-intensive applications are restricted to certain segments of the network.

Some commuter traffic is local. In this usage, the phrase *local traffic* suggests that the commuter could go from Point A to Point B without using a major highway. Likewise, some campus traffic is local. Campus traffic that does not enter the backbone and does not cross a router is considered local. Some commuter traffic is remote. In this situation, the phrase *remote commuter traffic* suggests that the traveler might need to travel a great distance to go from Point A to Point B and might need to use a major artery. Similarly, *remote campus traffic* refers to network traffic that needs to cross the network backbone or travel through a router. Understanding the traffic flow is important. Other design requirements such as scalability and security depend on knowing the traffic behavior in the network.

Server and Client End Stations

Enterprise servers and distributed servers generally support most campus applications. Enterprise servers support central functions such as e-mail, whereas distributed servers usually support local user groups. As up-and-coming software applications continue to place a greater demand on the network, enterprise servers have become the servers of choice for campus WAN design. Due to bandwidth requirements, many multimedia applications require a centralized server.

NOTE   The placement of the enterprise server is important. To ensure a consistent response to all users, place the enterprise server close to the network backbone.

To handle the ever-increasing quantity of traffic, some designers are now implementing super servers. Simply stated, super servers have two to three times the speed, memory, and data storage of a regular enterprise server.

NOTE   Replacing the enterprise server with a super server could introduce a single point of failure.

Applications such as Cisco IP/TV that deliver video to the desktop have entered the work environment. These applications demand that a certain quality of service be delivered to the desktop. The CCDP must ensure that network switch and router devices do not serve as a bottleneck to servers and high-power client end stations that have Fast Ethernet and Gigabit Ethernet capability.

Broadcast Traffic on Client/Server Networks

Server and client end stations run operating systems, applications, and protocols that generate broadcast traffic. Microsoft manufactures the most popular and widely used network operating systems, Windows 2000 and its predecessor, Windows NT. Both regularly use broadcasts to determine the presence of domain peers and services in the network neighborhood. The Novell networks use service advertising protocols (SAPs) to advertise the services available throughout the network. Reducing the protocols that generate broadcast traffic is one way of minimizing broadcast traffic. Using routers to create subnets is another way of controlling broadcast traffic. In addition to controlling broadcast traffic, the issue of broadcast radiation must be dealt with. Broadcast radiation can occur when the ambient level of broadcasts generated by the higher-layer protocols in the network restricts the number of nodes that the network can support. The effects of broadcast radiation can be so severe that an end station can spend all its CPU power on processing broadcasts.

Network Infrastructure

When choosing a network infrastructure, the CCDP has two basic choices: the distributed backbone and the collapsed backbone. Both choices have advantages and disadvantages. Knowing when each choice can and cannot deliver the desired result is a must for the CCDP.

The distributed backbone, shown in Figure 2-4, defines a router on each floor of a campus building. This design allows for maximum fault tolerance and ease of troubleshooting. The downside to this design is similar to the gotcha that dieters experience when eating a quart of butter pecan ice cream: This design is sweet and goes down good, but it's gonna cost you!

Figure 2-4   *Distributed Backbone*

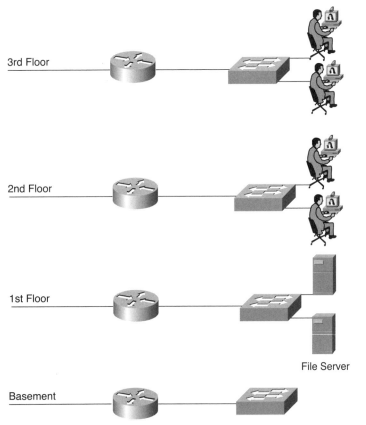

3rd Floor

2nd Floor

1st Floor

File Server

Basement

In contrast, the collapsed backbone has a single concentration point where all user traffic flows from each floor (see Figure 2-5). The collapsed backbone is less expensive but offers a single point of failure as a significant trade-off.

Figure 2-5   *Collapsed Backbone*

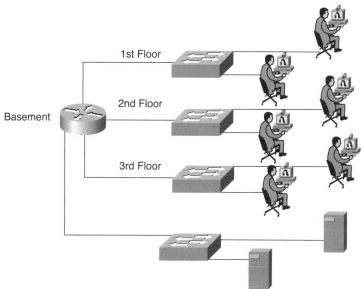

Choosing the right bandwidth is important. For the backbone, the CCDP must select a high-speed transport. ATM and Gigabit Ethernet are two examples.

Reliability and Resiliency

The grandest design will fail to meet expectations if it is *down*. A degree of redundancy should be installed on campus to ensure that the network will operate when it is needed.

The campus LAN designer should keep in mind several areas of redundancy:

- **Component redundancy**—Keeping backup or duplicate hardware
- **Server redundancy**—Keeping backups of data and applications
- **Network link redundancy**—Keeping alternate physical pathways available

Network Management

Two options are available for network management: centralized or distributed network management. For small to medium networks, centralized management usually works well. For larger networks, distributed management is recommended.

Network management comes in a variety of packages. In its simplest form, network management might involve a laptop loaded with protocol analyzer software monitoring network activity. In another scenario, network management might include a distributed database, auto-polling of network devices, and high-end workstations generating real-time graphical views of network topology changes and traffic.

The network management model is the primary means for understanding the major functions of network management systems. This model consists of five conceptual areas:

- Performance
- Configuration
- Accounting
- Fault
- Security

Business Concerns

Simply stated, business issues always revolve around cost. Even in the rarest of cases, where a network design project is blessed with what appears to be a virtually unlimited budget, there is still a point where cost becomes a constraining factor in the decision-making process. In addition to fixed equipment costs, recurring costs must be considered. Determining the total cost of ownership is critical to ensuring the network's long-term success.

NOTE   Cost is the metric against which all other design goals must be measured. You've got to *pay* to *play!*

For the CCDP, designing an internetwork can be a challenging task. Understanding the problem is the key to creating the optimum campus network design.

Determining how long the recommended design will remain viable with today's dynamic requirements will always be an art. When recommending a design, the CCDP should always think about future needs that will impact expandability, upgradability, and scalability.

Security

The CCDP should expect sensitive information to cross the campus network. The key buzzwords the CCDP should remember when designing for security are *identity* and *integrity*.

Identity is all about making sure the right person is accessing the data. Identifying the user is the most basic form of security. Access to network resources is granted based on who the user is and whether that user has authorization to access the information. Routers can be configured with access lists to provide intranetwork security. Because these types of filters provide limited firewall capability, they are sometimes referred to as a poor man's firewall. Firewalls block all users who are not authorized to access the network.

Integrity is all about making sure that the data is not intercepted or interfered with as it travels through the network. Encryption is the process of scrambling data so that it cannot be understood by anyone other than the sender or receiver. If a packet is intercepted, the scrambled contents render it unintelligible.

Change and Growth

There is one thing of which the CCDP can be certain: The network will always change. A necessary component of business is change and growth. Without it, the business will die. As the business changes and grows, the design requirements that support the business must change as well. Scalability, which is defined as the capability to keep up with changes and growth, is a critical component of network design.

Here are some of the changes the CCDP should anticipate for the campus LAN:

- An increase in the amount of traffic

- An increase in the number of supported applications

- An increase in the number of users

- An increase in the concern for security

Customer Availability Requirements

Customer availability *requirements* relate to performance metrics such as network reliability, traffic throughput, and host/client computer throughput speeds. When the CCDP asks a customer what they expect from a network, the CCDP is likely to be told to design and deliver a network that:

- Is *stable* and *manageable,* but easily upgradable

- *Can be scaled* to meet increased user and bandwidth demands

- Will deliver extremely *high reliability*

- Can seamlessly *integrate* new technologies along with the legacy equipment

- Can *quickly* and *easily accommodate* new services

- Is flexible enough to handle multimedia and other *quality-of-service* requirements

---

NOTE   Of course, all requirements should be delivered at the lowest possible cost.

Selecting the Right Device

Problems that a CCDP might be expected to solve include the following:

- Media contention

- Excessive broadcasts

- Protocols that don't scale well

- The need to transport new payloads

- The need for more bandwidth

- Overloaded backbone

- Network-layer addressing issues

- Security concerns

- The need to reduce congestion

BREAKING NEWS

We interrupt this chapter to report the following:

Users report that e-mail sent this morning was not received at the destination site. Sammy Sniffer reports via an unconfirmed trace that e-mail packets matching the description of the missing packets were last seen on a network segment four hops away. If you encounter these packets or have information concerning their whereabouts, take no action. Immediately contact the network administrator.

Many design solutions to problems caused by poor network performance can be found in the way devices are included in the network. When should the CCDP use a hub? A switch? A bridge? A router?

This also depends on the business and technical requirements and on what problems you are attempting to solve. As soon as the issues of cost and availability are resolved, the problems of performance at each segment must be addressed. See Figure 2-6.

Figure 2-6   *Network Problems*

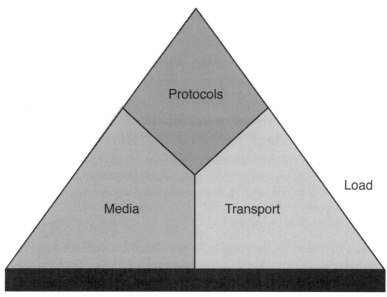

Although each network can face countless problems associated with performance, problems generally can be categorized into three areas:

- Media

- Protocols

- Transport

    — What's the problem?

        Slow performance on the network.

    — What's the cause?

        Too many collisions?

        Too many broadcasts?

        Too little transport?

Media

Media problems are usually caused by too much traffic on the network. A symptom of this problem might be excessive collisions on Ethernet or long waits for the token to pass in Token Ring. LAN switching is the recommended solution for congestion caused by media contention.

Switches can be used alongside hubs to provide the bandwidth required by power users or special applications.

Switches can provide the solution to media problems.

Protocols

Protocol problems are usually detected by excessive broadcasts on the network. Too many broadcasts happen when the wrong protocols are selected for a certain design. Although one protocol might be ideal for a small network, it might fail miserably when asked to perform for a large network.

Broadcasts become excessive when so many updates, announcements, and checkup services are running that there is not enough bandwidth remaining for the regular data payload to pass through. Desktop protocols, which were designed during the earliest days of campus LAN evolution, deliberately use multicasts and broadcasts for resource discovery and advertisement.

A flat network is a network that consists of one virtual LAN. Traditional bridges and switches that have not been segmented operate on a flat network. With a flat network, all the nodes are subject to the same amount of broadcast traffic.

In a flat network, there is a mathematical limit on the number of broadcasts that workstations on the network can tolerate before they become overwhelmed. When proprietary protocols such as IPX and AppleTalk were the standard for desktop protocols, controlling broadcasts was a major concern. Now that TCP/IP has become the de facto standard for desktop protocols, the CCDP can neutralize this problem by selecting TCP/IP as the operating protocol. All major network operating systems support TCP/IP. Microsoft and Novell, the two largest manufacturers of network operating systems, now use TCP/IP as their default protocol.

Routers can provide a remedy for excessive broadcasts and protocol problems.

NOTE   NetBEUI is an example of a protocol that works fabulously on a small network. In fact, NetBEUI might even be recommended on a home network. CCDPs who recommend NetBEUI for a large network might find their next design assignment at the unemployment office!

Transport

In the beginning, local- and wide-area communications remained logically separate. 80 to 90 percent of network access was done locally. New applications and the economics of supporting them, however, are forcing these conventions to change. In the near future, we should expect 80 to 90 percent of network access to be done remotely. Users who require multimedia to the desktop have shattered the conventional rules of design. Very soon, the majority of users will expect and demand voice and real-time video. The need to transport new payloads includes the need to offer voice, video, and data. These services will require more bandwidth.

Transport problems are usually caused when the network bandwidth is unavailable to deliver the payload that the applications request. Applications that are time-sensitive, such as voice and video, demand quality of service to ensure that their signal is delivered with integrity. For transport problems, the CCDP should select the fastest transport available. ATM and Gigabit Ethernet are good choices for getting the data from Point A to Point B.

ATM has emerged as one of the technologies integrating voice, video, and data. ATM can support any traffic type in separate or mixed streams, delay-sensitive traffic, or nondelay-sensitive traffic. It also can satisfy quality-of-service requirements.

80/20 Becomes 20/80

For the longest time, Cisco recommended that campus LANs be designed on the premise that 80 percent of the network traffic would be local and 20 percent would be remote. That recommendation was quite practical when most users accessed their applications via distributed servers and most of the traffic stayed within the local subnet. However, with the advent of the Internet, multimedia, and all of their bandwidth-hungry cousins, there has been a shift toward centralized servers. The pendulum is now swinging the other way, and conventional wisdom has changed. Now it is thought that 80 percent (if not more) of the network will be remote and only 20 percent (if not less) will be local. See Figure 2-7.

Figure 2-7   *Network Problem Solving*

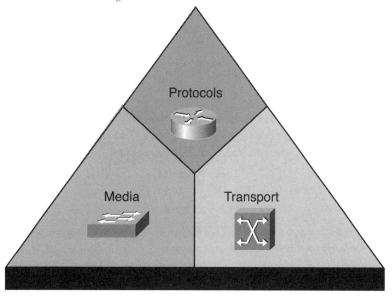

Foundation Summary

This section is a collection of tables and figures that provides a convenient review of many key concepts in this chapter. If you are already comfortable with the topics in this chapter, this summary might help you recall a few details. If you have just read this chapter, this review should help solidify some key facts. If you are doing your final preparation before the exam, these tables and figures are a convenient way to review the day before the exam.

As soon as you understand the business problem, you can achieve the solution to the problem by implementing the proposed design.

In new technology, the two largest factors in determining the network design are cost and availability. Budgetary considerations such as the cost of software, the cost of equipment, the cost of maintenance, and the recurring monthly costs play a huge role in determining what type of design will be implemented.

Defining the business requirements provides the necessary supporting data and financial models to support an internetwork's design and implementation. While cost savings should be an obvious benefit realized by the network design, other substantial benefits such as optimizing operations, innovating products and services, and providing better customer service should be realized as well.

The CCDP must be able to recognize the customer's primary campus LAN design issues and the driving forces in the dynamic environment. The CCDP must design with regard to the ongoing changes required by the network. Use switches to solve media contention problems. Use routes to solve protocol problems. Use ATM or some other high-speed transport protocol to solve transport problems.

Tables 2-2, 2-3, and 2-4 provide a quick reference for a number of important items covered in this chapter.

Table 2-2   *Cable Limitations for 10 Mbps Ethernet*

Cable Type	Topology	Type of Cable	Maximum Cable Length (in Meters)	Maximum Connections per Cable	Maximum Collision Domain (in Meters)
10Base5	Bus	Thick coax	500	100	2,500
10Base2	Bus	Thin coax	185	30	2,500
10BaseT	Star	UTP	100 from hub to station	2	2,500

NOTE   The maximum topology for all cable types subscribes to the 5-4-3 rule. Five segments and four repeaters are allowed per collision domain. Only three segments can have end systems.

Table 2-3 *Hubs, Bridges, Switches, and Routers*

Device	Does it Segment Bandwidth Domain?	Does it Segment Broadcast Domain?	Standard Usage	OSI Model
Hub	No	No	Connects devices in small LANs	Physical layer
Bridge	Yes	No	Connects networks	Data link layer
Switch	Yes	No	Connects individual devices or networks	Data link layer
Router	Yes	Yes	Connects networks	Network layer

Table 2-4 *Network Performance Parameters*

Function	Goal
Performance	Measure and make available various aspects of network performance so that internetwork performance can be maintained at an acceptable level.
Configuration	Monitor network and system configuration information so that the effects on network operation of various versions of hardware and software elements can be tracked and managed.
Accounting	Measure network-utilization parameters that the individual or group uses so that the network can be properly regulated. Regulation minimizes network problems and maximizes the fairness of network access across all users.
Fault	Detect, log, notify users of, and, where possible, automatically fix network problems to keep the network running effectively. Fault management is perhaps the most widely implemented of the ISO network management elements.
Security	Control access to network resources according to company guidelines so that the network cannot be sabotaged (intentionally or unintentionally) and sensitive information cannot be accessed by those without appropriate authorization.

Q&A

As mentioned in Chapter 1, the questions and scenarios in this book are more difficult than what you will experience on the actual exam. The questions do not attempt to cover more breadth or depth than the exam; however, they are designed to make sure that you know the answer. Rather than allowing you to derive the answer from clues hidden inside the question, the questions challenge your understanding and recall of the subject. Questions from the "Do I Know this Already?" quiz from the beginning of the chapter are repeated here to ensure that you have mastered this chapter's topic areas. Hopefully, these questions will help limit the number of exam questions on which you narrow your choices to two options and then guess. Be sure to use the CD and take the simulated exams.

The answers to these questions can be found in Appendix A.

1   What is the first step in campus network design?

_____

_____

_____

2   What two backbones are the recommended models for the campus LAN design?

_____

_____

_____

3   What business issues govern the design acceptance process?

_____

_____

_____

4   Into what three categories of problems do most networks fall?

_____

_____

_____

5   What are the two contrasting factors in determining network design?

_____

_____

_____

6 Why are desktop protocols least desirable for a large network?

_____

_____

_____

7 What solution should the CCDP employ when addressing a network with media contention?

_____

_____

_____

8 When might an ATM switch improve an internetwork's design and performance?

_____

_____

_____

9 What device should be used to filter broadcasts and multicasts?

_____

_____

_____

10 What is the difference between a broadcast domain and a bandwidth domain?

_____

_____

_____

11 What issues should you address when designing a campus LAN?

_____

_____

_____

12 How can a VLAN improve network performance?

_____

_____

_____

13 What device controls broadcasts and multicasts?

_____

_____

_____

14 Name two protocols that are not recommended for WAN design.

_____

_____

_____

15 What device terminates the bandwidth domain?

_____

_____

_____

16 What protocol is recommended for use on the Internet?

_____

_____

_____

17 What is media contention?

_____

_____

_____

18 What protocol is recommended for integrating voice, video, and data?

_____

_____

_____

19 True or false: Transport problems are usually caused when the network bandwidth is not available to deliver the payload that the applications request.

_____

_____

_____

20 Although broadcasts play an important function in network communications, excessive broadcasts can make the network inefficient. What can the CCDP do to remedy the problem of excessive broadcasts?

_____

_____

_____

21 List two applications that require high-speed quality-of-service transport.

_____

_____

_____

22 What Cisco IOS features can optimize core layer transport?

_____

_____

_____

23 What is the biggest trade-off of a distributed backbone?

_____

_____

_____

24 What is the 80/20 rule? Explain why some people now refer to it as the 20/80 rule.

_____

_____

_____

25 What devices terminate the broadcast domain?

_____

_____

_____

26 What is broadcast radiation?

_____

_____

_____

27 List five typical problems that the CCDP might be asked to solve.

_____

_____

_____

28 When would a multiprotocol backbone be recommended?

_____

_____

_____

29 What solution is recommended for solving congestion problems that are caused by media contention?

_____

_____

_____

Scenarios

Scenario 1

To help design the optimum solution and address the issues presented in each chapter, you have contracted with the design professionals at RouteitRight to help you.

RouteitRight's Key personnel are as follows:

Chief Executive Officer (CEO)	Billy Broadcast
Chief Information Officer (CIO)	Megg A. Bight
Senior Telecommunications Engineer	Peter Packett
Director of Sales	Freddy Forklift
Information Systems Manager	Harry Helpnot
Help Desk Manager	Millie Sekkons
Network Specialist	Roddy Routebegone

ZIP, the world famous university, is currently experiencing problems on its campus LAN network and would like to upgrade its campus LAN capabilities before the beginning of the fall semester, because it wants to compete more effectively in recruiting new students on campus. ZIP wants to give its students in the dormitory access to the campus LAN. The four dormitories on campus can accommodate 750 students. ZIP wants each student to be able to access his or her home directory files. In addition, each student should be able to upload and download regular files and e-mail to the main campus server, ZIP1. ZIP students currently access the Internet through their own dialup accounts. Therefore, there are no plans to provide access to the Internet from the dormitory to the campus LAN design.

The folks at RouteitRight are having a discussion about the ZIP LAN. Billy Broadcast, a 1971 graduate of ZIP, wants to make sure that the ZIP campus design solves the current performance problems. After a meeting with ZIP's president, Billy Broadcast identified the following objectives that ZIP would like to achieve:

- Increase enrollment by at least 10 percent each year

- Attract the caliber of athletes who are currently enrolling at SNAFU, the crosstown rival

- Allow students to connect to the campus network from their dormitory or home

- Maintain or decrease the overall amount being spent on network operations

After an interview with the Dean of Housing, Peter Packett noted that, on a questionnaire, students consistently listed poor performance of the dormitory network as a complaint. ZIP installed a 10 Mbps flat network in the dormitories two years ago. Initially, it worked fine and was well-received. For the past two years and, more specifically, since the release of DOOM version 8.2, it has been plagued by performance problems.

ZIP has an exclusive contractual agreement with Microhard to purchase and use its applications exclusively. Microhard's e-mail system, Inlook, is robust, but it uses lots of network bandwidth. Millie says that it is important to make sure that the e-mail system works properly. She says that e-mail is the most important service that a network can render. After a discussion with the ZIP help desk, Millie found out that ZIP allows its students to load whatever applications they want on their PCs.

Peter, who visited the ZIP network, thinks that minimizing broadcasts and collisions on a shared media network will be the key to success. He believes that this design is a perfect candidate for Layer 2 switching. Megg thinks that RouteitRight should complete a site survey at ZIP before discussing the technical requirements.

1 What technical issues must be taken into account when designing the network infrastructure between the dormitories and the main campus?

2 What backbone would you recommend for the dormitories? (Each dormitory has seven floors.) Why?

3 What changes should be made to ensure reliability and resiliency?

4 What type of cabling topology should be used to provide connectivity?

5 How can ZIP solve its performance problems?

6 How would you minimize broadcasts and collisions in your network design?

7 What protocol would you use for transport on the backbone between dormitories?

Scenario 2

For the past five years, ZIP has lost its homecoming game to SNAFU, its crosstown rival. After last year's loss, 45-0, ZIP's president commissioned a study to determine what might help recruiting at ZIP. One study recommended an upgrade of the facilities in the athletes' dormitory, including an upgrade of the computer networks. As part of the directive to improve the athletic quarters, the athletic director at ZIP, Joe Blough, has requested that the athletic dormitory have its own file server and network. In addition, all ZIP athletes will have high-speed connectivity to the Internet.

1 What upgrades would you recommend to facilitate these changes?

Scenario Answers

Answers to Scenario 1

1 What technical issues must be taken into account when designing the network infrastructure between the dormitories and the main campus?

Network contention is an issue. When the students at ZIP attach to the same segment, they share the segment's bandwidth. If the sharing is significant, the network will be impacted. The poor performance of the existing LAN is very likely due to users contending with other users for network bandwidth. These demands on a shared network cause collisions that result in overall poor performance for all users on the LAN. Collisions are inherent in Ethernet design. As collision rates increase, network response hits a point of diminishing returns, and user complaints increase. Also, collisions consume bandwidth.

Broadcasts are another issue on the shared LAN. Broadcasts consume bandwidth and impact CPU processor performance. Every computer on the segment must process each network broadcast.

2 What backbone would you recommend for the dormitories? (Each dormitory has seven floors.) Why?

Distributed backbone (see Figure 2-8). Distributed backbone lets each switch distribute signals to each campus floor. Because each floor has its own switch, troubleshooting is made simpler, and there is no single point of failure.

Figure 2-8   *Distributed Backbone*

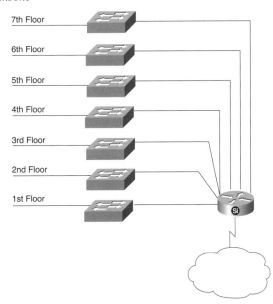

3 What changes should be made to ensure reliability and resiliency?

A second router running Hot Standby Routing Protocol (HSRP) could be employed at each dormitory (see Figure 2-9). HSRP automatically detects a network or router failure and switches to the alternative route. The ZIP students won't miss a click.

Figure 2-9 *Distributed Backbone with HSRP*

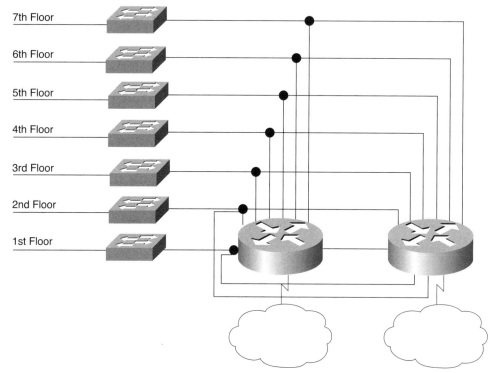

4 What type of cabling topology should be used to provide connectivity?

Cabling recommendations call for fiber-optic cable to be between floors of the dormitory and in the tunnels across campus. Fiber allows the bandwidth to be scalable while providing reliable links that are not susceptible to interference. Cat 5 UTP is recommended for wiring between the workstations and switches.

5 How can ZIP solve its performance problems?

LAN segmentation is recommended to increase bandwidth.

Segmentation with switches will provide dedicated bandwidth relief for the students at ZIP by increasing the network's available bandwidth. In addition, segmentation enables high-speed data exchanges. Switches will reduce the number of LAN collisions, improve network response and overall performance, and increase user productivity.

6 How would you minimize broadcasts and collisions in your network design?

By installing switches. Examples of Cisco LAN switches include the Catalyst 2900, 5000, and 6000 series. Switch selection depends on several factors: the number of ports required, scalability, and the budget allocated to the design solution.

7 What protocol would you use for transport on the backbone between dormitories?

ATM Transport or Gigabit Ethernet would ensure high-speed transport on the campus backbone.

Answers to Scenario 2

1 What upgrades would you recommend to facilitate these changes?

Collapsed backbone (see Figure 2-10) in the athletic dormitory represents a cost-effective approach to giving the athletes connectivity. Switches on each floor connect to the end workstations, and each switch attaches to a separate LAN interface on the router. If redundancy is required, a second router can be installed with HSRP.

Figure 2-10   *Collapsed Backbone for ZIP*

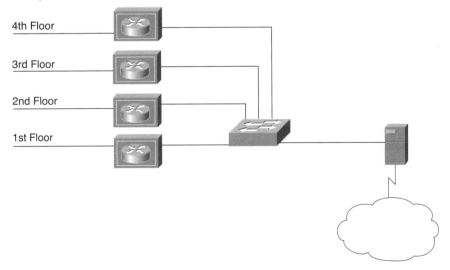

4th Floor

3rd Floor

2nd Floor

1st Floor

This chapter covers the following topics that you will need to master as a CCDP:

- **Examining campus LAN technologies**—This section discusses campus local-area network (LAN) technologies from a design perspective.

- **Defining LAN interconnection methods**—This section discusses the logical and physical connections that exist at the OSI Layer 2.

- **Defining VLANs**—This section defines virtual LANs (VLANs) and discusses their role in a successful campus LAN design strategy.

Cisco expects the successful CCDP candidate to be able to use campus LAN design models to render a cost-effective solution that will meet the client's requirements for scalability and stability. The CID exam tests your knowledge of how OSI Layer 2 functionality can be integrated into a successful network design.

Switched/Campus LAN Solutions

How to Best Use This Chapter

By following these steps, you can make better use of your study time:

- Keep your notes and the answers for all your work with this book in one place for easy reference.

- Take the "Do I Know this Already?" quiz and write down your answers. Studies show that retention is significantly increased through writing down facts and concepts, even if you never look at the information again.

- Use the diagram shown in Figure 3-1 to guide you to the next step.

Figure 3-1 *How to Use this Chapter*

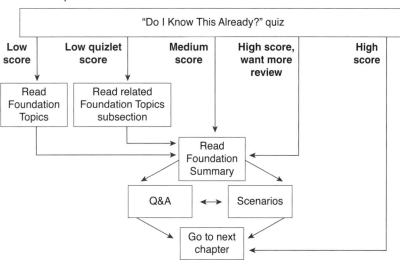

If you skip to the Foundation Summary, Q&A, and Scenarios sections and have trouble with the material there, you should go back to the Foundation Topics section.

"Do I Know This Already?" Quiz

The purpose of the "Do I Know this Already?" quiz is to help you decide what parts of this chapter to use. If you already intend to read the entire chapter, you do not necessarily need to answer these questions now.

This 15-question quiz helps you determine how to spend your limited study time. The quiz is divided into three smaller "quizlets" that help you select the sections of the chapter on which to focus. Figure 3-1 outlines suggestions on how to spend your time in this chapter. Use Table 3-1 to record your score.

Table 3-1 *Score Sheet for Quiz and Quizlets*

Quizlet Number	Foundation Topics Section Covering These Questions	Questions	Score
1	Examining campus LAN technologies	1, 7	
2	Defining LAN interconnection methods	2, 3, 4, 6, 8	
		9, 11, 12, 14, 15	
3	Defining VLANs	5, 10, 13	

1 Name four campus LAN technologies.

_____

_____

_____

2 State a major disadvantage of using Ethernet.

_____

_____

_____

3 List two LAN interconnection methods.

_____

_____

_____

4 What are two types of switching methods for Ethernet?

_____

_____

_____

5 State four goals that you can achieve by using switches in a campus LAN.

_____

_____

_____

6 Bridges operate at the _____ layer of the OSI model and forward _____.

_____

_____

_____

7 Name three primary types of cable used in LANs.

_____

_____

_____

8 Routers operate at the _____ layer of the OSI model and forward _____.

_____

_____

_____

9 List three types of wireless networks.

_____

_____

_____

10 How are traffic loops prevented on switches and routers?

_____

_____

_____

11 What cable is recommended for wiring between closet and campus buildings?

_____

_____

_____

12 What cable is recommended for transmitting data at very high speeds over long distances?

_____

_____

_____

13 What is the Cisco proprietary protocol for connecting Cisco switches?

_____

_____

_____

14 List three functions provided by routers.

_____

_____

_____

15 What are some benefits of designing a network with Thinnet?

_____

_____

_____

The answers to the "Do I Know this Already?" quiz are found in Appendix A. The suggested choices for your next step are as follows:

- **6 or fewer overall score**—Read the chapter. This includes the "Foundation Topics," the "Foundation Summary," and the "Q&A" sections, as well as the scenarios at the end of the chapter.

- **2 or less on any "quizlet"**—Review the subsection(s) of the "Foundation Topics" part of this chapter based on Table 4-1. Then move into the "Foundation Summary," the Q&A section, and scenarios at the end of the chapter.

- **7, 8, or 9 overall score**—Begin with the "Foundation Summary" section and then go to the Q&A section and scenarios at the end of the chapter.

- **10 or more overall score**—If you want more review on these topics, skip to the "Foundation Summary" section, then go to the Q&A section and scenarios at the end of the chapter. Otherwise, move on to the next chapter.

Foundation Topics

Once, 10 Mbps hubs were sufficient to meet the demands of LAN users. As the power of desktop processors and the requirements of client applications continue to increase, the demand for support beyond 10 Mbps has increased as well. The medium-to-large LANs of today demand greater bandwidth to support multimedia, videoconferencing, and quality of service (QoS) requirements. The CCDP should take advantage of the latest LAN technologies, such as Gigabit Ethernet and switching, to meet the greater demands of the network.

Examining Campus LAN Technologies

Much too often, campus LAN designers try to design their LANs simply using the fastest switch that supports the most bandwidth. Although this solution will probably solve most issues, it does not represent a cost-effective solution that matches a business requirement with a technical requirement. This section explores LAN technologies in an attempt to explain the issues and problems that are encountered in LANs today. This section will help you do more than just throw high-speed switches and maximum bandwidth at every problem you encounter.

LAN network technologies provide three types of switching:

- **Ethernet switching**—Provides Layer 2 switching and offers bandwidth domain segmentation using VLANs.

- **Token Ring switching**—Offers the same functionality as Ethernet switching but uses Token Ring technology. You can use a Token Ring switch as either a transparent bridge or a source-route bridge.

- **Fiber Distributed Data Interface (FDDI)**—Provides a LAN standard, defined by ANSI X3T9.5, specifying a 100 Mbps token-passing network using fiber-optic cable.

- **ATM switching technologies**—ATM switching offers high-speed switching technology for voice, video, and data.

Ethernet

Ethernet is the most widely used LAN technology, and the most widely used version of Ethernet technology is 10 Mbps twisted-pair. The 100 Mbps Fast Ethernet standard operates over twisted-pair and fiber-optic media. As the 100 Mbps standard becomes more widely adopted, hubs and computers are being equipped with interfaces that operate at both 10 Mbps and 100 Mbps. The most recent Ethernet standard, 1 Gigabit Ethernet, operates over twisted-pair and fiber-optic media at 1000 Mbps. Figure 3-2 shows an Ethernet network.

Figure 3-2 *Ethernet Network*

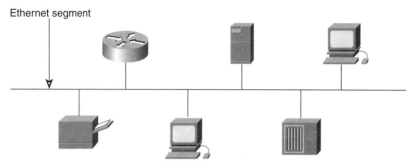

Ethernet workstations operate independently of all other stations on the network: There is no central controller. All stations attached to an Ethernet are connected to a logical bus topology. Every packet travels the length of the bus and is seen by every other device on the bus. To send data, a station first listens to the channel. If the channel is idle, the station transmits its data in the form of an Ethernet frame.

After each frame transmission, all stations on the network must contend equally for the next frame transmission chance. This ensures that access to the network channel is fair, and that no single station can lock out the other stations. Access to the shared channel is based on a system called Carrier Sense Multiple Access with Collision Detection (CSMA/CD). As traffic increases on the bus, the rate of collisions also increases. An excessive number of collisions reduces the available bandwidth. Ethernet is designed so that a normal collision does not result in lost data. In the event of a collision, the Ethernet interface waits for a period of time and then automatically retransmits the data.

A collision in and of itself is inherent to the design of Ethernet and is to be expected. However, the wise CCDP knows that too much of anything can be a bad thing. An excessive number of collisions reduces available bandwidth. If a design could be implemented using Ethernet that bypasses the potential for a large number of collisions, Ethernet could represent the ideal solution for a campus LAN environment. Ethernet switches provide the solution to the bandwidth/collision problem.

Standards for 10 Mbps Ethernet

IEEE published the 802.3 specification for running Ethernet over cable. This chapter looks at several standards for Ethernet topologies:

- 10BaseT
- 10Base2
- 10Base5
- 10BaseFL
- 100BaseX

10BaseT refers to an Ethernet network that uses unshielded twisted-pair (UTP) cable. 10BaseT uses a hub as the center of its Ethernet universe. All workstations acts as spokes and feed into the hub. You can make changes to workstations without impacting the network or other workstations. The maximum length of a 10BaseT segment is 100 meters (328 feet). Repeaters can be used to extend this cable length.

10Base2 refers to an Ethernet network that carries a 10 Mbps signal at approximately 2 times 100 meters—hence the name 10Base2. 10Base2 uses *Thinnet*, or thin coaxial cable. Thinnet has a maximum length of 185 meters. There is also a minimum cable length of at least 0.5 meters and a maximum limit of 30 computers per 185-meter segment.

A Thinnet network can have as many as five cable segments connected by four repeaters, but only three cable segments can have stations attached—thus, the 5-4-3 rule (five cable segments, four repeaters, three active cable segments).

10Base5 refers to an Ethernet that carries a 10 Mbps signal at approximately 5 times 100 meters—hence the name 10Base5. 10Base5 uses Thicknet, or thick coaxial cable. Thicknet can support up to 100 nodes per backbone segment. A Thicknet segment can be 500 meters long for a total of 2500 meters. The 5-4-3 rule applies with 10Base5 as well.

10BaseFL refers to an Ethernet that uses fiber-optic cable to carry Ethernet. 10BaseFL is optimum for long cable runs between campuses. The maximum distance for a 10BaseFL segment is 2000 meters.

100BaseX refers to an Ethernet that passes data at 100 Mbps. It is similar to 10BaseT in that all cables are attached to a hub. 100BaseX uses three media specifications:

- 100BaseT4
- 100BaseTX
- 100BaseFX

Ethernet Switches

When network traffic is not high, the choice of internetworking device is not as critical. Any bridge or router can segment the network. When traffic gets heavy, bridges and routers can become bottlenecks as the internetwork traffic increases. Ethernet switches can remove the bottleneck, enabling high-speed data exchanges, all while providing an increase in available bandwidth for each connected station. The Ethernet switch lets you increase the aggregate LAN bandwidth by creating dedicated network segments and interconnecting the virtual segments. As long as the switch's total bandwidth is not exceeded, each virtual segment added to the network increases the network's aggregate speed. Because they work at the second layer of the OSI model, switches are similar to bridges. However, switches can provide higher performance. Switches can connect two types of Ethernet segments interchangeably. Shared segments or single-station segments can be attached to any port on the switch. Ethernet switches use two types of switching methods:

- Cut-through

- Store and forward

Cut-through switching forwards the frame as soon as it is received. Cut-through switching is faster, but no error checking is performed. Because cut-through switching does not monitor for errors, the network might experience a higher number of errors and retransmissions.

Store and forward checks the frame integrity before passing the frame to its destination. Even though the latency rate for store and forward is lower than for cut-through switching, its overall throughput rate should be higher because store-and-forward switches minimize the potential for retransmissions.

Fast Ethernet

Fast Ethernet represents an upgrade from traditional 10 Mbps Ethernet. Fast Ethernet, or 100BaseT, is conventional Ethernet but is faster, operating at 100 Mbps. Data can move from 10 Mbps to 100 Mbps without protocol translation or changes to application and networking software. In addition, Fast Ethernet can also be run over 100BaseFX.

Fast Ethernet can run over a variety of media with 10BaseT, including UTP, shielded twisted-pair (STP), and 100BaseFX fiber. The Fast Ethernet specification defines separate physical sublayers for each media type:

- 100BaseT4 for four pairs of voice- or data-grade Category 5 UTP wiring

- 100BaseTX for two pairs of data-grade Category 5 UTP and STP wiring

- 100BaseFX for two strands of 62.5/125-micron multimode fiber and single-mode fiber

In most cases, organizations can upgrade to 100BaseT technology without replacing existing wiring. However, for legacy installations with Category 3 UTP wiring in their locations, four pairs must be available to implement 100BaseT4 Fast Ethernet.

CAUTION The use of 100BaseT4 is technically possible but is not recommended as a practical application.

Although the 100BaseTX and 100Base T4 specifications maintain the same 100-meter limit from the wiring closet to the desktop as 10BaseT, 100BaseFX can exceed the 100-meter limit because it uses fiber instead of UTP.

NOTE	Use 100BaseFX primarily between wiring closets and campus buildings to better leverage its support for longer cables.

Fast Ethernet supports full duplex, which means that 100 Mbps is available for transmission in each direction. You implement full-duplex communication by disabling the collision detection and loopback functions, which are necessary to ensure smooth communication in a shared network. Only switches can offer full duplex to directly attached workstations or servers. Shared 100BaseT hubs must operate at half duplex to detect collisions among end stations. Full duplex is defined by IEEE standard 802.3 and is not a function of Fast Ethernet, which is defined by IEEE standard 802.3u. Full duplex is a function of Ethernet switches that operate at 100 Mbps.

Gigabit Ethernet

Gigabit Ethernet runs at 1000 Mbps and represents an upgrade from Fast Ethernet. Gigabit Ethernet is perfect for deployment on the backbone between 10/100BaseT switches and as a connection to high-performance servers. With the addition of Gigabit Ethernet, Ethernet delivers a scalable solution from the desktop (10 Mbps) to the workgroup (100 Mbps) to the backbone (1000 Mbps). 1000BaseT still has the 100-meter limit on UTP. The IEEE standard for Gigabit Ethernet is 802.3z for copper and fiber. The standard for UTP is 802.3ab.

The next step for scaling the performance and functionality of design networks is combining multigigabit bandwidth and intelligent services to obtain scaled, intelligent, multigigabit networks. Since 1999, the Ethernet industry has been working on increasing the speed of Ethernet from 1 to 10 gigabits per second. This technology is very significant because not only will Ethernet run at 10 gigabits per second and serve as a LAN connection, but it will also allow Ethernet to operate in wide-area networks (WANs). With 10 Gigabit Ethernet, network managers can build LANs, MANs, and WANs using Ethernet as the end-to-end Layer 2 transport.

Token Ring

The *Token Ring* network protocol was originally developed by IBM. It is still IBM's primary LAN technology and is second only to Ethernet in general LAN popularity. When judged solely on its technical merits, Token Ring might be the logical choice. However, because Ethernet is less expensive and easier to install and maintain, it remains the predominant protocol of choice in non-IBM shops. Figure 3-3 shows a Token Ring network.

Figure 3-3 *Token Ring Network*

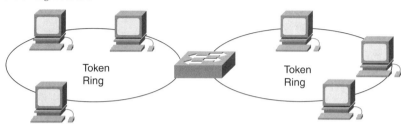

Token Ring Operation

The Token Ring network specifies a star, with all end stations attached to a device called a multistation access unit (MAU). Token Ring is a token-passing technology and is an alternative to Ethernet's collision-detection method. Token-passing networks operate at 4 or 16 Mbps and move a small frame, called a *token,* around the network. Possession of the token grants the right to transmit. If a node receiving the token has no information to send, it passes the token to the next end station.

Each station can hold the token for a determined maximum period of time. If a station possessing the token does have information to transmit, it seizes the token, alters one bit of the token (which turns the token into a start-of-frame sequence), appends the information it wants to transmit, and sends this information to the next station on the ring. While the information frame is circling the ring, no token is on the network (unless the ring supports *early token release*), which means that other stations wanting to transmit must wait. As a result, collisions cannot occur in Token Ring.

Token Ring networks generally have higher utilization of available bandwidth. Token Ring networks are ideal for applications where delay must be predictable and robust network operation is important. Individual Token Rings are interconnected with bridges. In recent years, wire-speed Token Ring switches have replaced the original slow and expensive bridges, making more rings with fewer stations attached to each ring an economical alternative for Token Ring users.

Why Use Token Ring Switches?

The traditional method of connecting multiple Token Ring segments is to use source-route bridging (SRB). Bridges can be used to link workgroup rings to the backbone ring. Bridges introduce congestion and reduce performance at the user's workstation. To maintain performance, the CCDP could use a collapsed backbone. Collapsed backbone routers can offer greater throughput than bridges and can interconnect a larger number of rings without becoming overloaded. However, routers have a relatively high price per port, and throughput typically does not increase as ports are added. As a collapsed backbone device, a Token Ring switch offers a lower per-port cost and can incur lower latency than a router. In addition, you can use the switch to directly attach large numbers of clients or servers, thereby replacing concentrators. The Cisco Catalyst 3900 and 5000 are examples of Token Ring switches commonly deployed in many networks.

FDDI

Fiber Distributed Data Interface (FDDI) is a high-speed backbone for mission-critical and high-traffic networks. It can transport data at a rate of 100 Mbps and can support up to 500 stations on a single network. FDDI was designed to run through fiber cables, but it can also run on copper as Copper Distributed Data Interface (CDDI) using electrical signals. Figure 3-4 shows an FDDI network.

Figure 3-4   *FDDI Network*

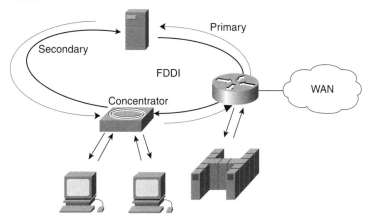

FDDI is highly reliable because FDDI networks consist of two counter-rotating rings. A secondary ring provides an alternative data path in case a fault occurs on the primary ring. FDDI stations incorporate this secondary ring into the data path to route traffic around the fault.

FDDI has seen its best days. It is being phased out in upgrade installations in favor of ATM and Gigabit Ethernet.

ATM Switches

ATM is a high-speed packet-switching technique that uses short fixed-length packets called cells. Fixed-length cells simplify the design of an ATM switch at the high switching speeds involved. Campus design that requires the capacity to handle multiservice traffic can take advantage of ATM switching. ATM switches can support all classes of traffic at high speeds.

Workgroup and Campus ATM Switches

Workgroup ATM switches can be used to deploy ATM to the desktop over low-cost ATM desktop interfaces. Campus ATM switches are generally used to link ATM routers or LAN switches. This use of ATM switches can minimize congestion while enabling the deployment of such new services as VLANs. Campus switches need to support a wide variety of both local backbone and WAN types while still commanding a respectable price/performance ratio for local backbone functionality.

Enterprise ATM Switches

Enterprise ATM switches are multiservice devices that are designed to form the backbones of large enterprise networks. They are intended to complement the role played by today's high-end multiprotocol routers. Like campus ATM switches, enterprise ATM switches can be used to interconnect workgroup ATM switches or other ATM-connected devices. Enterprise-class switches can serve as the single point of integration for all the multiservice technologies that can be found in enterprise backbones today. By integrating all of these services onto a common platform and a common ATM transport infrastructure, network designers can gain greater manageability while eliminating the need for multiple overlay networks.

Defining LAN Interconnection Methods

Network performance can be improved by dividing a segment into less-populated segments and connecting them with a bridge, switch, or router. Segmentation reduces traffic on each segment. The two methods of interconnecting a LAN segment are:

- Bridging/switching
- Routing

Bridging/Switching

A bridge is a device that connects one network to another. Bridges and switches are devices that operate principally at Layer 2 of the OSI reference model. They are referred to as *data-link layer devices*. Bridges connect and enable packet forwarding between different network segments.

A network bridge performs much the same function as a bridge that might be used in everyday traffic. Network bridges decide whether data is going to the LAN on the east wing of the campus or whether the data is crossing the bridge to the west wing. A bridge examines each message on a LAN and forwards the data that is destined to the other network. In bridging networks, addresses have no specific relationship to location. Therefore, messages are sent to every address on the network and are accepted only by the intended destination node. Bridges learn which addresses are on which network and develop a table so that future messages can be sent to the right network. A bridge works at the data-link level of a network, copying data from one network to the next along the communications path.

Several types of bridges exist:

- **Transparent bridging**—Found primarily in Ethernet environments. In transparent bridging, the device learns MAC addresses by remembering source MAC addresses in frames. Any incoming packet containing a destination address that is not found in the MAC table is forwarded.

- **Source-route bridging**—Found primarily in Token Ring environments. In source-route bridging, all forwarding decisions are based on the route information field.

- **Translational bridging**—Provides translation between Ethernet and Token Ring. Because Ethernet devices generally do not support source routing, and Token Ring devices generally do not support transparent bridging, translational bridging provides the connectivity link for Token Ring and Ethernet networks.

- **Source-route transparent bridging**—Combines transparent bridging and source-route bridging to enable communication in mixed Ethernet/Token Ring environments.

- **Source-route translational bridging**—Combines transparent bridging and source-route bridging and bridging between both networks.

Routing

Routers function at the third layer of the OSI model. Routers are used to extend a network across multiple links. Like a bridge, a router makes forwarding decisions based on information stored in its table. However, a router does not have the anonymity of a bridge. It is known to the workstations using its services, and a protocol must be loaded to connect it to those workstations.

Routing offers several advantages over bridging and switching:

- **Manageability**—The network manager can choose from among several protocols, giving the manager more control over path selection.

- **Functionality**—Routers have the means to provide flow control, error and congestion control, and fragmentation and reassembly services. They also can control the life of a packet.

- **Multiple active paths**—Routers can forward traffic through more than one path.

Cable Design Choices

A chain is only as strong as its weakest link, and in networking, a network connection is only as strong as its weakest cable. Cables have different limitations, depending on the topology. The CCDP should ensure that Layer 1, the physical layer, is not the weakest link of the network.

Choosing the right cable depends on several factors, including installation logistics, shielding, transmission speed, and security requirements.

When making design choices, the CCDP should ask the following questions:

- What distances must the cable cover?
- What are the network's security needs?
- How much bandwidth is required?
- What transmission speeds must be supported?

Types of Cable

There are three primary types of cable for Ethernet: coaxial, twisted-pair, and fiber-optic.

Coaxial Cable

During the first days of Ethernet, coaxial cable represented the de facto standard for LAN network cabling. Coaxial cable is composed of a core made of solid copper surrounded by insulation, a braided metal shielding, and an outer cover. A dual-shielded cable consists of one layer of foil insulation and one layer of braided metal shielding. Quad shielding, which consists of two layers of foil insulation and two layers of braided metal shielding, is also available. Shielding is the stranded mesh that surrounds the cable. Shielding protects transmitted data from being distorted by stray electronic signals. The core of a coaxial cable, which can be solid or stranded, carries the data. The core is surrounded by a dielectric insulating layer that separates it from the wire mesh. The braided wire drowns outs noise and other undesirable signals.

Coaxial cable has a copper core surrounded by wire mesh that absorbs noise and crosstalk. Figure 3-5 depicts coaxial cable.

Figure 3-5   *Coaxial Cable*

Although coaxial cable is a good choice for transmitting data, it is not used anymore in network deployments, due in large part to one undesirable trade-off: Coaxial cable can introduce a single point of failure throughout an entire LAN segment. One down node can cause each node on that segment to go down.

Two types of coaxial cable exist: Thicknet and Thinnet.

Thicknet is a relatively rigid coaxial cable about half an inch in diameter. It is sometimes called Standard Ethernet because it was the first type of cable used with the popular network architecture Ethernet. The copper core is thicker than a Thinnet core. The thicker the copper core, the farther the cable can carry signals.

Thicknet can carry signals farther than Thinnet. Thicknet can carry a signal for 500 meters (about 1640 feet). Because Thicknet can travel for longer distances, it is sometimes used as a backbone to connect several smaller Thinnet-based networks. A device called a *transceiver* connects the Thinnet coaxial to the larger Thicknet coaxial cable.

Thinnet is a flexible coaxial cable about a quarter-inch thick. Thinnet's flexibility makes it easy to work with, and it can be used in almost any type of network installation. Networks that use Thinnet have the cable connected directly to a computer's network adapter card. Thinnet coaxial cable can carry a signal up to approximately 185 meters (about 607 feet) before the signal starts to suffer from attenuation.

As a general rule, the thicker the cable, the more difficult it is to work with. Thick cable does not bend easily and is therefore harder to install. Thinnet cable is flexible, easy to install, and relatively inexpensive. This is a consideration when an installation calls for pulling a cable through tight spaces. Because of its versatility, most LAN networks that require coaxial cable use Thinnet. Thicknet's most significant advantage is that it carries a signal farther than Thinnet. For the most part, Thicknet cable is not employed in new Ethernet networks and can be found and discussed in only a historical context. Thicknet is not recommended as a preferred cable for campus LAN design.

Twisted-Pair Cable

Twisted-pair cable is available as shielded (STP) and unshielded (UTP). Not all twisted-pair cable is created equal. Unshielded twisted is available in five categories. Two of the most common categories are voice-grade, Category 3, and data-grade, Category 5. At a minimum, voice-grade cable needs to be able to carry voice conversations with reasonable intelligibility up to 10 Mbps, while data-grade cable must meet a tougher set of minimum specifications. Data-grade cable must ensure data transmission quality up to 100 Mbps. Category 5 UTP is the most popular type of cable for network installations. Figure 3-6 shows an example of twisted-pair cables.

Figure 3-6   *Twisted-Pair Cables*

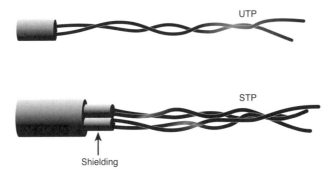

NOTE	At a distance, Category 3 cable and Category 5 cable look similar. Category 3 cable can handle data transmissions up to 10 Mbps. Category 3 cable should not be expected to deliver reliable, consistent, clean, secure computer data transmission. Install Category 5 cable as a minimum for all computer data networks.

Table 3-2 shows a comparison of Ethernet cabling technologies.

Table 3-2   *Ethernet Cabling Technologies*

Characteristic	10Base2 Thinnet	10Base5 Thicknet	10BaseT Twisted Pair	Fiber-Optic
Cost	More than twisted-pair	More than Thinnet	Least expensive	Most expensive
Recommended cable length	185 meters	500 meters	100 meters	2 kilometers
Transmission rates	10 Mbps	10 Mbps	4–100 Mbps	Greater than 100 Mbps
Ease of installation	Simple to moderate difficulty	Moderate difficulty	Simple	Moderate difficulty

Fiber-Optic Cable

Fiber-optic cable is faster and more secure than the other types of cable. Two types of fiber are popular for network design: multimode and single-mode. Multimode can handle distances up to 1 kilometer, and single-mode fiber can be used over longer distances. Fiber-optic cable is virtually untappable. Because fiber-optic is really a thin fiber of glass, it is immune to electromagnetic interference. The delicate nature of fiber-optic requires special expertise to install, which can be costly. Figure 3-7 depicts an example of fiber-optic cable.

Figure 3-7   *Fiber-Optic Network*

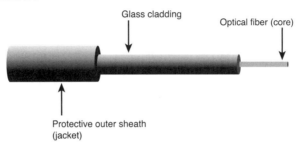

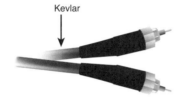

Wireless Networks

Cables are one way to transmit data between computers. Air is another medium that allows transmission between networks. Wireless networks can provide a missing ingredient of network design. Wireless networks can provide temporary connections to an existing network. Wireless networks can grant the user portability and can extend the physical length of the network. They might be the perfect solution for granting network access from lobbies and reception areas. Constantly mobile users would benefit from wireless networks because, no matter where they are in the building, they've got an instant LAN connection.

Infrared wireless networks function by using an infrared light beam to carry the data between devices. Because transmission signals are susceptible to interference, the system must generate strong signals. A infrared network can normally broadcast at 10 Mbps.

NOTE   Infrared is subject to interference from the strong ambient light found in most business environments. Infrared might not be effective beyond 100 feet.

Wireless networks use four methods of transmitting infrared signals:

- **Line-of-sight networks**—If the transmitter and receiver have a clear line of sight between them, transmission and reception can occur.

- **Scatter infrared networks**—The signals bounce off walls and ceilings and hit the receiver.

- **Reflective networks**—Optical transceivers transmit to receivers at a common location, which redirects signals to its ultimate destination.

- **Broadband**—Can handle high-quality multimedia and match cable networks.

Point-to-Point Transmission

Point-to-point technology is a bit different from the other wireless technologies in that it transfers data directly from one computer to another.

Point-to-point communicates directly from PC to PC through walls and ceilings. Point-to-point also supports data rates from 1.2 to 38.4 Kbps up to 200 feet indoors and up to a third of a mile outdoors.

Other Wireless Technologies

Laser technology is similar to infrared technology. Like infrared technology, laser technology requires a direct line of sight, and any object in the path of the laser beam blocks the transmission.

Narrow-band (single-frequency) radio does not require line of sight. The broadcast range is 5000 square feet. The signal's high-frequency components don't allow it to pass through steel or load-bearing walls.

Spread-spectrum radio broadcasts signals over a range of frequencies. The available frequencies are divided into channels, or hops. The spread-spectrum adapters tune to a hop for a predetermined interval and then switch to another hop for a predetermined interval. Transmitter and receiver must be synchronized with regard to the hopping sequence.

A wireless bridge can connect networks up to 3 miles apart. Long range can cover 25 miles using Ethernet and Token Ring topology. The cost can overcome or outweigh the need for leased line or T1, although T1 can provide a much faster transfer rate of 1.544 Mbps.

LAN Switches

A LAN switch typically consists of many ports that connect LAN segments, such as Ethernet and Token Ring, and a high-speed port, such as 100 Mbps Ethernet, FDDI, or 155 Mbps ATM. The high-speed port, in turn, connects the LAN switch to other devices in the network.

Figure 3-8 shows an example of a network with LAN switches.

Figure 3-8   *Ethernet Network Using LAN Switches*

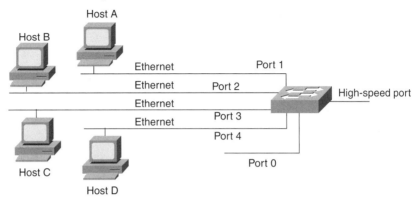

A LAN switch has dedicated bandwidth per port, and each port represents a different segment. For best performance, network designers often assign just one host to a port, giving that host a dedicated bandwidth allocation of 10 or 100 Mbps. When a LAN switch starts up and as the devices that are connected to it request services from other devices, the switch builds a table that associates the MAC address of each local device with the port number through which that device can be reached. Because they work like traditional bridges, a network built and designed with only LAN switches appears as a flat network topology consisting of a single broadcast domain.

Segmenting shared-media LANs divides the users into separate virtual LAN (VLAN) segments, reducing the number of users contending for bandwidth. Each switch port provides a dedicated 10/100 Mbps Ethernet segment or a dedicated 4/16 Mbps Token Ring segment. Switches deliver dedicated bandwidth to users through high-density group switched 10/100BaseT Ethernet, flexible 10/100BaseT Ethernet, fiber-based Fast Ethernet, Token Ring, and CDDI/FDDI.

Switches that enable communication between LANs while blocking other types of traffic interconnect segments. Switches have the intelligence to monitor traffic and compile address tables, which then allows them to forward packets directly to specific ports in the LAN. Switches also provide nonblocking service, which allows multiple conversations (traffic between two ports) to occur simultaneously.

NOTE   Switches allow for multiple collision domains but only a single broadcast domain.

The Role of LAN Switching Technology in Campus Networks

The CCDP can integrate switching devices into his or her existing shared-media networks to achieve the following goals:

- Reduce congestion and increase the available bandwidth for each user

- Organize users into logical workgroups

- Deploy multimedia applications across different switching platforms and technologies

- Reduce the costs of managing network operations

- Provide scalability, traffic control, and security

Layer 3 Switching

Layer 3 switches were developed to address the user's changing bandwidth requirements. The introduction of the Layer 3 switch has created a significant amount of debate with regard to the definitions of a switch and a router. Layer 3 switches do not adhere to the classic definition of a switch.

Depending on the vendor, there are Layer 3 switches available that function at Layer 3 of the OSI model and that have routing functionality equal to or greater than routers currently in use. These Layer 3 switches are designed to combine the speed of switching with the scalability of routing.

Layer 3 switches perform three major functions: packet switching, route processing, and provisioning of intelligent network services. Although they are specifically tailored for a campus LAN environment, Layer 3 switches actually perform most functions that routers have traditionally performed.

For CCDP test purposes, the term *switch* refers to hardware-based platforms that function at Layer 2.

Bridges and Switches

Although bridges and switches share many features at the data-link layer, there are significant differences between them. Because bridges switch in hardware, they are much faster than their software-switching counterparts. Switches can interconnect LANs of different bandwidths and can support higher fast-density ports than bridges. Switches can also support VLANs.

Switching technology has replaced bridging technology as the Layer 2 internetworking solution of choice. Switching implementations now dominate applications in which bridging technologies were implemented in prior network designs. Superior throughput performance, higher port density, lower per-port cost, and greater flexibility have contributed to the emergence of switches as replacement technology for bridges and as complements to routing technology.

Routing Technologies

Routing is a key technology for connecting LANs in a campus network. Routers interconnect at Layer 3 of the OSI model. A router's main job is to filter or forward packets. The device looks at the IP address of the destination packet and determines whether the packet should be forwarded. Routers use routing protocols to share information about routes and destinations.

Routing can be achieved by the use of Layer 3 switching or with traditional routers. Routers add functionality beyond bridges. Routers create collision and bandwidth domains. Routers prevent broadcasts from propagating across networks.

Routers provide the following functionality:

- Segment LANs and WANs
- Determine the best path to the destination based on the network layer protocol
- Communicate route information with other routers
- Send the data to other routers using the best path

Considerations for Scaling a Switched Network

The number of workstations that can be used on a flat network depends on the protocol:

- Avoid having more than 500 IP stations on a flat network.
- When using AppleTalk and NetBIOS, use no more than 200 stations.
- When using IPX, use no more than 300 stations.

Networks that rely heavily on broadcasts and multicast protocols should limit the maximum number of workstations.

Deploying VLANs

When a switch divides up a broadcast domain, a *virtual LAN (VLAN)* is created. A VLAN divides a single domain into several broadcast domains. A VLAN can be configured as a logical group of end stations with a common set of requirements. VLANs allow users in any location to participate in any VLAN. Switches can be connected to create a trunk. With a trunk, users can be separated by miles and still participate in the same VLAN.

VLANs allow logical network topologies to overlay the physical switched infrastructure such that any arbitrary collection of LAN ports can be combined into an autonomous user group or community of interest. The technology logically segments the network into separate Layer 2 broadcast domains, whereby packets are switched between ports designated to be within the same VLAN. By containing traffic originating on a particular LAN to the same VLAN, switched virtual networks avoid wasting bandwidth, a drawback inherent in traditional bridged and switched networks, in which packets are often forwarded to LANs that have no need for them.

Implementation of VLANs also improves scalability, particularly in LAN environments that support broadcast—or multicast-intensive protocols and applications that flood packets throughout the network. Figure 3-9 shows a traditional network with LAN segmentation and a segmented network using switches.

Figure 3-9 *LAN and VLAN Segmentation*

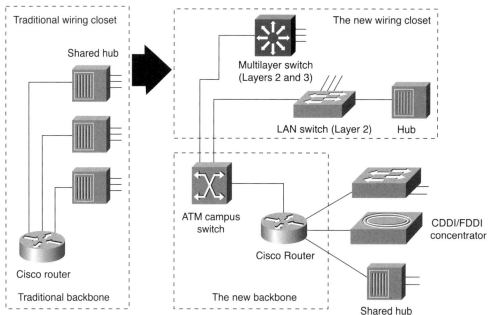

Communication Between VLANs

Communication between VLANs is accomplished through routing. The traditional security and filtering functions of the router can be used. Cisco IOS software provides network services such as security filtering, QoS, and accounting on a per-VLAN basis. As switched networks evolve to distributed VLANs, Cisco IOS provides key inter-VLAN communication and allows the network to scale.

Implementing VLANs

To connect different VLANs, several standards have been implemented. These standards permit connectivity for shared FDDI, Fast Ethernet, and ATM backbones:

- IEEE 802.10 is the standard for shared-medium backbones, such as FDDI, 10 Mbps Ethernet, Fast Ethernet, serial connections, and so on.

- Inter-Switch Link (ISL) is the Cisco proprietary standard for connecting Cisco switches.

- LAN Emulation is the ATM standard for providing services to ATM end stations.

- IEEE 802.1q is the multivendor standard for VLANs. It allows Cisco devices to interact with other vendors.

Foundation Summary

This section is a collection of tables that provide a convenient review of many key concepts in this chapter. If you are already comfortable with the topics in this chapter, this summary might help you recall a few details. If you have just read this chapter, this review should help solidify some key facts. If you are doing your final preparation before the exam, Tables 3-3 through 3-6 are a convenient way to review the day before the exam.

Table 3-3   *Comparing Store-and-Forward Features and Cut-Through Features*

Switching Mode	Latency	Error Checking	Catalyst Models	Comments
Store-and-forward	Medium	Yes	1900, 2800, 2600, 2820, 2900, 3000, 3900, 3920, 5000, 5500	As network speeds continue to increase, latency issues become more manageable. Required when using source and destination segments with different media.
Cut-through	Low	No	2600, 3000, 3900, 3920	Switch will allow bad frames to pass, which can waste bandwidth. Best bet for networks with low error rates.

Table 3-4   *Comparing Switching Technologies*

Switching Technology	Comments
Ethernet	Provides Layer 2 switching and broadcast domain segmentation.
Token Ring	Provides Layer 2 switching. Offers more bandwidth by reducing the size of the Token Ring domain.
Fiber Distributed Data Interface (FDDI)	Used largely as a campus backbone to consolidate Ethernet and Token Ring networks that contain FDDI devices.
Copper Data Distributed Interface (CDDI)	Operates on the same principles as FDDI while using copper. The use of copper represents a tremendous cost savings.
ATM	Workgroup ATM switches typically are connected to an Ethernet switch port and an ATM uplink to connect to a larger campus ATM switch. Campus ATM switches are generally used for small-scale ATM backbones. For example, campus ATM switches might link ATM routers or LAN switches. Enterprise ATM switches are designed to form the core backbones of large enterprise networks. Enterprise ATM switches are used to interconnect campus ATM switches.

Table 3-5   *Comparing 10Base IEEE Cable Standards*

IEEE Standard	Cable Type	Mode	Distance
10BaseT	Category 3, 5	Half duplex	100 meters
10BaseTX	Category 5	Half duplex, full duplex	100 meters
100BaseT4	Category 3	Half duplex	100 meters
100BaseT2	Category 3, 4, 5	Half duplex, full duplex	100 meters
100BaseFX	Multimode fiber	Half duplex, full duplex	400 meters for half duplex; 2000 meters for full duplex
100BaseFX	Single-mode fiber	Half duplex, full duplex	10,000 meters (10 kilometers)

Table 3-6   *Comparing Networking Devices*

Device	Collision Domains	Broadcast Domains	Comments
Repeater	One	One	All devices share the same bandwidth. Extends the length of a LAN segment up to the maximum distance defined by Ethernet.
Bridge	Can be numerous	One	Extends the length of a LAN while segmenting the network.
Switch	Can be numerous	Depends on the configuration	Can be configured to define multiple broadcast domains.
Router	Can be numerous	Can be numerous	Adds functionality beyond bridges and switches.

Q&A

As mentioned in Chapter 1, the questions and scenarios in this book are more difficult than what you will experience on the actual exam. The questions do not attempt to cover more breadth or depth than the exam; however, they are designed to make sure that you know the answer. Rather than allowing you to derive the answer from clues hidden inside the question, the questions challenge your understanding and recall of the subject. Questions from the "Do I Know This Already?" quiz from the beginning of the chapter are repeated here to ensure that you have mastered this chapter's topic areas. Hopefully, these questions will help limit the number of exam questions on which you narrow your choices to two options and then guess. Be sure to use the CD and take the simulated exams.

The answers to these questions can be found in Appendix A.

1 Name four campus LAN technologies.

_____

_____

_____

2 State a major disadvantage of using Ethernet.

_____

_____

_____

3 List two LAN interconnection methods.

_____

_____

_____

4 What are two types of switching methods for Ethernet?

_____

_____

_____

5 State four goals that you can achieve by using switches in a campus LAN.

_____

_____

_____

6 Bridges operate at the _____ layer of the OSI model and forward _____.

_____

_____

_____

7 Name three primary types of cable used in LANs.

_____

_____

_____

8 Routers operate at the _____ layer of the OSI model and forward _____.

_____

_____

_____

9 List three types of wireless networks.

_____

_____

_____

10 How are traffic loops prevented on switches and routers?

_____

_____

_____

11 What cable is recommended for wiring between closet and campus buildings?

_____

_____

_____

12 What are the four IEEE standards for 10 Mbps Ethernet5?

_____

_____

_____

13 What is the Cisco proprietary protocol for connecting Cisco switches?

_____

_____

_____

14 List three functions provided by routers.

_____

_____

_____

15 What are some benefits of designing a network with Thinnet?

_____

_____

_____

16 What type of cable is recommended to interconnect floors on the campus LAN backbone?

_____

_____

_____

17 What Ethernet switching method is fastest?

_____

_____

_____

18 List five types of bridging.

_____

_____

_____

19 What types of functionality do routers provide?

_____

_____

_____

20 True or false: Because bridges switch in hardware, they are much faster than switches, which rely on software to perform switching functions.

_____

_____

_____

21 What cable offers optimum security?

_____

_____

_____

22 What is the maximum number of IP stations that should be deployed on a flat network?

_____

_____

_____

23 List three advantages of configuring a Thinnet network.

_____

_____

_____

24 What is the 5-4-3 rule?

_____

_____

_____

25 What is the maximum segment length recommended for a 10BaseT network?

_____

_____

_____

26 Why would a designer want to segment a network?

_____

_____

_____

27 What types of cables can be used to connect computers on a Token Ring network?

_____

_____

_____

28 What considerations should you make when you're deciding which type of cable to select for a network?

_____

_____

_____

29 What type of cable is recommended for the desktop?

_____

_____

_____

30 Under what situations is unshielded twisted-pair cable not recommended?

_____

_____

_____

31 What cable is recommended for transmitting data at very high speeds over long distances?

_____

_____

_____

Scenarios

Scenario 1

To help design the optimum solution and address the issues presented in each chapter, you have contracted with the design professionals at RouteitRight to help you.

RouteitRight's key personnel are as follows:

Chief Executive Officer (CEO)	Billy Broadcast
Chief Information Officer (CIO)	Megg A. Bight
Senior Telecommunications Engineer	Peter Packett
Director of Sales	Freddy Forklift
Information Systems Manager	Harry Helpnot
Help Desk Manager	Millie Sekkons
Network Specialist	Roddy Routebegone

WeServeData is currently experiencing problems at its main branch. Users have reported delays on the network. They report that applications slow to a crawl and are essentially unusable during the middle of the day. Figure 3-10 shows the company's current topology.

Figure 3-10   *Present Topology at WeServeData*

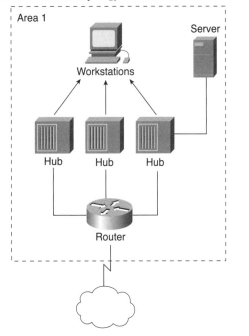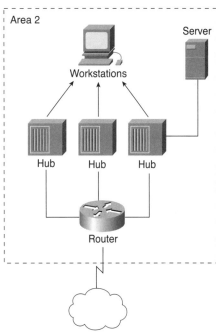

The folks at RouteitRight are having a discussion about WeServeData. Billy Broadcast has talked to the CEO of WeServeData, Herb Format, who has articulated a five-year business plan to expand into data warehousing.

Herb has identified the following business requirements for WeServeData:

- Increase service subscribers by 15 percent each year
- Reduce or trim network operating cost
- Provide users with quality service by maximizing network performance

Herb will make the business upgrade only when he believes his customers have confidence in WeServeData's ability to deliver services with the current technology. Roddy suggests that a traffic analysis be performed on the network to determine the cause of the bottlenecks. In addition, Roddy mentioned that a simulator might be used to determine latency, throughput, and packet loss on the network. Millie recommends an inventory of the applications to determine if the software is working properly. Peter thinks that the shared hubs should be replaced with LAN switches.

1 What requirements must you take into account when redesigning the network infrastructure for peak performance?

2 What is an advantage of the recommended change?

3 What changes could be made to ensure reliability and redundancy?

4 How can WeServeData address potential problems in the future?

Scenario 2

RouteitRight has been asked to review a design plan submitted by WeServeData for a client. WeServeData has contracted with Hook Me Up, a network cable installation company, to install network cable throughout its LAN. After a discussion, Hook Me Up has decided to implement 10BaseT Category 5 UTP wire for Hook Me Up's network.

1 Are there areas where the length exceeds the UTP cable length requirements?

2 In the areas where the length is OK, what other factors might determine the selection of a cable?

Use the following table to help determine the distances between locations and the length of cable required to reach between them.

Location	Distance	Location	Distance
1 to 2	50 feet	Hub to 1	400 feet
2 to 3	100 feet	Hub to 2	625 feet
3 to 4	150 feet	Hub to 3	800 feet
4 to 5	50 feet	Hub to 4	720 feet

continues

(Continued)

Location	Distance	Location	Distance
5 to 6	75 feet	Hub to 5	390 feet
6 to 7	80 feet	Hub to 6	400 feet
7 to 8	100 feet	Hub to 7	532 feet
8 to 9	125 feet	Hub to 8	389 feet
1 to 9	190 feet	Hub to 9	400 feet

Answers to Scenario 1

1 What requirements must you take into account when redesigning the network infrastructure for peak performance?

The original design at WeServeData assumed the traditional 80/20 design, where 80% of the network traffic is contained on the LAN. Performance problems at WeServeData quite likely started when new and existing user applications started moving to centralized sources of data storage and retrieval. No longer an 80/20 model, the traffic pattern has moved toward what is now referred to as the 20/80 model. In the 20/80 model, the new application requirements are considered because only 20% of the traffic is assumed to be local to the workgroup LAN, and 80% of the traffic is assumed to be leaving. The recommended design assumed the 20/80 model.

The performance of multilayer switching matches the requirements of the new 20/80 traffic model. The two components of multilayer switching on the Catalyst 5000 family are the RSM and the NetFlow feature card. The RSM is a Cisco IOS-based multiprotocol router on a card. Keep in mind that no performance penalty is associated with Layer 3 switching versus Layer 2 switching with the NetFlow feature card. The distribution layer consists of the Catalyst 5000 family of multilayer switches. The multilayer design takes advantage of the Layer 2 switching performance and features of the Catalyst family switches in the access layer and backbone and uses multilayer switching in the distribution layer. The multilayer model keeps the existing logical network design and addressing as in the traditional hub and router model. Access-layer subnets terminate at the distribution layer. From the other side, backbone subnets also terminate at the distribution layer. The distribution layer forms a broadcast boundary so that broadcasts won't be passed from area to area.

2 What is an advantage of this recommended change?

The greatest strengths of this model stems from its modular nature. It is modular because every part within a layer performs the same logical function. One key advantage of modular design is that different technologies can be deployed with no impact on the model's logical structure. For example, Fast Ethernet can be substituted for ATM LANE.

ATM LANE can be substituted for Gigabit Ethernet, and so on. Modularity makes both migration and integration of legacy technologies much easier. Troubleshooting is also easier because the whole design is highly deterministic in terms of performance, path determination, and failure recovery.

3 What changes could be made to ensure reliability and redundancy?

The distribution-layer switch shown in Figure 3-11 represents a point of failure at the building level. Users in Area 1 (the left side of the figure) could lose their connections to the backbone in the event of a power failure. If a link from a wiring closet switch to the distribution-layer switch is disconnected, all users on a floor could lose their connections to the backbone. Figure 3-12 shows a design that provides reliability and redundancy.

Figure 3-11 *Proposed Topology at WeServeData*

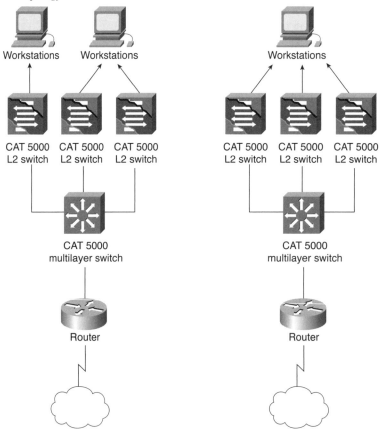

Figure 3-12   *Proposed Topology with Redundancy at WeServeData*

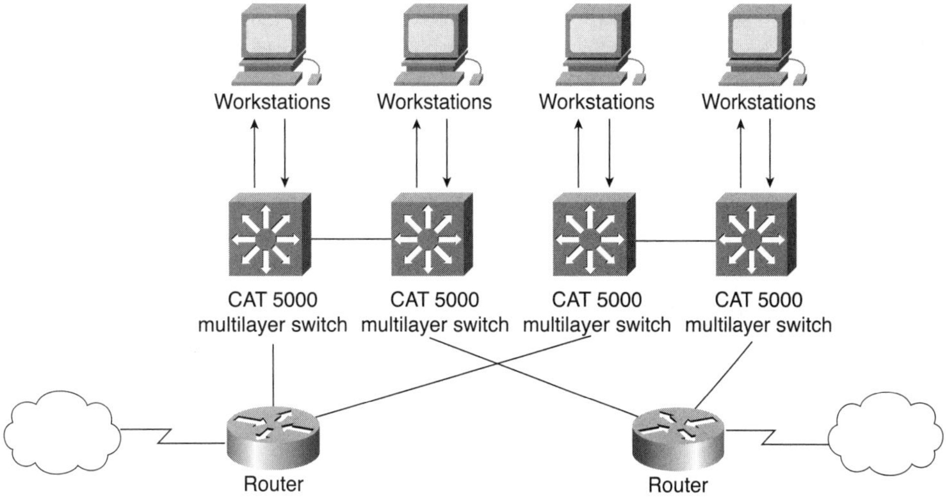

Multilayer switches A and B provide redundant connectivity. Redundant links from each access-layer switch connect to distribution-layer switches A and B. Redundancy in the backbone is achieved by installing two Catalyst switches in the core. Redundant links from the distribution layer provide failover as well as load balancing over multiple paths across the backbone. Redundant links connect access-layer switches to a pair of Catalyst multilayer switches in the distribution layer. Fast failover at Layer 3 is achieved with Cisco's Hot Standby Router Protocol (HSRP). The two distribution-layer switches cooperate to provide HSRP gateway routers for all the IP hosts in the building. Fast failover at Layer 2 is achieved by Cisco's UplinkFast feature. Load balancing across the core is achieved by intelligent Layer 3 routing protocols implemented in the Cisco IOS software.

4 How can WeServeData address potential problems in the future?

Because WeServeData expects growth, the company can definitely expect change. As the company grows and changes, so will the demands placed on the network. Business and Web applications will become more powerful and demanding as networks deliver more information to more users. The certainty of change makes flexibility a primary requirement for LAN solutions. To give WeServeData the technical liberty to change and grow, Cisco Systems offers a broad selection of best-of-class LAN solutions in desktop, stackable, and chassis-based models. Choose the right-size solution to meet today's requirements with the scalability and robustness for tomorrow's needs at WeServeData. As the LAN grows, connections and bandwidth can be added with clustering and stacking options.

Answers to Scenario 2

All of the distances to the hub exceed the maximum cable length of 328 feet specified by 10BaseT. Therefore, the hub-to-spoke solution will not work in these cases (see Figure 3-13). The maximum length of a 10BaseT segment is 100 meters (328 feet). Repeaters can be used to extend this cable length.

Figure 3-13   *WeServeData Client Network*

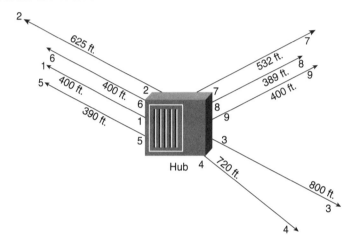

This chapter covers the following topics that you will need to master as a CCDP:

- **ATM protocols and specifications**—This section discusses the ATM protocol stack and how ATM uses virtual circuits for data transmission.

- **ATM routing in private networks**—This section discusses routing protocols and methods used in defining ATM addresses.

- **ATM design**—This section discusses show design models for ATM, which includes campus, LAN, and the WAN core.

CHAPTER 4

ATM Solutions

The evolving quality of service (QoS) and multiservice application integration requirements of voice, video, and data are driving the demand for ATM. As soon as you know the business, technical, and networking requirements, you can construct the appropriate ATM design solution. This chapter takes a closer look at how ATM technology can be used in high-performance workgroups and backbones.

ATM is a costly but all-purpose technology that can be implemented in campus-area networks (CAN) and global-area networks, as well as local- and wide-area networks. We discuss its many uses in this chapter.

Cisco expects the successful CCDP candidate to be able to use ATM design models to render an ATM solution that meets the client's requirements for performance. The CID exam tests your knowledge of how ATM can be integrated into a successful network design. It is expected that a CCDP will make design recommendations to improve performance utilizing ATM technologies.

How to Best Use This Chapter

By following these steps, you can make better use of your study time:

- Keep your notes and the answers for all your work with this book in one place for easy reference.

- Take the "Do I Know This Already?" quiz and write down your answers. Studies show that retention is significantly increased through writing down facts and concepts, even if you never look at the information again.

- Use the diagram shown in Figure 4-1 to guide you to the next step.

"Do I Know This Already?" Quiz

The purpose of the "Do I Know This Already?" quiz is to help you decide which parts of this chapter to use. If you intend to read the entire chapter, you do not necessarily need to answer these questions now.

This 15-question quiz helps you determine how to spend your limited study time. The quiz is divided into three smaller "quizlets" that help you select the sections of the chapter on which to focus. Figure 4-1 outlines suggestions on how to spend your time in this chapter. Use Table 4-1 to record your score.

Table 4-1 *Score Sheet for Quiz and Quizlets*

Quizlet Number	Foundation Topics Section Covering These Questions	Questions	Score
1	ATM protocols and specifications	1, 2, 3, 4	
2	ATM routing in private networks	6, 7, 8, 9, 10, 11, 12, 13	
3	ATM design	14, 15	

Figure 4-1 *How to Best Use This Chapter*

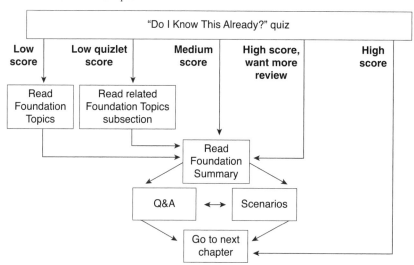

If you skip to the Foundation Summary, Q&A, and Scenarios sections and have trouble with the material there, you should go back to the Foundation Topics section.

1 What is the size of an ATM cell, and how do its fixed length and size contribute to low latency?

2 What are the two types of virtual circuits used by ATM?

_____

_____

_____

3 Name and describe the three layers of the ATM reference model.

_____

_____

_____

4 What layer of the OSI model closely relates to the ATM reference model?

_____

_____

_____

5 For each application listed, match the ATM adaptation layer best suited to it:

Data   AAL 1
Voice   AAL 2
SMDS   AAL 3/4
            AAL 5

_____

_____

_____

6 Name the four major components of ATM LANE.

_____

_____

_____

7 For what two LAN clients does ATM LANE provide emulation?

_____

_____

_____

8 What two types of interfaces are described in the ATM model?

_____

_____

_____

9 Name four alternate models for ATM internetworking.

_____

_____

_____

10 Name four networking areas where ATM could be implemented.

_____

_____

_____

11 What protocol controls the user cell stream between nodes and networks?

_____

_____

_____

12 How many characters comprise an NSAP address?

_____

_____

_____

13 What is Interim Local Management Interface (ILMI), and how is it used to connect end stations?

_____

_____

_____

14 Name four Cisco products that can form the building blocks of an ATM WAN.

_____

_____

_____

15 Name two business and technical requirements that might lead an engineer to select ATM as a design solution.

_____

_____

_____

The answers to the "Do I Know This Already?" quiz are found in Appendix A. The suggested choices for your next step are as follows:

- **6 or less overall score**—Read the chapter. This includes the "Foundation Topics," "Foundation Summary," and "Q&A" sections, as well as the scenarios at the end of the chapter.

- **2 or less on any quizlet**—Review the subsection(s) of the "Foundation Topics" part of this chapter based on Table 4-1. Then move into the "Foundation Summary," the "Q&A" section, and the scenarios at the end of the chapter.

- **7, 8, or 9 overall score**—Begin with the "Foundation Summary" section and then go to the "Q&A" section and scenarios at the end of the chapter.

- **10 or more overall score**—If you want more review on these topics, skip to the "Foundation Summary" section, and then go to the "Q&A" section and scenarios at the end of the chapter. Otherwise, move to the next chapter.

Foundation Topics

ATM Protocols and Specifications

For most people, ATM is short for Automatic Teller Machine. ATMs can be used at many locations throughout the world.

To some Ethernet lovers who have seen this highly touted technology protocol rise and fall in popularity, ATM stands for A Tragic Mistake.

To a CCDP, ATM stands for *Asynchronous Transfer Mode*. ATM is a technology that allows voice, video, and data transmission at gigabit speeds. Until the advent of Gigabit Ethernet, ATM was the only technology that could integrate all types of network traffic at higher speeds. ATM is still the only technology that provides multiservice integration with quality of service.

The ATM Forum is responsible for creating standards and specifications that ensure that ATM remains responsive to user needs. The ATM Forum was founded in October 1991 by Nortel Networks, Sprint Communications, Sun Microsystems, and Digital Equipment Corporation.

ATM switches small units of data called *cells*. The cell has a fixed length of 53 bytes—48 for data and 5 for the header. The small size of the cell makes ATM ideal for handling delay-sensitive traffic, such as voice and video. With the fixed length, the ATM switch doesn't have to be notified when the transmission is done. The switch knows when each cell ends and can process the data rapidly. ATM switches switch cells in hardware. An ATM switch doesn't waste overhead looking for information in software. ATM can move data *fast!* See Figure 4-2.

Figure 4-2   *ATM Data Frame*

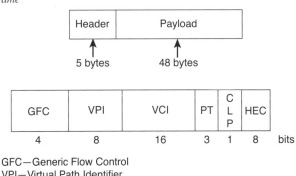

GFC—Generic Flow Control
VPI—Virtual Path Identifier
VCI—Virtual Channel Identifier
PT—Payload Type
CLP—Cell Loss Priority
HEC—Header Error Check

ATM Cell Format—Header and Payload

NOTE   If you feel the need for speed, ATM might be the answer. The small size of the ATM cells is the secret of ATM's velocity.

Because ATM is a connection-oriented protocol, there is a connection identifier in every cell header, which links a cell with a virtual channel on a physical link. The connection identifier consists of two subfields: the *Virtual Channel Identifier* (VCI) and the *Virtual Path Identifier* (VPI). VCIs and VPIs are used in multiplexing, demultiplexing, and switching a cell through the network. They are assigned at each link between ATM nodes when a connection is established, and they remain for the duration of the connection. ATM's flexibility allows it to run on permanent virtual circuits (PVC), as well as switched virtual circuits (SVC).

Permanent Virtual Circuits (PVCs)

PVCs are like leased lines. Once they're configured, they are always there. A PVC represents an end-to-end circuit that can be rerouted in the event of failure. Cisco requires subinterfaces to connect routers using PVCs. When configuring routers, note the VPI and the VCI number. Both ends of the VPI and the VCI must match. Think of the VCI as a highway and the VPI as a lane on that highway. For the sake of discussion, imagine a highway with five lanes (or paths). To create the circuit, if Router 1 is using highway 1, lane 4, then Router 2 should use highway 1, lane 4.

Same Highway---Same LaneConnection
Same Highway--Different LaneNo Connection
Different Highway- Different LaneNo Connection
1 0 5◆===============➡ 1 0 5

Figure 4-3 and Example 4-1 show an example of a PVC end-station configuration.

Figure 4-3   *ATM PVC Scenario*

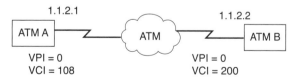

Example 4-1 *PVC Configuration Example*

```
hostname RtrA
!
interface ATM3/0
no ip address
!
interface ATM3/0.1 point-to-point
ip address 1.1.1.1 255.255.255.0
pvc 0/108
protocol ip 1.1.1.2
broadcast
encapsulation aal5snap
```

Switched Virtual Circuits (SVCs)

SVCs are temporary circuits. The SVC is set up, maintained, and freed by ILMI signaling
between the end-user device and the switch. When an ATM device wants to connect, it sends a
request packet from device to switch. After it's connected, it works like a PVC. When it's
finished, the circuit is torn down. Figure 4-4 shows a classic IP over ATM configuration (see
also Example 4-2).

Figure 4-4 *Classic IP Over ATM Configuration Using SVC*

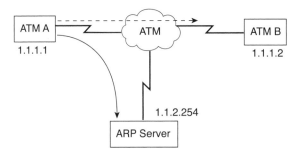

Step 1. Router ATM A wants to ping 1.1.1.2
Step 2. Router ATM A asks ARP server for NSAP matching 1.1.1.2
Step 3. Router ATM A creates SVC to router ATM B's NSAP

Example 4-2 *IP over ATM using SVC*

```
interface ATM3/0
no ip address
pvc 0/5 qsaal
pvc 0/16 ilmi
!
!
```

Example 4-2 *IP over ATM using SVC (Continued)*

```
interface ATM3/0
interface ATM3/0.1 multipoint
ip address 1.1.1.1 255.255.255.0
atm esi-address 777777777777.00
atm arp-server nsap 47.0091810000000001007386901.555555555555.00
RtrA#show arp
Protocol Address Age (min) Hardware Addr Type Interface
Internet 1.1.1.2 0 0 / 55 ATM ATM3/0.1
Internet 1.1.1.1 0 0 / 54 ATM ATM3/0.1
```

ATM Virtual Circuits

ATM virtual circuits operate in one of the following service categories:

- **Constant Bit Rate (CBR)**—CBR supports real-time applications that need a fixed amount of bandwidth. CBR supports applications that allow only a limited number of variations in delay. Voice and constant-bit-rate video are examples of two applications that require CBR.

- **Variable Bit Rate (VBR)**

  — Real-time Variable Bit Rate (rt-VBR)—rt-VBR supports time-sensitive applications that have constrained delay and delay variation requirements. Voice and variable-bit video are examples of two applications that might require rt-VBR.

  — Nonreal-time Variable Bit Rate (nrt-VBR)—nrt-VBR supports applications that have no constraints on delay and delay variations. Packet data transfers, terminal sessions, and file transfers fit the category of traffic that could utilize nrt-VBR.

- **Unspecified Bit Rate (UBR)**—The UBR service can be classified as a "best shot" service. It does not require constraints on delay and delay variations. It provides no specific quality of service. It provides no guarantees. Any traffic that does not require performance guarantees can be categorized under UBR.

- **Available Bit Rate (ABR)**—The ABR service distributes bandwidth among users. The objective of ABR is to make unused bandwidth available to end users in a fair and timely manner. ABR does not provide guarantees for delay variation. So real-time applications, such as voice and video, would not work well under ABR. Nonsensitive data traffic is the best fit for the ABR service.

ATM Reference Model and the OSI Model

The three layers of the ATM Reference Model are the *ATM physical layer,* the *ATM layer,* and the *ATM adaptation layers* (AAL). These three layers correlate to the physical and data-link layers of the OSI model. The ATM physical layer closely relates to the physical layer (Layer 1) in the OSI model. The ATM physical layer is responsible for tracking ATM cell boundaries, converting bits into cells, packaging cells into frames, and controlling the flow of bits between transmitting and receiving devices. The ATM layer establishes virtual connections and passes ATM cells through the ATM network. The ATM layer delivers the 48-byte payload on established connections. The AAL is responsible for allowing data conversions from multiple applications to and from the ATM cell. AAL translates higher-layer services, such as voice and video, into the size and format of an ATM cell. AAL also supports packet-based services, such as IP and Frame Relay. Figure 4-5 illustrates the relationship between the OSI model and the ATM model.

Figure 4-5   *OSI Model and ATM Model*

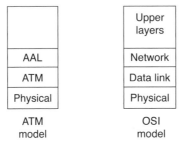

ATM Adaptation Layers (AAL)

The following sections discuss the five AALs. In addition to its other capabilities, ATM services provides functionality at five levels of support.

AAL1

The AAL1 protocol can transfer service data units received at a constant bit rate from the source and can deliver them at the same bit rate to the destination. AAL1 supports connection-oriented services that require constant bit rates and have specific timing and delay requirements. Voice and video are examples of applications that use AAL1.

AAL2

The AAL2 protocol supports ATM transport of connection-oriented variable-bit-rate applications that do not require constant bit rates.

AAL3/4

ATM combines AAL3 and AAL4 into a single unit called AAL3/4. AAL3/4 supports both connection-oriented and connectionless variable-bit-rate traffic, such as SMDS.

AAL5

The AAL5 protocol is used for data applications. AAL5 can provide a suitable solution for data applications, which are tolerant of delay and cell loss. AAL5 does not provide for error recovery and cell retransmission. This trade-off results in smaller bandwidth overhead and faster processing.

ATM Routing in Private Networks

Private Network Node Interface (PNNI) provides dynamic routing with QoS support. PNNI supports prefix routing for public and private networks and supports an address hierarchy. PNNI uses message flows to establish point-to-point and point-to-multipoint PVCs and SVCs. PNNI signaling controls the cell stream between nodes and networks.

The Interim Interswitch Signaling Protocol (IISP) is a protocol that is designed to provide signaling between switches from multiple vendors. The requirement to manually configure its prefix tables limits its applicability to networks with only a small number of nodes. The significance of IISP has diminished since the release of PNNI.

Designing an ATM Address Plan

Your ATM address plan is important for efficient operation and management. When designing ATM address allocation, keep in mind the following:

- ATM address prefixes must be globally unique.

- Addresses must be hierarchical and planned to match your network topology.

- Plan for future network expansion.

To create private ATM networks that can interoperate with a global ATM internetwork, all ATM addresses should be globally unique. To satisfy the uniqueness requirement, a number of registration authorities administer ATM addresses. ATM addresses are distributed in sets with a common prefix. The registration authority ensures the uniqueness of the prefix. The recipient allocates the remaining part of the ATM address to devise an addressing scheme that is appropriate for the private network. The recipient has to assign the remaining address part in a way that creates a set of unique addresses. If these guidelines are followed, private ATM networks can achieve global ATM interconnection without the need to renumber the addressing scheme.

ATM uses two types of addresses—one for private networks and one for public networks. For private networks, ATM uses Network Service Access Point (NSAP) addresses. For public networks, ATM uses E.164 addresses.

Private networks use a 20-octet or 40-hex character address at the UNI. The following is an example of an NSAP address:

```
47.009181000000001007386901.777777777777.00
```

Network Interfaces

ATM can be used for public carrier networks and within private networking products. ATM recognizes two types of interfaces: network-to-network interfaces (NNIs) and user-to-network interfaces (UNIs).

The UNI is an interface between the user and the network switch. An ATM UNI connects a user interface to a broadband terminal equipment interface (B-TE), a terminal adapter (TA), or a network termination (NT) device. The NNI is the interface between networks or switches. The network interface can be used for private or public networks.

A *c UNI* is used to interconnect an ATM user with an ATM switch in a public service provider's network. A *private UNI* is used to interconnect an ATM user with an ATM switch that is managed as part of the same network. The primary distinction between these two classes of UNI is physical reach. There are several differences between the interfaces, but the primary distinction between these two classes of UNI is the reach of the network. Both UNIs share a common ATM layer specification but may use different physical media. Facilities that connect users to switches in public central offices must be capable of covering long distances. Private switching equipment can use limited distance technologies and can often be located in the same room as the user device.

Controlling Congestion

What is congestion, and how do you control it? Everyone at one time or another has experienced congestion. Even without defining it, you know it when you see it, and it is always a bad thing. If you commute to work on a busy freeway, you have quite likely experienced congestion. If you work at home, you might have experienced congestion in checkout lines at the supermarket or at ticket lines at a movie theater. If you hear about these kinds of problems only from your chauffeur, butler, and hired staff, you might have experienced nasal congestion from a stuffy nose.

Congestion occurs when the demand exceeds the available resources. In the case of ATM, it occurs when bandwidth demand requests from the user exceed the available bandwidth. Whenever the total input rate is greater than the output link capacity, congestion occurs. When an ATM circuit is congested, the user does not get the quality of service that is described in the service contract.

There are several myths about the solutions for congestion control:

Myth: Congestion is caused by the shortage of buffer space. The problem will be solved when the cost of memory becomes cheap enough to allow for large quantities of memory.
Fact: Large buffers are valuable only for very short-term congestion. If a switch's total input rate is 1 Mbps and the capacity of the output link is 0.5 Mbps, the buffer will overflow after 16 seconds with 1 Mbps of memory and will also overflow after 1 hour with 225 Mbps of memory if the situation persists. This example shows that a larger buffer size can delay the discarding of cells but cannot prevent it. In addition, the long queue and long delay introduced by large memory might be undesirable for some applications.

Myth: Congestion is caused by slow links. The problem will be solved when high-speed links become available.
Fact: More bandwidth is not always the panacea. An increase in link bandwidth can actually aggravate the congestion problem if the higher-speed links make the network more unbalanced. Higher-speed links will shift the bottleneck to the switch and make the congestion condition worse.

Myth: Congestion is caused by slow processors. The problem will be solved when processor speed is improved.
Fact: This is another case of dynamic bottleneck. When faster processors transmit more data in unit time, the bottleneck shifts, and the target is overwhelmed.

Congestion is a dynamic problem. Any static solutions might not be sufficient to solve this problem. All the issues just presented—buffer shortage, slow links, and slow processors— might not be the sole cause of congestion. They might represent the symptoms of congestion. The CCDP knows that a design that renders a long-term solution does not treat the symptom. The CCDP must remember that adding buffers, processing power, and bandwidth might not address the root causes of congestion. A successful design uses a congestion-management strategy that addresses the root of the problem.

ATM Design

ATM is truly an all-purpose protocol. It can be a data-link protocol. ATM has many options available to the design process.

ATM can be used as the following:

- Local Area Network Emulation (LANE)

- A point-to-point data link

- A high-speed workgroup and backbone

- A router cluster backbone

- A wide-area network

ATM as a Local Area Network

LAN Emulation (LANE) is an ATM Forum standard that allows Ethernet and Token Ring clients to connect to an ATM network.

The LANE requirement makes ATM look like Ethernet or Token Ring. Therefore, an Ethernet client can send packets from endpoint to endpoint without realizing that it has traveled through an ATM network. ATM is connection-oriented, so it removes the connection requirements from the upper-layer protocols.

Emulated LANs (ELANs) have many of the same characteristics as virtual LANs (VLANs). ELANs rely on a group of ATM devices and Layer 2 LAN switches. Together, the devices comprise an independent broadcast domain. ELANs are interconnected by routing.

Living in the Fast Lane: A Tender Moment

There are millions of bits in the big city. This is a story about one of them. The names have been changed to protect the protocols. Delivering data on an Ethernet bus is a tough job, but someone's got to do it. On the Ethernet bus, there are no red lights, no stop signs. You travel at your own risk. The road is difficult at best. It's paved with hardships unforeseen. Every transmission is a new test. It is indeed a tough way to earn a living. The next time you open a document or send an e-mail, take a moment and say thanks to Billy Bitts.

Every day, Billy Bitts makes a living visiting ports up and down the Ethernet expressway. It is a life filled with uncertainty. Living a life of collisions is tough. But Billy's a dreamer. One day, he says, when he gets that promotion and raise, he won't have to put up with collisions every day.

After one especially tough week living in and out of the bit bucket, Billy finally got the break he was looking for. One day, he made a delivery to the VeeLan Cafe. While there, he met a waitress who took his clock pulse away. Her name was Daisy Chaine, and she told him about a place he could work where he would never have a collision, he would never hear customers complain about slow delivery, and he could spend his time cruising in the fast lane.

Daisy took Billy to the place. For Billy, it was love at first byte. Billy and Daisy shared A Tender Moment together and called the place she discovered A Tender Moment (ATM) Lane.

Billy had a lot of questions about ATM Lane. It was unlike any place he had ever seen on the Ethernet expressway. Billy asked Daisy:

- How would he find addresses on ATM Lane?
- How would new clients be welcomed to ATM Lane?
- How are packets broadcast?
- How are packets multicast?

Daisy explained that at ATM Lane, a LECS (LAN Emulation Configuration Server) welcome station welcomes new clients. Clients from Ethernet or Token Ring environments are greeted and assigned to an ELAN. Each client gets a visitor's badge and ID information. The badge and ID information consist of a unique address. The client can be identified by its address, which includes the ATM NSAP and MAC address. If the frame needs advice about how it will get to its destination, it goes to the LES (Lane Emulation Server) information booth.

The LES knows most of the places to see and visit on ATM Lane. It provides the destination address for the frame. In the event that the LES hasn't heard of the new destination, it contacts the BUS (Broadcast and Unknown Server). The BUS finds the destination. As soon as the client has the ID information and knows where the destination address is, it is ready to cruise at high speed.

Billy heard all he needed to know. He quit his job on the Ethernet bus. Since he's been working on ATM Lane, Billy says that life is so good, it's like living in a cloud.

LANE Components

ATM LANE allows for a translation and transition of data from Ethernet and Token Ring to ATM. Thanks to ATM LANE, users can receive high-speed, guaranteed, real-time information while using a legacy LAN network. The following sections define and describe the four logical components in the LANE specification.

LECS (LAN Emulation Configuration Server)

The LECS contains configuration information for all ELANs in the administrative domain. It is responsible for assigning each LEC to an ELAN. The LECS makes the ATM addresses available to the LES.

LES (LAN Emulation Server)

The LES manages the stations that comprise the ELAN. It performs address registration and resolution using the LAN Emulation Address Resolution Protocol (LE-ARP). When a device requests address information, it gets the information from the LES.

BUS (Broadcast and Unknown Server)

The BUS performs two major functions. When the LES does not know an address, it sends a broadcast to all stations to find the unknown client. Also, the BUS provides an important part of LAN emulation. Much of LAN traffic involves broadcasts and multicasts. To emulate the LAN, the BUS handles broadcasts and multicast requests across the ATM cloud.

LEC (LAN Emulation Client)

A LEC can be an ATM end station, a router, a switch, or a bridge. The LEC is responsible for data forwarding, address resolution, control functions, and emulating MAC functions to upper-layer protocols. The LEC registers its MAC and ATM addresses with the LES.

Routers can connect diverse LAN and WAN links to existing ATM internetworks. Routers can perform vital ATM services such as multicast server, ARP server, and LAN emulation server. A single Cisco router with compatible IOS features can serve as a LECS, a LES, a BUS, and a LEC. Figure 4-6 depicts a LAN emulation circuit.

Figure 4-6   *LAN Emulation Circuit*

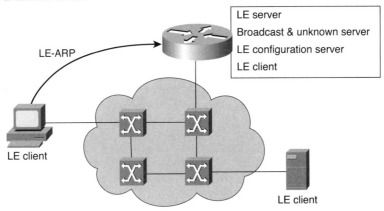

Figure 4-7 illustrates a high-speed workgroup and campus backbone application utilizing ATM as a high-speed protocol.

Figure 4-7   *ATM as a High-Speed Workgroup and Campus Backbone Application*

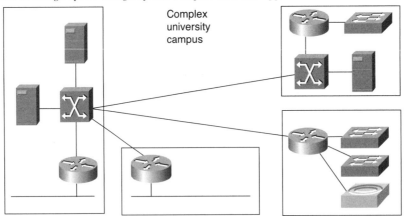

The campus buildings are connected by ATM, and the floors are connected by FDDI. This example uses a combination of routing and switching. ATM can be used as a point-to-point network. Figure 4-8 shows an example.

Figure 4-8   *ATM as a Point-to-Point Network*

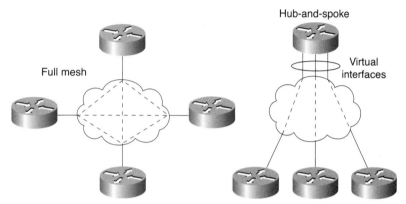

ATM can be configured as a full-mesh virtual circuit between routers. Each router can transmit directly to every other router over ATM. Figure 4-9 shows how ATM can be used as a router cluster backbone.

Figure 4-9   *ATM as a Router Cluster Backbone*

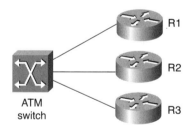

Routers can connect the LAN and WAN data links to ATM backbones.

ATM as a Wide-Area Network

The Cisco ATM products suited for WAN deployment include the following:

- Cisco/StrataCom IGX switch, which is well-suited for deployment in an enterprise WAN environment
- Cisco/StrataCom BPX/AXIS switch, which meets the needs of high-end enterprise WAN and service provider environments

- Cisco AIP for the Cisco 7500 and 7000 series of routers
- Cisco ATM Network Interface Module (NIM) for the Cisco 4700 and 4500 series of routers
- Cisco edge devices such as the Catalyst 5000 and Catalyst 3000 switches, which connect legacy LANs with an ATM network

Cisco/StrataCom BPX

The *Cisco/StrataCom BPX Service Node* is a standards-based, multiservice ATM switch designed to deliver the highest levels of network scalability, flexibility, and efficiency. The BPX achieves multiservice functionality, efficient use of bandwidth, high performance for all users, and guaranteed QoS for all traffic types through its advanced traffic-management features.

Advanced traffic-management features, together with an optimized hardware architecture, allow the switch to simultaneously support ATM, Frame Relay, Internet, voice, wireless communication, video, switched internetworking, and circuit emulation services.

The BPX also offers operational ease. With the BPX's 20-Gbps capacity of high-throughput, low-latency switching and support for multiple classes of service, service providers can deliver innovative revenue-generating data, voice, and video services. The BPX includes high-density Broadband Switch Module (BXM) cards that provide standard interfaces for connecting to cell-based customer premises equipment via ATM UNI or to non-Cisco networks via NNI.

The BXM cards support ATM-Frame Relay internetworking and service internetworking. They also allow you to configure PVCs or SVCs for the following defined service classes:

- Constant Bit Rate (CBR)
- Variable Bit Rate-Real-Time (rt-VBR-RT)
- Variable Bit Rate-Non-Real-Time (nrt-VBR-RT)
- Unspecified Bit (UBR)
- Available Bit Rate (ABR)

AXIS Interface Shelf

The AXIS interface shelf lets the BPX Service Node support a wide range of user services. AXIS modules adapt incoming data to 53-byte ATM cells using industry-standard ATM adaptation layers (AALs) for transport over the ATM network.

Because the AXIS interface shelf supports a range of services from a single platform, organizations can reduce equipment costs, fully utilize their investments in existing premises equipment, and rapidly deploy new services as required.

Services below 34 Mbps are provisioned on the AXIS shelf, and the following interfaces are supported:

- Frame Relay

- ATM Frame UNI
- SMDS
- T1/E1 ATM UNI
- n x T1/E1 inverse multiplexing for ATM (IMATM) UNI
- Circuit emulation
- ISDN switched access

Cisco/StrataCom IGX Family of Switches

The Cisco/StrataCom IGX family of switches provides the needed linkage to integrate high-speed LAN data and lower-speed voice and legacy data across the enterprise backbone in the most cost-effective manner. The IGX family of switches is specifically designed for enterprise integration.

The IGX family of ATM enterprise WAN switches includes the IGX8 (eight-slot switch), the IGX16 (16-slot switch), and the IGX32 (32-slot switch). The IGX family can provide the following enterprise WAN support:

- Voice
- Legacy data
- ATM
- Frame Relay
- Trunks

Benefits of the IGX

With the IGX switch, you can leverage ATM to save costs as follows:

- Apply utilization rates in your network design to source PVCs
- Combine multiple networks into one multiservice network
- Optimize the transmission network with design tools

By deploying IGX switches throughout the enterprise internetwork, you can obtain the following benefits:

- Integration of voice and data networks
- Improved performance for each type of traffic
- Better response times for new applications
- Reduced downtime
- Higher bandwidth utilization (a five-fold increase in traffic using existing trunks)
- Implementation of a scalable network that supports rapid deployment of new services
- Simplification of network design, with a reduction in management costs

Foundation Summary

This section contains tables that provide a convenient review of many key concepts in this chapter. If you are already comfortable with the topics in this chapter, this summary could help you recall a few details. If you have just read this chapter, this review should help solidify some key facts. If you are doing your final preparation before the exam, Tables 4-2 through 4-4 are a convenient way to review the day before the exam.

Table 4-2 *Components of ATM LANE*

Service	Function	Comments
LAN Emulation Client (LEC)	An endpoint that forwards data to the emulated ELAN	A single Cisco router or Catalyst switch can be a LEC, LES, BUS, and LECS simultaneously.
LAN Emulation Server (LES)	Provides mapping between ATM and LAN addresses	
Broadcast and Unknown Server (BUS)	Provides broadcasts for packets that have an unknown destination	
LAN Emulation Configuration Server (LECS)	Welcomes new users to the network	

Table 4-3 *Comparing ATM Addressing*

Address	Length	Used for PVC?	Used for SVC?	Comments
NSAP	40 hex characters	No	Yes	Address must be globally unique
VPI/VCI	24–28 bits in length	Yes	Yes	Address needs to be unique to only the local link

Table 4-4 *Comparing ATM Service Categories*

Service Category	Loss?	Delay Variance?	Bandwidth?	Preferred Applications
CBR	Yes	Yes	Yes	Voice, constant bit rate video
ABR	Yes	No	Yes	Nonsensitive data
UBR	No	No	No	High-performance file transfers

Table 4-4   *Comparing ATM Service Categories (Continued)*

RT-VBR	Yes	Yes	Yes	Voice, variable bit rate video
NRT-VBR	Yes	No	Yes	Terminal sessions, file transfers

ATM Network Components

The building blocks of an ATM internetwork may include the following:

- Routers with ATM interfaces

- Computers with a native ATM NIC

- LightStream 1010, Catalyst 5500 with ATM switch capability, or other ATM switches

- ATM physical layer, supporting Synchronous Optical Network (SONET) OC-3 with single or multimode fiber

- Transparent Asynchronous Transmitter/Receiver Interface (TAXI) with multimode fiber, or DS3/E3 with coaxial cable

- LAN switches with ATM interfaces

ATM works best if the design requires the following:

- Full support for Quality of Service (QoS)

- High-speed transport over long distances

- The potential for unlimited scalability and global reachability

ATM is a good choice if the following conditions exist:

- Network congestion must be relieved on the backbone

- Voice, video, and data must be consolidated to gain a business advantage

- Local-area network speed needs to exceed 100 Mbps

- Wide-area network speed needs to exceed T1 speed

Q&A

As mentioned in Chapter 1, the questions and scenarios in this book are more difficult than what you will experience on the actual exam. The questions do not attempt to cover more breadth or depth than the exam; however, they are designed to make sure that you know the answer. Rather than allowing you to derive the answer from clues hidden inside the question, the questions challenge your understanding and recall of the subject. Questions from the "Do I Know This Already?" quiz from the beginning of this chapter are repeated here to ensure that you have mastered this chapter's topic areas. Hopefully, these questions will help limit the number of exam questions on which you narrow your choices to two options and then guess. Be sure to use the CD and take the simulated exams.

The answers to these questions can be found in Appendix A.

1 What is the size of an ATM cell, and how do its fixed length and size contribute to low latency?

2 What are the two types of virtual circuits used by ATM?

3 Name and describe the three layers of the ATM reference model.

4 What layer of the OSI model closely relates to the ATM reference model?

5 For each application listed, match the ATM adaptation layer best suited to it:

Data   AAL 1
Voice   AAL 2
SMDS   AAL 3/4
          AAL 5

_____

_____

_____

6 Name the four major components of ATM LANE.

_____

_____

_____

7 For what two LAN clients does ATM LANE provide emulation?

_____

_____

_____

8 What two types of interfaces are described in the ATM model?

_____

_____

_____

9 Name four alternate models for ATM internetworking.

_____

_____

_____

10 Name four networking areas where ATM could be implemented.

_____

_____

_____

11 What protocol controls the user cell stream between nodes and networks?

_____

_____

_____

12 How many characters comprise an NSAP address?

_____

_____

_____

13 What is Interim Local Management Interface (ILMI), and how is it used to connect end stations?

_____

_____

_____

14 Name four Cisco products that can form the building blocks of an ATM WAN.

_____

_____

_____

15 Name two business and technical requirements that might lead an engineer to select ATM as a design solution.

_____

_____

_____

16 Why is congestion control a serious issue?

_____

_____

_____

17 What RFC allows multiple protocols to be multiplexed over a single PVC?

_____

_____

_____

18 Name four ATM layer service categories.

_____

_____

_____

19 Name four functions of the ATM physical layer.

_____

_____

_____

20 Name two types of addresses used by ATM.

_____

_____

_____

21 What is the function of the BUS?

_____

_____

_____

22 List three requirements of an efficient ATM address plan.

_____

_____

_____

23 True or false: A LAN Emulation client can be an ATM end station or router, but a switch or bridge cannot be configured as a LEC.

_____

_____

_____

24 True or false: Congestion is caused by slow links. The problem can always be solved by adding high-speed links.

_____

_____

_____

25 What is the function of the LAN Emulation Server?

_____

_____

_____

26 Describe the role that routers play in ATM internetworking.

_____

_____

_____

27 Name two Cisco ATM products suited for WAN deployment.

_____

_____

_____

28 What is one function of the ATM Forum?

_____

_____

_____

29 What is the function of the ATM layer?

_____

_____

_____

30 State two issues to consider when designing or expanding networks to include ATM.

_____

_____

_____

Scenarios

Scenario 1

To help design the optimum solution and address the issues presented in each chapter, you have contracted with the design professionals at RouteitRight to help you.

RouteitRight's key personnel are as follows:

Chief Executive Officer (CEO)	Billy Broadcast
Chief Information Officer (CIO)	Megg A. Bight
Senior Telecommunications Engineer	Peter Packett
Director of Sales	Freddy Forklift
Information Systems Manager	Harry Helpnot
Help Desk Manager	Millie Sekkons
Network Specialist	Roddy Routebegone

Distributed Learning, Inc., would like to teach Cisco routing throughout the country. In conversations with the CEO of Distributed Learning, Billy Broadcast has learned the business requirements that the network must meet:

- Deliver to the customers the services they require and demand.

- Make best use of the resources (bandwidth, people, and capital).

- Be capable of meeting the demand for growth in subscribers and bandwidth.

- Be able to support current and future applications, from telephony to multimedia.

- Have the reach to meet the needs of a global community into the new century.

In addition, Distributed Learning wants to set up remote access centers. At these remote access centers, students will access video terminals and connect to classrooms that are located at central sites. In this manner, students in rural and sparsely populated areas will be able to access the same information that students in metropolitan areas can. For example, a student in Soma, New Mexico, could access the same classroom resources as a student in Chicago.

Peter recommends that the design include ATM at the core and ATM to the desktop. Peter says that ATM is the best transport protocol for carrying voice, video, and data, and that currently it is the only protocol that includes built-in quality of service. Millie likes ATM. She knows that ATM has high performance. She believes that the students will be thoroughly satisfied with the performance of the ATM network. Megg wants the group to take a look at the cost of ATM. Megg has done some cost-benefit analysis for ATM in the past, and she knows that the benefits of ATM do not always justify the cost. In addition, she has heard that Gigabit Ethernet might be suitable for carrying the payload to the desktop. Roddy says that ATM can support longer distances than Gigabit Ethernet. In situations where two sites are connected by fiber, ATM is the better choice.

1 Is ATM a suitable transport protocol for Distributed Learning?

If so, design an enterprise ATM network for Distributed Learning using Cisco products. The design should allow Distributed Learning campuses at metropolitan sites to be connected to Distributed Learning campus remote sites.

Scenario 2

Fuster Bunn Video has contacted RouteitRight. Since Net Greeting was added to the network, some users have complained about performance. Fuster Bunn is very satisfied with the Net Greeting program, but it is concerned that the rest of the network's performance seems to be suffering as a result. After performing network analysis, Peter determined that when 10 Net Greeting connections were running simultaneously, the network was saturated and experienced serious performance problems. Repeated collisions were dropping network utilization to as low as 50 percent, an unacceptable level for customer satisfaction.

Fuster Bunn currently has an Ethernet network and a T-1 line to the Internet. Megg had a talk with their Sales Director and has identified the primary business requirement. Fuster Bunn would like to scale their existing network to provide video service while preserving their current investment in LAN technology. The folks at RouteitRight are having a discussion about this. Freddy says that Fuster Bunn might be able to go to ATM LANE. He knows that ATM LANE allows the current users and legacy Ethernet LAN users to take advantage of ATM's benefits without changes in their end-station hardware or software. Roddy says that adding an ATM switch as an ATM workgroup solution would work.

1 Is an ATM workgroup a workable solution for Fuster Bunn Video?

2 If so, design an ATM workgroup solution for Fuster Bunn Video.

Answer to Scenario 1

1 Is ATM a suitable transport protocol for Distributed Learning?

If so, design an enterprise ATM network for Distributed Learning using Cisco products. The design should allow Distributed Learning campuses at metropolitan sites to be connected to Distributed Learning campus remote sites.

ATM is the ideal choice as an enterprise transport protocol for the Distributed Learning network. ATM is recommended as the key core infrastructure technology because of ATM's guarantee of true multiservice capability with high-bandwidth efficiency and service quality across all services. ATM also addresses the broadband traffic demand within the Distributed Learning WAN backbone and provides the transport service for locations requiring only narrowband resources. Of equal significance are ATM's access and gateway devices, which can handle the classes of service needed for video with fairness and high quality.

As time passes, Distributed Learning will require applications that go beyond its current requirements of technical sophistication. ATM's scalability can provide support for today's and tomorrow's emerging applications needs with quality of service. ATM maps well to the existing IP Ethernet and Frame Relay network that Distributed Learning already maintains. In addition to connecting to workgroup ATM switches, ATM can be used to interconnect LAN switches. ATM can bridge existing legacy Ethernet switches with ultra-high-speed networks that can scale as high as 10 Gbps. High-speed ATM switches can be located at the core of the network. By integrating all of these services onto a common platform and a common ATM transport infrastructure, Distributed Learning can gain greater manageability while eliminating the need for multiple overlay networks. The Catalyst 5500 or the Lightstream 1010 can function effectively as an ATM workgroup switch. Workgroup ATM switches have an Ethernet switch port and an ATM uplink to connect to a Catalyst 5500 can serve as an ATM switch. The Catalyst 5500 LAN is a 13-slot switch. Slot 1 is reserved for the supervisor engine module, which provides switching, local and remote management, and dual Fast Ethernet uplinks. Slot 2 is available for a second, redundant supervisor engine, or any of the other supported modules. Slots 3 through 12 support any of the supported modules. Slot 13 can be populated only with a LightStream 1010 ATM Switch Processor (ASP). If an ASP is present in slot 13, slots 9 through 12 support any of the standard LightStream 1010 ATM switch port adapter modules (PAMs). The use of ATM switches minimizes potential backbone congestion while enabling the deployment of new VLANs. See Figure 4-10.

Figure 4-10   *ATM Network for Distributed Learning, Inc.*

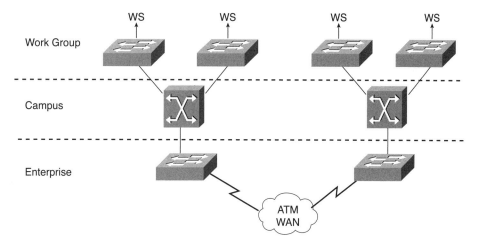

Answer to Scenario 2

1 Is an ATM workgroup a workable solution for Fuster Bunn Video?

2 If so, design an ATM workgroup solution for Fuster Bunn Video.

Fuster Bunn needs to increase its network's bandwidth and manageability while supporting the additional application requirements for Net Greeting. ATM's commitment to quality of service and its support for high throughput make it an ideal choice to support Net Greeting. The ATM workgroup solution provides an ATM workgroup switch that provides 25 Mbps ATM or 10 Mbps Ethernet switching connections to the Ethernet switches. The Ethernet switches can provide desktop users with 10 Mbps switched Ethernet connections. If you create an ATM workgroup, any bottleneck that previously existed will be removed from the network. ATM switches can offer the greater bandwidth required by the videoconferencing applications. The ATM workgroup will allow Fuster Bunn to protect its existing business investments and boost network performance with dedicated bandwidth to the desktop for each user. This ATM workgroup solution provides a state-of-the-art, robust, integrated solution that strikes an effective balance between upgrade costs and that meets Fuster Bunn's bandwidth needs, while providing the scalability to accommodate future growth. See Figure 4-11.

Figure 4-11 *Fuster Bunn ATM Workgroup Solution*

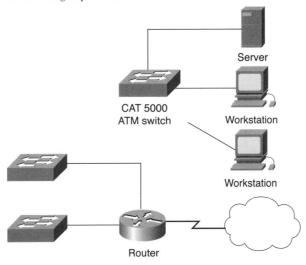

This chapter covers the following topics that you will need to master as a CCDP:

- **TCP/IP protocol and TCP/IP addressing**—Addressing choices and the decisions to be faced when designing a TCP/IP network are covered in detail in this section.

- **Classful and classless addressing**—This section defines classful and classless addressing and their role in optimizing TCP/IP design concerns.

- **Private network addressing**—Private network addressing and the methods that are used to conserve TCP/IP addressing space are discussed in this section.

Cisco expects the successful CCDP candidate to be able to use TCP/IP addressing fundamentals to render a cost-effective solution that will meet the client's requirements for scalability and stability. The CID exam tests your knowledge of how TCP/IP addressing can be integrated into a successful network design.

CHAPTER 5

IP Addressing

How to Best Use This Chapter

By following these steps, you can make better use of your study time:

- Keep your notes and the answers for all your work with this book in one place for easy reference.

- Take the "Do I Know This Already?" quiz and write down your answers. Studies show that retention is significantly increased through writing down facts and concepts, even if you never look at the information again.

- Use the diagram shown in Figure 5-1 to guide you to the next step.

Figure 5-1   *How to Best Use This Chapter*

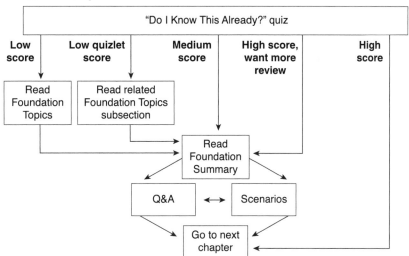

If you skip to the Foundation Summary, Q&A, and Scenarios sections and have trouble with the material there, you should go back to the Foundation Topics section.

"Do I Know This Already?" Quiz

The purpose of the "Do I Know This Already?" quiz is to help you decide what parts of this chapter to use. If you already intend to read the entire chapter, you do not necessarily need to answer these questions now.

This 15-question quiz helps you determine how to spend your limited study time. The quiz is divided into smaller "quizlets" that help you select the sections of the chapter on which to focus. Figure 5-1 outlines suggestions on how to spend your time in this chapter. Use Table 5-1 to record your score.

Table 5-1   *Score Sheet for Quiz and Quizlets*

Quizlet Number	Foundation Topics Section Covering These Questions	Questions	Score
1	TCP/IP Addressing	1, 2, 3, 5, 6, 7, 8, 12	
2	Classful and Classless Addressing	4, 9, 10, 11, 13, 14, 15	

1 What are the five IP address classes?

_____

_____

_____

2 What class of IP address is optimum for a small network?

_____

_____

_____

3 Which IP addresses are reserved for multicasting?

_____

_____

_____

4 What IP address class renders 254 hosts?

_____

_____

_____

5 Which IP addresses are reserved for experiments?

_____

_____

_____

6 What is NAT, and how can it help conserve IP addresses?

_____

_____

_____

7 List four benefits of address summarization.

_____

_____

_____

8 What subnet mask is ideal for connecting WAN links?

_____

_____

_____

9 Define classful routing.

_____

_____

_____

10 What is CIDR, and how does it offer greater flexibility in IP addressing?

_____

_____

_____

11 What is a discontiguous subnet?

_____

_____

_____

12 True or false: To support variable-length subnet masking and route summarization, a classless routing protocol must be incorporated into the design plan.

_____

_____

_____

13 Define classless routing.

_____

_____

_____

14 What is the prefix length of a Class A network?

_____

_____

_____

15 The network design requires 14 hosts. What network and subnet mask should be employed?

_____

_____

_____

The answers to the "Do I Know This Already?" quiz are found in Appendix A. The suggested choices for your next step are as follows:

- **6 or less overall score**—Read the chapter. This includes the "Foundation Topics," "Foundation Summary," and "Q&A" sections, as well as the scenarios at the end of the chapter.

- **2 or less on any quizlet**—Review the subsection(s) of the "Foundation Topics" part of this chapter based on Table 4-1. Then move into the "Foundation Summary," the "Q&A" section, and the scenarios at the end of the chapter.

- **7, 8, or 9 overall score**—Begin with the "Foundation Summary" section and then go to the "Q&A" section and scenarios at the end of the chapter.

- **10 or more overall score**—If you want more review on these topics, skip to the "Foundation Summary" section, and then go to the "Q&A" section and scenarios at the end of the chapter. Otherwise, move to the next chapter.

Foundation Topics

TCP/IP was initially developed by a Department of Defense (DOD) research project to provide interconnectivity between different branches and different computer networks within the DOD. TCP/IP was developed, in part, so that dissimilar systems in the military could communicate with each other. With technologies arising and then becoming obsolete in a few years, it is amazing that the original design concept of TCP/IP as a supernetwork has scaled well and continues to thrive with the explosion of the Internet.

Right now, TCP/IP is the universal protocol of choice for accessing information, products, and services. The global acceptance of IP is demonstrated in its ability to be deployed over all versions of data-link layer protocols. Now that the public Internet is used on a global scale, TCP/IP is the significant protocol in every major computer operating system. Machines at home, at work, or at play can connect to any other network using TCP/IP as a common medium. Thanks to TCP/IP, anyone can make their personal computer a host on the Internet. The casual browser can find, retrieve, view, and share information gathered from around the world.

TCP/IP Addressing

TCP/IP protocols fall under different layers of the OSI model. IP, which operates at the network layer of the OSI model, is responsible for moving packets of data from node to node. TCP, which operates at the transport layer of the OSI model, is responsible for verifying the correct delivery of data from client to server. Data can be lost in the intermediate network. TCP detects errors or lost data and retriggers retransmission until the data is correctly and completely received.

IP forwards each packet based on a 4-byte destination address. One of the most important design decisions a CCDP will make is the assignment of IP addresses. IP addressing represents the foundation of internetwork packet flow. One of the strengths of TCP/IP is its addressing scheme, which uniquely identifies every computer on the network. The public Internet address design is based on the premise that IP addresses are globally unique. If the design allowed duplicate IP addresses, there would be no way to ensure that a packet would know which duplicate address was the proper destination. The Internet Assigned Numbers Authority (IANA) assigns unique 32-bit IP addresses to organizations and companies. Globally unique addresses permit IP networks anywhere in the world to communicate with each other.

There are several ways to incorporate TCP/IP addressing. Efficient design requirements dictate that a choice be made with regard to which method is best for a given situation. The choices include the following:

- The use of automatic address assignment
- The use of public address space

- The use of address summarization
- The use of variable-length subnet masks
- The use of private address space

Prefix and Host Addressing

An IP address is divided into two parts: *prefix* and *host*. The prefix designates the network address, and the second part designates the host address. The IP address identifies a system location in the same manner that a street address identifies a house on a street. The network address identifies the systems that are located on the same physical network. The host address identifies the devices, such as workstation, server, and router, that are located on the network. Just as each house has a unique street and city address to ensure that mail is delivered efficiently, each system must have a unique network and host address to ensure that data is delivered efficiently. Figure 5-2 shows a 32-bit IP address, separated by prefix and host.

Figure 5-2   *Prefix and Host Addressing*

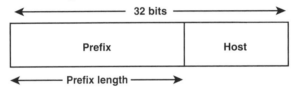

IP Network Classes

IP addressing supports five different network classes. *Class A* networks are intended mainly for use with networks that require a large number of hosts, because only 8 bits are provided for the network address field. *Class B* networks allocate 16 bits for the network address field, and *Class C* networks allocate 24 bits. Class C networks provide 8 bits for the host field, however, so the number of hosts per network (254) might be a limiting factor. In all cases, the leftmost bits indicate the network class. *Class D* is used for multicasting, and *Class E* is reserved for experimental operations. Table 5-2 shows IP address classes and the network addresses per class with standard subnet masks.

Table 5-2   *IP Address Classes*

Class	Network Address
A	1–126
B	128–191
C	192–223
D	224–239
E	240–254

Table 5-2   *IP Address Classes (Continued)*

Address	Class
10.1.1.1	A
180.171.2.1	B
201.211.1.4	C

Classful and Classless Routing

The original address design separated address groups into classes. *Classful routing protocols* were designed to make decisions based on the class of the IP address or the subnet mask that is associated with the interface. The design of classful networks assumes that the same major network will exist throughout the network. Classful routing observes the class address boundaries of Classes A, B, and C. Classful routing protocols cannot carry subnet mask information in their updates. Before a classful routing protocol sends out an update, it performs a check against the subnet mask of the network that is about to be advertised. If the subnet is different, the classful routing protocol drops the route. A classful routing protocol will not advertise routes out of an interface if those routes are on the same major network but have a different mask than that particular interface.

With the explosion of the Internet and the demand for more network address space, a solution had to be rendered to grant more network space. The number of entries in the routing tables of the Internet was reaching capacity. In addition, the amount of resources, CPU, and memory required to manage the large routing tables represented an ineffective use of router resources.

Classless interdomain routing (CIDR) has solved both of these issues for Internet routing. Classless routing protocols can read variable-length subnet mask information in their updates. Classless routing protocols provide greater flexibility in the IP addressing design plan. Figure 5-3 shows the prefix lengths of each class of IP address.

Figure 5-3   *Prefix Lengths*

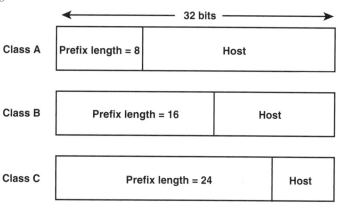

Classful routers accept only a few prefix lengths:

Class A   20.0.0.0/8
Class B   172.10.0.0/16
Class C   192.10.10.0/24

Classless routers accept any prefix length:

Classless   31.2.1.0 /10
Classless   172.20.0.0/20
Classless   192.10.10.0/28

Figure 5-4 shows an example of networks that use classless routing. Note that each network uses a different prefix length.

Figure 5-4   *Classless Routing and Variable Prefix Lengths*

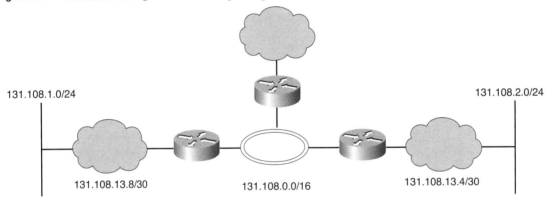

131.108.1.0/24   131.108.2.0/24

131.108.13.8/30   131.108.0.0/16   131.108.13.4/30

Network Addressing Guidelines

The host's network and address must be unique. If the network is connected to the public Internet, the network ID must be unique. If the network will not be used globally, the ID must be unique within the local environment. The host address must be unique to the local network ID.

The valid network ID cannot begin with the number 127. The number 127 is reserved for loopback testing.

In the case of a Class C network, the first octet cannot be set to 0 or 255. The host ID cannot be set to all 0s or all 1s. When the router sees a 0 address, it does not route the packet. When a router sees a 255 address in the rightmost byte of the address, it treats it as a broadcast.

For protocols such as OSPF, EIGRP, and RIP v2, the router can be configured to support classless routing. Classless routing allows the prefix to be increased from the fixed classful length. Classless routing allows prefixes to be greater than the classful specifications of 8, 16, and 24. Because different prefix lengths are available at different points, the concept has been defined as *variable-length subnet masking* (VLSM). VLSM relies on providing prefix length information clearly with each address. With classful routing, hundreds of addresses can go unallocated. With VLSM, IP address space can be used more efficiently. As an example, let's use a conventional classful address to configure a serial line and then compare it to an address that uses VLSM.

With the network 172.1.100.1/24, the address space from 172.1.100.1 to 172.1.100.254 is used. When the network 172.1.100.1/30 is used, the address space between 5 and 255 remains available for other networks. In this example, more than 250 addresses are conserved using VLSM! Distance vector routing protocols such as RIP and IGRP do not advertise classless prefixes in their routing protocol updates.

Classless Interdomain Routing (CIDR)

Classless interdomain routing (CIDR) allows for the reduction of the size of routing tables in the Internet by creating aggregate routes, or supernets. CIDR eliminates the concept of network classes and allows for better scalability when supporting the advertising of IP prefixes. CIDR allows routers to group routes to cut down on the quantity of routing information carried by the core routers. With CIDR, several IP networks appear to networks outside the group as a single, larger entity. CIDR completely changes the concept of address classes. It does not categorize a network by class. Instead, routes are viewed as a combination of addresses and masks. As long as the network has a common prefix, it doesn't matter where the boundary exists between network and host.

CIDR has the following advantages:

- One routing entry might match a block of host, subnet, or network addresses
- Routing tables can be shorter
- Switching performance is faster
- Routing protocol traffic is minimized

Route Summarization

Route summarization is also referred to as *supernetting* or *route aggregation*. Supernetting means extending the network prefix to the left. Instead of displaying all network entries in a routing table, a router announces a single network that shows the summarized prefix to its neighbor routers. When traffic is forwarded to the source router, the routers can switch packets to the appropriate subnet by applying the longest match rule. Summarization collapses the prefix to the left, and subnetting extends the prefix to the right. Figure 5-5 depicts this idea.

Figure 5-5 *Summarization and Subnetting*

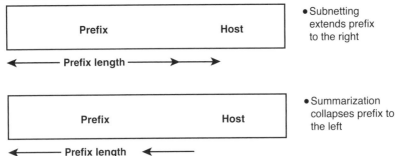

Extending IPv4 Address Space

The original RFC for IP was RFC 760. No concept of classes existed, and the address was an 8-bit network ID. RFC 791 introduced a segmentation of the address into classes. RFC 950 introduced subnetting and allowed for efficiency to exist with class addresses. RFCs 1517–1520 introduced CIDR, which is used primarily on the Internet routing tables.

NOTE   IPv6 stands for Internet Protocol Version 6. IPv6 will soon replace the current version, IPv4. IPv6 specifically addresses the growing shortage of IPv4 addresses, which are needed to support all new users who want to be added to the public Internet. Even though you shouldn't expect it to happen anytime soon, IPv6 is expected to gradually replace IPv4, with the two working side by side for a while during a transition period.

Discontiguous Subnets

A discontiguous network is comprised of a major network separated by another major network. In Figure 5-6, network 131.108.0.0 is separated by a subnet of network 137.99.0.0; 131.108.0.0 is a discontiguous network. Figure 5-5 is an example of a discontiguous subnet.

Figure 5-6 *Discontiguous Subnets*

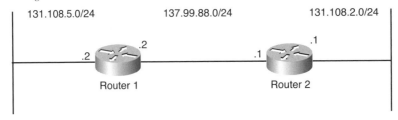

Subnetting

A *subnet* is a network in a multiple-segment environment that uses IP addresses derived from a single network ID. Dividing the network into subnets requires that each subnet use a different network ID. Partitioning the bits in the host ID into two parts, one for the extended network and one for the hosts, creates a unique subnet ID. A subnet mask blocks a portion of the IP address to separate the network ID from the host. A subnet mask specifies whether the host's IP address is located on a local network or needs to be routed. Even in cases where there is no subnetting, each host address requires a subnet mask.

Subnetting allows the CCDP to provide connectivity when the design must do the following:

- Mix different technologies, such as Ethernet and Token Ring

- Reduce network congestion by redirecting traffic and reducing broadcasts

- Exceed the maximum number of hosts per segment

To design a subnetted network, determine the number of required network IDs and the number of required host IDs for each subnet.

NOTE   If more than one route matches a particular destination, the longest prefix match is used. If several routers might match one destination, the longest matching prefix is always used. The route that has the longest match is considered the most-specific route.

NOTE   Save those addresses! Use the 255.255.255.252 "serial mask" 30-bit mask for efficient IP address allocation for WAN links. Table 5-2, shown earlier, lists subnet masks, the number of subnets, and the number of hosts per subnets associated with each subnet mask.

Calculating the Subnets and the Number of Hosts Per Subnet

A total of 32 bits comprise an IP address. An IP address A.B.C.D. consists of 8 bits per octet. In a network mask:

- If a bit is set to 0, it should be considered a host.

- If a bit is set to 1, it should be considered a network.

- If the first 8 bits in an IP address are set to 1, a Class A network is formed, and the subnet mask equals

    A.B.C.D. = 11111111 00000000 00000000 00000000

A.B.C.D = 255. 0. 0. 0.

- If the first 16 bits in an IP address are set to 1, a Class B network is formed, and the subnet mask equals

A.B.C.D. = 11111111 11111111 00000000 00000000

A.B.C.D = 255. 255. 0. 0.

- If the first 24 bits in an IP address are set to 1, a Class C network is formed, and the subnet mask equals

A.B.C.D. = 11111111 11111111 11111111 00000000

A.B.C.D = 255. 255. 255. 0.

NOTE

Remember: 1s equal network and 0s equal hosts.

Toggle only as many bits as you need. For more networks, start from the left, toggle that bit, and then move to the right until a sufficient number of bits have been toggled. For hosts, start from the right, toggle the bit to 0, and move to the left until a sufficient number of bits have been toggled. As an example, if a Class A needed 29 extra networks, 5 extra bits would be toggled to 1, providing $2^5 - 2$ networks, or 30 networks.

$2^5 - 2 = 30$

255.00000000.0.0 would become 255.11111000.0.0 or 255.248.0.0.

For example, if a Class C network needed 60 hosts, 6 bits would be toggled to 0, providing $2^6 - 2$ hosts, or 62 hosts.

    6 mask bits => 11111111 11111111 11111111 11000000 => 255.255.255.192
How many hosts does the following mask provide?

    13 mask bits => 11111111 11111111 10000000 00000000 => 255.255.255.128
Answer: 8190, because $2^{13} - 2 = 8190$

As an example, let's take a site that has been assigned the network 170.1.0.0. It requires 100 hosts per subnet. Future growth indicates 120 hosts per subnet.

1 Determine the bits required to support at least 100 hosts and future expansion to 120 hosts per subnet. Because $2^7 = 128$, 7 is the minimum number of bits required for 100–126 hosts. To determine hosts, start from the right and move left.

2 Determine the mask.

170.1.0.0/25, or 255.255.255.128

Table 5-5 lists the available network addresses for subnet mask .224.

Now take a look at Table 5-3.

Table 5-3   *Subnet Mask*

Subnet Mask	Number of Subnets	Number of Hosts Per Subnet
255.255.192.0	2	16,382
255.255.224.0	6	8190
255.255.240.0	14	4094
255.255.248.0	30	2046
255.255.252.0	62	1022
255.255.254.0	126	510
255.255.255.0	254	254
255.255.255.128	510	126
255.255.255.192	1022	62
255.255.255.224	2046	30
255.255.255.240	4094	14
255.255.255.248	8190	6
255.255.255.252	16,382	2

Table 5-4 lists the available network addresses for each subnet mask .192. The first and last addresses are unavailable. The first address is considered a local network, and the last address is used for broadcasting.

NOTE   These masks assume Class C networks.

Table 5-4   *Mask 192*

Network	Available Addresses	Local Address	Broadcast Address
0–63	1–62	0	63
64–127	65–126	64	127
128–191	129–190	128	191
192–255	193–254	192	255

Table 5-5 *Mask 224*

Network	Available Addresses	Local Address	Broadcast Address
0–31	1–30	0	31
32–63	33–62	32	63
64–95	65–94	64	95
128–159	129–158	128	159
160–191	161–190	160	191
192–223	193–222	192	223
224–255	225–254	224	255

NOTE   These masks assume Class C networks.

NOTE   The local address is not considered an available address. Cisco offers a feature called ip subnet-zero that allows a local address to be accessed. The concept of ip subnet-zero is beyond the scope of this chapter and is not discussed in this book

Table 5-6 lists the available network addresses for subnet mask .240.

Table 5-6 *Mask 240*

Network	Available Addresses	Network	Available Addresses
0–15 Local address: 0 Broadcast address: 15	1–14	128–143 Local address: 129 Broadcast address: 142 B142	129–142
16–31 Local address: 16 Broadcast address: 31	17–30	144–159 Local address: 145 Broadcast address: 158	145–158
32–47 Local address: 32 Broadcast address: 47	33–46	160–175 Local address: 160 Broadcast address: 175	161–174

Table 5-6   *Mask 240 (Continued)*

Network	Available Addresses	Network	Available Addresses
48–63 Local address: 48 Broadcast address: 63	49–62	176–191 Local address: 176 Broadcast address: 191	177–190
64–79 Local address: 64 Broadcast address: 79	65–78	192–207 Local address: 192 Broadcast address: 207	193–206
80–95 Local address: 80 Broadcast address: 95	81–94	208–223 Local address: 208 Broadcast address: 223	209–222
96–111 Local address: 96 Broadcast address: 111	97–110	224–239 Local address: 224 Broadcast address: 239	225–238
112–127 Local address: 112 Broadcast address: 127	113–126	240–255 Local address: 240 Broadcast address: 255	241–254

Table 5-7 lists the available network addresses for subnet mask .248.

Table 5-7   *Mask 248*

Network	Available Addresses	Network	Available Addresses
0–7 Local address: 0 Broadcast address: 7	1–6	136–143 Local address: 136 Broadcast address: 143	137–144
8–15 Local address: 8 Broadcast address: 15	9–14	144–151 Local address: 144 Broadcast address: 151	145–150
16–23 Local address: 16 Broadcast address: 23	17–22	152–159 Local address: 152 Broadcast address: 159	153–158
24–31 Local address: 24 Broadcast address: 31	25–30	160–167 Local address: 160 Broadcast address: 167	161–166

continues

Table 5-7   *Mask 248 (Continued)*

Network	Available Addresses	Network	Available Addresses
40–47 Local address: 40 Broadcast address: 47	41–46	168–175 Local address: 168 Broadcast address: 175	169–174
48–55 Local address: 48 Broadcast address: 55	49–54	176–183 Local address: 176 Broadcast address: 183	177–182
56–63 Local address: 56 Broadcast address: 63	57–62	184–191 Local address: 184 Broadcast address: 191	185–190
64–71 Local address: 64 Broadcast address: 71	65–70	192–199 Local address: 192 Broadcast address: 199	193–198
80–87 Local address: 80 Broadcast address: 87	81–86	200–207 Local address: 200 Broadcast address: 207	201–206
88–95 Local address: 88 Broadcast address: 95	89–94	208–215 Local address: 208 Broadcast address: 215	209–214
96–103 Local address: 96 Broadcast address:103	97–102	216–223 Local address: 216 Broadcast address: 223	217–222
104–111 Local address: 104 Broadcast address: 111	105–110	224–231 Local address: 224 Broadcast address: 231	225–230
112–119 Local address: 112 Broadcast address:119	113–118	232–239 Local address: 232 Broadcast address: 239	233–238
120–127 Local address: 120 Broadcast address: 127	121–126	240–247 Local address:240 Broadcast address: 247	241–246
128–135 Local address: 128 Broadcast address:135	129–134	248–255 Local address: 248 Broadcast address: 255	249–254

Table 5-8 lists the available network addresses for subnet mask .252.

Table 5-8   *Mask 252: The Serial Mask*

Network	Available Addresses	Network	Available Addresses
0–3 Local address: 0 Broadcast address: 3	1, 2	128–131 Local address: 128 Broadcast address: 131	129, 130
4–7 Local address: 4 Broadcast address: 7	5, 6	132–135 Local address: 132 Broadcast address: 135	133, 134
8–11 Local address: 8 Broadcast address: 11	9, 10	136–139 Local address: 136 Broadcast address: 139	137, 138
12–15 Local address: 12 Broadcast address: 15	13, 14	140–143 Local address: 140 Broadcast address: 143	141, 142
16–19 Local address: 16 Broadcast address: 19	17, 18	144–147 Local address: 144 Broadcast address: 147	145, 146
20–23 Local address: 20 Broadcast address: 23	21, 22	148–151 Local address: 148 Broadcast address: 151	149, 150
24–27 Local address: 24 Broadcast address: 27	25, 26	152–155 Local address: 152 Broadcast address: 155	153, 154
28–31 Local address: 28 Broadcast address: 31	29, 30	156–159 Local address: 156 Broadcast address: 159	157, 158
32–35 Local address: 32 Broadcast address: 35	33, 34	160–163 Local address: 160 Broadcast address: 163	161, 162
36–39 Local address: 36 Broadcast address: 39	37, 38	164–167 Local address: 164 Broadcast address: 167	165, 166

continues

Table 5-8   *Mask 252: The Serial Mask (Continued)*

Network	Available Addresses	Network	Available Addresses
40–43 Local address: 40 Broadcast address: 43	41, 42	168–171 Local address: 168 Broadcast address: 171	169, 170
44–47 Local address: 44 Broadcast address: 47	45, 46	172–175 Local address: 172 Broadcast address: 175	173, 174
48–51 Local address: 48 Broadcast address: 51	49, 50	176–179 Local address: 176 Broadcast address: 179	177, 178
52–55 Local address: 52 Broadcast address: 55	53, 54	180–183 Local address: 180 Broadcast address: 183	181, 182
56–59 Local address: 56 Broadcast address: 59	57, 58	184–187 Local address: 184 Broadcast address: 187	185, 186
60–63 Local address: 60 Broadcast address: 63	61, 62	188–191 Local address: 188 Broadcast address: 191	189, 190
64–67 Local address: 64 Broadcast address: 67	65, 66	192–195 Local address: 188 Broadcast address: 191	193, 194
68–71 Local address: 68 Broadcast address: 71	69, 70	196–199 Local address: 196 Broadcast address: 199	197, 198
72–75 Local address: 72 Broadcast address: 75	73, 74	200–203 Local address: 200 Broadcast address: 203	201, 202
76–79 Local address: 76 Broadcast address: 79	77, 78	204–207 Local address: 204 Broadcast address: 207	205, 206

Table 5-8   *Mask 252: The Serial Mask (Continued)*

Network	Available Addresses	Network	Available Addresses
80–83	81, 82	208–211	209, 210
Local address: 80		Local address: 208	
Broadcast address: 83		Broadcast address: 211	
84–87	85, 86	212–215	213, 214
Local address: 84		Local address: 212	
Broadcast address: 87		Broadcast address: 215	
88–91	89, 90	216–219	217, 218
Local address: 88		Local address: 216	
Broadcast address: 91		Broadcast address: 219	
92–95	93, 94	220–223	221, 222
Local address: 92		Local address: 220	
Broadcast address: 95		Broadcast address: 223	
96–99	97, 98	224–227	225, 226
Local address: 96		Local address: 224	
Broadcast address: 99		Broadcast address: 227	
100–103	100, 101	228–231	229, 230
Local address: 100		Local address: 228	
Broadcast address: 103		Broadcast address: 231	
104–107	105, 106	232–235	233, 234
Local address: 100		Local address: 232	
Broadcast address: 103		Broadcast address: 235	
108–111	109, 110	236–239	237, 238
Local address: 108		Local address: 236	
Broadcast address: 111		Broadcast address: 239	
112–115	113, 114	240–243	241, 242
Local address: 112		Local address: 240	
Broadcast address: 115		Broadcast address: 243	

continues

Table 5-8 *Mask 252: The Serial Mask (Continued)*

Network	Available Addresses	Network	Available Addresses
116–119	117, 118	244–247	245, 246
Local address: 116		Local address: 244	
Broadcast address: 119		Broadcast address: 247	
120–123	121, 122	248–251	249, 250
Local address: 120		Local address: 248	
Broadcast address: 123		Broadcast address: 251	
124–127	125, 126	252–255	253, 254
Local address: 124		Local address: 252	
Broadcast address: 127		Broadcast address: 255	

Here are the requirements for a variable-length subnetted mask:

- The routing protocol must be classless.

- It must carry the subnet mask in its updates.

- Summarized addresses must have the same high-order bits.

- Subnets can be used to address hosts or can be used for further subnetting.

Secondary Addressing: Several Subnets

Multiple IP addresses can be configured per interface. Secondary IP addresses can be used in a variety of situations. Use secondary IP addresses when:

- There might not be enough host addresses for a particular network segment. If subnetting allows up to 254 hosts per logical subnet, but on one physical subnet there are 300 host addresses, using secondary IP addresses on the routers or access servers would allow two logical subnets on the same physical subnet.

- There is a need to support discontiguous subnets. Two subnets of a single network might be separated by another network. A secondary network can act as a tunnel between two portions of the network that are not connected.

Figure 5-7 displays a network that uses secondary subnets.

Figure 5-7   *Secondary Subnets*

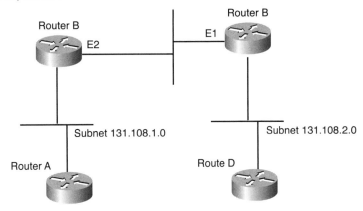

NOTE   Use secondary addressing only as a last resort. Secondary addressing increases network overhead, degrades throughput, and consumes router resources. When other options are exhausted, use secondary addressing as a temporary solution.

Private Networks

Users who do not want to use the public network may use private addresses. The RFC has defined a set of addresses that will never be assigned public. Any user can use these addresses privately. No user may use these addresses publicly.

NOTE   Use the 10.0.0.0 network as a private address. You'll never outgrow it!

Table 5-9 displays the private addresses that will never be routed onto the Internet.

Table 5-9   *Private Addresses*

Address	Class
10.0.0.0	A
172.16.0.0/16–172.31.0.0/16	B
192.168.0.0/24–192.168.255.0/24	C

Users who want to use private addressing and plan to have Internet access need to enable a translation method. To conserve public network addresses, Network Address Translation (NAT) was developed to allow private networks to access the Internet while using a limited amount of public addressing. In its simplest configuration, NAT operates on a router connecting two networks. One network, the private intranet, is addressed with either private or obsolete addresses that need to be converted into public addresses before packets are forwarded onto the public Internet. A single public address can serve as an alias for multiple sessions between multiple hosts on the intranet or Internet side of the NAT device. The goal of NAT is to provide functionality as if the private network had globally unique addresses and the NAT device was not present.

Reasons for using private addressing include the following:

- Security
- A shortage of addresses

Managing Addresses with DHCP

Dynamic Host Configuration Protocol (DHCP) manages IP addresses by automatically assigning IP addresses to hosts that are configured to use DHCP. When a DHCP client boots up, it requests IP addressing information from a DHCP server. When a DHCP server receives the request, it offers an address from a designated address pool to the DHCP client. The address can be leased for a specified period of time or leased indefinitely.

Using DHCP makes IP address management a snap. DHCP allows full-scale network addressing changes to be made without impacting the user. A new addressing plan can be implemented on Friday. When users boot up on Monday, they transparently receive the new addresses. With DHCP, it is not possible to configure duplicate addresses for hosts. Troubleshooting the IP network is made simpler because problems that are caused by typos are eliminated. Figure 5-8 shows a network that is managed by DHCP.

Figure 5-8   *DHCP*

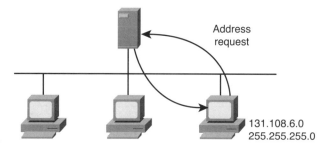

Address
request

131.108.6.0
255.255.255.0

NOTE	Use static addresses for fixed network devices such as servers, printers, routers, and managed hubs. Use DHCP for end stations and PCs.

DHCP Relay

You can configure DHCP relay on a Cisco router by configuring ip helper-address with the address of the DHCP server on the interface that will have DHCP clients. To prevent the forwarding of other broadcasts to the DHCP server, add ip forward-protocol udp bootpc to the router configuration.

Multicast Routing

Companies are beginning to see an increased benefit in using applications that send information to a large number of users at the same time. For example, video teleconferencing requires the capability to send video information to several teleconferencing sites at once. Unicast and broadcast networks cannot satisfy the demand for multimedia applications. *IP multicasting,* the transmission method that can send IP datagrams to multiple nodes in a logical group, is the answer. Multicasting can contain the multimedia requirements for one-to-many or many-to-many communications.

The *Internet's Multicast Backbone* (MBONE) was developed to handle multicast traffic across the Internet. Multimedia conferencing tools have been developed for multicasting across the network. These tools allow audio streams and/or video streams to be transmitted across the MBONE. Multimedia applications, desktop conferencing, and other up-and-coming applications will demand the capability to communicate from one to many or from many to many hosts. Multicast routing allows routers to communicate efficiently from one route to many routes.

How MBONE Works

If a client wants to join a multicast application, that client (or application) must inform the server that they want to join the multicast group and receive data from the multicast. The client will receive an address, allowing it to join and receive data. Routers need to know which stations should receive the multicast and which ones shouldn't. Routers use the *Internet Group Management Protocol* (*IGMP*) to determine which, if any, hosts on a segment belong to a particular group and need to receive the multicast traffic. If IGMP is not configured on the switch, the switch will essentially broadcast the multicast traffic to all ports.

NOTE   Configure IGMP on the switch to ensure efficient use of bandwidth.

As soon as the client has joined the multicast, the routers forward the data from server to client.

NOTE   Users can send data to a multicast server without joining the multicast group.

Users *must* belong to a multicast group to receive data from a multicast server.

Determining the Best Path

Because multicasts can consume large amounts of bandwidth, it is imperative that routers efficiently determine the best route from one point to all points. Several protocols are available to determine the best path for multicast routing. *Distance Vector Multicast Routing Protocol* (DVMRP) was the first multicast routing protocol to be widely accepted. As the name implies, DVMRP is a distance vector protocol. It has many similarities to RIP. DVMRP served the networking community well as a first-generation multicast routing protocol. Its periodic updates and hop count limitations disqualify it as the preferred protocol for today's internetworks. DVMRP should be employed in new designs only when backward compatibility to an existing infrastructure is a design concern.

To determine the best path for multicast routing, *protocol-independent multicast* (PIM) can be enabled on a Cisco router. PIM allows any unicast routing protocol to support IP multicast. PIM can be integrated into existing networks that are running IGRP, EIGRP, RIP, and OSPF. *Multicast Open Shortest Path First* (MOSPF) allows multicast traffic to be forwarded within an OSPF v2 unicast network.

Foundation Summary

This section is a collection of tables that provide a convenient review of many key concepts in this chapter. If you are already comfortable with the topics in this chapter, this summary might help you recall a few details. If you have just read this chapter, this review should help solidify some key facts. If you are doing your final preparation before the exam, Tables 5-10 through 5-12 are a convenient way to review the day before the exam.

Table 5-10   *Subnet Configuration*

Subnet Mask	Number of Subnets	Number of Hosts Per Subnet
255.255.192.0	2	16,382
255.255.224.0	6	8190
255.255.240.0	14	4094
255.255.248.0	30	2046
255.255.252.0	62	1022
255.255.254.0	126	510
255.255.255.0	254	254
255.255.255.128	510	126
255.255.255.192	1022	62
255.255.255.224	2046	30
255.255.255.240	4094	14
255.255.255.248	8190	6
255.255.255.252	16,382	2

Table 5-11   *RFC 1918 Private Network Addresses*

Class	Address	Comments
A	10.0.0.0–10.255.255.255	Provides unlimited growth and scalability
B	172.16.0.0–172.31.0.0	Best fit in medium-size networks
C	192.168.0.0–192.168.255.0	Great for small networks

Table 5-12   *IP Addresses: Decimal and Binary*

Decimal Address	Binary Address
10.1.1.1	00001010 00000001 00000001 00000001
172.16.32.2	10101100 00010000 00100000 00000010
201.245.221.214	11001001 11110101 11011101 11010110

Route summarization has several benefits:

- Reduces the size of the routing table

    — Smaller updates

    — Lower consumption of bandwidth

- Hiding network changes

    — No routing table changes for small network changes

- Network growth

    — Scalability

- Reduces router resource utilization

- Maximizes the use of IP addresses

Here are some things to consider when designing IP networks:

- Determine the number of hosts required on a network, present and projected

- Determine the number of subnets for an existing network, present and projected

- Determine interoperability issues with other vendor equipment and protocols

- Determine the appropriate location for a DHCP server

- Determine the security issues that need to be addressed

- Determine the method of Internet access

- Determine if private addressing will be used

Q&A

As mentioned in Chapter 1, the questions and scenarios in this book are more difficult than what you will experience on the actual exam. The questions do not attempt to cover more breadth or depth than the exam; however, they are designed to make sure that you know the answer. Rather than allowing you to derive the answer from clues hidden inside the question, the questions challenge your understanding and recall of the subject. Questions from the "Do I Know This Already?" quiz from the beginning of the chapter are repeated here to ensure that you have mastered this chapter's topic areas. Hopefully, these questions will help limit the number of exam questions on which you narrow your choices to two options and then guess. Be sure to use the CD and take the simulated exams.

The answers to these questions can be found in Appendix A.

1 What are the five IP address classes?

_____

_____

_____

2 What class of IP address is optimum for a small network?

_____

_____

_____

3 Which IP addresses are reserved for multicasting?

_____

_____

_____

4 What IP address class renders 254 hosts?

_____

_____

_____

5 Which IP addresses are reserved for experiments?

_____

_____

_____

6 What is NAT, and how can it help conserve IP addresses?

_____

_____

_____

7 List four benefits of address summarization.

_____

_____

_____

8 What subnet mask is ideal for connecting WAN links?

_____

_____

_____

9 Define classful routing.

_____

_____

_____

10 What is CIDR, and how does it offer greater flexibility in IP addressing?

_____

_____

_____

11 What is a discontiguous subnet?

_____

_____

_____

12 True or false: To support variable-length subnet masking and route summarization, a classless routing protocol must be incorporated into the design plan.

_____

_____

_____

13 Define classless routing.

_____

_____

_____

14 What is the prefix length of a Class A network?

_____

_____

_____

15 The network design requires 14 hosts. What network and subnet mask should be employed?

_____

_____

_____

16 Why is network 10.0.0.0 a popular private address?

_____

_____

_____

17 List three criteria for selecting a routing protocol.

_____

_____

_____

18 What is meant by the phrases "subnetting extends to the right" and "supernetting extends to the left"?

_____

_____

_____

19 To what IP address class would address 127.43.2.1 belong?

_____

_____

_____

20 What is secondary addressing, and when should it be utilized?

_____

_____

_____

21 How many hosts will a Class C network support with the default mask?

_____

_____

_____

22 What routing protocols should you avoid when using classless routing?

_____

_____

_____

23 What protocol ensures efficient use of bandwidth during multicasting?

_____

_____

_____

24 List five issues to consider when designing IP addressing schemes.

_____

_____

_____

25 List one disadvantage of using a classful routing protocol.

_____

_____

_____

26 What organization assigns public IP addresses?

_____

_____

_____

27 List two protocols that can be used to enact classless routing.

_____

_____

_____

28 What is meant by the sentence: "The router always looks for the longest match"?

_____

_____

_____

29 How is multicast traffic handled across the Internet?

_____

_____

_____

30 What applications require the use of multicasting?

_____

_____

_____

Scenario 1

To help design the optimum solution and address the issues presented in each chapter, you have contracted with the design professionals at RouteitRight to help you.

RouteitRight's key personnel are as follows:

Chief Executive Officer (CEO)	Billy Broadcast
Chief Information Officer (CIO)	Megg A. Bight
Senior Telecommunications Engineer	Peter Packett
Director of Sales	Freddy Forklift
Information Systems Manager	Harry Helpnot
Help Desk Manager	Millie Sekkons
Network Specialist	Roddy Routebegone

In discussions with Isaiah P. Freely, CEO and founder of Blue River Enterprises, Megg determined that Blue River needs to update its IP addressing scheme to comply with its recent merger with Yellow Stream. Blue River was granted an IP network of 183.100.0.0 from the Internet Assigned Numbers Authority. When the network administrator created the original addressing plan, no one envisioned that the company would need connectivity on a nationwide network. With the merger, Blue River is currently in 37 states. Blue River would like the network-addressing scheme to include the potential for expansion to all 50 states, as well as the District of Columbia. In addition, some address space should be reserved in the event that Blue River goes international. Peter wonders if this is a good time to implement NAT.

1   Using the Class B IP address of 183.100, design an addressing plan that summarizes to the state level. Why is it important to have an addressing plan?

2   Write out the addressing scheme in dotted decimal notation.

3   Blue River headquarters is located in Montgomery, Alabama. Design an IP addressing scheme for headquarters and the three regional offices located in Alabama.

4   Discuss another method for assigning addresses to Blue River.

Answer to Scenario

1   Using the Class B IP address of 183.100, design an addressing plan that summarizes to the state level. Why is it important to have an addressing plan?

The design methodology for Blue River is to develop the overall addressing scheme by assigning blocks of addresses to each state.

Each state would then assign blocks of addresses to each region. By assigning blocks of addresses to portions of the network, addressing and administration are greatly simplified. This hierarchical addressing results in very efficient summarization of routes throughout the network. This method should simply address administration and a scalable network. If the routing protocols used at Blue River use variable-length subnet masking, a true hierarchical addressing can be deployed. A 16-bit mask can be used at the core of the network backbone. A 24-bit mask can be used at the access layer for each state. If necessary, the network can be subdivided even further if business requirements dictate.

It is important to have an addressing plan because proper IP address management for Blue River would include allocating and documenting IP addresses and subnets in a network. IP addressing standards should define subnet size and subnet assignment. Recommending IP address management standards for Blue River minimizes the potential for overlapping or duplicate subnets, nonsummarization in the network, duplicate IP address device assignments, and wasted IP address space. See Figure 5-9.

Figure 5-9   *Private Networking for Blue River*

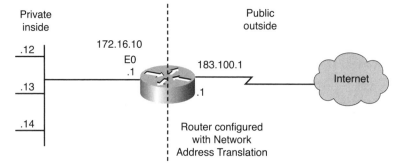

2 Write out the addressing scheme in dotted decimal notation.

State	Address
Alabama	183.100.1–4.0/24
Alaska	183.100.5–8.0/24
Arizona	183.100.9–12.0/24
Arkansas	183.100.13–16.0/24
California	183.100.17–20.0/24
Colorado	183.100.21–24.0/24
Connecticut	183.100.25–28.0/24
Delaware	183.100.29–32.0/24
District of Columbia	183.100.33–36.0/24
Florida	183.100.37–40.0/24
Georgia	183.100.41–44.0/24
Hawaii	183.100.45–48.0/24
Idaho	183.100.49–52.0/24
Illinois	183.100.53–56.0/24
Indiana	183.100.57–60.0/24
Iowa	183.100.61–64.0/24
Kansas	183.100.65–68.0/24
Kentucky	183.100.69–72.0/24
Louisiana	183.100.73–76.0/24
Maine	183.100.77–80.0/24
Maryland	183.100.81–84.0/24
Massachusetts	183.100.85–88.0/24
Michigan	183.100.89–92.0/24
Minnesota	183.100.93–96.0/24
Mississippi	183.100.97–100.0/24
Missouri	183.100.101–104.0/24
Montana	183.100.105–108.0/24
Nebraska	183.100.109–112.0/24
Nevada	183.100.113–116.0/24
New Hampshire	183.100.117–120.0/24

State	Address
New Jersey	183.100.121–124.0/24
New Mexico	183.100.125–128.0/24
New York	183.100.129–132.0/24
North Carolina	183.100.133–136.0/24
North Dakota	183.100.137–140.0/24
Ohio	183.100.141–144.0/24
Oklahoma	183.100.145–148.0/24
Oregon	183.100.149–152.0/24
Pennsylvania	183.100.153–156.0/24
Rhode Island	183.100.157–160.0/24
South Carolina	183.100.161–164.0/24
South Dakota	183.100.165–168.0/24
Tennessee	183.100.169–172.0/24
Texas	183.100.173–176.0/24
Utah	183.100.177–180.0/24
Vermont	183.100.181–184.0/24
Virginia	183.100.185–188.0/24
Washington	183.100.189–192.0/24
West Virginia	183.100.193–196.0/24
Wisconsin	183.100.197–200.0/24
Wyoming	183.100.201–204.0/24

3 Blue River headquarters is located in Montgomery, Alabama. Design an IP addressing scheme for headquarters and the three regional offices located in Alabama.

State	Address
Alabama	183.100.1–4.0/24
Montgomery	183.100.1.0/24
Mobile	183.100.2.0/24
Birmingham	183.100.3.0/24
Huntsville	183.100.4.0/24

A Class C address would be allocated to each location. This would allow 254 hosts in each office and the potential for subnetting within the branch offices.

4 Discuss another method for assigning addresses to Blue River.

The IANA has reserved three blocks of addresses for private networks. If Blue River exhausts the addresses in the 183.100.*x* range, it can use any of the address blocks reserved for private addressing without registering with any Internet authority. To ensure a standard of IP addressing across the nation, you recommend that each private address granted be unique within Blue River. Although address blocks are available in any class range, you recommend the Class B address range from 172.16.0.0 to 172.31.255.255.

This chapter covers the following topics that you will need to master as a CCDP:

- **Routing concepts**—This section discusses static and dynamic routing.

- **Path determination**—This section discusses path determination and how routing protocols use metrics to determine the best path.

- **Route redistribution**—This section discusses route redistribution between dissimilar protocols.

CHAPTER 6

IP Routing

Cisco expects the successful CCDP candidate to be able to understand the routing protocols, their metrics, and how they can be used to render a cost-effective solution that meets the client's requirements for scalability and stability. The CID exam tests your knowledge of how TCP/IP addressing can be integrated into a successful network design.

How to Best Use This Chapter

By following these steps, you can make better use of your study time:

- Keep your notes and the answers for all your work with this book in one place for easy reference.

- Take the "Do I Know This Already?" quiz and write down your answers. Studies show that retention is significantly increased through writing down facts and concepts, even if you never look at the information again.

- Use the diagram shown in Figure 6-1 to guide you to the next step.

"Do I Know This Already?" Quiz

The purpose of the "Do I Know This Already?" quiz is to help you decide which parts of this chapter to use. If you intend to read the entire chapter, you do not necessarily need to answer these questions now.

This 15-question quiz helps you determine how to spend your limited study time. The quiz is divided into three smaller "quizlets" that help you select the sections of the chapter on which to focus. Figure 6-1 outlines suggestions on how to spend your time in this chapter. Use Table 6-1 to record your score.

Figure 6-1 *How to Best Use This Chapter*

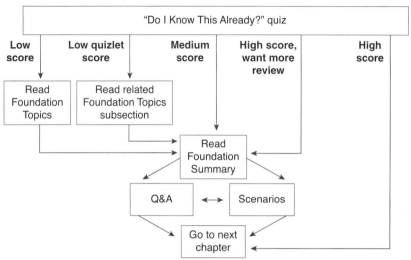

If you skip to the Foundation Summary, Q&A, and Scenarios sections and have trouble with the material there, you should go back to the Foundation Topics section.

Table 6-1 *Score Sheet for Quiz and Quizlets*

Quizlet Number	Foundation Topics Section Covering These Questions	Questions	Score
1	Routing concepts	1, 2, 3, 7, 8, 9, 11, 12, 13	
2	Path determination	4, 5, 6	
3	Route redistribution	8, 12, 15	

1 List five possible requirements for a routing protocol.

_____

_____

_____

2 What two tasks do routers perform?

_____

_____

_____

3 What is the simplest form of routing?

_____

_____

_____

4 What type of routing determines the best path?

_____

_____

_____

5 List four types of Interior Gateway Protocols.

_____

_____

_____

6 What is administrative distance?

_____

_____

_____

7 What protocol works primarily in the Internet?

_____

_____

_____

8 List three types of routing metrics.

_____

_____

_____

9 What is a classless protocol?

_____

_____

_____

10 List one disadvantage of classful routing protocols.

_____

_____

_____

11 List three types of switching methods used by Cisco routers.

_____

_____

_____

12 What is the routing metric for OSPF?

_____

_____

_____

13 List three requirements of route summarization.

_____

_____

_____

14 True or false: Secondary addressing is a recommended and preferred method of connecting discontiguous subnets.

_____

_____

_____

15 _____ is the exchange of routing information between two different routing processes.

_____

_____

_____

The answers to the "Do I Know This Already?" quiz are found in Appendix A. The suggested choices for your next step are as follows:

- **6 or less overall score**—Read the chapter. This includes the "Foundation Topics," "Foundation Summary," and "Q&A" sections, as well as the scenario at the end of the chapter.

- **2 or less on any quizlet**—Review the subsection(s) of the "Foundation Topics" part of this chapter based on Table 6-1. Then move into the "Foundation Summary," the "Q&A" section, and the scenario at the end of the chapter.

- **7, 8, or 9 overall score**—Begin with the "Foundation Summary" section and then go to the "Q&A" section and the scenario at the end of the chapter.

- **10 or more overall score**—If you want more review on these topics, skip to the "Foundation Summary" section, and then go to the "Q&A" section and the scenario at the end of the chapter. Otherwise, move to the next chapter.

Foundation Topics

The simplest form of routing is static routing. The chore of finding routes and propagating them throughout a network is beyond the scope of the static route. A router programmed for static routing forwards packets out of designated ports. After the link between a destination address and a router port is configured, there is no longer any need for a router to communicate its information about routes. Default static routes are entered as 0.0.0.0 and the next hop. A default router is one that all others look to for networks that are not in their tables. Any IP network address can be manually entered into the routing table. There are many benefits to using static routes. For instance, statically programmed routes can make for a more secure network. In addition, there is no overhead on the network for routing updates.

Dynamic routing happens when routers talk to neighboring routers, informing each other about what networks each router is currently connected to. Routing decisions are based on metrics. When a route goes down or changes, a dynamic route is automatically updated in a routing table. Routers that perform dynamic routing communication use a routing protocol, of which there are many to choose. Some of the dynamic routing protocols available for use include RIP, IGRP, EIGRP, and OSPF.

Distance-vector, link-state, and hybrid are three types of dynamic routing protocols. This chapter discusses the issues that relate to routing protocols in greater detail.

Static Versus Dynamic Routing

A stub is a section of the internetwork that can be accessed by one path. Because static routes do not change when a link goes down, they can effectively be used to connect to a stub. Static routes can save bandwidth if there is only one path to the network. A stub is a part of the internetwork that can be reached by a single route. Figure 6-2 shows an example of a static route to a stub network.

In addition, static routing is much more resource-efficient than dynamic routing. Static routing uses no bandwidth across the links and doesn't waste router resources. On the other hand, statically programmed routers cannot discover routes. Static routers lack the capacity to communicate routing information with other routers. Statically programmed routers can only forward packets using routes defined by a network administrator. As networks grow larger and add redundant paths to destinations, static routing can become an administrative nightmare. Any changes in the availability of routers or transmission facilities in the WAN must be manually programmed. Networks that have complex topologies that offer multiple potential paths require dynamic routing.

Figure 6-2   *Static Route to a Stub Network*

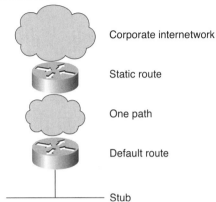

Corporate internetwork

Static route

One path

Default route

Stub

Types of Dynamic Routing Protocols

There are three categories of dynamic routing protocols:

* Distance-vector

* Link-state

* Hybrids

They are covered in the following sections.

Distance-Vector Routing

In distance-vector routing, routers pass copies of their routing tables to their immediate network neighbors at periodic intervals. Each recipient adds a distance vector, sometimes a hop count, to the table and forwards it to its immediate neighbors. This process results in each router's learning about other routers. For the most part, distance-vector protocols are simple protocols that are easy to configure, maintain, and use. They are quite useful in very small networks that have few redundant paths and no stringent network performance requirements. Distance-vector protocols are not recommended for larger networks because of their slow convergence time and limited diameter. RIP and IGRP are examples of distance-vector protocols.

Link-State Routing

Link-state routing algorithms, also known as *shortest path first (SPF)* protocols, maintain a complex database of the network's topology. Link-state protocols develop and maintain a full knowledge of the network's routers, as well as how they interconnect. Link-state routing uses events such as change to drive updates instead of sending intervals at fixed times. Link-state routing converges quicker than distance vectors, with less overhead. Link-state routing is best in larger, more complicated networks or in networks that must be highly scalable.

Link-state routing is both memory- and processor-intensive. In addition, more configurations and resources are required to support link-state routing than distance-vector routing. The cost of the routers that are configured for link-state routing is higher. These issues are not showstoppers and are easy to overcome with foresight, planning, and good design. OSPF, an example of a link-state protocol, uses cost as a metric.

Hybrid Routing

The hybrid routing protocols use distance-vector metrics but emphasize more accurate metrics than conventional distance-vector protocols. They also converge more rapidly than distance-vector protocols but avoid the overhead of link-state updates. Balanced hybrids are event-driven rather than periodic and thereby conserve bandwidth for real applications.

Currently, one hybrid protocol dominates internetworking—Cisco's proprietary protocol, the Enhanced Interior Gateway Routing Protocol (EIGRP). EIGRP was designed to combine the best characteristics of both routing protocols without incurring any of their performance limitations or penalties. EIGRP finds new networks like a distance-vector protocol while reacting to changes in topology like a link-state routing protocol.

Routing Metrics

Routing tables contain information that allow protocols to select the best route. How are routing tables built? When more than one route is available, how do protocols select a preferred route? Routing protocols use metrics to determine the best route. The following metrics can be used to determine the
best route:

- **Cost**—Some routing protocols allow arbitrary costs to be assigned to each network link. The cost metric is the sum of the costs associated with each link traversed.

- **Hop count**—Hop count counts the number of passes through a router that a packet must take to get from source to destination.

- **Reliability**—Reliability is an arbitrary value that indicates the link's dependability. Some network links might go down more often than others. After a network fails, certain network links might be repaired more easily or more quickly than others. Any factors that govern reliability can be factored into the reliability metric.

- **Delay**—Delay refers to the length of time required to move a packet from source to destination. Several factors affect delay, including the bandwidth of intermediate network links, the port queues at each router along the way, network congestion, and the physical distance to be traveled.

- **Bandwidth**—Bandwidth refers to a link's available traffic capacity. Although bandwidth is a rating of the maximum attainable throughput on a link, routes through links with greater bandwidth are not necessarily better than routes that pass through slower links. As an example, if a T-1 link is congested, the actual time required to send a packet to the destination on the T-1 could be greater than a 64 K line.

- **Load**—Load refers to the degree to which a network device is busy. Load can be calculated in a variety of ways, including CPU utilization and packets processed per second.

- **MTU**—The MTU setting acknowledges that media can support different sizes of packets. As an example, Ethernet, with a few exceptions, supports a maximum of 1500 bytes, while Token Ring can support much larger packets. MTU is used to avoid sending a frame that is too large in cases where the IP fragment bit is set. Though MTU is an included parameter, it has never been used in the calculation of metrics.

NOTE   The interstate highway (high-bandwidth) might look like the best and fastest path to take—until you discover that several lanes are blocked (delay) due to an accident.

Use bandwidth and delay when determining the best path.

IGRP and EIGRP can base route selection on multiple metrics. IGRP and EIGRP use five metrics to determine the best path:

- Bandwidth
- Delay
- Reliability
- Load
- MTU

Some people use the following mnemonic to help remember these metrics: Big Dogs Really Love Meat.

Table 6-2 shows the different metrics used by different routing protocols.

Table 6-2   *Routing Protocol Metrics*

Protocol	Metric
RIP V1	Hop count
IGRP	Bandwidth, delay, load, reliability, MTU
EIGRP	Bandwidth, delay, load, reliability, MTU
OSPF	Cost

Routing Algorithms

Link-state and hybrid protocols use routing algorithms to determine the best route. Routing algorithms can be categorized on several key characteristics. First, the particular goals of the algorithm designer affect the operation of the resulting routing protocol. Second, various types of routing algorithms exist, and each algorithm has a different impact on network and router resources. Finally, routing algorithms use a variety of metrics that affect the calculation of optimal routes.

Routing algorithms often have one or more of the following design goals:

- Optimality

- Simplicity and low overhead

- Robustness and stability

- Rapid convergence

Optimality refers to the capability of the routing algorithm to select the best route, which depends on the metrics and metric weightings used to make the calculation. One routing algorithm, for example, might use a number of hops and delays but might weight delay more heavily in the calculation. Naturally, routing protocols must strictly define their metric calculation algorithms.

The routing algorithm must offer its functionality efficiently, with minimum software and utilization overhead. Efficiency is particularly important when the software implementing the routing algorithm must run on a computer with limited physical resources.

Routing algorithms must be robust, which means that they should perform correctly in the face of unusual or unforeseen circumstances, such as hardware failures, high-load conditions, and incorrect implementations. Because routers are located at network junction points, they can cause considerable problems when they fail. The best routing algorithms are often those that have withstood the test of time and have proven stable under a variety of network conditions.

In addition, routing algorithms must converge rapidly. Convergence is the process of agreement, by all routers, on optimal routes. When a network event causes routes either to go down or to become available, routers distribute routing update messages that permeate networks, stimulating recalculation of optimal routes and eventually causing all routers to agree on these routes. Routing algorithms that converge slowly can cause routing loops or network outages.

A routing loop occurs when routers disagree. Routers disagree if their routing tables are not in agreement. This generally happens when the routes have changed and the routing algorithm from one protocol has not finished converging. Figure 6-3 shows an example of a routing loop.

Figure 6-3   *Routing Loop*

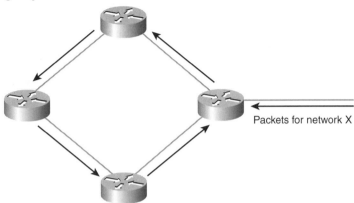

Packets for network X

Holddowns

Holddowns are used to prevent regular update messages from inappropriately reinstating a route that might have gone bad. When a router goes down, neighboring routers detect this via the lack of regularly scheduled update messages. These routers then calculate new routes and send routing update messages to inform their neighbors of the route change. This activity begins a wave of triggered updates that filter through the network. These triggered updates do not instantly arrive at every network device. So it is possible for a device that hasn't been informed of the change to send an update message with information stating that the route is still good to a device that already knows about the failure.

Holddowns tell routers to hold down any changes that might affect routes for some period of time. The hold-down period usually is calculated to be just greater than the period of time necessary to update the entire network with a routing change. Figure 6-4 shows an example of a network in holddown.

Figure 6-4   *Holddowns Prevent Routing Loops*

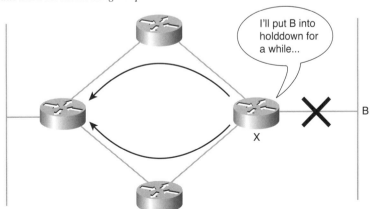

Enabling and Disabling Split Horizon for IP Networks

Normally, routers that are connected to broadcast-type IP networks and that use distance-vector routing protocols employ the split horizon mechanism to prevent routing loops. Split horizon blocks information about routes from being advertised by a router out any interface from which that information originated. This behavior usually optimizes communications among multiple routers, particularly when links are broken. However, with nonbroadcast networks such as Frame Relay and SMDS, situations can arise for which this behavior is less than ideal. Figure 6-5 depicts split horizon on an IP network.

Figure 6-5   *Split Horizon*

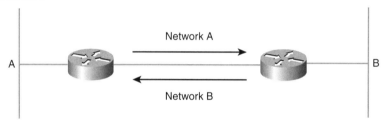

Switching and Path Determination

Routers have two distinct functions: switching packets and path determination.

Cisco routers can switch packets by fast switching or process switching. Process switching load-balances packet by packet. Fast switching load-balances destination by destination. Process switching is the most intensive switching operation the CPU can perform. Process switching involves transmitting entire frames to the router CPU. Frames are then repackaged for delivery to or from a WAN interface, and the router makes a route selection for each packet.

Figure 6-6 depicts the two router functions.

Figure 6-6   *Process Switching and Path Determination*

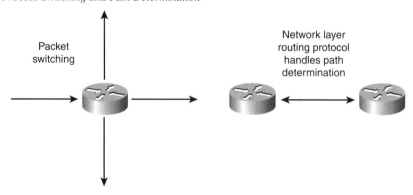

Path Determination

Path determination requires the use of dynamic routing, which involves the exchange of information between routers.

Dynamic routing protocols were created to overcome the shortcomings of static routing. Choosing the right routing protocol depends on the customer's business and technical requirements.

Routing protocols determine the best path to a destination network by exchanging routing metrics. When there are several ways to get to the same destination, the router uses metrics to calculate the best path. Figure 6-7 illustrates how path determination can be determined by metric.

Figure 6-7   *Path Determination*

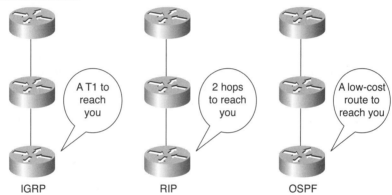

Load-Balancing Modes for IP

In addition to running routing protocols to develop a routing topology, a major function of a router is to switch packets from incoming interfaces to outgoing interfaces. Switching involves receiving a packet, determining how to forward the packet based on the routing topology and policy requirements, and switching the packet to the right outgoing interface.

Cisco supports several switching methods, offering varying speeds and behaviors. For the most part, the fastest switching method available should be selected for an interface type and protocol. Using a speedy switching mode is especially important on backbone and core enterprise routers. Fast switching is usually, but not always, the default setting. Check the version of IOS software to be sure.

NOTE   Check Cisco's documentation for more information about the methods supported for various router platforms, protocols, and interfaces. Documentation for Cisco products is available online at http://www.cisco.com/univercd/home/home.htm.

Process Switching

Process switching is the slowest of the switching methods. When a packet arrives at an interface, the system processor is interrupted for the time it takes to copy the packet from the interface buffer to system memory. The processor looks up the Layer 3 destination address for the packet in the routing table to determine the exit interface. The packet is rewritten with the correct header for that interface and is copied to the interface. At this time, an entry is also placed in the fast-switching cache so that subsequent packets for the destination address can use the same header. The first packet to a destination is always process-switched.

Fast Switching

Fast switching allows higher throughput by switching a packet using an entry in the fast-switching cache that was created when a previous packet to the same destination was processed. With fast switching, a packet is handled immediately, without scheduling an interrupt of the system processor.

Fast switching maximizes the volume of traffic that the router can handle by streamlining the router's queuing mechanisms. Fast switching deals with incoming frames in *processor interrupt mode* and minimizes the number of decisions that must be applied. Fast switching also precaches routes. As soon as an IP destination is process-switched, its route is cached and is associated with a specific interface. When an IP destination is precached, it is tied to a specific path.

Steps for Fast Switching

Use the following steps to implement fast switching:

1   A packet comes into an internetwork device.

2   The address or virtual circuit number is examined.

3   A table lookup operation determines where the packet or frame should be sent.

4   Header information might be changed.

5   The packet or frame is transmitted out an interface.

Autonomous Switching

Autonomous switching is available on Cisco 7000-series routers. It uses an *autonomous-switching cache* located on interface processors. Autonomous switching provides faster packet switching by allowing the *ciscoBus controller* to switch packets independently, without having to interrupt the system processor.

Silicon switching is similar to autonomous switching, but it speeds up autonomous switching through the use of a *silicon-switching cache* located on the Silicon Switch Processor (SSP) on some Cisco 7000-series routers.

Optimum Switching

Optimum switching is similar to fast switching but is faster due to an enhanced caching algorithm and the optimized structure of the *optimum-switching cache*. Optimum switching is available only on routers equipped with a Route/Switch Processor (RSP).

Distributed Switching

Distributed switching is supported on routers that have Versatile Interface Processor (VIP) cards or other interface cards that can receive route information from the master RSP to make their own autonomous, multilayer switching decisions. Distributed switching supports very fast throughput because the switching process occurs on the interface card.

NetFlow Switching

NetFlow switching identifies traffic flows between hosts and then quickly switches packets in these flows at the same time that it applies services. NetFlow switching also lets a network manager collect data on network usage to enable capacity planning and to bill users based on network and application resource utilization. The data can be collected without slowing down the switching process.

To maximize network scalability, a good design practice is to use NetFlow switching on the periphery of a network to enable features such as traffic accounting, QoS functionality, and security, and to use an even faster switching mode in the network's core. At the network's core, the switching mode should forward packets based on easily accessible information in the packet and generally should not spend time applying services.

Cisco Express Forwarding

Cisco Express Forwarding (CEF) is a Cisco-patented technique for switching packets very quickly across large backbone networks and the Internet. Rather than relying on the caching techniques used by classic switching methods, CEF depends on a *forwarding information base (FIB)*. The FIB allows CEF to be much less processor-intensive than other Layer 3 switching methods because the FIB tables contain forwarding information for all routes in the routing tables (whereas a cache contains only a subset of routing information).

CEF evolved to accommodate Web-based applications and other interactive applications that are characterized by sessions of short duration to multiple destination addresses. CEF became necessary when it became clear that a cache-based system is not optimized for these types of applications. CEF improves switching speed and avoids the overhead associated with a cache that continually changes through the use of the FIB, which mirrors the entire contents of the IP routing table.

CEF technology takes advantage of the distributed architecture of the high-end Cisco routers, such as the Cisco 7500. *Distributed CEF (DCEF)* provides each of the Cisco 7500 VIPs with an identical on-card copy of the FIB database, allowing them to autonomously perform CEF and therefore significantly increase aggregate throughput.

Tag Switching

Tag switching has a slightly different goal from the other switching methods covered. Whereas the other methods optimize the switching of a packet through a single router, tag switching optimizes packet switching through a network of tag switches.

Tag switching is an implementation of the IETF standard for *multiprotocol label switching (MPLS)*. The idea behind MPLS is that by labeling or tagging the first packet in a flow of data, subsequent packets can be expedited to the final destination. Tagging minimizes the processing required of a router and thus significantly reduces delay on packet and cell-based networks that include tag switches. In addition, packets can be tagged to travel along specified routes to implement load balancing, QoS, and other optimization features. Tag information can be carried in a packet as a small header inserted between the Layer 2 and Layer 3 headers, or as part of the Layer 3 header if the Layer 3 protocol supports it. (In IPv6, tag information can be included in the flow-label field.) Some Layer 2 implementations, such as ATM, support carrying the tag directly in the Layer 2 header.

Categories of Routing Protocols

Routing protocols can be categorized by how they are used. The uses listed here are covered in the following sections:

- Host Routing
- Interior Gateway Protocol (IGP)
- Exterior Gateway Protocol (EGP)

Host Routing

Host routing can be configured with a default gateway. In a basic configuration, if the gateway fails, the host loses connectivity to the network. To ensure that the host can maintain connectivity if the default gateway fails, Hot Standby Router Protocol (HSRP) can be implemented. With HSRP, two or more routers communicate on a virtual gateway address different from their interface address. If the primary router goes down, the secondary router becomes primary, utilizing the same gateway address. The change is transparent to the user, and the host traffic continues to be routed.

Using HSRP, a set of routers works in tandem to present the illusion of a single virtual router to the hosts on the LAN. This set is known as an HSRP group, or a standby group. A single router elected from the group is responsible for forwarding the packets that hosts send to the virtual router. This router is known as the active router. Another router is elected as the standby router. In the event that the active router fails, the standby assumes the packet-forwarding duties of the active router. Although an arbitrary number of routers may run HSRP, only the active router forwards the packets sent to the virtual router.

Hosts can also run the Gateway Discovery Protocol (GDP). The Internet Router Discovery Protocol (IRDP) is another method of dynamically determining a gateway router.

The following options are available to the designer but are not preferred or recommended. An option called proxy ARP lets you configure hosts with no default gateway so that the host always sends an Address Resolution Protocol (ARP) request for every destination. In this situation, the router is configured to respond to any ARP if it has a route in its routing table. Another even less-desirable option is having the hosts listen to Routing Information Protocol (RIP). This method requires RIP broadcasts and redistribution if other routing protocols are used.

Interior Gateway Protocols (IGPs)

IGPs are used within an autonomous system.

The following protocols are examples of IGPs that use the Internet Protocol (IP):

- Routing Information Protocol (RIP)
- Interior Gateway Routing Protocol (IGRP) and Enhanced IGRP (EIGRP)
- Integrated IS-IS
- Open Shortest Path First (OSPF)

IGPs fall into the category of link-state or distance-vector protocols. Distance-vector protocols such as RIP may send the entire routing table out at certain intervals, whereas EIGRP sends a partial update, conserving bandwidth. Link-state protocols such as OSPF send local link status information to peers. The LSA propagates to every peer router in the area. The routing table is built using an algorithm. After a router knows that its interfaces are functioning, it uses the OSPF Hello protocol to acquire neighbors, which are routers with interfaces to a common network. The router sends hello packets to its neighbors and receives their hello packets. In addition to helping acquire neighbors, hello packets also act as keepalives to let routers know that other routers are still functional. Table 6-3 shows how IGPs can be categorized by their use.

Table 6-3 *Categories of IGPs*

Protocol	Update	Hello	Type
RIP	Routes	No	Distance-vector
IGRP	Routes	No	Distance-Vector
OSPF	Links	Yes	Link-state
EIGRP	Routes	Yes	Hybrid

Exterior Gateway Protocols (EGPs)

EGPs are used to connect autonomous systems (ASs). Here's an example of an EGP: Border Gateway Protocol (BGP) is an Internet protocol that allows ASs to share routing information so that efficient, loop-free routes can be established. An AS is a set of routers, typically under a single technical administration, that uses an Interior Gateway Protocol and common metrics to route packets within the AS. It uses an Exterior Gateway Protocol to route packets to other ASs. BGP is commonly used within and between Internet service providers (ISPs). The BGP protocol is defined in RFC 1771.

A Cisco IP routing table is based on several factors:

- Static routing entries

- Local interface configuration

- Local interface status

- Dynamic routing protocols and routing metrics

- Redistribution between routing protocols

- Policy decisions implemented with access lists

The following paragraphs provide some analysis of how these factors interact.

Three processes are involved in building and maintaining the routing table in a Cisco router:

- Routing processes, which actually run a network (or routing) protocol, such as EIGRP, BGP, IS-IS, and OSPF

- The routing table itself, which accepts information from the routing processes and also replies to requests for information from the forwarding process

- The forwarding process, which requests information from the routing table to make a packet-forwarding decision

Figure 6-8 depicts the router's build-and-maintain process. This process is described in the following paragraphs.

Figure 6-8   *Router Build-and-Maintain Process*

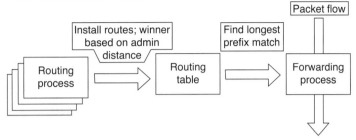

Decisions

When several routing processes provide information to the same router, the router must decide to which one it will listen. In a large network, some routing protocols and routers can be more reliable than others as sources of routing information. The routers listen to the protocol that has the lowest administrative distance. If administrative distance values are specified, the router can discriminate between sources of routing information.

An administrative distance can be defined as a rating of the trustworthiness of a routing information source. Numerically, an administrative distance is an integer between 0 and 255. The higher the value, the lower the trust rating. An administrative distance of 255 means that the routing information source cannot be trusted at all and should be ignored.

The router always uses the best routing source available: the routing source with the lowest administrative distance. Table 6-4 lists route types and the administrative distances associated with them.

Table 6-4   *Administrative Distances*

Route Type	Administrative Distance
Directly connected	0
Static route	1
EIGRP summary route	5
External BGP	20
Internal EIGRP	90
IGRP	100
OSPF	110
IS-IS	115
RIP	120
EGP	140

continues

Table 6-4 *Administrative Distances (Continued)*

Route Type	Administrative Distance
External EIGRP	170
Internal BGP	200
Unknown	255

Routing Convergence

Convergence is the time it takes for routers to arrive at a consistent understanding of the internetwork topology when a change takes place. Packets don't know for certain where the destination route is until convergence finishes. Convergence is a function of the size of the network and the complexity of the network design. Routing information that needs to propagate across a few routers obviously converges more quickly than routing information that needs to propagate across several hundred routers. Convergence is a critical design component for a time-sensitive protocol or application.

Convergence is composed of two factors:

- The time it takes to detect a link failure

- The time it takes to determine a new route

Link-state protocols were designed to converge faster than distance-vector protocols, which were designed first. For a small network, convergence might take only a few seconds. For larger networks, convergence can be impacted by several factors:

- The number of routing nodes in an area

- The number of networks in an area

- The number of areas

- How the address space is mapped

- Whether effective use of route summarization exists

- The stability of the links

Route Summarization

Route summarization, which is also referred to as aggregation or supernetting, is central to all routing protocols. Route summarization is the way to scale routed internetwork designs. Route summarization is most effective at the network's concentration points. Summarization reduces memory usage on routers and routing protocol network traffic. For summarization to work effectively, the following requirements must be met:

- Multiple IP addresses must share the same high-order bits.

- Routing protocols must carry the prefix length or subnet mask in a separate field, along with the 32-bit IP address.

- Routing tables and protocols must base their routing decisions on a 32-bit IP address with a prefix length that can be up to the entire 32-bit length of the field.

Figure 6-9 shows how classical distance-vector protocols perform route summarization. If a router has an interface on a major network, it tracks all the subnets of that major network in its routing table. If a router is not directly connected to a particular major network, it will not have any subnet information about that network. Only a single network route will appear in the routing table.

Figure 6-9   *Summarization of Classful Routing*

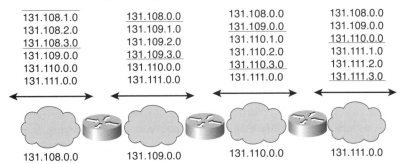

Configuration of route summarization with classless routing and VLSM is dependent on the routing protocol. All subnets might be automatically summarized at network boundaries by default. Manual configuration might be required to enforce this.

Figure 6-10 shows how summarization reduces routing tables.

Figure 6-10   *Summarization of Classless Routing*

131.108.1.0	131.108.0.0	131.108.0.0
131.108.2.0	131.109.1.0	131.109.0.0
131.108.3.0	131.109.2.0	131.110.1.0
131.108.4.4	131.109.3.0	131.110.2.0
131.108.4.8	131.109.4.4	131.110.3.0
131.108.4.12	131.109.4.8	131.110.4.4
131.109.0.0	131.109.4.12	131.110.4.8
131.110.0.0	131.110.0.0	131.110.4.12
131.111.0.0	131.111.0.0	131.111.0.0

131.108.0.0   131.109.0.0   131.110.0.0

When there is no summarization, all subnets are visible to all routers within a major network. When more subnets are added, the routing table continues to grow. With summarization, the routing table grows by only one network.

Route Redistribution

Route redistribution is the exchange of routing information between two different routing protocols. Translation between two environments using different routing protocols requires that routes generated by one protocol be redistributed into the second routing protocol environment. Route redistribution gives an organization the ability to run different routing protocols in workgroups or areas where each is particularly effective. Route redistribution is also used when Company A buys Company B and Companies A and B are running different routing protocols. Also, redistribution is effective when migrating to a new routing protocol. By allowing its users to employ more than one protocol, route redistribution minimizes cost while maximizing technical flexibility.

Cisco permits routing protocol redistribution between any of its supported routing protocols. Static route and directly connected information can also be redistributed. A default metric can be assigned so that all redistributed routes can use the same metric.

Cisco has enhanced its route redistribution features to improve administrative control over the methods by which routing information moves between routing domains. To ease configuration of route redistribution, Cisco created *route maps*. A route map is a set of instructions that tells the router how routing information is to be redistributed. Route maps contain an ordered list of match conditions. Each item in the list is matched in turn against any route that is a candidate for redistribution. When a match is found, an item performs an action associated with that match. The route can be permitted (redistributed) or not permitted (not redistributed), but the action also can mandate the use of certain administrative information (called *route tags*) that can be attached to routing data to augment routing decisions.

Route maps also can mandate the use of certain route metrics or route types and can even modify the route's destination in outgoing advertisements. Where different networks share similar redistribution needs, network administrators can conserve memory and save time by using the same route map for more than one protocol pair. Route maps give network managers control over the ways that routing information is propagated in their networks. Redistribution configuration files that use route maps are easy to create, understand, and modify. Using route maps, a CCDP can connect dissimilar networks with a great degree of control. Figure 6-11 shows route redistribution between protocols.

Figure 6-11   *Route Redistribution Between Protocols*

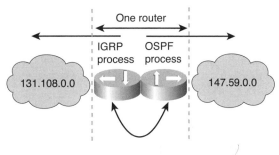

Route Redistribution Within the Same Network

Routes can also be redistributed within the same major network number. In Figure 6-11, you would block the IGRP advertisements from going to the RIP network and the RIP advertisements from going to the IGRP network using the passive interface command. Subnets are automatically redistributed between RIP and IGRP within the same major network. In other cases, subnet information might need to be forced with the subnets keyword. Figure 6-12 shows route distribution within the same major network.

Figure 6-12   *Same Network Route Redistribution*

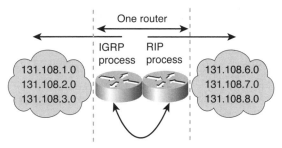

Different routing protocols have different limitations and different ways of determining things. When route redistribution is performed, information is lost. The CCDP must be sure that metric information is assigned during redistribution. RIP likes hops. OSPF likes cost. IGRP likes bandwidth and delay.

RIP and IGRP handle default routes differently. RIP uses network 0.0.0.0 as its universal default router. IGRP advertises and selects from a candidate default network. Because IGRP does not relate to the 0.0.0.0 route, the 0.0.0.0 route must be filtered when redistributing from RIP to IGRP.

Foundation Summary

This section contains tables and lists that provide a convenient review of many key concepts in this chapter. If you are already comfortable with the topics in this chapter, this summary could help you recall a few details. If you have just read this chapter, this review should help solidify some key facts. If you are doing your final preparation before the exam, Tables 6-5 and 6-6 are a convenient way to review the day before the exam.

Here are some of the technical requirements that might be expected of a routing protocol:

- Must adapt to change quickly and easily
- Does not create a great deal of traffic
- Scales to a large size
- Is compatible with existing hosts and routers
- Supports variable-length subnet masks and discontiguous subnets
- Supports policy routing
- Can be used between autonomous systems
- Is based on industry standards

Routing protocols consume network, CPU, and memory resources. The amount of bandwidth that is consumed depends on several issues:

- How often will the route be updated?
- How much of an update is being transmitted?
- How many others will receive the update?

Table 6-5 *Contrasting a RIP Protocol and an OSPF Protocol*

Feature	RIP V1 (Distance-Vector Protocol)	OSPF (Link-State Protocol)
Route learning	Learns about routes from its neighbor. Information gained is from one perspective.	Learns about routers based on the database of information provided by every router in the area. Every router in the area contains the same information.
Acknowledging updates	Does not acknowledge updates.	Acknowledges updates.
Routing updates	Sends the entire routing table at regular intervals.	Sends incremental routing updates and only when changes occur in the network.
Addressing	Uses classful addressing. Fixed-length subnet masks.	Uses classless addressing. Variable-length subnet masks.
Route advertisement	Uses broadcast addresses.	Uses multicast addresses.

Table 6-6   *IP Routing Protocols*

Protocol	Type	Updates	Metric	Comments
RIP V1	Distance-vector (IGP)	30 seconds	Hops (limited to 15)	Best for small networks. Supported by most network operating systems. Does not support variable-length subnet masking.
RIP V2	Distance-vector (IGP)	30 seconds	Hops (limited to 15)	Second-generation RIP. Improvements beyond RIP include the support of variable-length subnet masking.
OSPF	Link-state (IGP)	Triggered when there is a network change	$Cost = 10^8/BW$	Contains a link-state database. Uses link-state advertisements to announce network information.
IGRP	Hybrid (IGP)	90 seconds	Bandwidth Delay Reliability Load MTU	A Cisco proprietary protocol that contains link-state and distance-vector features. Does not support variable-length subnet masking.
EIGRP	Hybrid (IGP)	Triggered when there is a network change	Bandwidth Delay Reliability Load MTU	Second-generation IGRP. Improvements beyond IGRP include support of variable-length subnet masking and faster convergence time.
BGP	Path-vector (EGP)	Triggered when there is a network change	Cost	Concerned with interconnecting autonomous systems, primarily on the Internet.

Q&A

As mentioned in Chapter 1, the questions and scenarios in this book are more difficult than what you will experience on the actual exam. The questions do not attempt to cover more breadth or depth than the exam; however, they are designed to make sure that you know the answer. Rather than allowing you to derive the answer from clues hidden inside the question, the questions challenge your understanding and recall of the subject. Questions from the "Do I Know This Already?" quiz from the beginning of the chapter are repeated here to ensure that you have mastered this chapter's topic areas. Hopefully, these questions will help limit the number of exam questions on which you narrow your choices to two options and then guess. Be sure to use the CD and take the simulated exams.

The answers to these questions can be found in Appendix A.

1 List five possible requirements for a routing protocol.

_____

_____

_____

2 What two tasks do routers perform?

_____

_____

_____

3 What is the simplest form of routing?

_____

_____

_____

4 What type of routing determines the best path?

_____

_____

_____

5 List four types of Interior Gateway Protocols.

_____

_____

_____

6 What is administrative distance?

_____

_____

_____

7 What protocol works primarily in the Internet?

_____

_____

_____

8 List three types of routing metrics.

_____

_____

_____

9 What is a classless protocol?

_____

_____

_____

10 List one disadvantage of classful routing protocols.

_____

_____

_____

11 List three types of switching methods used by Cisco routers.

_____

_____

_____

12 What is the routing metric for OSPF?

_____

_____

_____

13 List three requirements of route summarization.

_____

_____

_____

14 True or false: Secondary addressing is a recommended and preferred method of connecting discontiguous subnets.

_____

_____

_____

15 _____ is the exchange of routing information between two different routing processes.

_____

_____

_____

16 List three ways that routing protocols can be characterized.

_____

_____

_____

17 What is a routing loop?

_____

_____

_____

18 What protocol has hybrid functionality, displaying the characteristics that resemble distance-vector and link-state protocols?

_____

_____

_____

19 What is a stub network?

_____

_____

_____

20 Two routing protocols, RIP and IGRP, are being redistributed. Design requirements state that RIP advertisements must be blocked from entering the IGRP cloud. What command should be implemented?

_____

_____

_____

21 What two factors determine convergence time?

_____

_____

_____

22 What is the routing metric for IP RIP?

_____

_____

_____

23 How can the Hot Standby Routing Protocol (HSRP) be used to provide redundancy?

_____

_____

_____

24 What three resources does routing consume?

_____

_____

_____

25 List two methods of filtering routes when redistributing.

_____

_____

_____

26 What protocols discussed in this chapter use the Hello protocol to update their routing tables?

_____

_____

_____

27 When redistributing protocols, why is it important to consider the metric differences of each protocol?

_____

_____

_____

28 What is the lowest administrative distance available to implement routing policy?

_____

_____

_____

29 What is the simplest form of switching path available on a Cisco router?

_____

_____

_____

30 What is split horizon?

_____

_____

_____

Scenarios

Scenario

To help design the optimum solution and address the issues presented in each chapter, you have contracted with the design professionals at RouteitRight to help you.

RouteitRight's key personnel are as follows:

Chief Executive Officer (CEO)	Billy Broadcast
Chief Information Officer (CIO)	Megg A. Bight
Senior Telecommunications Engineer	Peter Packett
Director of Sales	Freddy Forklift
Information Systems Manager	Harry Helpnot
Help Desk Manager	Millie Sekkons
Network Specialist	Roddy Routebegone

RouteitRight was recently contacted by Happy Routing. Happy Routing has just purchased regional outlets. To streamline business and administrative costs, the company would like to have one network protocol running through all of its sites. Currently, four protocols exist at the four different sites: OSPF at Memphis, IGRP at Atlanta, EIGRP at Charlotte, and RIP at Jacksonville. The networking group at Happy Routing cannot agree to standardizing on a single protocol. Peter Packett will talk to each network administrator to try to bring about a change to a common protocol. One of the sites, Memphis, is not using Cisco equipment and, therefore, cannot use IGRP or EIGRP.

Freddy Forklift will call the Memphis office. If he can sway them to implement a Cisco router in their segment of the WAN, the standardization process might be simplified. RouteitRight has recommended that Happy Routing redistribute the different protocols until a standard can be determined.

Look at the network topology, shown in Figure 6-13.

Figure 6-13 *Topology for Happy Routing*

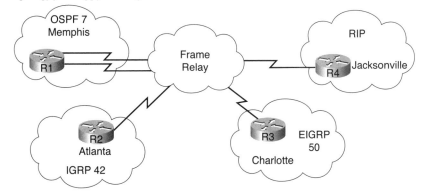

1 Is redistribution a good interim solution? If so, why?

2 What issues are involved with redistributing OSPF and RIP?

3 What issues are involved with redistributing IGRP and EIGRP?

4 Where might summarization assist in the redistribution process?

Answers to Scenario

1 Is redistribution a good interim solution? If so, why?

Redistribution is a good interim solution because it provides a way of passing the networks learned by one routing protocol to another. When the routing protocols share information, all the devices on the network that have privileges can connect to each other. Route redistribution appears simple on the surface. However, it can be loaded with complications. Understanding how the Happy Routing network processes work and interact is critical before implementing redistribution.

2 What issues are involved with redistributing OSPF and RIP?

RIP is a classful protocol. When you redistribute OSPF into a RIP environment, all subnet masks must be the same. RIP does not understand variable-length subnet masking. RIP only accepts information about a route that has a subnet that is the same as its own interface, or a mask that ends on a classful boundary. All OSPF routes that do not match the 24-bit subnet mask are not redistributed into RIP. When redistributing an OSPF route into RIP, include subnets. If subnets are omitted, subnetted routes are not included. Include the RIP metric of hops. If no metric is included, 16 is entered, and RIP considers the route unreachable. A default metric can be specified to designate the cost of all redistributed routes in RIP updates. All routes redistributed into RIP will have this default metric.

3 What issues are involved with redistributing IGRP and EIGRP?

IGRP is a classful protocol. When you redistribute EIGRP into an IGRP environment, all subnet masks must be the same. IGRP does not understand variable-length subnet masking. IGRP only accepts information about a route that has a subnet that is the same as its own interface, or a mask that ends on a classful boundary.

The metric calculation and the default metric value for IGRP and EIGRP are the same. By default, the composite metric is the sum of the segment delays and the lowest segment bandwidth for a given route. Although the default value can be adjusted with the `metric weights` command, the defaults provided usually offer excellent convergence and operation in most networks.

EIGRP can be added to an IGRP network (or vice versa) in two ways: using the same AS number, and using a new AS number.

If EIGRP uses the same AS number as IGRP, redistribution of IGRP into EIGRP and redistribution of EIGRP into IGRP occurs automatically. If EIGRP uses a different AS number, the network administrator needs to configure redistribution manually with the **redistribute** command. The redistribution of IGRP/EIGRP into another EIGRP/IGRP process doesn't require any metric conversion, so there is no need to define metrics or use the **default-metric** command during redistribution.

IGRP routes redistributed into EIGRP are marked as external. There are two caveats with EIGRP/IGRP redistribution within the same autonomous system: Internal EIGRP routes are always preferred over external EIGRP or IGRP routes, and external EIGRP route metrics are compared to scaled IGRP metrics.

4 Where might summarization assist in the redistribution process?

To ensure that connectivity is maintained during redistribution, all classless OSPF routes must be summarized to the same mask as the interface running RIP or to a classful boundary.

This chapter covers the following topics that you need to master as a CCDP:

- **Open Shortest Path First (OSPF) protocols and OSPF areas**—This topic discusses OSPF as a standard for IP routing and OSPF network types and categories.

- **OSPF summarization and scalable OSPF area internetworks**—This topic covers how OSPF propagates link-state advertisements with summarization and area definition. This topic also discusses the network design that maximizes stability and scalability.

- **OSPF backbone design and OSPF address mapping**—This topic discusses design models for the OSPF backbone.

- **Interior Gateway Routing Protocol (IGRP) and Enhanced IGRP (EIGRP) routing, characteristics, and convergence**—This topic discusses IGRP routing characteristics and how the IGRP metric works. In addition, this topic covers EIGRP and the enhancement features that make it superior to IGRP.

CHAPTER 7

OSPF, EIGRP, and IGRP

Cisco expects the successful CCDP candidate to be able to use OSPF, IGRP, EIGRP design models to render a cost-effective solution that will meet the client's requirements for scalability and stability. The CID exam tests your knowledge of how these interior gateway routing protocols can be integrated into a successful network design.

How to Best Use This Chapter

By following these steps, you can make better use of your study time:

- Keep your notes and the answers for all your work with this book in one place for easy reference.

- Take the "Do I Know This Already?" quiz and write down your answers. Studies show that retention is significantly increased through writing down facts and concepts, even if you never look at the information again.

- Use the diagram shown in Figure 7-1 to guide you to the next step.

"Do I Know This Already?" Quiz

The purpose of the "Do I Know This Already?" quiz is to help you decide which parts of this chapter to use. If you intend to read the entire chapter, you do not necessarily need to answer these questions now.

This 15-question quiz helps you determine how to spend your limited study time. The quiz is divided into four smaller "quizlets" that help you select the sections of the chapter on which to focus. Figure 7-1 outlines suggestions on how to spend your time in this chapter. Use Table 7-1 to record your score.

Table 7-1   *Score Sheet for Quiz and Quizlets*

Quizlet Number	Foundation Topics Section Covering These Questions	Questions	Score
1	OSPF Protocol and Area Assignments	1, 2, 3	
2	OSPF Summarization and Scalability	5, 9	
3	OSPF Backbone Design and Address Mapping	4, 6, 7, 8, 10, 11	
4	IGRP/EIGRP Routing, Characteristics, and Convergence	12, 13, 14, 15	

Figure 7-1 *How to Use This Chapter*

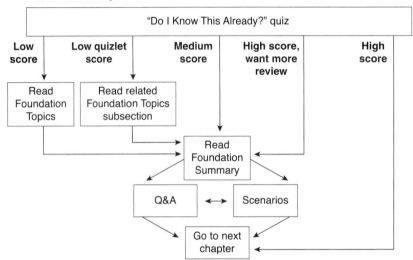

If you skip to the Foundation Summary, Q&A, and Scenarios sections and have trouble with the material there, you should go back to the Foundation Topics section.

1 What limitations of RIP, the first Internet routing protocol, was OSPF designed to overcome?

_____

_____

_____

2 What are the four types of connections for the OSPF routing protocol?

_____

_____

_____

3 Name the four classifications of OSPF routers.

_____

_____

_____

4 What are link-state advertisements? Name four types of link-state advertisements.

_____

_____

_____

5 True or false: All OSPF areas must be physically adjacent to the backbone.

_____

_____

_____

6 The following are OSPF routes. Perform summarization to one route. What configuration commands would be needed if the routes were external? What commands would be needed if the routes were internal?

- Route 1   172.26.30.0
- Route 2   172.26.31.0
- Route 3   172.26.32.0

_____

_____

_____

7 Compare and contrast stub, totally stubby, and not-so-stubby areas.

_____

_____

_____

8 List six rules for designing a scalable OSPF internetwork.

_____

_____

_____

9 How does OSPF route summarization save router resources?

_____

_____

_____

10 What is the meaning of cost, and how does OSPF calculate cost?

_____

_____

_____

11 What is the difference between an External Type 1 route and an External Type 2 route?

_____

_____

_____

12 Which routing protocols are supported by EIGRP?

_____

_____

_____

13 EIGRP updates are:

A periodic

B incremental

C A and B

D None of the above

_____

_____

_____

14 Name five values that IGRP and EIGRP use to determine metrics. Which metrics are used by default?

_____

_____

_____

15 Name two parameters that can be tuned by IGRP to allow faster convergence.

_____

_____

_____

The answers to the "Do I Know This Already?" quiz are found in Appendix A. The suggested choices for your next step are as follows:

- **6 or less overall score**—Read the chapter. This includes the "Foundation Topics," "Foundation Summary," and "Q&A" sections, as well as the scenarios at the end of the chapter.

- **2 or less on any quizlet**—Review the subsection(s) of the "Foundation Topics" part of this chapter based on Table 7-1. Then move into the "Foundation Summary," the "Q&A" section, and the scenarios at the end of the chapter.

- **7, 8, or 9 overall score**—Begin with the "Foundation Summary" section and then go to the "Q&A" section and the scenarios at the end of the chapter.

- **10 or more overall score**—If you want more review on these topics, skip to the "Foundation Summary" section, and then go to the "Q&A" section and the scenarios at the end of the chapter. Otherwise, move to the next chapter.

Foundation Topics

The Routing Information Protocol (RIP), which is defined in RFC 1058, was the first routing protocol for the Internet. In today's complex internetworking environments, RIP's limitations have made it virtually nonexistent. Today RIP exists, for the most part, in small networks where servers perform as low-end routers. Simple Windows NT networks can perform server-based routing scenarios. RIP's limited range, slow convergence, and susceptibility to routing loops have rendered it unacceptable in today's Internet environment. Open Shortest Path First (OSPF), defined in RFC 1583, was created to overcome the limitations of RIP. OSPF is now considered to be the de facto standards-based routing protocol for IP. OSPF is built on a ladder of network components. The highest level in the pecking order is the autonomous system (AS). An autonomous system is a group of networks that share the same routing and administration characteristics under the same domain.

An area represents a collection of adjacent routers that maintain the same link-state database. Areas limit the area to which routing advertisements are broadcast.

NOTE   OSPF is named after the *Dijkstra algorithm,* which is also called the *Shortest-Path Algorithm.*

OSPF addresses the following limitations of RIP:

- RIP has a hop-count limitation of 15. RIP always uses the lowest hop-count as the metric, regardless of a link's speed or reliability. OSPF is a link-state protocol, which means that it can consider metrics based on link speed when determining the best path to a destination network. In addition, OSPF has no hop-count limit.

- OSPF uses variable-length subnet masking, which provides for more efficient allocation. RIP uses fixed-length subnet masking (FLSM), which uses fixed network boundaries. RIP requires that all networks in the internetwork have the same subnet mask.

- OSPF has better network convergence. OSPF routes are propagated only during link-state changes. OSPF has reachability information for the whole area. RIP propagates every 30 seconds and must rely on its neighboring routers for reachability information.

OSPF Network Types

There are four types of OSPF router network connection types, three of which are shown in Figure 7-2:

- **Point-to-point network**—Joins a single pair of OSPF routers. ISDN and T1 connections are examples of point-to-point networks.

- **Broadcast multiaccess network**—Supports multiple routers and can address a single physical message to all attached routes. Ethernet, FDDI, and Token Ring are examples of broadcast multiaccess networks.

- **Nonbroadcast multiaccess (NBMA) network**—Supports multiple routers and does not address a single physical message to all routers. Frame Relay and X.25 are examples of NBMA networks.

- **Point-to-multipoint network**—Supports multiple routers. Designated and backup designated routers are not used with point-to-multipoint networks.

Figure 7-2   *OSPF Network Types*

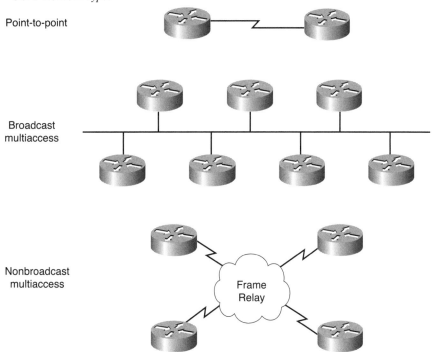

Point-to-point

Broadcast
multiaccess

Nonbroadcast
multiaccess

Frame
Relay

OSPF Classes of Routers

There are four classes of OSPF routers:

- **Internal router**—All routers that are completely contained within the same area.

- **Area Border Router (ABR)**—A router that attaches to more than one area.

- **Backbone router**—A router that connects to the backbone. The backbone router has at least one interface attached to Area 0. The ABR can also be a backbone router.

- **Autonomous System Boundary Router (ASBR)**—A router that exchanges routing information with routers that are not running OSPF (RIP, IGRP, EIGRP, and so on). ASBR routers inject external link-state advertisements into the OSPF database.

Figure 7-3 illustrates the router classifications for OSPF.

Figure 7-3 *OSPF Router Classifications*

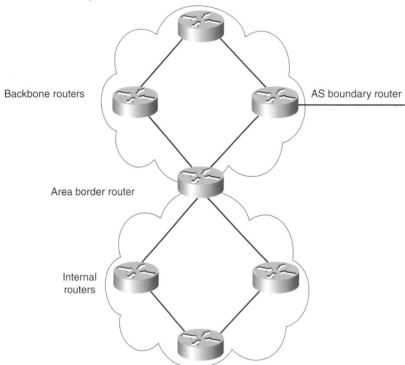

Link-State Advertisements (LSAs)

Every router in an area contains a link-state database, which consists of link-state advertisements (LSAs). LSAs describe the router's local state. All of the routers in an area have the same link-state database. The database consists of information gathered from all the LSAs received. The LSAs are sent to all routers in an area. The LSAs are produced by routers and include all the router's links, interfaces, state of links, and cost.

Types of Link-State Advertisements

LSAs present the state of the OSPF link. Different types of LSAs perform different assignments. An LSA can describe the state of the router interface inside a particular area. Some

LSAs are flooded only inside a router's area, and other LSAs advertise only interarea links. Other LSAs might show routes from external links. The following sections describe the different types of LSAs.

Type 1: Router LSA

Type 1 LSAs contain information about sending information to neighbor routers. Type 1 LSAs are transmitted in only a single area and are called router links. Type 1 LSAs have the following characteristics:

- Are originated by all routers
- Contain information about the number of links and the type of router interfaces
- Contain the link's metric

Type 2: Network LSA

Type 2 LSAs contain lists of routers connected to a network segment. Type 2 LSAs are usually sent by a designated router in a broadcast or nonbroadcast multiaccess network and are called network links. Type 2 LSAs have the following characteristics:

- Are originated by all designated routers
- Are flooded throughout a single area
- Contain lists of connected routers

Type 3: Summary LSA

Type 3 LSAs originate at area border routers and are sent into an area to advertise destinations outside the area. Type 3 LSAs refer to summary links. Type 3 LSAs have the following characteristics:

- Are originated by the ABR
- Contain summary route information

Type 4: Summary LSA (ASBR)

Type 4 LSAs originate as area system border routers. Type 4 LSAs advertise the ASBR router and refer to summary links. Type 4 LSAs have the following characteristics:

- Contain router links into the area
- Contain summary route information

Type 5: AS-External LSA

Type 5 LSAs contain information that describe routes to external (non-OSPF) routers. Type 5 LSAs refer to external links. Type 5 LSAs have the following characteristics:

- Are originated by ASBR

- Contain default routes for AS and advertise destinations external to the OSPF AS

Type 7: AS-External LSA

Type 7 LSAs originate from area system border routers that are connected between a not-so-stubby area (NSSA) and another AS. Type 7 LSAs are advertised only within an NSSA. These LSAs are converted to Type 5 LSAs by the ARB when leaving an NSSA. Type 7 LSAs have a lower priority than Type 5 LSAs.

Whenever a router changes state, LSAs propagate between routers with established adjacencies. Every router in the area gets at least one copy of the LSA. All routers within an area share the same link-state database.

Deciding on the Best Path

OSPF can decide on the best path to a destination using cost as a metric. OSPF uses less bandwidth than RIP. OSPF is a classless protocol that supports variable-length subnet masking, supernetting, summarization, and discontiguous subnets.

OSPF uses the Dijkstra algorithm and cost calculations to determine the shortest path. The algorithm places each router at the root of a tree and calculates the shortest path to each destination based on the cumulative cost required to reach the destination. The cost is a measure of the overhead required to send packets across an interface. The cost is inversely proportional to the interface's bandwidth. The higher the bandwidth, the lower the cost. The algorithm that calculates the shortest path to each destination inside an area uses lots of CPU processing cycles. As the number of link-state packets increases, the number of calculations increases exponentially.

Determining Cost

The cost is calculated using the following formula:

$$10^8 / BW$$

where 10^8 is 10 raised to the eighth power and BW is the bandwidth of the configured interface.

The following examples list the OSPF cost:

- **Fast Ethernet**—10^8 / 10^8 = 1

- **Ethernet**—10^8 / 10^7 = 10

- **T1**—10^8 / 1,544,000 = 65

Using the formula, the following costs have been derived:

- **56 Kbps serial link**—Default cost is 1785

- **64 Kbps serial link**—Default cost is 1562

- **E1 (2.048 Mbps serial link)**—Default cost is 48

- **4 Mbps Token Ring**—Default cost is 25

- **16 Mbps Token Ring**—Default cost is 6

- **FDDI**—Default cost is 1

The cost can be set by the following commands:

- **ip ospf cost**

- **bandwidth** *bandwidth*

- **auto-cost reference bandwidth**

The **auto-cost reference bandwidth** command is used to change the default of 10^8. Changing the default affects the cost of every OSPF interface on the router. The following command sets the reference bandwidth on a Cisco router:

```
RTR (config-router) #auto-cost reference bandwidth?
```

1–4294967 is the reference bandwidth in Mbps.

NOTE   To ensure stability, the backbone area should be as small as practicality will allow. All areas depend on the backbone to supply LSAs.

OSPF Summarization and Scalability

Summarization increases the network's stability and scalability. Summarization allows several subnetworks to be summarized at a bit boundary before being advertised to other areas. So, 16 subnet routes can be advertised with a single route. A benefit is that link-state changes on a subnetwork do not generate LSAs in the other area.

Specific routes within an area's summarized boundaries that change do not need to be changed in the backbone's routing tables or in other areas. Routers that received summarized routes have shorter routing tables and can provide faster routing lookups.

Summarization can occur at area borders, where a single summary LSA represents all the routes in a single area or at ASBR redistribution points where the summarized routes represent the external routes that are imported into OSPF. Route summarization procedures condense routing information. Without summarization, each router in a network must retain a route to every subnet in the network. With summarization, routers can reduce some sets of routes to a single advertisement, reducing both the load on the router and the perceived complexity of the network. The importance of route summarization increases with network size.

Summarization

There are two types of summarization:

- **Interarea route summarization**—Addresses can be summarized on an ABR into area 0 or from area 0.

- **External route summarization**—Addresses can be summarized into OSPF from external routing protocols on an ASBR.

Figure 7-4 shows OSPF interarea route summarization between Area 0 and Area 1.

Figure 7-4   *OSPF Interarea Route Summarization*

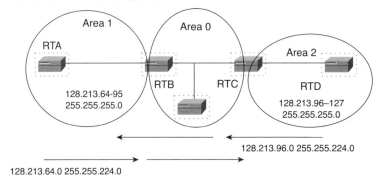

Figure 7-5 shows OSPF summarization of an external route imported from RIP.

Figure 7-5   *OSPF External Route Summarization*

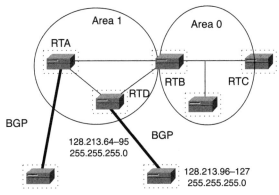

Scalable OSPF Internetworks

To design a scalable OSPF internetwork, make sure that the network conforms to the following:

- Has no more than six hops from source to destination
- Contains no more than 50 routers per area
- Connects all areas to Area 0
- Does not allow more than two areas per ABR
- Uses totally stubby areas
- Maximizes summarization
- Uses multiple-path redundancy instead of virtual links
- Does not overtax router memory
- Has available bandwidth

Security

OSPF protocol exchanges between adjacent routers can be configured to use authentication. Authentication provides added security for the routers that are on the network. Routers that do not have the password will not be able to gain access to the routing information because authentication failure prevents a router from forming adjacencies.

By default, routers use null authentication. Clear-text and Message Digest (MD5) authentication can be configured. The rules of implementing security for OSPF are simple. All routers in an area must have the same authentication key to form a neighbor and adjacency.

Simple password authentication exchanges clear-text passwords across the network and can be detected with a network sniffer.

NOTE   Always use MD5 authentication. MD5 authentication uses cryptography and does not exchange password information across the network.

Figure 7-6 shows an example of OSPF Clear-Text and Message Digest Authentication.

Figure 7-6   *OSPF Authentication*

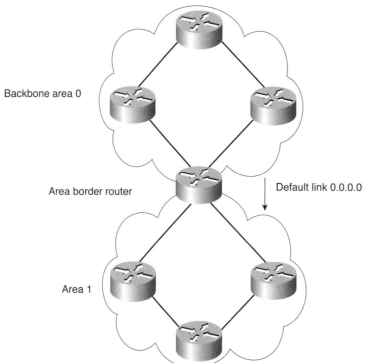

Creating Neighbors

Two OSPF routers do not become neighbors unless they share the following:

- **Area-id**—Routers that share a common segment must belong to the same area on that segment.

- **Authentication**—Routers that want to become neighbors must exchange the same password (the null password is exchanged by default).

- **Hello and dead intervals**—Routers must agree on the timing of the keepalive packets that are exchanged.

- **Stub area**—Routers must agree on the conditions of the stub area if an area is configured to be a stub.

"Howdy, Neighbor!"

OSPF is a right friendly protocol. It welcomes its new neighbors the way you would greet the family who just moved in next door. OSPF says "Hello!" OSPF sends its hello packets to the multicast address All SPF Routers. OSPF is a friendly protocol, and the first thing it wants to do is form an adjacency. As soon as the adjacency is established, OSPF shares all its information with its new neighbor. OSPF shares routing information and keeps a synchronized database with all its neighbors.

When an OSPF router detects a change in one of its interfaces, it modifies its topological database and multicasts the change to its adjacent neighbor, which in turn propagates the change to its adjacent neighbor until all routers within an area have synchronized topological databases. This results in quick convergence among routers. OSPF routes can also be summarized in LSAs.

Designated and Backup Designated Routers

On a broadcast network, OSPF routers don't form adjacencies with all their neighbors. The excessive traffic created by the link updates would be unacceptable. So OSPF elects designated routers (DR) and backup designated routers (BDR) to form the adjacencies.

In OSPF terminology, a broadcast network is any network that has more than two OSPF routers attached and supports the capability to address a single physical message to all the attached routers. The designated router can send LSAs to the rest of the routers on the network. The designated router is the router with the highest priority. The backup designated router is ready to step up in the event that the designated router becomes unavailable. To appoint a router to the office of designated router, be sure it has the highest priority (255). The routers with the two highest priorities are elected DR and BDR.

TIP   DR and BDR tasks require extra processing power that might overwhelm some low-end routers. To ensure that a low-end router never becomes a DR, it can be set to priority 0. If a router interface is set with a priority of 0, that router is ineligible to become the DR for that network. If all routers on a segment are set to 0, OSPF does not function on that segment.

Figure 7-7 illustrates an OSPF network using designated and nondesignated routers.

Figure 7-7   *OSPF Designated Routers*

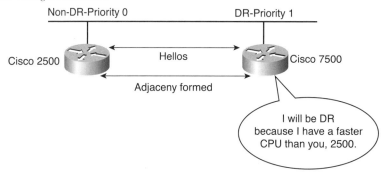

Stub Areas

To reduce the cost of routing, OSPF supports stub areas, in which a default route summarizes all external routes (Type 5 LSAs). For areas that are connected to the backbone by only one ABR (that is, the area has one exit point), there is no need to maintain information about external routes. Stub areas are similar to regular areas, except that the routers do not enter external routes in the area's databases.

To prevent flooding of external routes throughout the AS, you can configure an area as a stub when there is a single exit point from the area or when the choice of exit point need not be made on a per-external-destination basis. You might need to specify a stub area with no default cost if the area has more than one exit point.

In a stub area, routing to AS-external destinations is based on a per-area default cost. The per-area default cost is advertised to all routers within the stub area by a border router and is used for all external destinations.

Totally Stubby Area

A totally stubby area allows only the default summary link to be propagated into the area by the ABR. No redistribution can occur, and no other routing protocols can exist. No Type 3 and Type 5 LSAs are flooded into a totally stubby area. Only a single default route is sent.

NOTE   Not all vendors support the totally stubby feature. When including totally stubby as a design concept, be sure that it is supported if you expect your OSPF-area network to contain routers from other vendors.

Not-So-Stubby Areas (NSSAs)

Support for not-so-stubby areas (NSSAs) is described in RFC 1587. NSSAs allow you to treat complex networks similar to stub areas. This can simplify your network topology and reduce OSPF-related traffic.

NSSAs and Type 7 LSAs

NSSAs are similar to stub areas, except that they allow limited importing of autonomous system (AS) external routes. External routes carried into the backbone are not propagated into the area. Intra-area routes are propagated into the NSSA. NSSA is an area with an ASBR that allows external Type 7 LSAs into the OSPF network while retaining the characteristics of a stub area. The Type 7 LSA is generated by the ASBR in the NSSA. Type 7 LSAs are similar to Type 5 LSAs, except for the following:

- NSSAs can originate and import Type 7 LSAs. Like stub areas, NSSAs cannot originate or import Type 5 LSAs.

- Type 7 LSAs can be advertised only within a single NSSA. They are not flooded throughout the AS, as are Type 5 LSAs.

External Link Advertisement

OSPF classifies external routes into two types:

- External Type 1 routes use a metric that is the sum of the external metric and the collective internal cost of reaching the destination.

- External Type 2 routes use a metric that examines the external metric and does not take the internal cost into consideration.

The E1 metric is the sum of the internal and external metrics. The E2 metric does not add internal metrics.

Figure 7-8 illustrates OSPF stubby areas, and Table 7-2 discusses them in more detail.

Figure 7-8   *OSPF Stubby Areas*

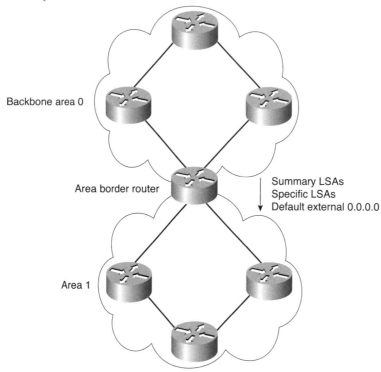

Table 7-2   *OSPF stubby areas*

Area Type	Interarea	Intra-area	External	Default
Stub	Yes	Yes	No	Yes
Totally stubby	No	Yes	No	Yes
Not-so-stubby	No	Yes	Yes	Yes
			NSSA has no External Type 5 route.	

Determining OSPF Convergence

When a change occurs in the network, it is the responsibility of the routing protocol to reroute traffic quickly. Convergence time defines the time it takes a router to recognize and recalculate a new route after a change in the network topology. OSPF convergence has three basic functions:

- Detect the failure
- Update the database
- Propagate the changed route information

Some changes are immediately detectable. For example, serial line failures that involve carrier loss are immediately detectable by a router. FDDI, Token Ring, and carrier detect (CD) failures can be detected instantaneously. Some types of network changes, however, are more difficult to detect. If a serial line becomes unreliable but the carrier is not lost, the unreliable link is not immediately detectable. In addition, some media (Ethernet, for example) do not provide physical indications such as carrier loss. When a router is reset, other routers might not detect this immediately. In general, failure detection is dependent on the media involved and the routing protocol used.

In general, OSPF convergence can range from 6 to 46 seconds, depending on the type of change, the timer settings, and the size of the network. The worst-case scenario for convergence exists when a routing node fails and the destination is still reachable because the 40-second default dead timer expires before the SPF is recalculated.

When a failure is detected, the routing protocol must select a new route. The mechanisms used to do this are protocol-dependent. All routing protocols must propagate the changed route.

Load Balancing with OSPF

The Cisco implementation of OSPF can support up to four equal-cost routes to a destination. If one route fails, OSPF uses the remaining paths as alternates. OSPF load balancing allows equal cost by default paths. The cost associated is determined by the interface bandwidth statement unless otherwise configured to maximize multiple-path routing.

OSPF Backbone Design and Address Mapping: Area 0

Area 0 is command center for all OSPF activity. All areas must have a connection to the backbone. If a physical connection is impossible, a logical connection can be configured. The importance of Area 0 makes it essential that the CCDP consider first and foremost which routers and devices should be included in Area 0. Do not place client workstations in Area 0. Keep all local workgroup traffic off the backbone. Use the backbone strictly as a transit area.

After Area 0 design issues have been considered, the remaining essential elements for successful design include the following:

- Determining the number of routers in an area
- Determining the number of neighbors for a single router

- Determining the number of areas supported by a single router
- Determining how many routers will serve as the designated router

---

NOTE   When a single router is connected to more than three areas, router memory and CPU resources might be overwhelmed. Limit the number of areas that connect to a single router to a maximum of three. A router with a high-speed CPU and lots of memory might be able to handle more areas.

Virtual Link

In an ideal design, all areas are physically connected to the backbone. If an area border router goes down, an area might become physically isolated from Area 0. In this situation, a virtual link can create a path through the transit area router to the backbone area. The ABRs at each end of the virtual link treat the path as a point-to-point link. A virtual link can extend a backbone area by joining two partitioned areas.

Figure 7-9 shows an example of an OSPF virtual link.

Figure 7-9   *OSPF Virtual Links*

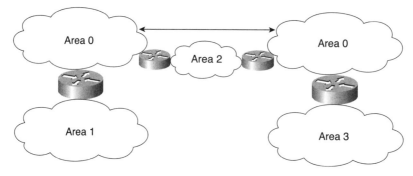

NOTE   Virtual links are not recommended as part of a good CCDP OSPF design strategy. Virtual links add a layer of complexity to the OSPF network. Use virtual links only as a last resort and only as a temporary fix.

OSPF Area Addressing

To reemphasize a point made earlier, the processes of OSPF can put a drain on router resources. Router memory and CPU usage are heavily utilized in large OSPF areas and domains. Using the techniques of summarization, the OSPF processing load on a router can be reduced. With summarization configured properly, there are fewer LSA packets to be sent and acknowledged. The following sections describe how bits can be split to efficiently summarize a major network number.

Bit-Splitting the Address Space

To efficiently summarize, networks should be assigned in bit boundaries. To divide a major network number across more than one area, use bit splitting. To divide the network into four areas, you need 2 bits. With 2 bits, the result is 00, 01, 10, and 11.

To differentiate 16 bits, split 4 bits. Table 7-3 shows the number of bits used. Bit splitting borrows subnet bits to designate areas. To differentiate two areas, split 1 bit.

Table 7-3   *Bit Splitting*

Area	Bits
4	2
8	3
16	4
32	5
64	6
128	7

Discontiguous Subnets

Subnets become discontiguous when they are separated by one or more subnets. When two major networks are separated by another major network, the network flow lacks continuity and becomes discontiguous. OSPF supports discontiguous subnets. The wise CCDP will avoid this design whenever possible.

Determining IGRP/EIGRP Routing, Characteristics, and Convergence

Cisco developed IGRP to be a proprietary protocol that was a simple, robust, and more scalable routing protocol than RIP. Although RIP worked fine in small, homogenous networks, it was found to be harshly restricted in larger internetworks because of its limit of 16 hop-counts. Indeed, the use of the hop-count as its only metric ensures that RIP will never have the flexibility it needs to perform successfully in a large, complex network. IGRP was intended to overcome the shortcomings and limitations of RIP. Because IGRP is a distance-vector protocol, it shares several features that are common to RIP. Like RIP, IGRP broadcasts its entire routing table to its neighbors periodically. Like RIP, IGRP is a classful protocol and summarizes at network boundaries.

IGRP has several features that differentiate it from RIP and allow it to have greater functionality:

- **Scalability**—IGRP can be configured for large internetworks. IGRP has a default network diameter of 100 hops and can scale up to 255 hops.

- **Fast response to network changes**—Unlike RIP and other distance-vector routing protocols, IGRP sends updates when route topology changes occur.

- **Sophisticated metric**—IGRP uses a composite metric that provides significant route selection flexibility. Internetwork delay, bandwidth, reliability, and load are all factored into the routing decision.

NOTE   By default, only bandwidth and delay are used.

- **Multiple paths**—IGRP can maintain up to four unequal paths between a network source and destination. Multiple paths can be used for redundancy or to increase available bandwidth.

IGRP Features

As mentioned in Chapter 6, IGRP by default uses a combination of bandwidth and delay as a routing metric:

IGRP metric = (C1 × bandwidth) + [(C2 × bandwidth) / (256-load) + (C3 × delay)]

C1, C2, and C3 are constants. By default, C2 = 0 and C1 and C3 = 1.

So, by default, IGRP metric = bandwidth + delay.

In addition to bandwidth and delay, IGRP can be configured to track the following metrics:

- Reliability
- Loading
- MTU (static)
- Hops (static)

IGRP Stability

IGRP provides a number of features that are designed to enhance its stability. These include holddowns and split horizon. The following sections discuss IGRP stability features.

IGRP Route Holddown

IGRP has a hold-down timer that prevents temporary routing loops during convergence. When a route is determined to be unreachable, it is considered to be a poisoned route and is placed in a hold-down state. A poisoned route is flagged and advertised with an unreachable metric. In the IP routing table, this route is listed as being possibly down. By default, the route remains in holddown for 280 seconds. This value equals 3×90 seconds (the update interval) plus 10 seconds. A poisoned route can be replaced in the routing table after holddown expires or when a reachable route is advertised. If the route remains poisoned after 630 seconds (10.5 minutes), it is flushed.

Fine-Tuning IGRP

IGRP can be tweaked for faster convergence by the following:

- Turning off or reducing holddown
- Reducing the update timer

IGRP has the following default values:

- **Update timer**—90 seconds
- **Invalid timer**—270 seconds
- **Holddown timer**—280 seconds
- **Flush timer**—630 seconds

Holddown and timer changes must be the same on every router in the autonomous system.

TIP   If you turn off holddown, IGRP converges faster. If you are doing IGRP routing over slow WAN links, it is better to reduce holddown than to eliminate it.

NOTE   To prevent count-to-infinity loops when holddown is disabled, IGRP poisons any destination network that shows an increase in hop-counts.

Split Horizon

When using physical interfaces on a broadcast network, it is not a good idea to send information about a route to the same router from which you learned it. Split horizon does not allow a router to propagate routes learned from an interface out the same interface. IGRP does not advertise network reachability to a neighbor from which the route was learned. Split horizon prevents routing loops.

When designing nonbroadcast multiaccess networks that use logical interfaces, such as Frame Relay , you might want to disable split horizon. If an interface is configured with secondary IP addresses and split horizon is enabled, updates might not be sourced by every secondary address. One routing update is sourced per network number, unless split horizon is disabled. Figure 7-10 shows an example of split horizon.

Figure 7-10   *Bit Splitting*

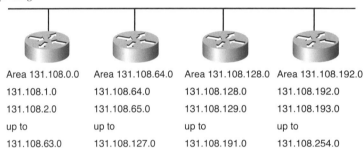

Area 131.108.0.0	Area 131.108.64.0	Area 131.108.128.0	Area 131.108.192.0
131.108.1.0	131.108.64.0	131.108.128.0	131.108.192.0
131.108.2.0	131.108.65.0	131.108.129.0	131.108.193.0
up to	up to	up to	up to
131.108.63.0	131.108.127.0	131.108.191.0	131.108.254.0

In this example, split horizon must be disabled for network 128.125.0.0 to be advertised into network 131.108.0.0, and vice versa. These subnets overlap at Router C, interface S0. If split horizon were enabled on serial interface S0, it would not advertise a route back into the Frame Relay network for either network.

IGRP Variance

IGRP variance is used to balance two links at different speeds. It is recommended that the links be similar in all respects, with the exception of speed. For example, the links should have the same encapsulation and the same maximum transmission unit size. IGRP supports up to four unequal-cost load-balancing paths at a time.

Determining EIGRP Routing, Characteristics, and Convergence

EIGRP is an enhanced version of IGRP. The same distance-vector technology found in IGRP is also used in EIGRP. All features in IGRP are available in EIGRP. However, EIGRP has enhancements that surpass the capabilities of IGRP. EIGRP can be viewed as a hybrid protocol because it contains features that are usually seen in link-state and distance-vector protocols.

One significant advantage that EIGRP delivers when compared to the other distance-vector protocols is updates. EIGRP does not send updates at regular intervals in the same fashion as IGRP and RIP. Not doing regular updates saves bandwidth and CPU resources. EIGRP uses link-state features to determine neighbor reachability. The convergence properties for EIGRP are better than IGRP. EIGRP provides compatibility and seamless interoperation with IGRP routers. EIGRP sends partial updates instead of the entire routing table. Updates are sent only to the neighbors that need it. EIGRP sends updates only when the network topology changes. EIGRP can be enabled without disruption to IGRP performance. An automatic redistribution mechanism allows IGRP and EIGRP to be imported and exported seamlessly. IGRP routes take precedence over EIGRP routes by default. This can be changed with a configuration command that does not require the routing processes to restart.

EIGRP dynamically learns about other routers on directly attached networks. EIGRP routers must also discover when their neighbors become unreachable or inoperative. This process is achieved with low overhead by periodically sending small hello packets. As long as hello packets are received, a router can determine that a neighbor is alive and functioning. As soon as this is determined, the neighboring routers can exchange routing information.

Each router keeps state information about adjacent neighbors. When a new neighbor is discovered, the neighbor's address and interface are recorded. This information is stored in the neighbor data structure. The router keeps a local routing table and an active routing table for each neighbor. Knowing the neighbor's routing table allows EIGRP to make fast routing decisions.

Components of EIGRP

To provide superior routing performance, EIGRP employs four key technologies that combine to differentiate it from other routing technologies:

- Neighbor discovery/recovery
- Reliable transport protocol (RTP)
- Diffusing Update Algorithm (DUAL) finite-state machine
- Protocol-dependent modules

Neighbor Discovery/Recovery

Neighbor discovery/recovery allows routers to dynamically learn about other routers on their directly attached networks. In addition to knowing when a neighbor is functioning, a router must also be able to determine when a neighbor is unreachable or unresponsive. Neighbor discovery/recovery is achieved with low overhead by periodically sending small hello packets. As long as hello packets are received, a router can determine that a neighbor is alive and functioning. As soon as this status is determined, the neighboring routers can exchange routing information.

Reliable Transport Protocol

The *reliable transport protocol* is responsible for guaranteed, ordered delivery of Enhanced IGRP packets to all neighbors. It supports intermixed transmission of multicast and unicast packets. Some Enhanced IGRP packets must be transmitted reliably, and others need not be. For efficiency, reliability is provided only when necessary. For example, on a multiaccess network that has multicast capabilities, such as Ethernet, it is not necessary to send hellos reliably to all neighbors individually. Therefore, Enhanced IGRP sends a single multicast hello with an indication in the packet informing the receivers that the packet need not be acknowledged. Other types of packets, such as updates, require acknowledgment, and this is indicated in the packet. The reliable transport has a provision to send multicast packets quickly when unacknowledged packets are pending. Doing so helps ensure that convergence time remains low in the presence of varying speed links.

DUAL Finite-State Machine

The *DUAL finite-state machine* is the decision-maker for all route computations. It tracks all routes advertised by all neighbors. DUAL uses the distance information to select efficient, loop-free paths. DUAL selects routes to be inserted into a routing table based on feasible successors. A successor is a neighboring router used for packet forwarding that has a least-cost path to a destination that is guaranteed not to be part of a routing loop. When there are no feasible successors, but there are neighbors advertising the destination, a recomputation must occur. The amount of time it takes to recompute the route affects the convergence time. Even though the recomputation is not processor-intensive, it is best to avoid recomputation when it's unnecessary. When a topology change occurs, DUAL tests for feasible successors. If there are feasible successors, it uses any it finds to avoid unnecessary recomputation.

Protocol-Dependent Modules

The protocol-dependent modules are responsible for network layer protocol-specific tasks. One example is the IP EIGRP module, which is responsible for sending and receiving EIGRP packets that are encapsulated in IP. It is also responsible for parsing Enhanced IGRP packets and informing DUAL of the new information received. IP EIGRP asks DUAL to make routing decisions, but the results are stored in the IP routing table. Also, IP EIGRP is responsible for redistributing routes learned by other IP routing protocols.

NOTE   When there are no feasible successors, but there are neighbors advertising the destination, EIGRP recounts the cost.

Automatic redistribution makes upgrading the network to EIGRP a snap:

- IP EIGRP automatically redistributes routes with IGRP in the same AS.

- AppleTalk EIGRP automatically redistributes with AppleTalk RTMP.

- IPX EIGRP automatically redistributes with IPX RIP and NLSP.

EIGRP Characteristics

EIGRP has several constructive characteristics that enhance network design:

- **Scalability**—Like IGRP, EIGRP can be configured for large internetworks. EIGRP can scale up to 255 hops.

- **Fast convergence**—EIGRP can converge within 1 second of detecting a link failure. EIGRP uses DUAL, which allows route filtering at any node and propagation to only the affected nodes, ensuring quick, loop-free convergence.

- **Sophisticated metric**—To ensure route-selection flexibility, EIGRP uses the same composite metric as IGRP. Internetwork delay, bandwidth, reliability, and load are all factored into the routing decision.

- **Multiple paths**—EIGRP can maintain up to four unequal paths between a network source and destination. Multiple paths can be used to increase available bandwidth or for route redundancy.

- **Supports mobile hosts**—EIGRP allows local mobility within the same major network.

By default, EIGRP uses a combination of bandwidth and delay as a routing metric. In addition to bandwidth and delay, EIGRP can be configured to track the following metrics:

- Reliability

- Loading

- MTU (static)

- Hop count (up to 255)

NOTE   By default, EIGRP uses no more than 50 percent of a link's bandwidth. When running EIGRP on a low-bandwidth WAN link, change the amount of bandwidth that EIGRP uses with the command **ip bandwidth-percent eigrp**.

EIGRP Supports Mobile IP

Mobile IP is most useful in environments where mobility is desired and the traditional landline dial-in model or Dynamic Host Configuration Protocol (DHCP) solutions are inadequate. If it is necessary or desirable for a user to maintain a single address while he makes the transition between networks and network media, Mobile IP can let him do this. Generally, Mobile IP is most useful in environments where a wireless technology is being utilized. This includes cellular environments and wireless LAN situations that might require roaming.

Each mobile node is always identified by an exception address. This address and route are propagated for a host that moves away from its subnet. Because the host route is more specific than the subnet route, the traffic is still routed to the host. The only devices that need to be aware of the movement of this node are the mobile device and a router serving the user.

EIGRP Supports VLSM

Like IGRP, EIGRP performs summarization by default automatically on network boundaries. However, EIGRP can be configured to advertise across a different major network.

Foundation Summary

This section contains tables and lists that provide a convenient review of many key concepts in this chapter. If you are already comfortable with the topics in this chapter, this summary could help you recall a few details. If you have just read this chapter, this review should help solidify some key facts. If you are doing your final preparation before the exam, Tables 7-4 through 7-8 are a convenient way to review the day before the exam.

OSPF Design Concepts

OSPF is the solution for designing complex multivendor networks. The CCDP should design the OSPF network with regard to scalability, compatibility, change, functionality, and cost.

Most WAN users have performance expectations that are defined by their Service-Level Agreements (SLAs). The network's design should ensure that the network will meet or exceed user expectations. The design must allow flexibility for organizational and technical changes. The design should allow for the organization to grow. A design that is ideal for a 50-user network might fail miserably when it needs to support 200 users. Route summarization allows the OSPF network to scale without putting an extra burden on router resources. The design must be flexible enough to allow for the dynamics of technology. Finally, the design should strike an effective balance between cost and performance.

Here are some reasons to use OSPF:

- Compatible with multivendor platforms
- Supports VLSM
- Uses network bandwidth efficiently
- Uses cost as a metric
- Supports large networks with different link speeds
- Supports authentication
- Supports discontiguous subnets
- Converges fast

For further review, consult tables 7-4 through 7-8.

Table 7-4 *OSPF Characteristics*

Term	Definition
OSPF	Open Shortest Path First protocol. a nonproprietary link-state routing protocol for TCP/IP. Developed in response to a need to overcome limitations of RIP, a distance-vector protocol.
Link-state protocol	A protocol that describes the state of the existing interface and link. A link-state database includes information about the interface's IP address, the type of network on which it resides, and information about neighboring routers.
Shortest Path First algorithm	An algorithm used by OSPF to determine the shortest path to each destination. This algorithm places each router at the root of a tree and calculates the shortest path to each destination based on the cost metric.
OSPF cost	A metric used by OSPF to determine overhead required to send a packet across an interface. The cost of an interface is inversely proportional to the interface's bandwidth. $\text{cost} = 10^8 / BW$
Area	A group of OSPF routers that contain the same link-state database.
Authentication	Security procedures that require passwords to be defined before a router can participate in area activity.
Backbone	Area 0 is the hub of all OSPF activity. All OSPF information must pass through Area 0.
Virtual link	A link used when an area cannot be physically connected to Area 0.
Neighbors	OSPF routers that share a common segment and common handshake information.

Table 7-5 *Six OSPF Packet Types*

Name	Type	Comments
Hello	1	
Database description	2	
Link-state request	3	Used to request full path information associated with a received database description packet.
Link-state update	4	Contains one or more link-state advertisements.
Link-state acknowledgment	5	Used to acknowledge the receipt of path information contained in link-state updates.
AS external link-state acknowledgment	7	Used by the ASBR to distribute external routing information throughout the NSSA.

Table 7-6   *OSPF Network Types*

Type	Comments
Point-to-point	Connects a single pair of routes over point-to-point serial links. Does not elect a DR or BDR. Dynamically establishes a neighbor relationship.
Broadcast	Connects two or more routers over broadcast media. Elects a DR and a BDR. Establishes adjacencies between each neighbor and the DR and BDR.
Nonbroadcast	Connects more than two routes. Requires manual configuration to establish neighbor relationships. Elects a DR and a BDR.
Point-to-multipoint	A configuration applied to NBMA networks. Connects more than two routers. Dynamically establishes a neighbor relationship. Does not elect a DR or BDR.

Table 7-7   *IGRP Features*

Feature	Comments
Scalability	Can be configured for large internetworks. Can scale up to 255 hops.
Sophisticated metric	Uses a composite metric of bandwidth, delay, reliability, load, and hop-count.
Multiple paths	Can maintain up to four unequal paths between source and destination.
Fast response	Sends updates when route topology changes.

Table 7-8   *EIGRP Characteristics*

Feature	Comments
Neighbor discovery	Routers dynamically learn about other routers on their directly attached networks. Routers also can discover when their neighbors become unreachable or inoperative.
Manual summarization	By default, EIGRP summarizes at the classful boundary. EIGRP can be configured to pass discontiguous subnets.
Redistributive compatibility with IGRP	Automatic redistribution when IGRP has the same autonomous system.
Supports VLSM	Allows flexibility in IP addressing.
Low use of bandwidth	EIGRP does not send updates unless hello packets detect a change in network topology.

Q&A

As mentioned in Chapter 1, the questions and scenarios in this book are more difficult than what you will experience on the actual exam. The questions do not attempt to cover more breadth or depth than the exam; however, they are designed to make sure that you know the answer. Rather than allowing you to derive the answer from clues hidden inside the question, the questions challenge your understanding and recall of the subject. Questions from the "Do I Know This Already?" quiz from the beginning of the chapter are repeated here to ensure that you have mastered this chapter's topic areas. Hopefully, these questions will help limit the number of exam questions on which you narrow your choices to two options and then guess. Be sure to use the CD and take the simulated exams.

The answers to these questions can be found in Appendix A.

1 What limitations of RIP, the first Internet routing protocol, was OSPF designed to overcome?

_____

_____

_____

2 What are the four types of connections for the OSPF routing protocol?

_____

_____

_____

3 Name the four classifications of OSPF routers.

_____

_____

_____

4 What are link-state advertisements? Name four types of link-state advertisements.

_____

_____

_____

5 True or false: All OSPF areas must be physically adjacent to the backbone.

_____

_____

_____

6 The following are OSPF routes. Perform summarization to one route. What configuration commands would be needed if the routes were external? What commands would be needed if the routes were internal?

- Route 1   172.26.30.0

- Route 2   172.26.31.0

- Route 3   172.26.32.0

_____

_____

_____

7 Compare and contrast stub, totally stubby, and not-so-stubby areas.

_____

_____

_____

8 List six rules for designing a scalable OSPF internetwork.

_____

_____

_____

9 How does OSPF route summarization save router resources?

_____

_____

_____

10 What is the meaning of cost, and how does OSPF calculate cost?

_____

_____

_____

11 What is the difference between an External Type 1 route and an External Type 2 route?

_____

_____

_____

12 Which routing protocols are supported by EIGRP?

_____

_____

_____

13 EIGRP updates are:

A periodic

B incremental

C A and B

D None of the above

_____

_____

_____

14 Name five values that IGRP and EIGRP use to determine metrics. Which metrics are used by default?

_____

_____

_____

15 Name two parameters that can be tuned by IGRP to allow faster convergence.

_____

_____

_____

16 As a rule of thumb, how many areas should be connected to a single router?

_____

_____

_____

17 What is the function of a designated router?

_____

_____

_____

18 What is a virtual link?

_____

_____

_____

19 What is an OSPF area?

_____

_____

_____

20 True or false: IGRP summarizes on network number boundaries but can be configured to support variable-length subnet masks.

_____

_____

_____

21 What is split horizon? In what situations might split horizon be useful to the network design?

_____

_____

_____

22 True or false: To ensure fast convergence for large internetworks, EIGRP keeps two routing tables, the local routing table and the active routing table, of any router three hops away.

_____

_____

_____

23 Why is EIGRP considered a hybrid protocol?

_____

_____

_____

24 What Cisco feature lets the percentage of bandwidth used by EIGRP be changed?

_____

_____

_____

25 What is the function of a designated router?

_____

_____

_____

26 Which protocols discussed in this chapter (OSPF, IGRP, and EIGRP) are classful by default?

_____

_____

_____

27 What provisions do OSPF and EIGRP make for security?

_____

_____

_____

28 Name three features that are supported by OSPF and EIGRP.

_____

_____

_____

29 What configuration command allows IGRP to support unequal-cost load balancing?

_____

_____

_____

30 Of the three routing protocols (OSPF, IGRP, and EIGRP), which protocol allows connectivity to routers not manufactured by Cisco?

_____

_____

_____

Scenarios

Scenario 1

To help design the optimum solution and address the issues presented in each chapter, you have contracted with the design professionals at RouteitRight to help you.

Shouting N' Routing would like an analysis of its Frame Relay network. Currently, all of the network is running OSPF, and all of the network is located in backbone Area 0. Shouting N' Routing has asked RouteitRight to optimize its OSPF configuration. See Figure 7-11.

Figure 7-11   *Shouting N' Routing Network Topology*

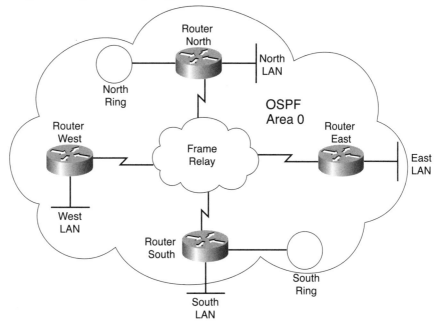

1 How would you reconfigure this network to optimize its use of OSPF?

2 Can a configuration be designed that will conserve router resources?

3 Is route summarization a consideration?

Scenario 2

The Corporation of International Scientists (CIS) contacted RouteitRight. CIS is merging with the Corporation of International Engineers (CIE) to expand its current operations. Both networks are running OSPF with a different backbone. In addition to connecting the two networks, CIS has requested that authentication be placed on the network for security. As soon as the new budget is approved, CIS and CIE will explore combining the network backbones into a single area. Until the budget is approved, CIS and CIE prefer to keep each backbone separate. Can you recommend a temporary solution for CIS and CIE?

Figure 7-12 shows the current CIS and CIE topologies.

Figure 7-12 *CIS and CIE Topology*

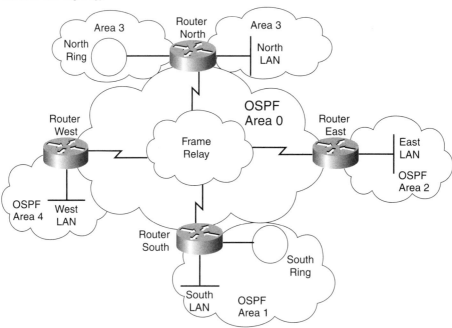

Answer to Scenario 1

The purpose behind the redesign of the OSPF network is to have faster convergence and response on the network. If the router uses fewer CPU and memory resources and has a smaller routing table, it can perform quicker route lookups. The edge routers do not need to know all of the WAN routes to make routing decisions. These routers could be configured as stub routers. In addition, routes can be summarized. Summarization is not an automatic process within OSPF. By default, all routes get advertised throughout the OSPF domain. Summarization can be configured on the ABR or the ASBR.

Given the following:

```
OSPF Route 1 172.168.70.0/24
OSPF Route 2 172.168.72.0/24
OSPF Route 3 172.168.74.0/24
```

Using the binary to decimal table below, perform the following steps to accomplish route summarization.

1 List the octets, 70, 72, and 74 in the right hand column.

2 Convert the octets, 70, 72, and 74 into binary.

3 Identify all the columns where the octets share common values.

4 Identify the first column where the octets do not share common values.

5 Summarize the block on the contiguous block of common values.

Binary Values								Decimal Values
128	64	32	16	8	4	2	1	
0	1	0	0	0	1	1	0	70
0	1	0	0	1	0	0	0	72
0	1	0	0	1	0	1	0	74

NOTE 172.168.64.0 MASK 255.255.240.0 summarizes the three addresses above. Note that all three addresses above. Note that all three addresses share the same binary values for their first four bits.

Routes can be summarized at 172.168.64.0/20 at the ABR or the ASBR.

Figure 7-13 shows a proposed OSPF network after optimization.

Figure 7-13 *Shouting N' Routing Optimized Network Topology*

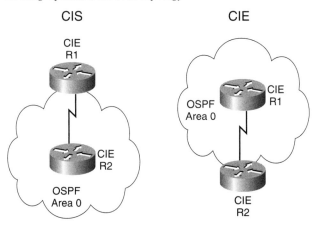

Answer to Scenario 2

OSPF allows for linking discontiguous parts of the CIS/CIE backbone using a virtual link. In the case of CIS and CIE, different Area 0s need to be linked because CIS and CIE need to merge two separate OSPF networks into one network with a common Area 0. A virtual link can be configured between separate ABRs that touch Area 0 from each side and that have a common area. This is illustrated in Figure 7-14.

Figure 7-14   *Revised CIS and CIE Topology*

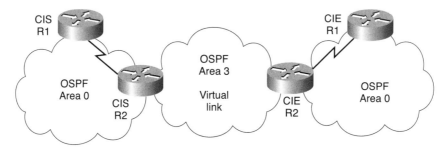

In Figure 7-14, two Area 0s are linked via a virtual link. In case a common area does not exist, an additional area, such as Area 3, could be created to become the transit area between CIS and CIE.

NOTE   Cisco recommends that virtual links be considered a temporary fix rather than a permanent solution.

This chapter covers the following topics that you will need to master as a CCDP:

- **AppleTalk protocol and AppleTalk routing**—This section discusses the AppleTalk protocol and considerations to remember when designing AppleTalk routing.

- **IPX protocol and IPX routing**—This section covers Novell's IPX routing and issues that relate to how SAP and RIP broadcasts are controlled on the network.

- **Windows Networking**—This section examines a client's requirements and constructs a design solution using Windows Networking.

CHAPTER 8

AppleTalk

How to Best Use This Chapter

By following these steps, you can make better use of your study time:

- Keep your notes and the answers for all your work with this book in one place for easy reference.

- Take the "Do I Know This Already?" quiz and write down your answers. Studies show that retention is significantly increased through writing down facts and concepts, even if you never look at the information again.

- Use the diagram shown in Figure 8-1 to guide you to the next step.

Figure 8-1 *How to Use This Chapter*

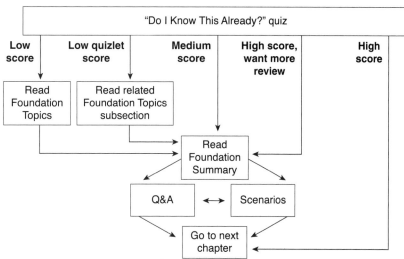

If you skip to the Foundation Summary, Q&A, and Scenarios sections and have trouble with the material there, you should go back to the Foundation Topics section.

"Do I Know This Already?" Quiz

The purpose of the "Do I Know This Already?" quiz is to help you decide which parts of this chapter to use. If you intend to read the entire chapter, you do not necessarily need to answer these questions now.

This 15-question quiz helps you determine how to spend your limited study time. The quiz is divided into three smaller "quizlets" that help you select the sections of the chapter on which to focus. Figure 8-1 outlines suggestions on how to spend your time in this chapter. Use Table 8-1 to record your score.

Table 8-1 *Score Sheet for Quiz and Quizlets*

Quizlet Number	Foundation Topics Section Covering These Questions	Questions	Score
1	AppleTalk protocol and AppleTalk routing	1, 2, 3, 4, 5	
2	IPX protocol and IPX routing	6, 7, 8, 9, 10, 15	
3	Windows Networking	11, 12, 13, 14	

1 In what situations is AppleTalk recommended?

_____

_____

_____

2 Name two AppleTalk protocols that operate at the network layer.

_____

_____

_____

3 What three elements comprise an AppleTalk network address?

_____

_____

_____

4 What method of AppleTalk configuration is recommended for LAN networks?

_____

_____

_____

5 Name three protocols that are used for AppleTalk routing.

_____

_____

_____

6 What two elements comprise a Novell network address?

_____

_____

_____

7 What routing protocol should be used on the WAN to conserve bandwidth?

_____

_____

_____

8 What is one method of controlling SAP and RIP broadcasts on the network?

_____

_____

_____

9 True or false: IPX clients on the network must have a dialup modem or have IP enabled on their workstations to access the Internet.

_____

_____

_____

10 What are the Novell and Cisco definitions for the four types of IPX encapsulation for Ethernet?

_____

_____

_____

11 What are the four methods used by Microsoft Windows to resolve host names?

_____

_____

_____

12 Name three things a designer should be mindful of when designing for DHCP.

_____

_____

_____

13 Why is NetBEUI not recommended for wide-area networks?

_____

_____

_____

14 What are the four domain models that are used in Microsoft Networking?

_____

_____

_____

15 How could IPX or AppleTalk be connected across an IP-only backbone?

_____

_____

_____

The answers to the "Do I Know This Already?" quiz are found in Appendix A. The suggested choices for your next step are as follows:

- **6 or less overall score**—Read the chapter. This includes the "Foundation Topics," "Foundation Summary," and "Q&A" sections, as well as the scenario at the end of the chapter.

- **2 or less on any quizlet**—Review the subsection(s) of the "Foundation Topics" part of this chapter based on Table 8-1. Then move into the "Foundation Summary," the "Q&A" section, and the scenario at the end of the chapter.

- **7, 8, or 9 overall score**—Begin with the "Foundation Summary" section and then go to the "Q&A" section and the scenario at the end of the chapter.

- **10 or more overall score**—If you want more review on these topics, skip to the "Foundation Summary" section, and then go to the "Q&A" section and the scenario at the end of the chapter. Otherwise, move to the next chapter.

Foundation Topics

If your customer is running Macintosh computers on the network and wants to install a protocol that is user-friendly and simple to configure and maintain on a small LAN, you should consider AppleTalk. If you need a protocol that scales to a large size, uses a minimum of bandwidth, and interoperates well with other protocols, well, you should not consider AppleTalk.

Suite of Protocols

AppleTalk is a suite of protocols that were developed by Apple Computer to work on local-area networks with Macintosh computers. Two versions of AppleTalk exist: AppleTalk Phase I and AppleTalk Phase 2. Most users have migrated to AppleTalk Phase 2.

The AppleTalk suite of protocols supports a full range of applications. This chapter discusses AppleTalk routing protocols later in greater detail.

The suite of protocols includes the following:

- **AppleTalk Address Resolution Protocol (AARP)**—Operates at the network layer and associates network addresses with hardware addresses. AARP is similar to ARP in IP.

- **Datagram Delivery Protocol (DDP)**—Operates at the network layer and provides a best-effort connectionless datagram service between AppleTalk sockets.

- **Name Binding Protocol (NBP)**—Operates at the transport layer and maps the addresses used at lower layers to AppleTalk names. The functionality of NBP is similar to the Domain Name Service (DNS) in TCP/IP.

- **Zone Information Protocol (ZIP)**—Maintains network number-to-zone name mappings in AppleTalk routes. A zone is a logical grouping of AppleTalk resources.

- **Routing Table Maintenance Protocol (RTMP)**—Responsible for establishing and maintaining routing tables for AppleTalk routers. RTMP is a distance-vector protocol and is quite similar to RIP in functionality.

- **AppleTalk Update-Based Routing Protocol (AURP)**—Allows two or more AppleTalk internetworks to be interconnected through a TCP/IP network to form a WAN. AURP encapsulates packets in UDP headers, allowing them to flow transparently through a TCP/IP network. AURP is designed to handle routing update traffic over WAN links more efficiently than RTMP. AURP does not replace RTMP in the LAN environment.

- **AppleTalk DataStream Protocol (ADSP)**—A session layer protocol that establishes and maintains full duplex communication between two AppleTalk sockets.

- **AppleTalk Transaction Protocol (ATP)**—A transport layer protocol that handles transactions between two AppleTalk sockets.

- **AppleTalk Filing Protocol (AFP)**—Implemented at the presentation and application layers of the AppleTalk protocol suite. AFP permits workstations to share files across a network.

- **Printer-Access Protocol (PAP)**—Allows a workstation to establish connections with print servers.

Figure 8-2 shows an AppleTalk suite of protocols.

Figure 8-2   *AppleTalk Protocol Suite*

IP network applications	AppleTalk network applications		Routing	Chooser
Mac TCP supports IP stack	Apple Talk higher layers			
	ATP	ADSP	RTMP ZIP	NBP
	DDP			AARP
	Physical and data link layers			

AppleTalk Addressing

AppleTalk uses addresses to identify and locate devices on a network in a manner similar to TCP/IP and IPX. A segment address must be unique. These addresses are composed of the following:

- **Network number**—A 16-bit value that identifies a specific network. This number roughly correlates to a class B IP network. There are 64,000 network numbers available. Network numbers in AppleTalk are also commonly called cable ranges.

  Network numbers should be administered in a way that makes logical sense. A logical numbering system aids in troubleshooting.

  Networks might be allocated by:

  — Building

  — Floor

  — Department

  — Division

- **Node number**—An 8-bit value that identifies a node attached to the network. The maximum number of hosts allowed per network is 253.

- **Socket number**—An 8-bit value that identifies an application.

Figure 8-3 shows numbers by location. Cable ranges are allocated by building number and floor. The Building 6 networks start with 6 and are followed by the floor number. So, network 6210 would be located in Building 6 on the second floor. By using known landmarks in the number, it is less likely that the names will overlap. Numbering by location also helps you administer future networks and isolate a faulty network.

Figure 8-3   *Allocating Numbers by Location*

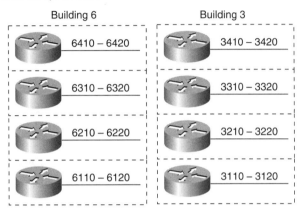

Use Instantly Recognizable Names for Nodes

If resources have recognizable names, users can locate them more efficiently on the network. If a simple convention for names exists, the user can quickly scan the list and identify a resource. NBP provides the name-to-address resolution. Figure 8-4 shows an example of how nodes can be identified by name. Users get the address from the name using the Chooser application and NBP. A Network Visible Entity (NVE) is a 32-character string that helps AppleTalk define devices on the AppleTalk network. To be an NVE, a device must have a network number, node number, and socket number.

Figure 8-4   *Identifying Nodes by Name*

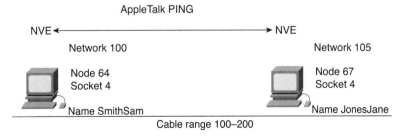

Use Expressive Names for Zones

Zone names should describe the functionality within the organization. A zone could represent the department it serves. Changing AppleTalk zone names is difficult. Routers must be reloaded to clear and reload routing tables. Whenever possible, design zone names in advance so that they relate to the task at hand. Figure 8-5 depicts a network that uses expressive names for zones.

Figure 8-5   *A Network with Expressive Names*

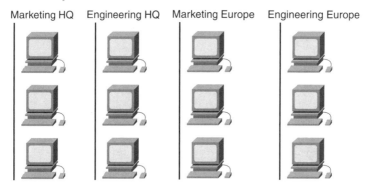

AppleTalk Filtering Options

There are four methods of filtering network and zone information in AppleTalk:

- **GetZoneList (GZL) filter**—Controls the zones seen on a network segment by AppleTalk workstations and has no effect on neighbor routers. GZL filtering must be implemented on all routers on the segment to work properly.

    — Filters ZIP information locally between a router and hosts.

    — Use to hide specific zones from users on specific networks.

    — Does not scale because each router must be configured.

- **Distribute list**

    — Controls RTMP broadcasts between routes.

    — Use to block cable ranges.

    — Do not use to hide zones.

- **ZIP reply filter**—Filters zone information between routers and control zones seen by neighbor routers and downstream routers. ZIP filters can hide zones from all AppleTalk devices on the network.

- **NBP filter**—Can reduce unnecessary overhead traffic. Access can be permitted or denied to a single device or multiple devices.

Configuring Cable Ranges

When multiple routers are connected to the same network, they may all be configured as a seed router with the same network range and zone name information. A router may start up as a nonseed and obtain configuration information from other routers that are already running. When they are running, there is no practical difference between a seed and a nonseed router. The following list explains the different ways an Apple router can be configured:

- **Hard seed**—The router configures the cable range without regard for the ranges used by other nodes. Hard seed can cause conflicts and should be used only during troubleshooting.

  A hard seed router can be configured with the local zone and local network information to be used when it starts up on the network segment to which it will be attached. A seed router maintains this configuration information even if it is in conflict with other routers on the same segment.

- **Soft seed**—This method is recommended for LAN networks. The router accepts a different cable range if AppleTalk discovery is enabled. The router disables the interface if it discovers a conflict.

  A soft seed configured with the local zone and local network information works almost like a hard seed router, with one significant difference. The difference between the hard seed and the soft seed router occurs at startup. When the soft seed router starts up, it also acquires the local zone and local network information from other routers attached to the same network. If the seeded information is in conflict with the acquired information, the soft seed router uses the acquired information rather than cause configuration problems on the network.

- **Nonseed**—The router receives the configuration from a seed router. A nonseed router acquires its local zone and local network information from other routers attached to the same network segment. For a nonseed router to acquire its network configuration properly, at least one other router running on that network segment must have the proper configuration information.

AppleTalk Routing Protocols

AppleTalk uses several dynamic routing protocols: RTMP, EIGRP, and AURP. This section discusses these protocols and provides information to help you determine the best protocol for each situation and circumstance.

NOTE	Floating static routes, although available for use as a backup route, are not recommended as an option. Use floating static routes only as a last resort.

RTMP

As mentioned earlier in this chapter, RTMP is responsible for establishing and maintaining routing tables for AppleTalk routers. RTMP is a distance-vector protocol and is quite similar to RIP in functionality. Like RIP, the maximum hop-count is 15. Like RIP, RTMP is chatty and consumes a great deal of bandwidth. It is recommended that RTMP not be used on WAN links, especially low-speed WAN links, because of its excessive bandwidth consumption. RTMP must be used on the LAN because AppleTalk workstations and servers rely on RTMP to pass AppleTalk information on the network. Like RIP, RTMP relies on split horizon. CCDPs who insist on using RTMP will not be able to use partial mesh as a design solution.

EIGRP

EIGRP supports AppleTalk routing and reduces routing traffic on the WAN. It saves bandwidth because it sends routing updates only when changes occur. IGRP has fast convergence time, converging within 1 second after a link failure.

AppleTalk devices use RTMP exclusively. Do not use EIGRP on the AppleTalk LAN. Do use EIGRP for routing in the WAN core. Figure 8-6 illustrates the quick convergence of EIGRP.

Figure 8-6 *EIGRP Convergence*

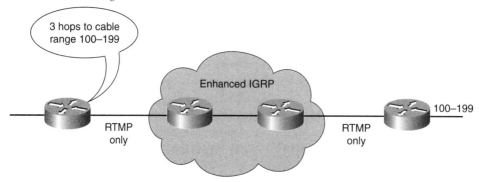

EIGRP:

- Overcomes 15 hop-count limitation
- Allows for a partial-mesh design when split horizon is disabled
- Does not send frequent routing updates

NOTE   AppleTalk EIGRP is different from IP and IPX EIGRP. IP and IPX EIGRP routers share a common autonomous system ID. When enabling AppleTalk EIGRP, each router must have a unique process ID.

AURP

AURP is an AppleTalk protocol that supports tunneling over point-to-point lines. AURP sends updates only when changes occur in the network. An AURP configuration is unique in that it does not require cable ranges or zones. Also, AURP allows for an extension of the hop-count. For example, a network that is 10 hops away with RTMP can appear to be two hops away via the AURP tunnel. Figure 8-7 shows a network using AURP.

Figure 8-7   *AURP*

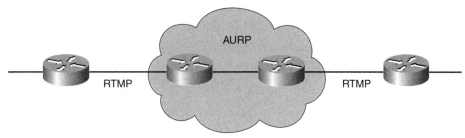

The benefits of using AURP are as follows:

- It reduces routing traffic.

- It grants a level of security and isolation from other networks.

IPX Protocol and IPX Routing

At one time, Novell NetWare was the most popular network operating system available for local-area networks. Even though it is still popular, Windows NT is replacing it in many new installations. Its prime-time protocol, IPX, is also being replaced by TCP/IP as the standard default protocol. Because many installations still use Novell and IPX, it is important that the CCDP understand the design features, functionalities, and capabilities of IPX. Cisco's implementation of IPX is certified to provide full IPX router functionality.

IPX Address Components

Like the other Layer 3 protocols, the Novell IPX addressing scheme is critical to the process of routing IPX data through an internetwork. Every network segment is assigned a unique network address. Routers rely on this address to know how to get a packet to its final destination network. Each host on a Novell IPX network has a unique 80-bit logical address.

The Novell IPX address is divided into two main parts: the network number, consisting of up to 32 bits, and the host number, usually the MAC address of the interface card.

IPX Address Format

The 80-bit Novell IPX address is grouped in a typical network.node format. The network number is a binary number that can be viewed as a hexadecimal number from 1 to FFFFFFFD and is the first 32 bits. The remaining 48 bits is the host number.

Whenever possible, use descriptive IPX network numbers. The hexadecimal numbers A, B, C, D, E, and F can be used creatively to define an IPX network. Network numbers should aid in administration and troubleshooting. If you're designing network numbers by geography, use a method that displays the most significant information on the left. Another popular method of using IPX address naming is to convert IP addresses to hexadecimal. For example, 170.50.10.0 would map to AA320A00.

Address fields can be used to distinguish:

- Media
- Encapsulation
- Phone number
- Office location
- Department
- Division

Encapsulation Types

When designing an IPX network, it is important that the Cisco router IPX encapsulation type match the encapsulation type of the Novell server.

Table 8-2 shows the IPX Ethernet encapsulation types that Cisco supports.

Table 8-2   *IPX Encapsulation Types for Ethernet*

Novell Term	Cisco Term
Ethernet_802.3 (default for Novell 3.x)	Novell-ether
Ethernet_SNAP	SNAP
Ethernet_802.2 (default for Novell 4.x)	SAP
Ethernet_II	ARPA

Table 8-3 shows the IPX Token Ring and FDDI encapsulations that are supported by Cisco routers.

Table 8-3   *IPX Encapsulation Types for Token Ring and FDDI*

Novell Term	Cisco Term
FDDI_SNAP	SNAP
FDDI_802.2	SAP
TOKEN-RING	Novell-tr
TOKEN-RING_SNAP	SNAP

To connect IPX networks with different encapsulations, use subinterfaces.

Novell Routing

Novell IPX uses Service Advertising Protocol (SAP) and RIP broadcasts to build a list of available services and routes.

Routing Information Protocols, or *RIPs*, carry information on the route to take to get to a specific network. RIP updates contain the destination network number, the hop-count, the delay, and the next-hop gateway information. As with SAP updates, a router listens to the RIP updates and builds a route table that lists all known routes.

RIP was Novell's first routing protocol. IPX RIP has many features that are similar to IP RIP. One significant difference between the two protocols is route determination. In addition to hop-count, IPX RIP uses delay as a metric. IPX RIP has the following features:

- 60-second update of routing tables
- 15 hop-count limit
- Split horizon issues require the use of a full mesh
- Delay as a metric

IPX RIP tracks delay as measured in ticks as well as hop count. By default, LAN hops are counted as one tick, and WAN links are counted as six ticks. The tick count can be adjusted with the **ipx delay** command. Table 8-4 shows the values that Cisco recommends for WAN links.

Table 8-4   *Recommended Values for WAN Links*

Bandwidth	Ticks
2.04 Mbps	6
1.544 Mbps	6
256 Kbps	6
128 Kbps	12
56 Kbps	18

Table 8-4   *Recommended Values for WAN Links (Continued)*

Bandwidth	Ticks
38.4 Kbps	24
19.2 Kbps	60
9600 bps	108

IPX SAP

Novell's *Service Advertisement Protocols (SAPs)* carry information on the type of service available, the name of the server, and its IPX address. SAP is an IPX protocol that provides a means of informing network clients, via routers and servers, of available network resources and services. These updates are sent out every 60 seconds by devices on the network that provide a service for others, such as file servers and print servers. A router listens to these SAP updates and builds a SAP table that shows all known services.

On networks with limited resources, SAP broadcasts are often undesirable because they consume bandwidth. The periodic broadcasts can overwhelm a slow link. The CCDP should consider filtering SAP broadcasts.

SAP timers can be modified so that SAPs are not broadcast every 60 seconds. To reduce traffic caused by RIP and SAP, implement incremental RIP and SAP.

NetWare Link-State Protocol

NLSP is a NetWare link-state routing protocol. Novell developed this protocol to take advantage of the features of link-state protocols and the demands of large internetworks. Link-state protocols adapt faster to topology changes than distance-vector protocols. NLSP has the following features:

- Faster convergence

- Can perform route summarization

- Uses less bandwidth than RIP

NSLP is a link-state protocol. It is most often compared to the Intermediate System-to-Intermediate System (IS-IS) protocol with just a backbone area. Because only one area is supported, the number of routers that can participate must be limited. Cisco recommends that the size of one NLSP process be limited to 400 routing nodes. NLSP works best when all the routing nodes are in the same geographic area. In a campus design, each separate campus should have its own NLSP process.

IPX EIGRP

IPX EIGRP reduces bandwidth consumption in Novell networks on the WAN by sending routing changes only when those changes occur. IPX EIGRP dramatically reduces RIP and SAP overhead in the WAN. Split horizon can be disabled with EIGRP. Partial-mesh Frame Relay circuits can have full connectivity.

IPX Access Lists

There are several types of access lists.

IPX traffic can be controlled with access lists. An effective design strategy would implement access lists at the distribution layer in the hierarchical model.

SAP access lists can be applied in three ways:

- Via input: **input-sap-filter**
- Via output: **output-sap-filter**
- Via source: **router-sap-filter**

When filtering, control SAP packets as close to the source as possible. Use SAP access lists based on SAP numbers rather than specific host addresses.

Get Nearest Server Queries

A router can respond to Get Nearest Server (GNS) queries on networks without a server. By default, the GNS response delay is zero.

IPX with NetBIOS

Because NetBIOS uses broadcasts, NetBIOS applications running over IPX do not pass through the router by default. The router must be configured to pass NetBIOS Type 20 broadcasts. The **ipx type-20-propagation** command forwards NetBIOS broadcasts while blocking other IPX broadcasts.

In addition, NetBIOS traffic can be filtered by name using the **ipx netbios input-access-filter** and **ipx -netbios-output-access-filter** commands.

By default, NetWare servers send keepalive messages in the form of watchdog packets to all clients every 5 minutes. Dialup costs can skyrocket if the line stays up, simply because watchdog packets are triggering the interface. The router can be configured to respond to watchdog packets. The command **ipx watchdog-spoof** allows the router to answer session keepalive locally, without activating a dialup line. In the same fashion, some applications require SPX keepalive packets. The routers can be configured to respond to keepalive packets with the command **ipx spx-spoof**.

IPX/IP Gateways

When you connect IPX clients to the Internet, you must install a TCP/IP gateway at a central location.

The IpeXchange IPX-to-IP gateway product requires only one IP address for all IPX clients in the network. The Cisco IpeXchange Internet gateway can be installed on a client or a server. The client runs on a typical Windows PC, and the server version can be loaded on a NetWare server.

Windows Networking

Windows Networking can be the most challenging of all for the CCDP. Windows relies heavily on the NetBIOS protocol. In addition to putting lots of broadcast traffic on the network, NetBIOS cannot be routed. In its native state, NetBIOS can be only bridged. Therefore, the CCDP must be familiar with Windows Networking techniques that allow NetBIOS to be encapsulated and passed across a routed network. In addition, Windows Networking uses the concepts of domains and workgroups, which you must understand if you are to successfully incorporate the Microsoft Network into your design. When this book refers to Windows Networking, it is referring to the networking system shared by the following Microsoft operating systems:

- Microsoft LAN Manager
- MS-DOS with LAN Manager client
- Windows for Workgroups
- Windows 95, 98, and Me
- Windows NT and 2000

Domains and Workgroups

Windows Networking has three concepts of a group of related computers: workgroups, domains, and a domain hierarchy. Workgroups can be any logical collection of computers; any computer on the network can join an existing workgroup or create a new one.

Domains are created and managed by a primary domain controller (PDC) process that runs on a Windows NT or Windows 2000 server. A domain has security and administrative properties that a workgroup does not. Each domain must have at least one NT or 2000 server that is responsible for the PDC process, user account information in the domain, and security within the domain. Windows Networking domains are not the same as the Internet domain names that are used by the Domain Name System (DNS). A domain hierarchy is a collection of domains organized into parent-child relationships. This convention, which is also known as Active Directory hierarchy in Windows 2000, enables easier searching through multiple domains.

Prior to Windows 2000, Windows Networking used the NetBIOS protocol for file sharing, printer sharing, messaging, authentication, and name resolution. A pure Windows 2000 installation would require NetBIOS only for interoperability with earlier versions of Windows Networking using the flat NetBIOS namespace. NetBIOS is a session-layer protocol that can run on any of the following transport protocols:

- NetBEUI (NetBIOS over LLC2)

- NWLink (NetBIOS over Internetwork Packet Exchange [IPX])

- NetBIOS over TCP (NBT)

Figure 8-8 depicts the protocols that can transport NetBIOS.

Figure 8-8   *NetBIOS-Supported Protocols*

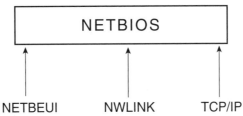

Although Microsoft recommends that clients use only one transport protocol at a time for maximum performance, NetBIOS over TCP is the default for Windows 2000. Pick a protocol to use for your entire network, preferably TCP/IP, and then turn off the other protocols, because the NetBIOS name service maintains information about computer names (a name space) separately for each transport. Name spaces do not interact with each other; each transport operates as a separate network.

It is recommended that you utilize NetBIOS over TCP (NBT) for most networks, or anytime the network includes a WAN. Because NBT uses TCP/IP, each computer must be configured to use a static IP address or to fetch an IP address dynamically with the Dynamic Host Configuration Protocol (DHCP). For ease of network administration, it is highly recommended that you use DHCP. For optimum network performance, it is highly recommended that you use a WINS (Windows Internet Name Service) server as well. A WINS server lets clients get browsing information without having to broadcast requests every time. There is a direct correlation between the number of broadcasts in a network and network performance. Broadcasts are necessary for a network to function, but minimizing them can be critical.

Cisco recommends that most customers use TCP/IP for Windows Networking.

NetBIOS Protocol

NetBIOS was created by IBM to interface with IBM LAN Server, Microsoft LAN Manager, and OS/2. Microsoft Windows uses NetBIOS for all of its operations. When a client connects to Network Neighborhood, NetBIOS makes access to the remote printer, client, or server possible. When it was initially designed, no one could have known that NetBIOS might be used beyond a local LAN. Therefore, NetBIOS has no Layer 3 addressing components and is not routable. NetBIOS relies on Layer 2 broadcasts to communicate. To get from Point A to Point B, NetBIOS must be transported across the network.

NetBIOS operates with a couple of other protocols quite nicely. NetBEUI, IPX, and TCP/IP all support NetBIOS transport. For IPX, the NWLink protocol encapsulates NetBIOS. For TCP/IP, NetBIOS over TCP/IP can be used.

NetBEUI Protocol

NetBEUI is a transport layer protocol. It uses the data-link layer to broadcast its requests to its clients. Once the default protocol of Windows NT in the early days of its development, NetBEUI is now a bench player at best. NetBEUI is the least scalable of the three protocols (NetBEUI, NWLink, and TCP/IP) because it must be bridged. NetBEUI is included only to support very old services, such as old versions of LAN Manager.

NetBEUI does not require any client address configuration. There is no fixed limit to the number of Windows clients you can have with NetBEUI, but it is common for this solution to run into performance problems as the number of clients in a single bridge group goes above 50 to 100 users. The flat topology and reliance on broadcasts do not scale, especially when traffic must traverse a WAN link.

For only the smallest of LANs, like the home-area network (HAN), and for legacy network operating systems still have value. Its main drawback is that it has no Layer 3 protocol and cannot be routed.

NWLink Protocol

NetBIOS over IPX is NWLink. NWLink is recommended only for networks already running IPX that cannot be upgraded to use TCP/IP. NWLink requires no client address configuration. NWLink uses IPX type-20 packets to exchange registration and browsing information. To forward type-20 IPX packets across Cisco routers, configure **ipx type-20 propagation** on each interface on every router on your network.

NetBIOS over TCP/IP (NBT)

TCP/IP communication relies on IP address as endpoint identifiers. Microsoft Windows communication relies on simple names as endpoint identifiers. TCP/IP workstations running Microsoft Windows use NBT, and Microsoft and Cisco recommend NBT for medium and large networks.

Name Resolution

In commands that require client and service access, Microsoft Windows uses NetBIOS names to communicate. NetBIOS names are created when services are started, when clients log in to the network, or when a NetBIOS application starts.

A client's or server's NetBIOS name is the computer name assigned during installation. This name can be viewed in Network Neighborhood when resources are accessed.

Before two NetBIOS hosts can communicate, the name must be resolved to an IP address. NetBIOS name resolution is the process of mapping a computer's name to an IP address. Microsoft uses several methods of resolving NetBIOS names:

- Broadcasts
- LMHOSTS
- WINS
- DNS

Broadcasts

By sending broadcasts on a subnet, Windows clients cause a browser election. The computer that is elected as browse master maintains a list of all the resources available. Because this method does not scale well, it is not recommended.

LMHOSTS

The LMHOSTS file is used to resolve NetBIOS names and IP addresses of remote computers outside the local subnet. The most common use of the LMHOSTS file is for locating remote servers for file, print, and RFC services. All clients are configured with an LMHOSTS file, which contains the name and IP address of their primary domain controller. Manual configuration tasks create an administrative burden and make the LMHOSTS option undesirable in medium to large networks.

WINS

Each WINS client is configured with the address of a WINS server. Upon startup, each client registers its name and address with the WINS server. When the client shuts down, the name and address are unregistered, and the WINS server database is updated dynamically. Client requests for name resolutions are sent directly to the server. The WINS server resolves the name and sends the IP address to the client, removing the need for a broadcast.

DNS

DNS is the classic TCP/IP application that resolves names to addresses. Whereas WINS uses NetBIOS names, DNS uses Internet names. Whereas Microsoft uses an LMHOSTS table to record its entries, DNS uses a HOSTS file.

Scaling to Larger Networks

Microsoft Networks give each user the ability to log in to the network with a single ID and password to any network resource that the user has permission to. Microsoft Networks has introduced two concepts, domains and trust, to allow the network to maintain security over resources while still allowing access to services, applications, and resources to anyone with connectivity and privileges. As mentioned earlier in this chapter, a domain is a logical group of users and computers organized for administrative purposes. The group can be organized with respect to organization, geography, or a common purpose. A trust is defined as a secure link between two domains (see Figure 8-9). With a trust relationship, Domain A can accept user accounts from users in Domain B and allow Domain B users to access Domain A resources. With Microsoft Networking, a user can log in to an enterprise account with one account and cross domain boundaries to use resources anywhere that a trusted domain relationship has been established. Without a trusted domain relationship, the domains are completely separate, and user access to a remote domain is impossible. The following sections describe the trust relationships and domain models available to the CCDP. When designing a Windows network, it is important to consider the right type of domain for your network. As you might expect, there are benefits and drawbacks for each domain model.

Figure 8-9   *Trusted Domain*

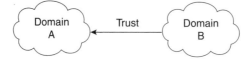

Single Domain

This domain model is the simplest because the network has only one domain. In the single domain model, all users and groups reside in one domain. Because only one domain exists, no trusts are necessary. A single domain is OK for small to medium networks that need centralized administration of accounts and resources. Theoretically, the user base can handle up to 40,000 users. In practical usage, the single domain model performs poorly if the number of users and groups in the domain overwhelm the server's resources. In addition, browsing is slower if the domain has a large number of servers.

Complete Trust

This model is designed for companies that do not have a centralized IS organization. For those who seek the ultimate in distributed management, complete trust is the answer. The complete trust model distributes the administration of users, groups, domains, and resources. The complete trust model is the easiest to understand, but it lacks security and can be the most difficult to manage. Everybody trusts everybody. Every domain in the network trusts every other domain. The following formula produces the number of trust relationships required to implement a complete trust:

$$n \, (n - 1) = \text{trust}$$

For example, $10 \, (10 - 1) = 10 \times 9 = 90$. In other words, 10 domains would require 90 trust relationships. Now that's a lot of trust!

NOTE   The number of trusts can be a factor in determining an appropriate domain structure because structures with the fewest number of trusts are the easiest to manage.

Figure 8-10 depicts the complete trust model.

Figure 8-10   *Complete Trust Model*

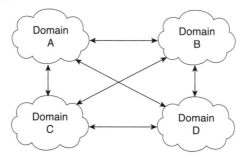

Master Domain

The single master domain model consists of at least two domains, which use the trust concept to implement communication between domains. In this model, all other domains trust a master domain. However, the master domain trusts no one. This option is advantageous when departments or divisions want administrative control over their own services and resources but still want to authenticate centrally. The master domain is a good choice for companies that have too many users for a single domain because of central server resources, but that still want their shared resources split into groups for management purposes. In the master domain model, user accounts can be located in the master (trusted) domain, and resources can be located in the resource (trusting) domain. Figure 8-11 depicts the master domain model.

Figure 8-11   *Master Domain Model*

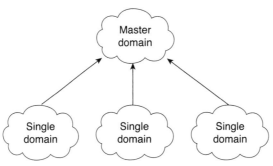

Multiple Master Domains

In a multiple master domain, each master domain is linked to every other master domain by a two-way trust. Every resource domain trusts each of the master domains but does not trust the other resource domains (see Figure 8-12).

Figure 8-12   *Multiple Master Domain Model*

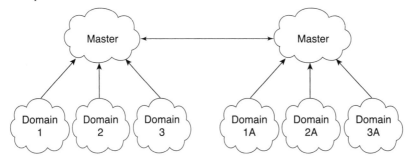

This model is designed to be a larger version of the master domain model. To restate, several master domains all trust each other, and each department in turn trusts each of the master domains. The following formula can be used to calculate the number of trusts in a multiple master domain model:

$$M \times (M - 1) + (R \times M)$$

where M is the number of master domains and R is the number of resource domains.

Figure 8-12 has two master domains and three resource domains, so

$$2 \times (2 - 1) + (3 \times 2) = 8$$

NOTE   The number of trusts can be a factor in determining an appropriate domain structure because structures with the fewest number of trusts are the easiest to manage.

DHCP

To solve the problems of manual addressing, the Internet Engineering Task Force (IETF) developed DHCP, the *Dynamic Host Configuration Protocol*. DHCP is designed to automatically provide clients with a valid IP address and related configuration information. Each range of addresses that a DHCP server manages is called a *scope*.

DHCP Scopes

Configure a range of addresses for every IP subnet where clients will request a DHCP address. Configure a DHCP server to serve several scopes because the DHCP server or servers do not need to be physically connected to the same network as the client. If the DHCP server is on a different IP subnet from the client, configure the DHCP relay to forward DHCP requests to your DHCP server.

DHCP Relay

DHCP relay typically runs on a router. Relay support is available on Windows NT Server version 4.0 and Windows 2000 Server. On Cisco 700 series routers, turn on DHCP relay with the **set dhcp relay** command.

DHCP centralizes, manages, and assigns IP addresses to network clients dynamically. Each time a DHCP client starts, it requests an IP address, a subnet mask, and a default gateway. Here are some of the advantages of using DHCP:

- Lower administrative overhead

- Mistakes made from incorrect configuration lessened

- Saves time

Routers must be configured to pass DHCP broadcasts across the network. The **ip helper address** command forwards broadcasts across the network and sends DHCP packets to the nearest DHCP servers.

When designing for DHCP, the CCDP should be mindful of the following:

- Address assignments

  — What IP address options will the client receive?

  — Which devices do not need to be DHCP clients?

  — Routers, switches, servers, hubs, printers

  — Have any IP addresses been reserved?

- DHCP lease length

- DHCP server redundancy

  — Are multiple servers on a subnet serving as DHCP servers?

  — Will a DHCP server supply addresses to multiple subnets?

Remote Design

Windows NT and Windows 2000 come with Microsoft's remote-access server (RAS), which uses the Point-to-Point Protocol (PPP). Windows supports TCP/IP, IPX, and NetBEUI for dial-in. Cisco access servers are the recommended choice for a remote design solution because its dial-in pools have better dial-in density and performance.

Foundation Summary

This section contains tables and lists that provide a convenient review of many key concepts in this chapter. If you are already comfortable with the topics in this chapter, this summary could help you recall a few details. If you have just read this chapter, this review should help solidify some key facts. If you are doing your final preparation before the exam, Tables 8-5 through 8-7 are a convenient way to review the day before the exam.

RTMP Design Considerations

When designing a network with RTMP, the CCDP is subject to many of the same constraints that the RIP design presents:

- The maximum hop-count is 15

- Routing updates occur every 10 seconds

- RTMP packets consume quite a bit of bandwidth

- The impact can be significant on a low-speed WAN link

- Split-horizon requirements mandate the use of a full-mesh topology

Refer to Tables 8-5 through 8-7 for further review.

Table 8-5 *Novell Frame Types*

Novell Frame Types	Cisco Equivalent
802.2	SAP
Ethernet 802.3_raw	Novell-ether
Ethernet_snap	SNAP
Ethernet II	ARP
Token Ring	SAP
Token_Ring_Snap	SNAP
Fddi_Raw	Novell-fddi
FDDI_802.2	SAP
FDDI_SNAP	SNAP

Table 8-6 *AppleTalk Protocols and the OSI Model*

OSI Model Layer	Apple Protocol
Application	AppleTalk Filing Protocol (AFP)
Presentation	AppleTalk Filing Protocol (AFP)

continues

Table 8-6 *AppleTalk Protocols and the OSI Model (Continued)*

OSI Model Layer	Apple Protocol
Session	AppleTalk Data Stream Protocol (ADSP)
	Zone Information Protocol (ZIP)
	AppleTalk Session Protocol (ASP)
	Printer Access Protocol (PAP)
Transport	Routing Table Maintenance Protocol (RTMP)
	AppleTalk Echo Protocol (AEP)
	AppleTalk Transaction Protocol (ATP)
	Name Binding Protocol (NBP)
Network	Datagram Delivery Protocol (DDP)
Data link	EtherTalk
	LocalTalk
	TokenTalk
	FDDITalk
Physical	Ethernet, Token Ring, LocalTalk, FDDITalk

Table 8-7 *Selecting the Right Domain Model for Microsoft Networking*

Feature	Single Domain	Master Domain	Multiple Master Domain
Users per domain	Up to 40,000 (depending on the equipment's resource capacity)	Up to 40,000 (depending on the equipment's resource capacity)	Handles more than 40,000 users per domain
Account management	Centralized	Centralized	Decentralized
Resource management	Centralized	Decentralized	Depends on the design
MIS	Centralized	Centralized	Depends on the design

Q&A

As mentioned in Chapter 1, the questions and scenarios in this book are more difficult than what you will experience on the actual exam. The questions do not attempt to cover more breadth or depth than the exam; however, they are designed to make sure that you know the answer. Rather than allowing you to derive the answer from clues hidden inside the question, the questions challenge your understanding and recall of the subject. Questions from the "Do I Know This Already?" quiz from the beginning of the chapter are repeated here to ensure that you have mastered this chapter's topic areas. Hopefully, these questions will help limit the number of exam questions on which you narrow your choices to two options and then guess. Be sure to use the CD and take the simulated exams.

The answers to these questions can be found in Appendix A.

1 In what situations is AppleTalk recommended?

2 Name two AppleTalk protocols that operate at the network layer.

3 What three elements comprise an AppleTalk network address?

4 What method of AppleTalk configuration is recommended for LAN networks?

5 Name three protocols that are used for AppleTalk routing.

6 What two elements comprise a Novell network address?

_____

_____

_____

7 What routing protocol should be used on the WAN to conserve bandwidth?

_____

_____

_____

8 What is one method of controlling SAP and RIP broadcasts on the network?

_____

_____

_____

9 True or false: IPX clients on the network must have a dialup modem or have IP enabled on their workstations to access the Internet.

_____

_____

_____

10 What are the Novell and Cisco definitions for the four types of IPX encapsulation for Ethernet?

_____

_____

_____

11 What are the four methods used by Microsoft Windows to resolve host names?

_____

_____

_____

12 Name three things a designer should be mindful of when designing for DHCP.

_____

_____

_____

13 Why is NetBEUI not recommended for wide-area networks?

_____

_____

_____

14 What are the four domain models that are used in Microsoft Networking?

_____

_____

_____

15 How could IPX or AppleTalk be connected across an IP-only backbone?

_____

_____

_____

16 What metrics does IPX RIP use to determine the best route?

_____

_____

_____

17 Design problem: Dialup lines stay up because keepalive traffic is triggering the line every 5 minutes. How should this be fixed?

_____

_____

_____

18 How many bits comprise a full Novell IPX address?

_____

_____

_____

19 What AppleTalk configuration is recommended only for troubleshooting?

_____

_____

_____

20 True or false: DHCP can assign addresses only to machines that use Microsoft Windows.

_____

_____

_____

21 Which routing protocol is highly recommended for the WAN but not for the LAN?

_____

_____

_____

22 What AppleTalk routing protocol supports tunneling?

_____

_____

_____

23 List four examples of how network numbers can be administered.

_____

_____

_____

24 Why is RTMP recommended for the LAN but not the WAN?

_____

_____

_____

25 List three benefits of using DHCP.

_____

_____

_____

26 Can a Cisco router be configured as a DHCP server?

_____

_____

_____

27 In what situations might NetBEUI still be a useful protocol?

_____

_____

_____

28 True or false: Like IP and IPX, AppleTalk routers use the same AS number on all routers in the domain.

_____

_____

_____

29 How can a Cisco router be configured to pass NetBIOS broadcasts?

_____

_____

_____

30 How can a router be configured to allow different types of encapsulation on the same interface?

_____

_____

_____

Scenarios

Scenario

To help you design the optimum solution and address the issues presented in each chapter, you have contracted with the design professionals at RouteitRight to help you.

Southwest Routing would like an analysis of its Bridgeport, New Mexico, branch location. The Bridgeport location has four departments located on four different floors:

- Sales and Marketing

- Service and Support

- Engineering

- Manufacturing

Each department needs to support AppleTalk, Novell, and NetBIOS applications. Each floor of the building has a router, and the computers are connected via Ethernet. In addition, corporate servers exist that use AppleTalk and IPX applications.

Design a set of AppleTalk and Novell addressing and naming conventions that will support the needs of Southwest Routing.

Network numbers can be allocated by department. These numbers are facilitated to help administration and troubleshooting. Note that the cable ranges (for AppleTalk) and the network numbers (for Novell) for each LAN are unique and do not overlap. In this scenario, the network numbers are used to designate the network's physical location. For example, Sales and Marketing is located on the first floor and has the first range of numbers. Here are the ranges of numbers:

Sales and Marketing	1000–1999
Service and Support	2000–2999
Engineering	3000–3999
Manufacturing	4000–4999

These numbers can be used for AppleTalk as well as Novell.

Answer to Scenario

An AppleTalk zone name can match the functional description of a division, department, or organization. So it makes sense to use the existing departments as zone names. In the case of Southwest Routing, SalesMarket, Engineering, Manufacturing, and ServeSupport are names that could be used. Using the division names makes it easier for users to identify and locate resources.

To assist users at Southwest Routing in distinguishing between different AppleTalk services, you can associate an AppleTalk address with a descriptive name using NBP. Each service can register an NBP object name and object type within a zone. For example, a deskjet printer could be registered as Southwest:LaserWriter@engineering, where Southwest is the object name, LaserWriter is the object type, and engineering is the zone name. Each of the object, type, and zone fields are limited to 32 characters in length. A Macintosh user at Southwest Routing should not encounter object and zone names. The Chooser takes care of looking up NBP types and mapping the results to AppleTalk addresses.

This chapter covers the following topics that you will need to master as a CCDP:

- **Determining which WAN technology to use**—This topic discusses the various options available and helps you choose the optimum technology to use.

- **Optimize core WAN availability**—This topic discusses the goals for designing the WAN core, including redundancy, partitioning, load balancing, and convergence.

- **Performance**—This topic discusses various performance-related options available in Cisco IOS in terms of design trade-offs such as compression, queuing, and Quality of Service (QoS).

- **WAN backbone design issues**—This topic discusses managing the backbone with single protocol versus multiprotocol. It also discusses tunneling features.

CHAPTER 9

WAN Design Considerations

This chapter lightly brushes over the business and technical reasons for designing an internetwork for a customer. This chapter also focuses on some of the issues facing designers today, including availability, performance, and redundancy. Technology topics mentioned in this chapter are more thoroughly discussed in other chapters.

Cisco expects design professionals to be able to provide a cost-sensitive solution that meets customers' requirements for redundancy and performance. This requires the design professional to analyze the business and technical requirements for wide-area network (WAN) designs and to provide the proper solution.

When you're designing most WAN implementations, reliability is the most important goal because the WAN is often a part of the internetwork.

The question to ask of the company is how important is it that the network be available 7/24/365?

Only from talking with your customers will you be able to make recommendations for equipment and design. WAN equipment and resources are expensive. The links that connect the sites are usually monthly recurring charges.

The CID exam tests your knowledge of how these technologies operate and interoperate.

It is expected that a design professional, given specific criteria, can make recommendations to improve performance utilizing Cisco IOS software features, such as compression, queuing, and Quality of Service (QoS).

Customers today all have concerns about their networks. Either reliability or availability is usually the most important, followed by cost. A good WAN design is typically a good balance of both.

Another concern is the amount of traffic traversing the WAN. What routing protocols are used across the WAN? Remember, typically WAN links are slow links, so you do not want to waste the available bandwidth with unnecessary routing updates. You also need to keep in mind whether you have to interface with legacy systems or standards.

The CID exam also tests your knowledge of how the WAN technologies operate and interoperate.

How to Best Use This Chapter

By following these steps, you can make better use of your study time:

- Keep your notes and the answers for all your work with this book in one place for easy reference.

- Take the "Do I Know This Already?" quiz and write down your answers. Studies show that retention is significantly increased through writing down facts and concepts, even if you never look at the information again.

- Use the diagram shown in Figure 9-1 to guide you to the next step.

Figure 9-1   *How to Use This Chapter*

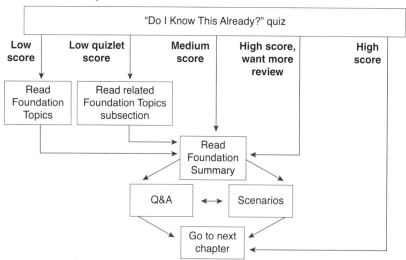

If you skip to the Foundation Summary, Q&A, and Scenarios sections and have trouble with the material there, you should go back to the Foundation Topics section.

"Do I Know This Already?" Quiz

The purpose of the "Do I Know This Already?" quiz is to help you decide which parts of this chapter to use. If you intend to read the entire chapter, you do not necessarily need to answer these questions now.

This 17-question quiz helps you choose how to spend your limited study time. The quiz is divided into four smaller "quizlets" that help you select the sections of the chapter on which to focus. Figure 9-1 outlines suggestions for how to spend your time in this chapter. Use Table 9-1 to record your score.

Table 9-1   *Score Sheet for Quiz and Quizlets*

Quizlet Number	Foundation Topics Section Covering These Questions	Questions	Score
1	Issues and concerns facing customers	1–4	
2	Optimize core WAN availability	5–8	
3	Performance	9–12	
4	WAN backbone design issues	13–17	

1 A customer needs a high-speed, cost-effective, low-latency network. Which technology should he choose?

   A Frame Relay

   B ISDN

   C Point-to-point

   D X.25

2 When designing networks for load sharing, what should you use between routers?

   A Equal hops

   B Equal latency

   C Equal bandwidth

   D Bandwidth on demand

3 Put the following in order of importance for a customer:

   A Redundancy

   B Single-protocol WAN

   C Reliability

   D Cost

   E Legacy system support

4 On what does a company base its purchasing decisions?

   A Reliability, cost, performance, redundancy

   B Cost, availability, redundancy, performance

   C Availability, scalability, performance, redundancy

   D Redundancy, availability, cost, performance

5 Which technology is used for low-volume intermittent traffic?

   A ISDN

   B Frame Relay

   C X.25

   D ATM

6 What Cisco feature enables the use of two ISDN bearer channels?

   A Bandwidth on demand

   B Dial on demand

   C Priority queuing

   D L2TP

7 What three objectives must the WAN design achieve?

_____

_____

_____

8 In a good design, what should the maximum number of hops be from endpoint to endpoint within a network?

_____

_____

_____

9 WAN designs in the core should be created with

   A An even number of routers

   B An odd number of routers

   C It doesn't matter

10 What methods can be used to optimize bandwidth utilization on the WAN?

_____

_____

_____

11 A round-robin type of queuing is called

   A Custom

   B CAR

   C CEF

   D Priority

12 What is the preferred queuing method for passing time-sensitive and delay-sensitive traffic?

_____

_____

_____

13 How many queues are available in custom queuing?

_____

_____

_____

14 What Cisco protocol encapsulates IP, CLNP, IPX, AppleTalk, DECnet Phase IV, XNS, VINES, and Apollo packets inside IP tunnels?

_____

_____

_____

15 With this switching method, the first packet that enters the router is copied to the system buffer.

_____

_____

_____

The answers to the "Do I Know This Already?" quiz are found in Appendix A. The suggested choices for your next step are as follows:

- **6 or less overall score**—Read the chapter. This includes the "Foundation Topics," "Foundation Summary," and "Q&A" sections, as well as the scenarios at the end of the chapter.

- **2 or less on any "quizlet"**—Review the subsection(s) of the "Foundation Topics" part of this chapter based on Table 9-1. Then move into the "Foundation Summary," the "Q&A" section, and the scenarios at the end of the chapter.

- **7, 8, or 9 overall score**—Begin with the "Foundation Summary" section and then go to the "Q&A" section and the scenarios at the end of the chapter.

- **10 or more overall score**—If you want more review on these topics, skip to the "Foundation Summary" section, then go to the "Q&A" section and the scenarios at the end of the chapter. Otherwise, move to the next chapter.

Foundation Topics

Understanding the issues and concerns that face the customer is a huge aspect of a successful WAN design. Although analyzing the amount of traffic crossing the WAN and dissecting the WAN's routing protocols are important, your first analysis should be an understanding of the business objectives. Customers know that if a network is cost-effective, reliable, and available, it will help them meet their bottom-line goals. For businesses that have profit as an objective, the network must help them achieve their goal of profitability. Nonprofit organizations will want the network to help them be more productive.

Here are some typical business goals a customer might want to achieve:

- Improve customer service
- Increase revenue and profit
- Reduce operating costs
- Provide new services
- Help employees and customers get the right information to make the right decisions

The customer will have internal political issues to address as they attempt to get the new design implemented and accepted within the organization. Understanding an organization's politics is important. In a perfect-world vacuum, the best technical solution would always be accepted. More often than not, the rendered real-world solution reflects a compromise between the technical, political, and organizational dynamics of the day. As an example, an organization might have policies regarding vendors, platforms, and technologies. For example, your favorite vendor and first choice, RouteitRight, might not be on the list of approved vendors. The CCDP must be prepared to address real-world constraints when rendering the original design concept. As soon as a customer's business objectives are understood, the CCDP should pursue the customer's technical objectives for a WAN design.

The WAN's design goals represent a unique challenge to the CCDP. Although the familiar LAN design themes of availability, scalability, reliability, and cost still apply, the CCDP who designs the WAN will find that they have less control over some of the WAN design variables.

Also, the CCDP will find that some variables play a more significant factor in WAN design than LAN design. As an example, latency plays a more important factor in WAN design. Because WAN bandwidth is typically slower than a LAN, a WAN and the traffic that travels on it are more sensitive to issues of latency. Cost plays a larger factor in WAN design than LAN design. The recurring monthly costs of the WAN do not exist in LAN design.

Reliability is the most important goal of WAN design because the WAN, as a part of the network backbone, impacts so many people. To add to the drama, much of the WAN's reliability and availability lie beyond the control of the CCDP and within the control of the vendor. Vendors in different geographical areas provide different capabilities. Issues that impact the last mile will vary from location to location. Nevertheless, certain areas of the WAN core can be controlled. This chapter discusses the tools and methods available to the CCDP to optimize the WAN for maximum reliability and availability.

The following sections discuss technologies available to the CCDP.

Determining Which WAN Technology to Use

Customers often ask which technology is best for their company. That's a difficult question to answer until the customer's technical requirements are analyzed. Table 9-2 lists some of the available WAN technologies, along with their advantages and disadvantages.

NOTE   X.25, Frame Relay, and ISDN technologies are covered in greater detail in later chapters.

Table 9-2   *Technology Advantages and Disadvantages*

Technology	Disadvantage	Advantage	Cost
Frame Relay (packet-switched)	Shared in cloud Nonsecure	Cost-effective mesh High speed, low latency Toll bypass	Inexpensive
X.25 (packet-switched)	Difficult to configure	Reliable WAN circuit	Expensive
ISDN (circuit-switched)	Nonstandard configurations	Flexible backup technology Support for voice, video, and data	Expensive in most areas
Leased lines	Not flexible	Low-cost connectivity in nonmesh Not shared	
ATM (packet-switched)	Difficult to configure	Speed, toll bypass	Expensive
DSL (leased line)	Not everywhere; limited availability	Speed	

The following list gives a few more details:

- Frame Relay

    — **Advantages**—Frame Relay is available just about everywhere. It has high speed and low latency. Recently, the introduction of voice over frame has become popular.

    — **Disadvantages**—It's "shared" in the Frame Relay network. Security could be an issue, depending on the provider. It has no error-checking capability.

    — **Cost**—It's relatively cheap.

- **X.25**

    — **Advantages**—It has guaranteed delivery and error-checking capability.

    — **Disadvantages**—It works at slow speeds and is difficult to configure.

    — **Cost**—It's expensive.

- **ISDN**

    — **Advantages**—It has a fast circuit setup time. It has great backup circuit technology. It supports voice, video, and data.

    — **Disadvantages**—It is difficult to configure and is distance-sensitive.

    — **Cost**—It's expensive in most areas.

- **Leased lines**

    — **Advantages**—They are secure. They support HDLC encapsulation. They are not shared.

    — **Disadvantages**—Point-to-point circuits are not flexible.

    — **Cost**—They are medium in cost compared to other alternatives.

- **ATM**

    — **Advantages**—It supports high speeds. It supports voice, video, and data. It has an inherent Quality of Service.

    — **Disadvantages**—It's difficult to configure.

    — **Cost**—It's expensive.

- **DSL**

    — **Advantages**—It's fast. You can use existing phone lines for connectivity.

    — **Disadvantages**—It isn't available everywhere. It is distance-sensitive.

    — **Cost**—It has the lowest cost.

Many WAN options are available. *Frame Relay* is probably the most popular. It is considered a packet-switched technology. The advantage of Frame Relay is the ability to connect multiple sites to a central site with only one physical serial interface on the central site router by using *subinterfaces*. Subinterfaces provide a flexible solution for routing various protocols over Frame Relay networks, as shown in Figure 9-2. A single physical interface can be logically divided into multiple virtual subinterfaces. The subinterface may be defined as either a point-to-point connection or a multipoint connection.

The *X.25* protocol suite maps to the lowest three layers of the OSI reference model, as shown in Figure 9-3. X.25 was designed for use in nonreliable physical layers. It implements reliability at Layer 2 with Link Access Procedure Balanced protocol. Today, with advancements being made in software applications and telephone line connectivity, the upper layers can guarantee delivery of packets using Frame Relay.

Figure 9-2   *Frame Relay*

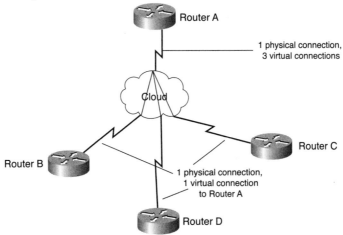

Figure 9-3   *X-25*

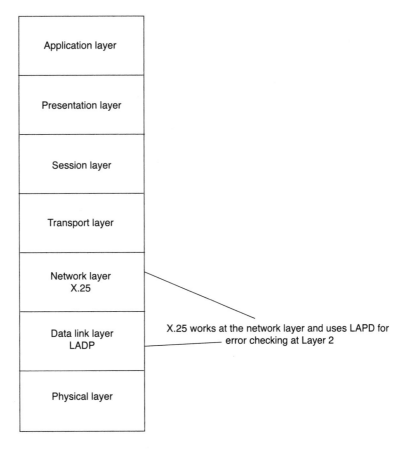

ISDN

ISDN was developed in the 1960s to provide a digital service for voice, video, and data. A circuit-switched technology, it is a great backup technology due to its ability to connect to multiple locations by using the Public Switched Telephone Network (PSTN). Select ISDN if you need a flexible backup solution or if you have a need for low-volume intermittent traffic (e-mail).

Leased lines are usually called point-to-point links. Leased lines eliminate the issues that arise with a shared connection, but they are costly.

ATM is a packet-switched technology that operates at very fast speeds. It is also very expensive, depending on which QoS is purchased. ATM has emerged as one of the technologies for integrating LANs and WANs. ATM has inherent QoS and can support any traffic type in separate or mixed streams, delay-sensitive traffic, and nondelay-sensitive traffic.

DSL, with its limited availability, could be considered a leased-line technology. Enterprises are increasingly turning to affordable DSL to expand the use of telecommuting, provide Internet-based services, and reduce spending.

WAN Availability

How often the network can be used defines its availability. Around-the-clock availability is sometimes described as 24/7/365, which suggests that the network is up 24 hours a day, 7 days a week, 365 days a year. The customer should be asked to specify availability requirements. These requirements will help you determine how much downtime is acceptable. An uptime of 99.999% is considered high availability. The design of connectivity in the core is crucial. The WAN core is often the most expensive and critical resource because it supports connectivity for the whole organization. Goals for designing the core should focus on the following:

- Maximization of throughput over WAN circuits

- Minimization of delay over WAN circuits

- Minimization of overhead traffic over WAN circuits

The following is a list of items that should be checked to ensure that the WAN circuits are optimized:

- Implement client/server applications that are not network-intensive.

- Tune protocol windows, and use larger packet sizes for maximum transport.

- Use bandwidth on demand to efficiently utilize links.

- Use filtering to block unnecessary traffic from the WAN.

- Use compression wherever possible to maximize efficiency.

- Use routing protocols such as EIGRP that update only when changes occur.

WAN Reliability

If the network has been determined to be available, it must also be reliable. Reliability is the most important goal of the WAN design. Reliability relates to accuracy, low error rates, and network stability. In addition, reliability describes the amount of time between failures and how quickly the network can recover from an outage. A WAN can be designed with additional links and equipment to maximize redundancy. In a perfect-world design vacuum, that would be the ultimate answer. In the real world, where high WAN costs are usually a constraint, the needs for redundancy must be weighed against the desire to have a cost-effective network that delivers a high return on investment.

A full mesh is an example of a network in which every router has a connection to all the other routers in the network (see Figure 9-4).

Figure 9-4   *Full Mesh*

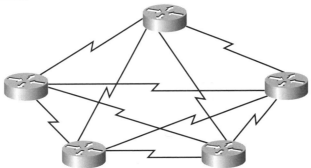

It is often too expensive to design a full-mesh WAN core. Because it can be prohibitively expensive to implement, a full mesh is usually reserved for network backbones. As a cost-effective compromise, companies elect to use a *hub-and-spoke design*. A hub and spoke can provide connectivity. However, there is usually a single point of failure (the hub site) that might result in connectivity loss between the sites. An example of a hub and spoke is shown in Figure 9-5.

Figure 9-5 *Hub and Spoke*

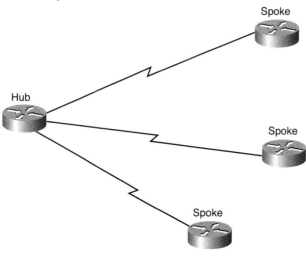

TIP   A full-mesh network eliminates the need for an extra router hop in case of network failure.

Convergence

When a topology change occurs, the time it takes for all routers to agree on network reachability is called *convergence*. Convergence time is a function of diameter and complexity. Routing information must propagate from one edge of the internetwork to the other. Convergence time in a 15-hop network can be quite long. As a rule of thumb, it is a good practice to design the internetwork so that there are no more than six hops from one end to the other. This way, the network's diameter can be consistent and small. If at all possible, use an even number of routers in your network for faster convergence and load balancing. Both link-state and distance-vector routing protocols converge faster over multiple equal-cost paths. Figure 9-6 shows that with an odd number of routers, the costs do not add up evenly, no matter which path is taken, due to the pentagon type of configuration. From Router A to Router E, the costs vary between 128 and 192 units.

RIP is a distance-vector routing protocol that makes routing decisions based on hop count. Convergence can take a lot of time because of the update intervals of 30 seconds upon which the full routing tables are broadcast. EIGRP combines the advantages of link-state-based routing protocols and distance-vector routing protocols and provides much faster convergence times in case of rerouting. EIGRP uses hellos between the adjacent routers and does not propagate the full routing tables on regular intervals (as do RIP and IGRP). Only the link-state changes are propagated.

Figure 9-6   *Convergence*

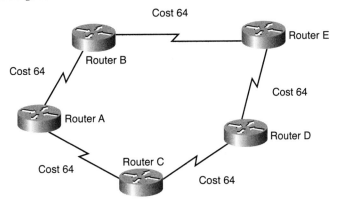

Load Balancing

Whether you load-balance on a packet-by-packet basis or on a destination basis depends on the switching mode used. *Process-switching* causes load balancing on a packet-by-packet basis, but there is more overhead on the CPU. *Fast switching* causes IP load balancing to be done on a per-destination or per-session basis. See Figure 9-7.

By default, most IP routing protocols use up to four equal-cost paths to do load balancing. Effectively balancing the load depends on which switching method you use.

Figure 9-7   *Load Balancing*

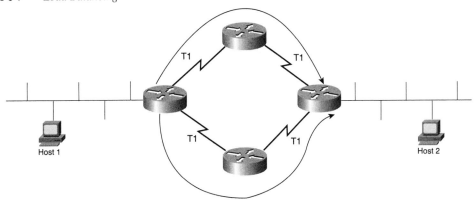

| **TIP** | Use equal-bandwidth links within each layer of the hierarchy for better load balancing. |

Design professional candidates need to know how and when to load-share across a WAN, whether there are equal-cost paths or unequal-cost paths. Load sharing works when there is more than one path to the destination, and it is used for routing packets, as shown in Figure 9-7. Packets from Host 1 to Host 2 load-balance with dynamic routing protocols. Dynamic routing protocols place routes in the routing table. EIGRP and IGRP can place unequal paths in routing tables. Other routing protocols (RIP, OSPF) can place only equal paths (same-cost or metric) in routing tables.

When using IPX, you need special commands such as **ipx maximum paths 2** for load balancing. If caching is turned on, per-link load sharing is provided. If it is turned off (no IP fast cache), per-packet load sharing is provided. An example of this is provided in the "Scenarios" section at the end of this chapter.

Which method of load balancing should you use?

As is often the case, it depends on the situation. The definition of equal-cost paths depends on the routing protocol. Keep the following in mind when designing for load balancing:

- OSPF exchanges link-state advertisements every 30 minutes, unless there is a topology change.

- EIGRP does not refresh the routing table unless there is a topology change.

- Both RIP and IGRP exchange routing updates regularly (RIP every 30 seconds and IGRP every 90 seconds).

If you use OSPF, EIGRP, and IGRP, loading sharing is enabled by default. If fast switching is enabled, the router will load-balance per session. If process-switching is used, the router will load-balance per packet.

The following are the keys to a good network design:

- Minimize the number of hops (try to keep it to six or less from endpoint to endpoint), as shown in Figure 9-8. Figure 9-8 shows a large network with 6000 routers that encompasses all 50 states in an all-OSPF network. All 50 states have a connection from their state capitol to the ATM backbone. The ATM backbone consists of three ATM switches fully meshed. Each state has an ATM router with the ATM interface in Area 0. The Ethernet interface is in the area number designated for each state. For example, Maryland OSPF Area 1 encompasses the state of Maryland. From the state capitol, spoke sites fan out throughout the state. From any spoke site, it would be at most six hops through the network to the Internet or any other spoke site.

- From endpoint to endpoint, there are no more than six hops.

- Sites that generate a lot of traffic should be directly connected. Use protocol-dependent metrics (variance and so on) to define equal-cost paths.

Figure 9-8   *Large OSPF Network*

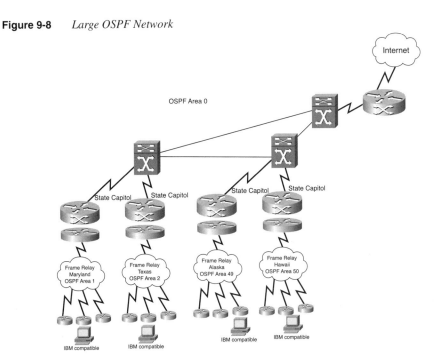

Quality of Service (QoS) Networking

QoS refers to the capability of a network to provide better service to selected network traffic. Some of the goals of QoS include dedicated bandwidth, controlled latency, and improved loss characteristics. Cisco IOS QoS technologies provide the capability to service a variety of networked applications and traffic types. Here are some of the benefits provided by the Cisco IOS QoS software:

- **Control over resources**—Bandwidth consumed over a backbone link by FTP transfers can be limited.

- **More efficient use of network resources**—By using Cisco's network analysis management and accounting tools (NetFlow), you will know what your network is being used for and that you are servicing the most important traffic to your business.

- **Tailored services**—Control and visibility allow service providers to offer carefully tailored grades of service differentiation to their customers.

- **Coexistence of mission-critical applications**—Cisco's QoS technologies make certain that the WAN is used efficiently by mission-critical applications.

To help you understand the role that bandwidth plays, let's take a look at the function of hot water in the shower:

In an apartment building, all the tenants share much of the same plumbing infrastructure. When all the tenants request hot water at the same time, the demand for hot water often outweighs the available supply. With only so much hot water available, someone has to take a cold shower or wait until hot water becomes available. The same is true of bandwidth.

When all the users request bandwidth at the same time, the demand for bandwidth often outweighs the available supply. With only so much bandwidth available, someone has to wait until bandwidth becomes available. Because network applications are continuing to grow and consume more bandwidth, Cisco has developed tools to ensure that bandwidth is conserved and that mission-critical data reaches its destination on time. Cisco's QoS tools allow complex networks to control when an application's data will arrive. Every network that carries mission-critical traffic needs QoS for optimum efficiency. QoS speeds the process of handling mission-critical applications while sharing network resources with noncritical applications. QoS also ensures available bandwidth and minimum delays required by time-sensitive multimedia and voice applications.

Priority Queuing and Custom Queuing

Many enterprises run Cisco networks with a mixture of SNA and client/server protocols. Networks in the near future will be designed to run voice, video, and data. Networks have traditionally operated on a best-effort delivery principle, which means that all traffic has equal priority and an equal chance of being delivered in a timely manner until congestion occurs. As a result, when congestion occurs, all traffic has an equal chance of being dropped. A key challenge when designing internetworks is to preserve the predictable response of sensitive traffic while ensuring that the network maintains its throughput requirements, even during periods of congestion.

If you think traffic volume or bandwidth limitations could cause performance degradations in the design of your network, this section is a must-read. Although attaching higher-speed lines to ensure enough bandwidth is a solution and an obvious remedy, it is not always cost-effective. A cost-effective design solution would implement queuing. Please keep in mind that the queuing techniques described in this chapter do not take effect unless there is congestion in the network.

Priority Queuing

Priority queuing gives strict priority to important traffic and guarantees that important traffic gets the fastest handling at each point where it is used. Priority queuing prioritizes according to protocol, incoming interface, packet size, and source/destination address. Each packet is placed in one of four queues based on an assigned priority: high, medium, normal, or low. High-priority traffic is always preferred over the other queues. When carrying time-sensitive traffic such as voice or mission-critical traffic such as SNA, priority queuing is preferred. If your design uses voice traffic, a priority queue would guarantee preferential treatment. When congestion occurs on the WAN, priority queuing guarantees that voice traffic will be sent first and foremost. When the voice queue empties, traffic on the next-highest-priority queue is transmitted.

Based on the assigned priority, packets can be classified and placed into one of the four output queues. Packets that are not classified by priority are considered normal.

Design Trade-Offs

If the queue for voice traffic is always full, other data packets in any other queues will be delayed or dropped. When priority queuing is used on a busy network, lower-priority traffic can be denied bandwidth in favor of higher-priority traffic. Priority queuing could result in lower-priority traffic never being sent. This is all because priority queuing introduces extra overhead. The system takes longer to switch packets because the processor card classifies the packets.

Configuring priority queuing is a manual process. It increases administrative overhead in a dynamic network, because priority queuing does not adapt to changing network conditions.

TIP

To avoid losing lower-priority traffic, use traffic shaping or committed access rate (CAR) to rate-limit the higher-priority traffic.

CAR is available only on selected hardware platforms—primarily the 7000 series.

Routers-a-GoGo: An Example of Priority Queuing

We are at the world-famous Routers-a-GoGo club. What a crowd! It's SNA Night, and the packets have really come out. My, would you just look at the crowd of packets lined up to get in! We've got voice, video, data. We've got big packets, small packets. They all want to get in to Routers-a-GoGo.

Dayta Link and the Fabulous Frames are playing tonight. They're doing a special salute to SNA, so we promised the SNA packets that they would be able to get in no matter what. Whenever a packet comes to the interface booth and shows the SNA header, it can get in first with no waiting. As long as there is a line at the door, the other packets must wait because tonight is SNA night. As soon as all the SNA packets are seated, the other packets will be seated. If any SNA packet shows up, it gets the preferential red-carpet treatment.

Example of Priority Queuing

Packets can be classified by the following: protocol or subprotocol type, interface, packet size, fragments, or access list. The following example assigns 1 as the arbitrary priority list number, specifies IP as the protocol type, and assigns a high-priority level to the IP packets transmitted on this interface:

```
priority-list 1 protocol ip high
```

The following example assigns a medium-priority level to every AppleTalk packet that has a size greater than 200 bytes:

```
priority-list 2 protocol apple medium gt 200
```

The following example assigns a high-priority level to traffic that matches IP access list 20:

```
priority-list 1 protocol ip high list 20
```

The following example assigns a low-priority level to Telnet packets:

```
priority-list 4 protocol ip low tcp 23
```

Figure 9-9 illustrates priority queuing. When a packet is to be sent out an interface, the priority queues on that interface are scanned for packets in descending order of priority. The high-priority queue is scanned first, then the medium-priority queue, and so on. The packet at the head of the highest queue is chosen for transmission. This procedure is repeated every time a packet is to be sent. The maximum length of a queue is defined by the length limit. When a queue is longer than the queue limit, all additional packets are dropped.

Custom Queuing

Custom queuing allows for a fairer approach to queuing. With custom queuing, every traffic or packet type has a chance of receiving at least a minimum level of service. Each queue is serviced in sequence. A percent of traffic in each queue is passed before the next queue is processed. Custom queuing guarantees that mission-critical data is always assigned a certain percentage of the bandwidth, but it also ensures predictable throughput for other traffic. The amount of bandwidth can be configured and reserved for each traffic type.

Custom queuing prioritizes multiprotocol traffic and allows for a maximum of 16 queues to be built. Each queue is serviced sequentially until the number of bytes sent exceeds the configurable byte count or the queue is empty. Custom queuing is designed for environments that want to ensure at least a bare minimum of service for all protocols. It allows protocols of different characteristics to share the media.

Figure 9-9   *Priority Queuing*

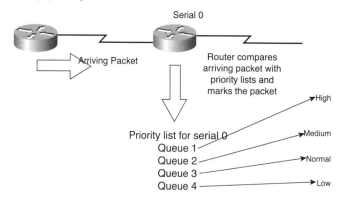

Example of Custom Queuing

As an example, a custom queuing design could reserve one-third of the bandwidth for IPX, one-third for IP, and one-third for other traffic. It does so because the default byte counts, the threshold at which the router will skip to the next queue, are 1500 per queue.

If there are no packets to be serviced in the other queues, one queue can get 100% of the bandwidth.

```
queue-list 1 protocol ipx 1 byte-count 500
queue-list 1 protocol ip 2 byte-count 500
queue-list 1 default 3 byte-count 500
int s 3/0
```

Figure 9-10 illustrates custom queuing. Custom queuing handles traffic by specifying the number of packets or bytes to be serviced for each class of traffic. It services the queues by cycling through them in round-robin fashion, sending the portion of allocated bandwidth for each queue before moving to the next queue. If one queue is empty, the router sends packets from the next queue that has packets ready to send.

TIP   Delay-sensitive traffic (voice and SNA traffic) should not be used for custom queuing.

Figure 9-10 *Custom Queuing*

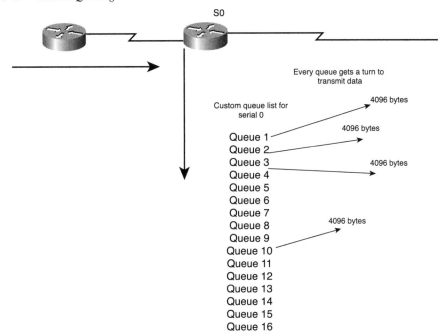

Process-switching

Process-switching is the simplest form of switching. Process-switching is defined by two essential concepts:

- The forwarding decision and information used to rewrite the MAC header on the packet are taken from a table.

- The packet is switched using the processor and a normal process running within the IOS.

With process-switching, the first packet that enters the router is copied to the system buffer. The packet is compared to a destination network address entry in the routing table located in main memory. The frame is then rewritten with the destination address and sent to the exit interface.

Fast Switching

The first packet of every session or connection is always process-switched. Fast switching stores the forwarding information in cache. This allows the entries in the route caches to be created. Subsequent packets are compared against the cached information. Fast switching enables higher throughput by switching a packet using a cache created by previous packets.

TIP

Disable fast switching when debugging and packet-level tracing. Packets that do not pass through the route processor cannot be captured. Disable fast switching when sending data to interfaces lower than T1. Congestion can occur when fast-switched packets are sent from a high-speed interface to a low-speed interface.

WAN Compression Techniques

Of all the features that the Cisco IOS software offers to maximize throughput and minimize WAN bandwidth bottlenecks, the most effective is compression.

Compression decreases the size of a frame while reducing the time the data takes to travel across the network. Compression works by identifying a redundant pattern in a data stream and providing a coding scheme at each end of a transmission link. These coding schemes allow characters to be removed from the frames of data at the sending side of the link and then be replaced correctly at the receiving side. Because the frames take up less bandwidth, more data can be transmitted.

Three types of compressions are a part of the Cisco IOS:

- Header
- Link
- Payload

The Cisco IOS header compression strategy subscribes to the Van Jacobson Algorithm defined in RFC 1144. It is highly effective on TCP/IP traffic, which consists of small packets with a few bytes of data, such as Telnet. TCP/IP header compression removes some of the redundant fields in the header of a TCP/IP connection. By keeping a copy of the original header on either side of the link, removing the redundant fields, and coding the remaining fields, the header can be compressed from 40 bytes to 5.

Compression Design Issues

Compression is effective in improving WAN transmission only when an application can accept the characteristics of compression being applied to it. When considering whether to use compression, keep these network characteristics in mind:

- Number of remote sites
- Increase in latency
- Router memory requirements
- Router CPU utilization

Each point-to-point connection must have dedicated memory to support the compression overhead. The greater the number of remote sites, the greater the requirement for memory. Each additional line increases CPU utilization, and the additional burden can increase latency. When compression is applied on the original data stream, the information must be processed and analyzed. As a result, latency is added to the input data before transmission. An increase in latency could affect transmission when protocols sensitive to added network latency are used over the WAN.

The amount of memory that the router must have and that the network manager must plan on varies according to the protocol being compressed, the compression algorithm, and the number of concurrent circuits on the router.

Cisco devices use the STAC (LZS) and Predictor data compression algorithms. The Cisco IOS software uses an optimized version of STAC that provides good compression ratios but is processor-intensive. The Predictor data compression algorithm was obtained from the public domain and optimized by Cisco engineers. When compared with STAC, it makes more efficient use of CPU cycles but requires more memory. The network manager must plan on additional memory for routers in a network utilizing data compression, regardless of the type of operation used.

TIP   The most recent releases in the Cisco IOS are recommended to ensure the best compression efficiency. Run the same version of IOS code on both sides of the WAN link to ensure compatibility.

Single-Protocol IP Backbone

For the sake of example, the administrators at RouteItFast know only IP, so they support only IP on their backbone. Branch site administrators have AppleTalk and IPX running at the edge of their WAN. The solution for RouteItFast would be to tunnel IP through the branch locations that specialize in AppleTalk and Novell IPX. For RouteItFast, staying with one protocol will make management of the WAN backbone less complicated. Their administrators don't have to learn the features, characteristics, and operating requirements of IPX or AppleTalk.

Cisco's *generic routing encapsulation (GRE)* multiprotocol carrier protocol encapsulates IP, CLNP, IPX, AppleTalk, DECnet Phase IV, XNS, VINES, and Apollo packets inside IP tunnels. By connecting multiprotocol subnetworks in a single-protocol backbone environment, IP tunneling allows expansion across an IP backbone environment.

NOTE	Custom and priority queuing are not supported on tunnels.

TIP	Because tunneling requires handling of the packets, it is faster to route protocols natively than to use tunnels. Tunneled traffic is switched at about half the normal process-switching rates. Routing updates, SAP updates, and other administrative traffic may be sent over each tunnel interface. It is easy to saturate a physical link with routing information if several tunnels are configured over it. Performance depends on the passenger protocol, broadcasts, routing updates, and bandwidth of the physical interfaces. It is also difficult to debug the physical link if problems occur.

Multiprotocol Backbone

If IP traffic does not constitute the overwhelming majority of traffic, it is wise to use multiple protocols. If problems occur with tunneling, a multiprotocol backbone should be used.

TIP	It takes more administrative know-how to configure multiple protocols. Different branches of an organization often control certain sections of the WAN. Each section must agree on a universal naming and addressing convention for each protocol.

When to Tunnel IP in IP

It is possible to tunnel IP inside IP. You might want to do this if you have legitimate IP addresses in the backbone, but not at the remote sites, or possibly if the same does not administer the remote sites group that manages the backbone.

Tunneling can put a lot of CPU overhead on the router, and that's not usually a good idea. Suppose five sites are connected, as shown in Figure 9-11. Router A is in San Diego and currently is running EIGRP on its LAN and WAN interfaces. Router B is located in San Jose and is running EIGRP and OSPF on Serial Interface 1. Router C is running only OSPF. Router D is running OSPF and EIGRP. Router E is running only EIGRP. The administrators have said that they need the EIGRP updates to travel from Router A to Router E, but the EIGRP routes cannot be seen in Router C. The administrators do not want the router to be overloaded by running two different routing processes on Router C. The overload can be avoided by using a tunnel—specifically, by using the command `tunnel mode ipip`—and configuring EIGRP in the tunnel.

The EIGRP updates will traverse through the tunnel, and neighbor adjacencies will form through the tunnel.

Figure 9-11   *IP-in-IP Tunneling*

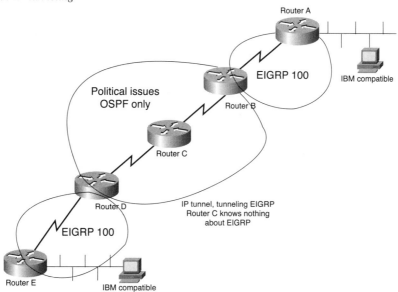

Foundation Summary

This section contains tables that provide a convenient review of many key concepts in this chapter. If you are already comfortable with the topics in this chapter, this summary could help you recall a few details. If you have just read this chapter, this review should help solidify some key facts. If you are doing your final preparation before the exam, these tables are a convenient way to review the day before the exam. Table 9-3 compares LAN and WAN characteristics.

Table 9-3 *Comparison of LAN and WAN Characteristics*

LAN	WAN
Fast interfaces	Slow interfaces
VLANs	No VLANs
Usually no tunneling	Tunneling is used
Not much compression used	Compression sometimes used
Usually not a lot of load balancing	Load balancing typically used
Cheaper interfaces	Expensive interfaces
Traffic usually not as sensitive to latency	Traffic is sensitive to latency

Quality of Service Commands

This section describes the function and displays the syntax of QoS commands. For more information about defaults and usage guidelines, see the corresponding chapter of the *Quality of Service Solutions Command Reference*.

priority-group

To assign the specified priority list to an interface, use the **priority-group** interface configuration command. To remove the specified priority group assignment, use the no form of this command.

```
priority-group list-number
no priority-group
```

list-number   Priority list number assigned to the interface. Any number from 1 to 16.

priority-list default

To assign a priority queue for packets that do not match any other rule in the priority list, use the **priority-list default** global configuration command. To return to the default or assign **normal** as the default, use the **no** form of this command.

```
priority-list list-number default {high | medium | normal | low}
no priority-list list-number default
```

Variable	Description
list-number	Any number from 1 to 16 that identifies the priority list.
high | medium | normal | low	Priority queue level.

priority-list interface

To establish queuing priorities on packets entering from a given interface, use the priority-list interface global configuration command. To remove an entry from the list, use the **no** form of this command with the appropriate arguments.

```
priority-list list-number interface interface-type interface-number {high | medium |
    normal | low}
no priority-list list-number interface
```

Variable	Description
list-number	Arbitrary integer from 1 to 16 that identifies the priority list selected by the user.
interface-type	Name of the interface.
interface-number	Number of the interface.
high | medium | normal | low	Priority queue level.

priority-list protocol

To establish queuing priorities based on the protocol type, use the **priority-list protocol** global configuration command. To remove a priority list entry assigned by protocol type, use the **no** form of the command, followed by the appropriate *list-number* argument and the **protocol** keyword.

```
priority-list list-number protocol protocol-name {high | medium | normal | low} queue-
    keyword keyword-value
no priority-list list-number protocol [protocol-name {high | medium | normal | low} queue-
    keyword keyword-value]
```

Variable	Description
list-number	Any number from 1 to 16 that identifies the priority list selected by the user.
protocol-name	Protocol type: **aarp, apollo, appletalk, arp, bridge** (transparent), **clns, clns_es, clns_is, compressedtcp, cmns, decnet, decnet_node, decnet_router-l1, decnet_router-l2, dlsw, ip, ipx, pad, rsrb, stun, vines, xns,** or **x25.**
high | medium | normal | low	Priority queue level.
queue-keyword keyword-value	Possible keywords are fragments, gt, list, lt, tcp, and udp.

priority-list queue-limit

To specify the maximum number of packets that can wait in each of the priority queues, use the **priority-list queue-limit** global configuration command. To select the normal queue, use the **no** form of this command.

```
priority-list list-number queue-limit [high-limit [medium-limit [normal-limit [low-
    limit]]]]

no priority-list list-number queue-limit
```

Variable	Description
list-number	Any number from 1 to 16 that identifies the priority list.
high-limit medium-limit normal-limit low-limit	(Optional) Priority queue maximum length. A value of 0 for any of the four arguments means that the queue can be of unlimited size for that particular queue.

queue-list default

To assign a priority queue for packets that do not match any other rule in the queue list, use the `queue-list default` global configuration command. To restore the default value, use the `no` form of this command.

```
queue-list list-number default queue-number

no queue-list list-number default queue-number
```

Variable	Description
list-number	Number of the queue list. Any number from 1 to 16.
queue-number	Number of the queue. Any number from 1 to 16.

queue-list interface

To establish queuing priorities on packets entering on an interface, use the **queue-list interface** global configuration command. To remove an entry from the list, use the **no** form of this command.

```
queue-list list-number interface interface-type interface-number queue-number

no queue-list list-number interface interface-type interface-number queue-number
```

Variable	Description
list-number	Any number from 1 to 16 that identifies the queue list.
interface-type	Name of the interface.
interface-number	Number of the interface.
queue-number	Any number from 1 to 16 that identifies the queue.

queue-list protocol

To establish queuing priority based on the protocol type, use the **queue-list protocol** global configuration command. To remove an entry from the list, use the no form of this command with the appropriate list number.

```
queue-list list-number protocol protocol-name queue-number queue-keyword keyword-value
no queue-list list-number protocol protocol-name queue-number queue-keyword keyword-
    value
```

Variable	Description
list-number	Number of the queue list. Any number from 1 to 16.
protocol-name	Required argument that specifies the protocol type: **aarp, apollo, appletalk, arp, bridge** (transparent), **clns, clns_es, clns_is, cmns, compressedtcp, decnet, decnet_node, decnet_routerl1, decnet_routerl2, dlsw, ip, ipx, pad, rsrb, stun, vines, xns,** or **x25.**
queue-number	Number of the queue. Any number from 1 to 16.
queue-keyword keyword-value	Possible keywords are **gt, list, lt, tcp,** and **udp.**

queue-list queue byte-count

To specify how many bytes the system allows to be delivered from a given queue during a particular cycle, use the **queue-list queue byte-count** global configuration command. To return the byte count to the default value, use the no form of this command.

```
queue-list list-number queue queue-number byte-count byte-count-number
no queue-list list-number queue queue-number byte-count byte-count-number
```

Variable	Description
list-number	Any number from 1 to 16 that identifies the queue list.
queue-number	Any number from 1 to 16 that identifies the queue.
byte-count-number	The lower boundary of how many bytes the system allows to be delivered from a given queue during a particular cycle.

queue-list queue limit

To designate the queue length limit for a queue, use the **queue-list queue limit** global configuration command. To return the queue length to the default value, use the no form of this command.

```
queue-list list-number queue queue-number limit limit-number
no queue-list list-number queue queue-number limit limit-number
```

Variable	Description
list-number	Any number from 1 to 16 that identifies the queue list.
queue-number	Any number from 1 to 16 that identifies the queue.

`limit-`*number*	Maximum number of packets that can be enqueued at any time. The range is from 0 to 32,767 queue entries. A value of 0 means that the queue can be of unlimited size.

show queue

To list fair queuing configuration and statistics for a particular interface, use the **show queue** privileged EXEC command.

`show queue` *interface-type interface-number*

Variable	Description
interface-type	The name of the interface.
interface-number	The number of the interface.

show queuing

To list all or selected configured queuing strategies, use the **show queuing** privileged EXEC command.

`show queuing` [custom | fair | priority | red]

Variable	Description
custom	(Optional) Status of the custom queuing list configuration.
fair	(Optional) Status of the fair queuing configuration.
priority	(Optional) Status of the priority queuing list configuration.
red	(Optional) Status of the Weighted Random Early Detection (WRED) configuration.

Q&A

As mentioned in Chapter 1, the questions and scenarios in this book are more difficult than what you will experience on the actual exam. The questions do not attempt to cover more breadth or depth than the exam; however, they are designed to make sure that you know the answer. Rather than allowing you to derive the answer from clues hidden inside the question, the questions challenge your understanding and recall of the subject. Questions from the "Do I Know This Already?" quiz from the beginning of the chapter are repeated here to ensure that you have mastered this chapter's topic areas. Hopefully, these questions will help limit the number of exam questions on which you narrow your choices to two options and then guess. Be sure to use the CD and take the simulated exams.

The answers to these questions can be found in Appendix A.

1 A customer needs a high-speed, cost-effective, low-latency network. Which technology should he choose?

   A Frame Relay

   B ISDN

   C Point-to-point

   D X.25

2 When designing networks for load sharing, what should you use between routers?

   A Equal hops

   B Equal latency

   C Equal bandwidth

   D Bandwidth on demand

3 Put the following in order of importance for a customer:

   A Redundancy

   B Single-protocol WAN

   C Reliability

   D Cost

   E Legacy system support

4 On what does a company base its purchasing decisions?

   A Reliability, cost, performance, redundancy

   B Cost, availability, redundancy, performance

   C Availability, scalability, performance, redundancy

   D Redundancy, availability, cost, performance

5 Which technology is used for low-volume intermittent traffic?

   A ISDN

   B Frame Relay

   C X.25

   D ATM

6 What Cisco feature enables the use of two ISDN bearer channels?

   A Bandwidth on demand

   B Dial on demand

   C Priority queuing

   D L2TP

7 What three objectives must the WAN design achieve?

_____

_____

_____

8 In a good design, what should the maximum number of hops be from endpoint to endpoint within a network?

_____

_____

_____

9 WAN designs in the core should be created with

   A An even number of routers

   B An odd number of routers

   C It doesn't matter

10 What methods can be used to optimize bandwidth utilization on the WAN?

_____

_____

_____

11 A round-robin type of queuing is called:

   A Custom

   B CAR

   C CEF

   D Priority

12 What is the preferred queuing method for passing time-sensitive and delay-sensitive traffic?

_____

_____

_____

13 How many queues are available in custom queuing?

_____

_____

_____

14 What Cisco protocol encapsulates IP, CLNP, IPX, AppleTalk, DECnet Phase IV, XNS, VINES, and Apollo packets inside IP tunnels?

_____

_____

_____

15 With this switching method, the first packet that enters the router is copied to the system buffer.

_____

_____

_____

16 Are custom and priority queuing supported on tunnels?

_____

_____

_____

17 List some benefits of Cisco's QoS.

_____

_____

_____

18 What is the most basic form of queuing?

_____

_____

_____

19 What is a method of controlling bandwidth into or out of an interface?

_____

_____

_____

20 Which technology supports both voice and video?

_____

_____

_____

21 Priority queuing is used for _____ WAN links.

_____

_____

_____

22 What type of compression is used for Telnet, LAT, and Xremote?

_____

_____

_____

23 What type of compression is used for point-to-point circuits?

_____

_____

_____

24 What type of compression is used for packet WAN?

_____

_____

_____

25 Which protocol should you use if you have to route IP, AppleTalk, and IPX in the core?

_____

_____

_____

26 Sites that generate a lot of traffic should be _____ connected.

_____

_____

_____

27 What technology was designed for use in nonreliable physical layers?

_____

_____

_____

28 What is a low-cost method of connecting two sites?

_____

_____

_____

29 Load sharing is on by default with which three routing protocols?

_____

_____

_____

30 RIP is a _____ routing protocol.

_____

_____

_____

31 _____ occurs when fast-switched packets are sent from a high-speed interface to a low-speed interface.

_____

_____

_____

Scenarios

Scenario 1

Administrator Yoko has been tasked with making Beetlenet more reliable. In its current configuration, the routers on Beetlenet are configured in a hub and spoke configuration, as shown in Figure 9-12. Router Ringo, Router George, and Router Paul must route their traffic to Router John.

Figure 9-12   *Beetlenet*

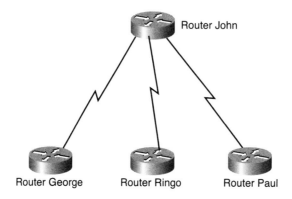

As the central hub and lead, Router John passes any data sent from one spoke router to the other spoke routers. As lead router, John likes controlling the show. John does a good job for the most part, but every now and then, after a wild night of routing, John has been known to throw up a packet or two the next morning. When that happens, Router John can become a single point of failure for the network. What are Ringo, George, and Paul to do?

1 How could you use load balancing to make Beetlenet more reliable?

2 Draw a proposed network diagram of Beetlenet with load balancing.

3 Verify that load balancing is occurring between networks.

4 What commands would you use? (Hint: Use **show** commands to verify that load balancing is occurring between networks.)

5 What routing protocols could be loaded?

Scenario 2

Router John and Router Ringo have unequal-cost paths. Router John's S0 is connected at 56 Kbps, and Router John's S1 is connected at T1.

How might load balancing be accomplished when the costs are unequal?

Answer to Scenario 1

Load balancing will make Beetlenet more efficient. Referring to Figure 9-13, if one path is unavailable, the routers on Beetlenet can take full advantage of an alternate path to a given destination. In this example, the paths are derived using EIGRP. However, the paths could have been derived statically or by using other dynamic protocols such as RIP, IGRP, and OSPF. If a router on Beetlenet receives and installs multiple paths with the same administrative distance and cost to a destination, load balancing will occur. The IGRP routing processes support unequal-cost load balancing. In this scenario, the variance command with IGRP is used to accomplish unequal-cost load balancing. Load balancing can also be configured to work per destination (fast switching) or per packet (process switching) on Beetlenet. If it's done by destination using the **ip route-cache** command on the serial interface, the router distributes the packets based on the destination address. Per-packet load balancing or process switching is configured with the no **ip route-cache** command on the serial interface. This means that Router Ringo will send one packet to Router John over the first path and the second packet for Router John over the second path.

Figure 9-13   *Scenario 1 Proposed Solution*

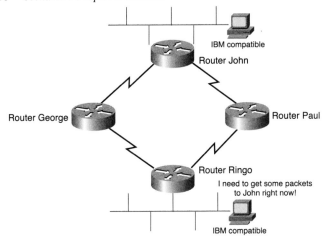

Answer to Scenario 2

IGRP can simultaneously use an asymmetric set of paths for a given destination. This feature is known as unequal-cost load balancing. Unequal-cost load balancing allows traffic to be distributed among multiple (up to four) unequal-cost paths to provide greater overall throughput and reliability. Alternative path variance (that is, the difference in desirability between the primary and alternative paths) is used to determine the feasibility of a potential route. An alternative route is feasible if the next router in the path is closer to the destination (has a lower metric value) than the current router and if the metric for the entire alternative path is within the variance. Only paths that are feasible can be used for load balancing and can be included in the routing table. These conditions limit the number of cases in which load balancing can occur but ensure that the dynamics of the network remain stable.

The following general rules apply to IGRP unequal-cost load balancing:

- IGRP accepts up to four paths for a given destination network.

- The local best metric must be greater than the metric learned from the next router. In other words, the next-hop router must be closer (have a smaller metric value) to the destination than the local best metric.

- The alternative path metric must be within the specified variance of the local best metric. The multiplier times the local best metric for the destination must be greater than or equal to the metric through the next router.

This chapter covers the following topics that you will need to master as a CCDP:

- **X.25 topologies**—This section offers a brief overview of the X.25 protocol, which is used extensively outside the United States.

- **Frame Relay**—This section discusses Frame Relay and some common terms used with it.

- **RFC 1490**—This section discusses multiprotocol over Frame Relay, Inverse ARP, and split horizon issues.

- **Frame Relay design options**—This section discusses four popular design alternatives with Frame Relay.

X.25/Frame Relay Topologies

The CCDP exam requires you to have an in-depth understanding of Frame Relay. Because X.25 actually came before Frame Relay, it is discussed in detail. X.25 is still used quite extensively in some parts of the world. If you will be working on networks outside North America, especially in Europe, the chance of your needing some X.25 knowledge is pretty good. You will eventually run into it, if you have not already. Although it will probably not be covered extensively on the test, it will probably be mentioned.

How to Best Use This Chapter

By following these steps, you can make better use of your study time:

- Keep your notes and the answers for all your work with this book in one place for easy reference.

- Take the "Do I Know This Already?" quiz and write down your answers. Studies show that retention is significantly increased through writing down facts and concepts, even if you never look at the information again.

- Use the diagram shown in Figure 10-1 to guide you to the next step.

Figure 10-1   *How to Best Use this Chapter*

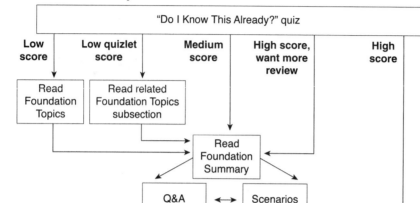

If you skip to the Foundation Summary, Q&A, and Scenarios sections and have
trouble with the material there, you should go back to the Foundation Topics section.

"Do I Know This Already?" Quiz

The purpose of the "Do I Know This Already?" quiz is to help you decide which parts of this
chapter to use. If you intend to read the entire chapter, you do not necessarily need to answer
these questions now.

This 15-question quiz helps you determine how to spend your limited study time. The quiz is
divided into four smaller "quizlets" that help you select the sections of the chapter on which to
focus. Figure 10-1 outlines suggestions on how to spend your time in this chapter. Use Table
10-1 to record your score.

Table 10-1   *Score Sheet for Quiz and Quizlets*

Quizlet Number	Foundation Topics Section Covering These Questions	Questions	Score
1	X.25 topologies	1–4	
2	Why Frame Relay?	5–8	
3	RFC 1490	9–12	
4	Design options	13–15	

1 X.25 uses what protocol at Layer 2?

2 X.25 uses what protocol at Layer 3?

3 At which layer do packet size and window size operate?

4 For what does AO/DI stand?

5 When the command **encapsulate frame relay** is applied to a serial interface, does that make the serial interface point-to-point or multipoint by default?

6 What range of DLCIs can be used on a serial interface encapsulated with Frame Relay?

7 Do most carriers charge for the local loop with dedicated lines? How about with Frame Relay?

8 If I have a measurement interval of .125 seconds, and I am guaranteed a CIR of 8K during that time period, what is my overall CIR?

_____

_____

_____

9 In a full-mesh environment, should Inverse ARP be disabled?

_____

_____

_____

10 Can split horizon be turned off for IPX RIP and AppleTalk RTMP?

_____

_____

_____

11 Does OSPF apply the split horizon rule?

_____

_____

_____

12 Name two good reasons to use subinterfaces.

_____

_____

_____

13 For what does NBMA stand?

_____

_____

_____

14 If four sites are fully meshed, how many links are needed?

_____

_____

_____

15 What two routing protocols are used for fast convergence?

_____

_____

_____

The answers to the "Do I Know This Already?" quiz are found in Appendix A. The suggested choices for your next step are as follows:

- **6 or less overall score**—Read the chapter. This includes the "Foundation Topics," "Foundation Summary," and "Q&A" sections, as well as the scenarios at the end of the chapter.

- **2 or less on any "quizlet"**—Review the subsection(s) of the "Foundation Topics" part of this chapter based on Table 10-1. Then move into the "Foundation Summary," the "Q&A" section, and the scenarios at the end of the chapter.

- **7, 8, or 9 overall score**—Begin with the "Foundation Summary" section and then go to the "Q&A" section and scenarios at the end of the chapter.

- **10 or more overall score**—If you want more review on these topics, skip to the "Foundation Summary" section, then go to the "Q&A" section and the scenarios at the end of the chapter. Otherwise, move to the next chapter.

Foundation Topics

This chapter examines scalable internetwork WANs using Nonbroadcast Multiaccess (NBMA) networks, partial mesh, and hierarchical mesh. We will discuss how to design a scalable, robust internetwork using hub and spoke technology, where and when to use subinterfaces, and so forth. The first part of this discussion concerns X.25 and how it works. The second part of the chapter focuses on why NBMA versus subinterfaces is an issue and looks at some of the most common designs using Frame Relay.

Carriers will be mentioned a lot throughout this chapter. Carriers can be like grains of sand on the beach—there are a lot of them. Each carrier might apply different rules to how it moves traffic throughout the network, and you pay for those services. We don't mention any carriers specifically, but we mention some of the differences or things to look for with carriers.

X.25

X.25 has been around for some time. It is a global protocol, available just about anywhere in the world. It was designed for use over unreliable analog circuits. X.25 is called a reliable service protocol. It has a reliable data-link layer that uses LAPB (Link Access Procedure Balanced), and it also provides reliability at the network layer, with the X.25 layer using what is called PLP (Packet-Level Protocol). Because of this, error checking is used at two different layers—Layer 2 and Layer 3—which provides for low throughput. LAPB is also flow control-oriented, which is explained in a moment.

X.25 devices are sometimes called Packet Assembler Devices (PADs). The reason for this term is that some legacy protocols send large packets of more than the 1500 bytes, such as 3000-byte packets. If these packets cross an Ethernet segment, they must be divided into smaller 1500-byte frames. As they arrive at their destination X.25 device, they must be reassembled back into a 3000-byte packet—hence the name Packet Assembler Device.

X.25 operates at Layer 3. Because it is a network layer protocol, you can route it similarly to the way IP is routed. In other words, a source and destination address are built into the packet, as shown in Figure 10-2. You also can encapsulate IP, IPX, and AppleTalk packets into an X.25 packet, a method commonly called *tunneling*. And, to make matters even more confusing, X.25 can be encapsulated into IP packets, a tunneling method referred to as XOT (X.25 over TCP/IP). This topic is discussed in this section.

Figure 10-2   *X.25 Addressing*

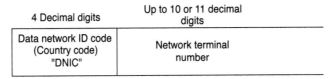

The first 4 digits denote country code and provider,
this address is refferred to as the "DNIC"

NOTE   With LAPB encapsulation, when an error occurs, the packet is retransmitted by the source. The extra error-recovery overhead in LAPB decreases performance, so you should use it only on lines that are prone to errors.

X.25 provides

- Cost-effective access

- Fairly inexpensive but low-speed transport

- International acceptance

You might end up working with companies in remote locations such as Singapore, Hong Kong, and South America. But distant locations aren't the only reason to use X.25. If you have noisy analog circuits, you should be thinking of using X.25 because of its built-in error-checking capability, which Frame Relay doesn't have. That noise factor makes X.25 an ideal candidate for satellite links. Airlines use X.25 extensively because airports exist internationally.

X.25 is most commonly configured as a transport for datagrams across an X.25 network. Layer 3 datagrams are reliably carried inside X.25 frames, as shown in Figure 10-3.

Figure 10-3 *X.25 Encapsulation*

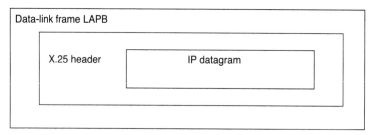

Datagram transport occurs between two hosts communicating over an X.25 network, as shown in Figure 10-4. You configure datagram transport by establishing a mapping on the encapsulating interface between IP and the X.121 address. (To avoid confusion, an X.121 address is applied with the command **x25 address**, not **x.121 address**.)

Figure 10-4 *X.25 Configuration*

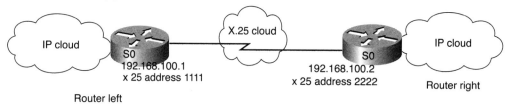

In Example 10-1, line 3 specifies a DCE interface. This indicates that the clock is being provided by this interface. One side of an X.25 connection must be a DCE, and the other side a DTE.

Example 10-1 *X25 Connection*

```
Router Left
1. interface Serial0
2.  ip address 192.168.100.1 255.255.255.0
3.  encapsulation x25 dce         ➡------"Logical" DCE
4. x25 address 1111               ➡------- This router's "x121" adress
5.  x25 map ip 192.168.100.2 2222 ➡-Mapping the remote x121 address with the
remote IP address
6. clock rate 2000000             ➡---Specifies clock rate 2000000 (The maximum
for X.25)
7. x25 route 2222 interface Serial 0 ➡---Maps the remote x25 address to the serial
port

Router Right
8. interface Serial0
9.  ip address 192.168.100.2 255.255.255.0
10.  encapsulation x25
```

Example 10-1 *X25 Connection (Continued)*

```
11.    x25 address 2222
12.    x25 map ip 192.168.100.1 1111
```

TIP   X.25 operates at Layer 3 of the OSI model, and LAPB operates at Layer 2.

Figure 10-5 shows two IP routers communicating over an X.25 link. Notice in the figure that the window size is not end-to-end but rather only between the router and the local X.25 switch. This window size negotiation happens on both sides of the cloud independently in this example. Flow control is also implemented locally, or between the router and the local X.25 switch. Flow control and window size negotiation also occur between the X.25 switches in the cloud via the X.75 protocol.

Figure 10-5   *X.25 in the WAN*

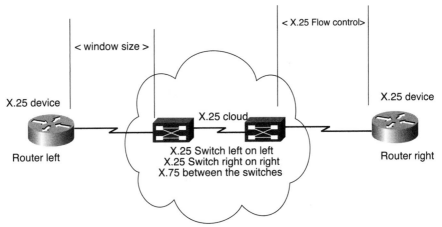

X.25 is packet-switched, so a packet goes in and gets switched between the X.25 switches across the network, as shown in Figure 10-5. Notice that the two X.25 switches communicate via the X.75 protocol. (Cisco does not support the X.75 protocol.)

Depending on your carrier, there might not be an X.25 switch in the carrier's network. The carrier might actually encapsulate the X.25 packets into IP, a technique known as XOT (X.25 over TCP/IP [RFC 1613, first available in Cisco IOS version 9.21]), as shown in Figure 10-6. In this example, X.25 packets are being encapsulated into TCP/IP by the routers. The IP network is transparent to the X.25 devices.

Figure 10-6   *Encapsulating the X.25 Packets into IP—XOT*

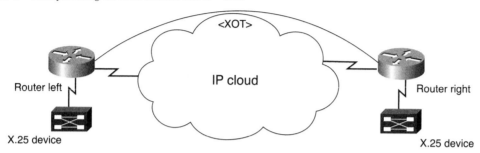

X.25 governs how your switch talks to the carrier. What the carriers do is up to them. Another possibility is using the STUN protocol to transport the X.25 traffic, which is a capability of the Cisco routers. X.25 acts like an overengineered data link. It is very robust, but you pay for the robustness with a little slowness.

TIP   When an interface is encapsulated with the **encapsulate x25** command, it becomes DTE by default. To make the interface a logical DCE (X.25 is required to make one end of a circuit a DCE), the command **encapsulate x25 dce** needs to be applied to the interface.

Also, the maximum clock rate of an X.25 port is 2000000.

The Cisco proprietary STUN protocol can encapsulate and transport X.25, Frame Relay, and other proprietary protocols. This is a very important tool for the CCDP to keep in mind when companies migrate to a total-IP backbone and still need to support their legacy protocols. Let's take a look at where STUN and XOT might work together on a large, complex network.

TIP   Each STUN tunnel occupies 32 K of memory.

Figure 10-7 shows a company using XOT over its ASN (Access Subnetwork) and STUN over its BSN (Backbone Subnetwork). STUN is a form of serial tunneling, in which data is encapsulated over a TCP tunnel. The endpoints of the STUN tunnel need to be defined. Using loopback interfaces is a good design practice for terminating tunnels because loopback interfaces will always be available.

Figure 10-7   *XOT and STUN in the Core*

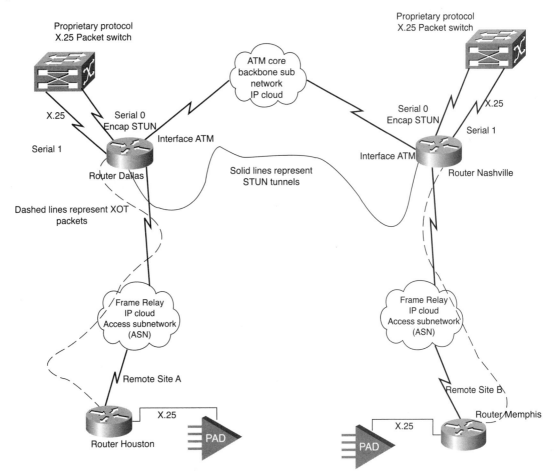

Follow the packet:

The X.25 PAD device at Remote Site A establishes an X.25 connection to the PAD at Remote Site B:

   1 The PAD makes an X.25 call setup request, and Router Houston accepts the call setup request via X.25.

   2 Router Houston establishes an XOT connection to Router Dallas at the core site, and Router Houston encapsulates the X.25 message into IP.

3 Router Dallas accepts the XOT connection, de-encapsulates the IP packets from Router Houston, and examines the X.25 source and destination addresses for the call setup request.

4 If the X.25 destination address is not local to Router Dallas, the router forwards it out S0 via X.25 to the X.25 packet switch.

5 The X.25 packet switch does an X.25 lookup and determines that the X.25 destination address is via Core Site B packet switch. The packet switches communicate via a proprietary protocol not supported by the Cisco routers.

6 The Cisco routers have created a STUN tunnel from their Serial 0 interfaces, encapsulating the proprietary protocol to let the packet switch devices communicate.

7 The Core Site B X.25 switch receives the call setup request over the STUN tunnel, does an X.25 table lookup, and determines that the address is out its X.25 connection to Router Nashville.

8 Router Nashville receives the X.25 call setup request, determines that the destination X.25 address is its XOT tunnel to Router Memphis, and encapsulates the X25 message into IP.

9 Router Memphis de-encapsulates the IP packet and sends the X.25 call setup request to the PAD, establishing the X.25 circuit from PAD to PAD.

TIP   Another difference between STUN and XOT is that when STUN tunnels are created, STUN constantly uses up CPU cycles to keep the tunnels up. With XOT, however, if the circuit to establish is an SVC, the tunnel is brought up only when needed. Hence, it requires fewer CPU cycles. If the XOT circuit is a PVC, CPU processor cycles are used again.

WARNING STUN tunnels can be very processor-intensive. STUN tunnels are process-switched, even if the router is using VIP cards that have their own processor.

NOTE   When creating tunnels, use TCP as the tunnel method if the end stations are sensitive to receiving frames in order. If the end stations are not sensitive to receiving frames in order, IP can be used as the transport method.

NOTE   It is possible to use the AUX port as an X.25 PAD on a Cisco router for testing purposes.

NOTE	Configure your AUX port so that you can dial in to your router. When you get the system prompt, type in **pad x121-address**, and you will get a PAD connection to your X.25 device.

Cisco routers can use X.25 in the following ways:

- As a transport medium (a backbone) using SNA or IP devices attached to remote Cisco routers

- With protocol translation, where X.25 is translated to TCP/IP to permit PAD users access to TCP/IP hosts

- With QLLC to give remote X.25-attached controllers access to a Token Ring-attached IBM host

NOTE	Window size and packet size belong to Layer 3 of the X.25 protocol.

WAN Data Links

From the router perspective, you typically will use either X.25 Switched Virtual Circuits (SVCs) or Permanent Virtual Circuits (PVCs) as WAN data links, as shown in Figure 10-8.

Figure 10-8   *X.25 PVC*

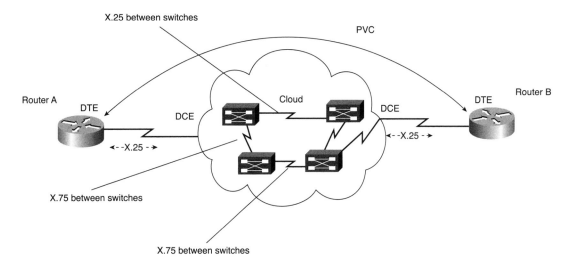

PVCs are nailed up from one endpoint to another. SVCs are brought up only when needed, similar to a person making a phone call.

The routers are the DTE end of the connection in X.25. The switch is DCE at the carrier providing the clock signal. The X.121 specification is the name of the addressing used in X.25.

In the figure, a PVC is being created from Router A to Router B. If your carrier is connected to another carrier, or from an X.25 switch to an X.25 switch, you are probably using the X.75 specification in the cloud.

Some parameters can be adjusted with X.25 to improve performance:

- **win** (windows in)—This value represents the number of packets that can be received without receiving an acknowledgment. The default is 2 bytes. Example:

  Router (config-if)#**X25 win** *packets*

  X25 win *packets*

- **wout** (windows out)—This value represents the number of packets that can be sent without sending an acknowledgment. The default is 2 bytes. Example:

  Router (config-if)#**x25 wout 5**

  X25 wout 5

- **ips**—This is the maximum input packet size. The default is 128 bytes. Example:

  Router (config-if)#**X25 ips** *bytes*

  X25 ips *bytes*

- **ops** (output packet size)—This represents the maximum output packet size. The default is 128 bytes. Example:

  Router (config-if)#**X25 ops** *bytes*

  X25 ops *bytes*

Let's take a look at another X.25 configuration example, shown in Example 10-2.

Example 10-2 *x.25 Configuration, Round Two*

```
Interface serial 0
Encapsulation x25
X25 address 123455555555555   ➡ - - - - - - - - - - - - - specifies address of interface
X25 ips 1024  ➡ - - - - - - - - - - - - - - - - - - - sets input packet size to 1024
X25 ops 1024  ➡ - - - - - - - - - - - - - - - - - - - sets output packet size to 1024
X25 win 5   ➡ - - - - - - - - - - - - - - - - - - - - - sets input window size to 7
X25 wout 5  ➡ - - - - - - - - - - - - - - - - - - - - - sets output window size to 7
```

Multiple SVCs

An issue that often comes up is what happens between the carriers in the X.25 cloud. The possibility exists that there could be multiple carriers and very low throughput, because it is hard to determine what path an X.25 circuit setup will take through the carrier's cloud.

The window size between carriers might be a low number, such as the default, which is 2. And, depending on your packet sizes, which could be as low as 128, your effective window is probably very small from end to end. Small window sizes mean low throughput, no matter what the bandwidth is. You can address this by setting up multiple switched virtual circuits between the routers.

As shown in Figure 10-9, you should use several SVCs between two destinations if you want to push more data through the X.25 cloud. (When the window closes on the first VC, you can still push data through the second VC.) This means that you'll be using more RAM.

Figure 10-9   *Multiple SVCs*

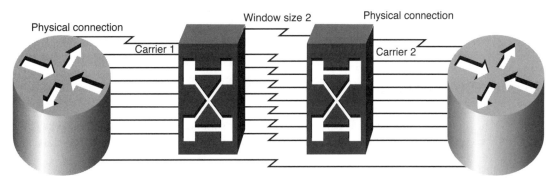

8 Virtual connections over 1 physical connection
Each router can send 16 packets
Carriers use a Window size of 2 by default

This is all done over one physical connection. You should check the frame size because larger is not always better. Naturally, if you are sending larger packets over noisy lines, and a large packet gets corrupted, you will be retransmitting a lot, so smaller packets might be better over noisy lines.

NOTE   A maximum of eight SVCs per protocol per destination are allowed.

Static Routing

Static routing is very common in X.25 networks. Because X.25 is a network layer protocol, X.25 can reroute around failures, which is not a characteristic of Frame Relay. One of the reasons to use static routing is that some businesses bill for their X.25 packets. This often is the case with airlines. Therefore, if you were to use a dynamic routing protocol such as IP to route around failures, the broadcast packets would add up into billable packets. X.25 does not use broadcast packets to locate resources.

All this means that a dynamic routing protocol isn't needed to give fault tolerance in an X.25 cloud. If you do this, you will have to set up a bunch of static X.25 routes. You still want to consider bandwidth arithmetic and some of the other factors, but you don't have to worry about broadcast overhead. There are networks that have as many as 1000 sites in a star topology using X.25.

You can connect so many sites to one central site because of the low speeds that X.25 uses. Remember, the highest speed that an X.25 interface supports is 2000000 bits per second. Usually X.25 circuits are very low-speed—typically 9.6 K or less. If you do the bandwidth arithmetic, there could be approximately 200 9.6 K circuits to a central site with a 2,000,000-bit X.25 interface. With lower-speed circuits, the number of remote sites can be even higher.

X.25 and Subinterfaces

Subinterfaces are always recommended for quality network designs. X.25 can use subinterfaces. Subinterfaces eliminate the need for split horizon issues in the network. This is probably a good idea because it makes all the circuits look like point-to-point protocols, and routing works correctly because point-to-point interfaces broadcast by default.

Multipoint subinterfaces are nonbroadcast by default. This provides robust, dynamic network layer routing and full connectivity with a partial mesh.

NOTE   Point-to-point networks are broadcast by default. Multipoint networks are nonbroadcast by default.

X.25 Packet Switch

Routers can act as X.25 packet switches but not as X.25 gateways. You might not normally want to use routers as packet switches, but some companies are using legacy public X.25 networks, and that can be very costly. If you have an alternate link in your network, you might consider carrying the X.25 traffic on your regular data network instead of paying for someone else to do it.

Figure 10-10 shows the routers doing local X.25 switching, so the router is switching an SVC call between two PADs.

Figure 10-10 *Cisco Routers as X.25 Packet Switches*

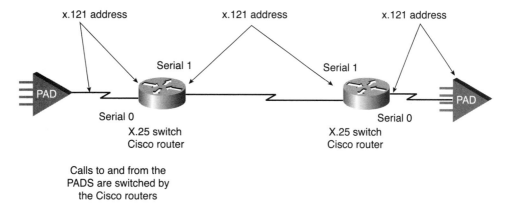

X.25 Over ISDN

It is possible to use X.25 over the Intergrated Services Digital Network (ISDN) (D Channel) to provide 9.6K connectivity. Because the ISDN D channel is "always on" and available, you can use it for X.25 purposes. This is known as AO/DI (Always On/Dynamic ISDN). Figure 10-11 shows how ISDN and X.25 work.

AO/DI offers ISDN telecommuting cost savings. Low-speed D channel services are typically more cost-efficient than the time-based tariffs applied to the B channels, which usually carry user data.

AO/DI is an on-demand service that is designed to make use of an existing Integrated Services Digital Network (ISDN) signaling channel (D channel) to transport X.25 traffic. This provides connectivity basically for free. Because the D channel is always up, why not use it? Depending on the region, some phone companies provide continuous service to locally connected sites working out of one central office. The X.25 D channel call is placed from the subscriber to the packet data service provider.

Notice that the use of PPP allows protocols to be encapsulated within the X.25 logical circuit carried by the D channel, not for authentication, for which PPP is also used. The bearer channels (B channels) use the multilink protocol without the standard Q.922 and X.25 encapsulations and invoke additional bandwidth as needed. You can also use the Bandwidth Allocation Control Protocol (BACP) to negotiate bandwidth allocation as required.

Figure 10-11 *X.25 Over ISDN*

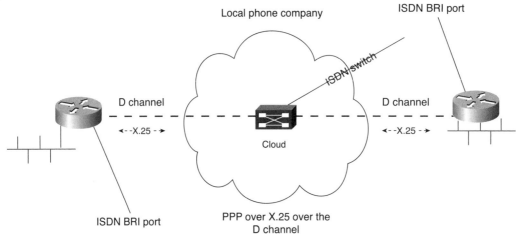

X.25 Design Tips

Here are some general design tips every CCDP should know about X.25:

- An X.25 interface can support 4095 PVCs because there are only 12 bits in the packet header to specify the Logical Channel Number (LCN).

- What is a large number of SVCs per interface? One hundred VCs is a rather common figure, although up to 600 VCs have been implemented successfully in an XOT environment.

- X.25 doesn't have any protocol overhead for PVC maintenance (unless XOT is involved).

- Typical bandwidth of X.25 interfaces is 64 Kbps. Sharing such a low bandwidth among many virtual circuits results in a very low figure per virtual circuit. This low figure must be compatible with user requirements.

- When applicable, an **X.25 map** or other commands are required to configure each virtual circuit. Repeating the same configuration pattern many times might cause a significant usage of NVRAM. Just count the bytes needed to configure one virtual circuit and do some multiplication to figure out the amount of NRAM available. NVRAM compression is sometimes available.

- X.25 is implemented at the process level (at least up to 11.1 IOS). The best routers to use for X.25 traffic are not necessarily the best routers to route IP. X.25 encapsulation is a CPU-intensive task because it involves sequence checking, flow control, and fragmentation.

- A safety factor needs to be applied to such figures, so it doesn't matter much if they don't match real measurements. Real results depend on many parameters. Network design cannot be based on 100% CPU utilization.

Why Frame Relay?

Let's talk about Frame Relay design. While doing that, one of our objectives will be to understand and review Frame Relay terminology. We will describe common components of Frame Relay networks such as LMI and BECN and look at various topology options in the design, including multipoint versus point-to-point interfaces. We will take a look at advantages and disadvantages, access devices and services, and switching operations together with the LMI. The discussion will include how Cisco routers fit into the picture, Cisco routers and RFC 1490, DLCI mapping and inverse ARP, and design ideas.

Frame Relay saves money. Figure 10-12 shows why you would use Frame Relay. Virtual circuits are the key. Figure 10-12 also shows a 64K point-to-point circuit from New York to Los Angeles. As you add a new circuit for Chicago, you have to add another port to the router at New York and another CSU/DSU. By adding circuits in this manner, the possibility exists that there will be a lot of redundancy. There also will be many port costs and circuit costs (which are the most expensive). Multiple access lines will go into the routers—a major portion of the circuit costs.

Another advantage of Frame Relay is that it operates at higher speeds than X.25. The higher speeds are achieved because Frame Relay does not do error checking. Frame Relay depends on the upper layers of the OSI model to guarantee delivery of data and do error checking. The disadvantage of Frame Relay as compared to X.25 is that Frame Relay can not reroute around network failures. It typically relies on IP to handle that. See Example 10-3.

Example 10-3 *Frame Relay*

```
hostname new-york
interface Serial0
 ip address 192.168.100.1 255.255.255.0
 encapsulation frame-relay
 no ip mroute-cache
 frame-relay map ip 192.168.100.2 102 broadcast
 frame-relay map ip 192.168.100.3 103 broadcast

new-york#sh ip rou
C    192.168.100.0/24 is directly connected, Serial0

hostname chicago
interface Serial0
 ip address 192.168.100.2 255.255.255.0
 encapsulation frame-relay
 frame-relay map ip 192.168.100.1 104 broadcast
 frame-relay interface-dlci 104
 no frame-relay inverse-arp
chicago#sh ip rou
C    192.168.100.0/24 is directly connected, Serial0



hostname LA
interface Serial0
 ip address 192.168.100.3 255.255.255.0
 no ip directed-broadcast
```

continues

Example 10-3 *Frame Relay (Continued)*

```
    encapsulation frame-relay
    no ip mroute-cache
    cdp enable
    frame-relay map ip 192.168.100.1 104 broadcast


LA#sh ip route
C    192.168.100.0/24 is directly connected, Serial0
```

Figure 10-12 *Frame Relay*

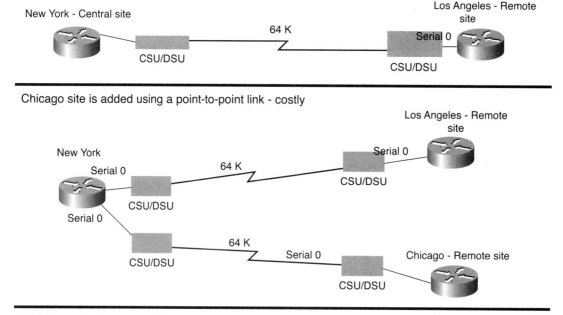

Chicago site is added using a point-to-point link - costly

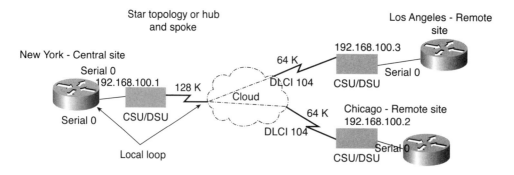

With Frame Relay, only 1 CSU/DSU and Serial port at central site for multiple remote sites.

Star topology is where everything goes back to a central hub point, as shown in Figure 10-13. Occasionally there is a tendency to tack short links onto an existing spoke router rather than adding another link to the existing star topology central site. This adds extra hops to the network, is not the most efficient design, and in general is not a good design practice. However, depending on the provider, it might be cheaper to take this approach.

Figure 10-13   *Star Topology with Additional Link*

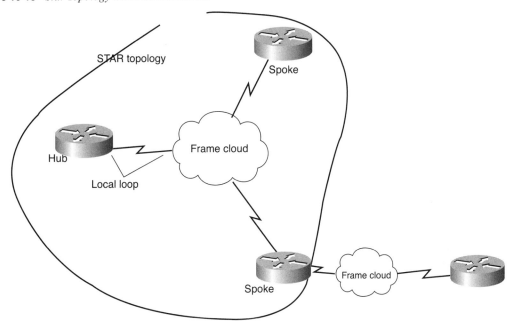

TIP	When a serial interface is applied to the **encapsulate frame relay** command, it becomes a multipoint interface by default, not a point-to-point.

Local Loop

By using Frame Relay, you can have one physical port with one CSU at the central site, saving money. But you can have multiple virtual circuits connected through the cloud. The beauty of this is that you can add sites by just placing a phone call to your vendor to get another circuit provisioned. In some cases, this might require an upgrade to the CSU/DSU.

Notice the local loop in Figure 10-13. This can be viewed as the wire from the central office to the local building. With most phone companies, this is a flat fee. In other words, no matter how far from the central office a company is, this will not cost any more money. So if you are 10 miles from the local central office, there's no extra fee. Frame Relay can be called "distance insensitive."

This isn't the case with dedicated leased lines. Leased lines are priced per mile and are quite expensive. The farther you are from the central office, the more it costs per month for the local loop. So now you might want to add another port only every 10 to 20 circuits or so, depending on oversubscription (see the later section "Oversubscription").

NOTE   Some states are considering subsidizing businesses that might want to build in a remote area of the state, where property is cheaper. But T3s and T1s are more expensive in those areas because the central office is some distance away, so they are hesitant to do so. Therefore, governors are offering subsidies to offset those costs.

Frame Relay Access Devices (FRADs)

Frame Relay Access Devices (FRADs) aren't often a test topic but are important nonetheless. There are many different ways of accessing Frame Relay networks, not just by Cisco routers. There are LAN FRADs and wide-area FRADs. *Wide-area FRADs* take serial line data in, tunnel it across the frame link, and deliver it out the other end as a serial line. *LAN FRADs* take an Ethernet frame, bridge it on a Frame Relay link, and bridge it out the other side as Ethernet. The idea behind FRADs is that they are low-cost Frame Relay access devices. You have to check each vendor specification to find out what they can or cannot do.

Remember that low-end Cisco routers are very cost-competitive. When interfacing FRADs with Cisco routers, use the IETF standard for signaling, because you will be intermixing different vendors:

```
frame-relay map ip 10.10.10.2 16 broadcast ietf
```

DLCI

Data Link Connection Identifier (DLCI) is the virtual circuit used to communicate with the Frame Relay switch. The DLCI is a value that specifies a PVC or SVC in the Frame Relay network. This value is configured on the Frame Relay switch and is obtained by the router via LMI signaling. When the router is powered up, it performs a full status inquiry to the Frame Relay switch and obtains a list of DLCIs assigned to the router's serial port. After this information is obtained by the router, there are four possible states the DLCI could be in:

- **Deleted**—The switch does not recognize the DLCI as a valid circuit. Look at it as though the switch in the provider's network is not sending a DLCI to the local router, or that the DLCI you configured under the subinterface on the router (such as DLCI 100) is not configured on the switch.

- **Inactive**—The switch recognizes the DLCI as a valid circuit, but it is not up and active end-to-end (perhaps it is not configured correctly, and so on). This can also mean that the DLCI is configured but the other side of the circuit (remote site) is either down or not configured.

- **Static**—This state is usually on the Frame Relay switch itself. It can mean that the DLCIs on the switch are statically configured.

- **Active**—The DLCI is configured in the local switch and recognizes that this circuit is connected end-to-end. It is ready to accept user traffic. All systems are go!

The DLCI is locally significant only. As shown in Figure 10-14, there could be a DLCI number at one end of a circuit and a different DLCI number at the other end.

Figure 10-14 *DLCI*

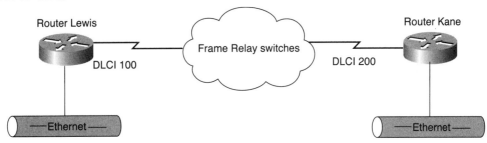

1. Router Lewis powers up
2. Router Lewis performs a full status inquiry to Frame Relay switch via the LMI protocol
3. Fram Relay switch provides router Lewis with DLCI 100
4. Router Lewis knows about only DLCI 100, not 200

An analogy would be an airport. Before you catch a flight into the clouds, you arrive at the airport and go to a gate—say, Gate 100. When you arrive at your destination, you arrive at Gate 200. Somewhere in the clouds, there was a connection from Gate 100 to Gate 200. This is typical Frame Relay; it's a good idea to design your network with certain rules. In other words, if you have a DLCI number of 107, it is a good design practice to make a subinterface of 107 to match it. This simplifies troubleshooting.

```
Int S0.107
Frame Relay Interface DLCI 107
```

Theoretically, the Frame Relay specification allows 10 bits for DLCI addressing, or 1024 DLCIs per interface (2^{10}). There are several reserved DLCIs (0–15 and 1007–1023). Therefore, Cisco routers support 992 DLCIs per interface. Some engineers recommend a maximum of 20 DLCIs per interface. This is based solely on the amount of traffic that will traverse the Frame Relay link and the amount of memory available on the router.

If you have a large Novell network, you have to duplicate the SAPs and RIPs for each DLCI, which causes a lot of overhead and results in lost packets. The recommendation of 20 DLCIs has come from trial and error in the field. You might want to use subinterfaces on the Frame Relay interfaces, which helps with this issue, but you need different network numbers for each subinterface, creating larger routing tables.

Frame Relay Service Characteristics

It's important to look at what happens to the DLCI in the Frame Relay cloud. Figure 10-15 shows this process. You send out a frame with a Frame Relay header on it from Router A. Inside that header is a DLCI number 100. There is no source or destination address, just the number 100. Think of a virtual circuit as pipes going through the Frame Relay carrier's cloud. Out of the cloud comes the circuit with a frame with 200 in the header that traverses to Router B. In the middle of the cloud, there could be many Frame Relay switches connecting the circuit from end to end. The end-station routers know about only their "local" DLCI, not about any of the others that might be involved in the connection. Because Frame Relay uses only this DLCI address, it cannot reroute around failures like X.25 can. Frame Relay must depend on IP to reroute around failures.

Figure 10-15 *Frame Relay Service Characteristics*

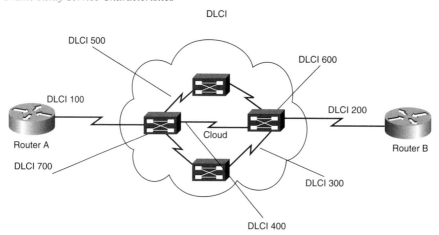

What happens in the cloud? The switch tracks the inbound port and the inbound DLCI number, saying if it comes in Port A carrying the number 100, put it out Port B, which is how the connection is made between the DLCIs.

The Frame Relay specification makes available the number of DLCIs as 0–1023 minus 16 on each side. That is because 0–15 are reserved on the low end, and 1008–1023 are reserved on the high end.

Frame Relay Configuration Parameters

This section discusses some common Frame Relay configuration parameters. Some common parameters were used in the mid-to-late '90s and might not be needed by carriers as much as they were before. Switches in the cloud have progressed to such a speed that it takes carriers more time to filter for FECN and BECN frames than it is worth. It is actually faster now to not look for them due to the fast switching equipment. But they might still be used in some places and are often the subject matter of tests, so it is still necessary to mention them.

Forward and Backward Explicit Congestion Notification

The carrier sets FECNs and BECNs. This means that your Frame Relay packets are running into congestion somewhere in your provider's network. These bits can be set in the Frame Relay header. The idea is that when a frame encounters congestion, the Frame Relay switch can set the FECN bit to notify the destination end that it encountered congestion. Hopefully the destination end notified the original sender that things are busy in the cloud and told it to please slow down.

If this congestion gets severe enough (each provider defines what severe is), your provider starts discarding packets that exceed the Committed Information Rate (CIR) and are marked discard-eligible. If the congestion gets even more severe (again, this is carrier-dependent), the provider's network might discard all packets regardless of whether they exceed the customer's CIR.

To test whether any traffic is getting lost, do an extended ping from the router when you see FECNs and BECNs incrementing on your router. This will tell you if all the pings get through. Other than this, you are at your provider's mercy, and you must go through them to get info on what is going on inside the Frame Relay cloud.

Extended ping is a very valuable tool for the CCDP to test the network design. By setting variables, you can conduct tests to ensure that not only the smaller 32-byte pings get through, but much larger packet sizes as well. Example 10-4 shows an example of extended ping. Simply type **ping** at the router prompt. Remember to answer yes to "Extended commands."

Example 10-4 *Extended Ping*

```
Router#ping   ➡----------Just type ping at the command prompt and press Enter
Protocol [ip]:   ➡-----------Select the protocol
Target IP address: 192.168.100.1  ➡---------Select the target IP address
Repeat count [5]:   ➡-------How many packets to send?
Datagram size [100]:   ➡----- The datagram will be 100 bytes
Timeout in seconds [2]:   ➡ The router will time out after two seconds, and a dot
is echoed back to the user.
Extended commands [n]: yes (these are more detailed commands).
Source address or interface: 192.168.100.2 ➡------Select which IP address will be
the source address for the ping
Type of service [0]:   ➡--- Select type of service
Set DF bit in IP header? [no]:  ➡-Select "Don't fragment" bit, which means do not
fragment this packet.
Validate reply data? [no]:
```

continues

Example 10-4 *Extended Ping (Continued)*

```
Data pattern [0xABCD]: ➔--- The data pattern in the payload field will be this
pattern repeated.
Loose, Strict, Record, Timestamp, Verbose[none]:
Sweep range of sizes [n]:
Type escape sequence to abort.
Sending 5, 100-byte ICMP Echos to 192.168.100.1, timeout is 2 seconds:
!!!!!
Success rate is 100 percent (5/5), round-trip min/avg/max = 56/58/60 ms
```

There are a few drawbacks to using FECN and BECN. The FECN and BECN bits get carried to the router, not to the end station or server. In many network protocols, there is no mechanism for the router to pass that information to the server. DECnet and CLNS will, but they are not common protocols. For DECnet and CLNS, you promote the FECN and BECN bits to the Layer 3 protocol. Remember that the Cisco router cannot throttle back the traffic; only the end hosts can. The protocol provides for end-host notification, and the router passes the notification along. Where it doesn't, you can either drop or defer the packet. If you drop the packet, you might as well transmit it on the off chance that the network will deliver it (because you will drop it anyway). If the packet is deferred, you need to decide how long it should stay around before it becomes "stale" and should be dropped from the queue.

Discard-Eligible and CIR

These two subjects are worth mentioning together. These values vary, depending on the carrier's switch and how the features were implemented. CIR is the "guaranteed" delivery rate, or Committed Information Rate. The access rate is the physical port speed. Normally, Burst Excess (Be) is the amount you are allowed to burst over CIR. The excess burst is like a highway. The speed limit is 65 mph, but you have been told that as long as no one else is on the highway, you can go 90 mph. So your CIR is 65 mph with an excess burst rate of 90 mph.

For example, you have a T1 for port access, but pay for a 128 Kbps CIR. The carrier guarantees that it will always be able to sustain a rate of 128 Kbps for my PVC.

The carrier lets up to 512 K be burst, and if it can, it will pass the data. But I only pay for a CIR of 128 K. Some carriers mark all traffic above CIR as discard-eligible (DE) but still transport all traffic up to port or burst speed if there is no congestion. However, other carriers allow you to exceed burst above your CIR for a fixed length of time only and then throw away anything in excess of your CIR. Still other carriers offer 0 CIR service, in which everything is marked as discard-eligible and by definition is all Be, but allow you to send traffic at the access rate. The only way to find out what your carrier allows is to ask the rep and to test your circuit after it is installed to make sure what he has told you is true.

TIP   If you have the Enterprise version of the Cisco IOS, use the TTCP utility to test throughput. At the router command prompt, type **ttcp**. This is a hidden command; you cannot view this command using the question mark.

If you subinterface each DLCI, you can then apply a DE list to each subinterface. A DE list is a method that allows you to decide which packets will get discarded within the Frame Relay network when there is congestion. If you mark some packets as DE, the carrier will discard those first rather than randomly guessing which packets to discard.

For example, if you have IP, IPX, and SNA on Frame Relay, usually you would decide to mark IP and IPX as DE to help make sure the SNA gets through. This would, of course, depend on your network and how you purchased Frame Relay.

There are several components to Frame Relay—access link (usually 56/64 KB or T1), port speed (56/64 for 56/64 K and 64 to 1.544 MB for T1 in increments of 64), and CIR.

If you buy a T1 access link with a 512 Kbps port speed and a 128 Kbps CIR, you can use up to 512 Kbps. The packets above 128 Kbps are randomly marked as DE. If some congestion arises on the carrier network, they are dropped. The DE list gives you a way to decide which packets will get dropped.

What happens if a frame is lost in the cloud? If a frame switch happens to throw away a frame, TCP/IP doesn't get an acknowledgment. It closes the window and goes into slow start or restart. The source can then drop back on the speed of retransmission, and hopefully the congestion will clear up. If a server at the central site is pumping out bits faster than the Frame Relay cloud can handle, the only way to relieve the congestion is to have the original sender slow down.

Practically speaking, there are performance issues that have to be dealt with on an individual basis. Obviously, the higher the CIR on the PVC, the more impact it will have on the individual interface's ability to handle the traffic. A T1 at the central site in Figure 10-16 could certainly be expected to handle 24 64 K PVCs with little problem. A T1 with 24 64 k PVCs equals about 1536 K of bandwidth. But if there is a lot of broadcast traffic, it could affect performance, because each broadcast would have to be replicated 24 times on the same interface at the central site. And if you try to put more than 24 64 K DLCIs into a T1 interface, the possibility of problems increases. This is known as oversubscription and is discussed later in this chapter.

The router uses the DE bit to mark frames that are eligible to be discarded if the frame switches encounter congestion.

In Example 10-5, the DLCI number is 100.

Figure 10-16 *Frame Relay CIR*

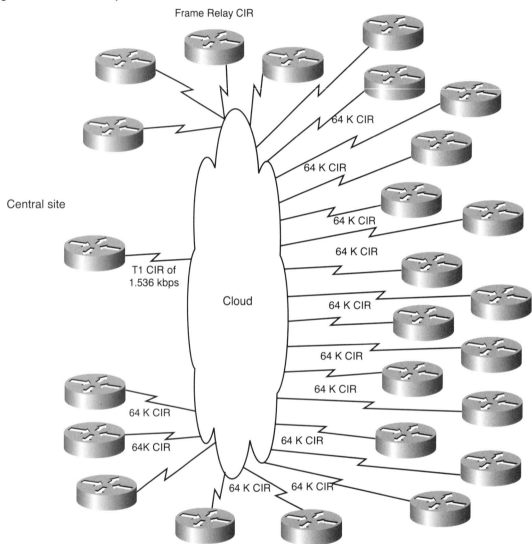

Frame Relay CIR

Central site

T1 CIR of
1.536 kbps

Cloud

64 K CIR

Example 10-5 *Discard Eligible Marking*

```
interface serial 0 ip address 192.168.1.1 255.255.255.0
encapsulation frame-relay
frame-relay de-group 1 100 ➡-----------Maps group 1 to DLCI 100
frame-relay map ip 192.168.1.2 100 broadcast ➡----Maps IP address to DLCI 100
frame-relay de-list 1 prot ip tcp http ➡- Marks HTTP as being discard eligible
```

This example means that when going over the 128K CIR, mark the HTTP frames as discard-eligible. The question remains, though: How do you know what is being discarded and how often by the provider? Does 50 percent of the traffic make it? Does 100 percent of the traffic make it?

Use the extended pings to test your configurations.

As mentioned earlier, Frame Relay switches have progressed to the point where it is actually beneficial to not look for the DEs because that becomes time-consuming for the switches. That means that there is no policing mechanism, and everybody's traffic is treated exactly the same way. It might depend on your carrier.

Oversubscription

In Figure 10-16, the T1 can handle the CIR from all remote sites. However, if all the remote sites can burst to 128 K, there are other issues. The combination of all the remote sites together bursting over the 64 K CIR results in too much data for the central site T1 to handle. This is common with Frame Relay; it's called *oversubscription*. You can risk oversubscription and simply assume that all the remote sites will not be busy at the same time. Most of the time, the traffic will get through, but this is a risk that needs to be thought out. For example, if the company sites are spread out around the world, the company can assume that due to the time differences between sites, some sites won't be very active at certain times because most work is performed between 8 a.m. and 5 p.m. at all the sites. The company can risk oversubscribing and feel confident that it will not cause any problems.

Measurement Interval

It is worthwhile to discuss how the CIR is measured. The CIR is measured in increments of time. Therefore, the more the measurements and the shorter their duration, the more accurate they are. If I have a CIR of 128 Kbps, would that mean the provider could provide for 32 Kbps in the first half-second and provide for 96 kbps in the second half-second, equaling 128 K, and thus and I'd meet my 128 K requirement for 1 second? No, this is where the measurement interval comes into play.

For example, if there is a 64 K CIR and I want the provider to measure every eighth of a second, I would have a CIR of 8 K every eighth of a second. This provides for more accuracy. Obviously, the more often you measure, the greater the chance that you'll get what you paid for. For example, if a measurement is made every sixteenth of a second, the provider needs to provide 4 K for a CIR of 64 K. Thus, it might be important to discuss how often your provider measures the intervals. If you hear "one-half second" in the same sentence you hear "measurement interval," you might want to reconsider your provider.

Frame Relay Operation: LMI

Frame Relay LMI is an interface specification that governs how the router talks to the switch. The Frame Relay LMI conveys the PVC status from the switch to you. The Frame Relay router talks to the Frame Relay switch using LMI. There are three standards. Two of them, the ANSI and the ITU, are very similar. The third standard, Cisco LMI, is a public specification by four companies in 1988, including Stratacom, Northern Telecom, Cisco, and DEC. They are commonly known as the Gang of Four.

LMI works a sort of double duty, sending signals back and forth between the Frame Relay switch and the router. This message is locally significant only, not end-to-end. Part of this signaling is keepalive, or status-inquiry messages every 10 seconds to make sure that the other end of the circuit is still there. The router needs to see a response to this short status inquiry to mark the line protocol as up.

Every 60 seconds, the router sends a full status inquiry, and the switch can respond with all the DLCI numbers assigned to that router's serial interface. This is when you should see the PVCs become active. If a change occurs in the PVC status, the router will not mark the PVC down until the next full status inquiry (every 60 seconds), unless you're using Cisco LMI on both the router and the switch and have configured asynchronous updates on the switch.

NOTE   Frame Relay LMI, as shown in Figure 10-17, is locally significant only. This means that even if Router B's circuit goes down, Router A's interface remains up but shows Inactive for DLCI 100 upon issuance of the command **show frame-relay pvc**.

Figure 10-17   *Frame Relay LMI*

1. Router A powers up and does a full status inquiry to the Frame Relay switch.
2. Frame Relay switch provides Router A with DLCI 100
3. Every 10 seconds keepalives are exchanged between router and switch

RFC 1490

Upper-layer protocols such as Novell and AppleTalk interoperate with Frame Relay with RFC 1490, which is simply a multiprotocol encapsulation method over Frame Relay. RFC 1490 is a specification for putting type codes into the Frame Relay headers and the ability to forward different protocols over Frame Relay. It covers both bridged and routed traffic. RFC 1490 was first supported in Cisco IOS version 10.3(1).

Frame Relay Mapping

Figure 10-18 shows how Frame Relay mapping works. A packet comes into Router A on the left, which is trying to reach 192.168.200.1. The router strips the data link header Ethernet encapsulation. It then looks at Layer 3 and recognizes it is an IP packet. The router looks at the IP header, finds a destination address of 192.168.200.1, and says it is not a directly connected interface. It looks in the IP routing table for the most explicit match, finds the next hop (in this case, Router B or 192.168.1.2), and an interface to send the data out on (Serial 0). This has to go via Frame Relay to Router B.

Figure 10-18 *Frame Relay Mapping*

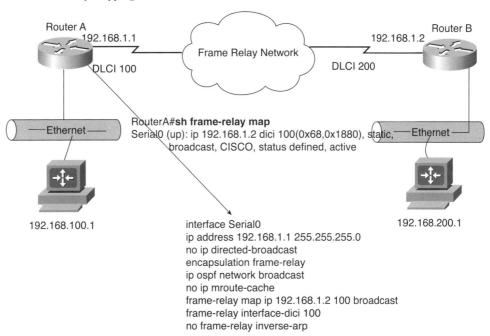

Router A starts to queue the packet, but it must first build the data-link Frame Relay header. It needs to put a DLCI 100 into the frame so that the switch knows to which virtual circuit it belongs. Somehow, Router A must get from "I have to send this to Router B" to "Which circuit do I use?" It looks in the Frame Relay map table and notices a direct mapping of the next hop 192.168.1.2 via DLCI 100 and puts it out on virtual circuit 100.

This is how Cisco routers mapped addresses up until Cisco IOS version 10.3. Because this required quite a bit of manual configuration, a solution to simplify the configuration was needed. Starting with version 10.3, a method called Inverse ARP was introduced, which eliminated the need for the manual mapping of addresses. (See Figure 10-18.)

Inverse ARP

Inverse ARP eliminates the need for manual configuration of Frame Relay map statements. When the router is powered up, it learns from the switch that the PVC is active. The router learns that DLCI 100 is active. The router sends out a frame with DLCI 100 and puts the IP address (192.168.1.1) of the interface into the body of the packet. It moves through the Frame Relay network, and the receiving router can say that Router A is at the other end of the PVC. Router B puts this into the Frame Relay mapping table. This same process happens from Router B to Router A.

WARNING   Inverse ARP should be disabled with AppleTalk, and also in a full-mesh environment. In a full-mesh environment, there is a possibility of obtaining the wrong Layer 3 address for a Layer 2 DLCI.

Interaction with Routing Protocols

If routers are to route traffic across the network, there needs to be routing protocols. This is where the rule of split horizon comes into play. Split horizon can be explained with this caveat: "Do not tell a joke back to the person who told you the joke." In Figure 10-19, Router A is advertising Network 200 to Router B. Normally Router B would not advertise this back out the same interface it learned the route from, due to the split horizon rule. If that were the case, Router C would never learn about Network 200 because you do not have a connection between Router A and Router C. One of the ways for Router C to learn that network 200 resides on Router A is to disable split horizon on Router B's serial interface. If Cisco's IGRP is being used, there is no need to disable split horizon because IGRP does that automatically. Unfortunately, with IPX RIP and AppleTalk RTMP, you cannot disable split horizon. DECnet has problems with split horizon as well.

Figure 10-19 *Frame Relay Hub and Spoke*

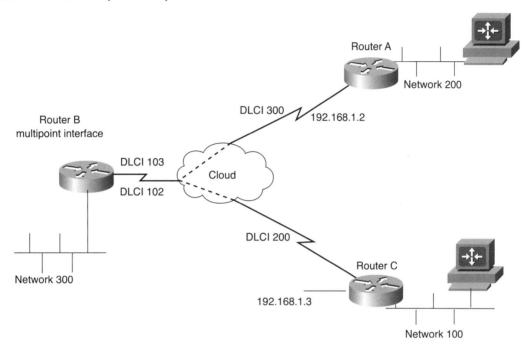

You can, however, disable split horizon with Cisco's EIGRP protocol.

NOTE   Notice that in the frame connections, all the addresses are on the same subnet because this is a multipoint network.

TIP   OSPF does not apply split horizon, so it does not have to be disabled in partial-mesh configurations. Because it is a link-state protocol, you don't need to disable it.

Subinterfaces

Another solution to the split-horizon problems is to create *subinterfaces*. A subinterface is a logical interface in the IOS. It is treated very much like a physical interface. In Figure 10-20, Serial 0.100 is a subinterface and is configured as a point-to-point circuit. Interface Serial 0.200 is also a point-to-point circuit to Router C. You can add logical interfaces to the physical interfaces on the router because you need them. The code in the router treats them as point-to-point or leased lines. Subinterfaces are definitely recommended. The trade-off is that, because with multipoint every router is on the same network, there are more routes in the routing table, because each subinterface has its own network. But it also makes troubleshooting easier, because split horizon issues are difficult to troubleshoot.

Figure 10-20 *Frame Relay Subinterfaces*

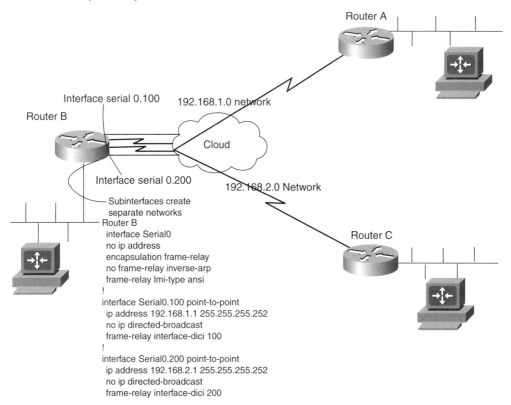

Design Options

This section discusses some design considerations to be used with Frame Relay. There are several topology options, including NBMA full mesh, hierarchical full mesh, and star (hub-and-spoke) networks. One of the major issues is, of course, split horizon and how the design addresses that.

Star networks (also called hub-and-spoke networks) are what most companies are implementing. Another important issue might be designing for redundancy with DDR. These are the most popular design considerations, so they are covered in this section.

Depending on what is going on in the router, taxing the processor at any given moment in time needs some consideration. For example, is any tunneling being performed on the router? How about DLSW activity? These things might affect the throughput across a Frame Relay network. The CPU utilization and processes need to be checked and tended, especially if CPU-intensive configurations are being used. The Cisco command **show process** is the CCDP's friend. It details the processes and shows how much CPU time the processes consume. If the processor shows high levels of utilization, it might be time to upgrade the router. See Example 10-6.

Example 10-6 *The* **show process** *Command*

```
Router#show process
CPU utilization for five seconds: 15%/11%; one minute: 13%; five minutes: 11%
 PID QTy       PC Runtime (ms)    Invoked   uSecs    Stacks TTY Process
   1 Csp  31E4C2E       47360      137744     343   732/1000    0 Load Meter
   2 ME   31672CC       24976         727   34354  2040/4000   18 Virtual Exec
   3 Lst  31D54F6     2161368      123031   17567  3704/4000    0 Check heaps
   4 Cwe  31DB6E6           0           1       0  3728/4000    0 Pool Manager
   5 Mst  315FE36           0           2       0  3696/4000    0 Timers
   6 Mwe  30F682A       37384        2519   14840  3636/4000
```

The number of hops across the network is an issue. Other things that need attention are the CIR, the number of access lines, the number of PVCs (which usually drive the cost), and so on.

Star topology

Star topology is probably the most common Frame Relay design. Usually there is a central site and a number of remote sites. Remember to provide enough bandwidth to the central site, and do the bandwidth arithmetic to make sure that oversubscription won't be a problem. A star topology is depicted in Figure 10-21. Here are some benefits of a star topology:

- Minimizes the number of PVCs
- Minimizes broadcast copying
- Easily managed

Notice the remote sites. They all have the same DLCI number, 100. This is very typical of Frame Relay providers. They assign the same DLCI to the remotes and different DLCI numbers at the central site. This makes troubleshooting easier because the engineers have to remember only one DLCI number for the remote sites.

Also notice that the remotes have a CIR of 64K. This means that the central site will need a CIR of at least 192 K to accommodate the remote sites if there is a need to avoid oversubscription.

Figure 10-21 *Frame Relay Hub and Spoke (Star)*

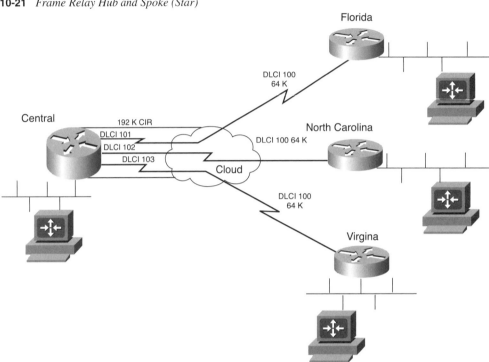

Full Mesh

NBMA, or full mesh, is not very common. It is a very expensive solution for connecting your sites. The best reason might be for implementing a voice over Frame Relay network or voice over IP network because there would be fewer delays from one site to another. The number of hops is one in a full mesh, which is good for voice traffic. Because full mesh can be expensive, some companies are asking for a CIR of 0 to offset their costs. The provider simply does not guarantee that any traffic will flow through the network at all. So, if you hear "voice" in the same sentence you hear "a CIR of 0," you might wind up disappointed.

A number of PVCs do not scale well in a full-mesh environment. The formula to determine the number of PVCs needed in a full-mesh environment is $n * (n - 1) / 2$, where n is the number of sites. This equates to a bill for 45 PVCs if you have 10 sites—not very cheap. Remember that circuits are monthly recurring costs. It should be your goal to keep that cost to a minimum while providing the company a quality WAN.

Here are some benefits of full mesh:

- Low latency, or a single-hop delay between sites

- Load balancing is a possibility between sites

- Good for voice because of the limited number of hops

Notice in Figure 10-22 that the circuit from the router Iowa to the router Idaho is 128 K. However, the other circuits, from router Iowa to Texas and router Tennessee, are 64 K. If the host PC on the right, Jackie, sends a large file to the host Harold PC, the file could be load-balanced across multiple links, depending on the routing protocol being used.

Figure 10-22 *Full Mesh with Multipoint Interfaces*

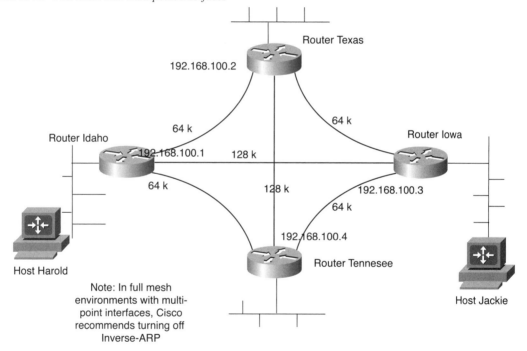

Hierarchical Mesh

Hierarchical mesh is a common design used for redundancy purposes. Notice in Figure 10-23 that there are six PVCs at NY1 and NY2. Each of these routers has a connection to all the remote routers. In this situation, if either of the central sites goes down, the remote sites still can get to the server. Be careful when doing bandwidth arithmetic not to shoot yourself in the foot.

Figure 10-23 *Frame Relay Hierarchical Mesh*

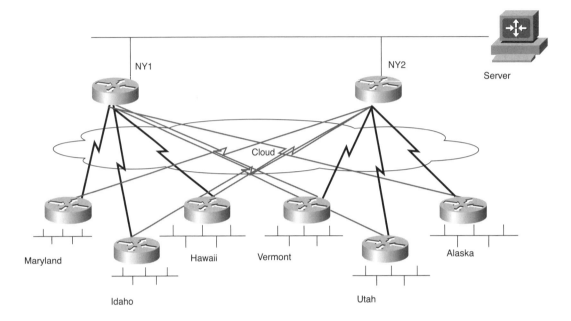

If Idaho has a connection to NY1 with a CIR of 64 Kbps, you should also make the redundant connection to NY2 64 Kbps. Companies have been known to make the redundant connection 0K CIR to save money. But when they lose their connection to the NY1 router, they can't move data through NY2 due to congestion in the Frame Relay network, preventing their users from getting to the server. Again, load sharing will probably happen here, depending on the routing protocol.

Here are some benefits of hierarchical mesh:

- Load balancing is a possibility between sites

- Availability

Dial-on-Demand Backup

There are a couple of choices for backing up Frame Relay circuits. The most popular is probably ISDN. Most companies usually rely on the remote sites to call the central site, as shown in Figure 10-24. NY is the central site in this case because the remote site has one PVC. Notice that the hub site has two PVCs. If one of the PVCs at the hub site loses its connection, the interface still receives and sends keepalive messages over the other PVC, which keeps the interface up.

Figure 10-24 *ISDN Backup*

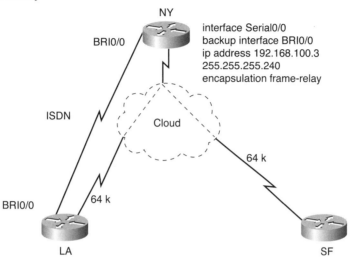

On the LA router, you put in a **backup interface BRI0** command on the serial interface, and when the serial link goes down or stops receiving keepalives from the Frame Relay switch, the router places an ISDN call to the New York router and brings up the link.

```
interface Serial0/0
backup interface BRI0/0  →-- When serial line fails, ISDN will activate
ip address 192.168.100.3 255.255.255.0
encapsulation frame-relay
```

ISDN is usually time-sensitive as far as price in most areas. Decisions need to be made to avoid high phone bills, and backup strategies need to be developed. Do you bring up the link, which is simple, or do you configure the dial-on-demand routing, which brings up the ISDN only as needed?

Here are some benefits of ISDN backup:

- Very fast circuit establishment

- Bandwidth on demand can be utilized

- Backup capabilities up to 128 K

Other decisions involve long-distance calls. In Figure 10-24, would it be more effective to have LA dial NY or SF? San Francisco is much closer to Los Angeles geographically, so long-distance charges probably are cheaper. Do you call SF and sacrifice some bandwidth by routing from NY to LA via SF? These are the decisions a CCDP must make. Sometimes there is no right answer—only different solutions with different trade-offs. With practice and experience, you will become an excellent Cisco Certified Design Professional.

Hardware

Frame Relay and X.25 use the standard 60-pin serial interfaces found on most Cisco routers. In some cases, when there is a need for many tunnels and serial interfaces on one router, a 7507 router with the VIP card might meet the need. The VIP is an interface processor for use with the Cisco 7000 series and Cisco 7500 series routers. It installs in the available slots in your Cisco 7000 series or 7500 series router. The VIP uses a single motherboard with up to two port adapters. The VIP port adapters provide the individual LAN, WAN, or LAN/WAN interface ports.

WARNING The VIP supports online insertion and removal (OIR), which allows you to remove and replace a VIP without first shutting down the system. Online insertion and removal maximizes router availability by letting you add or remove VIPs during system operation; however, the system might indicate a hardware failure if you don't follow proper procedures. Always shut down any ports on the port adapter cards before removing VIP or port adapters.

Tunneling is processor-intensive and should be activated cautiously when implementing STUN and XOT. Each VIP card can contain two port adapters. Each port adapter can support eight serial ports. That equals 16 serial ports per slot on the 7507, which has five slots available to the CCDP for ports. If one slot is used for redundant Ethernet cards, that leaves four slots of 16 port serial interfaces, for a total of 64 available serial ports.

Increasing demand for bandwidth-intensive services and wide-area network (WAN) connectivity requires that network administrators maximize the capacity and efficiency of network routers. Cisco Systems' four- and eight-port serial port adapters provide network administrators with flexible options for a broad range of port density requirements. Cisco's four- and eight-port serial port adapters enhance network performance at a low price per port, making them the most cost-effective solution for maximizing router efficiency.

NOTE Even though the port adapters have their own CPU, the tunneling of IP for STUN or XOT still has to interrupt the main RSP processor because tunnels are process-switched. CCDPs need to know what is process-switched and what is fast-switched.

Foundation Summary

This section is a collection of tables that provide a convenient review of many key concepts in this chapter. If you are already comfortable with the topics in this chapter, this summary could help you recall a few details. If you have just read this chapter, this review should help solidify some key facts. If you are doing your final preparation before the exam, Tables 10-2 through 10-3 are a convenient way to review the day before the exam.

Table 10-2   *Chapter Terms*

Term	Description
PAD	Packet Assembler/Disassembler. A device used to connect simple devices (such as character-mode terminals) that do not support the full functionality of a particular protocol to a network. PADs buffer data and assemble and disassemble packets sent to such end devices.
DLCI	Data-link connection identifier. A value that specifies a PVC or SVC in a Frame Relay network. In the basic Frame Relay specification, DLCIs are locally significant.
OSPF	Open Shortest Path First. A link-state, hierarchical IGP routing algorithm proposed as a successor to RIP in the Internet community. OSPF features include least-cost routing, multipath routing, and load balancing. OSPF was derived from an early version of the IS-IS protocol.
Frame Relay	An industry-standard switched data link layer protocol that handles multiple virtual circuits using HDLC encapsulation between connected devices. Frame Relay is more efficient than X.25, the protocol for which it is generally considered a replacement.
X.25	An ITU-T standard that defines how connections between DTE and DCE are maintained for remote terminal access and computer communications in PDNs. X.25 specifies LAPB, a data link layer protocol, and PLP, a network layer protocol.
LMI	Local Management Interface. A set of enhancements to the basic Frame Relay specification. LMI includes support for a keepalive mechanism, which verifies that data is flowing; a multicast mechanism, which provides the network server with its local DLCI and the multicast DLCI; global addressing, which gives DLCIs global rather than local significance in Frame Relay networks; and a status mechanism, which provides an ongoing status report on the DLCIs known to the switch.
FECN	Forward Explicit Congestion Notification. A bit set by a Frame Relay network to inform DTE receiving the frame that congestion was experienced in the path from source to destination. DTE receiving frames with the FECN bit set can request that higher-level protocols take flow-control action as appropriate.
BECN	Backward Explicit Congestion Notification. A bit set by a Frame Relay network in frames traveling in the opposite direction of frames encountering a congested path. DTE receiving frames with the BECN bit set can request that higher-level protocols take flow control action as appropriate.

continues

Table 10-2   *Chapter Terms (Continued)*

HDLC	High-Level Data-Link Control. A bit-oriented synchronous data link layer protocol developed by ISO. Derived from SDLC, HDLC specifies a data encapsulation method on synchronous serial links using frame characters and checksums.
Star (hub and spoke)	A LAN topology in which endpoints on a network are connected to a common central switch by point-to-point links.
Dual star	A redundant star network with the central sites connected via a common backbone, usually an Ethernet segment.
ISDN	Integrated Services Digital Network. A communication protocol offered by telephone companies that permits telephone networks to carry data, voice, and other source traffic.
X.121	An ITU-T standard describing an addressing scheme used in X.25 networks. X.121 addresses are sometimes called IDNs.

Table 10-3 contains detailed explanations of specific commands from this chapter that are important to the CCDP.

Table 10-3   *Show Processes*

Field	Description
CPU utilization for five seconds	CPU utilization for the last 5 seconds. The second number indicates the percent of CPU time spent at the interrupt level.
one minute	CPU utilization for the last minute.
five minutes	CPU utilization for the last 5 minutes.
PID	Process ID.
Q	Process queue priority. Possible values are H (high), M (medium), and L (low).
Ty	Scheduler test. Possible values are * (currently running), E (waiting for an event), S (ready to run; voluntarily relinquished processor), rd (ready to run; wakeup conditions have occurred), we (waiting for an event), sa (sleeping until an absolute time), si (sleeping for a time interval), sp (sleeping for a time interval (alternate call), st (sleeping until a timer expires), hg (hung; the process will never execute again), and xx (dead; the process has terminated but has not yet been deleted).
PC	Current program counter.
Runtime (ms)	CPU time the process has used, in milliseconds.
Invoked	Number of times the process has been invoked.
uSecs	Microseconds of CPU time for each process invocation.
Stacks	Low water mark/total stack space available, in bytes.
TTY	Terminal that controls the process.

Table 10-3   *Show Processes (Continued)*

Process	Name of the process.
5Sec	CPU utilization by the task in the last 5 seconds.
5Min	CPU utilization by the task in the last 5 minutes.

Q&A

As mentioned in Chapter 1, the questions and scenarios in this book are more difficult than what you will experience on the actual exam. The questions do not attempt to cover more breadth or depth than the exam; however, they are designed to make sure that you know the answer. Rather than allowing you to derive the answer from clues hidden inside the question, the questions challenge your understanding and recall of the subject. Questions from the "Do I Know This Already?" quiz from the beginning of the chapter are repeated here to ensure that you have mastered this chapter's topic areas. Hopefully, these questions will help limit the number of exam questions on which you narrow your choices to two options and then guess. Be sure to use the CD and take the simulated exams.

Unlike questions 1–15, which are directly out of the chapter, questions 16–30 might or might not be answered in this chapter. These questions are relevant to this chapter and can be researched using the Internet or http://www.cisco.com. The answers to questions 1–15 can be found in Appendix A.

1 X.25 uses what protocol at Layer 2?

_____

_____

_____

2 X.25 uses what protocol at Layer 3?

_____

_____

_____

3 At which layer do packet size and window size operate?

_____

_____

_____

4 For what does AO/DI stand?

_____

_____

_____

5 When the command **encapsulate frame relay** is applied to a serial interface, does that make the serial interface point-to-point or multipoint by default?

_____

_____

_____

6 What range of DLCIs can be used on a serial interface encapsulated with Frame Relay?

_____

_____

_____

7 Do most carriers charge for the local loop with dedicated lines? How about with Frame Relay?

_____

_____

_____

8 If I have a measurement interval of .125 seconds, and I am guaranteed a CIR of 8k during that time period, what is my overall CIR?

_____

_____

_____

9 In a full-mesh environment, should Inverse ARP be disabled?

_____

_____

_____

10 Can split horizon be turned off for IPX RIP and AppleTalk RTMP?

_____

_____

_____

11 Does OSPF apply the split horizon rule?

_____

_____

_____

12 Name two good reasons to use subinterfaces.

_____

_____

_____

13 For what does NBMA stand?

_____

_____

_____

14 If four sites are fully meshed, how many links are needed?

_____

_____

_____

15 What two routing protocols are used for fast convergence?

_____

_____

_____

16 Can there be different LMI types on subinterfaces?

_____

_____

_____

17 What is the maximum Frame Relay transmittable unit (MTU) size?

_____

_____

_____

18 When is LMI exchanged between the router and the carrier?

_____

_____

_____

19 Is there a limit to the number of subinterfaces that are allowed on a router when using Frame Relay?

_____

_____

_____

20 What does an increase in the number of FECN and BECN packets mean?

_____

_____

_____

21 For a DLCI on a subinterface to be "active," does the DLCI also have to be up at the remote end?

_____

_____

_____

22 With two subinterfaces on the same router, can there be two different Frame Relay encapsulations?

_____

_____

_____

23 Does OSPF use split horizon for an interface?

_____

_____

_____

24 For what is LMI used?

_____

_____

_____

25 By default, is a subinterface point-to-point or multipoint?

_____

_____

_____

26 Does LAPB provide error recovery?

_____

_____

_____

27 To which layer do the X.25 parameters *window size* and *packet size* belong?

_____

_____

_____

28 Does Frame Relay guarantee delivery of data?

_____

_____

_____

29 Does X.25 guarantee delivery of data?

_____

_____

_____

30 Which companies comprise the Gang of Four?

_____

_____

_____

Scenarios

RouteitRight has been assigned an address range of 199.198.197.0 by the InterNIC for addressing its network devices. Also, the address 1.1.1.1 has been assigned to the company for access to its ISP. This address range/subnet mask must accommodate only two valid IP addresses.

There are 50 users at the central site, 50 users at remote site 1, and 10 users at remote sites 2 through 4, as shown in Figure 10-25. Address these sites with the Class C address just mentioned. This is an IP addressing exercise only. Frame Relay DLCIs do not need to be addressed. Hint: Variable-length subnetting will need to be used.

Figure 10-25   *Scenario 1*

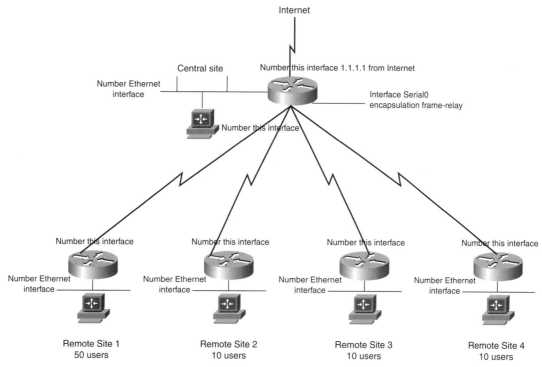

Scenario 1

1 RouteitRight has the following requirements:

— A central site with four remote sites

— Remote site 1 is 128 K CIR

— Remote site 2 is 64 K CIR

— Remote site 3 is 64 K CIR

— Remote site 4 is 64 K CIR

— There must be enough CIR at the central site to accommodate the remote sites.

— Network Address Translation must not be used.

— All hosts must have IP connectivity to the Internet.

Scenario 2

1 RouteitRight has grown and added voice requirements:

— The company has one central site and four remote sites, as shown in Figure 10-26.

— There must be any-to-any connectivity between sites for only voice purposes.

— There is no requirement for data connectivity.

— There must be enough bandwidth on the links so that the voice calls do not drop off.

— You are allowed to number the DLCIs between the sites. You must provide a numbering scheme that makes it practical and easier to troubleshoot.

Figure 10-26 *Scenario 2*

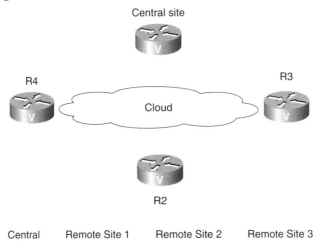

Scenario 3

1 RouteitRight has the following requirements:

— The company has two central sites and four remote sites, as shown in Figure 10-27.

— If one of the central sites goes down, the other central site will provide full connectivity to the Internet and company servers at the central site.

— The company needs vendor redundancy for the Frame Relay circuits to each site.

Figure 10-27 *Scenario 3*

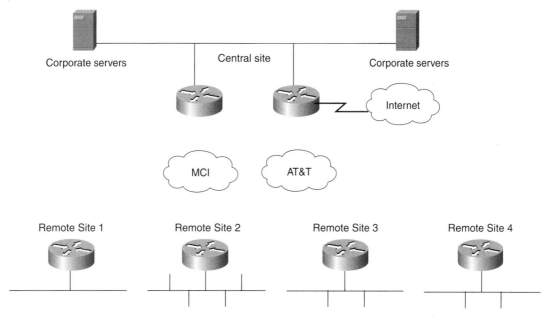

Scenario Answers

Answer to Scenario 1

Figure 10-28 shows one solution. There are other ways of meeting the company's requirements. This is only a recommended solution that meets the requirements placed on the CCDP.

Figure 10-28   *Suggested Solution for Scenario 1*

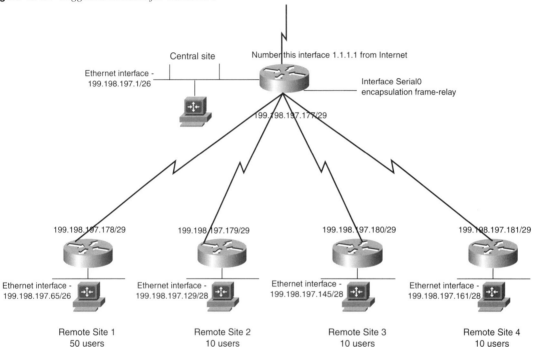

1   The IP address assigned to the central site is 1.1.1.1. Meeting the requirement would require a 30-bit subnet mask, or 255.255.255.252, which leaves you with two valid IP addresses, 1.1.1.1 and 1.1.1.2. (1.1.1.0 and 1.1.1.3 are unusable with this 30-bit mask.) The 1.1.1.2 address must be the ISP's address because 1.1.1.1 is being used at the local company router. It often happens that a customer knows only their IP address (1.1.1.1) and not the ISP's address. The engineer needs to determine by the network mask what the IP address is at the ISP.

   — **Central site:** Notice in Figure 10-28 that the IP address range used for the central site is 199.198.197.0-64.

   That has been determined because a 26-bit mask or 255.255.255.192 is being used. This effectively leaves about 61 addresses for devices, more than meeting the customer's requirement.

The CIR has been determined to be 320K at the central site. This was determined by adding up the remote site CIR (128 Kbps + 64 Kbps + 64 Kbps + 64 Kbps = 324 K).

— **Remote sites**—Let's address the requirements for remote site 1. About 50 users are working out of this office. Using the assigned block of addresses, it has been determined that another block of 64 addresses can be used. The address range 199.198.197.65–127 with a mask of 255.255.255.192 (or 26, because 26 bits make the mask) has been determined and is now available for addressing hosts. The CIR assigned to this site is 128K, which is the most bandwidth of the four remote sites. Notice that this site has the most users as well.

TIP   A rule of thumb some engineers use is to multiply the number of users by 4 K to determine the amount of bandwidth needed on the Frame Relay links. If that rule is applied here, 4 K multiplied by 40 is 160 K.

The company has decided that it will purchase and pay for a 128 K CIR, and if that is not enough, it can always increase the CIR later. Also, this traffic needs to be monitored regularly because network traffic doubles about every year or year-and-a-half. That has been consistent for the last six years.

— **Remote site 2**—The address range for this site has been determined to be 199.198.197.128–143 and a mask of 255.255.255.240 (or a 28-bit mask). The .129 address is being used by the router's Ethernet port. This leaves 130–142 as effective host addresses, or about 12 to use.

— **Remote site 3**—The address range for this site has been determined to be 199.198.197.144–159 with a mask of 255.255.255.240 (or a 28-bit mask), with 145 being assigned to the router's Ethernet port. This leaves 146–158 as effective host addresses, satisfying the requirement for 10 users.

— **Remote site 4**—The address range for this site has been determined to be 199.198.197.160–175 and a mask of 255.255.255.240 (or a 28-bit mask), with 161 being assigned to the Ethernet port. This leaves 162–174 as effective host addresses, satisfying the requirement for 10 users.

The Frame Relay links are numbered with the address range 199.198.197.176–183 and a mask of 255.255.255.248 (or a 29-bit host mask). Because this example is a multipoint Frame Relay interface, all IP addresses should be on the same subnet.

Answer to Scenario 2

1 Figure 10-29 is one possible solution for scenario 2. There are other ways of meeting the company's requirements. This is only a recommended solution that meets the requirements placed on the CCDP.

Figure 10-29 *Suggested Solution for Scenario 2*

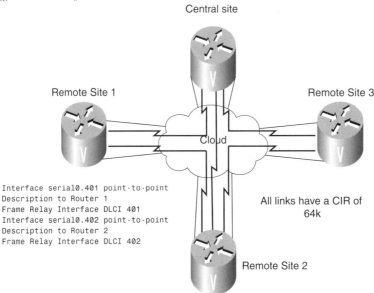

```
Interface serial0.401 point-to-point
Description to Router 1
Frame Relay Interface DLCI 401
Interface serial0.402 point-to-point
Description to Router 2
Frame Relay Interface DLCI 402
```

The requirements for any-to-any connectivity for voice purposes can be met with a full-mesh solution. This solution has a direct PVC from every site to every site.

WARNING   These PVCs are for voice only! In most designs like this, separate PVCs are used for data, which could double your cost.

If you use the full-mesh formula for calculating how many links are in the network, the total is 6.

Each link has a CIR of 64 K, which guarantees that at least 64 K of bandwidth will be available for the voice calls.

Number scheme solution:

From Router 1, the local DLCIs are 104, 102, and 103. Let's look at an example:

```
Interface serial0.104
Description to Router 4
Frame Relay Interface DLCI 104
Interface serial0.102
Description to Router 2
Frame Relay Interface DLCI 102

Interface serial0.103
Description to Router 3
Frame Relay Interface DLCI 103
```

The significance of the 1 is that you start with Router 1. The significance of the 0 is that the Frame Relay network (represented by the cloud) is the 0. The 4 represents the router that the DLCI is going to. You simply repeat this from router to router.

Let's look at Router 4:

```
Interface serial0.401
Description to Router 1
Frame Relay Interface DLCI 401
Interface serial0.402
Description to Router 2
Frame Relay Interface DLCI 402

Interface serial0.403
Description to Router 3
Frame Relay Interface DLCI 403
```

As you can see, the provider has connected these DLCIs in the provider network with the Frame Relay switches. For example, DLCI 104 is connected to 401 in the Frame Relay network. See Figure 10-29.

This is not the only way this scheme could be accomplished. If you figured out a solution to this scenario, you are on your way to understanding and designing Frame Relay.

Answer to Scenario 3

1 There are other ways of meeting the company's requirements. This is only a recommended solution that meets the requirements placed on the CCDP.

Figure 10-30 depicts a recommended solution. There are four remote sites. Each router has a connection to two different service providers. This is common in redundant Frame Relay networks and is called a *hierarchical mesh*. Let's take a look at what happens from Router A's standpoint. If Router A loses a serial link from S0, all traffic will be directed over S1 through Service Provider B. The same thing would happen with Routers B, C, and D. If a problem developed in one of the service provider networks and the whole Frame

Relay network became unavailable, the other service provider should remain unaffected, and traffic should route through there. Load balancing would be a good idea in the configuration specified in the figure, so choose your routing protocol wisely.

Figure 10-30 *Suggested Solution for Scenario 3*

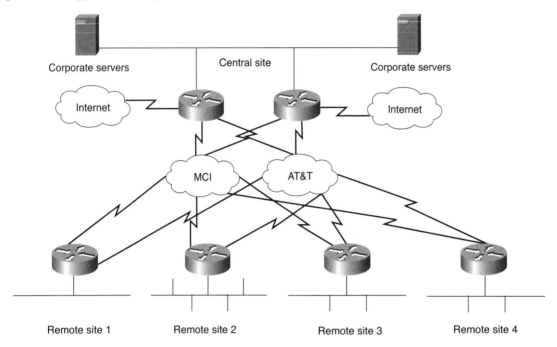

The requirement that the Internet can be reached will be met, because if one of the central sites becomes unavailable, traffic will travel through the other central site.

For the Internet providers, you also can use two different ones, as shown in the figure, with Internet connections from both central site routers. If Provider A has a problem, traffic can flow through the other provider. These decisions are determined by availability concerns.

This chapter covers the following topics you will need to master as a CCDP:

- **Remote access issues**—This section discusses analog and ISDN services, as well as the common methods of access remote node and remote control.

- **Point-to-Point Protocol (PPP)**—This is the most popular protocol used for remote access. This section discusses some of the features that are available for this protocol.

- **Equipment**—Many options are available for routers and remote access servers. This section describes where remote access equipment fits into a network design, as well as other Cisco equipment.

CHAPTER 11

Remote Access

The CCDP exam requires you to have an in-depth understanding of remote access technology. Remote access is essential to any network today, when there are more ways to access a network than ever before. The CCDP candidate must constantly keep up with new technology in this area but stay familiar with older technologies as well.

This chapter discusses older technologies, including ISDN. Newer technologies such as cable and DSL will be briefly mentioned, and some of the Cisco features used with ISDN, including IP unnumbered, will be discussed.

How to Best Use This Chapter

By following these steps, you can make better use of your study time:

- Keep your notes and the answers for all your work with this book in one place for easy reference.

- Take the "Do I Know This Already?" quiz and write down your answers. Studies show that retention is significantly increased through writing down facts and concepts, even if you never look at the information again.

- Use the diagram shown in Figure 11-1 to guide you to the next step.

Figure 11-1 *How to Best Use this Chapter*

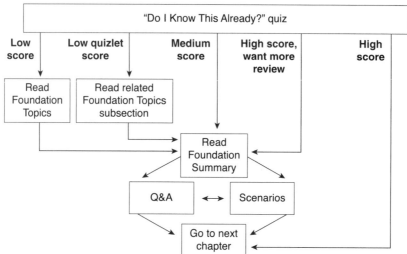

If you skip to the Foundation Summary, Q&A, and Scenarios sections and have trouble with the material there, you should go back to the Foundation Topics section.

"Do I Know This Already?" Quiz

The purpose of the "Do I Know This Already?" quiz is to help you decide which parts of this chapter to use. If you already intend to read the entire chapter, you do not necessarily need to answer these questions now.

This 15-question quiz helps you choose how to spend your limited study time. The quiz is divided into three smaller "quizlets" that help you select the sections of the chapter on which to focus. Figure 11-1 outlines suggestions on how to spend your time in this chapter. Use Table 11-1 to record your score.

Table 11-1 *Score Sheet for Quiz and Quizlets*

Quizlet Number	Foundation Topics Section Covering These Questions	Questions	Score
1	Remote access issues	1–5	
2	PPP	6–10	
3	Equipment	11–15	

1 Does IPX use the unnumbered feature?

_____

_____

_____

2 Is IP unnumbered a standard in the industry?

_____

_____

_____

3 Can you use IP unnumbered on a Frame Relay interface?

_____

_____

_____

4 Is a T1 full duplex or half duplex?

_____

_____

_____

5 What are the pinouts of a T1 interface used with an RJ-45 jack?

_____

_____

_____

6 Is it possible to bundle four ISDN BRI connections to one logical channel (bundle) using multilink PPP?

_____

_____

_____

7 Against what type of attack does CHAP provide protection?

_____

_____

_____

8 Does MLPPP affect routing tables?

_____

_____

_____

9 Name three dialer interfaces that MLPPP supports.

_____

_____

_____

10 What remote access protocol was used prior to PPP?

_____

_____

_____

11 Which series of router provides for cable modem access?

_____

_____

_____

12 What series of router can share modular cards with the 1600, 2600, and 3600 routers?

_____

_____

_____

13 Which remote access server in the 5000 series supports a T3 connection?

_____

_____

_____

14 Which processor do the 2600 and 3600 routers use?

_____

_____

_____

15 What is the Stack Group Bidding protocol?

_____

_____

_____

The answers to the "Do I Know This Already?" quiz are found in Appendix A. The suggested choices for your next step are as follows:

- **6 or less overall score**—Read the chapter. This includes the "Foundation Topics," "Foundation Summary," and "Q&A" sections, as well as the scenarios at the end of the chapter.

- **2 or less on any quizlet**—Review the subsection(s) of the "Foundation Topics" part of this chapter based on Table 11-1. Then move into the "Foundation Summary," the "Q&A" section, and the scenarios at the end of the chapter.

- **7, 8, or 9 overall score**—Begin with the "Foundation Summary" section and then go to the "Q&A" section and scenarios at the end of the chapter.

- **10 or more overall score**—If you want more review on these topics, skip to the "Foundation Summary" section, and then go to the "Q&A" section and scenarios at the end of the chapter. Otherwise, move to the next chapter.

Foundation Topics

Remote access design is becoming more and more popular on the CCDP test. This chapter focuses on analog and ISDN access, along with a discussion of the most popular remote access protocol, PPP. Finally, selecting equipment to be deployed at branch offices, regional offices, and central sites is always important.

Remote access security is discussed in Chapter 15.

Remote Access Issues

The network architect has to think about connecting remote users in a number of ways. There are increasing numbers of remote users, whether they are end users, sales force, support staff, or vice presidents. There are small office/home office (SOHO) connections for the employee who needs to work from home. There are also mobile users who travel worldwide and need to access corporate resources.

There are at least five major concerns to address when designing for remote access:

- **Bandwidth**—Users today need speed. The various methods to obtain it are discussed in this chapter.

- **Cost**—Price drives everything!

- **Distance from the office**—Distance can be a factor when determining the solution for SOHO with sensitive media such as ISDN and DSL.

- **Availability**—Dependability is a must with remote access.

- **Security**—With more and more e-commerce transactions being performed, security is more important today than ever.

Accessing a corporate site over the Internet is a viable option today. With the appropriate Internet access security features enabled, this form of access is very convenient for mobile users who are on the move.

When you're doing remote access, you want to do it right up front. When companies rush things and end up with something that does not scale or is ineffective, it causes a lot of headaches and more money the second time around. Do it right the first time!

Setting realistic expectations is important also. One of the biggest costs is doing it over. In other words, don't expect to do video over dialup links. If your users are expecting that, they will be disappointed when they can't. If a customer wants to do multicast over a dialup link, you need to make sure they understand the consequences or persuade them to look at another option.

Analog Review

Most everyone is familiar with dialing into their ISP from home to connect to corporate resources or to browse the Internet. Today, modem speeds can reach 56 K, but as recently as 1994, modem speeds reached only 2.4 K or 9.6 K.

Most users connect over the Public Switched Telephone Network (PSTN). Transmitting data over the PSTN has some issues. Computer data must be converted from digital to analog form by the modem, transmitted over the PSTN, and then converted back to digital by the modem on the receiving end. The PSTN was designed for the transmission of analog voice messages, not digital messages. Many of the telephone lines that exist today were installed in the 1960s, which can mean poor transmission quality.

With the price of leased lines coming down, companies do not connect their sites via modems very often anymore. However, everything has its place. Analog modems fit into the picture as backup links very well, as shown in Figure 11-2.

Figure 11-2   *An Analog Backup Line*

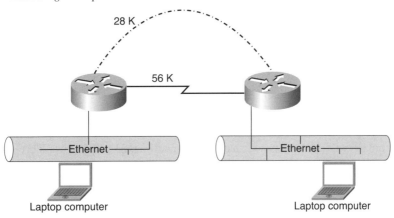

Telephone companies offer two different types of links between sites over the telephone network—leased lines and dialup lines:

- Leased lines are more economical for transmitting large amounts of data over a long period of time, and they generally are available 24 hours a day, seven days a week.

- Dialup lines are used as a form of redundancy in the event of a leased line failure.

Leased lines can be either two- or four-wire. With a two-wire link, transmit and receive are on the same pair of wires, or half duplex. With a four-wire link, each pair of wires is dedicated to one direction of data flow, or full duplex. Most are four-wire. Figure 11-3 shows a four-wire T1 circuit using pins 1 and 2 for transmit and pins 4 and 5 for receive. Pins 3, 6, 7, and 8 are not used.

Figure 11-3 also shows a 64 K pinout of 1, 2, 7, and 8. Again, 1 and 2 are for transmit, with 4 and 5 for receive.

Figure 11-3 *Pinouts T1/64 K*

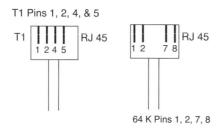

Analog modems are usually used in an emergency, such as when a company is relocating part or all of its business. The company might plan and expect a frame relay or dedicated connection at a certain date, but for one reason or another, the phone company can't deliver the circuit, and the company is left to establish some kind of temporary connection, usually analog, until the data circuit is installed. Analog modems might also be used for the following:

- Intermittent faults or possibly when testing the main connection

- When the network is down

- Intermittent retrieval of data (e-mail)

TIP   When using an external modem with a router, you need an EIA/TIA-232 DTE serial transition cable to connect the modem to the router's serial interface. Another method would be to use the auxiliary port on the router, or multiple auxiliary ports in a bundled situation.

CCDP candidates must be careful when using analog modems for backup. For example, would you really want to back up a 1.544 circuit with a 56 K modem? No. But you could possibly bundle several modems together to guarantee a bandwidth of 112 K, as shown in Figure 11-4, which might be enough to at least get critical information through until service is restored. You could also prioritize traffic in that situation so that only critical data gets through and noncritical traffic does not consume the 112 K link.

Figure 11-4   *Analog Bundled Backup*

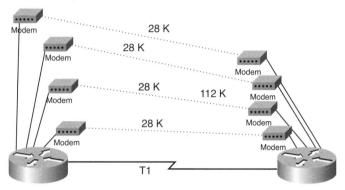

TIP   Always make sure there is enough bandwidth capacity for backup circuits.

ISDN Overview

One of the other alternatives to analog dialup for accessing corporate networks or providing for redundancy is ISDN (Integrated Services Digital Network). ISDN supports two different types of interfaces—Basic Rate Interface and Primary Rate Interface:

- **Basic Rate Interface (BRI)**—The BRI is made up of two bearer channels and one delta channel. This is written as 2B+D. The BRI delta channel operates at 16 Kbps, and the bearer channels each operate at 64 Kbps to the local central office. The total user data rate on the BRI is 128 Kbps. (As mentioned in Chapter 10, you could use 9.6 Kbps of the delta channel for X.25 data.)

- **Primary Rate Interface (PRI)**—The PRI is made up of 23 bearer channels and one delta channel (64 k) in the United States and Japan, usually terminated into an RJ-45. The total user data rate on the PRI is approximately 1472 K.

ISDN is a digital network standard and can provide a wide range of user services. ISDN is also a great backup technology with a very fast circuit setup time. Costs vary throughout the world. Developed in the 1960s, ISDN never had the success that was predicted due to inconsistent switch configurations used by the telephone companies. Had a simpler standard been put into place, it might have had much more success. Nevertheless, ISDN is still widely available and is used by companies (and SOHO users as well) worldwide. Its main drawback is that it is considered difficult to configure. Another drawback is cost. Throughout the United States, each regional Bell operating company charged different rates for the same service, adding more confusion to this digital service. Due to its ability to call multiple sites upon failure, it is a versatile technology. ISDN can offer a maximum bit rate of about 2 Mbps in Europe or about 1.5 Mbps in the USA and Japan.

ISDN services are targeted at both businesses and private residential users. Residential users might occasionally use ISDN for videoconferencing or possibly teleconferencing in a company meeting. Although even 128 K would be a slight throughput problem for video, 384 K or bundling six 64 K bearer channels together would provide much better-quality video.

ISDN can allocate transmission bandwidth on a demand basis, which means that it suits the bandwidth to the particular data being transmitted. A computer network often transmits data in irregular bursts.

In addition to providing a suitable transmission medium for very different services, ISDN guarantees a specific quality of service. It guarantees fast connection setup, low bit-error rates, and short end-to-end delays between messages.

Common services that use ISDN are graphics and voice, which might require up to 128 Kbps (two B channels), as compared to a text transfer, which might need as little as 4.8 Kbps.

NOTE   The CCITT/ITU-T is the body primarily responsible for producing international ISDN standards.

ISDN Terminology

It's important to review ISDN terminology because it's often the subject of test material.

ISDN has what are called function and reference points. Terminal Endpoint Identifiers (TEIs) are used to identify the equipment. Terminal equipment (TE) refers to the end-user devices—the equipment actually used by the customer. Examples of TE devices are ISDN-capable workstations, routers, or ISDN telephones.

Functions are basically representations of hardware components:

- **TE1**—A device that has an ISDN component built into it, such as an ISDN external modem.

- **TE2**—A device without an ISDN component, such as a laptop.

- **TA**—A terminal adapter, which converts computer electrical signals into ISDN signals. An example is an ISDN internal modem in a PC.

- **NT1**—The termination point for the two-wire local loop. This device also converts the signals from the two-wire local loop to four-wire ISDN.

- **NT2**—Network termination equipment type 2 (NT2). These are also called ISDN switches or multiplexers. Examples of NT2 devices include PBXs, Madge ISDN switches, and the Adtran 800 switch.

Four ISDN reference points define communication between the different hardware devices. They are known as R, S, T, and U reference points:

- **R**—Represents a device that has no ISDN capability. It defines the interface between a TE2 and a TA. An example is a PC without any ISDN capability or a Cisco 2500 series router without any ISDN ports.

- **S**—Defines the reference points between user terminals and an NT2. An example is an ISDN telephone that has a connection to a digital PBX.

- **T**—Represents the interface between NT1 and NT2 devices. An example is the PBX connection to the NT1.

- **U**—Defines the two-wire interface between the NT1 and the PSTN.

In Figure 11-5, notice the NT2 device, a PBX switch. The ISDN phone attempts to seize an outside line and contacts the PBX switch. The PBX switch then checks to see if it can accommodate the ISDN phone and access one of the ISDN channels from the central office. The ISDN central office is often called the *local exchange carrier*, or LEC.

Figure 11-5   *Functions and Reference Types*

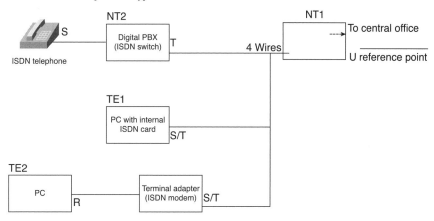

Notice that, in the other examples, the S/T is collapsed. This is because there is no need for a PBX or ISDN switch in those situations.

NOTE   In the absence of an NT2 or PBX device, the user network interface is called the S/T reference point.

Figure 11-5 shows several devices all accessing an ISDN channel from the central office. There the PC is using the R interface to access an ISDN channel from the central office. It has a terminal adapter or ISDN modem connected to its serial port on the PC.

The terminal adapter is connected to the NT1 device, which provides the access to the channel. Some of the low-end routers do have NT1 built into them; the routers would have to be sold with the U interface, which designates an internal NT1.

ISDN Basic Rate Interface (BRI)

ISDN uses time division multiplexing (TDM) to provide several logical channels on a single physical wire. Under TDM, each logical channel is given exclusive use of the wire for a duration of time. Think of three lanes of cars being squeezed into one lane. All the cars still get to their destination, but they get there more slowly. The channels are swapped in and out of the wire, which is sort of a weaving method. ISDN access interfaces comprise a D channel for signaling and a number of B channels for user services.

- The D channel operates at 16 Kbps and carries signaling information between the user and the network using the LAPD protocol.

- The B channel is 64 K to the central office and carries user services, including voice, video, and data signals.

NOTE   ISDN B channels are guaranteed only 64 K between the local site and the central office.

Because some central offices use robbed bit signaling, ISDN is not guaranteed to be 64 K between the central offices and might actually be 56 K.

ISDN Primary Rate Interface (PRI)

There are a number of different configurations of the PRI. In the United States and Japan, the PRI consists of 23 to 64 K channels and one shared signaling channel.

In a PRI, the D channel operates at 64 Kbps, in contrast to the BRI, where it operates at 16 Kbps. The North American PRI is based on the T1 carrier. It operates at a total bit rate of 1.544 Mbps, of which 1.536 Mbps is user data. A 30B+D PRI is based on the E1 carrier. It operates at 2.048 Mbps, of which 1.984 Mbps is user data.

Because the PRI contains more channels than individual devices would need, it is typically used for handling switching functions. For example, it might be used in a PBX or to connect a host computer to remote terminals.

A common use of ISDN PRIs is connecting multiple remote sites using ISDN BRI ports to a central site with a PRI port. At the central site, common ISDN equipment would be a Cisco 4000, 7000, or maybe an AS5300, as shown in Figure 11-6.

Figure 11-6 shows three remote sites connecting to the central site. All the remotes use two 64 K BRIs.

Figure 11-6   *Remote Sites*

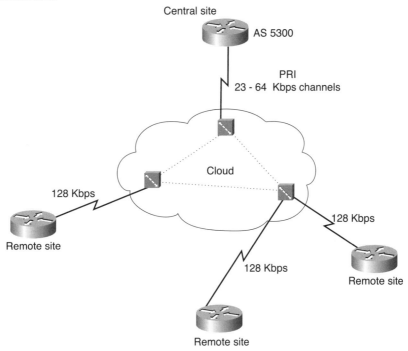

NOTE   New VIP cards are available that have eight RJ-45 ports. These ports can be used as either ISDN PRI ports or serial T1 ports.

IP Unnumbered

The Cisco feature IP unnumbered is mentioned here because it goes hand-in-hand with ISDN. It seems this feature is often misunderstood on many networks, so that is why it will be discussed here in detail. It is not a standard, so you could not have a Cisco router talk to another vendor router using unnumbered interfaces. Many companies use IP unnumbered to conserve address space, but there are other benefits as well.

First, it is important to talk about the basic mechanics of IP unnumbered. For any point-to-point serial link or point-to-point subinterface, IP unnumbered lets you borrow the address of a LAN interface to use as a source address for routing updates and packets from that interface. In Figure 11-7, a ping is sent from Host Nick to Host Erik. On Cisco Router A, every IP network interface not residing on a common "wire" must belong to a unique subnet. Based on network information contained in the IP routing table on Router A, the network 1.1.1.0 is not directly attached to Router A. It can be reached by forwarding a packet to a next-hop address obtained from the IP routing table—in this case, 1.1.1.1.

Figure 11-7   *IP Unnumbered*

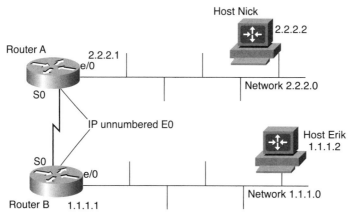

Figure 11-7 assumes that there is a routing protocol between the two routers. When the final destination network is on an interface directly attached to the destination Router B, the packet can simply be delivered to the end host Erik.

Let's take a look at what happens under the hood. Router B receives an update from Router A. Normally Router B would use the source address of the routing update as the next hop, because it is directly connected to the router sending the update. In this case, Router A has borrowed 2.2.2.1 as its address for the source update. Instead of simply entering a next-hop address based on the source address of the update, Router B enters the IP routes learned on the IP unnumbered interface into the routing table as interface routes:

```
Router A#
SH IP ROUTE
Network 2.2.2.0 learned via Interface S0
```

The invalid next-hop address is bypassed in favor of interface S0, from which you received the update. Because of this, IP unnumbered only makes sense for point-to-point links. The attraction is saving subnet addresses.

The trade-off with this feature is that it is a little more difficult to troubleshoot network problems with the unnumbered feature. You don't have a way to ping or monitor the interface through SNMP because the interface basically uses another interface's IP address.

Loopback interfaces are popular with IP unnumbered. When using a real interface, such as Ethernet, for your unnumbered configuration, if the Ethernet interface goes down, you lose the whole connection between the routers. The loopback interface will always stay up (even when your Ethernet is down), except when your router is powered off.

TIP   When designing addressing for networks, design your loopback interfaces from the start to fit into summarization schemes and so on. Then, you can use them for peer connections, unnumbered interfaces, router IDs, and so on.

IP Unnumbered and ISDN

Normally, when an ISDN call is placed, an address is associated to the BRI port. For example, in Figure 11-8, Router A calls Router B with ISDN. Address 1.1.1.1 on Router A calls Router B at address 1.1.1.2. This works fine because they are on the same subnet.

Figure 11-8   *ISDN Call*

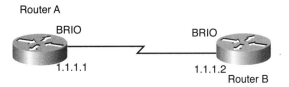

Now take a look at Figure 11-9, where Router A has address 1.1.1.1.

Figure 11-9   *ISDN Call: A Second Look*

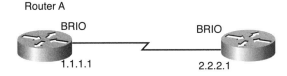

Calling Router B with address 2.2.2.1 on the ISDN interface will not work because the addresses are on different subnets. Data will not be able to be exchanged between routers.

Now look at Figure 11-10. IP unnumbered has been brought into the picture. Define the BRI port with the command **ip unnumbered Ethernet 0,** which uses the IP address of the Ethernet port for the BRI interface as the source. Because there are unnumbered interfaces, this will work as soon as the ISDN link is brought up. The routers exchange routing updates, and Router A puts in the routing table "to get to net 1.1.1.0, go out interface BRI0." Router B installs in its routing table "to get to network 2.2.2.0, go out interface BRI0."

Figure 11-10 *IP Unnumbered*

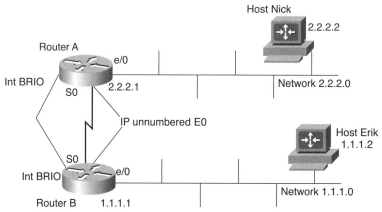

This unnumbered feature adds a huge advantage to backup capabilities. It means that you can configure the ISDN routers to call different sites. Normally, IP addresses would be assigned to these interfaces, preventing the ISDN router from calling another router that might be in a different subnet. The unnumbered feature removes that restriction. In Figure 11-11, Router Nashville backs up the serial link with ISDN to reach headquarters in Washington, D.C., via the Atlanta regional office router. If the Atlanta regional router becomes unavailable, when the Nashville router dials the Atlanta office, there is no response. Using the unnumbered feature, first configure Nashville to dial into Atlanta. If there is no response, you can configure a second dial map statement to dial into Dallas. In this situation, it is a good idea to use a routing protocol that supports discontiguous subnets—preferably EIGRP. OSPF supports discontiguous subnets, but the configuration of areas could be rather difficult to design and maintain.

NOTE   AppleTalk and IPX do not use the unnumbered feature.

Figure 11-11 *ISDN Backup Using the Unnumbered Feature*

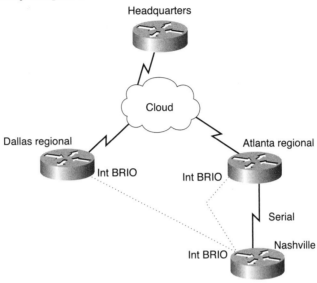

Remote LAN Access

Two methods of remote LAN access, remote control and remote node, are discussed in this section.

Remote Control

A typical example of remote-control LAN access is the popular program PC Anywhere. With this program, an engineer can dial into a PC at headquarters and assume control over the PC as if they were actually sitting at the PC at headquarters. With this type of remote access, security is a natural concern because the PC at headquarters must be left on at all times to be able to accept calls.

Another drawback of remote-control LAN access is the overhead required when transferring Windows images across the dialup connection. In Figure 11-12, the user dials into the corporate PC and assumes control of the desktop.

Figure 11-12 *Remote Control*

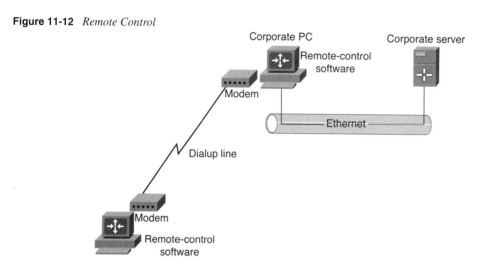

Remote Node

Remote-node LAN access seems to be more popular than remote-control LAN access. In this type of setup, shown in Figure 11-13, the remote node appears to be a network node on the LAN. The only hardware needed is an access device, and no special programs need to be run on the PC. The user dials into the access server, which is connected to the corporate Ethernet segment. This method usually involves a logon account from corporate. Disk drive mappings are typically provided upon logon to the network. After logging in, the user can use the Windows Explorer program to map disk drive letters to server locations, provided that the proper permissions have been created for the user. More admin overhead is required than with remote-control LAN access because you have to support the remote user with personnel at corporate headquarters.

Figure 11-13 *Remote Node*

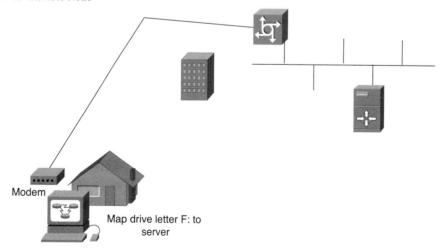

PPP

PPP (Point-to-Point Protocol) is by far the most popular remote connectivity protocol because it supports authentication with Challenge Handshake Authentication Protocol (CHAP) and Password Authentication Protocol (PAP).

PPP was created as a solution to remote access connectivity problems. It was not the first method for transmitting datagrams over serial point-to-point links, though—that was SLIP (Serial Line Internet Protocol). SLIP has many shortcomings that PPP addresses. PPP provides router-to-router and host-to-network connections over both synchronous and asynchronous circuits. Other PPP duties include assignment and network protocol multiplexing, link configuration, link quality testing, error detection, data compression, and address negotiation. PPP also supports IPX and DECnet, whereas SLIP supports only IP packets.

The only absolute requirement imposed by PPP is the provision of a duplex circuit that can operate in either asynchronous or synchronous bit-serial mode. PPP physical connections operate across any DTE/DCE interface.

PPP transmits datagrams over serial point-to-point links. There are three components—LCP, HDLC, and network control protocols:

- **LCP (Link Control Protocol)**—LCP initiates and performs a handshake function that establishes the connection, as shown in Figure 11-14.

Figure 11-14 *Link Control Protocol*

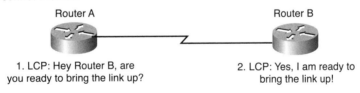

Router A   Router B

1. LCP: Hey Router B, are you ready to bring the link up?

2. LCP: Yes, I am ready to bring the link up!

3. Okay, let's do it!

- **HDLC (High-Level Data Link Control)**—PPP uses HDLC to encapsulate datagrams over a point-to-point link.

- **Network Control Protocols**—These initiate and perform a handshake function at Layer 3, configuring the link for different network protocols, as shown in Figure 11-15.

Figure 11-15 *Network Control Protocols*

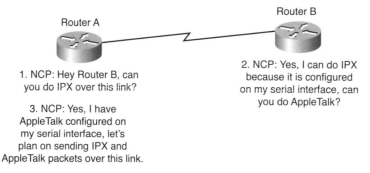

Router A

Router B

1. NCP: Hey Router B, can
you do IPX over this link?

2. NCP: Yes, I can do IPX
because it is configured
on my serial interface, can
you do AppleTalk?

3. NCP: Yes, I have
AppleTalk configured on
my serial interface, let's
plan on sending IPX and
AppleTalk packets over this link.

LCP

To establish communication over a serial link, the originating station first sends LCP frames at Layer 2 to configure and test the link. Two routers must agree to "bring the link up." This is a handshake that must happen before you can ever get to the PPP negotiation process, which happens between Layer 2 and Layer 3.

The basic mechanics of LCP are that it goes through three different phases:

1   Establish the link and negotiate the configuration.

2   Determine link quality.

3   After a successful handshake and agreement at Layer 2, perform negotiation at the network layer.

Before any packets can be transferred between two devices, LCP must establish a connection. Using what is called a configuration acknowledgment frame, LCP negotiates configuration parameters. After LCP does this and determines the link quality, network-layer protocols can be brought up and taken down at any time. If a link is closed by LCP, the network-layer protocols are informed so that they can take appropriate action.

After the link has been established, the originating PPP device sends NCP frames to figure out which network protocols are to be used over the link. When this decision is made, packets from the chosen network-layer protocol can be sent over the link. LCP retries allow a reestablishment of the connection if it should fail. This reestablishment allows for missed or incorrect negotiation.

HDLC Versus LAPB

Two other methods of encapsulation at Layer 2 are HDLC and LAPB. HDLC is Cisco's proprietary protocol. It assumes a point-to-point link, developed from IBM's HDLC.

The difference between Cisco and IBM HDLC is that the IBM version can carry only one protocol, TCP/IP. Cisco's modified version can carry multiprotocol traffic, even at the same time.

No error recovery is available with Cisco HDLC. If there's an error, the packet is dropped. As mentioned in Chapter 10, when an error occurs with LAPB encapsulation, the packet is retransmitted. The extra error recovery overhead in LAPB decreases performance, so you should use LAPB only on lines that are prone to errors.

Multilink PPP (MLPPP)

MLPPP was first introduced in Cisco IOS Release 11.0(3) and is referenced by RFC 1990 (replacing RFC 1717). It specifies multivendor interoperability. MLPPP is a data-link protocol. It sits between PPP and the Network Control Protocol. The sending peer receives protocol data units (PDUs) from the network control layer above it.

MLPPP converts the PDUs into packets for transmission by adding addressing information and MLPPP headers.

MLPPP also lets you aggregate the bandwidth across multiple interfaces, usually ISDN interfaces. For example, a 64 K BRI can combine with a 64 K serial link, totaling 128 K of bandwidth into one logical pipe. For example, if a customer needed more bandwidth but did not want to affect the existing network, this method would be a solution. Design engineers can increase bandwidth without affecting routing tables on the network. This means that network designers can use MLPPP to simplify fault management and build redundancy into the network without affecting users. Therefore, it reduces the effort and cost of maintaining a network.

MLPPP provides load balancing over dialer interfaces, including

- ISDN interfaces
- Synchronous interfaces
- Asynchronous interfaces

Before the introduction of MLPPP, two or more ISDN B channels could not be used in a standardized way while ensuring sequencing. MLPPP solves several of the problems associated with load balancing across multiple serial links.

Bundles

During LCP negotiation, a router can indicate to another router that it can combine multiple physical links into what is known as a bundle. MLPPP uses packet sequencing and load calculation to negotiate the maximum received reconstructed unit (MRRU) option during the PPP LCP negotiation. The MRRU option is used to negotiate the size of information fields in reassembled packets. This negotiation indicates that MLPPP is controlled by the addition of a

2-, 4-, or 8-byte sequencing header in the PPP frame. The header indicates the sequencing of the fragments. The routers must be able to receive and reconstruct upper-layer protocol data units (PDUs). The routers must also be able to receive PDUs of an agreed-upon size. Transmission channels in a bundle do not need to be the same type. Asynchronous and synchronous links can be used to simultaneously transmit fragments of one datagram.

Figure 11-16 shows a serial link with 64 Kbps of bandwidth, an ISDN B channel with 64 Kbps, and a dialup link of 9.6 Kbps. MLPPP bundles the three channels for a total bandwidth of 137 K.

Figure 11-16 *MLPPP-1*

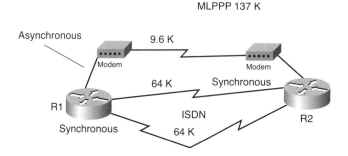

MLPPP is also interoperable with routers that conform to RFC 1990. It is recommended for use with applications in which bandwidth requirements are dynamic.

For example, it would be recommended for use with remote LAN access applications used by telecommuters or SOHO environments. Transmission channels in a bundle do not need to be the same type. Asynchronous and synchronous interfaces can be used to simultaneously transmit fragments of one datagram, as illustrated in Figure 11-16. PPP is the standard networking protocol for connecting WAN links. PPP's major disadvantage, however, is that it can handle only one physical link at a time, unlike MLPPP.

Using MLPPP, each end system has access to the combined bandwidth of all the links in the bundle. Packets generated by one system can be sent across any of the links to the remote address, which prevents delays in transmission and provides faster data throughput.

MLPPP can split packets and send the fragments simultaneously down separate links to the same remote address. This is known as *packet fragmentation*. Each fragment negotiates the fastest route to the remote address. Packet fragmentation can mean that the fragments arrive at the remote address out of sequence. MLPPP can reconfigure the packets into the correct sequence.

MLPPP has the following features in common with PPP:

- It can negotiate configuration options.

- It can support a variety of different network layer protocols.

- It can include options such as authentication and compression.

MLPPP is the first protocol to fully exploit multichannel services.

For example, you could use MLPPP to combine a Frame Relay circuit with one or more ISDN channels. Data from one system can travel across several channels at once to reach the destination address, as depicted in Figure 11-17.

Figure 11-17 *MLPPP-2*

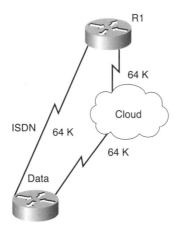

Multichassis MLPPP (MMP)

Cisco equipment also supports multichassis MLPPP (MMP). When an ISDN BRI interface connects to an ISP, the first BRI, BRI:0, might connect to an AS5300, such as access server A. The second BRI on the interface, BRI:1, might actually connect to access server B. There needs to be some form of communication between the access servers to synchronize the traffic. That is done with the Stack Group Bidding protocol. One of the access servers needs to be in control of who will bind the links together. This is done through a bidding process; the parameters are configured on the access server. An example of this is shown in Figure 11-18.

Figure 11-18 *MMP*

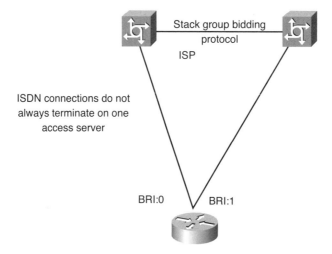

To run MPP, connect a stack of access servers with a switch. In Figure 11-18, the remote site dials into the ISP. The ISP receives the calls, but two different access servers receive them. One of the access servers needs to bind the two channels as a 128 Kbps circuit to the remote site, which is accomplished via the Stack Group Bidding process. MMP protocol goes into a bidding process.

Remote User Access Equipment

One of the hardest tasks for a CCDP is determining which equipment to recommend for a solution. It's difficult to remember all the features of a particular router, so finding the best router for your purposes is potentially very difficult. To help you find a suitable router from its product range, Cisco has designed a selection tool at its Web site:

```
http://www.cisco.com/public/products_prod.shtml
```

To build a remote access network, you need to select the proper routing equipment for each site. You also need to identify what additional interface equipment might be required—for example, modems, NT1s, or CSU/DSU devices. There are various user categories with remote access equipment. There is the occasional telecommuter or SOHO type of access. And, of course, there's the mobile user, who travels a lot. There's also equipment for large-scale access using the AS5000 series.

The router you select for your WAN connection must supply the interfaces that will be able to meet the customer's needs. There are many types of interfaces on Cisco routers. Let's review a few of the WAN interfaces:

- **Asynchronous serial**—Typically used with modems. Supports asynchronous dialup connections.

- **Synchronous serial**—Supports leased lines, Frame Relay, HDLC, and X.25.

- **BRI**—Supports ISDN connections.

- **Channelized T1 and E1**—Support leased lines, dialup, ISDN PRI, and Frame Relay.

- **T3 or E3**—T3 and E3 ports provide direct connectivity to T3 lines for full duplex communications at the DS3 rate of 44.736 MHz.

No discussion about remote access would be complete without addressing the various equipment choices available to a CCDP. Let's start with the smaller access routers and work our way up to the larger-capacity routers.

BRI Routers

The Cisco 1003, Cisco 2503, Cisco 2504, Cisco 2516, and Cisco 2517 products deliver single-port ISDN BRI service. The Cisco 4000 series with one BRI network processor module (NPM) delivers either four or eight BRI ports.

NOTE	End of life for the 4000 series has been announced. This will occur roughly around the end of 2003, at which point Cisco will no longer provide support for this device.
	The end of life for the 4500 series was also recently announced. This will occur around 2005. The CCDP needs to maintain an up-to-date record of devices and how long they can be of value to a company.

PRI Routers

For PRI services, the Cisco 4000 series offers one PRI per NPM, and the Cisco 7000 series offers up to eight PRIs per Versatile Interface Processor (VIP). Those same eight PRI ports (RJ-45) can actually be converted to serial ports with the 12.x IOS.

Telecommuter Routers

Cisco provides a choice of telecommuter site equipment, including the 700, 800, 900, 1000, and 1600 series. The telecommuter site needs a router that supports an ISDN BRI connection to an ISDN network. It must also support an Ethernet connection. Many Cisco routers meet both these requirements. BRI modules and BRI WAN interface cards have either a BRI S/T or BRI U interface. An S/T interface requires an external NT1 in the United States and Japan. A U interface has a built-in NT1. A straight-through patch cable (RJ-45-to-RJ-45 cable), supplied by the ISDN service provider, is used to connect the ISDN BRI interface to the ISDN network.

- The Cisco 700 series, which is designed for telecommuters, is an inexpensive, easy-to-manage, multiprotocol ISDN router. Originally created by a company called Combinet, it has a different IOS than most other routers. Because it supports standards, it can connect to any network that supports ISDN and IP/IPX routing.

- The Cisco 800 series routers are Cisco's cheapest routers that operate using the regular Cisco IOS software. The 800 series is popular as ISDN access routers because it offers secure, manageable, high-performance solutions for Internet and corporate LAN access. This series is usually used by SOHOs and telecommuters.

- The Cisco 900 series comes in several varieties:

    — The Cisco UBR900 series products are commonly referred to as *cable modems*. They are designed to let cable companies expand their service to customers.

    — The Cisco UBR924 cable access router is an integrated cable modem and Cisco IOS router all in one box. It offers Voice-over-IP (VoIP) and Virtual Private Networks (VPNs).

    — Cisco UBR914 cable access routers are finding their way into malls. Malls use these devices to connect to the outside world using the cable broadband network instead of traditional telco-based WAN connectivity options such as leased lines. Then mall management sells bandwidth to the stores in the mall by providing them an Ethernet connection to the network, thereby making a profit.

- The Cisco 1000 series is designed for remote-office networking where there is a need for Cisco IOS software, high performance, and WAN options. This is an early version of the 1600 router. It is hard to upgrade because the internal components, such as memory, are unique and hard to find.

Branch Office Routers

Cisco provides many options when it comes to selecting branch office router equipment. One of the first available routers for branch offices is the popular 2500 series router, known as the "bread and butter" router because it was very successful for Cisco. The 2500 series routers can have fixed configurations with permanent fixed interfaces. There is no way to add WAN interface cards or network modules, as compared to the modular models. If you choose a fixed-configuration router, you receive the router with preset interfaces on the hardware.

Typical branch office router solutions include the following:

- **Cisco 1600 series**

    The Cisco 1600 series has become very popular for small branch offices and small businesses. The Cisco 1600 series routers have functionality similar to the Cisco 1000 series routers, but they also have a slot for a WAN interface card. The cards used by the 1600 are also used by the 1700, 2600, and 3600 series and will be shared in modular branch office products in the future. Ethernet ports can only be 10 Mbps Ethernet, not Fast Ethernet.

A few of the nice features that come with the 1600 include advanced security, including optional integrated firewall, encryption, and VPN software. The 1600 also supports end-to-end quality of service (QoS) and multimedia support. It is considered easy to deploy and manage.

- **Cisco 1700 series**

    The Cisco 1720 modular access router has two modular WAN slots and delivers a flexible, integrated data access solution for branch offices and small- and medium-sized businesses. The 1720 access router can handle 1600, 2600, and 3600 data WAN interface cards. It also features an auto-sensing 10/100 Mbps Fast Ethernet LAN port. (The 100 Mbps Ethernet port will not support ISL.)

    The Cisco 1720 access router delivers multiple capabilities in a modular, integrated platform with two modular slots. With the 1720, customers can build an access solution that offers the flexibility and performance they need to maintain a competitive edge in today's Internet-driven economy.

- **Cisco 1750 router**

    The Cisco 1750 modular access router is very similar to the 1720, offering three modular slots. It delivers investment protection with modularity, features, and performance to support services such as multiservice, voice/data integration, VPNs, and broadband access. It is designed for small branch offices and small- and medium-sized businesses. The Cisco 1750 provides a cost-effective solution that supports a variety of applications.

- **Cisco 2500 series**

    By far one of the most popular Cisco routers, the 2500s have a fixed configuration with many variations of interfaces, with two exceptions—the 2524 and the 2525. These accept up to three WAN modules in plug-in slots. All 2500s except the 2524 and 2525 usually have a minimum of two of the following interfaces:

    — Ethernet

    — Token Ring

    — Synchronous serial

    — Asynchronous serial

    — ISDN BRI

These are "run from Flash" routers and often do not require a lot of RAM because the IOS executes from Flash. Normally the IOS is stored in Flash memory and is loaded from there into RAM memory, where it is executed. However, with the 2500 series, the IOS executes from Flash. Two models have plug-in modules available. The 2524 and 2525 accept up to three WAN modules. The 2500 series uses Motorola processors. Newer models might actually run from RAM. It might be worthwhile to check.

- **Cisco 2600 series**

    The 2600 series modular-based routers extend enterprise-class versatility, integration, and power to branch offices. As new services and applications become available, these routers offer a branch office solution that provides the versatility needed to adapt to changes in network technology. The Cisco 2600 series shares modular interfaces with the Cisco 1600, 1700, and 3600 series, providing a cost-effective solution to meet today's branch office needs for applications, including:

    — Analog and digital dialup access services

    — VPN access

    — Inter-VLAN routing with the 2621 model

    The 2621 comes with 100 Mbps Ethernet interfaces that can be encapsulated with the ISL protocol, allowing the router to route between VLANs.

Regional

The Cisco 4500 and 4700 series access routers are high-performance, modular, central-site routers that support a broad range of LAN and WAN technologies. They are intended for large regional offices that don't need the number of LAN and WAN connections that Cisco's 7200 series provides.

Cisco 7200 routers are very high-performance, modular, regional or central-site routers that support a variety of LAN and WAN technologies using convenient modular plug-in boards. They are the only routers that support ATM CES cards, which provide circuit emulation services. The CES port adapter is an ATM access concentrator on a card that provides the concentration of voice, video, and data traffic over a single ATM trunk.

The 7200 is targeted at large regional offices that might spoke out to branch offices, as depicted in Figure 11-19.

Figure 11-19 *Typical Net*

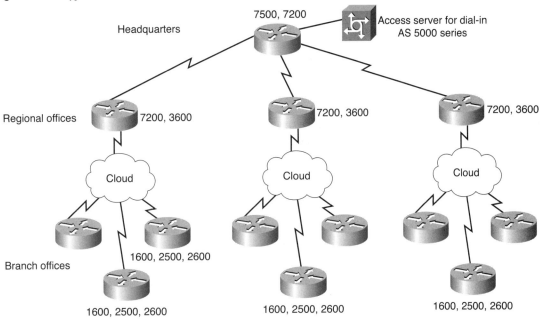

This figure represents equipment found at central, regional, and branch offices. It does not mean that this is the only equipment that can reside there. Rather, it's a practical approach.

Notice that the central site contains the larger routers and access servers, the regional sites contain the larger multiservice routers, and the branch sites contain the lower-end routers.

Central Site (Headquarters)

Central site routers often consist of the 7500 series. 7500 series routers are rather large and come in five-slot, seven-slot, ten-slot, and 13-slot models. The 7576 model is actually two 7500 routers in one cabinet used for redundancy purposes.

7500

The market leader for high-performance routers remains the Cisco 7500 series. This is due to its advanced support for LAN/WAN services, redundancy, reliability, and performance. The 7500 series with the new RSP8 processor can process-switch between 25,000 to 30,000 packets per second, equivalent to the 7200 NPM-400 processor.

One of its key components is called a VIP (Versatile Interface Processor). The VIPs make the 7500 a very scalable device by distributing the workload across multiple cards. Each VIP has its own processor, which is capable of switching IP data packets and providing network services. In addition to performing packet switching, the VIPs also can provide a set of distributed IP network services, including access control, QoS, and traffic accounting (NetFlow).

WARNING NetFlow can be a dangerous thing to do on a core router because it is CPU-intensive. Try to perform NetFlow activities on another device that is not your main router.

NOTE Anything that must be process-switched on the router must still be done at the RSP and is not performed by the VIP. The VIP is used with fast-switching activities.

With the VIPs offloading these IP switching and service functions from the RSP, the RSP can devote all its CPU cycles to handling other essential tasks, such as any process-switched activity.

Since its launch, the Cisco 7500 series router has seen huge improvements in performance and its ability to scale. Besides its larger number of interfaces (port adapters) for both LAN and WAN connectivity, this platform has the latest high-end RSP8 CPU and VIP4 module, which means that it continues to deliver market-leading performance.

The central site is often the home of the AS5000 series access devices. These come in 5100, 5200, 5300, and, recently, the 5800, which offers T3 access capability. Only the noncarrier class access devices are discussed here.

AS5100

The 5100 series access server was quite nice for its time. The Cisco AS5100 is the first access server to offer a versatile data communications platform that combines in one chassis the functions of an access server, a router, and analog and digital modems. Companies that need to centralize processing capabilities for mobile users and telecommuters typically use this device. The AS5100 is optimized for high-speed modem access and is ideally suited for all traditional dialup applications, such as access to a host, e-mail, file transfer, and dial-in access to a local-area network.

AS5200

The newer models are similar to the 5100 but provide a more powerful CPU. The Cisco AS5200 universal access server is a versatile data communications platform that provides the functions of an access server, a router, modems, and terminal adapters (TAs) in a modular chassis.

AS5300

The AS5300 is the next step in Cisco's award-winning AS5x00 family of universal access servers. The big difference in this access server is the ability to terminate ISDN, 56 K analog modem, fax, and VoIP calls on the same interface. The Cisco AS5300 universal access server is intended for telecommunications carriers and other service providers, as well as large enterprises that require consistent high-density connectivity for subscribers and telecommuters connecting to the Internet and corporate intranets. It also acts as a VoIP gateway, which makes it a very attractive choice when migrating customers to VoIP.

AS5800

The 5800 series can connect to the phone company with a channelized T3. (A T3 connection is equal to 28 T1s, or 45 Mbps with HEC-formatted frames, and 40 Mbps with PLCP-formatted frames.)

The Cisco AS5800 provides the highest concentration of modem and ISDN terminations available in a single remote access server product. Typically, this is a carrier class access server, but it can be used within very large companies. Additionally, the Cisco AS5800 Voice Gateway enables highly scalable deployment of toll-quality voice and fax service over packet networks.

Cisco 3600 Series Routers

The Cisco 3600 series is a family of modular, multiservice access platforms for medium- and large-sized offices. The 3600 series multiservice access servers and routers provide a modular solution for dialup and permanent connections over asynchronous, synchronous, and ISDN lines. The 3600 routers use RISC processors. As many as six network-module slots are provided for LAN and WAN requirements. The 3620 provides for two slots, the 3640 four slots, and the 3660 six slots. The Cisco 3600 family provides solutions for data, voice video, hybrid dial-in access, VPNs, and multiprotocol data routing. The 3600 series can process-switch 8000 packets per second, which is approximately one-fourth the power of a 7200 series with the NPM-400 processor.

Cisco MC3810 Multiservice Router

The Cisco MC3810 series multiservice access concentrator accepts data, voice/fax, and video signals as inputs to the router. It can connect to ATM, Frame Relay, and leased-line networks.

This platform of routers lets organizations integrate all traffic, whether it be LAN, legacy, voice, fax, or video, over a single network backbone. The Cisco MC3810 supports a variety of user interfaces, including Ethernet LAN, T1/E1 trunks, analog telephones, and ISDN services. MC3810s have standard interfaces that come with the router: two administrative ports (one console and one auxiliary), one Ethernet port, and two synchronous serial ports.

There are many optional interfaces, including:

- T1/E1 trunk port
- BRI S/T backup port
- Four ISDN QSIG BRI voice ports
- Up to six analog voice ports:
    - **FXS**—Foreign Exchange Station port
    - **FXO**—Foreign Exchange Office port
    - **Digital voice port**—Supports one digital T1/E1 voice port
    - **E&M**—Analog port for a two-wire or four-wire interface to PBX

Foundation Summary

This section contains a table that provides a convenient review of many key concepts in this chapter. If you are already comfortable with the topics in this chapter, this summary could help you recall a few details. If you have just read this chapter, this review should help solidify some key facts. If you are doing your final preparation before the exam, Table 11-2 is a convenient way to review the day before the exam.

Table 11-2   *ISDN Terms*

TE1	A device that has an ISDN component built into it, ie an ISDN external modem.
TE2	A device without an ISDN component, ie a Laptop.
TA	Terminal Adapters convert computer electrical signals into ISDN signals.
NT1	A termination point for a 2 wire local loop.
NT2	An ISDN switch, ie PBX, Madge ISDN switch, Adtran 550

Table 11-3   *ISDN Reference Points*

R	Represents a device with no ISDN capability, ie a PC or Laptop, a 2500 router without any ISDN interfaces.
S	Defines the reference points between user terminals and a NT2, an example being an ISDN telephone
T	Represents the interface between NT1 and NT2 devices. An example is the PBX connection to the NT1
U	Defines the two-wire interface between the NT1 and the PSTN.

Table 11-4   *Remote LAN Access*

Remote Control	Think of PC Anywhere. A PC is always left on at Headquarters to dial into - insecure.
Remote Node	Think of dialing into Headquarters, logging on to a server, and using Windows Explorer to map disk drives – more secure than Remote Control.

Table 11-5   *Routers and where they fit*

Telecommuter Routers	700, 800, 900, 1000, and 1600 Series
Branch Office Routers	1600,1700, 2500, 2600 , 3800 Series routers
Regional Office Routers	4500, 4700, 3600, 7200, AS 5000 Series
Central Site	7200, 7500, 7000, AS 5000 Series

Q&A

As mentioned in Chapter 1, the questions and scenarios in this book are more difficult than what you will experience on the actual exam. The questions do not attempt to cover more breadth or depth than the exam; however, they are designed to make sure that you know the answer. Rather than allowing you to derive the answer from clues hidden inside the question, the questions challenge your understanding and recall of the subject. Questions from the "Do I Know This Already?" quiz from the beginning of the chapter are repeated here to ensure that you have mastered this chapter's topic areas. Hopefully, these questions will help limit the number of exam questions on which you narrow your choices to two options and then guess. Be sure to use the CD and take the simulated exams.

The answers to these questions can be found in Appendix A.

1 Does IPX use the unnumbered feature?

_____

_____

_____

2 Is IP unnumbered a standard in the industry?

_____

_____

_____

3 Can you use IP unnumbered on a Frame Relay interface?

_____

_____

_____

4 Is a T1 full duplex or half duplex?

_____

_____

_____

5 What are the pinouts of a T1 interface used with an RJ-45 jack?

_____

_____

_____

6 Is it possible to bundle four ISDN BRI connections to one logical channel (bundle) using multilink PPP?

---

7 Against what type of attack does CHAP provide protection?

---

8 Does MLPPP affect routing tables?

---

9 Name three dialer interfaces that MLPPP supports.

---

10 What remote access protocol was used prior to PPP?

---

11 Which series of routers provides for cable modem access?

---

12 What series of router can share modular cards with the 1600, 2600, and 3600 routers?

---

13 Which remote access server in the 5000 series supports a T3 connection?

_____

_____

_____

14 Which processor do the 2600 and 3600 routers use?

_____

_____

_____

15 What is the Stack Group Bidding Protocol?

_____

_____

_____

16 Is a four-wire 64 K circuit full duplex or half duplex?

_____

_____

_____

17 Would a 2500 series router be a TE1 or a TE2?

_____

_____

_____

18 A PBX is which type, NT1 or NT2?

_____

_____

_____

19 What reference point interface connects to the local loop?

_____

_____

_____

20 Name at least three protocols that can be used over PPP.

_____

_____

_____

21 Does MLPPP provide for load balancing?

_____

_____

_____

22 What are the pinouts of a 64 K circuit used with an RJ-45?

_____

_____

_____

23 What processor does the Cisco 2500 series use?

_____

_____

_____

24 What is one of the primary differences between the AS5200 and the AS5300?

_____

_____

_____

25 Which router would you use to meet the following requirements: ten users at a branch office, multiservice, voice/data integration, VPNs, and broadband access?

_____

_____

_____

26 Into what slot would an RSP8 module fit in a Cisco 7500 router?

_____

_____

_____

27 Which series of routers has a totally different OS than the other routers?

_____

_____

_____

28 Which series of routers will no longer be supported by Cisco past 2005?

_____

_____

_____

29 Into which router would an NPM fit?

_____

_____

_____

30 Is it possible to have a 100 Mbps Ethernet port in a Cisco 1600 router?

_____

_____

_____

Scenarios

Scenario 1

RouteitRight has the following requirements:

- The company has one central headquarters site, two regional offices, and three remote sites for each regional office.

- All branch offices must have a Frame Relay link with ISDN backup circuits to the regional sites.

- The branch sites must be able to survive a total regional site outage.

Scenario 2

RouteitRight has the following requirements (and uses the topology shown in Figure 11-20):

- The company has no backup circuit requirement. If the branch offices lose connectivity, that is OK until the problem is fixed.

- The company has obtained free ISDN service, so more than 64 K must be available to the branch offices.

- No extra money may be spent to obtain this goal. It must be accomplished using existing equipment (no CSUs, interfaces for routers, and so on).

Scenario 3

RouteitRight has decided to build a new network. The company has the following requirements:

- The network architect should recommend equipment for all the sites.

- The central site needs a router that can efficiently handle traffic from 13 regional sites.

- The central site router must be able to support at least half of the regional offices if there is a carrier outage.

- The regional site routers must be able to handle the ten branch office routers connected to the regional sites. They must also have T1 backup capability to the central office.

- The regional offices' routers must be scalable and flexible to support any other needs that might come up in the near future.

- The branch office routers must be able to support ten users, with a 100 Mbps Ethernet port on the router for future use with VPN services and ISDN backup to the regional offices.

Answer to Scenario 1

There are other ways of meeting the company's requirements. This is only a recommended solution that meets the requirements placed on the network architect.

Figure 11-20 depicts a recommended solution. There are six branch sites at the bottom of the figure. The branch sites each have a Frame Relay connection to their regional office. If the Frame Relay link should fail, the ISDN Link will come up and connect them to their respective regional office. What if a catastrophe hits the regional office in Dallas, for example? Let's take a look at what happens:

- The branch office Irving loses its Frame Relay connection to the regional office.

- The ISDN link kicks in and calls the Dallas regional office.

- The Dallas regional office is not there to respond.

Figure 11-20   *Scenario 1 Suggested Solution*

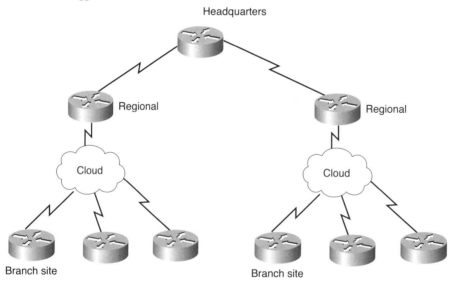

The customer's requirement that the branch office be able to survive a regional office outage can be met with the IP unnumbered feature. If you implement this feature with the routing protocol EIGRP, you can configure the branch office to dial in to any regional office. And the BRI interface can actually be configured to try different regional offices.

For example, suppose the Atlanta region has an outage. The Nashville router first attempts to dial into Atlanta. After receiving no response, the Nashville router dials into Dallas and gets an answer. The EIGRP protocol forms a neighbor relationship, and for 30 to 35 seconds the route to Nashville is known to the rest of the network as going through Dallas.

TIP   This would be more difficult to configure using OSPF because of area configuration issues. It is much easier using EIGRP.

Answer to Scenario 2

This solution is not the only solution; other ways of meeting the company's requirements are possible. This is only a recommended solution that meets the requirements placed on the network architect.

Figure 11-21 depicts a recommended solution. The requirement that more bandwidth be added to the remote sites without spending more money on interfaces, CSUs/DSUs, and so on can be met by using the Multilink PPP protocol. This protocol binds the ISDN 64 k link to the Frame Relay 64 k link and creates a virtual link of 128 k. You can do this starting with 11.2 Cisco IOS using the virtual template interface. This is another reason to use IP unnumbered because if the ISDN link has an IP address as well as a Frame Relay interface, that would not work.

Figure 11-21 *Scenario 2 Suggested Solution*

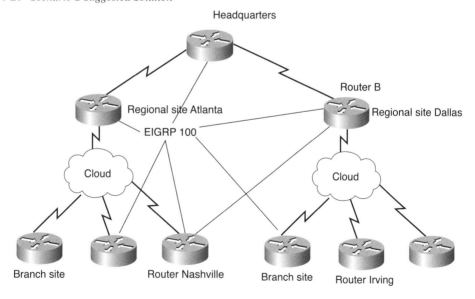

The virtual template is a pattern for making virtual access interfaces. The virtual access interfaces are actually used to handle traffic. All of the virtual access interfaces are made from the same virtual template via copying. Therefore, if you specify an IP address on the virtual template, your router might have problems because multiple interfaces will have the same IP address when your router has multiple virtual access interfaces. That is why you should use **ip unnumbered** on your virtual template.

Answer to Scenario 3

This solution is not the only solution; there are other ways of meeting the company's requirements. This is only a recommended solution that meets the requirements placed on the contractor.

Figure 11-22 depicts a recommended solution. At the central site:

- A Cisco 7507 router can support all the sites. To meet the T1 backup circuit requirement, a VIP 250 with up to eight PRI interfaces could be installed. If the requirement was for all 13 sites to be backed up at the same time in case of a full outage, there could be two VIPs, making a total of 16 T1 backup circuits.

- At the regional sites, one option would be to use Cisco 7200 routers. They would be able to support the ten branch offices, and also a PRI for the backup link to the central site.

- At the branch offices, Cisco 1700 routers meet the requirement for VPN capability.

- They would need the ISDN backup card. The 1700 series also comes with a 100 Mbps Ethernet port.

WARNING   Even though the 1700 comes with a 100 Mbps Ethernet port, it does not support ISL trunking capability.

Figure 11-22   *Scenario 3 Suggested Solution*

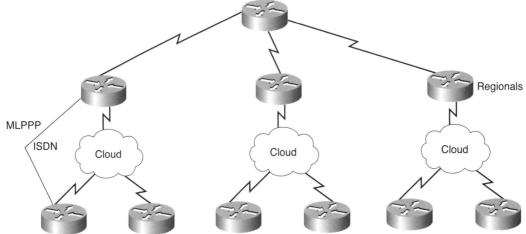

Regionals

MLPPP

ISDN

Cloud   Cloud   Cloud

Branch offices

This chapter covers the following topics you need to master as a CCDP:

- **SNA overview**—This section introduces IBM network technologies.

- **SNA gateways**—This section discusses the types of gateways available in the SNA arena.

- **LLC2**—This section covers the LLC2 connection-oriented protocol.

- **SDLC**—This section covers the SDLC connection-oriented protocol, frame types, and so on.

CHAPTER 12

SNA Technology

The CCDP exam requires you to have an in-depth understanding of Systems Network Architecture (SNA) technology. This chapter focuses on several topics, including the types of gateways used and the two types of connections that are primarily used in an SNA environment: SDLC and LLC2. The main components that make up the SNA network are also discussed, including mainframes, front-end processors (FEPs), node types, cluster controllers, and physical and logical units.

One of the amazing things about SNA is its ability to predict response times. Even though the networks of today have faster processors, they still cannot guarantee the response time of the older SNA networks with slower processors.

How to Best Use This Chapter

By following these steps, you can make better use of your study time:

- Keep your notes and the answers for all your work with this book in one place for easy reference.

- Take the "Do I Know This Already?" quiz and write down your answers. Studies show that retention is significantly increased through writing down facts and concepts, even if you never look at the information again.

- Use the diagram shown in Figure 12-1 to guide you to the next step.

Figure 12-1   *How to Use This Chapter*

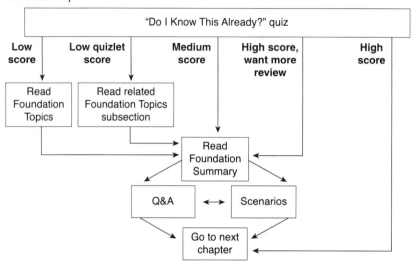

If you skip to the Foundation Summary, Q&A, and Scenarios sections and have trouble with the material there, you should go back to the Foundation Topics section.

"Do I Know This Already?" Quiz

The purpose of the "Do I Know This Already?" quiz is to help you decide which parts of this chapter to use. If you already intend to read the entire chapter, you do not necessarily need to answer these questions now.

This 15-question quiz helps you choose how to spend your limited study time. The quiz is divided into four smaller "quizlets" that help you select the sections of the chapter on which to focus. Figure 12-1 outlines suggestions on how to spend your time in this chapter. Use Table 12-1 to record your score.

Table 12-1   *Score Sheet for Quiz and Quizlets*

Quizlet Number	Foundation Topics Section Covering These Questions	Questions	Score
1	SNA overview	1–4	
2	Token Ring gateways	5–8	
3	LLC2	9–12	
4	SDLC	13–15	

1 Hosts are what physical unit type?

_____

_____

_____

2 The fifth layer of the SNA model is called the _____ layer.

_____

_____

_____

3 Software that runs on a front-end processor is called _____.

_____

_____

_____

4 Transmission groups are physical links that connect what?

_____

_____

_____

5 What types of routes are used to get from a source to a destination in an SNA network?

_____

_____

_____

6 Novell's SAA Gateway would be considered what type of gateway?

_____

_____

_____

7 What is a TIC?

_____

_____

_____

8 Locally administered addresses are almost always used in Token Ring shops to improve what?

_____

_____

_____

9 Which three timers are involved in an LLC2 session?

_____

_____

_____

10 When an SSCP-to-PU session is created, what type of units signal between the devices?

_____

_____

_____

11 A PU finds the gateway by using what type of frame?

_____

_____

_____

12 Which SNA communications protocol was designed to run over Token Ring?

_____

_____

_____

13 What are the three SDLC frame types?

_____

_____

_____

14 Name the two types of SDLC link stations.

_____

_____

_____

15 Name the two types of secondary link state operation.

_____

_____

_____

The answers to the "Do I Know This Already?" quiz are found in Appendix A. The suggested choices for your next step are as follows:

- **6 or fewer overall score**—Read the chapter. This includes the "Foundation Topics," "Foundation Summary," and "Q&A" sections, as well as the scenarios at the end of the chapter.

- **2 or less on any quizlet**—Review the subsection(s) of the "Foundation Topics" part of this chapter based on Table 12-1. Then move into the "Foundation Summary," the "Q&A" section, and the scenarios at the end of the chapter.

- **7, 8, or 9 overall score** —Begin with the "Foundation Summary" section and then go to the "Q&A" section and scenarios at the end of the chapter.

- **10 or more overall score** —If you want more review on these topics, skip to the "Foundation Summary" section, and then go to the "Q&A" section and the scenarios at the end of the chapter. Otherwise, move to the next chapter.

Foundation Topics

SNA is often troublesome for most design-professional candidates. This chapter examines the components that make up an SNA design, what each component does, various methods and benefits of each design, and also how Cisco routers fit into the design.

SNA is host-centric and hierarchical—everything revolves around the mainframe. Because it uses polling and is connection-oriented, this technology has managed to outlast a host of others and is still considered a worthwhile investment even though it was introduced in 1974. This chapter discusses some of the fundamental roles of SNA hardware and software and where Cisco routers fit into the SNA picture. SNA is certainly not a new technology, but it is still widely used for a variety of purposes and will probably continue to be for some time. Design professionals need to know which considerations to watch out for.

SNA Overview

In the early 1970s, IBM developed a hierarchical product consisting of a mainframe computer connected to multiple terminals. The mainframe computer polled the terminals, asking each one if it was ready to send data. This is how polling technology began.

An example of this can be found in a local department store, in which the cashiers use dumb terminals that connect to a central mainframe computer. It is the mainframe's job to poll the terminals in the store and then accept transactions and do all the processing. Another example would be a racetrack, which might have anywhere from 200 to 600 terminals for people to place their bets. After you place your bet, the machine notifies the mainframe that it has a transaction to process. The mainframe processes the information and signals the machine to print the ticket for you.

SNA Model

Because SNA was developed before the OSI model, the definition of the layers differs slightly from that of the OSI model. It might make sense to first compare the SNA model to the OSI model and discuss some of the general differences between TCP/IP and SNA before going on with the rest of the chapter. The SNA model is described in Table 12-2. It is functionally equivalent to the OSI model.

Table 12-2   *The SNA Model*

SNA Stack	OSI Model
7. Transaction services layer	7. Application layer
6. Presentation services layer	6. Presentation layer
5. Data-flow control layer	5. Session layer
4. Transmission control layer	4. Transport layer

Table 12-2   *The SNA Model (Continued)*

SNA Stack	OSI Model
3. Path control layer	3. Network layer
2. Data-link control layer	2. Data link layer
1. Physical control layer	1. Physical layer

The following list describes the layers:

- **Transaction services**—Provides application services, such as databases and document interchange.

- **Presentation services**—Organizes data for presentation media and coordinates resource sharing.

- **Data-flow control**—Synchronizes data flow, groups data into units, and correlates data exchange.

- **Transmission control**—Controls data exchanges to match processing capabilities (pacing), tracks session status, controls sequencing, provides error correction, and encrypts data if security is needed.

- **Path control**—Controls routing of data and controls traffic in the network. Transmission groups, explicit routes, and virtual routes all operate at this layer. Path control is also responsible for sending messages.

- **Data-link control**—Transmits data between nodes—SDLC and LLC2.

- **Physical control**—Connects nodes physically and electrically.

When you compare the SNA and OSI models as described in Table 12-2, they might look almost the same. But there are several differences between TCP/IP and SNA networks:

- SNA does not have any feature equivalent to OSI's X.25 packet-level acknowledgment.

- SNA does use the concept of an X.25 permanent or virtual circuit.

- SNA headers differ from OSI headers.

- SNA flow control differs from OSI flow control.

- SNA command structures differ from OSI command structures.

- TCP/IP networks are an unreliable, connectionless packet delivery system. SNA networks are connection-oriented and provide reliable data transfer.

- TCP/IP networks are peer-to-peer networks with no one particular device in control of the network. Traditional SNA networks are hierarchical, with the mainframe being in control of the network. The mainframe and the software within it (VTAM) control all the devices in the network.

NOTE   Throughout this chapter, you'll see the terms APPN and subarea. In subarea SNA networks, physical units need a VTAM to establish and maintain sessions. In APPN SNA networks, the VTAM is not needed.

SNA Components

For SNA to work properly, it requires a means to provide services to move information through the network between nodes and to allow the network to be managed and controlled. Those means are called network addressable units (NAUs). These consist of physical units, logical units, and system service control points. All of these components are discussed in the following sections.

Network Addressable Units

NAUs are a major component of the SNA network. Think of NAUs as having unique addresses and symbolic names. NAUs send and receive messages and communicate with other NAUs in the SNA network. NAUs consist of physical units, logical units, and control points. They communicate with each other via a path control network, as shown in Figure 12-2. The path control network is responsible for reliable, ordered transfer of data between NAUs.

Figure 12-2   *Path Control Network*

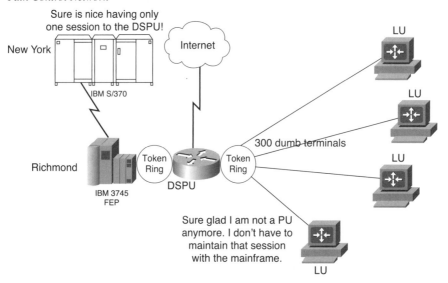

Physical Units

Physical units (PUs) are depicted in Figure 12-3. They represent a set of functions. PUs are comprised of software, hardware, and microcode; think of a PC or a 3174 front-end processor. Also, software such as VTAM could be classified as a PU. There are five types of PUs: 5, 4, 2, 1, and 2.1. These physical units represent actual devices and their associated resources in the SNA network:

- **PU type 5**—Referred to as a subarea node, this type contains an SSCP and is usually a mainframe.

- **PU type 4**—Referred to as a subarea node, this type does not contain an SSCP and is usually a front-end processor.

- **PU type 2**—These are referred to as peripheral nodes user-programmable end nodes, and are typically cluster controllers. PU 2 nodes provide networking services to logical units. PU 2 nodes have greater processing capabilities than PU 1.0 nodes and are user-programmable. They are configured with the address of the SNA PU 4 or PU 5 that provides a boundary function. An SNA boundary function is the equivalent of the default gateway in a TCP/IP network.

- **PU type 1**—Referred to as peripheral nodes, these are not user-programmable and have fewer capabilities than PU 2s. PU type 1s are almost always printers.

- **PU type 2.1**—These PUs are used in APPN networks and can provide APPN network node or end node functions. Even though they are APPN nodes, they still can attach to subarea SNA networks. An example of a PU 2.1 node is the downstream physical unit (DSPU), discussed later in this chapter.

Figure 12-3   *Physical Units*

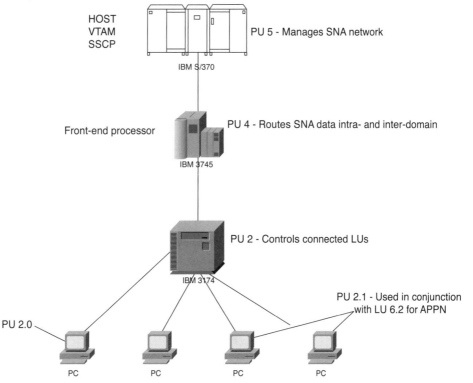

Logical Units

Users access the network through logical units (LUs). Each LU type is made up of a subset of SNA functions. Logical units define a set of services and transmission capabilities that are assigned users. SNA defines seven LU types: 0, 1, 2, 3, 4, 5, and 6.2. There are many LU types because memory and processing on SNA devices is expensive. IBM decided to create several types that allowed specific functions to be associated with the end user so that only the minimum processing and memory would be required for a particular device.

Of these LU types, LU 4 and LU 5 were never implemented and are no longer in use. LU 0, LU 1, and LU 3 are not considered test topics. We will discuss the two most important—LU 2 and LU 6.2.

Table 12-3 describes the LU types.

Table 12-3   *Types of Logical Units*

LU Type	Description
0	Application-to-terminal
1	SNA character-stream devices: printers
2	Application-to-display, such as 3270 terminals
3	Application-to-printer
4, 5	Not implemented or not used
6.2	APPC (Advanced Program-to-Program Communication)

NOTE   LU 6.2 works in the APPN environment and includes program-to-program communication (APPC) and peer-to-peer communication between peripheral nodes.

System Service Control Points

SSCPs reside on the host or mainframe and coordinate the activity in an SNA domain by activating and deactivating SNA resources and initiating and terminating LU sessions. An SNA domain consists of all the resources managed by an SSCP. A domain usually has more than one subarea. (Subareas are discussed in the following section.)

SSCPs coordinate network resources, activate and deactivate links, and manage startup and shutdown of the network. SSCP is required to activate a session between two logical units. A session between two logical units is called a LU-LU session, which is how devices communicate in an SNA network. In Figure 12-4, for the two FEPs to communicate in the SNA domain CCDP, the SSCP must initiate and control the LU-LU session.

Figure 12-4   *System Series Control Point*

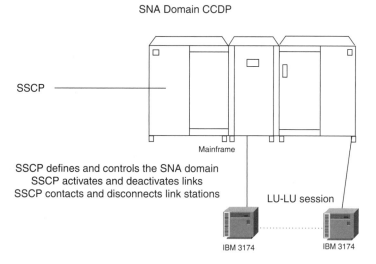

SNA Domain CCDP

SSCP

Mainframe

SSCP defines and controls the SNA domain
SSCP activates and deactivates links
SSCP contacts and disconnects link stations

LU-LU session

IBM 3174   IBM 3174

NOTE   All SNA communication is between NAUs.

Subareas

When SNA was developed, the architecture of SNA subareas was introduced. Later, another concept called APPN was developed to improve communications in the SNA network. APPN is discussed in the next chapter. This section discusses the concepts of SNA subareas, along with some of the differences with APPN.

A subarea consists of a subarea node and all the peripheral nodes attached to it, similar to a domain concept. Subarea nodes are mainframes and front-end processors. An example of a peripheral node is a cluster controller.

Subarea SNA resources are controlled from a central location, usually the mainframe. A mainframe connected to a FEP would not be considered a subarea because the FEP is not a peripheral node; it is a subarea node. A subarea consists of one subarea node (think mainframe) and all the resources it controls. A subarea node is a node (think mainframe, front-end processors) that can communicate with other subarea nodes (think front-end processors) and its own peripheral nodes (think cluster controllers, PCs, printers, and so on). Figure 12-5 shows several subareas, each controlled by a subarea node.

Figure 12-5 *Subarea Concepts*

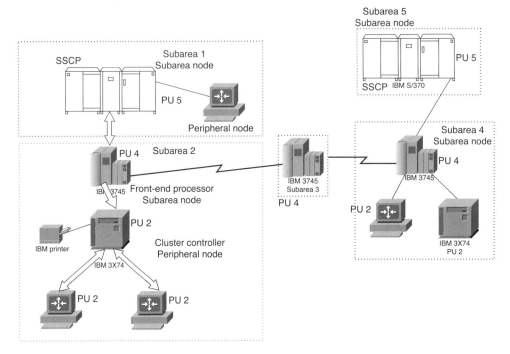

Subarea Nodes

Subarea nodes are either PU type 5 or 4. The main components in an SNA domain are the mainframe (5) and the FEP (4). Subarea nodes can communicate with other subarea nodes and their peripheral devices, but peripheral nodes can communicate only with the subarea node to which they are connected.

There are two main types of subarea nodes: host (or mainframe) and FEP:

- **Host or mainframe**—This type of node sits at the top of the network and contains the CPU. This device is in charge of the network and is sometimes referred to as the master. This is from where all resources in the network are controlled. Software that runs on the mainframe is called VTAM. The mainframe typically is connected to a FEP by a channel. A channel can be copper bus and tag or fiber ESCON connector:

    — **VTAM (Virtual Telecommunications Access Method)**—A software package developed by IBM that runs on the mainframe. It directly controls the transmission of data to and from the network.

    — **ESCON (Enterprise System Connection)**—The ESCON Channel Port Adapter provides a single channel attachment interface for connecting Cisco 7200-series routers to an ESCON director or to a mainframe channel. This interface can eliminate the need for a separate front-end processor (FEP). The

ESCON Channel Port Adapter contains an ESCON I/O connector, which is a single female duplex connector.

- **FEP**—This type of node is a programmable device that sits between the mainframe and the cluster controller. FEPs also act as routers between SNA domains, as shown in Figure 12-5. The software that runs on these devices is known as a network control program. FEPs are sometimes referred to as slaves and can assist the mainframe with its duties by taking over character handling and polling. Keep in mind when designing that this device is not mandatory in an SNA network.

Let's take a quick look at how these two nodes operate in a real environment. Once a week, probably on Sunday morning, a sysgen function is performed on the mainframe, and new devices are added to the network. sysgen then updates VTAM, which automatically passes the information to the Network Control Program (NCP) that runs on the FEP. These newly added devices are now ready to communicate within the network. The FEPs will be able to poll the new devices and take care of character handling. Remember that even the new devices still need the SSCP on the mainframe to initiate and control communications in an SNA subarea network.

Peripheral Nodes

Peripheral nodes are PU type 2 nodes. Peripheral nodes can be printers, PCs, and cluster controllers. Peripheral or PU 2 type nodes always attach to a PU 4 or PU 5 node.

- 3270 terminals are terminal types used to access data from IBM mainframe applications. When data is accessed, a Primary Logical Unit-Secondary Logical Unit (PLU-SLU) session is established between the mainframe and the terminal. This is a key concept that will be discussed in later sections of this chapter. 3270 terminals are fairly dumb terminals, with most of the smarts located on the cluster controller.

- A cluster controller is a peripheral node in SNA. Cluster controllers provide the ability to aggregate many PCs and printers in a hierarchical fashion. Cluster controllers are IBM device type 3x74. The 3270 terminals just mentioned attach to the cluster controller, as shown in Figure 12-6.

Figure 12-6 *Peripheral Nodes*

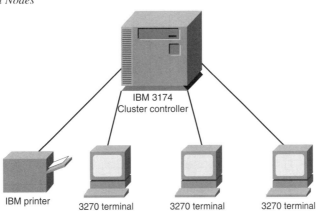

IBM 3174
Cluster controller

IBM printer   3270 terminal   3270 terminal   3270 terminal

NOTE When a 3270 terminal accesses an application on the host computer, a PLU-SLU session is established.

Establishing a LU-LU Session

As mentioned previously, end users or terminals access the network through logical units. For example, a 3270 terminal communicates with the mainframe via Logical Unit-Logical Unit (LU-LU) sessions that are controlled by the SSCP. A secondary logical unit (SLU) initiates the session. A primary logical unit (PLU) activates the session.

Let's look at what must happen for LU-LU session establishment. Figure 12-7 depicts this concept. It is explained in the following steps:

1 The SLU, a cluster controller in this example, requests a session with a PLU on the host.

2 The SLU sends a LOGON to the SSCP. The LOGON is a request that a LU-LU session be established between the SLU and PLU.

3 The SSCP contacts the PLU with session parameters.

4 The SSCP sends an initiate to the PLU, which asks the PLU to activate a session with the SLU.

5 The PLU establishes the LU-LU session with the SLU.

Figure 12-7   *LU-LU Session Establishment*

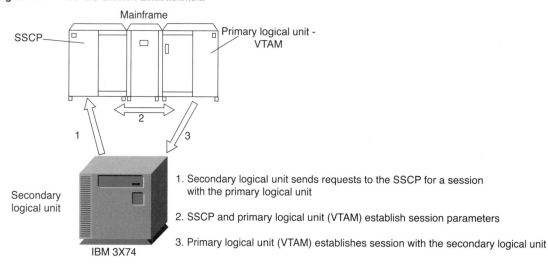

Dependent and Independent LUs

In your SNA travels, you will probably run across logical-unit terms other than SLU and PLU. Logical units can be either dependent on or independent of an SSCP. The protocols the LU uses to initiate a session is what makes it dependent or not dependent on an SSCP. In Figure 12-8, PU 2 needs to communicate with an SSCP.

Figure 12-8 *Dependent and Independent LUs*

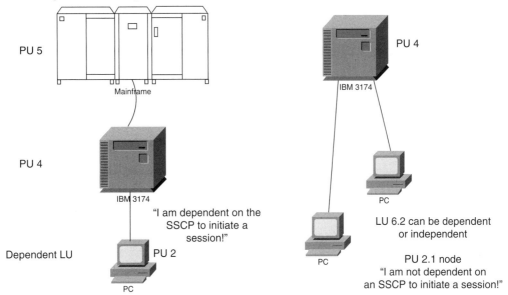

Boundary Nodes

Before discussing boundary nodes, the types of path information units (PIUs) used to communicate between physical units should be covered. Communication between subarea nodes is usually done with these PIUs. PIUs can be segmented for transmission between subarea nodes. The adjacent link station reassembles the PIU. This causes a lot of overhead and should be avoided.

There are two types of FID frames: format identifier 4 (FID4) and format identifier 2 (FID2).

- FID4 are the frame types used to communicate between subarea nodes only: FEP to FEP, mainframe to mainframe, and mainframe to FEP. The address field in the PIU FID4 consists of two parts:

    — **Subarea number**—The subarea component identifies the subarea to which a NAU belongs, similar to a subnet in IP.

— **Element number**—The element component identifies the particular NAU within the subarea, similar to a host in IP. See Figure 12-9.

Figure 12-9　*Network Address*

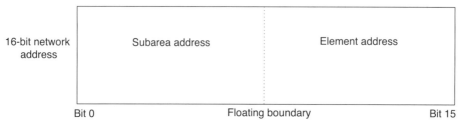

16-bit network address | Subarea address | Element address

Bit 0　　　　　Floating boundary　　　　Bit 15

Boundary nodes communicate with peripheral nodes with FID2 PIU packets.

• FID2 are the frame types used to communicate between a cluster controller and a FEP.

In Figure 12-10, the boundary node segments the large Token Ring frames into small SDLC frames.

Figure 12-10　*Path Information Units*

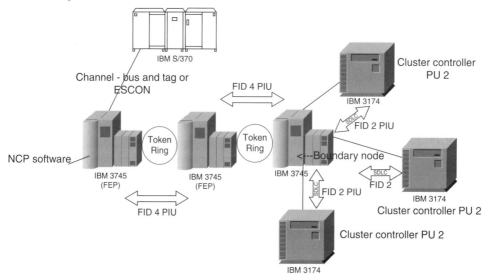

Some SNA networks might have a number of FEPs connected, with Token Ring between the mainframe and the cluster controllers. The boundary device is the last subarea node (FEP) where the node type 2 (cluster controller) is attached. The main function of this device is to convert a local address into a full network address when a message unit passes from a peripheral node to a subarea node. Figure 12-11 depicts the boundary node concept. In Figure 12-11, the boundary node for the remote PU 2 is the PU 4 in the 3745 FEP. If there were not a 3745 FEP, VTAM would assume the boundary function on the mainframe. When VTAM performs the boundary function, the boundary function is a PU 5, which is shown in the figure where the PU 2 is directly connected to the mainframe by a channel.

Figure 12-11 *Boundary Function*

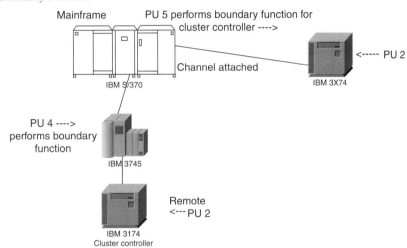

Path Control Layer

The path control layer operates at Layer 3 of the SNA model. The path control layer handles data addressing and routing, controls data flow, and transmits data over specified links. The path control layer performs the following functions:

- **Addressing**—Translates local addresses into complete network addresses when message units pass from peripheral nodes to subarea nodes. The network administrator assigns the local address, and the system assigns the network address.

- **Sending messages**—Builds a transmission header for each message.

- **Segmenting**—Segments messages. Messages are broken into smaller segments if they are too large or are combined to form larger blocks if they are too small.

- **Routing**—Determines the next node through which the message will pass and over which transmission groups it will flow.

- **Sequencing**—Provides message unit sequencing because units can travel over different links in the same transmission group.

- **Network control**—Detects congestion and regulates flow control.

There are several ways to get from a source to a destination in an SNA network using the path control layer. These "routes" are different from the TCP/IP routes used with Cisco routers, so they need to be discussed in detail:

- **Explicit routes**—You can use explicit routes to get from a source to a destination in an SNA network. Explicit routes provide a path between two subarea nodes. These are equivalent to static routes in an IP network. Like IP static routes, they must be configured in both directions because they are half-duplex paths mapped to physical communication lines connecting the nonadjacent subareas. Figure 12-12 depicts this. Explicit routes need to be statically defined in all the subarea nodes they cross. For mainframe A to communicate with mainframe B, explicit routes must be configured in both directions.

Figure 12-12 *Explicit Routes*

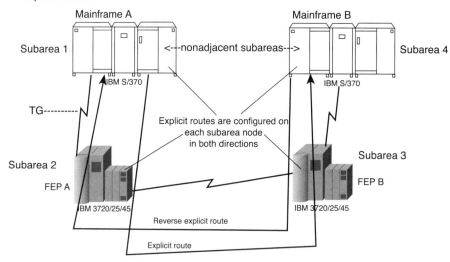

- **Virtual routes**—These are full-duplex paths between two subareas that can be adjacent or nonadjacent. This is considered a fixed path between subarea nodes. An analogy is an SVC, or a logical connection between the nodes. Virtual routes can be assigned priorities of high, medium, or low (not to be confused with Cisco router priority queuing). When there are messages to send, they can be prioritized so that the most important messages will be in the high-priority queue. They are dependent on the explicit routes being configured in both directions first.

- **Transmission groups**—The link between the subarea nodes in Figure 12-12 is called a transmission group (TG). A TG consists of one or more links between two adjacent nodes. No matter how many links make up a TG, it appears to the path control layer as a single link between two adjacent subarea nodes. This provides for availability. In Figure 12-13, if one of the links fails in either TG 1 or TG 255, the TG remains operative. The range for TGs is from 1 to 255.

Figure 12-13 *Transmission Groups*

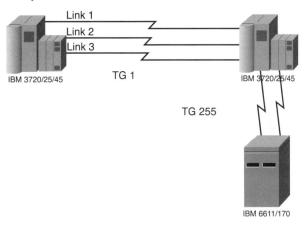

Transmission groups are the physical links that connect subarea nodes.

Team SNA

Let's sum all this up into something you can easily understand. If SNA were a football team, the head coach, Mr. VTAM (a rather large PU 5), needs to make sure everyone in his domain is on the same page. Mr. VTAM carries with him his organizer (SSCP), which keeps track of everybody and their skills. This requires him to have a session (LU 2.0) with every ballplayer on the team (the PU 2s). This task of having these daily sessions has been wearing heavily on Mr. VTAM, so he decides to offload some of his processing to the assistant coach, NCP (PU 4-FEP). The assistant coach decides to pass Mr. VTAM's game plan on to the quarterback (still a PU 2.0 but now a cluster controller). We might want to call him a clusterback. He will control all the sessions in the huddle and will pass the assistant coach's information to the players. All the players still have a session with the PU 5, but they do not have to bother the head coach anymore. Keep in mind that all the players might be in session with Mr. VTAM, but they have no sessions with and cannot talk to each other. For the players to be able to communicate with other without Mr. VTAM's knowledge is called Advanced Peer-to-Peer Networking (APPN), discussed in the next chapter.

Token Ring Gateways

A computer attached to a Token Ring network must go through a gateway to access SNA resources, as shown in Figure 12-14.

Figure 12-14 *Token Ring Gateways*

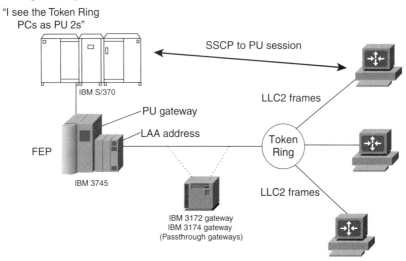

A gateway converts Token Ring LLC2 frames into SNA. Workstations on the Token Ring segment access host applications through the 3745 (FEP) gateway by using the locally administered address (LAA) assigned to the Token Interface Coupler as the destination address. (LAA is defined later in this chapter.) Token Ring devices can appear as either PU type 2 or as an LU, depending on the type of gateway selected. This section discusses the two categories of gateways, along with LAAs. We will also look at a device called a Downstream Physical Unit, often the subject of test material with SNA environments.

Another popular method is using a 3174 as the passthrough PU gateway. However, the 3174 is a cluster controller, not a FEP, so the burden of converting addresses that are destined for nodes on the Token Ring is now on the host. Figure 12-15 depicts this. Notice in the figure that each node has a session with the SSCP.

There are two categories of gateways:

- **PU gateway**—The Token Ring gateway device appears as PU node type 2, as shown in the preceding two figures.

- **LU gateway**—The Token Ring gateway device appears to be a LU, as shown in Figure 12-16. An application such as Novell's SAA Gateway can appear as a PU node type 2 on the same gateway device.

Figure 12-15 *Passthrough Gateways*

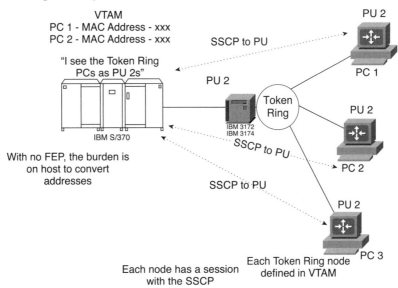

Figure 12-16 *LU Gateways*

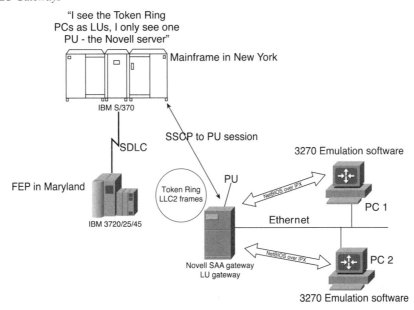

NOTE	Netware for SAA is a gateway for Novell Netware users to access IBM resources via SNA protocols. Systems Application Architecture (SAA) is an IBM standard for developing distributed applications.

PU Gateways

A passthrough gateway, shown in Figure 12-15, is just what its name implies—passthrough. The IBM 3172 cluster controller is invisible to the Token Ring attached PCs and the SNA host. Therefore, every node must be defined in VTAM, creating an SSCP session to every node type 2 on the ring. This creates a lot of overhead on the host. Also, another drawback is that PCs are usually turned off at 5 p.m. When they are powered up in the morning, they are all visible to the IBM 3172, creating much explorer traffic in the network.

LU Gateways

Logical unit (LU) gateways are available from several vendors. They are called logical because an application that runs on the device performs session functions. For example, suppose you take a Novell Server and load Novell's SAA Gateway software on it, as depicted in Figure 12-16. You would also load some type of client 3270 emulation software on the users' PCs, which would allow them to connect to the SAA gateway server. LU gateways reduce overhead on the host because the SSCP is only in session with the PU in the SAA gateway. The SAA gateway is in session with the terminals. This reduces the required definition on the host. Notice that the PCs are connected via Ethernet and use NetBIOS over IPX as the transport protocol. The SAA gateway converts the Ethernet frames into Token Ring LLC2 frames.

Locally Administered Addresses

Locally administered addresses (LAAs) are almost always used in Token Ring networks to improve manageability. Token Ring network interface cards are assigned a 12-digit burned-in universally administered address (UAA) by the vendor. It is set in the card's ROM memory and is commonly referred to as its burned-in address (BIA). This UAA can be overridden with an LAA. The LAA is an assigned address given to LAN administrators from the design team. This will now be the 12-digit number that will be the hardware address for the physical device on the LAN. LAAs begin with a hex of 40 to identify them as LAAs. This gives the CCDP several benefits and one major drawback.

In Figure 12-17, the PCs in the Accounting department have been administered an LAA of 2222 in the second octet. In the Payroll department, the PCs have been administered an LAA of 1111 in the second octet. This helps with troubleshooting because you can identify addresses with departments and their location in the network hierarchy. Another benefit is that the network interface cards on the PCs can be swapped out without changing any definitions or purging any cached MAC addresses. The last benefit is that multiple Token Ring interface couplers (TICs) can be assigned the same MAC address. This allows redundant TICs to be configured.

Figure 12-17 *Locally Administered Addresses*

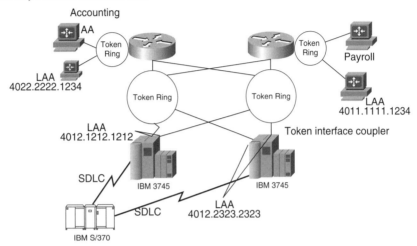

The only drawback is the administration that is needed to configure the device addresses. Redundant addresses might occur if mistakes are made in configuration. It is almost impossible to have redundant addresses using UAA.

NOTE   Cisco routers allow Ethernet interfaces to be assigned LAAs.

The upside of all this is that a MAC address can be divided into fields that describe the location or department. This helps with troubleshooting. All LAAs begin with a hex number of 4 for the MAC address.

Downstream Physical Units (DSPU)

It is important to discuss where Cisco routers can be used as gateways. This is very similar to the earlier example of the LU gateway with the Novell SAA gateway. An available feature in the Cisco IOS is called DSPU. This feature lets the router function as a PU gateway for SNA PU type 2 nodes, as shown in Figure 12-18. The advantage of using this feature is that configuring PU gateways at the router simplifies the task of configuring the host with PU definitions. The DSPU feature lets you define downstream PU type 2 devices in the router. DSPU simplifies host configuration by letting you replace multiple PU definitions that represent each downstream device with one PU definition that represents the router. In Figure 12-18, the Cisco router appears as the only PU to the host; the four PCs are viewed as LUs by the host. In Figure 12-18, the router is configured for the Token Ring PCs as a PU, not the host.

Figure 12-18 *DSPU*

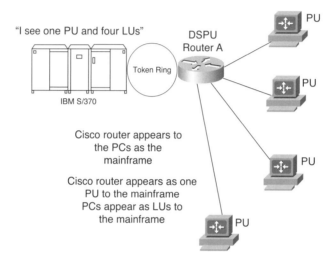

A big advantage of this is, because you define the downstream PUs at the router rather than at the host, you isolate the host from changes in the downstream network topology. Therefore, you can insert and remove downstream PUs from the network without making any changes on the host.

Another major benefit of concentrating downstream PUs at the router is that this reduces network traffic on the wide-area network (WAN) by limiting the number of sessions that must be established and maintained with the host. Terminating downstream sessions at the router ensures that idle session traffic does not appear on the WAN. See Figure 12-18.

LLC2

This section looks at Logical Link Control (LLC) type 2 frames (see Figure 12-19) and how they perform session establishment. There are three types of LLC frames:

- Type 1 provides unacknowledged connectionless service.

- Type 2 provides connection-oriented service.

- Type 3 provides acknowledged connectionless service.

Figure 12-19 *LLC Frame Format*

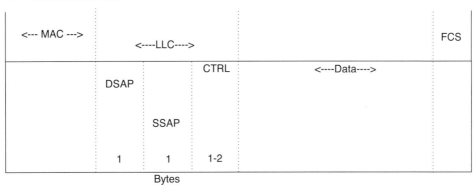

SNA, being a connection-oriented protocol, prefers type 2. LLC type 2 (LLC2) service establishes virtual-type circuits between the sender and receiver and is therefore connection-oriented. LLC2 acknowledges data upon receipt.

The three key fields in Figure 12-19 are the destination service access point (DSAP), the source service access point (SSAP), and the control field (CTRL).

LLC2-speaking stations can communicate by sending exchange of identification (XID) frames to each other. These frames identify the stations at a higher level than the MAC address and also can contain information about the station's configuration. These frames are typically sent only during setup and configuration periods when it is deemed that sending them is useful.

Two stations communicating with LLC2 do the following:

- Open and close sessions with each other before and after sending data.

- Acknowledge the receipt of any frames the other station sends.

- Control the flow of data between them by limiting the number of frames that may be sent by one before the other acknowledges any of them.

- Recover from errors and inform the other station of this.

LLC2 stations communicate in an *asynchronous balanced mode* (ABM). LLC2-speaking stations are considered *peers* and may send data to other LLC2 stations at any time. This ability to send data at any time is called being *asynchronous. Balanced mode* means that each station can send to others without permission.

All frames used in LLC2 communication have both a source and a destination address. LLC2-speaking stations usually communicate over a local-area network (LAN) on which many stations communicate. As such, each station needs its own address. Because the LLC2 protocol runs at the data link layer, the MAC address is typically used.

Session Establishment

Now you are ready to create an LLC2 session from a Token Ring terminal. Let's take a look at exactly how a session is established from the terminal (SLU) and logs on to a host (PLU). First of all, the DSPU starts the process by initiating a session toward the host. Follow along in Figure 12-20.

Figure 12-20 *LLC2 Session Establishment*

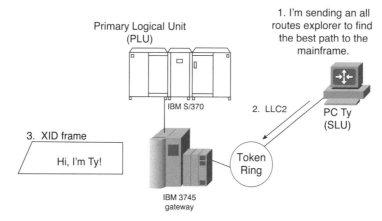

1 The PU (PC Ty) is powered up and finds the gateway (FEP) by sending an LLC2 test frame as an all-routes explorer frame. All-routes explorer frames take all possible paths to a destination and report back to PC Ty which is the best path to take.

2 The PU identifies itself to VTAM by sending an XID frame.

3 VTAM establishes the session with the PU PC Ty. (If there were a DSPU in this example between the PCs and the FEP, the DSPU would send the all-routes explorer frames to the FEP gateway, and the PCs would send their all-routes explorer to and be replied to by the DSPU and not the FEP.)

At this point, the user at the SLU should be able to log on to the host. You have successfully created an SSCP-to-PU session, and LLC2 request/response units are starting to flow.

NOTE   LLC type 2 service establishes logical connections between sender and receiver and is therefore connection-oriented.

Session Establishment and LU Gateways

If every terminal powers up in the morning and sends out these all-route explorer frames and establishes a session with the host, there will be a lot of traffic on the network at one time and also across the WAN, as shown in Figure 12-21. You can provide a solution to decrease the traffic by implementing an LU gateway, which could be a Novell server, as mentioned previously in this chapter. The attraction of this is that the session is established to the gateway one time, and if it stays powered up, that's all that is needed, as shown in Figure 12-22. When each terminal is powered up, they need to establish a session only with the SAA gateway, not the host. This eliminates complete round trips of traffic from every PC to the host. LU gateways are probably necessary if there are more than 25 PUs at a location.

Figure 12-21 *LU Session Establishment*

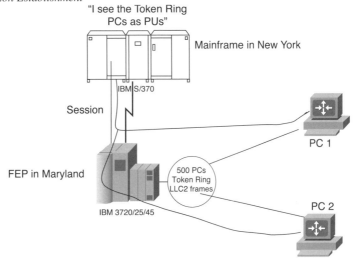

Figure 12-22 *LU Session Establishment, Part 2*

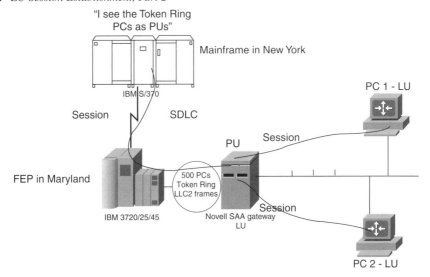

LLC2 Timers

As soon as the session is established, take a look at the timers that are functioning during this period. Connection-oriented protocols always have some kind of timer to let the sender and receivers know that each other are still alive. Because LLC2 is a connection-oriented protocol, at any given moment during a session there are three timers that a design professional needs to be aware of: the T1, the T2, and the Ti (inactivity timer).

The T1 timer is typically 1 to 3 seconds long and starts when any LLC2 frame is sent from the source to the destination, as shown in Figure 12-23. The T2 timer is a pacing timer, in effect preventing slow devices from a fast response. In the figure, the PC has transmitted a frame and will wait up to 3 seconds for a response. If there is no response within that time period, the PC starts its timer inactivity, which is set to 60 seconds. The T1 timer is an inactivity timer—it is in effect when T1 and T2 are not. After 3 seconds, if the PC has not heard back from the destination, it starts the timer inactivity. There also is a RETRY parameter, which means that the T1 interval is repeated as many times as specified before breaking the session. A typical setting is seven retries. In this example, the session would break after 21 seconds, or approximately seven intervals of 3 seconds. If there is a 60-second timer inactivity to that, the session would not break until 60 or 81 seconds.

Figure 12-23 *LLC2 Timers*

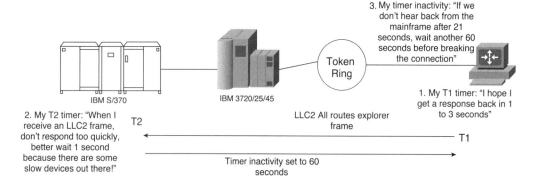

When a session does break, you might see the following message on a router:

```
UTC: %LLC-4-T1_ERR: LLC2: INCREASE LLC TIMERS
```

This error indicates that the T1 timer broke. Increasing the acknowledgment timers (T1) should decrease the likelihood of a failure.

Synchronous Data Link Control (SDLC) Sessions

The other connection-oriented data link in SNA is IBM's proprietary SDLC, developed in 1975. LLC2 was modeled after SDLC, and the two are very similar. See Figure 12-24.

Figure 12-24 *SDLC*

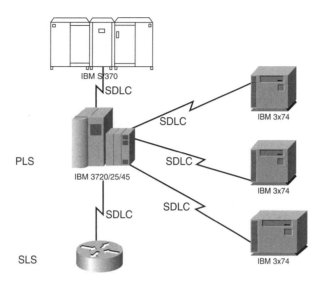

Think of SDLC as being used over point-to-point or multipoint leased lines to devices at remote sites, whereas LLC2 is used locally over a LAN connection. SDLC provides reliable transport and sliding window flow control. SDLC links were originally designed to run over low-speed serial lines and can be used to run over various media, including telephone lines, fiber optic links, microwave links, and satellite links, among others. LLC2 was designed for fast LAN connections such as Token Ring.

With traditional SNA, there are two types of SDLC link stations: Primary Link Stations (PLSs) and Secondary Link Stations (SLSs). Primary nodes poll secondary nodes in a predetermined order. Secondary nodes then transmit any outgoing data. When configured as primary and secondary nodes, your routers are established as SDLC stations.

Primary Link Station

The PLS is in charge. It is responsible for issuing commands and is also responsible for error recovery. It controls the link and also receives responses. The SLS can be considered a slave station. There are at least four ways to connect a PLS station to one or more secondary stations:

- **Point-to-point**—An example of this is a FEP connected over a serial link to a cluster controller. In Figure 12-24, the cluster controllers can communicate with each other.

- **Multipoint**—This is similar to hub and spoke in Frame Relay, with the FEP acting as the hub. The spokes would be cluster controllers. However, in this situation, the spokes would not be able to communicate with each other but with only the FEP (PLS). See Figure 12-25.

- **Loop**—This is all devices connected in a circle, with the FEP (PLS) having serial connections to only the first and last cluster controllers (SLS).

Figure 12-25   *SDLC Multipoint*

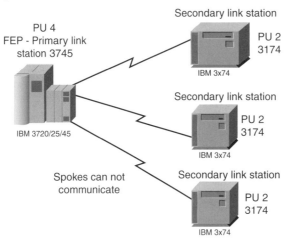

Secondary Link Station

The SLS is the slave. It receives commands and returns responses. The physical layer can be full duplex or half duplex, and it can be leased or dialup. The frame type can be FID2 or FID4. Because it is a slave, it waits for the line protocol to be initiated by the PLS. There are two types of SLS operation:

- **Two-way simultaneous**—This device can both transmit and receive at the same time.

- **Two-way alternate**—This device can either send or receive data, but not both at the same time. Two-way alternate can send data and wait while the other link station sends.

When you configure Cisco routers as the PLS, these options must match between the router and the SDLC device.

Physical Layer Between Link Stations

The leased line can be full duplex or half duplex between the PLS and SLS. The four-wire full-duplex circuit is more expensive but more efficient. It is a good design practice is to connect all the FEPs with full duplex, and any connections from the FEP to cluster controllers should be half duplex. Each drop is controlled by a line-sharing device (LSD).

NOTE   *Full datamode* is when the PLS is full duplex and the SLS is full duplex. *Half datamode* is when the PLS is full duplex and the SLS is half duplex.

SDLC Frames

There are three types of frames to discuss with SDLC: the U-frame, the I-frame, and the S-frame. These operate in the control field of the SDLC frame, as shown in Figure 12-26.

Figure 12-26 *SDLC Frame Format*

Flag 8 bits	Address 8 bits	Control field 8 or 16 bits I-frames - 00000000 U-frames - 11000000 S-frames - 10000000	Info length varies	FCS 16 bits	Flag 8 bits

- **Unnumbered frames (U-frames)**—These frames are primarily used for controlling the data link, diagnostics, initializing procedures, and transferring data.

- **Supervisory frames (S-frames)**—A 1 in bit position 1 and a 0 in bit position 2 designates S-frames. S-frames are used for control functions such as acknowledging the receipt of information frames, requesting polls, and reporting status.

- **Information frames (I-frames)**—Information frames send and receive counts to ensure proper ordering. Information frames are designated by a 0 in bit position 1 of the control field. I-frames are primarily used for sending user data, although some control information is allowed.

Foundation Summary

This section contains tables that provide a convenient review of many key concepts in this chapter. If you are already comfortable with the topics in this chapter, this summary could help you recall a few details. If you have just read this chapter, this review should help solidify some key facts. If you are doing your final preparation before the exam, these tables are a convenient way to review the day before the exam.

Table 12-4 reviews some terms from this chapter.

Table 12-4 *Chapter Terms Defined*

Term	Description
NAU	The SNA term for an addressable entity. Examples include LUs, PUs, and SSCPs. NAUs generally provide upper-level network services.
APPN	Advanced Peer-to-Peer Networking. An enhancement to the original IBM SNA architecture. APPN handles session establishment between peer nodes, dynamic transparent route calculation, and traffic prioritization for APPC traffic.
APPC	Advanced Program-to-Program Communication. IBM SNA system software that allows high-speed communication between programs on different computers in a distributed computing environment. APPC establishes and tears down connections between communicating programs. It consists of two interfaces: a programming interface and a data-exchange interface. The former replies to requests from programs requiring communication; the latter establishes sessions between programs. APPC runs on LU 6.2 devices.
Cluster controller	Generally, an intelligent device that provides the connections for a cluster of terminals to a data link. In SNA, a programmable device that controls the input/output operations of attached devices. Typically, an IBM 3174 or 3274 device.
FEP	Front-end processor. A device or board that provides network interface capabilities for a networked device. In SNA, typically an IBM 3745 device.
Host	SNA subarea node that contains an SSCP.
PLU	Primary LU. The LU that initiates a session with another LU.
LU	Logical unit. The primary component of SNA, an LU is an NAU that lets end users communicate with each other and gain access to SNA network resources.
PU 2.1	Physical Unit type 2.1. The SNA network node used to connect peer nodes in a peer-oriented network. PU 2.1 sessions do not require that one node reside on VTAM. APPN is based on PU 2.1 nodes, which can also be connected to a traditional hierarchical SNA network.
DLU	Dependent LU. An LU that depends on the SSCP to provide services for establishing sessions with other LUs.
TIC	Token Ring Interface Coupler. The controller through which an FEP connects to a Token Ring.
XID	Exchange identification. Request and response packets exchanged prior to a session between a router and a Token Ring host. If the parameters of the serial device contained in the XID packet do not match the host's configuration, the session is dropped.

Table 12-6 compares SDLC with LLC2.

Table 12-5   *SDLC Compared with LLC2*

Protocol	SDLC	LLC2
Speed	9600 bps to 1.5 Mbps	4, 16, and 25 Mbps
Medium	Serial links	Token Ring
Frames	265 bytes or 512 bytes	512 bytes up to 4470 bytes
Window	8 frames	128 frames
Mode	Normal response	Async balanced

Q&A

As mentioned in Chapter 1, the questions and scenarios in this book are more difficult than what you will experience on the actual exam. The questions do not attempt to cover more breadth or depth than the exam; however, they are designed to make sure that you know the answer. Rather than allowing you to derive the answer from clues hidden inside the question, the questions challenge your understanding and recall of the subject. Questions from the "Do I Know This Already?" quiz from the beginning of the chapter are repeated here to ensure that you have mastered this chapter's topic areas. Hopefully, these questions will help limit the number of exam questions on which you narrow your choices to two options and then guess. Be sure to use the CD and take the simulated exams.

The answers to these questions can be found in Appendix A.

1 Hosts are what physical unit type?

_____

_____

_____

2 The fifth layer of the SNA model is called the _____ layer.

_____

_____

_____

3 Software that runs on a front-end processor is called _____.

_____

_____

_____

4 Transmission groups are physical links that connect what?

_____

_____

_____

5 What types of routes are used to get from a source to a destination in an SNA network?

_____

_____

_____

6 Novell's SAA Gateway would be considered what type of gateway?

_____

_____

_____

7 What is a TIC?

_____

_____

_____

8 Locally administered addresses are almost always used in Token Ring shops to improve what?

_____

_____

_____

9 Which three timers are involved in an LLC2 session?

_____

_____

_____

10 When an SSCP-to-PU session is created, what type of units signal between the devices?

_____

_____

_____

11 A PU finds the gateway by using what type of frame?

_____

_____

_____

12 Which SNA communications protocol was designed to run over Token Ring?

_____

_____

_____

13 What are the three SDLC frame types?

_____

_____

_____

14 Name the two types of SDLC link stations.

_____

_____

_____

15 Name the two types of secondary link-state operation.

_____

_____

_____

16 Name the two communication protocols in an SNA network.

_____

_____

_____

17 What are boundary nodes?

_____

_____

_____

18 Where are FID2 frames used?

_____

_____

_____

19 Where are FID4 frames used?

_____

_____

_____

20 What is one advantage of the DSPU feature of a Cisco router?

_____

_____

_____

21 Which type of frames do two LLC2 stations use to communicate with each other?

_____

_____

_____

22 What are channels?

_____

_____

_____

23 Name the two types of physical connectors for FEPs.

_____

_____

_____

24 The ability of end stations to initiate communication without permission is called what?

_____

_____

_____

25 Name a drawback of using LAA.

_____

_____

_____

26 When a mainframe communicates with another mainframe, what type of session is created?

_____

_____

_____

27   LAA MAC addresses begin with which hexadecimal numbers?

_____

_____

_____

28   Full datamode is when the PLS is full duplex and the SLS is _____.

_____

_____

_____

29   An AS400 is similar to what?

_____

_____

_____

30   The path control layer of the SNA stack is equivalent to what layer of the OSI model?

_____

_____

_____

Scenarios

RouteitRight has a mainframe in New York that 200 users access from Baltimore via 3270 terminals on their desktops connected via Token Ring, as shown in Figure 12-27. The 200 users also have PCs on their desktops that they use to access a Novell server via Ethernet for common everyday applications, the Internet, and so on. RouteitRight's Richmond location has 300 users with only 3270 terminals. This is where only the Payroll department resides. Figure 12-27 shows the current environment.

Figure 12-27 *Scenario 1 Current Environment*

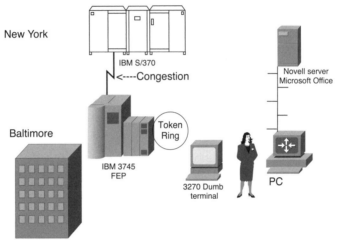

Scenario 1: Baltimore

RouteitRight has the following requirements:

- Simplify the desktop by consolidating the two devices (the 3270 terminal and desktop computer) into one device.

- Eliminate the expensive Token Ring segment to the users.

- The company has noticed some congestion on the WAN link. Decrease the amount of explorer traffic traversing the WAN link to New York.

- All users must still be able to perform the same duties they currently perform from their desktops.

Scenario 2: Richmond

Currently, Richmond exists as shown in Figure 12-28.

Figure 12-28 *Scenario 2 Current Environment*

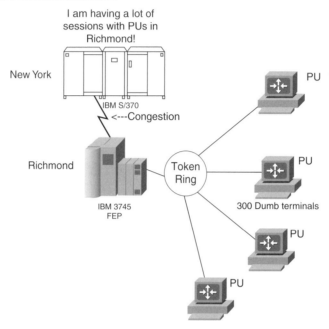

RouteitRight has the following requirements:

- Decrease WAN traffic.

- Possibly add the Internet to the site.

- No Novell gateways must be installed.

Answer to Scenario 1

There are other ways of meeting the company's requirements. This is only a recommended solution that meets the requirements placed on the CCDP. Figure 12-29 depicts the recommended solution.

Figure 12-29 *Scenario 1 Suggested Solution*

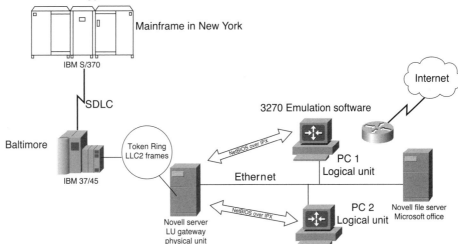

The CCDP has decided to meet the requirement to simplify the desktop by doing a number of things:

- Installing 3270 emulation software on the desktop PCs. This allows the company to eliminate the 3270 terminals that were cluttering up the user desktops.

- Installing a Novell Netware SAA server. This is needed so that the PCs can attach to it for SNA access. The PCs would be a LU from the mainframe's viewpoint. The PCs will access it via the NetBIOS-over-IPX protocol. This solution also meets the requirement to decrease WAN traffic to the mainframe by allowing the PCs to establish a session with the SAA Gateway and not to the mainframe.

- Installing an Ethernet card in the SAA gateway. This allows the CCDP to eliminate the expensive Token Ring segment to the users' dumb terminals.

Answer to Scenario 2

There are other ways of meeting the company's requirements. This is only a recommended solution that meets the requirements placed on the CCDP. Figure 12-30 depicts the recommended solution.

Figure 12-30 *Scenario 2 Suggested Solution*

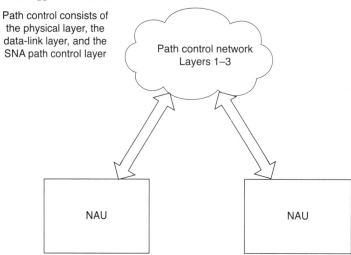

Path control consists of the physical layer, the data-link layer, and the SNA path control layer

Path control network
Layers 1–3

NAU

NAU

The CCDP meets the requirements by installing a single Cisco router at the company's site. This meets the customer's requirements by doing the following:

- Decreasing the WAN traffic by adding a Cisco router and configuring it as a DSPU. This allows the terminals to establish a session with the DSPU and not the host, thus decreasing WAN traffic.

- The CCDP has also provided the company with a future Internet connection with the Cisco router.

This chapter covers the following topics you will need to master as a CCDP:

- **SNA internetworking**—This section discusses the basic fundamentals of SNA.

- **Serial Tunnel (STUN)**—This section discusses serial tunneling of SDLC and some of the transport protocols for the SDLC frames.

- **SDLLC**—This section discusses converting SDLC frames into Token Ring frames and presenting those frames to the mainframe.

- **Data-link switching (DLSw+)**—This section discusses the evolution of DLSw+ and some of its options.

- **Advanced Peer-to-Peer Networking (APPN)**—This section discusses second-generation SNA.

- **Channel Interface Processor (CIP)**—This section covers some of the CIP features and terminology.

CHAPTER 13

SNA Internetworking

The CCDP exam requires you to have an in-depth understanding of Systems Network Architecture (SNA) technology. This chapter focuses on SDLLC, APPN, DLSw+, and the STUN protocol. SNA is not a new technology by any means, but you still might be called upon either to create a new design or to upgrade an existing legacy network.

The purpose of this chapter is not just to discuss the basics of these technologies, for there are other Cisco Press books that examine that in detail, but rather to discuss some of the SNA options that might be on the exam, and also what you should keep in mind when designing complex SNA networks.

How to Best Use This Chapter

By following these steps, you can make better use of your study time:

- Keep your notes and the answers for all your work with this book in one place for easy reference.

- Take the "Do I Know This Already?" quiz and write down your answers. Studies show that retention is significantly increased through writing down facts and concepts, even if you never look at the information again.

- Use the diagram shown in Figure 13-1 to guide you to the next step.

Figure 13-1   *How to Best Use this Chapter*

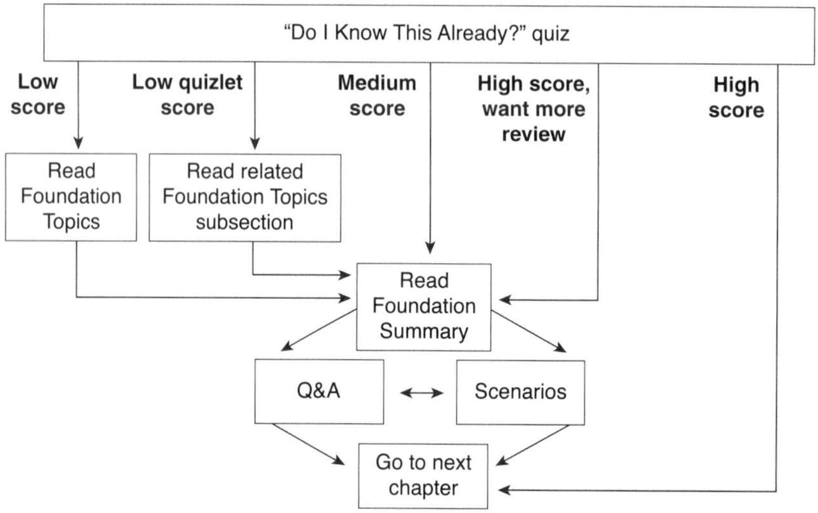

If you skip to the Foundation Summary, Q&A, and Scenarios sections and have trouble with the material there, you should go back to the Foundation Topics section.

"Do I Know This Already?" Quiz

The purpose of the "Do I Know This Already?" quiz is to help you decide which parts of this chapter to use. If you already intend to read the entire chapter, you do not necessarily need to answer these questions now.

This 14-question quiz helps you choose how to spend your limited study time. The quiz is divided into six smaller "quizlets" that help you select the sections of the chapter on which to focus. Figure 13-1 outlines suggestions for how to spend your time in this chapter. Use Table 13-1 to record your score.

Table 13-1   *Score Sheet for Quiz and Quizlets*

Quizlet Number	Foundation Topics Section Covering These Questions	Questions	Score
1	SNA Internetworking	1–3	
2	STUN	4–6	
3	SDLLC	7–8	
4	DLSw+	9–11	
5	Advanced Peer-to-Peer Networking	12–13	
6	Cisco Channel Interface Processor	14	

1 What SNA device performs a routing-like function?

_____

_____

_____

2 Which method of encapsulation of LLC2 frames provides for local acknowledgment?

_____

_____

_____

3 What does virtual multidrop mean?

_____

_____

_____

4 With STUN, which encapsulation method should be used for serial links?

_____

_____

_____

5 What does STUN connect?

_____

_____

_____

6 What is SDLLC?

_____

_____

_____

7 What is a benefit of local acknowledgment with SDLLC?

_____

_____

_____

8 What are dynamic peers?

_____

_____

_____

9 What does promiscuous mean?

_____

_____

_____

10 Of border peers, border groups, load balancing, and on-demand peers, which three are provided with DLSw+?

_____

_____

_____

11 Name the two methods that APPN network nodes use for routing updates.

_____

_____

_____

12 What is a composite network node?

_____

_____

_____

13 The CIP processor is supported on which Cisco routers?

_____

_____

_____

14 Name the six sources of traffic that SNA delivers to the mainframe from.

_____

_____

_____

The answers to the "Do I Know This Already?" quiz are found in Appendix A. The suggested choices for your next step are as follows:

- **6 or fewer overall score**—Read the chapter. This includes the "Foundation Topics," "Foundation Summary," and "Q&A" sections, as well as the scenarios at the end of the chapter.

- **2 or less on any quizlet**—Review the subsection(s) of the "Foundation Topics" part of this chapter based on Table 13-1. Then move into the "Foundation Summary," the "Q&A" section, and the scenarios at the end of the chapter.

- **7, 8, or 9 overall score**—Begin with the "Foundation Summary" section and then go to the "Q&A" section and scenarios at the end of the chapter.

- **10 or more overall score**—If you want more review on these topics, skip to the "Foundation Summary" section, and then go to the "Q&A" section and scenarios at the end of the chapter. Otherwise, move to the next chapter.

Foundation Topics

This chapter starts out with business and technical requirements and then moves into a look at Token Ring, followed by serial networking and how to tunnel SNA traffic using Cisco routers. This is followed by a discussion of protocol translation SDLLC, where serial SDLC traffic is converted into Token Ring LLC2 traffic. The modern standard variant of that, data-link switching (DLSw), is discussed, along with IBM-centric networking, or APPN (Advanced Peer-to-Peer Networking) and the CIP processor for the 7000 series routers.

Mainframe data centers have centralized computing, separate PC/mini/mainframe strategies, interactive terminal-oriented applications, and centralized management. The mainframe is often considered a corporate data repository that can support large-scale client/server applications. Expensive communication equipment such as front-end processors is now being replaced with Cisco routers. As more and more data centers are integrated with networks, a mainframe can be facilitated as a high-speed file server, SNMP mail server, or even as a Web HTTP server. So instead of having separate networks, one IBM-centric and one multiprotocol-centric, you can combine them and give new life to the mainframe. The mainframe does have high-speed access via ATM or Gigabyte Ethernet, and high availability.

SNA Token Ring Internetworking

As recently as the early 1990s, companies had deployed SNA networks and IP networks with no interaction between them. They were considered separate networks. As technology progressed and routers became smarter, the convergence of these two protocols was inevitable. When Frame Relay became widely known about 1994, the two environments became closer than ever before. Cisco seized this opportunity to develop software for its routers that could handle this explosive arena. The routers and mainframes can now process more information than ever before, and mainframes even have other uses never considered in the early days of SNA. For example, using the mainframe as a Web server has its advantages. It allows for migrating from legacy applications to modern-day applications.

TIP   Any media type that can be connected to a Cisco router can be connected to the mainframe.

This saves money by utilizing the existing investment in infrastructure costs. Cisco invested heavily in developing a router product that could help alleviate the need for the amount of IBM hardware a company would support by replacing the IBM equipment with Cisco routers.

Before Cisco routers were introduced to the network, front-end processors were performing a routing-like function between different SNA domains, as illustrated in Figure 13-2. There were also lots of leased SDLC lines, which are costly, slow-speed links. There also were varying amounts of Token Ring in the SNA domains.

Figure 13-2   *Pre-Cisco Routers*

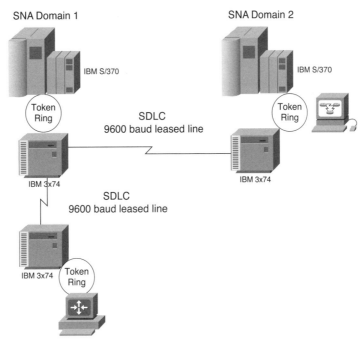

The first step in migrating from SNA to IP networks is to establish confidence in TCP/IP and Cisco routers. The routers are installed throughout the network. Using the Cisco tunneling feature DLSw+, layer 2 Token Ring LLC2 frames are encapsulated into IP datagrams back to the data center, as shown in Figure 13-3.

This figure illustrates a Token Ring PC communication with a mainframe. LLC2 frames are received on Ring 1 from the PC and are encapsulated into IP packets. Using the Cisco DLSw+ feature, they are transported across the non-Token Ring medium to their destination, R1. As soon as R1 receives them, it de-encapsulates the IP packets, and the LLC2 frames can now traverse Ring 2 toward their destination. Another possibility would be SDLC frames encapsulated into DLSw+ across the non-Token Ring medium, as shown in Figure 13-4.

An alternative method of migrating from SNA to IP networking is to use Frame Relay as the transport mechanism at Layer 2, as shown in Figure 13-5. This method does not involve DLSw+. Frame Relay provides cost savings over leased 9600-baud lines by enabling the use of other protocols over one physical connection. Begin by putting in routers until a stable network is in place.

Figure 13-3 *SNA Tunnels*

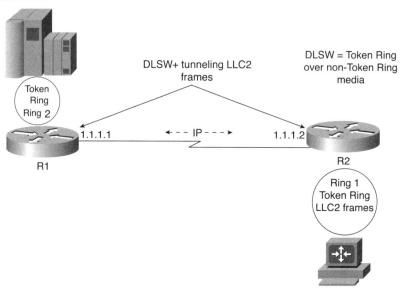

Figure 13-4 *SDLC Tunneled into DLSw+*

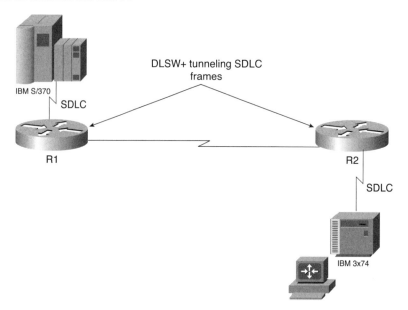

Figure 13-5   *SNA with Frame Relay*

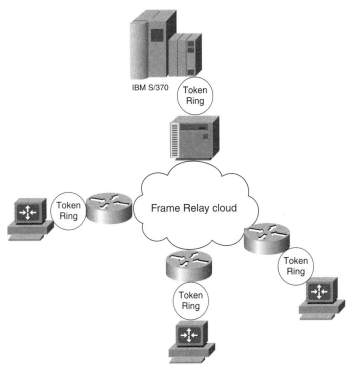

Then continue connecting the SNA devices. Thoroughly check router processes and buffers to make sure the routers are not being overworked. Migrating from SNA FEPs to Cisco routers might leave the customer with extra front-end processors (FEPs) and nothing to do with them. In some cases, the FEPs might be able to be sold back to IBM, or possibly another customer of IBM, because FEPs are quite expensive. The CCDP could make enough money for the company to pay for the routers, and even make some profit from the whole transaction for the company.

Migrating from FEPs to Cisco routers also saves money in support costs. It is more cost-effective to support Cisco routers than IBM FEPs. Another possibility is for cost savings in multiple mainframe environments where an abundance of cross-domain traffic is implementing the APPN feature of the Cisco IOS. APPN is discussed in more detail later in this chapter.

APPN should be used near the data center because it does not scale well. Using DLSw+ for remote site connectivity from the central site would be a good idea. Be concerned about the amount of memory needed to implement APPN. It can be substantial.

SNA does not have the same ability to reroute around link failures as IP does. In Figure 13-6, if the SDLC link between FEP A and FEP B fails, the SNA traffic will not reroute around FEP A and FEP C. If you have an IP network and you lose the wide-area link, IP will route around it. If the network converges quickly, SNA won't notice. There is one source of vulnerability: If you set up a tunnel between two routers and you lose that tunnel, you have to reestablish the session over the redundant link, possibly deleting the user's previously established session.

Figure 13-6   *SNA Link Failure*

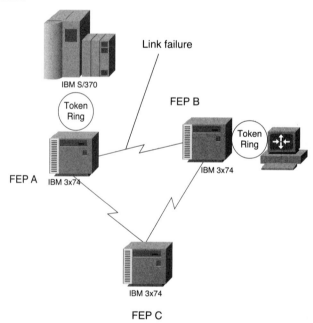

Serial Tunnel (STUN)

STUN was mentioned briefly in Chapter 10. STUN provides the ability to connect FEPs and cluster controllers across a multiprotocol backbone or any HDLC-based protocol, such as X.25. It also can be encapsulated into IP packets. With the IBM product line, STUN encapsulates both the FID4 and FID2 SNA path information units. In Figure 13-7, the FID4 frames between the

FEPs are encapsulated into IP packets across the STUN tunnel. STUN tunneling is always performed on serial ports, as shown in the figure.

Figure 13-7   *STUN FEP to FEP*

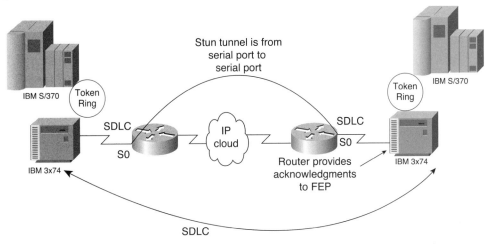

In Figure 13-7, the tunnel is created using a TCP connection between the routers. The command **stun route all TCP 1.1.1.1** is applied to the serial interface and creates the tunnel. The advantage of using TCP is that it lets the router provide the TCP acknowledgments locally versus across the WAN. Acknowledging locally can increase throughput.

STUN Transport Protocols

STUN has three transport protocols available as choices for the CCDP:

- TCP for local acknowledgment. It has the most overhead, but it also supports the most features, including local acknowledgment. Choose this method if there are multiple routers between endpoints of the STUN tunnels or if the redundancy and availability requirements are critical. Figure 13-8 illustrates the TCP method for STUN.

Figure 13-8 *STUN Using TCP Encapsulation*

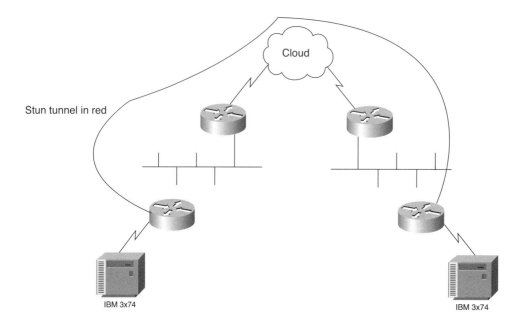

- HDLC for serial links. This method offers the best performance of the three methods because of the low overhead. Use this method if only two sites are connected over a leased line. The drawback is that this can be used only as a single link. This is not a very robust method; redundancy is hard to achieve. Figure 13-9 illustrates the HDLC method.

Figure 13-9 *STUN with HDLC Encapsulation*

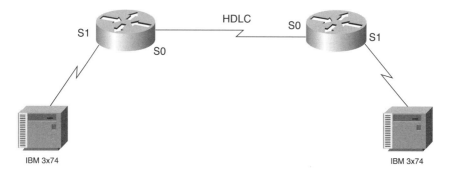

- Serial direct is used to connect local controllers to the router. An example of this is a FEP connected to one port of a Cisco router and a cluster controller connected to another port of the same router, as shown in Figure 13-10. This is not a very popular method.

Figure 13-10 *Serial Direct*

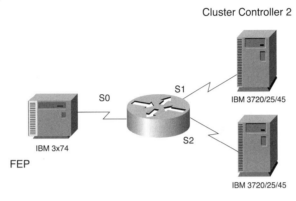

Cluster Controller 2

IBM 3720/25/45

S0

S1

S2

IBM 3x74

FEP

IBM 3720/25/45

Cluster Controller 1

Local Acknowledgment for STUN

Local acknowledgment with STUN is a good idea, especially if you have a congested WAN. Choose local acknowledgment for TCP STUN connections in cases where congestion and delay in the WAN cause SNA sessions to drop. However, keep in mind that local acknowledgment can create more overhead on the CPU, and STUN is already processor-intensive.

Remember, STUN is not just for IBM devices. Any HDLC-based protocol can be encapsulated with STUN. For example, a Nortel DPN-100 (an X.25 packet switch from the late 1970s) can have its proprietary protocol encapsulated over a STUN connection to communicate with another DPN-100 because the DPN-100 Netlink protocol is based on HDLC.

NOTE   X.25 is based on the HDLC protocol.

If the tunnels are carrying critical data, it might be necessary to implement a form of QoS such as Class-Based Weighted Fair Queuing (CBWFQ) on the routers. This can prioritize the STUN packets and also guarantee a certain amount of bandwidth for the connection through the routers. Because SDLC is typically used with slow links (slow links meaning 128 KB or less), the SDLC timers are more patient before timing out.

TIP   When classifying STUN packets as important through a QoS mechanism such as CBWFQ, do it as close as possible to the source.

SDLLC

SDLLC can convert remote SDLC frames to Token Ring frames on the mainframe side and pass them as true Token Ring traffic to the mainframe, as shown in Figure 13-11. Router A terminates LLC2 on the Token Ring interface and terminates SDLC on the SDLC interface. This has the potential to save money if there are many serial SDLC links in the network. By using a Cisco router and adding a high-speed Token Ring, you can consolidate expensive links into a Frame Relay network, as illustrated in Figure 13-12. Performance would be increased if you used the DLSw+ protocol (see the next section) and the local acknowledgment feature of Cisco IOS. LLC2 frames travel across the WAN links via IP packets and terminate on Routers B, C, and D. The hub router, Router A, must possess enough CPU horsepower to be able to withstand the stress of terminating multiple DLSw+ tunnels. This would be a slight trade-off from converting the LLC2 frames to SDLC frames on Router A.

Figure 13-11 *SDLLC*

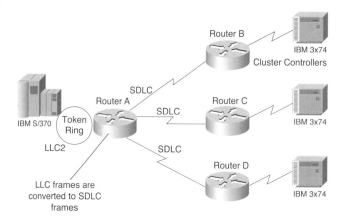

Figure 13-12 can be broken into three different sections if you use local acknowledgment. There would be an LLC2 session between the mainframe and Router A. Router A would acknowledge the LLC2 frames, which would provide for less overhead over the WAN medium.

There would also be a TCP session across the WAN Frame Relay network from Router A to Routers B, C, and D. Routers B, C, and D acknowledge the SDLC frames toward the cluster controllers. Again, you should monitor CPU utilization very closely.

Figure 13-12 *LLC2 Frames*

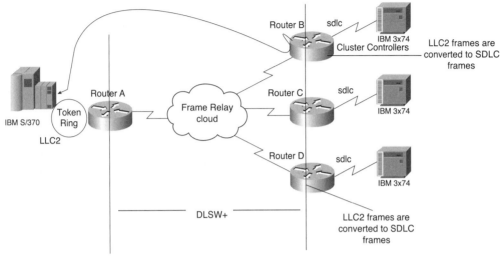

NOTE   Processor utilization thresholds can vary. For example, a 7206 with an NPM 400 processor module can easily withstand a steady 80% utilization rate. However, a less-powerful CPU on the 3600 series router might be susceptible to dropping packets at a steady 80% utilization rate.

Data-Link Switching (DLSw)

DLSw is a method of transporting SNA and NetBIOS traffic over a campus network or WAN with TCP/IP. Think of DLSw as Token Ring over non-Token Ring media. The end systems can attach to the network over Token Ring, Ethernet, SDLC, QLLC, or FDDI.

NOTE   QLLC is LLC2 frames over X.25 media. This is not discussed in this book.

Supported by IBM, Cisco, 3Com, Nortel, and others, DLSw uses TCP for reliable transport. It also supports direct encapsulation over Frame Relay or serial links. If there is a + after the letters DLSw, the + represents Cisco's own proprietary version of DLSw. DLSw supports STUN and SDLLC capabilities. This first version of DLSw, as specified in RFC 1434, has the following features:

- Provides for load balancing

- Allows for backup of peer routers

- Supports RIF termination
- Supports LLC2 termination

Cisco Enhanced DLSw+ Features

DLSw currently is in its third iteration. In the early 1990s, IBM was the first to introduce DLSw with RFCs 1434 and 1495. Then, a year or two later, IBM introduced RFC 1795 as the DLSw standard. RFC 1795 is known as version 1. DLSw version 2 added some scalability enhancements and is known as RFC 2166. Then Cisco developed its own flavor of DLSw called DLSw+, which added even more enhancements to the protocol. The improvements made by Cisco help with scaling, availability, and usability. DLSw+ can divide one large group of full-meshed peers into smaller groups. This decreases overhead on the Cisco routers, as shown in Figure 13-13. DLSw+ can also elect routers to speak on behalf of peer groups; these are known as border peers. Border peers communicate with each other and represent a group of spoke routers. Instead of having all the spoke routers talk to each other as a full mesh, as shown in Figure 13-13, a spoke router talks to only its border peer. The border peer communicates with the other border peer, and that border router updates its group of routers.

Figure 13-13 *DLSw+ Border Peers*

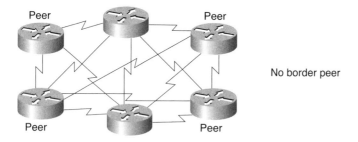

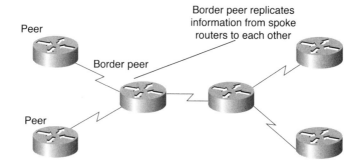

Another feature is on-demand peers, where the connection is made when there is a demand for it. On-demand peers require very little configuration. The router must be in promiscuous (listening) mode to receive the connection request.

The following are some scalability benefits of DLSw version 2 as specified in RFC 1795:

- Peer groups
- Border peers
- On-demand peers
- Backward compatibility with RSRB
- Backward compatibility with STUN
- Local and remote caching
- RIF termination
- Preferred/capable peers
- Backup peers
- Duplicate TIC address support

Choose a Transport Protocol for DLSw+

The transport connection between DLSw+ peer routers can vary according to needs.

Cisco supports four transport protocols between DLSw+ peers:

- **TCP/IP**—One of the main differences from TCP encapsulation is that it is process-switched and therefore uses more CPU power than either FST or Direct encapsulation. TCP transports SNA and NetBIOS traffic across WANs, where local acknowledgment is required to minimize unnecessary traffic and prevent data-link control timeouts and where nondisruptive rerouting around link failures is critical. A Cisco 4700 router running DLSw+ can switch up to 8 Mbps of data, so TCP will meet most of the requirements.

  If higher throughput is desired, consider adding more routers or using alternative methods to encapsulate the data.

- **FST/IP**—Usually used over high-speed links such as 256 Kbps or higher. Because FST is fast-switched, this encapsulation allows DLSw+ to process more packets per second than TCP. FST transports SNA and NetBIOS traffic across WANs with an arbitrary topology. This solution allows rerouting around link failures, but recovery might be disruptive, depending on the time required to find an alternative path. This option does not support local acknowledgment of frames. FST is supported only when the end systems are Token Ring, whereas TCP is supported if one of the end systems is on Ethernet. Load balancing is not recommended with FST because frames might arrive out of order.

- **Direct**—Direct encapsulation is fast-switched. Direct transports SNA and NetBIOS traffic across a point-to-point or Frame Relay connection, where the benefits of an arbitrary topology are unimportant and where nondisruptive rerouting around link failures is not required. This option does not support local acknowledgment of frames. Like FST, Direct is supported only when the end systems reside on Token Ring.

- **DLSw Lite**—Otherwise known as LLC2 encapsulation, DLSw Lite is processed-switched and can process approximately the same amount of traffic as TCP. DLSw Lite transports SNA and NetBIOS traffic across a point-to-point connection where local acknowledgment and reliable transport are important but where nondisruptive rerouting around link failures is not required.

Avoiding Timeouts with LLC2 Termination

Because LLC2 is a connection-oriented data-link protocol, the end stations involved in the LLC2 connection must periodically check that the LLC2 connection is still active. The great thing about DLSw is that, unlike RSRB, you can terminate LLC2 connections locally. The DLSw standards eliminate the requirements for LLC2 acknowledgments and keep messages flowing across the WAN alive. Because routers acknowledge frames locally, LLC2 timeouts should never occur.

Advanced Peer-to-Peer Networking (APPN)

A significant step from the original SNA architecture from IBM is APPN, shown in Figure 13-14. It provides peer-to-peer SNA routing. Instead of defining all the network resources on the mainframe, you can define local resources on the nodes (routers), and they pass this information around in the form of a distributed database. This is similar to what Cisco routers do by defining the networks connected to the interfaces. The routers pass around the information from those networks as in OSPF. In the same manner, the routers pass the SNA network information to each other. Sessions can be established between any two logical units in the network without involving a mainframe.

Figure 13-14   *APPN*

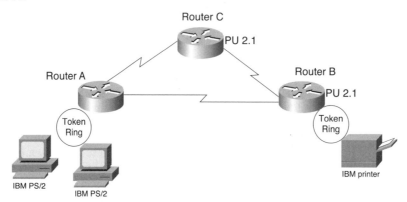

Second-Generation SNA: APPN

APPN was designed by IBM to meet the following requirements:

- Provide an effective routing protocol to allow SNA traffic to flow natively and concurrently with other protocols

- Allow sessions to be established between end users without the involvement of the mainframe

- Reduce requirements for predefined resources and paths

- Maintain and enhance Class of Service (COS) to provide prioritization within SNA traffic

- Provide an environment that supports both legacy and APPN traffic

APPN Terminology

It is important to define APPN terms before moving on to the rest of this section. APPN has what is known as a network node, usually defined as a Cisco router. The network node is a PU 2.1 in IBM terminology. Network nodes typically have control points (CPs) that communicate with neighboring network node control points and exchange information. There are also end nodes, which could be PU 2.1. End nodes provide end-user services and are usually located on the outskirts of the APPN network. A third type of node is called the low entry node (LEN), which represents dumb nodes. LENs were developed before APPN, and they need to have resources defined to them. The fourth and final type of node is the mainframe, which is called a composite network node.

Control points activate resources in a node. Control points are also where local resources are defined.

The question arises: What routing protocol is used to propagate this SNA information from router to router? Two routing protocols are used. The first one, developed by IBM, was intermediate session routing (ISR). The new development is high-performance routing (HPR).

ISR and HPR

End stations can use two methods to communicate over the routers. The first is intermediate session routing (ISR). A single session is divided into stages, as shown in Figure 13-15. Each session has a unique identifier, called the Local-Form Session Identifier (LFSID). In Figure 13-15, there is a session 123 between the Token Ring PC and the router. There is also a unique session between the two routers, labeled 456. As a message traverses the routers, the entire message must be buffered. Error detection, error correction, flow control, and resegmentation might occur at each point, not at the end stations. At each router, the incoming unique LFSID is swapped for the outgoing unique LFSID. So the only things that must be remembered are the label and port in both directions. The major drawback of ISR is that it is very much like IP static routing and cannot reroute around failures. In addition, much checking and verifying are done at each stop rather than just at the connection's endpoints.

Figure 13-15 *Session Stages*

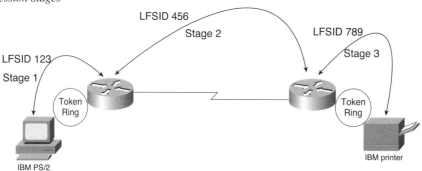

With high-performance routing (HPR), APPN dynamically reroutes around link failures without disrupting SNA sessions. Also, HPR does error checking at the end stations and not all the intermediate hops as ISR does. In Figure 13-16, the PC on Router B can print to the printer on Router A if either of the serial links connected to Router A fails. HPR accomplishes this by using two networking layers. The first protocol to discuss is a connectionless layer called Automatic Network Routing (ANR), which has some similarities to IP. ANR HPR has a second reliable connection-oriented layer called Rapid Transport Protocol (RTP), which provides end-to-end functionality and guarantees delivery of data. RTP is a transport layer protocol similar to TCP. It provides functions including error recovery, packet resequencing, segmentation, and flow control.

Figure 13-16 *HPR*

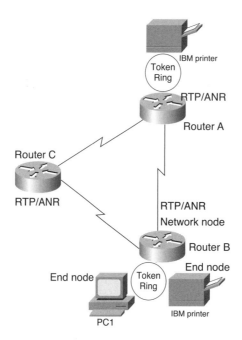

In intermediate nodes, processing occurs at the ANR level, significantly reducing latency, which is important in high-speed environments.

Virtual Nodes

On a Token Ring LAN, there is no need to go through the network node if two devices reside on the same LAN. In Figure 13-16, if PC1 wants to send information to the printer on the Token Ring LAN, a feature is needed that permits that to happen without disturbing the router. This is where virtual nodes come in.

After a virtual node is defined, all routing occurs through the virtual node, not the network node. Every end node still has a CP-CP session with the network node, but sessions with another resource on the LAN do not pass through the network node. Each network node defines two connections—one to the network node and one to the virtual node.

When the network node receives a session request, it recognizes both end nodes as being on the same medium and selects a route that directly connects the two through the virtual node rather than through the network node.

Dependent LUs

When APPN was first defined in the mid-1980s, it supported LU 6.2 applications only. Because most applications were 3270 applications, the corporate world did not embrace it right away. However, in VTAM release 4.2, a feature known as dependent LUs was introduced. This feature allowed the use of APPN for any application in the network.

In APPN, the concept of primary and secondary LUs does not exist; there is no concept of upstream or downstream devices. Primary and secondary roles are negotiated by the nodes. Dependent Logical Units (DLUs) are legacy LUs—types 0, 1, 2, 3, and so on. They cannot initiate sessions without the intervention of VTAM, and they lack the ability to actively participate in a peer-to-peer session initiation.

APPN no longer has the concept of a primary and secondary end of a session. Either end can initiate a session and become the primary; the primary then sends the BIND to set up the session. In APPN, there is no concept of a node that cannot send a BIND. Special support has been added to APPN to permit legacy LUs to participate. This support is called Dependent Logical Unit Requester/Server (DLUR/DLUS), where the server is implemented in VTAM 4.2 and the requester can be in a network node or end node in the network. DLUR is implemented in the Cisco router.

Cisco IOS Support

Let's finish this topic by looking at how the Cisco IOS functions here. APPN support became available in Cisco release 11.0. Features included ISR routing, support for nodes on a LAN, DLU support, and APPN routing across the channel using the CIP card. A Cisco router can support LENs as well as DLUs. Because the LENs do not establish CP-CP sessions with their adjacent network node, the LEN must be predefined to the network node. A Cisco IOS configuration command provides this function. Because APPN nodes have a full PU image, they are known to VTAM and Netview and can be managed by SNA management services as well as SNMP.

Cisco Channel Interface Processor

The Channel Interface Processor (CIP) feature of the Cisco IOS is available on the 7000 and 7500 series routers. More recently, the 7200 has a port adapter that can perform CIP functions. The CIP passes TCP/IP, SNA, and APPN traffic to the mainframe over the mainframe channel. CIPs replace the function of the IBM 3172 and eliminate the need for a separate FEP. One advantage of using the CIP is the ability to attach ATM or Gigabit Ethernet to the mainframe. Another added benefit is the ability to route IP packets to the CIP router from remote sites. Probably the major cost savings comes into effect when you consider the ability to replace FEPs with CIP routers. A CIP router is depicted in Figure 13-17.

Figure 13-17 *Channel Interface Processor*

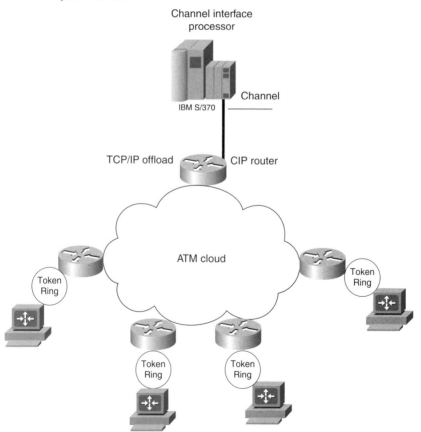

Notice in Figure 13-17 the phrase "TCP/IP Offload." TCP/IP Offload is a handy Cisco IOS feature that offloads the building of IP headers and TCP headers from the mainframe to the router, saving mainframe CPU cycles. However, the need for a TCP/IP stack on the mainframe still exists.

CIP SNA

Another feature that the CIP card supports is CIP SNA (CSNA). CSNA lets the CIP talk directly to the VTAM on the host and gives customers a way to replace their channel-attached FEPs. CSNA delivers traffic to and from the mainframe from a variety of sources, including DLSw+, DSPU, APPN, RSRB, SDLLC, and QLLC.

LAN and WAN Interconnectivity with the CIP

The Cisco CIP, with the range of function and power of the Cisco 7000 and 7500 series, is a high-performance data center internetworking product with broad connectivity that is easy to manage. Many LAN and WAN technologies are supported, including 10 Mbps Ethernet, 100 Mbps Ethernet, Gigabit Ethernet, low- and high-speed serial links, Frame Relay, ATM, High-Speed Serial Interface (HSSI), and ISDN.

Foundation Summary

This section contains tables that provide a convenient review of many key concepts in this chapter. If you are already comfortable with the topics in this chapter, this summary could help you recall a few details. If you have just read this chapter, this review should help solidify some key facts. If you are doing your final preparation before the exam, these tables are a convenient way to review the day before the exam.

Table 13-2 compares the APPN model with the OSI model.

Table 13-2   *APPN Model Versus the OSI Model*

SNA/APPN	OSI Reference Model
Application	Application layer
APPC/LU 6.2	Presentation layer
APPN path control	Session layer
APPN path control	Transport layer
APPN path control	Network layer
Data link control layer	Data link layer
Physical control layer	Physical layer

In Table 13-3, match the following components with their description.

Table 13-3   *SNA Components*

1. LLC1	A. Supports border peers and border groups
2. DLSw+	B. Distributed directory services
3. APPN	C. Connectionless without acknowledgment
4. DLUR	D. Attaches the router directly to a mainframe
5. SDLLC	E. Always used for SNA and NetBIOS sessions
6. LLC2	F. Should be implemented in a network with few alternative paths
7. FST encapsulation	G. Connects FEPs across a multiprotocol backbone
8. CIP	H. Controls RSRB explorers
9. STUN	I. Developed for legacy LUs
10. Proxy Explorer	J. Converts SDLC into Token Ring frames

Q&A

As mentioned in Chapter 1, the questions and scenarios in this book are more difficult than what you will experience on the actual exam. The questions do not attempt to cover more breadth or depth than the exam; however, they are designed to make sure that you know the answer. Rather than allowing you to derive the answer from clues hidden inside the question, the questions challenge your understanding and recall of the subject. Questions from the "Do I Know This Already?" quiz from the beginning of the chapter are repeated here to ensure that you have mastered this chapter's topic areas. Hopefully, these questions will help limit the number of exam questions on which you narrow your choices to two options and then guess. Be sure to use the CD and take the simulated exams.

The answers to these questions can be found in Appendix A.

1 Which method of encapsulation of LLC2 frames provides for local acknowledgment?

_____

_____

_____

2 What does virtual multidrop mean?

_____

_____

_____

3 With STUN, which encapsulation method should be used for serial links?

_____

_____

_____

4 What does STUN connect?

_____

_____

_____

5 What is SDLLC?

_____

_____

_____

6 What is a benefit of local acknowledgment with SDLLC?

_____

_____

_____

7 What are dynamic peers?

_____

_____

_____

8 What does promiscuous mean?

_____

_____

_____

9 Of border peers, border groups, load balancing, and on-demand peers, which three are provided with DLSw+?

_____

_____

_____

10 Name the two methods that APPN network nodes use for routing updates.

_____

_____

_____

11 What is a composite network node?

_____

_____

_____

12 The CIP processor is supported on which Cisco routers?

_____

_____

_____

13 Name the six sources that CSNA delivers traffic to the mainframe from.

_____

_____

_____

14 Which process offloads routers' CPU cycles by having the workstation be the tunnel peer?

_____

_____

_____

15 In APPN, a router is known as what?

_____

_____

_____

16 What is used so that legacy SDLC controllers can connect to TIC-attached FEPs?

_____

_____

_____

17 What should you use for RIF termination and on-demand peers for greater scalability?

_____

_____

_____

18 What special support was added for legacy secondary logical units that cannot issue a BIND?

_____

_____

_____

19 APPN is used for what purpose?

_____

_____

_____

20 Name two benefits of DLSw+.

_____

_____

_____

21 With DLSw+, the RIF terminates where?

_____

_____

_____

22 Name two reasons to use SDLLC.

_____

_____

_____

23 Name two reasons to use local acknowledgment with STUN.

_____

_____

_____

24 Name two reasons to integrate the mainframe into the data center.

_____

_____

_____

25 Which encapsulation method provides for local acknowledgment?

_____

_____

_____

26 Why is load balancing not recommended with FST encapsulation?

_____

_____

_____

27 Promiscuous mode means the peer will accept connections from whom?

_____

_____

_____

28 If you have only one Token Ring path to a destination, what type of RIF cache could you use?

_____

_____

_____

29 What does the command **source-bridge proxy-explorer** do?

_____

_____

_____

30 What does NCIA stand for?

_____

_____

_____

Scenarios

RouteitRight has offices in four locations: New York, Livermore, Chicago, and Annapolis. Currently, the company is paying substantial money for the leased lines used to connect their legacy X.25 network. The legacy network consists of an X.25 switch at each location connected via 256 Kbps links. The company also uses Cisco 7500 series routers to route its IP traffic. These routers are connected via an ATM backbone that provides a total throughput of 40 Mbps.

NOTE	An ATM DS3, when formatted with Physical Layer Convergence Protocol (PLCP), which is the standard, ends up being 40 Mbps and not 45 Mbps due to the overhead of the PLCP format. PLCP is widely used in the United States and provides for 96,000 cells per second, which equals about 40 Mbps. PLCP adds 4 bytes of data as overhead to every cell, thereby decreasing the throughput to about 40 Mbps for a DS3. The 4 bytes of overhead per cell are used as pointers by the PLCP to identify the cell location in the PLCP frame.

The current ATM backbone is not overly subscribed, and plenty of bandwidth is available.

Scenario 1

Figure 13-18 represents RouteitRight's current network configuration.

RouteitRight has the following requirements for the CCDP:

- Cut costs by eliminating the expensive leased-line serial links between the four locations.
- CIP cards for the routers are not an option.
- Although it is legacy traffic, it is very important traffic because it generates revenue. This traffic should be treated as mission-critical traffic.
- There need to be redundant paths for the legacy traffic.

Figure 13-18 *Scenario 1*

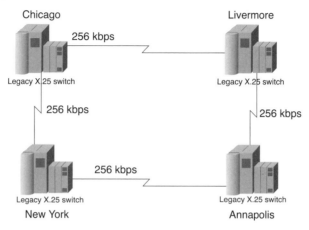

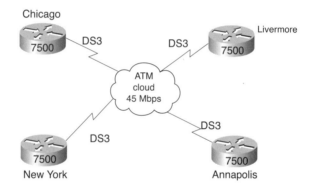

Scenario 1 Suggested Solution

There are other ways of meeting the company's requirements. This is only a recommended solution that meets the requirements placed on the CCDP.

The CCDP decides to meet the requirement to eliminate the costly leased lines by implementing the STUN protocol between the routers to transport the legacy traffic.

In Figure 13-19, the legacy X.25 switches have two paths through the network for redundancy. Let's take a look at the commands used to perform STUN:

Command	Description
`interface Loopback1`	Creates a loopback interface
`ip address 1.1.1.1 255.255.255.0`	Use this address for the STUN peer name

continues

Command	Description
`stun peer-name 1.1.1.1`	The router STUN identifier
`stun protocol-group 1 basic`	Assign this group one of the serial interfaces
`stun protocol-group 2 basic`	Assign this group to the second serial interface
`interface Serial0/0`	
`no ip address`	Notice that no IP address is needed on the serial interface
`encapsulation stun`	Applies the STUN protocol to the interface
`stun group 1`	Applies the STUN group to the interface
`stun route all tcp 3.3.3.3`	On this interface route, all the traffic to STUN peer 3.3.3.3

Figure 13-19 *Recommended Solution*

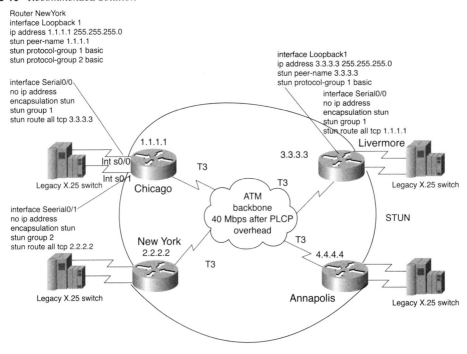

NOTE Local acknowledgment cannot be used with STUN basic routes.

```
r1(config-if)# stun route all tcp 2.2.2.2 local-ack
```

By encapsulating the HDLC-based X.25 traffic into IP packets, there is some redundancy. If one of the core site routers fails, the traffic takes an alternate path from the legacy X.25 switch at the functioning sites. In other words, if router Chicago fails, the switch at New York will still be able to get to Livermore via router Annapolis.

By implementing Quality of Service, the STUN packets can be given priority on the network. There are many ways to configure QoS. A practical method in this example might be to configure Class-Based Weighted Fair Queuing. CBWFQ is a good choice because when you use extended access lists, the STUN traffic can be prioritized. You can also guarantee a certain amount of bandwidth per STUN tunnel.

This chapter covers the following topics you will need to master as a CCDP:

- **Reliable SNA internetworks**—This section discusses some common Token Ring designs.

- **DLSw+ design topologies**—This section discusses various DLSw+ designs and methods of controlling broadcasts with border peers.

- **QoS and DLSw**—This section discusses various methods for implementing Quality of Service with DLSw+.

- **DLSw tuning**—This section describes the different timers available to the CCDP and when it might be practical and effective to apply them.

SNA Topologies

The CCDP exam requires you to have an in-depth understanding of SNA technology. This is the third of three chapters on this topic. In this chapter, the discussion focuses on several topics, including some common Token Ring and DLSw+ designs with border peers. As with any time-sensitive protocol, quality of service (QoS) needs to be applied to help the traffic receive the priority it needs so that it does not time out. Various QoS methods are discussed. Finally, another important aspect of DLSw+ is the many timer options available to the CCDP. The timer's default values are listed, along with reasons for changing them.

How to Best Use This Chapter

By follow these steps, you can make better use of your study time:

- Keep your notes and the answers for all your work with this book in one place for easy reference.

- Take the "Do I Know This Already?" quiz and write down your answers. Studies show that retention is significantly increased through writing down facts and concepts, even if you never look at the information again.

- Use the diagram shown in Figure 14-1 to guide you to the next step.

Figure 14-1 *How to Use This Chapter*

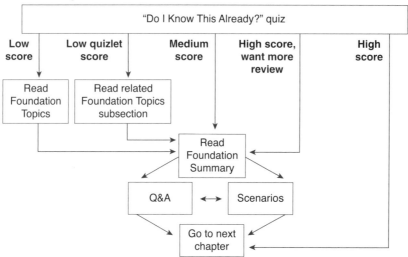

If you skip to the Foundation Summary, Q&A, and Scenarios sections and have trouble with the material there, you should go back to the Foundation Topics section.

"Do I Know This Already?" Quiz

The purpose of the "Do I Know This Already?" quiz is to help you decide what parts of this chapter to use. If you intend to read the entire chapter, you do not necessarily need to answer these questions now.

This 15-question quiz helps you choose how to spend your limited study time. The quiz is divided into four smaller "quizlets" that help you select the sections of the chapter on which to focus. Figure 14-1 outlines suggestions on how to spend your time in this chapter. Use Table 14-1 to record your score.

Table 14-1 *Score Sheet for Quiz and Quizlets*

Quizlet Number	Foundation Topics Section Covering These Questions	Questions	Score
1	Reliable SNA internetworks	1–3	
2	DLSw+ design topologies	4–7	
3	QoS and DLSw	8–11	
4	DLSw tuning	12–15	

1 What are two frame types that SNA networks transport?

_____

_____

_____

2 What type of explorer packet takes every possible path through the network?

_____

_____

_____

3 In SNA networks, should the convergence time be less than the session expiration time?

_____

_____

_____

4 Does an explorer ever visit the same Token Ring twice?

_____

_____

_____

5 For what is Proxy Explorer used?

_____

_____

_____

6 What is a method of transporting SNA and NetBIOS frames over an IP network?

_____

_____

_____

7 What type of DLSw+ encapsulation can be used on Token Ring ports but not Ethernet?

_____

_____

_____

8 Which type of encapsulation uses more CPU cycles to support it, Local Acknowledgment or Direct?

_____

_____

_____

9 Name three methods of controlling CANYOUREACH explorer frames in DLSw+ networks.

_____

_____

_____

10 How many times must a border peer replicate a broadcast if it is configured for nine peers in its group and two other border peers?

_____

_____

_____

11 Which type of QoS provides guaranteed service end-to-end across a network?

_____

_____

_____

12 Name one reason why ISPs do not like to implement RSVP.

_____

_____

_____

13 How many bits are in the IP header's Type of Service field?

_____

_____

_____

14 How many bits make up the IP Precedence portion of the Type of Service field?

_____

_____

_____

15 What is the only command that is absolutely necessary on a router if it is to participate in DLSw+ in listening mode?

_____

_____

_____

The answers to the "Do I Know This Already?" quiz are found in Appendix A. The suggested choices for your next step are as follows:

- **6 or less overall score**—Read the chapter. This includes the "Foundation Topics," "Foundation Summary," and "Q & A" sections, as well as the scenarios at the end of the chapter.

- **2 or less on any "quizlet"**—Review the subsection(s) of the "Foundation Topics" part of this chapter based on Table 14-1. Then move into the "Foundation Summary," the "Q&A" section, and the scenarios at the end of the chapter.

- **7, 8, or 9 overall score**—Begin with the "Foundation Summary" section and then go to the "Q&A" section and the scenarios at the end of the chapter.

- **10 or more overall score**—If you want more review on these topics, skip to the "Foundation Summary" section, then go to the "Q&A" section and the scenarios at the end of the chapter. Otherwise, move to the next chapter.

Foundation Topics

Unfortunately, there really is no perfect SNA design. You must look at several different methods in any SNA design, and there are multiple ways of accomplishing the same goal. Some methods are better than others. In this chapter, we put together the last two chapters and apply them to common SNA design models. We will talk about how to design reliable SNA networks with redundancy. We will also discuss DLSw+ designs and how to apply QoS features to DLSw+. By the end of this chapter, you should have a solid understanding of some of the topics on the exam.

Reliable SNA Internetworks

The heart and soul of SNA is predictable and reliable data links. When designing complex SNA networks with Cisco routers and transporting LLC2 and SDLC frames, it is important that the convergence time is less than the session expiration time. Otherwise, timeouts might occur. As long as this is done, you will have the predictability and reliability needed to maintain the SNA session. Let's discuss some of the methods commonly used in SNA to maintain that reliability.

Redundancy and Load Balancing

Let's start off with one of the most common methods—using dual front-end processors (FEPs) (see Figure 14-2). The key to this design is that the same locally administered MAC address appears on both FEPs. In this design, explorers from hosts 1 through 4 find multiple paths to the FEPs by configuring the routers as DSPUs or gateways. Half of the hosts have MAC address A, and the other half have MAC address B. Half of the PCs should connect to FEP right, and the other half should connect to FEP left. This method provides not only load balancing, but redundancy as well.

NOTE   In this scenario, the Token Rings connected to the FEPs have to be numbered differently. In other words, both rings cannot be Token Ring 10—they are 10 and 20.

Figure 14-2   *Dual FEPs*

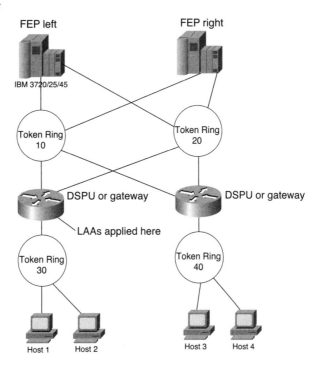

Dual-Backbone Token Ring Design

Dual-backbone Token Ring design is another common technique used in IBM environments. Remember that the basic mechanic of source route bridging is explorer control. Because an all-routes explorer takes every possible path through a network, you will have explorers multiplying in the network if you are not careful with your design.

Figure 14-3 depicts a practical design for controlling explorers. Start with a dual Token Ring backbone. In Figure 14-3, the mainframes are connected to the backbone rings (the vertical rings in this example). Servers are also attached to the backbone rings in most cases. Clients reside on the horizontal rings.

Figure 14-3 *Dual Backbones*

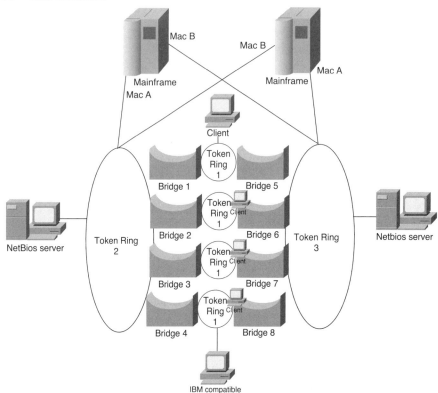

You can now limit the number of explorers by limiting the hop-count to one hop, because after one hop they will have arrived at their destination. Clients can now talk to servers or mainframes that are one hop away but not to clients on other rings, which would be two hops away. To curtail the explorer replication even further, it is a good idea to give the Token Rings the same number because an explorer never visits the same ring twice. However, in this situation, the bridge numbers would have to be different. Confusion would set in if they were numbered the same.

NOTE   You might want to use a different limit of hop counts for spanning explorers than those of all-routes explorers. The reason behind this is that mainframes are typically arranged in a hierarchical fashion, and NetBios servers usually are distributed. As a result, there might need to be more hop-counts for SNA because there might be more hops to the SNA mainframes than the hop-counts for NetBios servers, which are probably distributed around the rings.

Dual Collapsed Backbone

Dual collapsed backbone, depicted in Figure 14-4, is an alternate method to the conventional dual-backbone Token Ring design. The backbone Token Rings are collapsed into the backplane of two routers. Each router has an internal virtual ring 7 that is bridged to the client rings. In this case, there are four client rings. This method provides for redundancy and controls explorer looping by making the virtual ring the same number (7). As a result, explorers from the client rings do not traverse ring 7 twice because the rule is to never visit the same ring twice.

Figure 14-4   *Dual Collapsed Backbones*

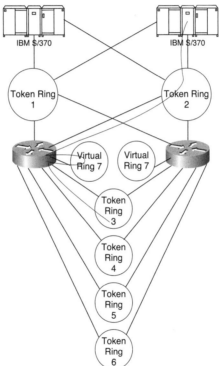

Proxy Explorer

Proxy Explorer also enables explorer control without using duplicate Token Ring Interface Coupler (TIC) addresses. You should use it if SNA explorer packets are destined for a single FEP on only a single ring, as depicted in Figure 14-5. This design feature creates an explorer-packet reply cache on the router. The entries are reused when subsequent explorer packets need to find the same host. There is no possibility of redundant paths.

Figure 14-5 *Proxy Explorer*

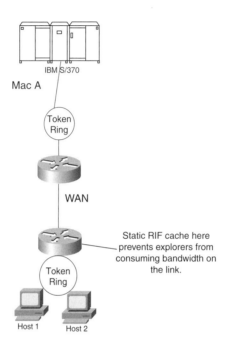

Proxy Explorer functionality is very useful in traditional SNA configurations because most explorer packets are destined for a single FEP on a single ring. However, if the host to be reached is a FEP on two rings (with a single locally administered address duplicated on both rings), this feature selects a single path without the possibility of redundant paths from a single router.

DLSw+ Design Topologies

Data Link Switching (DLSw+) is a popular subject within SNA networks. DLSw+ can be described as Token Ring over non-Token Ring media, or a means to transport SNA and NetBIOS over an IP backbone. DLSw+ is a second-generation RSRB (Remote Source Route Bridge). In the early 1990s, companies that deployed IP and SNA networks were on totally separate networks—two trains on two tracks. IBM realized that these two networks would eventually have to merge onto the same track. In 1993, IBM introduced its first attempt at standardizing a formal IP encapsulation of SNA protocol, RFC 1434, as a formal specification for DLSw, which would be one of the mechanisms used (Cisco has many proprietary flavors) to merge these two technologies. About two years later, in 1995, IBM made some improvements and introduced RFC 1795 as DLSw version 1. Around that time, Frame Relay networks were exploding. Coupled with DLSw, they would provide a path for SNA/IP integration.

SNA applications have always been known to provide mission-critical business functions but only to SNA equipment over SNA communication devices. IBM noticed the rapid growth of the Internet in the mid-'90s and realized it must make SNA applications more IP-friendly and accessible to the IP community. This paradigm shift can be compared to the migration of the voice world to voice over IP today. Organizations needed to make adjustments to the SNA/IP paradigm shift similar to the paradigm shift of VoIP.

DLSw version 1 required full-mesh connectivity between peers. This requirement was eliminated with the introduction of DLSw version 2, RFC 2166. DLSw 2 also added several other benefits:

- One TCP session instead of two between peers

- The use of UDP unicast instead of TCP

Finally, Cisco developed its own proprietary version of DLSw called DLSw+. DLSw+ differs from DLSw primarily in the types of encapsulations that can be used. DLSw+ peers may be connected via TCP, Fast Sequence Transport (FST), or Direct. FST and Direct are Cisco's own methods.

You might need to read Chapters 12 and 13 or have some understanding of DLSw+ before you attempt to read this chapter. In the early days of DLSw+, there probably was a full-mesh configuration connecting all the peers. Full-mesh configurations have many drawbacks. Like most protocols, DLSw+ works best in a hierarchical topology. This section discusses a method of dealing with a DLSw+ hierarchical structure called *border peers*. Border peers provide a hierarchical structure similar to a default gateway function in IP and eliminate unnecessary traffic that can be compared to the way a router blocks broadcasts. This section also discusses some of the key components of DLSw+ design and eliminating unnecessary traffic. Some of the key components include design rules and the border-peer design theory of operation. Border peers help reduce the number of physical connections in a full-mesh environment.

DLSw+ is sometimes called an any-to-any (full-mesh) network.

Hierarchical

Let's take a look at some of the key components involved in supporting a DLSw+ network:

- The number of physical units is a driving factor. Because an SNA physical unit has either an SDLC or LLC2 connection to another device, it must send keepalive messages at regular intervals. Keepalive messages can be processor-intensive. If there are many connections, this could affect router selection.

NOTE   A Cisco 4700 router can handle about 4000 physical units.

- Transaction rate is important. A typical transaction rate is one transaction per logical unit per minute. By doing some arithmetic, you can determine the number of logical units per physical units on average, which can give you an average approximation. To determine router utilization requirements, you must understand transaction rates and requirements.

NOTE   Transaction message size is about 40 bytes inbound and 1000 bytes outbound.

- The type of encapsulation is important. Each type of encapsulation impacts router performance differently. If you choose an encapsulation that provides for local acknowledgment, that puts more overhead on the processor. Of the four types of encapsulation used with DLSw+, two provide for local acknowledgment (TCP and LLC2). The other two types, FST and Direct encapsulation, can run in pass-through mode over fast, reliable networks and require very little router-processing overhead. However, more bandwidth is consumed across the links.

WARNING   FST encapsulation can be used only on Token Ring ports; there is no support for Ethernet.

NOTE   If there is a lot of unused bandwidth between sites, use DLSw in pass-through mode, which does not require local acknowledgments. This decreases the router overhead, as shown in Figure 14-6. In the figure, the two end stations send acknowledgments that must traverse the WAN.

Figure 14-6   *Passthru*

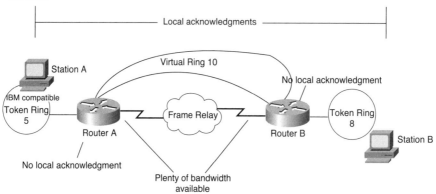

- You need to consider the number of remote-site routers peering to the central site. More remote-site routers might necessitate more central-site routers to alleviate the processing burden on the central-site router. More remote peers means more central-site routers.

- If connection requests are initiated from remote peers, that should not be a problem. However, if they are initiated from the central site, that could be a problem due to the amount of CPU usage needed to generate a session.

- The types of explorers, whether they be NetBIOS or SNA, can affect performance.

Peering Router Placement

As soon as you have determined the number of DLSw+ routers, you need to determine their placement. Peer placement usually depends on a combination of traffic load, multiprotocol traffic volumes, backup scenarios, and encapsulation types. Let's take a look at four typical methods to peer the routers:

- **All-in-one (DLSw+, IP, and WAN)**—Peer all remote routers to the central site, as shown in Figure 14-7. The central site typically has a 7500 or 7200 router with a CIP card installed and directly attached to a mainframe. In this situation, the router performs several functions:

    — WAN encapsulations with the serial port connected to the WAN. Other functions performed by the router include DLSw+ signaling to the remote sites and communication with the mainframe. This is a solution for small SNA networks— 30 to 60 branches maximum. Because this solution represents the fewest components, it is also the least-costly solution.

Figure 14-7   *All-in-One*

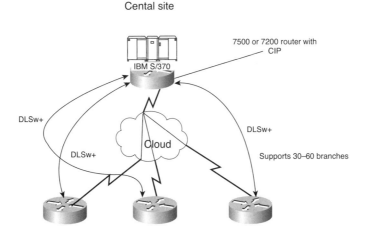

- **CIP and DLSw+ together**—This solution can scale up to 200 remote branches with offloading of the WAN encapsulation function to another router. Peer all remote sites to the central site, similar to the first solution, only this time the serial ports connected to the WAN will be on a separate router, as shown in Figure 14-8. This solution may also include a separate peering router connected to the WAN for redundancy purposes. In the event of a failure of one of the routers, the other router should be able to handle the load.

Figure 14-8   *CIP and DLSw+*

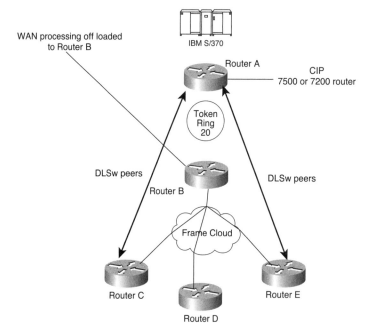

- **WAN and DLSw+ combined**—This option offers some of the best advantages. Using DLSw+, peer all remote sites to the WAN-attached router, as shown in Figure 14-9. The attraction of this is that if a FEP is connected to the mainframe, it could be used instead of the CIP router to connect the Token Ring to the mainframe. Then peering to the WAN-connected router is an option. This is a good solution for medium-to-large networks. Another attraction is that if remote network peer requirements continue to grow, low-end Cisco routers can be added to provide the necessary scale.

- **Dedicated DLSw+**—This option offers various rewards. Finally, peer all routers to a router at the central site that is neither WAN-connected nor CIP-connected, as shown in Figure 14-10. Although this solution is more costly, it offers redundancy and load balancing. This option separates the DLSw+ and WAN processing from the CIP router. It also separates DLSw+ and CIP functions from the WAN attached router.

Figure 14-9   *WAN and DLSw+*

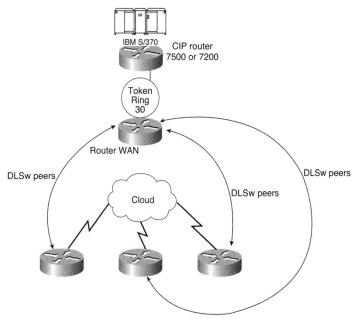

Figure 14-10   *Dedicated DLSw+*

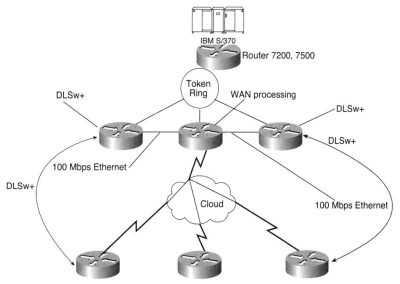

Backup Strategies

This section discusses some DLSw+ redundancy alternatives. With DLSw+, losing a session and recreating it around backup links can be disruptive to end systems, depending on the encapsulation method used. Recovery can be dynamic and nondisruptive with TCP encapsulation. Let's take a look at two different backup strategies: link recovery and central-site router recovery:

- **Link recovery**—By using TCP encapsulation with local acknowledgment and providing alternative paths for traffic, failures in the WAN can be recovered. When a failure occurs, the routers spoof the acknowledgments, giving the routing protocol time to establish a new path, as shown in Figure 14-11. With FST encapsulation, which does not provide for local acknowledgment, acknowledgments might time out before a new path is found. This can be disruptive to an end system.

Figure 14-11 *Link recovery*

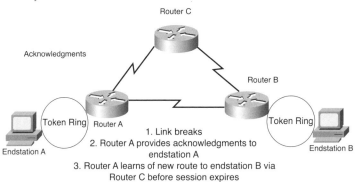

- **Central-site router recovery**—Losing a central-site router is usually disruptive. There are two ways to minimize this risk: You can use multiple backup peers or a single backup peer:

  — **Multiple backup peers**—If remote-site peers concurrently connect to multiple central-site peers, loss of a central site should cause the remotes to reestablish connectivity over the other central-site peers, as shown in Figure 14-12. The figure shows concurrent sessions between Router C and the central-site routers.

  — **Single backup peer**—If remote peers connect to a single central-site peer, a backup peer can be specified in case the primary peer fails.

NOTE DLSw supports load balancing up to four ports.

Figure 14-12 *Central-Site Router Recovery*

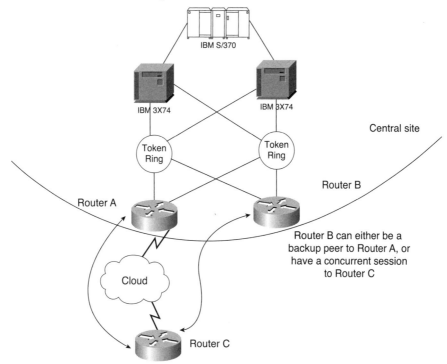

Explorer Control

The name of the game with SNA is explorer control. Explorer traffic volumes can severely impact router CPU and network throughput. With DLSw+, routers send CANUREACH explorer frames to each neighbor. This can result in extensive broadcast traffic trying to locate resources. There are many different options for CCDPs to control broadcasts:

- **Filtering**—The most common method for minimizing explorer traffic is to filter unnecessary protocols and explorers. Cisco access lists in the 200 range have parameters for addressing explorer traffic.

- **Static**—Another possibility is to use static configurations. This is effective depending on the size of the network. Static configurations eliminate broadcasts by allowing a router to set up circuits without sending explorers. Another option if the network is large is to statically configure only the key resources. The Cisco command **icanreach** is typically used to configure static resources.

- **Virtual ring numbering**—Virtual ring numbering prevents inbound explorers from being replicated back to the WAN by using a common ring number because the explorer cannot travel through the same ring twice.

- **Explorer firewall**—This type of firewall permits only one explorer for a certain MAC address destination to be sent across the WAN at a time. All other explorers trying to reach the same destination must wait until a response is received from the first explorer. This prevents the start-of-day explorer storm that many networks experience.

- **Caching**—Frequently requested NetBIOS names can be statically defined on the router. DLSw+ reduces broadcasts and improves scalability by supporting local, remote, and peer group caching.

Border Peers

Border peers and peer groups are advanced features of DLSw+ developed for full-mesh topologies that also help limit explorer traffic. Full-mesh networks are difficult to support and troubleshoot because all routers must have a physical connection using a static configuration to all other routers on the network. To find the number of links, use the formula from previous chapters, $n(n-1)/2$, where n is the number of routers. For example, 10 routers means 45 connections. DLSw+ solves this problem by providing a hierarchical structure using border peers.

Instead of a single branch router sending a query to every branch router in its group, the branch router E sends only a single CANUREACH broadcast to its border peer, as shown in Figure 14-13. Before the border peer forwards the explorer from Router E, it checks its local, remote, and group cache. If the destination resource is not found, the border peer propagates the broadcast within its group and to other border peers. The other border peers in turn flood the broadcast within their group. In this case, Border Peer A must make five broadcasts to its neighbors if the address is not located in the cache.

Here are the benefits of border peering:

- Simplified configuration because static routes don't have to be put on all the routers

- Reduced explorer traffic

- Minimized processor overhead for maintaining TCP connections

- Enhanced scalability

Figure 14-13 *Border Peers*

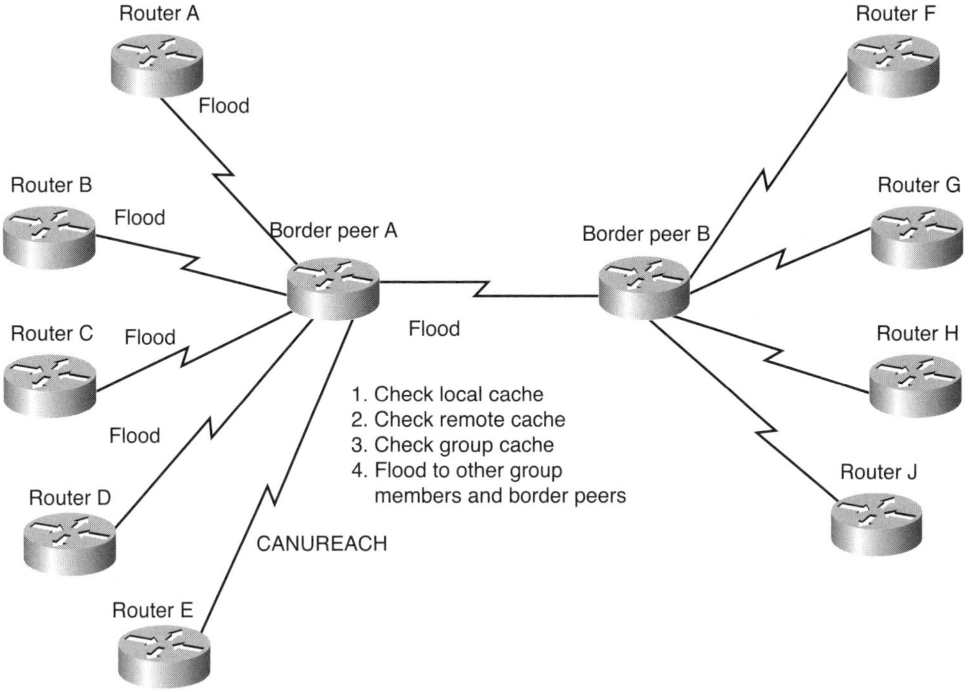

Design Rules

The following rules should be applied in any DLSw+ design situation that calls for multiple active border peers:

- All border peers in a group must peer to each other.

- Try to have multiple active border peers for redundancy, not load balancing. Border peers do not provide for load balancing.

- Within a group, every group member must peer to every border peer in its group.

- Border peer routers should be in the 7200 or 7500 series to support the large amount of broadcast and explorer traffic.

- Try to position border peers at distribution or central sites. The sole function of a border peer is to replicate the broadcast of branch routers. Because these routers are at the heart of the DLSw+ network and must handle many broadcasts, they should be the more powerful routers and should be located at regional or central sites.

When designing for high availability, keep these rules in mind:

- TCP encapsulation provides nondisruptive recovery from link failures between peers.

- Multiple active peers or ports allow for fast dynamic recovery from loss of peer, TIC, or FEP.

- Use backup peers for disaster recovery sites or where dual paths are cost-prohibitive.

When designing for very large networks, try to implement "promiscuous" peers where possible. The following are the benefits of promiscuous peers:

- Configurations at the central site are reduced because fewer commands are needed with promiscuous peers.

- NVRAM requirements are minimized because the only command needed is the promiscuous command.

- When adding remote sites, there is no need to configure or change the configuration of the central site.

TIP   Each page is worth about 2 K of NVRAM when you do a **show run** command. For example, if the router has 32 K of NVRAM, it will display roughly 16 pages at the most of configuration information. CCDPs need to know their NVRAM limitations!

Designing Peer Group Size (50 or More)

When deciding how large peer group sizes should be, remember that a single broadcast by a peer router must be replicated to every peer in the group and to all border peers. For example, in Figure 14-14, Border Peer Doug must replicate any broadcast by Router Greg to Laurie and Jeff. Border Peer Doug must in turn replicate to Border Peer Connie, who replicates to Holly, Melissa, and Mike. Router Connie replies that it can reach Resource Mike. That makes for three broadcasts (one each to Connie, Greg, and Jeff) by Router Doug if the resource is not found in cache. As a rule of thumb, a router with 50 or fewer peers can probably be all in one group. It is when scaling higher—say, 1000—that a single peer group is not a good idea. Each broadcast would have to be replicated 999 times.

Figure 14-14 *Replication*

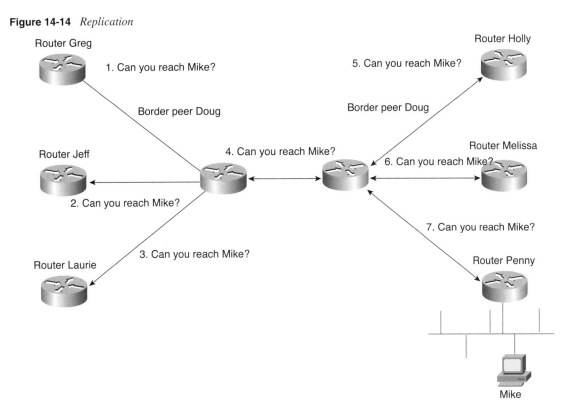

Figure 14-15 shows 250 peers in each group, which means there would be 249 broadcasts within the group and three broadcasts to border peer routers, totaling 252 broadcasts.

So the thought here is that designers should divide groups, ensuring that border peers can support the amount of broadcast replication that any single router can perform. Typically, border peer routers should be a higher-end class Cisco router in the 7200–7500 range. Depending on the network's size, a 3600 might be appropriate as well.

Figure 14-15   *252 Broadcasts*

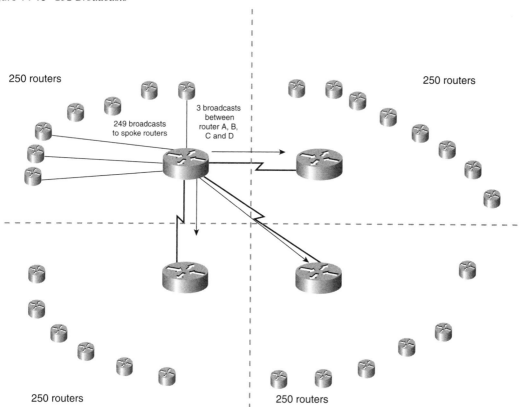

Minimizing Explorer Replication in Border-Peer Design

Branch-to-branch traffic in a DLSw+ design is minimal and rarely impacts border peer design. The resources accessed every day by branch offices are usually at the central site.

To avoid unnecessary explorer forwarding to central-site resources, you can configure all remote branch routers to peer to both their border peer and a data-center router. The attraction of this is that if the **dlsw icanreach** command is added to Router Treva in Figure 14-16, when the capabilities exchange is done between remote Router Reggie and Router Treva, Remote Router Reggie will learn it can reach the mainframe. It will not have to send out an explorer for the mainframe.

Figure 14-16 *Central-Site Peering*

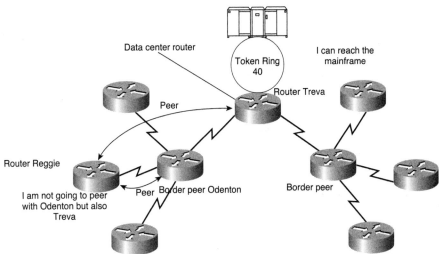

So instead of forwarding the circuit setup request to the border peer Odenton, Router Reggie forwards the circuit setup request directly to Router Treva, avoiding any broadcasts to the border router and the other branch routers—a very nice solution, indeed.

Promiscuous Mode

Promiscuous mode is defined in central-site routers. It allows central-site routers to make peering connections with remote DLSw peers without having to configure each peer on the hub router. Each remote peer is configured to connect to the hub router.

QoS and DLSw+

DLSw+, like any SNA protocol, is sensitive to network delay. DLSw+ uses Quality of Service (QoS) to manage network traffic, optimize performance, and improve the overall network design. There are different levels of QoS in Cisco IOS:

- **Best effort**—An example of best-effort traffic is usually the Internet or HTTP protocol. There are no guarantees for end-to-end service. Cisco IOS uses the first-in-first-out (FIFO) queuing algorithm for best-effort traffic.

- **Differentiated service**—An example of this type of QoS is using the IP Precedence field of the IP packet to declare that the data in this packet is important and should be given priority. This basically means that some of the traffic, depending on the IP Precedence field, can be treated with more urgency than other packets. This also involves queuing algorithms such as custom and priority queuing.

- **Guaranteed service**—This type of service usually means a guaranteed bandwidth from one end of the network to the other for an application (RSVP protocol, for example). This means that along the path from end to end, routers need to reserve buffer space, queuing disciplines to ensure that specific traffic gets a specific service level.

NOTE   It is not uncommon to find businesses defining the levels of service as follows and referencing them with the maximum amount of delay:

- **High availability**—150 milliseconds or less response time

- **Normal availability**—1-second response time

- **Low availability**—2-second response time

- **Best effort**—5-second response time

Much of the first part of this section focuses on DLSw+ prioritization, the steps needed to configure prioritization, and the ports that TCP uses to distinguish traffic. The end of this section discusses the use of Cisco IOS queuing algorithms—priority queuing, custom queuing, and weighted fair queuing—to provide differentiated services and meet service-level requirements.

Prioritizing Traffic

DLSw+ encapsulates all SNA and NetBIOS traffic into TCP packets. This makes it difficult to identify the traffic. For that reason, DLSw+ supports opening four separate TCP connections and then places traffic based on priority directly from the input queue into one of these four pipes. Then, at the output interface, traffic is prioritized among these four TCP connections based on its TCP port number.

To specify the traffic and activate the four TCP connections (ports 2065, 1981, 1982, and 1983), a priority keyword must be used on a remote-peer statement.

In Figure 14-17, by default, DLSw+ assigns certain traffic to specific TCP ports as follows:

- **TCP port 2065**—Defaults to high priority. This port carries all circuit administration frames, peer keepalives, and capabilities exchange.

- **TCP port 1981**—Defaults to medium priority. In the absence of any other configuration, this port does not carry any traffic.

- **TCP port 1982**—Defaults to normal priority. In the absence of any other configuration, this port carries information frames.

- **TCP port 1983**—Defaults to low priority. In the absence of any other configuration, this port carries broadcast traffic.

Figure 14-17   *Prioritizing Traffic*

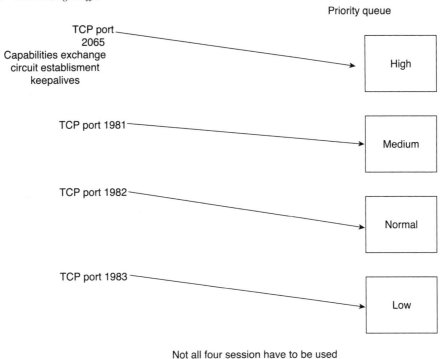

Not all four session have to be used

NOTE	If you specify priority on the remote-peer statement and do nothing else, all steady traffic goes in TCP port 1982 by default. Circuit establishment and capabilities exchange are still done over port 2065.

Configuring Traffic Priority

When designing large DLSw+ networks, you will probably need to specify traffic priority and configure it. Three steps are required for configuring traffic priority:

Step 1   Configure the priority keyword on the appropriate DLSw+ remote-peer statements.

Step 2   Classify the packets on the incoming port and assign the traffic to the appropriate TCP connection.

Step 3   Assign traffic to the appropriate queue based on protocol, TCP port number, or message size, and define the queuing technique to be used on the interface.

TIP   Queuing does not occur until the total number of packets exceeds the capacity of the outbound link.

Queuing Algorithms

After priority traffic has been assigned to TCP ports, you can use a variety of Cisco IOS queuing algorithms to improve QoS. Priority and custom queuing come to mind, as well as WFQ. These subjects were discussed in Chapter 9, and they apply here too.

Priority and Custom Queuing for DLSw+

If you have many slow links or less than 56 K in your network, you might want to use priority queuing. This queuing technique is somewhat drastic. It is easy to shoot yourself in the foot. Priority queuing is drastic because traffic in the lower queues is not sent until the high queue is empty, which can be unfair to the lower queues. If you absolutely must have DLSw traffic as the first priority, this is the approach to take. If so much DLSw traffic goes through that your IP traffic can't get through, you might lose your routing updates, which is not a good idea. A less-drastic method is custom queuing. Priority queuing was designed to provide strict, absolute priority to the most important traffic on the network.

WARNING   Be careful with priority queuing. If there is enough priority traffic, it might keep your routing updates from getting through.

Custom Queuing

Custom queuing was discussed in Chapter 9, but it applies to DLSw+ as well. Custom queuing is particularly important for time-sensitive protocols such as SNA, which requires predictable response times. As mentioned, priority queuing can be unfair. Custom queuing can be considered fair, because you can define up to 16 queues. The queues are serviced in a round-robin fashion, so even the lower queues get serviced. An added benefit is that a byte weight can be applied to each queue so that many of the bytes get through before another queue is served.

NOTE   Earlier IOS versions supports only up to ten custom queues.

Weighted Fair Queuing

This type of QoS can be stated as "WFQ favors low-volume conversations." An analogy would be an amusement park in which large groups of people are waiting to get on a ride that has only a few seats available. The park attendants search for one or two people to fill the seats, neglecting the people who have been waiting in line the longest. Low-volume traffic streams, which comprise the majority of network traffic, get preferential treatment. This ensures that user applications receive satisfactory response. Batch file transfers (FTP, for example) would share the remaining bandwidth.

With standard WFQ, packets are classified by flow. Packets with the same IP address, destination address, or source or destination TCP or UDP port belong to the same flow. WFQ allocates an equal share of the bandwidth to each flow. Flow-based WFQ is also called fair queuing because all flows are equally weighted.

How is it configured?

WFQ requires no configuration and is on by default.

Class-Based Weighted Fair Queuing

Class-Based Weighted Fair Queuing (CBWFQ) uses the 3 bits in the IP Precedence field to define what traffic should be favored even further. Traffic must first be classified as important using extended access lists, which define which traffic gets the IP Precedence bits set.

IP Precedence

The *IP Precedence* field has been around since IP was developed, but now new schemes are finally utilizing this field.

IP Precedence lets administrators establish service classes using the three precedence bits in the Type of Service field in the IPv4 header. The attraction of this is that administrators can use the existing queuing mechanisms (WRED, WFQ) and don't have to change existing applications or any part of the network infrastructure.

IP Precedence uses the Type of Service field in the IP header. This is an 8-bit field at the front of the IP packet (see Figure 14-18). Seven of these bits enable classification of traffic across an IP network. The eighth bit is not used and is set to 0. The first three bits are used to set precedence. The next four bits specify the type of service (ToS). Up to six classes of service can be partitioned using the ToS bits. As soon as this traffic is classified as important, queuing technologies in the network use these bits to apply the appropriate expedited handling across the network.

Figure 14-18 *IP Precedence*

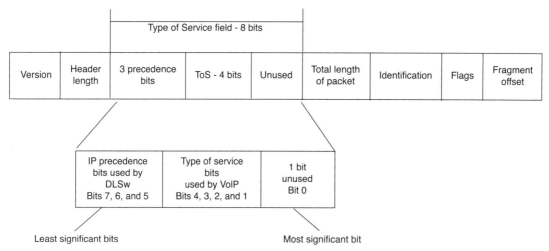

Network architects use extended access lists to classify the traffic. The use of these access lists offers considerable flexibility for precedence assignment, down to the user or application level. Another option is to classify packets by source and destination, source subnet, and so on. Normally, this is done closest to the source, whether at the edge or near the core.

TIP   Set IP Precedence bits closest to the source.

Field Values

IP Precedence is specified in RFC 791. IP Precedence can use parameters such as high, normal, and low priorities to classify traffic into service-level criteria. When packets are classified from the endpoint, they keep their service-level definitions as they move from network hop to network hop.

NOTE	The IETF has created a working group to define "An Architecture for Differentiated Service" (RFC 2475). This IETF work is defining the use of IP Precedence to deliver scalable, differentiated services across the Internet.

Table 14-2 shows the values of the IP Precedence bits and their corresponding definitions. Cisco routers use only bits 0 through 5. Bits 6 and 7 are not used.

Table 14-2 *IP Precedence Bits and Their Corresponding Definitions*

Value	Definition
Network	Matches packets with network-control precedence (7)
Internet	Matches packets with internetwork-control precedence (6)
Critical	Matches packets with critical precedence (5)
Flash-Override	Matches packets with flash-override precedence (4)
Flash	Matches packets with flash precedence (3)
Immediate	Matches packets with immediate precedence (2)
Priority	Matches packets with priority precedence (1)
Routine	Matches packets with routine precedence (0)

How TCP Ports Map to DLSw

Table 14-3 lists DLSw+ priority queues and IP Precedence default mapping. Notice that TCP port 2065 maps directly to the High queue, which is equivalent to the Critical value or Bit 5 in the IP Precedence field.

When the **priority** keyword option is used on the **dlsw** remote-peer command, DLSw automatically does the following things:

- Activates the four TCP ports to the remote peer
- Sets IP Precedence values
- Assigns traffic to the specific ports according to the extended access list

Table 14-3 *DLSw+ Priority Queues and IP Precedence Default Mapping*

TCP Port	DLSw+ Priority Queue	IP Precedence	IP Precedence Value
2065	High	Critical	5
1981	Medium	Flash override	4
1982	Normal	Flash	3
1983	Low	Immediate	2

If it was not turned on, DLSw+ would queue this traffic on the router's outbound ports. As soon as the traffic started traversing an internetwork, the service classifications would be lost.

If there is a reason to change the default values, you can override them using the command **dlsw tos map** or by using policy-based routing. For example, you could use this command:

```
dlsw tos map high 5 medium 2 normal 1 low 0
```

Policy-Based Routing

CCDPs must know where and when to use Policy-Based Routing (PR). Policy-Based Routing could be called Static Routes Version 2, because in essence it is another flavor of static routing. Policy routing is the ability to specify the path that traffic will take through the network based on user-specific parameters. An added bonus is that the priority packets can be modified.

Policy Routing classifies packets through the use of extended access lists. ACLs, IP Precedence, queuing, and other QoS capabilities work together to carry out the network management policy framework. CCDPs can control the traffic path using extended ACLs, bypassing the lookup in the routing table.

Policy Routing comes in handy when you have transmission lines between two points that have different characteristics. Figure 14-19 shows a low-bandwidth terrestrial link from Router A to Router B and a high-bandwidth, high-propagation-delay satellite link. Policy routing is also used in a particular situation in which the need is to route based on the source address and the traditional destination address.

Figure 14-19   *Policy-Based Routing*

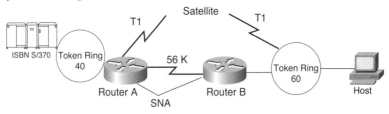

SNA traffic would best be served by being directed over the low-propagation delay link.

RSVP

RSVP is an IETF standard (RFC 2205) for allowing an application to dynamically reserve network bandwidth. RSVP lets an application dynamically reserve network bandwidth from endpoint to endpoint. DLSw+ supports the use of RSVP to reserve bandwidth for TCP connections between DLSw+ peers. This is usually not the first choice for QoS. Cisco usually recommends trying CBWFQ before trying RSVP.

Many ISPs do not want to reserve bandwidth for customers. For one thing, once the bandwidth is reserved, no one else can use it.

Simply put, as soon as RSVP is configured on the two-endpoint routers, the routers in between all check to see if they can supply the memory and buffers for a specific traffic flow. If they can, the RSVP path is set up. If they can't, the path is not set up. For example, Routers A and D ask the middle routers, B and C, if they have enough buffer and memory to help provide a 384 K pipe between the endpoint routers. If they do not, the path is not set up. If they do, the 384 K pipe is established from endpoint router to endpoint router. If the endpoint routers do not send any traffic, Routers B and C cannot use the 384 K reserved space and have only roughly 1160 K between them to use because the 384 K is reserved from router A all the way through Router D.

The attraction of using RSVP is that 384 K can be guaranteed to DLS+ (or another example is video) at all times. The user can specify the amount of RSVP reserved bandwidth in three different ways:

- **Globally**—By using the **dlsw rsvp** command, DLSw+ uses the configured parameters to initiate RSVP to all its peers. As soon as the global command is in place, the user must enable RSVP to all its peers.

- **Per peer**—When the command **dlsw remote peer tcp** is configured on a router, DLSw+ configures the RSVP parameters specifically for this peer connection.

- **Type of peer connection**—When either DLSw+ **peer-on-demand-defaults** or **dlsw prom-peer defaults** is configured, DLSw+ uses the configured RSVP parameters for peer-on-demand and promiscuous connections, respectively.

For RSVP to work, all the devices between the start and endpoint of a connection need to support RSVP. Because there is a sender and a receiver in the RSVP path, RSVP commands must be configured on the endpoint routers. However, commands need not be configured on the routers that are in the IP routed path between two DLSw+ peers, B and C. The devices between the peers prioritize the packets belonging to the DLSw+ session according to the IP ToS settings. However, if the devices in the middle do not support RSVP, end-to-end bandwidth is not guaranteed.

DLCI Priority with Frame Relay

DLCI prioritization is another way to prioritize traffic. Prioritizing by DLCI is an expensive option because you need extra PVCs. For this reason, it is not used extensively. Data-link connection identifier prioritization is a process in which different traffic types are placed on separate DLCIs so that a Frame Relay network can provide a different CIR for each traffic type. Custom queuing and priority queuing can also be used in conjunction with DLCI prioritization to provide bandwidth management control over the Frame Relay link.

Figure 14-20 depicts this activity. In this example, SNA traffic is shown on DLCI 17, Telnet is on DLCI 18, and FTP is on DLCI 19. Traffic is differentiated on up to four DLCIs with this feature. DLCI 16 is high priority, and DLCI 17 is medium priority.

Figure 14-20   *DLCI Prioritization*

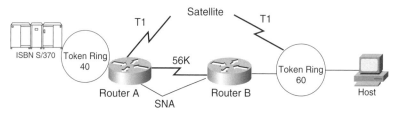

Using this technique, there can be different CIRs for each DLCI. For example, the Telnet DLCI CIR could be 0, because Telnet is very low-bandwidth traffic, and the DLCI 16 could have a CIR of 56 K.

DLSw Tuning

When designing for DLSw+ networks, CCDPs must know the tunable parameters if they are to make the network really purr. This section discusses some of the major tunable parameters and the impact that the commands can have.

IP MTU Path Discovery

This parameter specifies the largest packet size that may traverse the network. This is determined during peer establishment. The maximum IP frame size then dictates the maximum number of SNA bytes that can be stored in one frame. The default is 1450 bytes for a TCP/IP network. Changing this value can result in better performance. A good example is to increase the serial MTU to 4096 bytes to allow larger frame sizes to traverse the serial link and, therefore, carry more SNA data.

The Cisco IOS global command for setting IP MTU path discovery is

```
ip tcp path-mtu-discovery
```

TCP Window Size

Another adjustment is to increase the TCP window size to allow more outstanding requests. This command can also minimize packet fragmentation, because creating larger packets means fewer smaller ones.

Initial window sizes are set during connection establishment and usually do not change during the transfer of data.

NOTE   If the window size changes to 0, this means the sender should stop sending data.

Explorer Queue Depth

The explorer queue depth is important because it allows explorers to be handled on a queue separate from real data. Explorers are used to find resources in DLSw+ and on LANs. This helps reduce broadcast storms with Token Ring environments. The problems are that when there is an excessive amount of broadcast traffic, the explorers arrive at a rate faster than DLSw+ can process them.

Using the explorer queue depth in DLSw+ configuration helps control this activity. It also does the following:

- Sets up a queue specific to explorer traffic. This is where you configure limits on explorer traffic.

- Minimizes the risk of broadcast storms.

- Dropping explorer packets is better than dropping user data. Another advantage is that CPU utilization is minimized.

Idle Time

You should implement a larger LLC2 idle timer value when there is a large number of LLC2 sessions. Increasing the LLC2 idle time when supporting a large number (thousands) of sessions significantly decreases router CPU utilization.

Router Startup

The input hold queue can be used to hold off input frames from LAN interfaces (Token, Ethernet) that are waiting to be placed in a system buffer. Protocols such as DLSw+ that are traffic-intensive at startup might require that the input hold queue be increased. Increasing this timer lets the router buy some time, so to speak, and allocate system buffers in a more favorable manner.

Typically, APPN would fall into this type of category. Many small packets are involved with APPN startup, and it is not uncommon to see a buildup in the input hold queue.

NOTE   If there are many constant drops in the input hold queue, increasing the input hold queue will not make much difference. There might be a problem in the network, however.

Foundation Summary

This section is a convenient review of many key concepts in this chapter. If you are already comfortable with the topics in this chapter, this summary could help you recall a few details. If you have just read this chapter, this review should help solidify some key facts. If you are doing your final preparation before the exam, Table 14-4 is a convenient way to review the day before the exam.

Table 14-4 *Five methos of controlling explorers*

Caching	Statically define frequent NetBIOS names.
Explorer Firewall	Limit the amount of explorers that can travel across a link at one time.
Virtual Ring Numbering	Prevent explorers from being replicated.
Filtering	Filter unnecessary traffic.
Static	Allows a router to setup circuits without sending resources.

Table 14-5 *Availability and response times for traffic*

High Availability	150 milliseconds or less.
Normal Availability	1 Second or less.
Low Availability	2 Second response time.
Best Effort	5 Second response time.

Table 14-6 *DSLw+ TCP Ports*

TCP Port 2065	High priority—Circuit administration frames, keepalives, capabilities exchanges
TCP Port 1981	Medium priority
TCP Port 1982	Normal priority—Information frames
TCP Port 1983	Low priority—Broadcast frames

Q&A

As mentioned in Chapter 1, the questions and scenarios in this book are more difficult than what you will experience on the actual exam. The questions do not attempt to cover more breadth or depth than the exam; however, they are designed to make sure that you know the answer. Rather than allowing you to derive the answer from clues hidden inside the question, the questions challenge your understanding and recall of the subject. Questions from the "Do I Know This Already?" quiz from the beginning of the chapter are repeated here to ensure that you have mastered this chapter's topic areas. Hopefully, these questions will help limit the number of exam questions on which you narrow your choices to two options and then guess. Be sure to use the CD and take the simulated exams.

The answers to these questions can be found in Appendix A.

1 What are two frame types that SNA networks transport?

_____

_____

_____

2 What type of explorer packet takes every possible path through the network?

_____

_____

_____

3 In SNA networks, should the convergence time be less than the session expiration time?

_____

_____

_____

4 Does an explorer ever visit the same Token Ring twice?

_____

_____

_____

5 For what is Proxy Explorer used?

_____

_____

_____

6 What is a method of transporting SNA and NetBIOS frames over an IP network?

7 What type of DLSw+ encapsulation can be used on Token Ring ports but not Ethernet?

8 Which type of encapsulation uses more CPU cycles to support it, Local Acknowledgment or Direct?

9 Name three methods of controlling CANYOUREACH explorer frames in DLSw+ networks.

10 How many times must a border peer replicate a broadcast if it is configured for nine peers in its group and two other border peers?

11 Which type of QoS provides guaranteed service end-to-end across a network?

12 Name one reason why ISPs do not like to implement RSVP.

13 How many bits are in the IP header's Type of Service field?

_____

_____

_____

14 How many bits make up the IP Precedence portion of the Type of Service field?

_____

_____

_____

15 What is the only command that is absolutely necessary on a router if it is to participate in DLSw+ in listening mode?

_____

_____

_____

16 NetBIOS is transported in what type of frame?

_____

_____

_____

17 If the **priority** command is specified on the DLSw+ command and nothing else, what TCP port will the traffic use?

_____

_____

_____

18 What would be a good routing choice if you needed to specify a path that traffic should take?

_____

_____

_____

19 What does Weighted Fair Queuing favor?

_____

_____

_____

20 What does DLSw+ encapsulate?

_____

_____

_____

21 What router platforms are a good choice for a very large DLSw+ network?

_____

_____

_____

22 What is an example of differentiated service?

_____

_____

_____

23 What is an example of guaranteed service?

_____

_____

_____

24 On what TCP port do circuit establishment, keepalives, and capability exchanges occur?

_____

_____

_____

25 What is Class-Based Weighted Fair Queuing?

_____

_____

_____

26 Which type of encapsulation provides for Local Acknowledgment?

_____

_____

_____

27 What does the + in DLSw+ mean?

_____

_____

_____

28 Over how many ports can DLSw+ load-balance?

_____

_____

_____

29 What three cache types does DLSw check for before flooding broadcasts?

_____

_____

_____

30 Do border peers provide for load balancing?

_____

_____

_____

Scenarios

Scenario 1

RouteitRight has the following requirements:

- A mainframe at the central site and three remote sites

- Three remote sites have a total bandwidth of 128 K

- Three DLCIs to each remote site exist

- SNA traffic must have 64 K

- FTP must have 64 K

- Telnet and best-effort traffic can coexist

- A Token Ring connection to the mainframe

List some advantages and disadvantages of your solution.

Scenario 2

RouteitRight has the following requirements:

- A mainframe must reside at the central site with no Token Ring connection.

- The router connected to the mainframe must not use the DLSw+ protocol.

- Three remote sites must be able to access the mainframe at the central site via DLSw+.

List some advantages and disadvantages of your solution.

Scenario 3

RouteitRight has the following requirements:

- A border peer router must reside at the central site.

- The border peer router has no configuration for remote peers.

List some advantages and disadvantages of your solution.

Scenario Answers

Answer to Scenario 1

The customer requirements can be met by placing a 7200 router at the central site with the CIP processor module. Also, install three DLCI circuits to each remote site and specify that the circuits get 64 K CIR. The third circuit for Telnet has a CIR of 0, and Telnet traffic will get through unless the WAN is severely congested.

Configuring the remotes to peer with the 7200 router satisfies the DLSw+ requirement.

Figure 14-21 shows the suggested solution.

Figure 14-21 *Scenario 1 Solution*

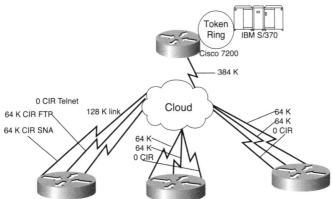

Advantage: If you use only one router at the central site, there will be fewer routers to maintain.

Advantage: Cost. There is no CIP router to maintain and expense at the central site.

Disadvantage: One central-site router is susceptible to failure.

Disadvantage: If traffic exceeds the remote link's capacity, Telnet might not get through.

Disadvantage: Cost, due to the need to pay for three DLCIs at the remote sites.

Answer to Scenario 2

Place a CIP 7200 router with a CPA adapter at the central site and a separate router connected to the WAN. The 7200 CIP router does not have to peer with the remote routers; that is the job of the WAN router.

Figure 14-22 shows the suggested solution.

Figure 14-22 *Scenario 2 Suggested Solution*

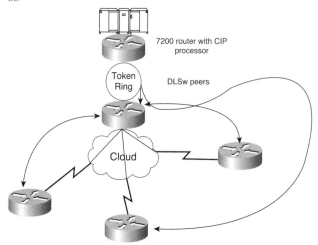

Advantage: There is no DLSw+ processing on the CIP router.

Disadvantage: There are two routers to maintain at the central site.

Answer to Scenario 3

Configuring the central site router as promiscuous meets the requirement. The reason is that by being promiscuous, the border router accepts connections from any remote peer. This eliminates the need to place manual configuration commands on the border router pointing to the remote peers.

Figure 14-23 shows the suggested solution.

Figure 14-23 *Scenario 3 Suggested Solution*

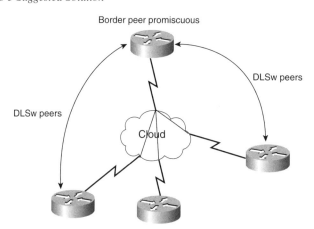

This chapter covers the following topics you will need to master as a CCDP:

- **Security overview**—This introductory section examines the underlying security technologies and their components.

- **Firewall design**—This section discusses some of the common firewalls available and where they fit into a corporate design. Cisco IOS features for firewalls are also covered.

- **IPSec**—This section explains the concept of IPSec and some of the algorithms it uses, including DES and SHA encryption technologies.

- **VPNs**—This section covers VPN concepts and the tunneling mechanisms L2TP, L2F, and PPTP.

CHAPTER 15

Network Security Technologies

The CCDP exam requires you to have an in-depth understanding of firewall technologies. In this chapter, the discussion focuses on an overview of security technologies and some of the major components in today's network designs. Security technologies commonly used to establish identity (public and private keys) are described, and so are methods of ensuring some degree of data integrity and confidentiality.

How to Best Use This Chapter

By following these steps, you can make better use of your study time:

- Keep your notes and the answers for all your work with this book in one place for easy reference.
- Take the "Do I Know This Already?" quiz and write down your answers. Studies show that retention is significantly increased through writing down facts and concepts, even if you never look at the information again.
- Use the diagram shown in Figure 15-1 to guide you to the next step.

Figure 15-1 *How to Best Use this Chapter*

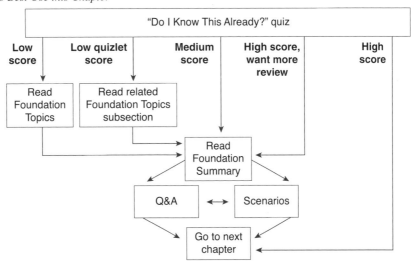

If you skip to the Foundation Summary, Q&A, and Scenarios sections and have trouble with the material there, you should go back to the Foundation Topics section.

"Do I Know This Already?" Quiz

The purpose of the "Do I Know This Already?" quiz is to help you decide which parts of this chapter to use. If you intend to read the entire chapter, you do not necessarily need to answer these questions now.

This 15-question quiz helps you choose how to spend your limited study time. The quiz is divided into five smaller "quizlets" that help you select the sections of the chapter on which to focus. Figure 15-1 outlines suggestions on how to spend your time in this chapter. Use Table 15-1 to record your score.

Table 15-1   *Score Sheet for Quiz and Quizlets*

Quizlet Number	Foundation Topics Section Covering These Questions	Questions	Score
1	Security overview	1–4	
2	Firewall design	5–8	
3	IPSec	9–12	
4	VPNs	13–14	
5	Hardware	15	

1 What is a bastion host?

_____

_____

_____

2 Name four services to turn off on the (perimeter) router that interfaces with the Internet.

_____

_____

_____

3 Can a Cisco 2500 router be used as a firewall?

_____

_____

_____

4 What are network security policies?

_____

_____

_____

5 On what router platforms is CBAC available?

_____

_____

_____

6 What is a "choke" router?

_____

_____

_____

7 At what layer of the OSI model do stateful filters work?

_____

_____

_____

8 What network layer addresses should always be blocked from entering your network from the outside?

_____

_____

_____

9 Of the two key similar exchange mechanisms Diffie-Hellman and Oakley, which is considered superior?

_____

_____

_____

10 For what does PKI stand?

_____

_____

_____

11 What does SHA authenticate?

_____

_____

_____

12 Does ESP encrypt the IP Header?

_____

_____

_____

13 Does L2F support multiprotocol?

_____

_____

_____

14 Does L2TP support multiprotocol?

_____

_____

_____

15 What is the name of the product that replaced NetRanger?

_____

_____

_____

The answers to the "Do I Know This Already?" quiz are found in Appendix A. The suggested choices for your next steps follow:

- **6 or less overall score**—Read the chapter. This includes the "Foundation Topics," "Foundation Summary," and "Q&A" sections, as well as the scenarios at the end of the chapter.

- **2 or less on any "quizlet"**—Review the subsection(s) of the "Foundation Topics" part of this chapter based on Table 15-1. Then move into the "Foundation Summary," the "Q&A" section, and the scenarios at the end of the chapter.

- **7, 8, or 9 overall score**—Begin with the "Foundation Summary" section and then go to the "Q&A" section and the scenarios at the end of the chapter.

- **10 or more overall score**—If you want more review on these topics, skip to the "Foundation Summary" section, then go to the "Q&A" section and the scenarios at the end of the chapter. Otherwise, move to the next chapter.

Foundation Topics

Vast quantities of security technologies exist. The hardest challenge for a CCDP sometimes is to design a single network-wide security policy that meets all the customer requirements. The goals of this chapter are to understand how and why modern network security works, to learn how the PIX firewall works in comparison to other firewalls, and to learn the technologies that are implemented in the PIX firewall. This chapter also introduces security rules that should be followed with every network design. The topics covered here are very important to the average network, from the placement of access lists to the new features offered in Cisco IOS, including CBAC and TCP Interceptor. PIX Firewall is covered, along with the new Internet IPSec standard. With Virtual Private Networking, L2F and L2TP are discussed, along with the advantages and disadvantages of each.

Security Overview

The security challenge facing CCDPs today is evaluating a multitude of products and technologies and choosing the right combination for the customer. It is not the lack of technology that makes this difficult, but rather the choices available that can complicate the issues.

One of those choices is the *firewall*. A firewall can be thought of as any one of several ways to protect a network. It can be accomplished in a variety of ways. In most cases, you either permit traffic to flow through a network or deny traffic into the network. Cisco routers can act as firewalls, but they do not have the performance capability of devices made to perform firewall-only functions, such as the PIX 520 firewall. Some firewalls place more emphasis on permitting traffic, and others place more emphasis on blocking traffic. If you have a choice, you might want to lean toward a solution that requires the least amount of processing overhead.

TIP   A *bastion host,* shown in Figure 15-2, is a UNIX device or secure gateway that supports a limited number of applications used by outsiders. It usually resides in the demilitarized zone (DMZ) area and holds data that outsiders access, typically WWW pages. Outsiders can access only these pages.

Figure 15-2   *Bastion Host*

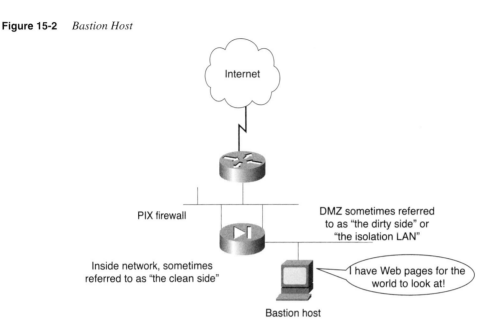

What Is a Firewall?

By definition, a *firewall* is a system or group of systems that enforce a security policy or control policy between two different networks. Because this definition is very generic, any network access control mechanism can be a firewall. Firewalls can set up access control lists on routers, application proxies, or a dedicated piece of hardware such as the PIX 520.

Why Use Firewalls?

Firewalls were developed because a customer cannot make global networks follow their own security policy. A customer can't make the Internet behave in a certain way. In the early days of the Internet, an installation might have had 1000 UNIX systems connected to the Internet without a firewall. When a security hole was discovered in the UNIX system, 1000 devices had to be upgraded, as illustrated in Figure 15-3.

Firewalls have made this job a bit easier. Now, only a few devices must be upgraded. The 1000 devices are protected behind the firewall. It is much easier to monitor one box rather than 1000. Also, today's networks have many more devices running other operating systems, such as Windows, Novell, and so on, that have their own security weaknesses. Firewalls are not the best solution because they add an element of delay and must be monitored extensively. Using firewalls together with securing systems is the best solution for now.

Figure 15-3   *Before Firewalls*

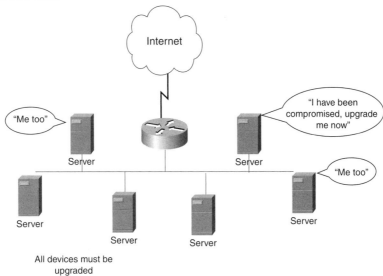

Identify the risks to your network, and make the proper security decisions.

Security Policy Requirements

The most important step for the CCDP is to identify the company's policy requirements to protect the network thoroughly. Network security policies have well-documented rules about what activities are permitted on the network. If no security policy is in place, create one.

TIP   One enterprise, one security policy. If a large company has several different regions, it is better to have one global network security policy that pertains to all regions rather than having each region specify its own security policy.

The CCDP needs to ask the most important questions first:

- What are the objectives of the security system?

- What are the requirements for monitoring, redundancy, and control?

- Where is the information that needs to be protected?

Often there is a trade-off between redundancy, availability, and cost. Good security reduces costs.

WARNING   You do not have network security if it is undocumented in any way or if no designated person has the time and authority to enforce policies.

Security policies define the type of security put into place. They are identified by several different terms:

- **Permissive or open**—Everything that is not explicitly prohibited is allowed. This is similar to a highway where all traffic is permitted, except where the signs say "no trucks allowed." All other traffic flows normally—except the trucks, of course.

- **Restrictive or closed**—Everything that is not explicitly allowed is prohibited. This is similar to backstage passes at major concerts. At the end of the show, people are allowed to enter the star's dressing room only if their names appear on the security guard's backstage pass list. All others are explicitly denied entrance to the star's dressing room.

Security Issues

Firewalls are a major piece of the security puzzle. Other pieces are remote-access users, such as mobile users, telecommuters, and SOHO users. All of these access users need to be authenticated somehow—usually by a password. The goal is to keep security as simple as possible while providing a flexible and secure network.

Network security issues involve technology weaknesses, configuration weaknesses, and policy weaknesses:

- **Technology weaknesses**—TCP/IP has many weaknesses that can be exposed by attackers, including session hijacking, in which a user monitors traffic between two hosts and injects traffic as if it were one of the hosts, stealing the session. Because UNIX and Windows NT servers use TCP/IP, they are vulnerable to these types of attacks. Figure 15-4 shows a *denial-of-service (DoS)* attack. With denial of service, an attacker deliberately overwhelms a server with too many requests or too much data, thereby denying service to legitimate users. This problem is very hard to solve because the affected system cannot determine whether the person is a legitimate user or an attacker. Other weaknesses include:

  — **IP spoofing**—Spoofing is pretending to be someone you are not by providing false information to gain unauthorized access.

— **Ping of death**—A DoS type of attack that involves sending many small packets that are reassembled by the server into large IP packets, consuming the server's resources.

— **Mail flooding**—A DoS type of attack that floods a server with e-mail and consumes the server's resources. Other indications of this type of attack are bandwidth consumed on the WAN links and an increase in router CPU process utilization.

- **Configuration weaknesses**—These weaknesses involve misplaced passwords, easily guessed passwords, misconfigured equipment, and unsecured user accounts. Probably the most common configuration weakness is with access lists—either misconfigured or improperly placed on the router interfaces.

- **Policy weaknesses**—These involve political constraints, lack of written policies, shortage of administrative people, and so on. Most often, unauthorized changes to the network topology or the installation of unapproved applications can create security holes.

Figure 15-4 *A Denial-of-Service Attack*

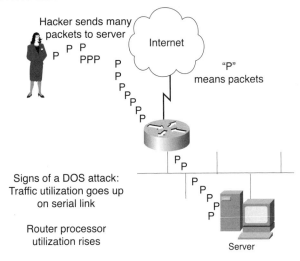

Hacker sends many packets to server

P P P
P PPP
P
P
P
P
P
P
P
P

Internet

"P" means packets

Signs of a DOS attack:
Traffic utilization goes up
on serial link

Router processor
utilization rises

P P
P
P
P
P
P

Server

TIP

Without the firewall feature set, Cisco routers support filtering by TCP or UDP ports and inbound or outbound access lists. Within the Firewall feature set is *content-based access control* (CBAC). CBAC has many other features, such as Java applet filtering, DoS detection and prevention, TCP/UDP transaction logs, and real-time alerts. CBAC is available only with the Firewall feature set. Engineers often assume that CBAC comes with the IP PLUS Feature set, but it does not.

Good Security

A good security solution reduces the total cost of a network's implementation and operation. The CCDP's challenge can be to consolidate a company's many different security technologies so that there are just a few. This saves the company personnel training costs by limiting the devices on which those personnel need to be trained. It also reduces ongoing administrative costs of needing people to monitor logs and so on. Another advantage is that applications once considered unsafe can be implemented, enabling extranet-type applications to link the company more closely with partners and suppliers. The Internet will be a more accessible global access medium.

Firewall Design

There is no "best" firewall. Which one is best depends on the situation in which the firewall is required. At least three different types of firewalls are commonly used in today's networks:

- Packet-filter routers (Cisco IOS serves as a packet filter in a router)

- Dual-homed gateways (application proxies)

- Stateful filters

Each of the three are discussed in detail in this section. Network Address Translation is also discussed.

Packet-Filter Routers

If you configure routers with packet filters, traffic can be allowed in or out of the perimeter routers. A perimeter router is the router that interfaces with the Internet, or the exit point from a customer's network, as shown in Figure 15-5.

Figure 15-5   *A Perimeter Router*

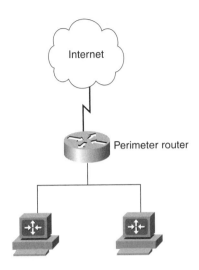

NOTE	The perimeter router can be referred to as the "front door" router.

Packet-filtering rules or access lists restrict access to network services and applications. If internal users need access to Internet services, allow all TCP outbound traffic initiated from inside the customer network, as shown in Figure 15-6.

Figure 15-6   *Packet Filtering*

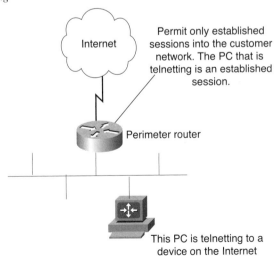

Packet filtering can be done by permitting only "established connections" to enter from the outside back in to the customer network. Because TCP requires an acknowledgment (ACK) to be set, as soon as the internal user initiates a connection at the workstation, the returning packet should have the ACK bit set and can continue on its way to the host PC. Any connection initiated from the outside would not have the ACK bit set and would be denied entry into the network. This is quite common. Packet filtering is integrated in all the Cisco routers but has limited functionality. The router can be set to filter by the following:

- Source and destination network address
- Source and destination port number
- Protocol type

TIP   Place extended access lists closest to the source. Place standard access lists closest to the destination.

Packet-filtering firewalls have other benefits. They do the following:

- Support network address translation (NAT)
- Log access-list violations
- Filter multiprotocol (IP, IPX, DECnet, AppleTalk, and others)

TIP   Secure the perimeter router. This is a good idea as a first line of defense and to guard against denial-of-service attacks.

Packet-filtering firewalls also have disadvantages:

- Complex rules are difficult to configure, implement, and manage.
- Some applications (those that require dynamic ports) cannot be secured completely.
- Packet-filtering firewalls do not scale well.

TIP   A design rule of thumb is to block all UDP traffic from the Internet, unless a specific service needs to be allowed in.

Disable All Unnecessary Features on Packet-Filter Routers

CCDPs should limit the number of services on the perimeter router, as shown in Figure 15-7. Because the perimeter router is closest to the Internet, there are design rules to follow to limit its vulnerability:

- **Disable Telnet access**—Deny anyone from the Internet access to this device. All access can be done through the console port.

- **Turn off Cisco Discovery Protocol (CDP) broadcasts**—The service provider does not need to hear CDP broadcasts from the perimeter router. Information obtained from the CDP broadcast packets can expose a customer's network.

- **Use static routing only if connected to only one service provider**—Usually Border Gateway Protocol (BGP) is needed only when there are a minimum of two connections to the Internet.

- **Do not use this router as a Trivial File Transport Protocol (TFTP) server**—No one should be obtaining images from this router.

- **Disable the finger service with the command no service finger**—If the finger service is enabled, someone could get a list of the users on the router. The information would include the processes running on the system, the line number, connection name, idle time, and terminal location.

- **Disable IP redirects with the command no icmp redirects**.

- **Disable IP route caching with the command no ip route-cache**.

- **Disable source-route bridging with the command no ip source-route**—Do not leave the ability for someone to determine his route through the network.

- **Use the TCP Intercept tool**—This tool comes with the IOS Firewall and is a CBAC component. It protects against syn flooding and DoS attacks.

- **Log events to a Syslog server**—This is extremely important. The events should be monitored on a daily basis.

- **Block RFC 1918**—Block private addresses in the source address from coming in.

- **Block 127.0.0.0 in the source address from coming in.**

- **Block inside networks in the source address from coming in**—No one should enter the customer network with a source address that resides internally to the customer network.

Figure 15-7 *Perimeter Router Filtering*

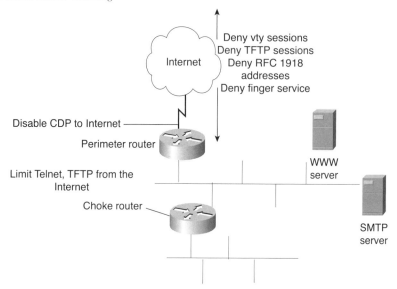

Here are some more guidelines for configuring your packet-filter router:

- When setting passwords for privileged access to the router, use the **enable secret** command rather than the **enable password** command, which does not have as strong an encryption algorithm. Beware: Even **enable secret** can be compromised in a short amount of time with the high-speed CPUs now in existence.

- Put an alphanumeric password on the console port. Configure the **login** command with a username.

- Think about access control *before* you connect a console port to the network in any way, including attaching a modem to either the auxiliary or console port. Be aware that a BREAK on the console port might give total control of the packet-filter router, even with access control configured.

- Apply access lists and password protection to all virtual terminal ports. Use access lists to limit who can Telnet into your router. Do not use the privilege-level commands. Don't enable any local service (such as SNMP or NTP) that you don't use. Cisco Discovery Protocol (CDP) and Network Time Protocol (NTP) are on by default. You should turn them off if you don't need them.

To turn off CDP, enter the **no cdp run** global configuration command. To turn off NTP, enter the **ntp disable** interface configuration command on each interface not using NTP.

If you must run NTP, configure NTP only on required interfaces, and configure NTP to listen only to certain peers.

Any enabled service could present a potential security risk. A determined hostile party might be able to find creative ways to misuse the enabled services to access the firewall or the network. For local services that are enabled, protect against misuse. Protect by configuring the services to communicate only with specific peers, and protect by configuring access lists to deny packets for the services on specific interfaces.

- **Protect against spoofing**—Protect the inside network from being spoofed from the outside network. You can protect against spoofing by configuring input access lists at all interfaces to pass only traffic from expected source addresses and to deny all other traffic, but this method would probably be overkill considering that access lists are processed-switched, which decreases the router's performance.

  You should also disable source routing. For IP, enter the **no ip source-route** global configuration command. Under no circumstances should **ip source-route** be used, unless Token Ring is being used.

  You should also disable minor services. For IP, enter the **no service tcp-small-servers** and **no service udp-small-servers** global configuration commands.

- Normally, you should disable directed broadcasts for all applicable protocols on your firewall and on all your other routers. For IP, use the **no ip directed-broadcast command**. Rarely, some IP networks do require directed broadcasts; if this is the case, do not disable directed broadcasts. Directed broadcasts can be misused to multiply the power of denial-of-service attacks, because every denial-of-service packet sent is broadcast to every host on a subnet.

- Configure the **no proxy-arp** command to prevent internal addresses from being revealed. (This is important to do if you don't already have NAT configured to prevent internal IP addresses from being revealed.)

- Keep the packet-filter router in a secured (locked) room.

TIP   Proxy ARP is on by default. Turn it off.

Application Proxies

This type of firewall commonly runs on general-purpose operating systems such as UNIX or Windows NT servers and is considered slower than the other types of firewalls. The reason for the slowness is that the application proxies can do more application-level filtering than the other types. A common example of this is a Web proxy server. The application proxy is a server with two NIC cards that acts as if it is a host attached to two networks, as shown in Figure 15-8. There is no IP routing between the NIC cards, but rather a static configuration of IP routes.

Figure 15-8 *Application Proxy*

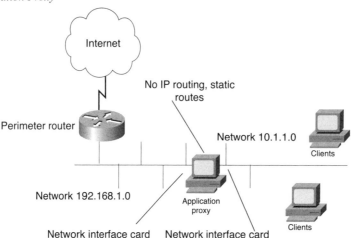

Proxy-type firewalls have a number of benefits:

- **Good auditing capabilities**—Application proxies typically have programs for auditing user transactions that are superior to those of regular types of firewalls. As soon as users are logged into an account, their transactions to the Internet can be monitored and logged.

- **Permissions**—You can control users by placing access permissions on their accounts. Filtering by permissions is a way to restrict what Web sites internal users can access on the Internet.

- **Application layer filtering of data**—Packet-filter routers and other types of firewalls usually do not look into a packet higher than Layer 4. Application proxies can look into the layers all the way up to Layer 7.

Proxy-type firewalls also have disadvantages:

- **Low throughput and high latency**—This occurs because the application proxy must go further into the packet than the other types of firewalls. The application proxy looks into the upper layers—specifically, Layers 5 through 7. A rule of thumb is that the higher the layer, the more time it takes to filter.

- **It's difficult to add new services**—Adding new services might require software patches to be added to some of the currently installed software programs. Another possibility is that the system might have to be taken offline, creating an inconvenience for users.

Stateful Filters

Stateful filters were designed to replace application proxies. PIX firewalls are an example of stateful filtering. Stateful filters evolved from packet-filter routers but do not filter by packets. Rather, they work at Layer 4 of the OSI model and are based on connections from endpoint to endpoint. They can extract connection data from packets that go through the stateful filter firewall and remember which connections are open and are still going through the device. PIX firewalls do not have routing tables because they do not route IP packets. Rather, PIX firewalls use *state tables* to grant a packet access to networks through the PIX firewall.

Based on this state table they keep in memory, they can distinguish every packet as belonging to a certain connection (see Figure 15-9) and not allow potential hostile packets into the network from nonexistent connections. Stateful filtering can place an extensive amount of information about a data packet into the table and use that information to grant the following packets access to either the inside, outside, or DMZ networks.

Figure 15-9   *Stateful Filtering*

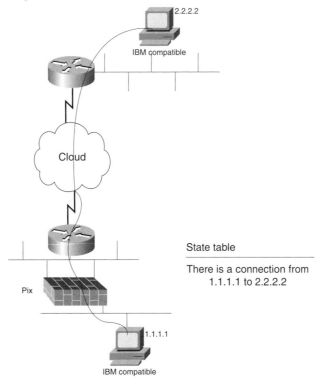

State table
_____

There is a connection from
1.1.1.1 to 2.2.2.2

Stateful filters have the following benefits:

- Rich set of security features

- High performance because they work at Layer 4

- A command structure similar to that of the Cisco IOS on Cisco routers

- Higher security against low-level attacks because they identify connections from endpoint to endpoint

Disadvantages of stateful filters include the following:

- It's difficult to analyze the content of upper layers because the PIX operates at Layer 4.

- Auditing capabilities. Other application programs would be necessary to maintain auditing of user transactions through the PIX.

Demilitarized Zone (DMZ)

When you're designing security for customers, the term DMZ usually comes up when firewalls are discussed. DMZ is also called the *screened subnet,* the *dirty LAN,* and the *isolation LAN.* The demilitarized zone is a buffer between the customer internetwork and the outside world, as shown in Figure 15-10. This is known as a three-layer firewall system—the inside network, the outside network or Internet, and the DMZ area. The DMZ is usually where the customer's WWW servers reside and is usually all that is visible to the outside world. The DMZ is not visible to the inside or clean networks either.

Figure 15-10 *DMZ*

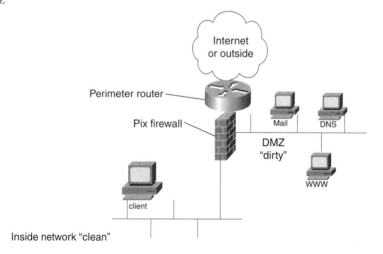

The following services are available to the outside world in the DMZ:

- Anonymous FTP servers

- World Wide Web servers

- Domain Name Service

- E-mail servers

- E-business servers

The choke router shown in Figure 15-7 should also be restricted with services. The choke router separates the inside network from the DMZ for customers who might want to establish another layer of security. It should allow only established sessions back into the inside network, and perhaps mail and WWW traffic. If someone breaks into the public area (DMZ), the internal users are still secure.

TIP When designing for security through the perimeter router, allow only specific services to specific hosts on the DMZ area.

Network Address Translation (NAT)

NAT was designed to provide IP address conservation and for internal IP networks that have private IP addresses. NAT translates these private IP addresses into public addresses at the firewall. Only public addresses can route through the Internet. NAT also can be configured to advertise only one address for the entire internal network to the outside world. This is called Port Address Translation (PAT). This provides security by effectively hiding the entire internal network from the world.

Avoid IP Spoofing

Another design rule is to deny packets from outside your network that claim to have a source address from inside your network. This type of attack is known as *IP spoofing*.

The idea behind this type of attack is that an attacker uses a trusted machine address in conjunction with a mechanism that does address-based authentication. An example of this are the UNIX tools rsh and rlogin. These protocols allow an administrator to establish a list of trusted remote hosts whose users do not need to supply a password.

The point here is that along with blocking the IP network ranges 10.0.0.0, 172.16.00 through 172.16.31.0, and 192.168.0.0 from entering your network from the outside, it might be necessary to block your internal networks from entering from the outside. There should not be any users with these source addresses trying to enter your network.

Inbound and Outbound Access Lists

CCDPs always need to be aware of the consequences of misplaced access lists. Misplaced access lists can cause utilization of bandwidth. In Figure 15-11, the idea is to prevent the desktop PC connected to R1, R2, and R3 from accessing the server on R4. It would be better to place the access lists on R1, R2, and R3 rather than R4 because if you place the lists closer to the source, unnecessary traffic is limited from crossing the WAN links and absorbing bandwidth. This should be evaluated on a case-by-case basis and the proper design put into place.

Figure 15-11 *Access-list placement*

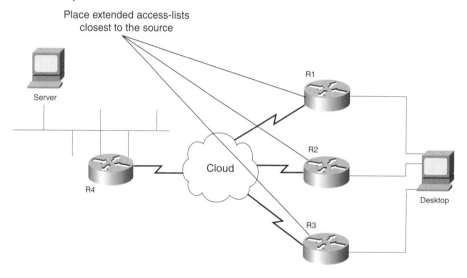

TIP When an access list is applied to an interface, the default direction is outbound if the **inbound** or **outbound** keywords are not used.

Content-Based Access Control (CBAC)

Cisco Firewall IOS provides an extensive set of security features. The CCDP has the option of configuring simple or elaborate firewalls. As mentioned earlier, ordinary Cisco IOS is limited in its capability when trying to protect a network. If a company is prone to denial-of-service attacks and wants to stop being vulnerable, it needs a solution. Enter CBAC. CBAC examines not only network layer and transport layer information, but also the application layer protocol information (such as FTP information) to learn about the state of TCP and UDP connections. CBAC maintains connection state information for individual connections similar to that of PIX firewalls. This state information is used to make intelligent decisions about whether packets should be permitted or denied, and it dynamically creates and deletes temporary openings in the firewall.

Without CBAC, traffic filtering is limited to access list implementations that examine packets at the network layer, or, at most, the transport layer. This allows support of protocols that involve multiple channels created as a result of negotiations in the control channel. Most of the multimedia protocols as well as some other protocols (such as FTP, RPC, and SQL*Net) involve multiple channels. For example, FTP uses ports 20 and 21, one port for control and one port for data, as shown in Figure 15-12.

Figure 15-12 *FTP Control and Data*

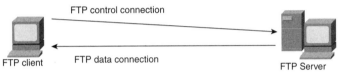

The CBAC feature is supported on the following platforms:

*   Cisco 1600 series

*   Cisco 2500 series

IP Security (IPSec)

IPSec (RFC 2041) is considered by many to be a complex topic. This section provides an overview and discusses some of the basic mechanisms utilized with IPSec. IPSec works at the network layer. It is a set of protocols and algorithms that work together to secure data between endpoints. IPSec consists of two authentication protocols, Encapsulation Security Payload (ESP) and Authentication Header (AH), and two protection modes, tunnel and transport. Public and private encryption keys are also discussed, including the Diffie-Hellman method of key exchange. CCDPs need to know the basic mechanics of IPSec and its advantages and disadvantages in large enterprise networks.

ESP

Encapsulation Security Payload (ESP) is used to provide confidentiality of the data. It encrypts the data but does not manipulate the addressing portion of the packet. It leaves the header alone, so it does not provide for data origin authentication. What ESP does is scramble the data in the packet so that if the packet is intercepted, the attacker cannot get the information in the packet. ESP can be in two modes—transport or tunnel. Transport mode is used within a network where hiding IP addresses is not important. Tunnel mode is commonly used in conjunction with VPN services, where a remote user appears to be within a local network.

● **Transport mode**—The ESP header is inserted after the IP header and before the upper-layer protocol header. Figure 15-13 shows the transport-mode packet.

Figure 15-13 *Transport Mode*

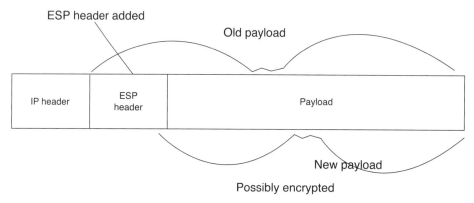

● **Tunnel mode**—With tunnel mode, a new tunnel IP header and ESP header are added before the original IP header and payload, as shown in Figure 15-14. The tunnel method offers protection similar to that of AH by protecting the header from being exposed.

Figure 15-14 *Tunnel Mode*

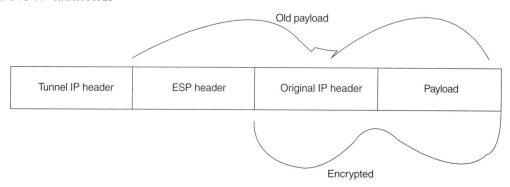

Authentication Header (AH)

The IP *Authentication Header (AH) protocol* (RFC 2402) protects the entire datagram by embedding the header into the data or payload portion of the packet and creating a new header. It is important to understand that AH authenticates only that the packet is from who sent it, as shown in Figure 15-15. AH can be applied alone or in combination with the IPSec ESP to increase security. The principal differences between ESP and AH is that ESP does not protect any IP header fields unless those fields are encapsulated in ESP tunnel mode.

Figure 15-15 *Authentication Header*

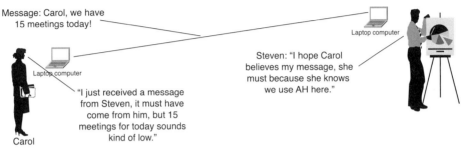

NOTE   IPSec is supported on the 1600, 2x00, 36x0, 4x00, 5x00, and 7x00 platforms.

Keys

Encryption *keys* are used to verify that a packet came from the real sender of the packet and not from an impostor. Encryption keys do not scramble the payload data, but rather make the IPSec connection secure by providing security association management with the exchange of session keys. In Figure 15-16, Carol is sending Steven a message that no one else must see. This encrypted message or data is then sent to the destination device, and the key is applied at the other end, which applies the secret key and decrypts the data, turning it back into cleartext. Public keys and private keys are used with encryption technologies.

Figure 15-16 *Encryption*

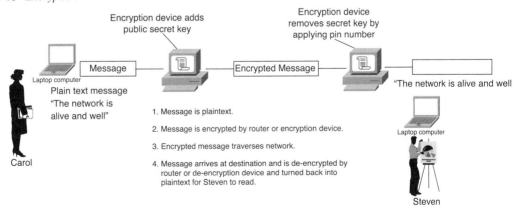

Public Key Technology

Public key encryption was invented by Diffie-Hellman. Using this encryption method, a message is encrypted at the source end with a public key and is decrypted at the destination with a private key. An analogy for this is an Automatic Teller Machine (ATM) and ATM card. The ATM card could be the public key—everybody has one. But only the holder of the card and the receiver of the message know the PIN (Personal Identification Number)—the private key. At each end of the ATM transaction, the end devices know the private key and use it to complete the transaction. If someone steals your ATM card, he needs to know your PIN (private key) before he can access your account and get money. This is why PINs (private keys) are guarded very closely.

In Figure 15-16, Carol is encrypting a message using Steven's public key (credit card). The only way Steven can decrypt this message is to use his PIN (private key). So, using this method, you only need the other person's credit card number (public key) to send him an encrypted message. He probably will not give you his PIN, though, which is okay. The manual method of obtaining keys does not scale well because everyone would need to know everyone else's public keys and send them to each other. Enter *Public Key Infrastructure (PKI)*. The credit cards (public keys) are published on the Internet for the senders to use when sending to a person. This is called Public Key Infrastructure (PKI).

Digital Signatures

Let's take a look at some other variations of the preceding theme. Carol can encrypt her message with her PIN (private key) instead of Steven's credit card number (public key). At Steven's end, her message is then decrypted with her credit card number (public key). Steven knows how to obtain her public key from the Internet, and he knows that this message must be from Carol and not an impostor. The drawback of this is that anyone at the receiving end could obtain the public key from the Internet and read the message. This approach is called a *digital signature* or *digital certificate*.

Finally, if Carol encrypts a message with Steven's public key and then encrypts it a second time with her private key, the result is a two-tiered encryption that means the message must have come from Carol. Using this method, only Steven can read it this time, because he needs to apply his private key to the message to decrypt it. This is the most secure method of the three discussed.

The necessary commands to define the keys on the Cisco routers are called **crypto map** commands.

Hashing Algorithms

By using keys, you can feel comfortable that your message came from the person who sent it, and not an impostor. However, the keys only protect the packet as it traverses the network for authentication, not the actual payload or data in the packet. If the packet is intercepted, the attacker can then try to manipulate the data field. Fortunately, there is a safeguard: hash codes. Just as hash is made by grinding up a pig, a hash code is made by "grinding" up the code. The resulting "hash" is sent across the wire to the destination, and hash is reassembled into code. IPSec can use two hash functions, MD5 and SHA.

- **MD5 (Message Digest 5)**—Message digest hashing is a form of digital signature and encryption that ensures that a message has not been altered as it traverses a network. MD5 produces a fixed-length signature from plain-text messages. The hashing function is performed on the packet as it enters the router. It produces a 128-bit hash of the packet.

- **SHA (Secure Hash Algorithm)**—Another form of digital signature developed by the National Institute of Standards and Technology, this hash algorithm is used to authenticate packet data.

NOTE   IPSec uses Diffie-Hellman/Oakley algorithms, and Diffie-Hellman/Oakley uses hash functions MD5 and SHA.

Public Key Infrastructure

IPSec scalability, the ability to deploy large (greater than 100 nodes) IPSec networks, has been one of the greatest challenges facing early implementers of network-layer encryption. Digital certificate technology lets devices easily authenticate each other in a manner that scales to very large networks. Many organizations are currently implementing a public key infrastructure (PKI) to manage digital certificates across a wide variety of applications, including virtual private networks (VPNs), secure e-mail, secure Web access, and other applications that require security. Cisco's implementation of IPSec is interoperable with several leading PKI vendors.

Diffie-Hellman

This is the well-known and widely used algorithm for establishing session keys to encrypt data. (Oakley could be considered an enhanced Diffie-Hellman.) IPSec is a public-key method of key exchange that uses the Diffie-Hellman/Oakley mechanisms to allow the end devices to come up with a common shared key dynamically, rather than preconfiguring all the public/private key parameters on all the routers. They accomplish this by exchanging a complicated set of numbers.

Internet Key Exchange (IKE)

Routers need to be able to negotiate their neighbor relationships. Otherwise, all routers would need to have crypto map statements pointing to each other. That's where the *Internet Key Exchange* (IKE) comes in. IKE is the process of exchanging keys with IPSec. IKE enhances IPSec by providing additional features, flexibility, and ease of configuration for the IPSec standard, along with authenticating each peer in an IPSec transaction. IKE was formerly known as ISAKMP/Oakley and is a hybrid of three key exchange mechanisms:

- **Oakley key exchange**—Oakley is superior to Diffie-Hellman and uses *modes* to describe a series of key exchanges.

- **Skeme key exchange**—A key exchange protocol that provides anonymity with rapid key refreshment.

- **ISAKMP framework**—ISAKMP (Internet Security Association and Key Management Protocol) was developed at the National Security Agency and is the protocol used by IPSec to manage keys.

NOTE   ISAKMP is the manager, and Oakley/Diffie-Hellman and Skeme all work for him. And ISAKMP reports to IKE.

IKE has the following benefits:

- Eliminates the need to manually specify all the IPSec security parameters in the crypto maps at both peers.

- Allows you to specify a lifetime for the IPSec security association.

- Allows encryption keys to change during IPSec sessions.

- Allows IPSec to provide anti-replay services.

NOTE   VeriSign, Inc., is the leading provider of digital certificate solutions for extranets and intranets, including IPSec. VeriSign OnSite for IPSec lets organizations easily issue certificates and build their own virtual private networks (VPNs) using the IPSec capabilities built into Cisco products.

Data Encryption Standard (DES) Encryption

DES is a widely used encryption standard that works on the data itself. By performing an algorithm, DES can turn clear-text messages into cipher text at the source. The destination restores the cipher text back to data. Keys called *shared secret keys* enable this to happen.

Virtual Private Networks (VPNs)

With the advent of the Internet, corporate networks must seriously consider VPN technology. VPNs enable the creation of private networks across the Internet, enabling tunneling and privacy of non-TCP/IP protocols and saving money in the process. In some cases, TCP/IP is tunneled as well.

A typical example of the use of VPN occurs whenever a corporate user on a travel assignment dials into a local service provider for a popular online service. The user can access company information over a virtual tunnel through the Internet, without fear of someone's intercepting the data as it transits the unsecured Internet. The user could be using an IP-based workstation or a Macintosh AppleTalk workstation because the AppleTalk traffic can be tunneled through IP. Figure 15-17 shows an example of a VPN.

Figure 15-17 *VPN*

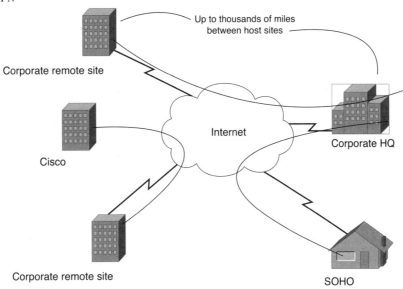

The sites shown in Figure 15-17 are separated by thousands of miles. Leased lines between the sites would be expensive, and Frame Relay might not be available in this area. The solution is to purchase a VPN service from a provider. In this example, all traffic between sites is encrypted for confidentiality. This is accomplished through the use of tunneling, of which there are three main types: L2F, L2TP, and IPSec. The figure shows three different VPNs. The SOHO user is accessing corporate resources (e-mail and servers) from the Internet. There is LAN-to-LAN or remote-site connectivity through the Internet. And a remote site is performing some extranet activity with one of its successful partners.

TIP   To determine how much money you can save your customer with your CCDP VPN design, access the VPN calculator at http://www.cisco.com/warp/public/779/largeent/learn/technologies/vpn/vpn_calc/vpnstart.html.

L2F

Cisco's own proprietary implementation is called *Layer 2 Forwarding,* or L2F. The L2F protocol focuses on providing a tunneling mechanism for transporting link-layer frames (for example, HDLC, PPP, SLIP) of higher-layer protocols. Using such tunnels, it is possible to separate the location of the initial dialup to the local ISP from the location at which the dialup protocol connection is terminated and the location at which access to the network is provided (usually a corporate gateway).

TIP　　　　L2F transports link-level frames, so it does not support multiprotocol tunnels.

Layer 2 Tunneling Protocol (L2TP)

In late 1999, the IETF committee created L2TP, a media-independent multiprotocol technology. Using L2TP tunneling, an ISP can create a virtual tunnel to link customers' remote sites and remote users with corporate home networks. At the ISP, there is a device called a *Local Access Concentrator* (LAC). The LAC exchanges Point-to-Point Protocol messages with remote users and communicates by way of L2TP requests and responses with the customers' L2TP network server (LNS) to establish the tunnels.

TIP　　　　Because L2TP is multiprotocol, this means that IP, IPX, AppleTalk, and other protocols can be tunneled through L2TP tunnels.

L2TP Access Concentrator (LAC)

A LAC can be a Cisco network-access server connected to the public switched telephone network (PSTN), as shown in Figure 15-18. The LAC need only implement media for operation over L2TP. A LAC can connect to the LNS using a local-area network or wide-area network, such as public or private Frame Relay. The LAC is the initiator of incoming calls and the receiver of outgoing calls.

Figure 15-18　*Layer 2 Access Concentrator*

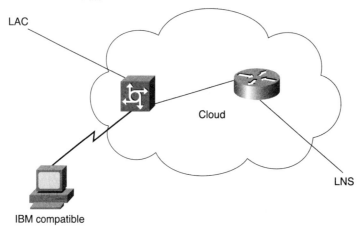

Foundation Summary

This section is a convenient review of many key concepts in this chapter. If you are already comfortable with the topics in this chapter, this summary could help you recall a few details. If you have just read this chapter, this review should help solidify some key facts. If you are doing your final preparation before the exam, Table 15-2 is a convenient way to review the day before the exam.

Table 15-2   *Key Concepts*

Term	Description
Bastion host	A secure gateway that supports a limited number of outsiders
Restrictive	Network security policies are well-documented rules about what activities are permitted on the network
DES	56-bit encryption
Permissive	Everything that is not explicitly prohibited is allowed
CBAC	Filters Java applets
Stateful filters	Filter at Layer 4 of the OSI stack
DMZ	Screened subnet
NAT	Hiding internal network from the world
SHA	Authenticates packet data
NetRanger	Intrusion detection system
L2TP	IETF standard—multiprotocol
L2F	Cisco proprietary
PPTP	Microsoft's VPN solution—multiprotocol

Q&A

As mentioned in Chapter 1, the questions and scenarios in this book are more difficult than what you will experience on the actual exam. The questions do not attempt to cover more breadth or depth than the exam; however, they are designed to make sure that you know the answer. Rather than allowing you to derive the answer from clues hidden inside the question, the questions challenge your understanding and recall of the subject. Questions from the "Do I Know This Already?" quiz from the beginning of the chapter are repeated here to ensure that you have mastered this chapter's topic areas. Hopefully, these questions will help limit the number of exam questions on which you narrow your choices to two options and then guess. Be sure to use the CD and take the simulated exams.

The answers to these questions can be found in Appendix A.

1 What is a bastion host?

_____

_____

_____

2 Name four services to turn off on the (perimeter) router that interfaces with the Internet.

_____

_____

_____

3 Can a Cisco 2500 router be used as a firewall?

_____

_____

_____

4 What are network security policies?

_____

_____

_____

5 On what router platforms is CBAC available?

_____

_____

_____

6 What is a "choke" router?

_____

_____

_____

7 At what layer of the OSI model do stateful firewalls work?

_____

_____

_____

8 What network layer addresses should always be blocked from entering your network from the outside?

_____

_____

_____

9 Of the two key similar exchange mechanisms Diffie-Hellman and Oakley, which is considered superior?

_____

_____

_____

10 For what does PKI stand?

_____

_____

_____

11 What does SHA authenticate?

_____

_____

_____

12 Does ESP encrypt the IP Header?

_____

_____

_____

13 Does L2F support multiprotocol?

_____

_____

_____

14 Does L2TP support multiprotocol?

_____

_____

_____

15 What is the name of the product that replaced NetRanger?

_____

_____

_____

16 Where would the local network server be located—at the ISP or on the customer's property?

_____

_____

_____

17 What does the authentication header protect?

_____

_____

_____

18 How many bits does the MD5 hash encrypt with?

_____

_____

_____

19 What are the router commands that are used for exchanging keys called?

_____

_____

_____

20 Name three layers that CBAC examines.

_____

_____

_____

21 Which has the stronger authentication mechanism—**enable secret** or **enable password**?

_____

_____

_____

22 With CBAC, which feature is needed to prevent denial-of-service attacks?

_____

_____

_____

23 Where should extended access lists be applied—closest to the source or the destination?

_____

_____

_____

24 What is a perimeter router?

_____

_____

_____

25 For what does ISAKMP stand?

_____

_____

_____

26 What RFC is NAT?

_____

_____

_____

27 Why is stateful filtering considered faster than application proxies?

_____

_____

_____

28 Without CBAC, can Cisco routers filter TCP and UDP ports?

_____

_____

_____

29 Name three network security weaknesses.

_____

_____

_____

30 What IOS feature set is required for CBAC?

_____

_____

_____

Scenarios

Scenario 1

RouteitRight has decided to connect its headquarters to the Internet and has purchased a 2500 router. The company has determined the following requirements. It is up to you to implement them.

- No DMZ is needed because there are no Web servers.

- The ISP cannot receive Layer 3 address information from CDP packets.

- Users will be able to telnet from inside the network to the Internet but not from the Internet to the inside network.

Scenario 2

RouteitRight has decided to implement a Web server but has been receiving many denial-of-service attacks. The company has purchased a second router as a precautionary measure to protect its internal users from the Internet. The company has determined the following requirements. It is up to you to implement them.

- A feature must be implemented that blocks DoS attacks.

- If the DMZ becomes compromised, the internal users are still protected from the Internet.

- RFC 1918 addresses can be used inside the network.

Scenario 3

RouteitRight has added more bastion hosts to the DMZ and needs a better solution. The company has determined the following requirements. It is up to you to implement them.

- Stateful firewall to the DMZ should be put into place.

- Site A must connect to Site B for LAN-to-LAN data flow without any Layer 2 connections between the two sites.

Scenario Answers

Answer to Scenario 1

The requirements placed on the CCDP can be met by turning off CDP broadcasts at the serial interface on the perimeter router. Because no DMZ area or choke router will be in place, it would be a good idea to place access lists that permit only certain traffic (ports) through to the servers inside. Another idea would be to deny unnecessary traffic. Permitting only established sessions from the Internet to enter the inside network meets the Telnet requirement. See Figure 15-19.

Figure 15-19 *Scenario 1 Suggested Solution*

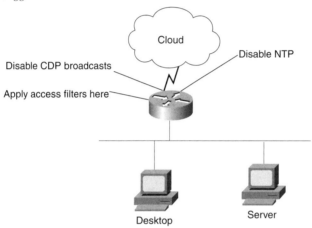

Answer to Scenario 2

By implementing CBAC and the TCP Interceptor tool that comes with it, you can prevent DoS attacks from entering the customer's network. By installing the choke router behind the perimeter router, anyone trying to compromise the DMZ will be denied access through the choke router. By implementing the NAT feature on the perimeter router, the CCDP can meet the RFC 1918 requirement. See Figure 15-20.

Answer to Scenario 3

Figure 15-21 shows a suggested solution for Scenario 3.

Figure 15-20   *Scenario 2 Suggested Solution*

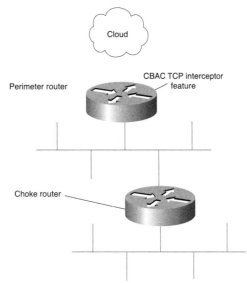

Figure 15-21   *Scenario 3 Suggested Solution*

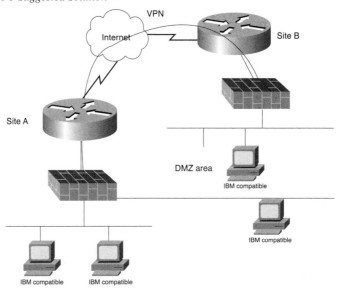

By implementing the solution shown in Figure 15-21, the CCDP can meet the customer's requirements. Stateful firewall is put into place by using the PIX firewall.

Also, by implementing a VPN tunnel between the PIX firewalls, you can meet the LAN-to-LAN requirement.

This chapter covers the following topics that you will need to master as a CCDP:

- **Traditional voice environment**—This section provides a review of the traditional voice environment.

- **Designing voice over data**—This section addresses the challenges that the design professional faces when engineering voice over data.

- **Quality of Service for voice**—This section addresses QoS for voice and discusses why voice traffic needs guarantees to ensure timely delivery.

CHAPTER 16

Voice Techniques

As soon as you know the business, technical, and networking requirements, you can construct the appropriate voice-design solution. The evolving Quality of Service (QoS) and multiservice application integration requirements of voice, video, and data are critical factors in a successful design network. This chapter takes a closer look at how voice can be designed to work over data networks.

Cisco expects the successful CCDP candidate to be able to use design models to render a voice over data solution that will meet the client's requirements for performance. The CID exam tests your knowledge of how voice can be integrated into a successful network design. It is expected that a CCDP will make design recommendations to improve performance utilizing voice over data.

How to Best Use This Chapter

By following these steps, you can make better use of your study time:

- Keep your notes and the answers for all your work with this book in one place for easy reference.

- Take the "Do I Know This Already?" quiz and write down your answers. Studies show that retention is significantly increased through writing down facts and concepts, even if you never look at the information again.

- Use the diagram shown in Figure 16-1 to guide you to the next step.

Figure 16-1 *How to Use This Chapter*

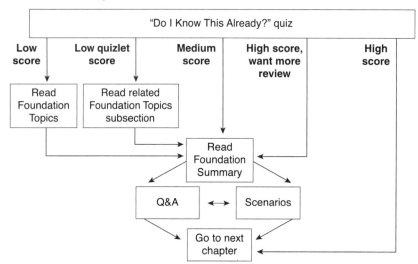

If you skip to the Foundation Summary, Q&A, and Scenarios sections and have trouble with the material there, you should go back to the Foundation Topics section.

"Do I Know This Already?" Quiz

The purpose of the "Do I Know This Already?" quiz is to help you decide which parts of this chapter to use. If you intend to read the entire chapter, you do not necessarily need to answer these questions now.

This 15-question quiz helps you determine how to spend your limited study time. The quiz is divided into three smaller "quizlets" that help you select the sections of the chapter on which to focus. Figure 16-1 outlines suggestions on how to spend your time in this chapter. Use Table 16-1 to record your score.

Table 16-1 *Score Sheet for Quiz and Quizlets*

Quizlet Number	Foundation Topics Section Covering These Questions	Questions	Score
1	Traditional voice environment	1, 2, 11, 12, 13	
2	Designing the voice over data network	3, 4, 7, 10, 15	
3	Quality of Service for voice	5, 6, 8, 9, 14	

1 What challenge does the CCDP face when merging voice onto a data network?

_____

_____

_____

2 What are three different types of voice interfaces used on a Cisco router?

_____

_____

_____

3 What two types of digital signaling are available?

_____

_____

_____

4 What is a dial plan?

_____

_____

_____

5 List three benefits of a dial plan.

_____

_____

_____

6 What must a successful QoS voice over data network design ensure?

_____

_____

_____

7 List four factors that have a significant impact on voice quality in a network.

_____

_____

_____

8 List three types of delay that, by design, are inherent in voice networks.

_____

_____

_____

9 For good voice quality, what does Cisco recommend as the maximum amount of delay (one-way) from end to end?

_____

_____

_____

10 What is handling delay? Provide an example of handling delay in a voice network.

_____

_____

_____

11 True or false: QoS should start in the LAN. The largest bottlenecks are usually found on the campus network.

_____

_____

_____

12 What three areas of concern should be addressed at the router?

_____

_____

_____

13 What three protocols can provide transport for voice?

_____

_____

_____

14 What three processes must occur before voice can be passed from the PBX to the router?

_____

_____

_____

15 What four components comprise the H.323 family?

_____

_____

_____

The answers to the "Do I Know This Already?" quiz are found in Appendix A. The suggested choices for your next step are as follows:

- **6 or less overall score**—Read the chapter. This includes the "Foundation Topics," "Foundation Summary," and "Q&A" sections, as well as the scenario at the end of the chapter.

- **2 or less on any "quizlet"**—Review the subsection(s) of the "Foundation Topics" part of this chapter based on Table 16-1. Then move into the "Foundation Summary," the "Q&A" section, and the scenario at the end of the chapter.

- **7, 8, or 9 overall score**—Begin with the "Foundation Summary" section and then go to the "Q&A" section and the scenario at the end of the chapter.

- **10 or more overall score**—If you want more review on these topics, skip to the "Foundation Summary" section, then go to the "Q&A" section and the scenario at the end of the chapter. Otherwise, move to the next chapter.

Foundation Topics

For a long time, voice and data were viewed as different resources. Typically, the telecommunications division managed the voice network, and the LAN-support division supported the data operations. Businesses and enterprises that supported voice and data had to bear the two separate expenses of a voice infrastructure and a data infrastructure. Figure 16-2 shows an example of separate voice, video, and data networks.

Figure 16-2 *Voice, Video, and Data Networks*

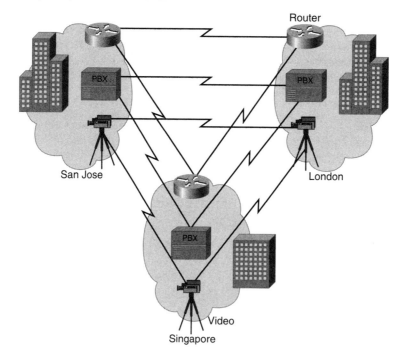

Recently, as businesses continue to pursue strategies to reduce operating costs, voice over data design has emerged as a way to save expenses. Voice over data allows the consolidation of the costs of administering and maintaining both networks by converging voice and data onto one network. Using the same infrastructure for voice and data results in significant cost savings. Savings come from the elimination or reduction of voice-only circuits and services. Savings come from the costs associated with the administration and maintenance of dual systems. Last, but not least, the recurring costs of supporting two systems are reduced as well.

Voice over data, which is a component of multiservice networking, is emerging as a strategically important issue for enterprise and public service provider infrastructures alike.

Multiservice networking suggests that voice, video, and data can travel over a single packet-cell-based infrastructure.

The benefits of multiservice networking are reduced operational costs, higher performance, greater flexibility, integration and control, and faster new application and service deployment. Although most discussion of a multiservice converged network focuses on voice, video, and data, this chapter focuses specifically on the issues that govern voice over data. Although the voice-over-data solution is wonderful in that it allows network managers to access the Internet as an alternative to the more-costly toll solutions, there are issues associated with the convergence. Data networks and protocols were not designed to handle the special requirements of voice. Voice is sensitive to time and delay. Merging voice and data offers a significant opportunity for savings but also presents a significant challenge to the network designer. The goal of a well-designed voice-over-data network is to achieve a convergence of the voice and data infrastructures in a single multiservice network. Figure 16-3 shows a multiservice network converging voice, video, and data.

Figure 16-3   *Multiservice Network*

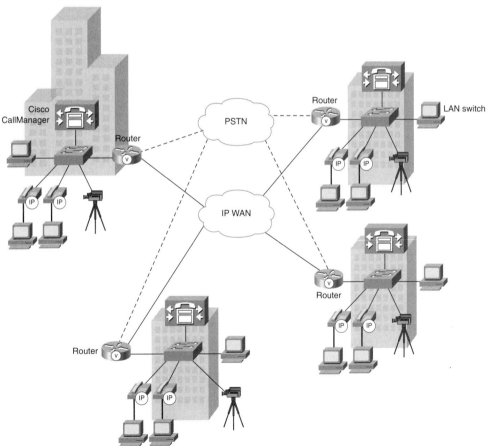

Traditional PBX Environment

In a traditional business environment, devices such as private branch exchanges or key systems handle telephone connections between the customer equipment and the central office.

Key Systems

Key systems are switches that allow multiple phones to share a common pool of external phone lines. All users in the key system share up to four external lines for long-distance dialing. A key system gives the user a choice of three or four external lines to use when dialing. While punching a designated line, the user connects his phone to that line. The line lights up to indicate to other users that it is unavailable. Key systems can include features such as hold, transfer, and speed dial. Key systems are ideal for small office environments. Key systems are phone switches with less-complex capabilities. Figure 16-4 shows a typical key system.

Figure 16-4   *Key System*

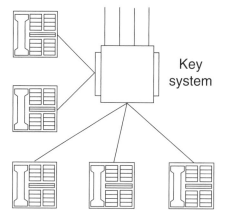

PBX

Private branch exchanges (PBXs) are common in offices with more than 25 phone lines. With PBXs, each phone has a unique extension number. For interoffice communication, PBXs can connect to other PBXs via a trunk connection. Many multisite businesses have trunk lines, which are also known as *tie-lines,* between each office to allow users to use intercom dialing. The trunk lines between offices create a private voice network within the enterprise. Using tie-lines is cost-effective in that it allows the company to bypass the long-distance per-call charge. A line connection refers to a connection between a telephone switch and a PBX.

When businesses consider integrating voice and data, the first phase of migration considered is toll bypass. Toll bypass lets businesses send their intraoffice voice and fax calls over their existing data network.

Figure 16-5 shows an example of legacy PBX-to-PBX connectivity. The connections are from the PBX to the local exchange carrier, and then to a tandem switch. Then the connection is made to an interexchange carrier's point of presence.

Figure 16-5 *Private Branch Exchange (PBX)*

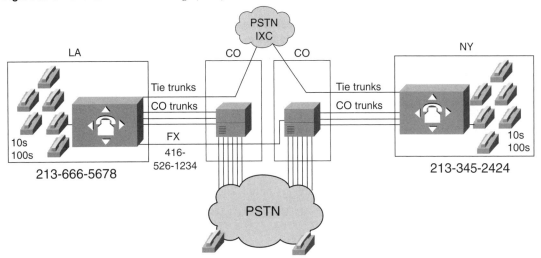

Designing Voice-over-Data Networks

The requirements that drive the design issues when running voice over data are similar to the other design issues that have been discussed throughout this book.

If the business requirement is to lower overall communications costs, a potential design solution places voice over data. The cost savings result from not having to run a separate network for voice and a separate network for data. For the design to be considered a success, the voice over data network must successfully deliver the quality and performance of the existing voice network. Data and voice networks were designed with different objectives. A traditional data network allows and expects bursty data flow. Data comes in packets and grabs as much bandwidth as it can at any given time. Data networks tolerate bursty data flow and first-come, first-served access. In addition, the data rate adapts to network conditions and can tolerate small delays.

In contrast, voice traffic does not flow in bursts. The packets are equally spaced. Voice packets need a reserved amount of bandwidth. They don't need much; sometimes as little as 8 K is enough. Whatever they need must be available during the duration of the call.

When e-mail is slow, the problem of receiving e-mail slowly is usually tolerated. When voice traffic is slow and delayed, however, the result is unacceptable. If voice traffic runs over a network that is optimized for data, the result could be choppy and unintelligible voice traffic. Unlike data traffic, which tends to be bursty, voice traffic tends to be constant. Although the amount of bandwidth per call is not as large as with data traffic, the bandwidth needs to be guaranteed and without delay.

In voice transmission, delay is intolerable. The actual words spoken carry only a part of the meaning. When individuals carry a conversation, meaning is also conveyed in inflection, intonation, and pace. A tiny pause has as much meaning as a verbalized part, and its timing must be preserved. Voice networks must be designed to transport the voice conversation, reliably and in synchronization with the originator's intent.

Regular phone service provides 99.999% reliability and availability. Failures within the traditional phone network are extremely unusual. Cell phone users might accept and acknowledge unintelligible voice traffic from time to time because of the convenience that a cell phone offers. Computer users tolerate slow access to a Web site or a network's being down. (Some look forward to it because it means extra time off!) However, regular phone users have become accustomed to a 99.999% reliability and availability standard for voice quality, and they will not (and should not) tolerate anything less.

Path Basics

Signaling, addressing, and routing are the major functions of a voice over data network. Each is discussed in detail in the following sections.

Analog and Digital Signaling

The purpose of signaling in a voice network is to establish a connection. Mapping PBX signaling to your data network requires an understanding of how the PBX handles PBX-to-PBX signaling. The first PBXs used simple analog lines to achieve voice-band information. Analog signaling has become outdated and has largely been replaced by less-expensive and more-effective digital signaling.

Two methods can be employed for digital signaling:

- Channel Associated Signaling (CAS), or Robbed-Bit Signaling
- Common Channel Signaling (CCS)

In CAS, the signaling information is conveyed within the voice channel. CAS is sometimes called robbed-bit because, in every sixth frame, a bit is stolen from the voice channel to signal information. In North America, the standard for digital transmission is T1. T1 uses 24 time slots for a total speed of 1.544 Mbps. In North American CCS, a signaling channel is designated on the T1, and the signaling bits for all the other T1 channels are transmitted across the single CCS channel.

In Europe and in most other parts of the world, the standard for digital transmission is E1. E1 uses 32 time slots for a total speed of 2.048 Mbps. The channel maintains synchronization and passes control information; the 16th channel passes signaling information. Both CAS and CCS use time slot 16. The difference between the two is their use of messages to pass signaling information. In CAS, the signaling is conveyed in channel 16, and the signaling associated with each channel is maintained via a fixed relationship. CCS eliminates the requirement for the signaling to maintain a fixed relationship with the voice channel. In CCS, signaling is passed in messages between processors that control the terminating switches.

NOTE   For CAS or CCS, Cisco can translate the voice signals and carry them over the data network.

Signaling is a three-step process:

> **Step 1**   The line is seized.
>
> **Step 2**   A path is established across the network.
>
> **Step 3**   A remote peer acknowledges the call.

For a telephone call to be completed, signaling must occur. The instant the receiver is lifted from the cradle, an off-hook signal is sent to the PBX. In an exchange that is defined as Station Loop Signaling, the PBX responds with a dial tone and receives digits from the user phone. As soon as the PBX receives the digits, decisions occur at the PBX. What is the call's destination? Is the call local to the PBX? If not, how can the call best be routed? Should the call be placed to the telephone company central office (CO) or on an internal network to another PBX via a tie-line?

In the first scenario, the PBX signals to seize a trunk to the CO. Depending on the services, the signaling might be analog or digital. If the facilities are analog, the PBX might use E&M signaling. If the call is established, the same signaling then occurs at the remote end of the network. The CO seizes a line to the PBX and forwards the digits. The PBX selects the appropriate station and signals an alert to the station. The PBX makes the call-routing decision based on its best-match voice routing table. Enterprise PBXs communicate with each other through industry-standard protocols or proprietary protocols. These specialized protocols let PBXs offer enhanced services between sites.

NOTE   Cisco does not support proprietary protocols. When considering integration with the PBX, verify the standard protocol features that Cisco supports.

It is often impractical to interconnect every PBX. As this book has discussed in earlier chapters, the full-mesh scenario can be quite costly. One alternative is the use of tandem PBXs.

Tandem Switching

A *tandem PBX* is a main PBX that accepts all inbound calls to an organization. It has a directory number and can connect other PBX stations to the public network for both incoming and outcoming calls. A tandem switch connects one trunk to another. A tandem switch is an intermediate switch or connection between an originating telephone call location and the final destination of the class.

Signaling System 7

Signaling System 7 (SS7) is important for Voice over IP (VoIP) because it provides a common protocol for signaling, messaging, and interfacing VoIP and PBX traffic. SS7 uses out-of-band signaling to establish the appropriate path for the call through the carrier network before establishing the actual transmission path. Many modern PBXs directly support the SS7 signaling protocol. This allows each PBX to make and process requests from the telephone company network.

After a call has been established, the transmission path does not change for the duration of the call. Networks with these inherent signaling characteristics are called connection-oriented networks.

Addressing

For any telephone network to function, each telephone must be identified by a unique address. Voice addressing relies on a combination of international and national standards, local telephone company practices, and internal customer-specific codes.

The International Telecommunications Union ITU-T recommendation E.164 defines the international numbering plan for ISDN. In addition, E.164 has the country codes used for dialing internationally. The international telephone service-numbering plan is a subset of this numbering plan. Each country's national numbering plan must conform to the E.164 recommendation and work in conjunction with the international numbering plan. Providers of Public-Switched Telephone Networks (PSTNs) must ensure that their numbering plan aligns with the E.164 recommendation and that each of their customers' networks conform.

Users and PSTN providers employ alternative numbering schemes. Exceptions to the E.164 recommendation include *Carrier Identification Code (CIC)*, a prefix to select different long-distance carriers; prefixes to select tielines, trunk groups, and WATS lines; and private number plans, such as seven-digit dialing. When you integrate voice and data networks, you need to consider each of these numbering plans. The ITU-T has provided the international public telecommunication numbering plan. It can be found on the Internet at http://www.itu.int. Table 16-2 provides examples of randomly selected country code assignments.

Table 16-2   *E.164 Country Code Assignments*

Code	Country
1	United States
242	Congo
34	Spain
503	El Salvador
81	Japan
90	Turkey
966	Saudi Arabia
20	Egypt
27	South Africa

Routing

Routing is closely related to the numbering plan and signaling just described. Routing allows the establishment of a call from the source telephone to the destination telephone. However, most routing is much more sophisticated. It lets subscribers select services or divert calls from one subscriber to another. Dialing tables and SS7 are used for routing.

Routing occurs as a result of establishing a set of tables or rules within each switch. As each call arrives, the path to the desired destination and the types of services available are derived from these tables or rules. It is important to know just how the routing and the associated features are accomplished in the voice network because these functions might have to be provided in an integrated voice-data network.

Dial Plans

A dial plan is a set of rules for routing incoming and outgoing calls and accessing voice calls from one system to another. All calls are routed based on the configured dial plan. The dial plan is a required configuration on the switch, PBX, or key system.

Here are the benefits of a dial plan:

- Controls the behavior of the voice system
- Enables reliability and security
- Enables cost savings

- Toll call control

- Least-cost routing

Whenever you use a phone in an office situation, it is very likely that a dial plan governs the flow of voice traffic. The internal extensions are mapped to direct in-house numbers. Interoffice calls typically require you to enter four digits to reach an extension. The plan might require you to dial 9 to get access to the outside network. It might require dialing 8 to get access to long-distance calls. The plan might require access codes to make long-distance calls. Some phones might not be able to access the outside network. Dial plans typically create a number of *Class of Service (CoS)* groups. CoS assigns privileges to users. A class can contain one or many users. CoS can also restrict access during specified times.

To describe a typical dial plan, let's take a look at a small voice network with four remote sites and a central site. Users at all sites can dial three-digit extensions to reach other users at the local site. To call between sites, the users must use a trunk access code to connect the phone switch to the remote site. After receiving a second dial tone, users can dial a three-digit extension. In this example, users from Site A must dial 2 to reach site B, 3 to reach site C, and 4 to reach site D. Table 16-3 depicts the dial plan for a small network. The dial plan allows for scalability up to 1000 connections.

Table 16-3   *Network Dial Plan*

Source	Destination	Dialed Numbers
From Site 1	To Site 1	001–999
From Site 1	To Site 2	2001–2999
From Site 1	To Site 3	3001–3999
From Site 1	To Site 4	4001–4999
From Site 2	To Site 2	001–999
From Site 2	To Site 1	1001–1999
From Site 2	To Site 3	3001–3999
From Site 2	To Site 4	4001–4999
From Site 3	To Site 3	001–999
From Site 3	To Site 1	1001–3999
From Site 3	To Site 2	2001–3999
From Site 3	To Site 4	4001–4999
From Site 4	To Site 4	001–999
From Site 4	To Site 1	1001–1999
From Site 4	To Site 2	2001–2999
From Site 4	To Site 3	3001–3999

Class of Service groups:

- CoS1Lobby phone: No outside access; 1–800 only
- CoS2Admin phone: Local only and 1-800 service
- CoS3Sales phone: Local, long-distance
- CoS4Manager's phone: No restrictions

Handling incomplete calls, voice mail, redirected calls, and 911 calls are also the responsibility of an efficient dial plan.

Figure 16-6 shows adding and stripping digits for a dial routing plan.

Figure 16-6   *Dial Routing Plan*

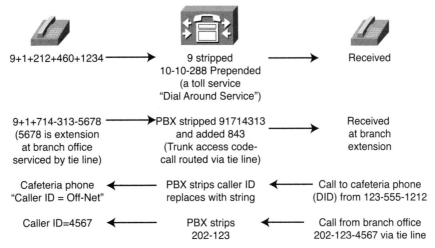

Examine the figure in regards to outgoing calls in the first example:

- Strips digits or adds access codes to call the PSTN.
- Caller keys in 9-1-212-460-1234.
- PBX strips the 9 and adds 10-10-288 to rout the signal to dial around the long-distance service.

Look again at Figure 16-6 for the second example:

- Strips and adds digits on a network call.
- Caller keys 9-1-714-313-1234 (1234 is the extension at the branch office serviced by the tie-line).
- PBX strips 91714313 and adds 843 (843 is the trunk access code to route the signal through the tie-line).

Incoming calls:

- Strips extra digits coming from the PSTN.

- Cafeteria phone receives an outside call.

- Caller ID is stripped and replaced with the string "off-net call"

- Strips or adds digits coming from a PBX.

In a call from a remote branch with company-wide extensions, PBX can strip all the leading digits, which leaves the remaining four digits to be passed to the phone number.

Two major classes of dial plans are available:

- Multinational

- National enterprise

Voice-over Technologies

Thanks to advances in technology, the transmission of voice can now be transmitted over traditional public networks. Using three different protocols, Cisco provides three ways of providing voice services over data connections:

- Voice over ATM

- Voice over Frame Relay

- Voice over IP

All packet-voice systems follow a common model. The packet-voice transport network may be based on IP, Frame Relay, or ATM. At the edges of the network are devices to change the voice information from its traditional telephony form to a form suitable for packet transmission. The network then forwards the packet data to a voice agent serving the destination.

Transport Versus Translate

There are two basic models for integrating voice over data: *transport* and *translate*. Transport is the transparent support of voice over the existing data network. Simulation of tie-lines over ATM using circuit emulation is a good example. Translate is the translation of traditional voice functions by the data infrastructure. An example is the interpretation of voice signaling and the creation of SVCs within ATM. Translate networking is more complex than transport networking, and its implementation is a current topic within many standards committees today. The appropriate platform and protocol should be selected based on cost, availability, and technical considerations.

Voice over ATM

ATM can transport voice in an efficient and flexible manner. A number of approaches are available to the CCDP. Some methods are established, whereas other practices are continually evolving as technology becomes more sophisticated.

The design of ATM technology provides the capability to efficiently transmit voice traffic patterns that are variable in terms of information rate. Simply stated, ATM standards are tailor-made for the requirements of voice. The range of standards now available allows a variety of voice networking applications to be addressed. If you include VoATM in the design of the modern multiservice network, a complete range of voice and data services can be merged into a single network.

The ATM Forum and the ITU have specified different classes of service to represent different possible traffic types for VoATM. Different ATM adaptation types have been developed for different traffic types, each with its benefits and detriments. ATM Adaptation Layer 1 (AAL1) is the most common adaptation layer used with constant bit-rate services.

Unstructured AAL1 takes a continuous bit stream and places it within ATM cells. This is a common method of supporting a full E1 byte stream from end to end. The trade-off with this method is that a full E1 may be sent, regardless of the actual number of voice channels in use. Structured AAL1 contains a pointer in the payload that allows the DS0 structure to be maintained in subsequent cells. This allows the network to be more efficient by not using bandwidth for unused DS0s. The remapping option allows the ATM network to terminate structured AAL1 cells and remap DS0s to the proper destinations. This eliminates the need for PVCs between every possible source and destination. The big change with this method is that a PVC is not built from edge to edge.

Constant bit rate (CBR) and variable bit rate (VBR) classes have provisions for passing real-time traffic and are suitable for guaranteeing a certain level of service in a voice network. CBR, in particular, allows the amount of bandwidth, end-to-end delay, and delay variation to be specified during the call setup. The method of transporting voice channels through an ATM network is dependent on the nature of the traffic.

VoATM Signaling

PVCs are created for both signaling and voice transport. First, a signaling message is carried transparently over the signaling virtual circuit (VC) from end station to end station. Second, coordination between the end systems allows the selection of a VC to carry the voice communication between end stations. The ATM network is generally transparent with regard to interpreting the signaling that takes place between end stations. However, some products understand CAS signaling and can prevent the sending of empty voice cells when the end stations are on-hook. A signaling request from an end station causes the ATM network to create a switch virtual circuit (SVC) with the appropriate QoS to the desired end station. The creation of an SVC versus the prior establishment of PVCs is clearly more advantageous from three aspects:

- SVCs are more efficient users of bandwidth.

- QoS for connections do not need to be constant, as with PVCs.

- The ability to switch calls within the network can lead to the elimination of the Tandem PBX and potentially the edge PBX.

VoATM Addressing

ATM standards support both a private and public addressing scheme. Both schemes are 20 bytes in length.

VoATM Routing

ATM uses a private network-to-network interface (PNNI), a hierarchical link-state routing protocol that is scalable for global usage. In addition to determining reachability and routing within an ATM network, it is also capable of call setup. As soon as the connection is established, voice traffic flows between end stations as if a leased line exists between the two. This specification spells out routing in private networks.

VoATM and Delay

ATM has several mechanisms for controlling delay and delay variation. ATM's QoS capabilities allow the specific request of constant bit-rate traffic with bandwidth and delay variation guarantees. The use of VC queues allows each traffic stream to be treated uniquely. In the case of voice traffic, priority can be given to its transmission. The use of small fixed-size cells reduces queuing delay and the delay variation associated with variable-sized packets.

Voice over Frame Relay

VoFR is a popular choice for implementing toll bypass. Because standards for VoFR have been in place for several years, vendor interoperability and functionality have been better tested than the emerging VoIP standards.

Here are some of the benefits of using VoFR:

- Frame Relay costs for tie-line functionality are relatively low when compared to the costs of other WAN circuits.

- Frame Relay is readily available.

- Frame Relay can be oversubscribed.

The following sections discuss VoFR signaling and VoFR addressing.

VoFR Signaling

At the outset of Frame Relay, call setup processes varied with the vendor. As a result, there were interoperability issues between different vendors. Frame Relay Forum FRF.11 Implementation Agreement establishes a standard for call setup, coding types, and packet formats for voice over Frame Relay and will provide the basis for interoperability between vendors in the future.

VoFR Addressing

Address mapping is handled through static tables—dialed digits mapped to specific PVCs. How voice is routed depends on which routing protocol is chosen to establish PVCs and the hardware used in the Frame Relay network. Voice is routed to the configured PVCs. The PVCs are then routed by the Frame Relay network. Routing can be based on bandwidth limits, hops, delay, or some combination of these, but most routing implementations are based on maximizing bandwidth utilization.

The methods for designing a VoFR network are as follows:

- A full mesh of voice and data PVCs minimizes the number of network transit hops and maximizes the ability to establish different Qualities of Service. This network minimizes delay and improves voice quality at a huge cost.

- To reduce costs, both data and voice segments can be configured to use the same PVC, thereby reducing the number of PVCs required. In this design, the central site switch serves as a tandem switch and reroutes voice calls.

A number of mechanisms can minimize delay and delay variation on a Frame Relay network. The presence of long data frames on a low-speed Frame Relay link can cause unacceptable delays for time-sensitive voice frames. To reduce this problem, some vendors implement smaller frame sizes by fragmenting large data frames to help reduce delay and delay variation.

To ensure compatibility between vendor platforms, FRF.12 proposes an industry-standard approach to address delay and delay variation.

FRF.12 is an Implementation Agreement defined to help support voice and other real-time (delay-sensitive) data on lower-speed links. It accommodates the variation of frame sizes in a manner that allows the mixture of real-time and non-real-time data. To ensure voice quality, the Committed Information Rate (CIR) on each PVC must be set.

Voice over IP

Of the emerging technologies, voice over IP is the most sensitive. Voice design sets the standard for engineering and quality in a network. Demand for voice over IP is leading the movement for QoS in IP environments. It will ultimately lead to the use of the Internet for fax and voice telephony services. Voice over IP will ultimately be a key component of the migration of telephony to the LAN and WAN infrastructure.

VoIP Signaling

VoIP signaling has three major areas:

- Signaling from the PBX to the router
- Signaling between routers
- Signaling from the router to the PBX

The user's phone is connected to the PBX. When the user picks up the handset, an off-hook condition is generated. The off-hook condition generates a signal from the PBX to the router. The connection between the PBX and the router appears as a trunk line to the PBX, which signals the routers to seize the trunk. Signaling from the PBX may be any of the common signaling methods used to seize a trunk line, such as FXS or E&M signaling. In the future, digital signaling such as CCS or QSIG will become available. The PBX then forwards the dialed digits to the router in the same manner the digits would be forwarded to a telephone company switch. Within the router, the dial plan mapper maps the dialed digits to an IP address and signals a Q.931 Call Establishment Request to the remote peer that is indicated by the IP address. Meanwhile, the control channel is used to set up the Real-Time Protocol (RTP) audio streams, and the RSVP protocol is used to request a guaranteed quality of service.

When the remote router receives the Q.931 call request, it signals a line seizure to the PBX. After the PBX acknowledges, the router forwards the dialed digits to the PBX and signals a call acknowledgment to the originating router.

In connectionless network architectures such as IP, the responsibility for session establishment and signaling reside in the end stations. To successfully emulate voice services across an IP network, enhancements to the signaling stacks are required. For example, an H.323 agent is added to the router for standards-based support of the audio and signaling streams. The Q.931 protocol is used for call establishment and teardown between H.323 agents or end stations. The Real-Time Control Protocol (RTCP) is used to establish the audio channels themselves. A reliable session-oriented protocol, TCP, is deployed between end stations to carry the signaling channels. RTP, which is built on top of UDP, is used to transport the real-time audio stream. RTP uses UDP as a transport mechanism because it has lower delay than TCP and because actual voice traffic, unlike data traffic or signaling, tolerates low levels of loss and cannot effectively exploit retransmission.

VoIP Addressing

In an existing corporate intranet, an IP addressing plan is in place. To the IP numbering scheme, the voice numbers appear as additional IP hosts, either as an extension of the existing scheme or with new IP addresses.

The dial plan mapper performs translation of dial digits from the PBX to an IP host address. The destination telephone number, or some portion of the number, is mapped to the destination IP address. When the number is received from the PBX, the router compares the number to those mapped in the router table. If a match is found, the call is routed to the IP host. After the connection is established, the corporate intranet connection is transparent to the subscriber.

VoIP Routing

One of the strengths of IP is the maturity and sophistication of its routing protocols. A modern routing protocol such as EIGRP can take delay into consideration in calculating the best path. EIGRP can typically converge in less than a second, which allows voice traffic to take advantage of the self-healing capabilities of IP networks. Advanced features such as policy routing and access lists make it possible to create highly sophisticated and secure routing schemes for voice traffic.

The Resource Reservation Protocol (RSVP) can be automatically invoked by Cisco's VoIP gateways to ensure that voice traffic can use the best path through the network. This can include segments of arbitrary media, such as switched LANs or ATM networks. Some of the most interesting developments in IP routing are the development of Tag Switching and other IP switching disciplines. Tag Switching provides a way to extend IP routing, policy, and RSVP functionality over ATM and other high-speed transports. Another benefit of Tag Switching is its traffic-engineering capabilities, which are needed for the efficient use of network resources. Traffic engineering can be used to shift traffic load based on different predicates, such as time of day.

RSVP

RSVP is an internetwork end-to-end protocol that can reserve the necessary resources for the different classes of service by making the most of each underlying network type. RSVP lets the participants advise the network of their needs, allowing the network to configure itself to meet those needs. For example, an application can signal the network about the level of service it requires. To guarantee this level across the entire flow of the application, RSVP lets the network reserve resources from end to end, using Frame Relay techniques on Frame Relay networks, ATM techniques on ATM, and so on. RSVP is beneficial when occasional bandwidth needs to be reserved for non-voice applications. If priority queuing is enabled for voice at all checkpoints, RSVP might not add value to your QoS configuration.

VoIP and Delay

IP networks offer a unique challenge in controlling delay and delay variation. Typically, IP traffic has consisted of data traffic, which was variable in nature, allowing large file transfers to monopolize network bandwidth. Voice networks must support traffic that is more sensitive to delay and delay variation. RSVP allows the end station to reserve resources in the network. This allows you to allocate queues for different types of traffic, helping you reduce delay and delay variation inherent in current IP networks.

Weighted Fair Queuing (WFQ) or priority queuing allow the network to put different traffic types into specific QoS queues. This is designed to prioritize the transmittal of voice traffic over data traffic. This reduces the potential of queuing delay.

H.323 Family

H.323 defines a set of standards and protocols for multimedia approved by the ITU that defines how audiovisual data is transmitted across networks. In a typical setting, H.323 lets users participate in the same audio or video conference even though they are using different videoconferencing applications.

H.323 standards identify four components that form a point-to-point or point-to-multipoint multimedia communications service. Figure 16-7 illustrates an H.323 network.

Figure 16-7   *H.323 Network*

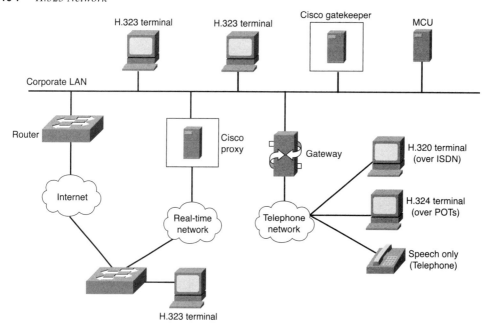

The components are as follows:

- **Gatekeeper**—The gatekeeper is the most important component. The gatekeeper controls the H.323 zone and determines how calls may proceed and whether a zone can initiate or receive calls. The gatekeeper converts E.164 destination addresses into IP destination addresses to pass a VoIP packet to its next destination. Gatekeepers provide a means to manage dial plans and call routing in a VoIP network. Without a gatekeeper, each VoIP gateway would have to be directly mapped to every other destination. For large networks, this could amount to thousands of dial-peer statements in each router, which would of course be impractical. The gatekeeper allows for tandem switching. Gatekeepers provide a central point for administration and resource allocation.

- **Gateways**—Provide services that translate protocols and convert different information formats, allowing connectivity with non-H.323 devices such as traditional telephone networks. A Cisco router with a voice interface that is connected to the PSTN is an example of an H.323 gateway. Gateways manage the call-signaling conversion and the media-signaling conversion when connecting the dissimilar network.

- **Terminals**—Provide real-time two-way multimedia communications. All endpoints must support voice.

- **Multipoint control units**—Provide conference bridging support for multiconferencing.

H.323 Protocol Stack

H.323 relies on several protocols to do its business. They are defined as follows:

- **IP Internet protocol**—Routes packets through the Internet.

- **TCP protocol**—Ensures that the packets are properly sequenced.

- **UDP connectionless protocol**—Sends data from one device to another. Used by voice packets.

H.225

H.225 provides the signaling needed to establish connectivity between an H.323 terminal and an H.323 gatekeeper. In addition, H.225 provides location and discovery services and RAS functionality, which includes registration, administration, and status information between the two devices.

NOTE   As of version IOS 12.1.3, Cisco allows the router to also function as a gatekeeper. Check the gatekeeper documentation for new software releases on CCO to verify the current state of gatekeeper functionality.

Cisco IOS Gatekeeper

Cisco offers a Voice over IP gatekeeper called the *Multimedia Conference Manager*, which is an H.323-compliant program implemented as part of the Cisco IOS software. The following sections describe the main functions of a gatekeeper:

- Zone and subnet configuration
- Terminal name registration
- Interzone communication

A zone is defined as the set of H.323 nodes controlled by a single gatekeeper. Gatekeepers that coexist on a network can be configured so that they register endpoints from different subnets. Endpoints attempt to discover a gatekeeper, and consequently what zone they are members of, using the RAS message protocol. The protocol supports a discovery message that may be sent multicast or unicast. If the message is sent multicast, the endpoint registers nondeterministically with the first gatekeeper to respond. Any endpoint on a subnet that is not enabled for the gatekeeper is not accepted as a member of that gatekeeper's zone. If the gatekeeper receives a discovery message from such an endpoint, it sends an explicit reject message.

Gatekeepers recognize one of three types of terminal names:

- H.323 identifiers (IDs), which are arbitrary, case-sensitive text strings
- E.164 addresses, which are telephone numbers
- E-mail IDs

If an H.323 network deploys interzone communication, each terminal should at least have a fully qualified e-mail name as its H.323 ID, such as ccdp@ciscopress.com. The domain name of the e-mail ID should be the same as the configured domain name for the gatekeeper of which it will be a member. The domain name would be ciscopress.com.

To allow endpoints to communicate between zones, gatekeepers must be able to determine which zone an endpoint is in and locate the gatekeeper responsible for that zone. If DNS is available, you can associate a DNS domain name to each gatekeeper. If AAA is enabled on the gatekeeper, the gatekeeper emits an accounting record each time an endpoint registers or unregisters, or each time a call is admitted or disconnected.

Three types of address destinations are used in H.323 calls. The destination can be specified using an H.323 ID address (a character string), an E.164 address (a string containing telephone keypad characters), or an e-mail ID (a character string). How interzone calls are routed by the Cisco IOS gatekeeper depends on the type of address being used.

- With H.323 ID addresses, interzone routing is handled through the use of domain names. For example, to resolve the domain name ccdp@ciscopress.com, the source endpoint's gatekeeper finds the gatekeeper for ciscopress.com and sends the location request for target address ccdp@ciscopress.com to that gatekeeper. The destination gatekeeper looks in its registration database, sees ccdp registered, and returns the appropriate IP address to get to ccdp.

NOTE	Although H.225 does not require the use of a domain name with H.323 IDs, the Cisco IOS gatekeeper does.

- With E.164 addresses, call routing is handled through means of zone prefixes and gateway type prefixes, also called technology prefixes. The zone prefixes, which are typically area codes, serve the same purpose as domain names in H.323 ID address routing. Unlike domain names, however, more than one zone prefix can be assigned to one gatekeeper, but the same prefix cannot be shared by more than one gatekeeper. With Cisco IOS release 12.0(3)T and later, interzone routing can be configured using E.164 addresses.

- With e-mail IDs, interzone routing is handled through the use of domain names—just as it is with H.323 IDs. Again, the source endpoint's gatekeeper finds the gatekeeper for the specified domain and sends the location request for the target address to that gatekeeper.

Cisco CallManager Version 3.0

Cisco has introduced a new Voice over IP-based telephone to complement the existing range of VoIP solutions. Cisco CallManager is a client/server application that resides on a Windows NT server and performs all the functionality that normally resides on a traditional PBX. Think of Call Manager as a new and improved PBX for IP. Call Manager can support up to 5000 phones on a single server, and it relates well to H.323-compliant gateways. Cisco CallManager is the software-based call-processing component of the Cisco IP telephony solution, part of Cisco AVVID (Architecture for Voice, Video, and Integrated Data). The software extends enterprise telephony features and functions to packet telephony network devices such as IP phones, media processing devices, VoIP gateways, and multimedia applications. Additional data, voice, and video services such as unified messaging, multimedia conferencing, collaborative contact centers, and interactive multimedia response systems interact with the IP telephony solution through Cisco CallManager's open telephony application programming interface (API).

Cisco CallManager is installed on the Cisco Media Convergence Server (MCS). The Cisco CallManager software product includes a suite of integrated voice applications that perform voice conferencing, manual attendant, bulk administration, and simple billing and quality monitoring functions. Supplementary and enhanced services such as hold, transfer, forward, conference, multiple-line appearances, automatic route selection, speed dial, last-number redial, and other features are extended to IP phones and gateways. Because it is a software application, enhancing its capabilities in production environments is a matter of upgrading software on the server platform, thereby avoiding expensive hardware upgrade costs.

Furthermore, Cisco CallManager and all phones, gateways, and applications may be distributed across an IP network, providing a distributed, virtual telephony network.

The benefit of this architecture is improved system availability and scalability. Call admission control ensures that voice QoS is maintained across constricted WAN links and automatically diverts calls to alternative PSTN routes when WAN bandwidth is unavailable. Cisco CallManager is installed on the Cisco high-availability server platforms, the MCSs. A Web-browsable interface to the configuration database is available for remote device and system configuration. HTML-based online help is available for users and administrators.

Cisco CallManager Version 3.0(4) significantly enhances the scalability, distributability, and availability of the enterprise IP telephony solution. Multiple Cisco CallManager servers are clustered and managed as a single entity. The capability to cluster multiple call-processing servers on an IP network is unique in the industry and highlights the industry-leading architecture of Cisco AVVID. Scalability for up to 10,000 users per cluster is provided. By interlinking multiple clusters, system capacity can be increased to up to tens of thousands of users per multisite system. Clustering aggregates the power of multiple distributed Cisco CallManagers, enhancing the scalability and accessibility of the servers to phones, gateways, and applications. Triple server redundancy improves overall system availability. TAPI (Microsoft's telephone application interface) and JTAPI (Java's application programming interface for Java-based computer-telephony applications) interfaces allow a rich set of Cisco and third-party vendor IP-enabled voice applications to augment base system capabilities.

NOTE   The New Feature Release Notes section of the CCO is an excellent source of information and is a good starting point to learn about new technologies and features supported in Cisco routers.

Quality of Service for Packetized Voice

QoS lets a network provide optimum service to voice and data traffic. QoS ensures that voice traffic is prioritized over data and will always be delivered ahead of data. Cisco IOS offers a broad range of QoS features. These features provide predictable network service by the following:

- Supporting dedicated bandwidth
- Improving loss characteristics
- Avoiding and managing network congestion
- Shaping network traffic
- Setting traffic priorities across the network

These features can be categorized as follows:

- **Best effort**—Best effort is essentially no QoS. It provides only basic connectivity on a best-effort basis, with no guarantees.

- **Differentiated service**—Some traffic can be treated better than other traffic. Differentiated service supports intelligent queuing schemes that can prioritize and classify traffic types based on network and application requirements. IP precedence is often used to implement this level of service.

- **Guaranteed network**—This feature guarantees the reservation of network resources. This QoS feature is recommended for voice. The goal of the guaranteed network is to provide a virtual certainty that certain types of traffic will pass if the network is functional. Figure 16-8 shows Cisco end-to-end QoS services.

Figure 16-8   *Cisco End-to-End QoS Services*

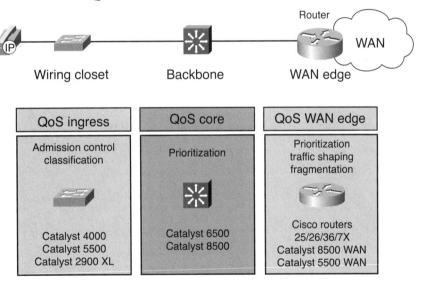

The following components are necessary to deliver QoS across a multiservice network:

- QoS within a single network element, which includes queuing, scheduling, and traffic-shaping features

- QoS signaling techniques for coordinating QoS from end to end between network elements

- QoS policing and management functions to control and administer end-to-end traffic across a network

QoS starts in the WAN. Often, much consideration is given to campus design speed and router selection without giving regard to the WAN. Remember that a network chain is no stronger than its weakest link. Most designers ignore the carrier because, for the most part, what the carrier does is beyond the designer's control. Designing a VoIP network for QoS is tough because the network designer does not have control over all the elements. The designer has no control over the service provider network. All this increases the significance of the importance of tweaking the QoS parameter by an order of magnitude. Cisco provides QoS tools to give the network designers what they need to control the bandwidth, delay, jitter, and packet loss that can combine to deprive the network of a consistent level of voice quality.

Not all QoS techniques are appropriate for all network routers. Because edge routers and backbone routers in a network do not necessarily perform the same operations, the configured assignments for QoS should be expected to vary. To configure an IP network for real-time voice traffic, consider the functions of both edge and backbone routers in the network.

In a general sense, edge routers perform packet classification, admission control, and configuration management, whereas backbone routers might be expected to perform congestion management and congestion avoidance.

The foundation of any voice-over-data network is a QoS-enabled infrastructure.

The biggest challenge in designing a packet or cell network to support voice is providing the same level of quality that the user had in the original voice network.

The following factors have the largest impact on voice quality in a network:

- Delay
- Delay variation
- Loss
- Echo

Delay

Three types of delay are inherent in voice networks:

- Propagation
- Handling
- Queuing

The largest factor in delay is the distance between points in a network. In a phone call across town, the delay due to distance is hardly noticeable because the signals travel at the speed of light. In a phone call to someone 100,000 miles away, the delay can be perceptible. The time required for the signal carrying voice to travel the distance across the physical network medium is called propagation delay. When distances are short, propagation delay is negligible. As distances increase, delay also increases.

The expected propagation delay can be estimated by simply dividing the distance by the speed of light. Light travels in a vacuum at a speed of 186,000 miles per second. Electrons travel through copper or fiber at 125,000 miles per second. Devices that forward the packet add to the delay while handling the packets. In integrated networks, delay can contribute significantly to voice degradation. Effective voice communication is all about timing. Voice information has characteristic timing. A particular syllable of a word is uttered with an interval of time between it and the following syllable. Sometimes a speaker pauses for effect. If a voice network is impacted by unacceptable delay, the speech becomes corrupted.

NOTE	For good voice quality, Cisco recommends that no more than 150 ms of one-way end-to-end delay should occur.

NOTE	Delay can degrade a voice signal in two ways:
	• Delay in an absolute sense can interfere with the byplay of human conversation and the rhythm of communication with tone and inflection.
	• Delay variations, which are sometimes called jitter, can create unexpected pauses between speech patterns. Jitter is the more serious problem that packet voice networks must address. Voice networks expect consistent and predictable real-time delivery. If the packets arrive at an unexpected rate, the network can be described to be in a state of jitter. Jitter is particularly disruptive to audio communications because it can cause pops and clicks that can be heard on the audio line.

If the one-way delay is greater than 250 ms, talker overlap can become a problem. One user starts talking without realizing that the other person hasn't finished (because the other person's conversation is late in arriving). This might be acceptable for walkie-talkie conversation or for long-distance satellite communications, but it is unacceptable for voice networks.

Delay also causes echo. Echo is caused by the signal reflections of the speaker's voice from the far-end telephone equipment back into the speaker's ear. Echo can become a problem when the round-trip delay becomes greater than 50 ms. Voice over data networks must address the echo problem.

As you know, communication among humans is quite different from communication among computers. When delay is introduced to data traffic, the packet can be retransmitted. A protocol ensures that the packet is placed in the proper sequential order and that the data is delivered. When delay is introduced to voice traffic, the packet cannot be retransmitted. If a voice packet is retransmitted, this will only confuse the listener, because the user expects to hear conversation in real time. Unexpected pauses will puzzle the listener.

Poorly Tuned Voice Network

Under perfect conditions, there are problems with understanding and interpreting what is said. Imagine how communications might suffer on a poorly tuned voice network. Here is an example. At Acme Law, a lawyer is calling a client about a pending divorce case. The network does not have QoS for voice. Here is an excerpt from the conversation:

Lawyer: What are the grounds for your divorce?

Client: A home located on about two acres near the county line.

Lawyer: No, what is the foundation for your case?

Client: It is made of concrete, brick, and mortar.

Lawyer: Do you have a grudge?

Client: No. We have a two-car carport and have never really needed one.

Lawyer: Is there any infidelity in your marriage?

Client: Yes. Both my son and daughter have stereo sets in need of replacement.

Lawyer: Have you ever beat your wife up?

Client: Yes. About twice a week I get up earlier than she does—although on the weekends she usually beats me up.

Lawyer: Why does your wife want a divorce?

Client: Who knows? Ever since I got this new voice over data network, she thinks I have a problem communicating.

Handling delay is caused by all the components that must handle the voice traffic during its transmission. In a typical voice-over-data network, the following components might handle the signal in some way, thereby adding to the delay time:

- Packetization and depacketization of voice traffic
- Queuing of packetized voice
- Coding and decoding of digital voice signals

- Transmission delay over the serial link
- Queuing delay and serialization delay over each device in the network path

Loss

As stated earlier in this chapter, packet loss is acceptable and expected in data networks. Packet loss in voice networks has a deleterious impact on voice quality and should be kept to a minimum.

Echo

Echo is the result of speech signals from one direction reflecting into the opposite direction. Some echo is a good thing. A little echo should always be present because it helps the end user hear his or her own voice. Too much echo is undesirable. Talker echo occurs when the speech signal travels toward the destination and is reflected into the return path at a point near the destination. A talker hears the reflected signal as an echo. If the echo signal is reflected, the listener hears the echoed signal.

Delay

Queuing *delay* is a function that occurs during the transmission that increases delay. Queuing delay is also called transmission delay. Simply stated, queuing delay is the amount of time required to put data on the wire. It is sometimes called serialization delay for a single packet.

Router Design Concerns

Three areas of concern should be addressed at the router: prioritization, slow-speed links, and traffic shaping.

Simply stated, prioritization is making sure the voice packets maintain top priority in the packet food chain. Voice packets belong in the top sirloin section of the supermarket. Large data frames that take a long time to clock out can create delays. To a voice packet, a delay is the kiss of death.

Prioritization involves two steps: classification and queuing.

IP Precedence

The *IP Precedence* bits are the three high-order bits in the Type of Service (ToS) field of the IP header. Table 16-4 shows the values for each setting of IP Precedence. Cisco recommends that voice traffic be set at IP Precedence bit value 5.

Table 16-4   *IP Precedence Bit Values*

Bit Value	Priority
0	Normal traffic
1	Priority
2	Immediate
3	Flash
4	Flash override
5	Critical
6	Internet
7	Network

Class-Based Weighted Fair Queuing

Class-Based Weighted Fair Queuing (CBWFQ) is the preferred queuing mechanism for voice. With CBWFQ, priority queues get established for voice, so voice queues get served before other data queues. CBWFQ is recommended over WFQ because WFQ is too fair to the other processes and allows other traffic to flow ahead of voice. CBWFQ combines the best features of priority, custom, and weighted fair queuing.

Here are the steps to implement CBWFQ:

Step 1   Define traffic classes to specify the classification policy.

Step 2   Apply policies to classes.

Step 3   Attach policies to interfaces.

CBWFQ allows the exact amount of bandwidth to be allocated for a specific class of traffic. Taking into account available bandwidth on the interface, 64 classes can be configured. CBWFQ allows the use of access control lists and protocols or input interface names to define how traffic will be classified, thereby providing coarser granularity. Packets satisfying the match criteria meet the traffic class. These packets are assigned characteristics such as bandwidth, weight, and maximum packet limit. The policies are then assigned to an interface. Figure 16-9 shows an example of CBWFQ.

NOTE   A number of QoS features are scattered over various IOS releases. It is important to audit the existing hardware platforms to determine whether the hardware supports the features that are needed.

Figure 16-9   *Class-Based Weighted Fair Queuing*

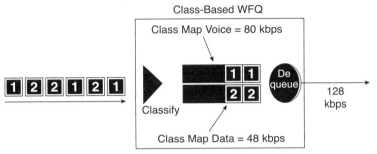

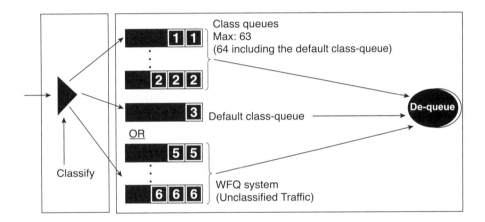

Traffic Engineering

This section explains how the number of trunks and ports can be calculated to provision the amount of necessary bandwidth. Traffic engineering can be defined as the process of determining the number of trunks necessary to carry an organization's voice and data traffic calls.

As you know, there are two main types of connections: lines and trunks. Leased lines provide a dedicated, nonswitched, point-to-point connection. A communication path between any two points is a line. For example, the communication path between the central office (CO) and your house is a line. The communication path between two or more central office switches is a truck. Because it would be impractical to have a different line for every possible connection, trunks are used to connect switches. The following are the most common types of trunk routes:

- Tie-lines connect two PBXs

- CO trunks connect a PBX to the CO

- Direct Inward Dialing (DID) trunks connect a CO to a PBX. DID trunks allow outside callers to reach an internal company extension directly by dialing a seven-digit number (and the area code, if applicable).

NOTE   Because DID trunks do not provide a dial tone, they cannot be used for outgoing calls from the PBX to the CO.

Wide-area transmission service (WATS) trunks provide toll-free service (in the United States with 800 numbers) for users who make frequent calls to the same geographic area. Outgoing WATS (OUTWATS) trunks are used exclusively for outgoing toll-free calls from a PBX to a defined area or organization, and incoming WATS (INWATS) trunks are used exclusively for incoming toll-free calls from a defined area or organization to the PBX.

When measuring network traffic, it is important to consider all of the following types of traffic:

- **Automatic call distribution (ACD)**—High-priority traffic that is typically sent over dedicated trunks

- **Incoming (non-ACD) traffic**—Traffic that originates in the PSTN and does not pass through an ACD call center

- **Outgoing off-net (non-ACD) traffic**—Traffic that originates in the network and terminates in the PSTN

- **On-net incoming and outgoing traffic**—Traffic that originates and terminates within the same network

- **Voice mail**—Traffic that consists of spoken messages that are stored on a voice-messaging system

- **Data traffic**—Traffic that originates from computer systems and is passed to other computer systems

Traffic Measurement Units

In the United States, voice traffic is typically measured in one of two ways—Centum call seconds or Erlang:

- **Centum call seconds (CCS)**—A unit that expresses the amount of time that a particular line is in use. The CCS measurement is made per 100 seconds of usage. For example, a telephone with 9 CCS per hour means that it is off-hook (in use) 900 seconds per hour (15 minutes).

- **Erlang**—A unit that expresses one hour of traffic on a trunk or trunk group in one hour. For example, five calls of 1-hour duration equal five Erlangs of traffic, whereas five 12-minute calls equal 1 Erlang of traffic.

So, 1 Erlang equals 36 CCS per hour, which is 3600 seconds.

NOTE   When troubleshooting voice networks, remember that the telephone company only responds to problems beyond the demarcation point (the jack or other connection that ties your system to the telephone company).

Consider the following issues when planning the voice aspects of your converged network:

- Identify communities of interest. Identify groups or teams in your organization that tend to exchange phone calls frequently.

- Centralize digital service units (DSUs). Keeping DSUs in a centralized location makes it easier to manage network connectivity. This approach also potentially shortens the distance between nodes, reducing the cost of cable runs.

- Use high-bandwidth media. Packetized voice traffic is highly sensitive to network problems such as delay and congestion.

- Install or upgrade to the fastest possible medium that you can afford—preferably fiber-optic cable.

NOTE   If the cost of laying additional cable is prohibitive, a wireless networking solution might be appropriate. Contact your Cisco sales representative for additional information.

Traffic Engineering Process

Traffic engineering for a VoIP network consists of the following steps, which are described in the following sections:

Step 1   Forecast growth.

Step 2   Gather voice traffic data.

Step 3   Categorize traffic by group.

Step 4   Calculate the number of trunks.

Step 5   Choose the proper combination of trunks.

Step 6   Convert PSTN traffic to IP traffic.

Forecasting Growth

To ensure that your system can keep pace with your organization's needs, determine how many phones are needed now and in the future.

Complete the following steps to forecast growth:

Step 1   Determine how many phones are currently in use.

Step 2   Determine how many employees are on campus.

Step 3   Calculate the ratio of phones to employees by dividing the number of phones by the number of employees.

Step 4   Forecast the annual growth rate by projecting the number of employees who are hired each year (expressed as a percentage over the next five years).

Step 5   Use the annual growth rate forecast to calculate how many employees the company might expect to have at the end of each year for the next five years.

Step 6   Calculate the number of phones that are expected to be required at one-year intervals by multiplying the projected number of year-end employees by the forecasted annual growth rate.

Gathering Voice Traffic Data

Step 1   Contact the telephone service provider to get the following information for two to three weeks of traffic:

Step 2   Peg counts (measurements of switch events) for incoming calls, abandoned calls, and blocked calls (due to busy trunks).

Step 3   Grade of Service (GoS) rating for trunk groups. GoS represents the percentage of busy signals that you are willing to accept.

Step 4   Total traffic carried per trunk group.

Step 5   Carrier rates (from phone bills).

Step 6   Obtain Call Detail Records (CDRs) or traffic reports from legacy PBXs. CDRs typically record incoming calls but do not provide information on calls that were blocked because all trunks were busy.

Growth Forecast Example

The following example shows how to define and forecast growth for a small company:

- Number of phones: 150

- Number of employees: 200

- Ratio of phones to employees (PE): 0.75

- Annual growth rate: 10 percent

Number of employees:

- One year from now: 220 (200 employees × 10% = 20. 200 + 20 = 220.)

- Two years from now: 242

- Three years from now: 266

- Four years from now: 293

- Five years from now: 322

Projected phone requirements:

- One year from now: 165 (220 employees × 0.75 PE = 165 phones)

- Two years from now: 182

- Three years from now: 200

- Four years from now: 220

- Five years from now: 242

Categorizing Traffic by Group

In most large businesses, it is cost-effective to apply traffic engineering to groups of trunks serving a common purpose. For example, place inbound customer service calls into a trunk group that is separate from general outgoing calls.

Start by separating traffic according to its direction (inbound or outbound). Next, group outbound traffic in terms of the distance (such as local, local long-distance, intrastate, interstate, and so on). Organizing traffic by distance is important, because most tariffs are based on distance.

Determine the purpose of the calls. Categories could include fax, modem, call center, 800 customer service, 800 voice mail, and telecommuter.

Calculating the Number of Trunks

This section explains how to calculate how many trunks might be needed:

Step 1   Calculate CCS (per user).

Step 2   Identify a target Grade of Service (GoS). A GoS of 0.01 is standard for most calls. Use 0.05 for tie-line services and 0.10 for long distance.

Step 3   Calculate the number of Erlangs as follows:

Number of users × CCS = total CCS

Total CCS / 36 = number of Erlangs

Step 4   Based on these calculations, determine how many trunks are needed.

NOTE   CCS is typically dependent on what type of business you are in. The hotel and hospital industries, for example, use a CCS of 4, and finance companies use a CCS of 8. If the CCS is unknown, use a value of 6.

New System Example

Suppose that you expect the following traffic patterns:

- 40 percent inbound traffic (IT)

- 40 percent outbound traffic (OT)

- 20 percent station-to-station calls (S)

Assuming that you have 75 end users and that you are using the default CCS (6), make the following calculations:

75 users × 6 CCS = 450 CCS
450 / 36 = 12.5 Erlangs (E)

Assuming that you are using a GoS value of 0.01 for DID and CO lines, you calculate that you need 11 IT lines and 11 OT lines, for a total of 22 lines:

40%IT
40% × 12.5E = 5.00 E
11 DID lines
40%OT
40% × 12.5E = 5.00 E
11 CO lines
Totals:
10.00E
22 analog lines

Based on the Erlang B table, approximately 18 trunks will be needed, and one T1 "supertrunk" with DID must be provisioned along with CO, and long-distance services, or 18 analog trunks.

Legacy System Busiest Hour

If you have some traffic information, but it is not broken down according to the busiest hour, you can extrapolate this information from your weekly or monthly traffic bill. The following example shows how to calculate the number of Erlangs (E):

Average hourly traffic on the monthly bill = 1700 hours = 1700 E
Average number of business days in a month = 22
Average hourly traffic on an average day = 1700 / 22 = 77.27 E
Average daily busy-hour traffic (17% of the total) = 77.27 × 17% = 13.14 E

Using the Erlang B table, looking up 13.14 E with a GoS of 0.01, you calculate that you will require 28 or 29 trunks (depending on whether you round up or down from 13.14).

Choosing the Proper Combination of Trunks

Finding a combination of trunks that is right for your organization is more of an economic decision than a technical decision.

Cost per minute is the most commonly used measurement for determining whether to add trunks. Ensure that all cost components are considered, such as accounting for additional transmission, equipment, administration, and maintenance costs.

Consider the following two rules when optimizing the network for cost:

* Use average-usage figures instead of the busy hour, which would overstate the number of call minutes.

* Use the least-costly circuit until the incremental cost becomes more expensive than the next-best route.

Knowing how much traffic you have to deal with at peak loads (in Erlangs) and how the traffic flows will determine how many and what type of trunks are required to support your organization's calls. If the calling pattern suggests only local calls, you might require direct connection to the central office (CO). Extensive long-distance dialing might require a dedicated T1 connection to an Interexchange Carrier (IEC or IXC) for long-distance services. An inbound call center that generates revenue or provides customer service and support might also require a dedicated T1 connection. Or, several small companies sharing a leased facility might require several small groups of COs.

Converting PSTN Traffic to IP Traffic

The last calculation you need to make is to equate Erlangs of carried traffic to packets per second (pps). (If your system includes Asynchronous Transfer Mode [ATM] links, this calculation is made in cells per second [cps] instead of packets per second.) The following example illustrates one way to do this:

1 Erlang = 1.44 million packets (20-byte packets) or 400 pps

Next, apply modifiers to these figures based on the actual conditions. Types of modifiers to apply include packet overhead, voice compression, voice activity detection (VAD), and signaling overhead. Packet overhead can be used as a percent modifier. For example:

> 20 bytes for IP
> 8 bytes for User Datagram Protocol (UDP)
> 12 to 72 bytes for Real-Time Transport Protocol (RTP)

Without using Compressed Real-Time Protocol (CRTP), the amount of overhead is unrealistic. The actual multiplier is 3. CRTP can reduce the overhead further, generally from 4 to 6 bytes. Assuming it is 5 bytes, the multiplier changes to 1.25. Assuming that you are running 8 Kb of compressed voice, you cannot get below 10 Kbps if you allow for overhead.

Voice compression and voice activity detection are also treated as multipliers. For example, use a 0.125 multiplier for conjugate structure algebraic code excited linear prediction (CS-ACELP [8 Kbps]). For VAD, use a 0.6 or 0.7 multiplier.

Signaling overhead is an additional consideration. In particular, you need to factor in the Real-Time Control Protocol (RTCP) and H.225 and H.245 connections.

PSTN-to-IP Traffic Conversion Example

With the information you have collected, you can apply traffic distribution to the trunks to see how that distribution affects bandwidth. Traffic distribution is based on busy-hour and average-hour calculations.

Suppose that for the busy hour and the average hour, the distribution of traffic per trunk is 2.64 Erlangs and 2.2 Erlangs, respectively. If one pulse code modulation (PCM) voice channel requires 64 Kbps, the busy hour will have the following amount of traffic:

> 2.64 Erlangs $\times$ 64 Kbps = 169 Kbps

and traffic during an average hour will be:

> 2.2 Erlangs $\times$ 64 Kbps = 141 Kbps

Therefore, 2.2 Erlangs of traffic carried over IP using voice compression requires the following bandwidth:

> 141 Kbps $\times$ 0.125 (8 Kb voice) $\times$ 1.25 (overhead using CRTP) = 22 Kbps

---

NOTE   The CCDP must account for other modifiers as well, such as call setup and teardown signaling overhead, Layer 2 overhead, and voice activity detection (if used).

Foundation Summary

This section is a collection of tables that provide a convenient review of many key concepts in this chapter. If you are already comfortable with the topics in this chapter, this summary could help you recall a few details. If you who have just read this chapter, this review should help solidify some key facts. If you are doing your final preparation before the exam, Tables 16-5 through 16-7 are a convenient way to review the day before the exam.

Table 16-5   *Voice Network Recommendations*

Location	Recommended Equipment
Wiring closet	Catalyst 2900 XL
	Catalyst 4000
	Cisco 2600, 3810
Backbone	Catalyst 6500
	Catalyst 8500
	Cisco 3600, 7200
WAN edge	Cisco Routers 7200, 7500
	Catalyst 5500
	Catalyst 8500

Table 16-6   *ISO Reference Model and H.323 Standards*

OSI Protocol Layer	ITU H.323 Standard
Application	E.164 phone number
Presentation	G.711, G.729, G.729a, and so on
Session	H.323, H.245, H.225, RTCP
Transport	RTP, UDP
Network	IP, RSVP, WFQ
Data Link	PPP, Frame, ATM

Serialization delay is especially a problem on low-speed links. Table 16-7 shows the relationship between link speed and frame size. Note that a 1 KB frame requires 144 ms on a 56 Kbps circuit. The delay for that circuit, in and of itself, exceeds the target delay budget of 150 ms.

NOTE   Time is listed in units of seconds. Micro = microseconds, and milli = milliseconds.

Table 16-7   *Frame Relay Serialization Delay Matrix*

Link Size	Frame Size						
	1 byte	64 bytes	128 bytes	256 bytes	512 bytes	1024 bytes	1500 bytes
56 Kbps	143 micro	9 milli	18 milli	36 milli	72 milli	144 milli	214 milli
64 Kbps	125 micro	8 milli	16 milli	32 milli	64 milli	128 milli	187 milli
128 Kbps	62.5 micro	4 milli	8 milli	16 milli	32 milli	64 milli	93 milli
256 Kbps	31 micro	2 milli	4 milli	8 milli	16 milli	32 milli	46 milli
512 Kbps	15.5 micro	1 milli	2 milli	4 milli	8 milli	16 milli	23 milli
768 Kbps	10 micro	640 micro	1.28 milli	2.56 milli	5.12 milli	10.24 milli	15 milli
1536 Kbps	5 micro	320 micro	640 micro	1.28 milli	2.56 milli	5.12 milli	7.5 milli

Q&A

As mentioned in Chapter 1, the questions and scenarios in this book are more difficult than what you will experience on the actual exam. The questions do not attempt to cover more breadth or depth than the exam; however, they are designed to make sure that you know the answer. Rather than allowing you to derive the answer from clues hidden inside the question, the questions challenge your understanding and recall of the subject. Questions from the "Do I Know This Already?" quiz from the beginning of the chapter are repeated here to ensure that you have mastered this chapter's topic areas. Hopefully, these questions will help limit the number of exam questions on which you narrow your choices to two options and then guess. Be sure to use the CD and take the simulated exams.

The answers to these questions can be found in Appendix A.

1   What challenge does the CCDP face when merging voice onto a data network?

_____

_____

_____

2   What are three different types of voice interfaces used on a Cisco router?

_____

_____

_____

3   What two types of digital signaling are available?

_____

_____

_____

4   What is a dial plan?

_____

_____

_____

5   List three benefits of a dial plan.

_____

_____

_____

6 What must a successful QoS voice over data network design ensure?

_____

_____

_____

7 List four factors that have a significant impact on voice quality in a network.

_____

_____

_____

8 List three types of delay that, by design, are inherent in voice networks.

_____

_____

_____

9 For good voice quality, what does Cisco recommend as the maximum amount of delay (one-way) from end to end?

_____

_____

_____

10 What is handling delay? Provide an example of handling delay in a voice network.

_____

_____

_____

11 True or false: QoS should start in the LAN. The largest bottlenecks are usually found on the campus network.

_____

_____

_____

12 What three areas of concern should be addressed at the router?

_____

_____

_____

13 What three protocols can provide transport for voice?

_____

_____

_____

14 What three processes must occur before voice can be passed from the PBX to the router?

_____

_____

_____

15 What four components comprise the H.323 family?

_____

_____

_____

16 What is the main function of a gatekeeper?

_____

_____

_____

17 What three types of terminal names are recognized by a gatekeeper?

_____

_____

_____

18 What product has Cisco released that envelopes the total VoIP solution?

_____

_____

_____

19 What is a key switch?

_____

_____

_____

20 What is a PBX?

_____

_____

_____

21 What is a tandem switch?

_____

_____

_____

22 List three major functions of a voice over data network.

_____

_____

_____

23 What is the first step in establishing connectivity between a router and a phone switch?

_____

_____

_____

24 True or false: VoFR and VoATM allow tandem call routing. VoIP does not.

_____

_____

_____

25 What feature automatically dials a predetermined number when a user goes off-hook?

_____

_____

_____

26 List one business requirement that would be satisfied by designing a voice over data network.

_____

_____

_____

27 Define jitter.

_____

_____

_____

28 List some metrics that will define success on the voice-over-data design project.

_____

_____

_____

29 What is the name of the signaling standard that is used to perform out-of-band signaling in the PSTN?

_____

_____

_____

30 What problems can be experienced in running a voice-over-data network with no QoS?

_____

_____

_____

31 What conditions exist on a data network that would be intolerable for voice traffic?

_____

_____

_____

32 True or false: Fax calls are less sensitive to latency than voice calls.

_____

_____

_____

Scenarios

Scenario 1

To help design the optimum solution and address the issues presented in this chapter, you have contracted with the design professionals at RouteitRight to help you.

Championship Soccer, Inc. has contacted RouteitRight. Its MIS director has heard that it might be possible to save money on its communications network. Its current network has a separate voice network and a separate data network. The company locations consist of headquarters and four branch locations. The voice network is connected via the PSTN. The data network is connected via a T1 link.

Freddy Forklift recommends that Championship Soccer, Inc. replace their existing phone lines with a VoIP solution. Freddy has read about CallManager, a Cisco VoIP solution. Peter Packett agrees that the ultimate solution could be end-to-end VoIP. However, Peter thinks that RouteitRight should recommend a phased-in solution, starting with toll bypass. Megg A. Bight says that the cost savings that would be realized from turning off the tie-lines would be significant. Even if the data circuit had to be increased to acknowledge the aggregate of traffic, the cost of the increased bandwidth would be less than the cost of two separate circuits. Roddy says that the converged solution will result in an overall lower total cost of ownership. In addition to savings that result from sharing the same line, the costs of adding, moving, and changing phone lines will go to zero.

Figure 16-10 depicts the Championship Soccer network as a separate voice and data network.

Figure 16-10 *Championship Soccer Voice and Data Network*

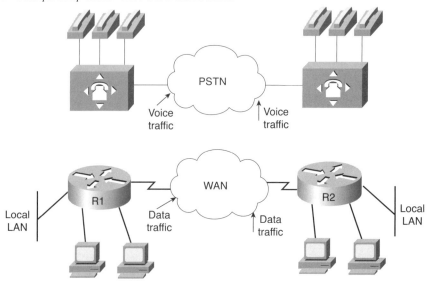

The experts at RouteitRight agree that converging the two networks is the way to go. There are several ways to do this. What would you recommend? How would you plan the conversion?

Answer to Scenario 1

Getting Championship Soccer's network ready for voice and data should happen in stages. The first stage, toll bypass, allows voice traffic to bypass the PSTN and be routed to the IP network. Both PBX and routers remain in place as the network is migrated in phases from voice and data to one voice/data network. The second stage is the IP telephony phase: IP phones, voice-capable computer applications, and Web-based multimedia applications that integrate voice and data to the desktop.

What type of voice over packet should be used for Championship Soccer, Inc.? VoIP? VoFR? VoATM?

In this case, you aren't running ATM. So VoATM can't be considered. This leaves you with VoFR and VoIP.

VoFR is the circuit that most interoffices have adopted to carry voice traffic. The standards for VoFR have been in place for several years. So VoFR in general has greater vendor interoperability and is a better-tested product. VoFR uses less bandwidth than VoIP. A call that has been compressed using G.729A uses about 8 Kbps. When the FR overhead is added, the bandwidth consumption increases to just under 11 Kbps. VoFR is an excellent WAN transport technology, but it cannot be deployed over LANs or to the desktop.

You should select VoIP because it is the only choice that can be completely deployed to the desktop for the final stage. VoIP can leverage the Internet and intranet infrastructure in terms of routing and making any-to-any calls over the Internet. Leveraging the emerging employee productivity, customer care, e-commerce, and business efficiency multimedia applications requires VoIP.

Figure 16-11 shows the Championship Soccer network after the first phase of toll bypass.

Figure 16-11 *Championship Soccer Network with Toll Bypass*

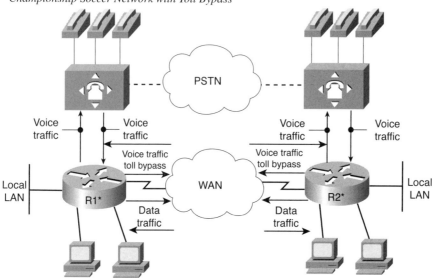

* Router carries voice traffic

Figure 16-12 illustrates the Championship Soccer network after end-to-end IP telephony has been installed.

Figure 16-12 *Championship Soccer with End-to-End IP Telephony*

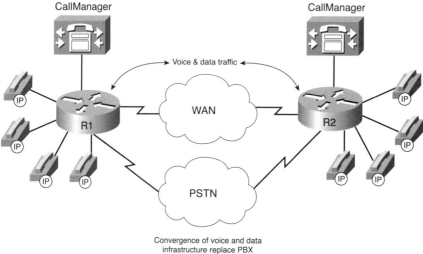

Convergence of voice and data
infrastructure replace PBX

Answers to Review Questions

Chapter 1

1 What are the goals of an internetwork design?

Functionality.

Scalability.

Adaptability.

Manageability.

Cost-effectiveness.

2 What are the seven steps for designing an internetwork?

Gather information.

Analyze requirements.

Develop internetwork structure.

Estimate network performance.

Assess costs and risks.

Implement.

Monitor.

3 What trade-off is present in every network design?

Cost versus availability.

4 What are the three layers of the hierarchical model?

Core.

Distribution.

Access.

5 What benefits can be gained by using the hierarchical model?

Scalability.

Ease of troubleshooting.

Protocol support.

Manageability.

6 Name two methods of redundancy that are available to the CCDP.

Backup hardware.

Fault-tolerant media.

7 Where should redundancy be prioritized?

The primary focus of redundancy should be on the WAN link. Configure the WAN as a top priority for maximum availability.

8 Name a Cisco router that can be employed at each layer of the hierarchical model.

Core—Cisco 7000 and 12000 series routers.

Distribution—Cisco 4000 series routers.

Access—Cisco 1000 and 2500 series routers.

9 Explain the processes involved in gathering information.

Data gathering involves defining the problem. The CCDP should learn about the corporate structure and the decision-making process. Gathering data includes discovering what applications are being used and what plans exist in the future for change.

10 What layer acts as the intermediate layer in the hierarchical model?

The distribution layer is the intermediate layer between the core layer and the access layer. The distribution layer is the recommended place for access lists and security functions.

11 What tools can be used to estimate network performance?

Network simulation and modeling tools are available to estimate network performance.

12 What are two methods of reducing bandwidth on a remote access link?

Snapshot routing and static routing.

13 True or false: After implementing the network, the CCDP should consider the task complete.

False. After the implementation phase, the network must be monitored. During the monitoring phase, the customer should concur that the network is functioning according to design specifications.

14 Why is a partial mesh more cost-effective than a full-mesh design?

The partial mesh design allows for fewer dedicated links, thus reducing the recurring circuit costs. The full-mesh design requires all-to-all connectivity. As the number of links increases, a full-mesh design can become cost-prohibitive.

15 What layer of the network is primarily concerned with high-speed transport of data?

Core.

16 How have the latest technology advances changed the 80/20 rule?

Originally, the 80/20 rule stated that 80 percent of the traffic should remain local. With the advent of the Internet and other centralized servers, 20 percent of the traffic is now accessed from the local network. With the advent of the Internet, other centralized servers, and high-speed networking, 80 percent of the traffic now travels outside the local network.

17 At what step of designing the internetwork should a protocol be selected?

Step 3: Developing the internetwork structure.

18 What Cisco router is recommended for the Core layer?

Cisco 7000 and above.

19 List five elements of strategic internetwork design.

Capacity planning.

Overall internetwork topology.

Budget.

Network applications.

Network management.

Policy decisions.

20 What is the simplest internetwork design model?

Flat-earth design.

21 Where can information on network design be found?

Cisco provides information on the Cisco Connection documentation CD and at http://www.cisco.com/univercd/home/home.htm.

22 True or false: To save the customer money, an immediate cutover is recommended as the first option of implementation.

False. Phased-in implementation is always recommended.

23 What is the most significant cost component of an internetwork over time?

Internetwork support is the most significant cost component for an internetwork over time.

24 What area of the network usually is the most dominant cause of latency in the wide-area network? What area usually contributes the least?

WAN links usually cause the most latency in the WAN. Switches and routers contribute the least amount of latency.

25 When provisioning hardware, what do you need to consider in addition to node capacity?

You need to consider the capacity of links in addition to node capacity.

26 Why is protocol selection important with regard to network design?

Protocols can consume large quantities of bandwidth due to broadcasts. If a station spends too much time processing broadcasts, the network can become efficient.

27 What is typically the largest cost not related to support?

The recurring costs of the WAN links.

28 Your design will require compression, congestion, control, and security. At what layer should this be implemented?

Distribution.

29 Why has the hierarchical layer been a successful factor in network design?

Hierarchical models can make complex network problems simpler. By assigning specific functions to each tier, the hierarchical model aids in manageability and scalability. In addition, it allows for ease of troubleshooting.

30 What Cisco IOS features can improve WAN utilization and performance?

Header, link, and payload compression.

Priority queuing and bandwidth reservation.

Proxy services between the router and clients.

Encapsulation and tunneling across the WAN core.

Chapter 2

1 What is the first step in campus network design?

Identifying the business and technical requirements.

2 What two backbones are the recommended models for the Campus LAN design?

Distributed and collapsed.

3 What business issues govern the design acceptance process?

Business issues are governed by cost. In addition to fixed equipment costs, recurring costs must be considered. Determining the total cost of ownership is critical to ensuring the long-term success of the network.

4 What three categories of problems do most networks fall into?

Most problems can be attributed to media, protocols, or transport.

5 What are the two contrasting factors in determining network design?

Cost and availability.

6 Why are desktop protocols least desirable for a large network?

Desktop protocols tie up large quantities of bandwidth with broadcasts. Excessive broadcasts can render the network inefficient.

7 What solution should the CCDP employ when addressing a network with media contention?

Switches.

8 When might an ATM switch improve an internetwork's design and performance?

For networks that require Quality of Service delivery.

9 What device should be used to filter broadcasts and multicasts?

Router.

10 What is the difference between a broadcast domain and a bandwidth domain?

A bandwidth domain consists of all traffic associated with a single port on a bridge or switch. A broadcast domain consists of all traffic associated with a single port on a router.

11 What issues should you address when designing a campus LAN?

Server and client end stations.

Network infrastructure.

Network management.

Business concerns.

12 How can a VLAN improve network performance?

A VLAN isolates bandwidth segments. So, one user or a group of users who require large amounts of bandwidth will not impact network performance for the rest of the network.

13 What device controls broadcasts and multicasts?

Router.

14 Name two protocols that are not recommended for WAN design.

NetBEUI and AppleTalk.

15 What device terminates the bandwidth domain?

Switch.

16 What protocol is recommended for use on the Internet?

TCP/IP.

17 What is media contention?

Media contention relates to excessive collisions on Ethernet or long waits for the token on a Token Ring network.

18 What protocol is recommended for integrating voice, video, and data?

ATM.

19 True or false: Transport problems are usually caused when the network bandwidth is not available to deliver the payload that the applications request.

True.

20 Although broadcasts play an important function in network communications, excessive broadcasts can make the network inefficient. What can the CCDP do to remedy the problem of excessive broadcasts?

The CCDP should ensure that routers are strategically placed in the campus LAN network to minimize the impact of broadcast traffic.

21 List two applications that require high-speed Quality of Service transport.

Voice and video.

22 What Cisco IOS features can optimize core layer transport?

Compression and queuing.

23 What is the biggest trade-off of a distributed backbone?

Cost.

24 What is the 80/20 rule? Explain why some people now refer to it as the 20/80 rule.

The 80/20 rule allows for 80 percent of the network traffic to remain on the local subnet. Some people call it the 20/80 rule because now only 20 percent of the network traffic is expected to be on the local network.

25 What devices terminate the broadcast domain?

Router.

26   What is broadcast radiation?

Broadcast radiation is a problem when the ambient level of broadcasts generated by the higher-layer protocols in the network restricts the number of nodes that the network can support. The effects of broadcast radiation can be so severe that an end station can spend all its CPU power on processing broadcasts.

27   List five typical problems that the CCDP might be asked to solve.

Media contention.

Excessive broadcasts.

Nonscalable protocols.

Security.

Overloaded backbones.

28   When would a multiprotocol backbone be recommended?

When other campus LANs use protocols other than IP. The router introduces latency when tunneling IP. So, to optimize the design, multiple protocols are preferred over tunneling.

29   What solution is recommended for solving congestion problems that are caused by media contention?

Switching.

Chapter 3

1   Name four campus LAN technologies.

Ethernet, Token Ring, FDDI, ATM.

2   State a major disadvantage of using Ethernet.

Ethernet allows collisions to occur on the network. An excessive number of collisions reduces available bandwidth.

3   List two LAN interconnection methods.

Bridging, switching and routing.

4   What are two types of switching methods for Ethernet?

Cut-through and store and forward.

5   State four goals that you can achieve by using switches in a campus LAN.

Reducing network congestion while increasing the available bandwidth.

Organizing users into logical workgroups.

Reducing the costs of managing network operations.

Providing scalability, traffic control, and security.

6 Bridges operate at Layer ___ of the OSI model and forward _____.

2, frames.

7 Name three primary types of cable used in LANs.

Coaxial, twisted-pair, fiber-optic.

8 Routers operate at Layer ___ of the OSI model and forward _____.

3, packets.

9 List three types of wireless networks.

Infrared, laser, point-to-point transmission.

10 How are traffic loops prevented on switches and routers?

STP, split horizon, poison reverse.

11 What cable is recommended for wiring between closet and campus buildings?

Fiber-optic.

12 What are the four IEEE standards for 10 Mbps Ethernet5?

10Base2, 10BaseT, 10Base5, 10BaseFL.

13 What is the Cisco proprietary protocol for connecting Cisco switches?

ISL.

14 List three functions provided by routers.

Segmenting LANs and WANs.

Determining the best path to the destination.

Communicating route information with other routers.

15 What are some benefits of designing a network with Thinnet?

Relatively inexpensive.

Easy to install.

Easy to configure.

16 What type of cable is recommended to interconnect floors on the campus LAN backbone?

Fiber-optic.

17 What Ethernet switching method is fastest?

Cut-through.

18 List five types of bridging.

Transparent.

Source-route.

Translational.

Source-route transparent.

Source-route translational.

19 What types of functionality do routers provide?

Routers, filters, and forward packets.

20 True or false: Because bridges switch in hardware, they are much faster than switches, which rely on software to perform switching functions.

False. Switches are faster than bridges.

21 What cable offers optimum security?

Fiber. Fiber-optic cable cannot be tapped, because the data is transmitted in the form of light.

22 What is the maximum number of IP stations that should be deployed on a flat network?

500.

23 List three advantages of configuring a Thinnet network.

Relatively inexpensive.

Easy to install.

Easy to configure.

24 What is the 5-4-3 rule?

A Thinnet network can combine as many as five cable segments connected by four repeaters, but only three segments can have stations attached.

5 segments.

4 repeaters.

3 trunks with stations attached.

25 What is the maximum segment length recommended for a 10BaseT network?

100 meters.

26 Why would a designer want to segment a network?

Segmentation reduces traffic on the network. Reduced traffic helps high-bandwidth applications perform better.

27 What types of cables can be used to connect computers on a Token ring network?

Token Ring cables use IBM Type 1, 2, and 3 cabling.

28 What considerations should you make when you're deciding which type of cable to select for a network?

What distances must the cable cover?

What are the network's security needs?

How much bandwidth will be required?

What transmission speeds must be supported?

29 What type of cable is recommended for the desktop?

CAT 5.

30 Under what situations is unshielded twisted-pair cable not recommended?

Unshielded twisted-pair cable is susceptible to interference. If data must be transmitted great distances at high speeds, unshielded twisted-pair cable is not the recommended choice of cabling.

31 What cable is recommended for transmitting data at very high speeds over long distances?

Fiber-optic cable is not susceptible to interference. Use fiber to transmit data at very high speeds over long distances.

Chapter 4

1 What is the size of an ATM cell, and how do its fixed length and size contribute to low latency?

The ATM cell has a fixed length of 53 bytes—48 for the data and 5 for the header. With the fixed length, the ATM switch doesn't have to be notified when the transmission is done. So, the ATM switch doesn't waste overhead looking for information in software.

2 What are the two types of virtual circuits used by ATM?

ATM's flexibility allows it to run on permanent virtual circuits and switched virtual circuits.

3 Name and describe the three layers of the ATM reference model.

The three layers of the ATM reference model are the ATM physical layer, the ATM layer, and the ATM adaptation layer (AAL). These three layers correlate to the physical and data link layers of the OSI model. The AAL is responsible for allowing data conversions from multiple applications to and from the ATM cell.

4 What layer of the OSI model closely relates to the ATM reference model?

The ATM physical layer closely relates to the physical layer (Layer 1) in the OSI model.

5 For each application listed, match the ATM Adaptation Layer best suited to it:

Voice _____

AAL 1

SMDS_____

AAL 2

Data _____

AAL 3/4

_____

AAL 5

Voice _____

AAL 1

SMDS_____

AAL 3/4

Data _____

AAL 5

6 Name the four major components of ATM LANE.

LECS (LAN Emulation Configuration Server).

LEC (LAN Emulation Client).

LES (LAN Emulation Server).

BUS (Broadcast and Unknown Server).

7 What two LAN clients does ATM LANE provide emulation for?

Ethernet and Token Ring.

8 What two types of interfaces are described in the ATM model?

User Network Interface (UNI).

Network-to-Network Interface (NNI).

9 Name four alternative models for ATM internetworking.

Local Area Network Emulation (LANE).

A point-to-point data link.

A high-speed workgroup and backbone.

A router cluster backbone.

10 Name four networking areas where ATM could be implemented.

Campus, local area, wide area, metropolitan.

11 What protocol controls the user cell stream between nodes and networks?

Private Network-Node Interface (intranetwork) or Private Network-Network Interface (internetwork)(PNNI).

12 How many characters comprise an NSAP address?

20 octet or 40 hex.

13 What is Interim Local Management Interface (ILMI), and how is it used to connect end stations?

ILMI allows two systems to exchange ATM information. LECs use ILMI to locate the LECs and to determine their own address.

14 Name four Cisco products that can form the building blocks of an ATM WAN.

Cisco/StrataCom IGX switch, which is well-suited for deployment in an enterprise WAN environment.

Cisco/StrataCom BPX/AXIS switch, which meets the needs of high-end enterprise WAN and service provider environments.

Cisco AIP for the Cisco 7500 and 7000 series of routers.

Cisco ATM Network Interface Module (NIM) for the Cisco 4700 and 4500 series of routers.

15 Name two business and technical requirements that might lead an engineer to select ATM as a design solution.

Business requirement: Distance learning and training.

Business requirement: Video on demand.

Technical requirement: Single multiservice enterprise solution granting voice, data, and video with Quality of Service.

Technical requirement: Greater bandwidth on demand to satisfy bandwidth-intensive applications.

16 Why is congestion control a serious issue?

Congestion control is a serious issue because one cell loss means loss of the whole frame. If a frame is lost, many cells must be retransmitted. Congestion control helps guarantee the Quality of Service specified in the service contract.

17 What RFC allows multiple protocols to be multiplexed over a single PVC?

RFC 1483.

18 Name four ATM layer service categories.

Constant Bit Rate (CBR).

Variable Bit Rate (VBR).

Unspecified Bit Rate (UBR).

Available Bit Rate (ABR).

19 Name four functions of the ATM physical layer.

Tracking of ATM cell boundaries.

Conversion of bits into cells.

Packaging of cells into frames.

Control of transmission and receipt of data.

20 Name two types of addresses used by ATM.

For private networks, ATM uses Network Service Access Point (NSAP) addresses and E.164 addressing for public networks.

21 What is the function of the BUS?

The BUS is the Broadcast and Unknown Server. It is a multicast server that provides information to the LES. If the LES does not know the location of a destination address, the BUS discovers the address by broadcasting a request for information.

22 List three requirements of an efficient ATM address plan.

Address prefixes must be globally unique.

Addresses must be hierarchical and planned to match your network topology.

The address plan must allow for future network expansion.

23 True or false: A LAN Emulation Client can be an ATM end station or router, but a switch or bridge cannot be configured as a LEC.

False. Catalyst 5000 can be configured as a LEC.

24 True or false: Congestion is caused by slow links. The problem can always be solved by adding high-speed links.

False. An increase in link bandwidth can actually aggravate the congestion problem if the higher-speed links make the network more unbalanced. Depending on the configuration, higher-speed links can shift the bottleneck and make the congestion condition worse.

25 What is the function of the LAN Emulation Server?

The LES provides a registration facility for LECs to register unicast and multicast addresses. The LES requests and maintains a list of LAN destination MAC addresses.

26 Describe the role that routers play in ATM internetworking.

Routers can connect diverse LAN and WAN links to existing ATM internetworks. Routers can perform vital ATM services such as multicast server, ARP server, and LAN emulation server. A single Cisco router with compatible IOS features can serve as LES, BUS, and LEC.

27 Name two Cisco ATM products suited for WAN deployment.

Cisco/StrataCom IGX switch, which is well-suited for deployment in an Enterprise WAN environment.

Cisco ATM Network Interface Module (NIM) for the Cisco 4700 and 4500 series of routers.

28 What is one function of the ATM Forum?

The ATM Forum is responsible for creating standards and specifications that ensure that ATM remains responsive to user needs.

29 What is the function of the ATM layer?

The ATM layer establishes virtual connections and passes ATM cells through the ATM network. The ATM layer is responsible for payload delivery, virtual connections, and cell identification.

30 State two issues to consider when designing or expanding networks to include ATM.

Quality of service (QoS).

Multiservice (voice, video, and data) integration.

Chapter 5

1 What are the five IP address classes?

Classes A, B, C, D, and E.

2 What class of IP address is optimum for a small network?

Class C.

3 Which IP addresses are reserved for multicasting?

224.0.0.0 to 239.255.255.255.

4 What IP address class renders 254 hosts?

Class C.

5 Which IP addresses are reserved for experiments?

240.0.0.0 to 254.255.255.255.

6 What is NAT, and how can it help conserve IP addresses?

Network Address Translation (NAT) allows unregistered addresses in a private domain to be translated to a registered public address.

7 List four benefits of address summarization.

Reduces the size of the routing table.

Hiding network changes.

Network growth.

Reduces router resource utilization.

8 What subnet mask is ideal for connecting WAN links?

255.255.255.252 (/30) mask. It provides two hosts. On the WAN, serial lines require only two host addresses.

9 Define classful routing.

Classful routing observes the class address boundaries of Classes A, B, and C. Classful routing protocols cannot carry variable-subnet mask information in their updates.

10 What is CIDR, and how does it offer greater flexibility in IP addressing?

Classless interdomain routing (CIDR) allows for the reduction of the size of routing tables by creating aggregate routes, or supernets. CIDR eliminates the concept of network classes and allows for better scalability when supporting the advertising of IP prefixes in the Internet.

11 What is a discontiguous subnet?

A discontiguous subnet is two or more portions of a major network that are separated by another major network.

12 True or false: To support variable-length subnet masking and route summarization, a classless routing protocol must be incorporated into the design plan.

True.

13 Define classless routing.

Classless routing allows the prefix to be increased from the fixed classful length. Classless routing allows prefixes to be greater than the classful specifications of 8, 16, and 24.

14 What is the prefix length of a Class A network?

8 bits.

15 The network design requires 14 hosts. What network and subnet mask should be employed?

255.255.255.240.

16 Why is network 10.0.0.0 a popular private address?

Network 10.0.0.0 provides a large amount of address space for assigning subnetted networks and hosts. It allows for lots of scalability.

17 List three criteria for selecting a routing protocol.

Support for variable-length subnet masks (VLSM).

Interoperates with other systems and supports redistribution.

Scalable to support present and future needs.

18 What is meant by the phrases "subnetting extends to the right" and "supernetting extends to the left"?

Subnetting extends the prefix to the right of the classful boundary, and supernetting extends the prefix to the left of the classful boundary.

19 To what IP address class would address 127.43.2.1 belong?

The 127 address belongs to no IP address class. The 127 address is reserved for testing.

20 What is secondary addressing, and when should it be utilized?

Secondary addressing can be used when a single subnet runs out of available host addresses.

21 How many hosts will a Class C network support with the default mask?

254.

22 What routing protocols should you avoid when using classless routing?

RIP, IGRP.

23 What protocol ensures efficient use of bandwidth during multicasting?

IGMP.

24 List five issues to consider when designing IP addressing schemes.

Determining the number of hosts required on a network, present and projected.

Determining the number of subnets for an existing network, present and projected.

Determining interoperability issues with other vendor equipment and protocols.

Determining the appropriate location for a DHCP server.

Determining the security issues that need to be addressed.

25 List one disadvantage of using a classful routing protocol.

All interfaces must use the same network mask..

26 What organization assigns public IP addresses?

The Internet Assigned Numbers Authority (IANA) assigns unique 32-bit IP addresses.

27 List two protocols that can be used to enact classless routing.

OSPF, EIGRP.

28 What is meant by the sentence "The router always looks for the longest match"?

If more than one entry in the routing table matches a particular destination, the longest prefix match in the routing table is used. The route with the longest match is considered to be the most specific route.

29 How is multicast traffic handled across the Internet?

The Internet's Multicast Backbone (MBONE) has been developed to handle multicast traffic across the network.

30 What applications require the use of multicasting?

Multimedia, desktop conferencing.

Chapter 6

1 List five possible requirements for a routing protocol.

Should adapt to change easily and quickly.

Does not create a lot of traffic.

Scales to a large size.

Based on industry standards.

Compatible with existing hosts and routers.

2 What two tasks do routers perform?

Switching frames and path determination.

3 What is the simplest form of routing?

Static routing.

4 What type of routing determines the best path?

Dynamic routing.

5 List four types of interior gateway protocols.

RIP, OSPF, IGRP, EIGRP.

6 What is administrative distance?

Administrative distance can be defined as a rating of the trustworthiness of a routing information source. Numerically, an administrative distance is an integer between 0 and 255. The higher the value, the lower the trust rating.

7 What protocol works primarily in the Internet?

BGP.

8 List three types of routing metrics.

Hop count, delay, bandwidth.

9 What is a classless protocol?

Classless protocols support VLSMs and include network masks in their routing updates. Classless protocols are not restricted by class boundaries.

10 List one disadvantage of classful routing protocols.

The whole network must use the same network class mask.

11 List three types of switching methods used by Cisco routers.

Process switching, fast switching, autonomous switching.

12 What is the routing metric for OSPF?

Cost.

13 List three requirements of route summarization.

Multiple IP addresses must share the same high-order bits.

Routing protcols must carry the prefix length or subnet mask in a separate field along with the 32-bit IP address.

Routing tables and protocols must base their routing decisions on a 32-bit IP address with a prefix length that can be up to the entire 32-bit length of the field.

14 True or false: Secondary addressing is a recommended and preferred method of connecting discontiguous subnets.

False. Secondary addressing consumes resources. Use secondary addressing as a last resort and as a temporary resort.

15 _____ is the exchange of routing information between two different routing processes.

Route redistribution.

16 List three ways that routing protocols can be characterized.

Distance vector, link state, hybrid.

17 What is a routing loop?

A routing loop occurs when routers disagree. Routers disagree if their routing tables are inconsistent.

18 What protocol has hybrid functionality, displaying the characteristics that resemble distance-vector and link-state protocols?

EIGRP.

19 What is a stub network?

A stub network is a part of the network that can be accessed via only one route.

20 Two routing protocols, RIP and IGRP, are being redistributed. Design requirements state that RIP advertisements must be blocked from entering the IGRP cloud. What command should be implemented?

Passive interface.

21 What two factors determine convergence time?

The time it takes to detect a link failure.

The time it takes to determine a new route.

22 What is the routing metric for IP RIP?

Hop count.

23 How can the Hot Standby Routing Protocol (HSRP) be used to provide redundancy?

With HSRP, two or more routers communicate on a single gateway address. If the primary router goes down, the secondary router becomes primary, utilizing the same gateway address.

24 What three resources does routing consume?

CPU, memory, network.

25 List two methods of filtering routes when redistributing.

Route maps, access lists.

26 What protocols discussed in this chapter use the Hello protocol to update their routing tables?

OSPF, EIGRP.

27 When redistributing protocols, why is it important to consider the metric differences of each protocol?

Different protocols have different methods of determining the best route. When one route is redistributed into another, it must adopt the metric standards of the protocol it is being distributed to. If metrics are not taken into consideration, the protocol receiving the redistribution will not enter the distributed routes properly.

28 What is the lowest administrative distance available to implement routing policy?

Directly connected.

29 What is the simplest form of switching path available on a Cisco router?

Process switching.

30 What is split horizon?

Split horizon helps prevent routing loops. It tells a router not to broadcast a learned route back through a port from which it received the learned information.

Chapter 7

1 What limitations of RIP, the first Internet routing protocol, was OSPF designed to overcome?

Limited range of 15 hops.

Slow convergence.

Susceptibility to routing loops.

2 What are the four types of connections for the OSPF routing protocol?

Point-to-point.

Point-to-multipoint.

Broadcast.

Nonbroadcast.

3 Name the four classifications of OSPF routers.

Internal.

Area border router (ABR).

Area system border router (ASBR).

Backbone router.

4 What are link-state advertisements? Name four types of link-state advertisements.

Link State Advertisements (LSAs) advertise the state of the link to other OSPF routers.

Router LSA—Type 1 LSAs contain information about router links, interfaces, state of links, and cost.

Network LSA—Type 2 LSAs contain lists of routers connected to a multiaccess network segment.

Summary LSA—Type 3 LSAs originate at area border routers and are sent into an area to advertise networks that have been summarized into a single route.

Summary LSA (ASBR)—Type 4 LSAs originate as area system border routers and are sent to networks that have been summarized into a single route to the OSPF network to advertise the ASBR.

AS-external LSA—Type 5 LSAs contain information that describes destinations external to the OSPF AS.

5 True or false: All OSPF areas must be physically adjacent to the backbone.

False. Virtual links can connect areas that are not physically attached to the backbone.

6 The following are OSPF routes. Perform summarization to one route. What configuration commands would be needed if the routes were external? What commands would be needed if the routes were internal?

Route 1 _____
172.26.30.0

Route 2 _____
172.26.31.0

Route 3 _____
172.26.32.0

External routes: **summary address 172.26.0.0 255.255.192.0**

Internal routes: **area 1 range 172.26.0.0 255.255.192.0**

7 Compare and contrast stub, totally stubby, and not-so-stubby areas.

In a stub area, a default route summarizes all external routes. Stub areas are similar to regular areas, except that the routers do not enter external routes in the area's databases. Type 3 LSAs are still flooded into the area.

A totally stubby area only allows the default summary link to be propagated into the area by the ARB. Type 3 LSAs are not flooded into the area.

Not-so-stubby areas are similar to stub areas, except that they allow limited importing of external routes.

8 List six rules for designing a scalable OSPF internetwork.

No more than six hops from source to destination.

50 routers per area.

All areas connect to Area 0.

Do not allow more than two areas per ABR.

Use totally stubby areas.

Maximize summarization.

9 How does OSPF route summarization save router resources?

Summarization reduces the memory and the CPU processing load on the routers.

10 What is the meaning of cost, and how does OSPF calculate cost?

Cost is the metric that OSPF uses to determine the shortest path. The metric is added from source to destination over all outgoing links. OSPF defines cost as 10 E8/BW.

11 What is the difference between an External Type 1 route and an External Type 2 route?

External Type 1 routes use a metric that is the sum of the external metric and the collective internal cost of reaching the destination.

External Type 2 routes use a metric that examines the external metric and does not take the internal cost into consideration.

12 Which routing protocols are supported by EIGRP?

IP, IPX, AppleTalk.

13 EIGRP updates are

A. periodic

B. incremental

C. A and B

D. None of the above

Answer is B, incremental

14 Name five values that IGRP and EIGRP use to determine metrics. Which metrics are used by default?

By default, IGRP metric = bandwidth + delay.

In addition to bandwidth and delay, IGRP can be configured to track the following metrics:

Reliability.

Loading.

MTU (static).

15 Name two parameters that can be tuned by IGRP to allow faster convergence.

Turning off or reducing holddown.

Reducing the update timer.

16 As a rule of thumb, how many areas should be connected to a single router?

If a single router is connected to lots of areas, router memory and CPU resources might be overwhelmed. Limit the number of areas that connect to a single router to three. A router with high-speed CPU and lots of memory might be able to handle more areas.

17 What is the function of a designated router?

The designated router can send LSAs to the rest of the routers on the multiaccess subnetwork. The designated router is the router with the highest priority.

18 What is a virtual link?

A virtual link is a logical link between Area 0 and another area that is not physically connected to the backbone.

19 What is an OSPF area?

Areas are logical groups of OSPF networks that share information about routes. Each router in the area shares the same database information.

20 True or false: IGRP summarizes on network number boundaries but can be configured to support variable-length subnet masks.

False.

21 What is split horizon? In what situations might split horizon be useful to the network design?

Split horizon prevents a router from sending information out the interface from which it originated. Split horizon might be desirable in networks that use logical subinterfaces on the same physical interface, such as Frame Relay or ATM.

22 True or false: To ensure fast convergence for large internetworks, EIGRP keeps two routing tables, the local routing table and the active routing table, of any router three hops away.

False. EIGRP keeps its own local routing table, which is formed from communications with neighbors, and the active routing table of each adjacent neighbor. This allows a faster way for EIGRP to determine a route change.

23   Why is EIGRP considered a hybrid protocol?

EIGRP is considered a hybrid protocol because it has properties of link-state and distance-vector protocols. EIGRP overcomes the typical limitations of distance-vector protocols. EIGRP uses less bandwidth than most distance-vector protocols by sending updates only when the network topology changes. EIGRP uses hello packets to determine neighbor reachability.

24   What Cisco feature lets the percentage of bandwidth used by EIGRP be changed?

ip bandwidth-percent eigrp

25   What is the function of a designated router?

The designated router can send LSAs to the rest of the routers on the multiaccess subnetwork. The designated router is the router with the highest priority.

26   Which protocols discussed in this chapter (OSPF, IGRP, EIGRP) are classful by default?

IGRP and EIGRP are classful by default. EIGRP can be configured to examine class by using the **no auto-summary** command.

27   What provisions do OSPF and EIGRP make for security?

EIGRP and OSPF support router authentication. A router can be configured to accept routing updates only from trusted sources. Both EIGRP and OSPF support MD5 and clear-text authentication.

28   Name three features that are supported by OSPF and EIGRP.

Variable-length subnet masking.

Support for summarization.

Support for discontiguous networking.

Support for authentication.

29   What configuration command allows IGRP to support unequal-cost load balancing?

The **variance** command.

30   Of the three routing protocols (OSPF, IGRP, EIGRP), what protocol allows connectivity to routers not manufactured by Cisco?

OSPF. OSPF is an IP standards-based routing protocol that has been adopted by all vendors. IGRP and EIGRP are Cisco-proprietary.

Chapter 8

1 In what situations is AppleTalk recommended?

AppleTalk is recommended when the goal is to design a small network to support Apple computers that is easy to use, configure, and maintain.

2 Name two AppleTalk protocols that operate at the network layer.

AppleTalk Address Resolution Protocol (AARP).

Datagram Delivery Protocol (DDP).

3 What three elements comprise an AppleTalk network address?

Network number, node number, socket number.

4 What method of AppleTalk configuration is recommended for LAN networks?

Soft seed.

5 Name three protocols that are used for AppleTalk routing.

AppleTalk Update-Based Routing Protocol (AURP).

Routing Table Maintenance Protocol (RTMP).

Enhanced Interior Gateway Routing Protocol (EIGRP).

6 What two elements comprise a Novell network address?

Network number and node number.

7 What routing protocol should be used on the WAN to conserve bandwidth?

Enhanced Interior Gateway Routing Protocol (EIGRP).

8 What is one method of controlling SAP and RIP broadcasts on the network?

SAP and RIP broadcasts can be controlled with access lists.

9 True or false: IPX clients on the network must have a dialup modem or have IP enabled on their workstations to access the Internet.

False. An IPX-to-IP gateway can be configured. All IPX clients can access the Internet through the gateway.

10 What are the Novell and Cisco definitions for the four types of IPX encapsulation for Ethernet?

Ethernet 802_3 _____
Novell-ether.

Ethernet_SNAP _____
SNAP.

Ethernet 802_2 _____
SAP.

Ethernet_II_____
ARPA.

11 What are the four methods used by Microsoft Windows to resolve host names?

LMHOSTS.

Broadcasts.

DNS.

WINS.

12 Name three things a designer should be mindful of when designing for DHCP.

Address assignments, lease length, server redundancy.

13 Why is NetBEUI not recommended for wide-area networks?

NetBEUI is not routable.

14 What are the four domain models that are used in Microsoft Networking?

Single domain model.

Master domain model.

Multiple master domain model.

Complete trust domain model.

15 How could IPX or AppleTalk be connected across an IP-only backbone?

Tunneling.

16 What metrics does IPX RIP use to determine the best route?

Hop count and delay.

17 Design problem: Dialup lines stay up because keepalive traffic is triggering the line every 5 minutes. What command will fix this?

ipx watchdog-spoof.

18 How many bits comprise a full Novell IPX address?

80.

19 What AppleTalk configuration is recommended only for troubleshooting?

Hard seed.

20 True or false: DHCP can assign addresses only to machines that use Microsoft Windows.

False. DHCP can assign address to other machines, including Cisco routers.

21 Which routing protocol is highly recommended for the WAN but not for the LAN?

Enhanced Interior Gateway Routing Protocol (EIGRP).

22 What AppleTalk routing protocol supports tunneling?

AURP.

23 List four examples of how network numbers can be administered.

By building, floor, department, or division.

24 Why is RTMP recommended for the LAN but not the WAN?

AppleTalk devices on the LAN require RTMP to communicate. RTMP packets consume a lot of bandwidth. RTMP routers broadcast their AT routing tables every 10 seconds. The impact could be significant on a low-speed WAN.

25 List three benefits of using DHCP.

Saves time, reduces the administrative burden, minimizes the potential for configuration errors.

26 Can a Cisco router be configured as a DHCP server?

Yes.

27 In what situations might NetBEUI still be a useful protocol?

Small networks where routing is not required.

28 True or false: Like IP and IPX, AppleTalk routers use the same AS number on all routers in the domain.

False. AppleTalk routers require unique AS numbers for all routers in the domain.

29 How can a Cisco router be configured to pass NetBIOS broadcasts?

ipx type-20-propagation.

30 How can a router be configured to allow different types of encapsulation on the same interface?

Subinterfaces.

Chapter 9

1 A customer needs a high-speed, cost-effective, low-latency network. Which technology should he choose?

Frame Relay
ISDN
Point-to-point
X.25

Frame Relay

2 When designing networks for load sharing, what should you use between routers?

Equal hops
Equal latency
Equal bandwidth
Bandwidth on demand

Equal hops

3 Put the following in order of importance for a customer:

Redundancy
Single-protocol WAN
Reliability
Cost
Legacy system support

Reliability
Cost
Redundancy
Single-protocol WAN
Legacy system support

4 What does a company base its purchasing decisions on?

A. Reliability, cost, performance, redundancy.

B. Cost, availability, redundancy, performance.

C. Availability, scalability, performance, redundancy.

D. Redundancy, availability, cost, performance.

Answer: Reliability, cost, performance, redundancy.

5 Which technology is used for low-volume intermittent traffic?

ISDN
Frame Relay
X.25
ATM

ISDN

6   What Cisco feature enables the use of two ISDN bearer channels?

Bandwidth on demand
Dial on demand
Priority queuing
L2TP

Bandwidth on demand.

7   What three objectives must the WAN design achieve?

Maximizing throughput, minimizing delay, minimizing overhead traffic.

8   In a good design, what should the maximum number of hops be from endpoint to endpoint within a network?

6.

9   WAN designs in the core should be created with

An even number of routers
An odd number of routers
It doesn't matter.

An even number of routers.

10   What methods can be used to optimize bandwidth utilization on the WAN?

Compression and queuing.

11   A round-robin type of queuing is called:

Custom
CAR
CEF
Priority

Custom.

12   What is the preferred queuing method for passing time-sensitive and delay-sensitive traffic?

Priority queuing.

13   How many queues are available in custom queuing?

16.

14   What Cisco protocol encapsulates IP, CLNP, IPX, AppleTalk, DECnet Phase IV, XNS, VINES, and Apollo packets inside IP tunnels?

Cisco's Generic Routing Encapsulation (GRE).

15 With this switching method, the first packet that enters the router is copied to the system buffer.

Process switching.

16 Are custom and priority queuing supported on tunnels?

No. Custom and priority queuing are not supported on tunnels.

17 List some benefits of Cisco's QoS.

Control over resources.

More efficient use of network resources.

Tailored services.

Coexistence of mission-critical applications.

18 What is the most basic form of queuing?

FIFO.

19 What is a method of controlling bandwidth into or out of an interface?

Committed Access Rate (CIR).

20 Which technology supports both voice and video?

ISDN.

21 Priority queuing is used for _____ WAN links.

Slow.

22 What type of compression is used for Telnet, LAT, and Xremote?

Header.

23 What type of compression is used for point-to-point circuits?

Link compression.

24 What type of compression is used for packet WAN?

Payload.

25 Which protocol should you use if you have to route IP, AppleTalk, and IPX in the core?

EIGRP.

26 Sites that generate a lot of traffic should be _____ connected.

Directly.

27 What technology was designed for use in nonreliable physical layers?

X.25.

28 What is a low-cost method of connecting two sites?

A point-to-point link.

29 Load sharing is on by default with which three routing protocols?

IGRP, EIGRP, OSPF.

30 RIP is a _____ routing protocol.

Distance vector.

31 _____ occurs when fast-switched packets are sent from a high-speed interface to a low-speed interface.

Congestion.

Chapter 10

1 X.25 uses what protocol at Layer 2?

LAPB.

2 X.25 uses what protocol at Layer 3?

X.25 PLP (Packet-Level Protocol).

3 At which layer do packet size and window size operate?

At the X.25 layer or Layer 3.

4 What does AO/DI stand for?

Always On Dynamic ISDN.

5 When the command **encapsulate frame relay** is applied to a serial interface, does that make the serial interface point-to-point or multipoint by default?

Multipoint.

6 What range of DLCIs can be used on a serial interface encapsulated with Frame Relay?

16–1007. The range defined is 0–1023, but 0–15 and 1008–1023 are reserved.

7 Do most carriers charge for the local loop with dedicated lines? How about with Frame Relay?

Most carriers charge extra for distance with dedicated lines, but with Frame Relay they do not.

8 If I have a measurement interval of .125 seconds, and I am guaranteed a CIR of 8k during that time period, what is my overall CIR?

64k (.125 = 8 intervals of 8k).

9 In a full-mesh environment, should Inverse ARP be disabled?

Yes.

10 Can split horizon be turned off for IPX RIP and AppleTalk RTMP?

No.

11 Does OSPF apply the split horizon rule?

No. Every router has a copy of the database.

12 Name two good reasons to use subinterfaces.

So that different parameters can be applied to each subinterface

Split horizon issues are hard to troubleshoot.

13 What does NBMA stand for?

Nonbroadcast multiaccess.

14 If four sites are fully meshed, how many links are needed?

6. Using the formula $n \times (n-1) / 2$, $4 \times (4-1) / 2 = (4 \times 3) / 2 = 12 / 2 = 6$.

15 What two routing protocols are used for fast convergence?

OSPF and EIGRP.

16 Can there be different LMI types on subinterfaces?

No. LMI types are set on the physical interfaces, not the subinterfaces.

17 What is the maximum Frame Relay transmittable unit (MTU) size?

1500 bytes. Frame Relay sends packets up to this size without fragmentation and reassembly. To test if packets of various sizes are being fragmented, use Cisco's Extended IP ping, pick a packet size, and set the don't fragment (DF) bit. This makes the ping fail if Frame Relay is trying to fragment the packet, and you can find the true MTU packet size for your Frame Relay circuit.

18 When is LMI exchanged between the router and the carrier?

LMI keepalives are exchanged every 10 seconds. Full status inquiries are exchanged every 60 seconds.

19 Is there a limit to the number of subinterfaces that are allowed on a router when using Frame Relay?

Because there can be only 992 DLCIs, you would reach that limit before the subinterface limit.

20 What does an increase in the number of FECN and BECN packets mean?

The provider is probably experiencing congestion in the network.

21 In order for a DLCI on a subinterface to be "active," does the DLCI also have to be up at the remote end?

Yes. The remote DLCI must be up in order for a DLCI on a subinterface to be active.

22 With two subinterfaces on the same router, can there be two different Frame Relay encapsulations?

No. The parent interface can be configured with only one encapsulation.

23 Does OSPF use split horizon for an interface?

OSPF does not use split horizon, because it is a link-state routing protocol.

24 What is LMI used for?

The Frame Relay LMI conveys the DLCI status from the switch to the router.

25 By default, is a subinterface point-to-point or multipoint?

Multipoint.

26 Does LAPB provide error recovery?

Yes. However, this slows down performance. Cisco's HDLC does not do error recovery. It simply drops the packet. But performance is faster.

27 To which layer do the X.25 parameters *window size* and *packet size* belong?

Layer 3 of the X.25 spec.

28 Does Frame Relay guarantee delivery of data?

No. Frame Relay relies on upper-layer protocols to correct errors.

29 Does X.25 guarantee delivery of data?

Yes. It relies on the LAPB protocol to check for errors on the line and request retransmission for errors on the link.

30 Which companies comprise the Gang of Four?

Stratacom, Northern Telecom, Cisco Systems, Digital Equipment Corporation.

Chapter 11

1 Does IPX use the unnumbered feature?

No.

2 Is IP unnumbered a standard in the industry?

No. It is not a standard and will not work with other vendor routers.

3 Can you use IP unnumbered on a Frame Relay interface?

Yes. IP unnumbered assumes a point-to-point environment, so it will work if you use a point-to-point subinterface at both ends.

4 Is a T1 full duplex or half duplex?

Full duplex.

5 What are the pinouts of a T1 interface used with an RJ-45 jack?

A T1 uses pins 1, 2, 4, and 5 with an RJ-45 jack.

6 Is it possible to bundle four ISDN BRI connections to one logical channel (bundle) using multilink PPP?

Yes. For point-to-point connections, use the Cisco IOS feature **ppp multilink**, which is described in RFC 1717 and is available starting in Cisco IOS 11.0(3).

7 What type of attack does CHAP provide protection against?

Playback attacks.

8 Does MLPPP affect routing tables?

No. MLPPP operates at Layer 2.

9 Name three dialer interfaces that MLPPP supports.

ISDN, asynchronous, synchronous.

10 What remote access protocol was used prior to PPP?

Serial Line IP (SLIP).

11 Which series of routers provides for cable modem access?

The 900 series.

12 What series of router can share modular cards with the 1600, 2600, and 3600 routers?

The 1700 series routers.

13 Which remote access server in the 5000 series supports a T3 connection?

The AS5800 series can support a T3 connection.

14 Which processor do the 2600 and 3600 routers use?

The RISC processor.

15 What is the Stack Group Bidding Protocol?

It is a protocol used between access servers to determine who should do the processing for remote-access connections.

16 Is a four-wire 64k circuit full duplex or half duplex?

Full duplex.

17 Would a 2500 series router be a TE1 or a TE2?

TE2. TE2 devices have no ISDN hardware and need a terminal adapter.

18 A PBX is which type, NT1 or NT2?

NT2.

19 What reference point interface connects to the local loop?

The U interface.

20 Name at least three protocols that can be used over PPP.

IP, IPX, AppleTalk.

21 Does MLPPP provide for load balancing?

Yes.

22 What are the pinouts of a 64k circuit used with an RJ-45?

Pins 1, 2, 7, and 8.

23 What processor does the Cisco 2500 series use?

The Motorola processor.

24 What is one of the primary differences between the AS5200 and the AS5300?

The 5300 can be used as a VoIP gateway.

25 Which router would you use to meet the following requirements: ten users at a branch office, multiservice, voice/data integration, VPNs, and broadband access?

The Cisco 1720 or 1750 would meet these needs.

26 Into what slot would an RSP8 module fit in a Cisco 7500 router?

The processor slot.

27 Which series of routers has a totally different OS than the other routers?

The 700 series was purchased from a company called Combinet and has a completely different OS.

28 Which series of routers will no longer be supported by Cisco past 2005?

The 4500 series.

29 Which router would an NPM fit into?

The 4000 series.

30 Is it possible to have a 100 Mbps Ethernet port in a Cisco 1600 router?

No. 1600s only come with a fixed 10 Mbps port.

Chapter 12

1 Hosts are what physical unit type?

5.

2 The fifth layer of the SNA model is called the _____ layer.

Data flow.

3 Software that runs on a front-end processor is called _____.

Network control program.

4 Transmission groups are physical links that connect what?

Subarea nodes.

5 What types of routes are used to get from a source to a destination in an SNA network?

Explicit routes.

6 Novell's SAA Gateway would be considered what type of gateway?

Logical unit gateway.

7 What is a TIC?

Token Ring Interface Coupler.

8 Locally administered addresses are almost always used in Token Ring shops to improve what?

Manageability.

9 Which three timers are involved in an LLC2 session?

T1, T2, Ti.

10 When an SSCP-to-PU session is created, what type of units signal between the devices?

Request/response.

11 A PU finds the gateway by using what type of frame?

All-routes explorer frame.

12 Which SNA communications protocol was designed to run over Token Ring?

LLC2.

13 What are the three SDLC frame types?

Unnumbered, information, supervisory.

14 Name the two types of SDLC link stations.

Primary and secondary.

15 Name the two types of secondary link state operation.

Two-way simultaneous, two-way alternate.

16 Name the two communication protocols in an SNA network.

SDLC, LLC2.

17 What are boundary nodes?

The boundary device is the last subarea node (FEP) where the node type 2 (cluster controller) is attached.

18 Where are FID2 frames used?

Between the FEP and PU 2s.

19 Where are FID4 frames used?

Between FEPs or PU 4 to PU 4.

20 What is one advantage of the DSPU feature of a Cisco router?

You can insert and remove downstream PUs from the network without making any changes on the host.

21 Which type of frames do two LLC2 stations use to communicate with each other?

XID frames.

22 What are channels?

Channels connect FEPs to mainframes.

23 Name the two types of physical connectors for FEPs.

Copper, bus and tag fiber, ESCON.

24 The ability of end stations to initiate communication without permission is called what?

Asynchronous balanced mode.

25 Name a drawback of using LAA.

Addresses must be configured manually.

26 When a mainframe communicates with another mainframe, what type of session is created?

An SSCP-to-SSCP session.

27 LAA MAC addresses begin with which hexadecimal digits?

40.

28 Full datamode is when the PLS is full duplex and the SLS is _____.

Full duplex.

29 An AS400 is similar to what?

A mainframe.

30 The path control layer of the SNA stack is equivalent to what layer of the OSI model?

The network layer.

Chapter 13

1 What does the command **source-bridge proxy-explorer** do?

It configures a dynamic RIF cache on the router.

2 What does NCIA stand for?

Native Client Interface Architecture.

3 Which method of encapsulation of LLC2 frames provides for local acknowledgment?

TCP encapsulation.

4 What does virtual multidrop mean?

It is a method of using one physical SDLC connection to a router. The router has several SDLC connections to cluster controllers.

5 With STUN, which encapsulation method should be used for serial links?

HDLC. This method offers the best performance of the three methods because of the low overhead.

6 What does STUN connect?

FEPs and cluster controllers across a multiprotocol backbone.

7 What is SDLLC?

SDLLC converts remote SDLC frames to Token Ring frames on the mainframe side.

8 What is a benefit of local acknowledgment with SDLLC?

It improves performance, because routers accept the full SDLC window without delay.

9 What are dynamic peers?

They are configured remote peers that are connected only when circuits are using them.

10 What does promiscuous mean?

It means that the peer is in a "listen-only" mode and will accept connections from any other peer.

11 Of border peers, border groups, load balancing, and on-demand peers, which three are provided with DLSW+?

Border peers, border groups, on-demand peers.

12 Name the two methods that APPN network nodes use for routing updates.

ISR and HSR.

13 What is a composite network node?

In APPN, a composite network node is a mainframe.

14 The CIP processor is supported on which Cisco routers?

The 7500 and the 7000.

15 Name the six sources that CSNA delivers traffic to the mainframe from.

DLSW+, DSPU, APPN, RSRB, SDLLC, QLLC.

16 Which process offloads routers' CPU cycles by having the workstation be the tunnel peer?

Native client interface architecture.

17 In APPN, a router is known as what?

A network node.

18 What is used so that legacy SDLC controllers can connect to TIC-attached FEPs?

SDLLC.

19 What should you use for RIF termination and on-demand peers for greater scalability?

DLSW+.

20 What special support was added for legacy secondary logical units that cannot issue a BIND?

Dependent Logical Unit Requester (DLUR).

21 APPN is used for what purpose?

To allow sessions to be established between end users without the involvement of the mainframe.

22 Name two benefits of DLSw+.

It minimizes the number of concurrent peer connections.

Dynamic on-demand peer relationships.

23 With DLSw+, the RIF terminates where?

In the virtual ring.

24 Name two reasons to use SDLLC.

To conserve FEP ports.

To connect remote SDLC controllers.

25 Name two reasons to use local acknowledgment with STUN.

Prevents session loss over periodically congested WAN.

Improves performance, because routers accept the full SDLC window without delay.

26 Name two reasons to integrate the mainframe into the data center.

Facilitates the mainframe as a high-speed file server.

Supports new business applications.

27 Which encapsulation method provides for local acknowledgment?

TCP.

28 Why is load balancing not recommended with FST encapsulation?

Because packets might arrive out of order.

29 Promiscuous mode means the peer will accept connections from whom?

Any other peer.

30 If you have only one Token Ring path to a destination, what type of RIF cache could you use?

A static RIF cache.

Chapter 14

1 What are two frame types that SNA networks transport?

SDLC and LLC2.

2 What type of explorer packet takes every possible path through the network?

An all-routes explorer.

3 In SNA networks, should the convergence time be less than the session expiration time?

Yes. If a link goes down, the routers need to converge on a new path to the destination before an SNA session will time out.

4 Does an explorer ever visit the same Token Ring twice?

No. Explorers should visit a Token Ring only one time.

5 What is Proxy Explorer used for?

It creates an explorer reply cache on the router.

6 What is a method of transporting SNA and NetBIOS frames over an IP network?

DLSw+.

7 What type of DLSw+ encapsulation can be used on Token Ring ports but not Ethernet?

Fast Sequenced Transport (FST).

8 Which type of encapsulation uses more CPU cycles to support it, Local Acknowledgment or Direct?

Local Acknowledgment encapsulation provides for Local Acknowledgement, which creates more work for the CPU.

9 Name three methods of controlling CANYOUREACH explorer frames in DLSw+ networks.

Filtering, statically, virtual ring numbering, caching, explorer firewalls.

10 How many times must a border peer replicate a broadcast if it is configured for nine peers in its group and two other border peers?

11 broadcast replications must be done—two for the border peers and nine for the members of the group that it is border peering for.

11 Which type of QoS provides guaranteed service end-to-end across a network?

Resource Reservation Protocol (RSVP).

12 Name one reason why ISPs do not like to implement RSVP.

It permanently ties up bandwidth, even when there is no traffic flow.

13 How many bits are in the IP header's Type of Service field?

8.

14 How many bits make up the IP Precedence portion of the Type of Service field?

3.

15 What is the only command that is absolutely necessary on a router if it is to participate in DLSw+ in listening mode?

dlsw local-peer peer-id x.x.x.x promiscuous.

16 NetBIOS is transported in what type of frame?

NetBIOS is transported in an LLC2 frame.

17 If the **priority** command is specified on the DLSw+ command and nothing else, what TCP port will the traffic use?

The normal port, or 1982.

18 What would be a good routing choice if you needed to specify a path that traffic should take?

Policy routing.

19 What does Weighted Fair Queuing favor?

Low-volume conversations.

20 What does DLSw+ encapsulate?

SNA and NetBIOS traffic.

21 What router platforms are a good choice for a very large DLSw+ network?

The 7500, 7200, and possibly the 3600.

22 What is an example of differentiated service?

Custom and priority queuing.

23 What is an example of guaranteed service?

Resource Reservation Protocol (RSVP).

24 On what TCP port do circuit establishment, keepalives, and capability exchanges occur on?

TCP port 2065.

25 What is Class-Based Weighted Fair Queuing?

CBWFQ is when WFQ uses the IP Precedence bits to classify which conversation flows get more priority.

26 Which type of encapsulation provides for Local Acknowledgment?

TCP encapsulation.

27 What does the + in DLSw+ mean?

It means that this is Cisco's proprietary version of DLSw.

28 How many ports can DLSw+ load-balance over?

Four.

29 What three cache types does DLSw check for before flooding broadcasts?

Local, remote, group cache.

30 Do border peers provide for load balancing?

No.

Chapter 15

1 What is a bastion host?

A bastion host can be considered a Web server or a secure gateway that supports a limited number of applications for use by outsiders.

2 Name four services to turn off on the (perimeter) router that interfaces with the Internet.

CDP, finger, tcp-small-servers, udp-small-servers.

3 Can a Cisco 2500 router be used as a firewall?

Yes. The 2500 router can be used as a firewall and also supports CBAC!

4 What are network security policies?

Network security policies are well-documented rules about what activities are permitted on the network.

5 On what router platforms is CBAC available?

The Cisco 1600 and 2500 series.

6 What is a "choke" router?

The choke router sits behind the perimeter router on the customer side of the network, blocking the DMZ from the internal network.

7 At what layer of the OSI model do Stateful firewalls work?

Layer 4.

8 What network layer addresses should always be blocked from entering your network from the outside?

127.0.0.0, 192.168.0.0, 172.16.16–31.0, 10.0.0.0, and any inside network layer addresses.

9 Of the two key similar exchange mechanisms Diffie-Hellman and Oakley, which is considered superior?

Oakley is superior, but Diffie-Hellman might be used more.

10 What does PKI stand for?

Public Key Infrastructure.

11 What does SHA authenticate?

SHA authenticates packet data.

12 Does ESP encrypt the IP Header?

No. Authentication Header protocol encrypts the header of the IP packet. ESP encrypts only the payload portion.

13 Does L2F support multiprotocol?

No. Cisco's L2F is a Layer 2 tunneling protocol.

14 Does L2TP support multiprotocol?

Yes.

15 What is the name of the product that replaced NetRanger?

Intrusion Detection System (IDS).

16 Where would the local network server be located—at the ISP or on the customer's property?

At the customer's location. The L2TP Access Concentrator is located at the ISP.

17 What does the authentication header protect?

It protects the entire datagram by embedding the header into the payload portion of the packet.

18 How many bits does the MD5 hash encrypt with?

128.

19 What are the router commands that are used for exchanging keys called?

Crypto maps.

20 Name three layers that CBAC examines.

Network, Transport, Application.

21 Which has the stronger authentication mechanism—**enable secret** or **enable password**?

enable secret.

22 With CBAC, which feature is needed to prevent Denial of Service attacks?

TCP Interceptor.

23 Where should extended access lists be applied—closest to the source or the destination?

Extended access lists should be placed closest to the source.

24 What is a perimeter router?

The perimeter router is the router that is closest to the exit point of a customer's network—usually the Internet.

25 What does ISAKMP stand for?

Internet Security Association Key Management Protocol.

26 What RFC is NAT?

RFC 1918.

27 Why is stateful filtering considered faster than application proxies?

Because the firewall only needs to look at Layer 4. As the firewall unwraps the packet, it would be more work to have to unwrap more layers than necessary. Application proxies work at the Application layer.

28 Without CBAC, can Cisco routers filter TCP and UDP ports?

Yes. Regular Cisco IOS can filter TCP or UDP ports, as well as source and destination IP addresses and networks.

29 Name three network security weaknesses.

Policy, Configuration, Technology.

30 What IOS feature set is required for CBAC?

The Firewall feature set.

Chapter 16

1 What challenge does the CCDP face when merging voice onto a data network?

Data networks tolerate delay. Voice networks do not tolerate delay, and the packets must be delivered in a real-time predictable order.

2 What are three different types of voice interfaces used on a Cisco router?

Foreign Exchange System (FXS).

Foreign Exchange Office (FXO).

Ear and Mouth (E&M).

3 What two types of digital signaling are available?

Channel Associated Signaling (CAS).

Common Channel Signaling (CCS).

4 What is a dial plan?

A dial plan is a set of rules for routing incoming and outgoing calls and accessing voice features from one system to another.

5 List three benefits of a dial plan.

Enables reliability and security.

Enables cost savings.

Controls the behavior of the voice system.

6 What must a successful QoS voice over data network design ensure?

A QoS design must ensure that voice is prioritized over data and will always be delivered ahead of data.

7 List four factors that have a significant impact on voice quality in a network.

Delay.

Delay variation.

Packet loss.

Echo.

8 List three types of delay that, by design, are inherent in voice networks.

Propagation delay.

Handling delay.

Queuing delay.

9 For good voice quality, what does Cisco recommend as the maximum amount of delay (one-way) from end to end?

150 ms.

10 What is handling delay? Provide an example of handling delay in a voice network.

Handling delay is caused by all the components that must handle the voice traffic during its transmission. Packetization and depacketization of voice traffic are examples of handling delay.

11 True or false: QoS should start in the LAN. The largest bottlenecks are usually found on the campus network.

False. QoS should start in the WAN.

12 What three areas of concern should be addressed at the router?

Prioritiziation.

Slow-speed links.

Traffic shaping.

13 What three protocols can provide transport for voice?

Frame Relay.

ATM.

IP.

14 What three processes must occur before voice can be passed from the PBX to the router?

Signaling must be passed from the PBX to the router.

Signaling must be passed between routers.

Signaling must be passed from the router to the PBX.

15 What four components comprise the H.323 family?

Gatekeeper.

Gateways.

Terminals.

Multipoint Control Units.

16 What is the main function of a gatekeeper?

Zone and subnet configuration.

Terminal name registration.

Interzone communication.

17 What three types of terminal names are recognized by a gatekeeper?

H.323, E.164 addresses, e-mail IDs.

18 What product has Cisco released that envelops the total VoIP solution?

Call Manager.

19 What is a key switch?

A key switch allows multiple phones to share a common pool of external phone lines.

20 What is a PBX?

PBX allows interoffice communications and provides connectivity to the PSTN for medium to large offices. PBXs are common in offices with more than 25 users.

21 What is a tandem switch?

A tandem switch is a device that accepts all calls and reroutes them to another destination. Tandem switches are often located at the central office or at the headquarters site to reroute calls made from site to site.

22 List three major functions of a voice over data network.

Signaling, addressing, routing.

23 What is the first step in establishing connectivity between a router and a phone switch?

Ensuring hardware and signaling compatibility.

24 True or false: VoFR and VoATM allow tandem call routing. VoIP does not.

True. VoIP requires the configuration of an H.323 gateway.

25 What feature automatically dials a predetermined number when a user goes off-hook?

Private Line Automatic Ring-Down (PLAR).

26 List one business requirement that would be satisfied by designing a voice over data network.

Cost savings.

27 Define jitter.

Jitter is caused when packets arrive at different rates due to changes in the flow of network traffic.

28 List some metrics that will define success on the voice over data design project.

Cost-effectiveness, functionality, scalability, manageability, interoperability.

29 What is the name of the signaling standard that is used to perform out-of-band signaling in the PSTN?

Signaling System 7 (SS7).

30 What problems can be experienced in running a voice over data network with no QoS?

"Choppy" or unintelligible voice.

Gaps in speech.

Disconnected calls.

Poor caller inactivity.

31 What conditions exist on a data network that would be intolerable for voice traffic?

Bursty data flow.

Network outages.

Delay based on changes in network condition.

32 True or false: Fax calls are less sensitive to latency than voice calls.

False. A fax call expects a response from the receiving machine. If it does not receive that call in a specified time frame, it retransmits the whole call.

INDEX

Numerics

2B+D, 393
10Base2, 79
10Base5, 79
10BaseFL, 79
10BaseT, 79
10 Gigabit Ethernet, 81
24-7-365 availability, 298
30B+D PRI, 396
80/20 rule, 59
100BaseT, 80-81
100BaseX, 79
3270 terminals, 441
7000 series routers
    autonomous switching, 192
    CIP, 494
7500 series routers (CIP), 494

A

AAL (ATM Adaptation Layers), 119-120
AAL1 (ATM Adaptation Layer 1), 120, 605
AAL2 (ATM Adaptation Layer 2), 120
AAL3 (ATM Adaptation Layer 3), 120
AAL4 (ATM Adaptation Layer 4), 120
AAL5 (ATM Adaptation Layer 5), 121
AARP (AppleTalk Address Resolution Protocol), 259
ABM (asynchronous balanced mode), 453
ABR (Available Bit Rate), 119
ABRs (Area Border Routers), 219
access layer, 25
access lists, 561
    IPX, 269
    placement, 570
access routers
    branch office routers, 410-412
    BRI routers, 409
    central site routers, 413-415
    Cisco 3600 series, 415
    PRI routers, 409
    regional office routers, 412-413
    telecommuter routers, 409-410
ACD (automatic call distribution), 622
active state (DLCI), 349

adaptation layers (ATM), 119–120, 605
address allocation, private ATM networks, 121-122
    network interfaces, 122
address field, FID4 frames, 443
addressing
    AppleTalk, 260
        AURP, 265
        cable ranges, configuring, 263
        EIGRP, 264
        filtering options, 262
        name-to-address resolution, 261
        RTMP, 264
        zones, 262
    DHCP, 277
    IPX, 265
    name resolution, 273
    VoATM, 606
    VoFR, 607
    voice over data networks, 600-601
    VoIP, 609
    X.121, 340
adjacencies (OSPF), forming, 226
administrative distance, 197
ADSP (AppleTalk DataStream Protocol), 259
advertisements
    LSAs, 220
        AS-External LSAs, 222
        network LSAs, 221
        router LSAs, 221
        summary LSAs, 221
        Type 7, 229
AFP (AppleTalk Filing Protocol), 260
aggregation, 198
AH (Authentication Header), 572
all-routes explorers, hop counts, 514
analog backup links, 391, 393
analog signaling, 598-599
analyzing customer design requirements, 10
ANR (Automatic Network Routing), 492
any-to-any networks, DLSw+
    hierarchical topology, 517-526, 529
    promiscuous mode, 529
    QoS, 529-532
    queuing algorithms, 532-533
AO/DI (Always On/Dynamic ISDN), 343
AppleTalk, 259
    addressing, 260
        cable range configuration, 263

B

J-K

L

M

N

S

W

X

Z

CCIE Professional Development

Cisco LAN Switching

Kennedy Clark, CCIE; Kevin Hamilton, CCIE

1-57870-094-9 • AVAILABLE NOW

This volume provides an in-depth analysis of Cisco LAN switching technologies, architectures, and deployments, including unique coverage of Catalyst network design essentials. Network designs and configuration examples are incorporated throughout to demonstrate the principles and enable easy translation of the material into practice in production networks.

Advanced IP Network Design

Alvaro Retana, CCIE; Don Slice, CCIE; and Russ White, CCIE

1-57870-097-3 • AVAILABLE NOW

Network engineers and managers can use these case studies, which highlight various network design goals, to explore issues including protocol choice, network stability, and growth. This book also includes theoretical discussion on advanced design topics.

Large-Scale IP Network Solutions

Khalid Raza, CCIE; and Mark Turner

1-57870-084-1 • AVAILABLE NOW

Network engineers can find solutions as their IP networks grow in size and complexity. Examine all the major IP protocols in-depth and learn about scalability, migration planning, network management, and security for large-scale networks.

Routing TCP/IP, Volume I

Jeff Doyle, CCIE

1-57870-041-8 • AVAILABLE NOW

This book takes the reader from a basic understanding of routers and routing protocols through a detailed examination of each of the IP interior routing protocols. Learn techniques for designing networks that maximize the efficiency of the protocol being used. Exercises and review questions provide core study for the CCIE Routing and Switching exam.

Cisco Press   **www.ciscopress.com**

Cisco Career Certifications

Cisco CCNA Exam #640-507 Certification Guide
Wendell Odom, CCIE

0-7357-0971-8 • AVAILABLE NOW

Although it's only the first step in Cisco Career Certification, the Cisco Certified Network Associate (CCNA) exam is a difficult test. Your first attempt at becoming Cisco certified requires a lot of study and confidence in your networking knowledge. When you're ready to test your skills, complete your knowledge of the exam topics, and prepare for exam day, you need the preparation tools found in *Cisco CCNA Exam #640-507 Certification Guide* from Cisco Press.

CCDA Exam Certification Guide
Anthony Bruno, CCIE & Jacqueline Kim

0-7357-0074-5 • AVAILABLE NOW

CCDA Exam Certification Guide is a comprehensive study tool for DCN Exam #640-441. Written by a CCIE and a CCDA, and reviewed by Cisco technical experts, *CCDA Exam Certification Guide* will help you understand and master the exam objectives. In this solid review on the design areas of the DCN exam, you'll learn to design a network that meets a customer's requirements for perfomance, security, capacity, and scalability.

Interconnecting Cisco Network Devices
Edited by Steve McQuerry

1-57870-111-2 • AVAILABLE NOW

Based on the Cisco course taught worldwide, *Interconnecting Cisco Network Devices* teaches you how to configure Cisco switches and routers in multi-protocol internetworks. ICND is the primary course recommended by Cisco Systems for CCNA #640-507 preparation. If you are pursuing CCNA certification, this book is an excellent starting point for your study.

Designing Cisco Networks
Edited by Diane Teare

1-57870-105-8 • AVAILABLE NOW

Based on the Cisco Systems instructor-led and self-study course available world-wide, *Designing Cisco Networks* will help you understand how to analyze and solve existing network problems while building a framework that supports the functionality, performance, and scalability required from any given environment. Self-assessment through exercises and chapter-ending tests starts you down the path for attaining your CCDA certification.

Cisco Press

Cisco Press Solutions

Enhanced IP Services for Cisco Networks
Donald C. Lee, CCIE

1-57870-106-6 • **AVAILABLE NOW**

This is a guide to improving your network's capabilities by understanding the new enabling and advanced Cisco IOS services that build more scalable, intelligent, and secure networks. Learn the technical details necessary to deploy Quality of Service, VPN technologies, IPsec, the IOS firewall and IOS Intrusion Detection. These services will allow you to extend the network to new frontiers securely, protect your network from attacks, and increase the sophistication of network services.

Developing IP Multicast Networks, Volume I
Beau Williamson, CCIE

1-57870-077-9 • **AVAILABLE NOW**

This book provides a solid foundation of IP multicast concepts and explains how to design and deploy the networks that will support appplications such as audio and video conferencing, distance-learning, and data replication. Includes an in-depth discussion of the PIM protocol used in Cisco routers and detailed coverage of the rules that control the creation and maintenance of Cisco mroute state entries.

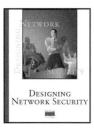

Designing Network Security
Merike Kaeo

1-57870-043-4 • **AVAILABLE NOW**

Designing Network Security is a practical guide designed to help you understand the fundamentals of securing your corporate infrastructure. This book takes a comprehensive look at underlying security technologies, the process of creating a security policy, and the practical requirements necessary to implement a corporate security policy.

Cisco Press

www.ciscopress.com

Cisco Press

Committed to being your long-term learning resource while you grow as a Cisco Networking Professional

Help Cisco Press **stay connected** to the issues and challenges you face on a daily basis by registering your product and filling out our brief survey. Complete and mail this form, or better yet ...

Register online and enter to win a FREE book!

Jump to **www.ciscopress.com/register** and register your product online. Each complete entry will be eligible for our monthly drawing to win a FREE book of the winner's choice from the Cisco Press library.

May we contact you via e-mail with information about **new releases, special promotions,** and **customer benefits?**

❒ Yes ❒ No

E-mail address _____

Name _____

Address _____

City _____ State/Province _____

Country_____ Zip/Post code _____

Where did you buy this product?

❒ Bookstore   ❒ Computer store/Electronics store   ❒ Direct from Cisco Systems
❒ Online retailer   ❒ Direct from Cisco Press   ❒ Office supply store
❒ Mail order   ❒ Class/Seminar   ❒ Discount store
❒ Other_____

When did you buy this product? _____ **Month** _____ **Year**

What price did you pay for this product?

❒ Full retail price   ❒ Discounted price   ❒ Gift

Was this purchase reimbursed as a company expense?

❒ Yes ❒ No

How did you learn about this product?

❒ Friend   ❒ Store personnel   ❒ In-store ad   ❒ cisco.com
❒ Cisco Press catalog ❒ Postcard in the mail   ❒ Saw it on the shelf ❒ ciscopress.com
❒ Other catalog   ❒ Magazine ad   ❒ Article or review
❒ School   ❒ Professional organization ❒ Used other products
❒ Other_____

What will this product be used for?

❒ Business use   ❒ School/Education
❒ Certification training ❒ Professional development/Career growth
❒ Other_____

How many years have you been employed in a computer-related industry?

❒ less than 2 years   ❒ 2–5 years   ❒ more than 5 years

Have you purchased a Cisco Press product before?

❒ Yes ❒ No

Cisco SYSTEMS

Cisco Press

c i s c o p r e s s . c o m

How many computer technology books do you own?
❐ 1   ❐ 2–7   ❐ more than 7

Which best describes your job function? (check all that apply)
❐ Corporate Management   ❐ Systems Engineering   ❐ IS Management   ❐ Cisco Networking
❐ Network Design   ❐ Network Support   ❐ Webmaster   Academy Program
❐ Marketing/Sales   ❐ Consultant   ❐ Student   Instuctor
❐ Professor/Teacher   ❐ Other _____

Do you hold any computer certifications? (check all that apply)
❐ MCSE   ❐ CCNA   ❐ CCDA
❐ CCNP   ❐ CCDP   ❐ CCIE   ❐ Other _____

Are you currently pursuing a certification? (check all that apply)
❐ MCSE   ❐ CCNA   ❐ CCDA
❐ CCNP   ❐ CCDP   ❐ CCIE   ❐ Other _____

On what topics would you like to see more coverage?

_____

_____

Do you have any additional comments or suggestions?

_____

_____

Thank you for completing this survey and registration. Please fold here, seal, and mail to Cisco Press.

Cisco CID Exam Certification Guide (1-58720-033-3)

Indianapolis, IN 46278-8046
P.O. Box #781046
Customer Registration—CP050227
Cisco Press

Place
Stamp
Here

ciscopress.com
Indianapolis, IN 46290
201 West 103rd Street
Cisco Press